D1606647

Encyclopedia of Contemporary Writers and Their Work

GEOFF HAMILTON
and BRIAN JONES

Facts On File
An imprint of Infobase Publishing

Encyclopedia of Contemporary Writers and Their Work

Facts On File, Inc.
An imprint of Infobase Publishing
132 West 31st Street
New York NY 10001

Library of Congress Cataloging-in-Publication Data

Hamilton, Geoff.
Encyclopedia of contemporary writers and their works / Geoff Hamilton and Brian Jones.
p. cm.
Includes bibliographical references and index.
ISBN 978-0-8160-7578-2 (acid-free paper) 1. English fiction—20th century—Bio-bibliography—Dictionaries. 2. American fiction—20th century—Bio-bibliography—Dictionaries. 3. Commonwealth fiction (English)—Bio-bibliography—Dictionaries. 4. English fiction—21st century—Bio-bibliography—Dictionaries. 5. American fiction—21st century—Bio-bibliography—Dictionaries. 6. Authors, English—20th century—Biography—Dictionaries. 7. Authors, American—20th century—Biography—Dictionaries. 8. Authors, Commonwealth—Biography—Dictionaries. 9. Authors, English—21st century—Biography—Dictionaries. 10. Authors, American—21st century—Biography—Dictionaries. I. Jones, Brian. II. Title.
PR881.H34 2010
823'.9140903—dc22 2009022546

Facts On File books are available at special discounts when purchased in bulk quantities for businesses, associations, institutions, or sales promotions. Please call our Special Sales Department in New York at (212) 967-8800 or (800) 322-8755.

You can find Facts On File on the World Wide Web at http://www.factsonfile.com

Text design by Erik Lindstrom
Composition by Hermitage Publishing Services
Cover printed by Sheridan Books, Ann Arbor, Mich.
Book printed and bound by Sheridan Books, Ann Arbor, Mich.
Date printed: May 2010
Printed in the United States of America

10 9 8 7 6 5 4 3 2 1

This book is printed on acid-free paper.

CONTENTS

Introduction   v

Entries A to Z   1

Bibliography of Major Works by Major
Contemporary Fiction Writers   397

Bibliography of General Secondary Sources   403

Index   405

INTRODUCTION

This encyclopedia is intended as a guide to contemporary fiction writers in English, "contemporary" meaning, for our purposes, writers born after 1959. From that pool we selected those writers who have received the highest literary acclaim. Some of them, such as David Foster Wallace, Chang-rae Lee, and Sherman Alexie, already have well-established reputations and have become fixtures on college syllabi. Others, such as Nell Freudenberger, Z. Z. Packer, and David Mitchell, are now just beginning to claim a wide audience and an institutional foothold.

At first glance, the staggeringly rich and diverse amalgam of literary talent gathered under the rubric "Contemporary Literature in English" would appear to defy any attempt at overall characterization. While no author here came of literary age before the 1980s, and while most are currently residing in Britain or America, their roots stem from countries and histories scattered all over the Western world, from the endless, debilitating stasis of Daniel Alarcón's Peru and the brutal misery of Edwidge Danticat's Haiti, to the weird nowhereland of Douglas Coupland's Canada and throughout that vast and self-contradictory abstraction known as the British Commonwealth. Even in Britain and America they give voice to a swarm of ethnicities, religions, classes, and walks of life.

Indeed, if we hold in mind, almost as a thought experiment, the vestigial profile of the canonic Western literary sensibility (the CWLS)—that white, middle-class, Christian, Anglo-Saxon male who even to this day fights a stubborn rearguard action, largely in spite of himself, in the halls of academia—we can discover the first characteristic defining (roughly but in the main) the authors here assembled. With few exceptions—and they mostly prove the rule—they are natives or landed immigrants of a country one might call Somewhere Else Entirely. Even those, such as Bret Easton Ellis, Rick Moody, or David Foster Wallace, who were born near the very epicenter of that canonic sensibility, seem inevitably to have gained an early citizenship in this strange world.

However, and this may be taken as a second characteristic of the species, for all the diversity of their homogeneous origins, an overwhelming number were "schooled" in the art of writing, in ways and at establishments that were and still are profoundly shaped by the canonical sensibility they defy. Indeed, a surprising number graduated with M.F.A.'s—those modern, seemingly oxymoronic degrees in academic creativity—from a single creative writing program: the Iowa Writers' Workshop, founded in 1936 by Wilbur Schramm, who received an M.A. in American civilization at Harvard University and a Ph.D. in English at the University of Iowa and who had no creative background at all but was known by the somewhat ominous title of "the father of communications." The result, at times, seems a strange sort of uniformity, as if one wandered through an enormous department store that sold a seemingly infinite variety of the same thing.

Those who truly did come from somewhere else entirely, like Danticat and Alarcón, or Sherman Alexie—born and raised on the Spokane Indian Reservation in Wellpinit, Washington (pop. 1,100)—in many ways, ironically, preserve the best and strongest traits of the CWLS, writing with passionate engagement, unmediated by ironic distance or hyper-sophistication, of worlds rich in experience and human resonance, for all the appalling circumstances they often narrate. Whereas—and this may serve as a third characteristic of the species—the nearer we approach the (vestigial) epicenter of the CWLS, now Somewhere Else Entirely, the more we encounter an almost suffocating, metaphysical irony, feeding unhealthily on itself for want of other food. Nowhere, perhaps, is this more or more sadly evident than in the case of the late David Foster Wallace, who committed suicide in 2008 and whose 1,096-page *Infinite Jest,* an epochal touchstone of contemporary literature in English, may be seen as a relentless yet doomed attempt to escape the ironic through an excess of irony. "The next real literary 'rebels' in this country," Wallace wrote in his essay "*E Unibus Pluram*" (From the ones the many), "might well emerge as some weird bunch of *anti*-rebels, born oglers who dare somehow to back away from ironic watching, who have the childish gall actually to endorse and instantiate single-entendre principles. Who treat plain old untrendy human troubles and emotions in U.S. life with reverence and conviction. Who eschew self-consciousness and hip fatigue" (81).

This preoccupation with irony may be the single most definitive quality of the literature here assembled; evident even—perhaps most vividly— in instances where the author attempts to overcome it, as in *What Is the What: The Autobiography of Valentino Achek Deng, A Novel,* the harrowing tale of a Sudanese "lost boy," told by Dave Eggers, native of the middle-class Chicago suburb of Lake Forest and graduate of the University of Illinois in Urbana-Champaign.

The rise of irony deserves at least a summary historical sketch. Excepting those authors who were born and raised entirely outside the Anglo-American milieu, virtually all our authors came of literary age in the 1980s. And with the elections of Thatcher and Reagan, in '78 and '80 respectively, it was as if a well-heeled 1950s couple had returned to their suburban ranch estate to find the brutally hung-over remains of a generation-long house party—and cleaned house. The jaded, drug-addled cynicism, apathy, and quietism of the '70s was swept into the trash, and new rules laid down for living in this house. An entire generation of youth was put on permanent curfew and denied the car keys. Neatness, propriety, and presentability became the norm, and rebellion and entropic passion in all its forms became a matter for the bedroom and the basement. Little wonder that irony attained a kind of apotheosis: with nowhere to go, and not much to do, confined and baffled by restrictions and expectations long despised, Somewhere Else Entirely was the only place to be.

We may very roughly distinguish, then, three subspecies within the broader species of contemporary literature in English: (1) this latter true and troubled vestige of the CWLS; (2) the new, "anti-rebels," who, like the Goths and Vandals of old, come to Rome from the outside and recover its original virtues in a new and vigorous form; and (3) a varied host of authors who continue, on a modest but by no means unrewarding scale, the traditional praxis of the CWLS, telling good stories, exploring contemporary concerns with sensitivity and skill, and holding an old but trusty mirror up to nature.

Perhaps the single most dominant theme of this literature as a whole is that of intersection or hybridity, whether it be racial, familial, psychological (especially surrounding questions of personal identity), ethnic, geographical, cultural, aesthetic, or linguistic (as in the Ebonics of Ricardo Cortez Cruz's *Straight Outta Compton*). Hybrid anatomies, unstable intersections, gaps and fissures proliferate; countless narratives revolve around them like stars around black holes, forming a literature of the 21st century.

Absurdistan Gary Shteyngart (2006)

Satire might be defined as art in reverse. Rather than revealing pearls of beauty buried in the scummy details of our daily existence, it reveals hidden ugliness lurking beneath life's most shimmering and smiling surfaces. But the present moment—in which the world, as Thomas Friedman informs us, is flat, and everything in it, as Ivan Karamazov foretold, is permitted—seems to present few reliable distinctions between the sacred and profane, between theology and marketing, between treasure and rubbish. (Perhaps this problem is nothing new; the Roman satirist Juvenal was so exasperated with the superficiality of life in the first century that he found it "harder *not* to write satire.") If it has become increasingly easy to tell a joke, it has become increasingly difficult to have it really mean anything.

In GARY SHTEYNGART's first novel, *The RUSSIAN DEBUTANTE'S HANDBOOK*, the recurring metaphor for any such facile enterprise was "hunting cows." Its scene was the supposedly blithe decade following the fall of the Berlin Wall, in which the world "with the exception of the nascent slaughter in the Balkans, the African Horn, the ex-Soviet periphery, and of course the usual carnage in Afghanistan, Burma, Guatemala, the West Bank, Belfast, and Monrovia . . . was a sensible place" (*RDH* 221). His sophomore effort, *Absurdistan*, hunts more dangerous game in the even more senseless decade that follows. *Absurdistan* is a term that Eastern Bloc dissidents like Václav Havel used to designate a hopelessly dysfunctional situation, and Shteyngart occasionally relapses into hunting cows: *Absurdistan*'s Timofey, for example, cherishes an electric iron as *Debutante*'s Rybakov cherished an electric fan, and the novel laughs at a Petersburg thug's frustrated attempts to register the internet domain "www.ruslan-the-enforcer.com" (65). However, *Absurdistan* offers a number of more challenging satiric profanities, for instance a marketing survey that analyzes the "oversaturation of the Holocaust brand" (269) but offers hope for its revival because it is "better documented" than the average genocide (267), or a Halliburton accounting trick in which the greedy chieftains of two rival ethno-religious sects are convinced to stage an artificial civil war.

Shteyngart even verges on the ultimate profanity for a post-9/11 Manhattanite: a slapstick redestruction of the World Trade Center. In a scene describing the bombing of an American-built skyscraper in the fictional oil fiefdom of Absurdisvanï, which is linked in an earlier ode to the "invincible" Twin Towers (29), he observes that "the West, when stripped bare" is "essentially a series of cheap plastic components, pneumatic work chairs, and poorly framed motivational posters" (285). Yet Shteyngart has expressed bafflement at *Absurdistan*'s failure to create satiric friction. "I expected a lot of State Department people to hate me, a lot of Azerbaijani people to hate me, a lot of . . . society people to hate me," he tells *Atlantic Monthly*, "I wanted all of them to come out for a public lynching, but it didn't happen."

Although both novels chronicle a forced exile from New York, what friction *Absurdistan* does achieve comes by reversing the dilemma of *Debutante*'s anemic antihero Vladimir Girshkin, who lusts for the fortune that will buy him upward social mobility. *Absurdistan*'s Misha Vainberg, "son of the 1,238th-richest man in Russia" (3), has unlimited wealth and status but nothing useful to do with it. As various characters chorally inform him in each chapter, he is "a sophisticate and a melancholic" who should content himself with his vague "multi-culturalist" humanism—he hatches plans to provide bottled water and snacks to Cuban boat refugees" (67) and "airlift twenty progressive social workers" into the Petersburg slums (104)—and leave the world's ethical grownups to their own devices.

Misha's father, Boris, is the most psychologically and narratively salient of those grownups, a prosperous New Russian mobster universally renowned for selling Halliburton a useless "eight-hundred kilogram screw" (116). His fanatical Zionism and the "cloying" and suggestively pedophilic "Russian affection" (vii) he directs toward his son represent the historical shackles from which the resolutely cosmopolitan Misha cannot buy his escape. Just before Misha begins his freshman year of college, Boris arranges for his circumcision in a Chinatown hospital "reeking of mildew and fried rice" (34), which is gruesomely botched by reveling Hasids who have baled a bathtub of onion-flavored vodka with plastic party cups.

The novel as a whole is a delirious nightmare of wrenching juxtapositions: a pidgin R&B musical staged at a Halliburton barbecue by Absurdi prostitutes, a tank assault on a McDonald's in which Ronald and Grimace become "human shields" (147), a street gang of religious fanatics who loot an upscale perfumery that sells "the odour of the Bronx" (118) and dream of a "violent, sexy life . . . in the Los Angeles metropolitan area" (265). Unfortunately, the war is not "exciting enough" (254) to capture the fickle attention of the Western media, yet in one of its sharpest ironies, the tale ends on September 11, 2001, when, for Shteyngart, the West itself will become Absurdistan.

Misha, alias Snack Daddy, an "incorrigible fatso" (3) in the tradition of Rabelais's Gargantua, also betters *Debutante*'s third-person narrator

in his ability to convey an absurd world's sumptuous feast of tastes and smells. His father's widow smells of a "strong British breath mint, and the sulfuric undercurrent of lamb's tongue" (85), and an Absurdi warlord's daughter like "ripe green papaya" (199), while his "multicultural" Bronx sweetheart Rouenna (33) has "fast-food breath" and "caramelized summertime breasts" (x). Even the "buckwheat kasha and used underwear" of the Hasids' cramped apartment (20), and the "sweet and sickly and masculine" scent of "spent rocket fuel," (253) are comestible, and given Misha's synesthesia—he is at one point aroused by a particularly orange towel—so too is "the morning glare of foam and pollution" that renders the Caspian Sea the "bruised pink color of corned beef" (180).

Though Shteyngart is a contributing editor to *Travel + Leisure*—the source of *Absurdistan* can be found in an article he wrote for the magazine describing a jaunt to the Azerbaijani capital, Baku—the travel and leisure of his enormously sympathetic and perceptive protagonist imply the ethical bankruptcy of globalized hedonism. Vainberg laments his "impotence and collusion in everything around" him (37), and fears that "there's no way to be good" in a world that is "all wrong, wrong, wrong" (157). The unbridgeable gap between consumerism and active goodness is typified by the rationalization of his own pornography habit: "I wanted to go back to my room and look at the poor girls on the internet some more. I wanted to tear their tormentors apart with both hands" (161).

But at the same time, Vainberg represents Shteyngart's defiant rejection of any attempt to sanctify renunciation, which concentrates in his disgust for Orthodox Judaism's "codified system of anxieties" (88). The broader implication here is that both capitalism and jihad misunderstand the true nature of pleasure, which inheres, like satire, in perverse bursts of iconoclasm—Misha fondly recalls the pre-perestroika poverty in which he and Boris would "trap the neighbor's anti-Semitic dog in a milk crate and take turns peeing on it" (25)—and in isolated and tenuous acts of iconic construction.

This sensitivity to the anatomy of pleasure, and its relation to both goodness and well-being, is a kind of shared thematic thread weaving through the work of an otherwise staggeringly diverse host of influences that Shteyngart explicitly cites in the novel, among them Ivan Goncharov, Isaac Babel, Ivan Turgenev, Fyodor Dostoyevsky, Lev Tolstoy, Raymond Carver, Herman Melville, William Dean Howells, and Joseph Heller.

Bibliography

Day, Barbara. "Small War in Absurdistan." *Spectator,* 26 August 1989, p. 28.

Gritz, Jennie. "Same Planet, Different Worlds." Atlantic Monthly (June 15, 2006). Available online. URL: http://www.theatlantic.com/doc/200606u/shteyngart. Accessed May 11, 2009.

Juvenal. *Sixteen Satires.* Translated by Peter Green. New York: Penguin, 1999.

Shteyngart, Gary. *Absurdistan.* New York: Random House, 2006.

———. "Exploring Azerbaijan." Travel + Leisure (September 2005). Available online. URL: http://www.travelandleisure.com/articles/frontier/and/1/. Accessed October 16, 2009.

———. *The Russian Debutante's Handbook.* New York: Riverhead, 2002.

—Aaron Winter

Adichie, Chimamanda Ngozi (1977–)
Nigerian novelist and short story writer

Adichie is the author of two critically acclaimed novels, PURPLE HIBISCUS (2003) and HALF OF A YELLOW SUN (2006), as well as dozens of short stories. Her fiction has won respect in both Nigeria and the West for offering vivid portraits of modern Nigeria and for providing nuanced depictions of sensitive topics like child abuse, government corruption, and war.

Born in Enugu, Nigeria, to Igbo parents Grace Ifeoma and James Nwoye Adichie, Chimamanda Adichie grew up in the university town of Nsukka. When she was seven, her family moved into the house once occupied by Igbo novelist Chinua Achebe, whom she cites as the most important influence on her work. Adichie claims that by writing about Nigeria, Achebe showed her that she too could write about her world (McGrath).

At the age of 19, Adichie gave up her study of medicine and pharmacy at the University of Nigeria for a scholarship to Drexel University in Philadelphia. She studied communications at Drexel for two years before moving to Connecticut to live with her sister. Adichie received her degree from Eastern Connecticut State in 2001, graduating with a major in communications and a minor in political science. It was during her senior year that she started work on her first novel, *Purple Hibiscus.*

Since completing her undergraduate degree, she has received a master's degree in creative writing from Johns Hopkins, and a Hodder fellowship at Princeton for the 2005–06 academic year, which allowed her to work on her second novel, *Half of a Yellow Sun.* Currently, Adichie is working toward a degree in African studies at Yale, and she continues to divide her time between Nigeria and the United States.

Adichie's earliest publications include a volume of poetry, *Decisions* (1998), and a play, *For Love of Biafra* (1998), which first evidenced her enduring interest in Biafran history. Since then, she has turned her energy to fiction; award-winning short stories include: "You in America," "Half of a Yellow Sun" (which she developed into the novel of the same name), and "The American Embassy."

Her debut novel, *Purple Hibiscus,* was a popular and critical success, earning Adichie the Commonwealth Writer's Prize and the Hurston/Wright Legacy Award. *Purple Hibiscus* opens with the phrase, "Things started to fall apart at home," echoing her predecessor Achebe's well-known novel, *Things Fall Apart,* offering him tribute but also inviting readers to make connections. Adichie's novel might be read as an update of Achebe's work. Where his novel focused on the colonial encounter between British and Igbo culture, hers explores the legacy of this encounter in modern Nigeria. Adichie's characters show how Nigerians navigate this inheritance in different ways. Papa Eugene, the patriarch of the family, allies himself with British culture and rejects his father, who retains Igbo culture. Eugene's sister, Ifeoma, attempts a compromise, blending elements of both cultures. The other major update is the focus on female experience; Adichie tells her story through the eyes of the 15-year-old Kambili, and the story is the record of her coming of age, of her growing understanding of the abuse she is suffering at the hands of her religiously fanatic father, and her development of a voice. While Adichie sets this story in her childhood hometown of Nsukka, the violent family dynamic is not based on her own experiences.

Adichie followed the success of *Purple Hibiscus* with the Orange Broadband winner *Half of a Yellow Sun,* which revisits the Biafran War. The title refers to the Biafran flag, and the story chronicles the war that split Nigeria in the late 1960s, leaving Igbos to fight for an independent republic of Biafra. In order to capture the details that would make the story authentic, Adichie did a great deal of oral research, interviewing the previous generation of Nigerians, including her father, about their memories of the war. With chapters that alternate between the perspective of the young houseboy Ugwu, the upper-class Igbo Olanna, and the British writer Richard, Adichie is able to create a complex picture of events and emotions. Within the novel, Adichie addresses the question of who has the right to tell the story of the war, and in interviews she admits she was nervous about how readers would react to her telling a story that happened before she was born and that represents a painful chapter of Nigeria's history. But her deft handling of the material has received widespread praise from Nigerians, including Achebe (Gonzalez).

Adichie plans to focus her next novel on Nigerian immigrant experience. Her own crossing of borders has sparked debates about how to classify her work. She has been grouped with other young Nigerian writers, Helon Habila and Ike Oguine, as third-generation Nigerian writers. She has also been categorized with African women writers in Nigeria, predecessors such as Flora Nwapa and Buchi Emecheta. Even more broadly, her attention to violence against women has been compared by the literary critic Heather Hewett to the work of Yvonne Vera, EDWIDGE DANTICAT, and Tsitsi Dangarembga. Adichie acknowledges her part in "a real renaissance in Nigerian writing" ("Author Profile" 5) but has resisted the idea that she needs to pick one identity to represent her writing as Nigerian, or African, or African-American, hoping that instead of worrying so much about the labels, readers will appreciate the stories she has to tell.

Bibliography

Adichie, Chimamanda. *Half of a Yellow Sun.* New York: Random House, 2006.

———. *Purple Hibiscus.* Chapel Hill, N.C.: Algonquin Books, 2003.

"Author Profile: Chimamanda Ngozi Adichie." *World Literature Today* 80, no. 2 (2006): 5–6.

Gonzalez, Susan. "In her novel, student tells human story of Biafran War." Yale Bulletin and Calendar (30 March 2007). Available online. URL: http://www.yale.edu/opa/arc-ybc/v35.n23/story4.html. Accessed May 11, 2009.

Hewett, Heather. "Coming of Age: Chimamanda Ngozi Adichie and the Voice of the Third Generation." *English in Africa* 32, no. 1 (2005): 73–97.

McGrath, Charles. "A Nigerian Author Looking Unflinchingly at the Past." New York Times on the Web (23 September 2006). Available online. URL: http://query.nytimes.com/gst/fullpage.html?res=9900E0DD1E31F930A1575AC0A9609C8B63 &sec=&spon=&pagewanted=2. Accessed May 11, 2009.

—Laura White

Alarcón, Daniel (1977–) *Peruvian novelist, short story writer*

Alarcón is the author of one short story collection, WAR BY CANDLELIGHT, and one novel, *Lost City Radio.* Many of his stories take place in Alarcón's native Peru, often focusing on that country's violent history and its effect on the present, from the perspective of those most haunted by the past. Like his short stories, *Lost City Radio* concerns violence, memory, and family, and offers an unsparing view of the poverty and violence of present-day Latin America, a region it portrays as haunted by its bloody past. Alarcón also writes about the effects of economic and cultural globalization on Latin American society, often in *Etiqueta Negra,* the Spanish-language magazine of which he is associate editor.

Alarcón was born in Lima, Peru, in 1977. In 1980, his family fled the rising political violence in Peru, settling in a suburb of Birmingham, Alabama. Later he attended Columbia University in New York, graduating with a bachelor's degree in anthropology. In 2001, he received a Fulbright scholarship to Peru, where he taught photography to students in San Juan de Lurigancho, a shanty-town in Lima. He began many of the stories collected in *War by Candlelight* during this time, setting them in Lima's marginal neighborhoods. The next year he returned to the United States to study at the Iowa Writers' Workshop, graduating with a master of fine arts degree in 2004.

In 2003, his short story "City of Clowns" was published in *The New Yorker,* and since then his stories and nonfiction have appeared in *Harper's, Virginia Quarterly Review,* and *n+1,* as well as in the *Best American Non-Required Reading* anthologies for 2004 and 2005. His essay "What kind of Latino am I?" concerning his reception as a successful, young Latino writer, appeared in the online magazine Salon.com in 2005. He has received Guggenheim and Lannan Fellowships, a Whiting Award, and a National Magazine Award. *War by Candlelight* was a finalist for the 2006 PEN/Hemingway Foundation Award.

Reviewers have compared Alarcón's fiction to that of JHUMPA LAHIRI, another writer whose spare style recounts often-heartbreaking stories of migration and loss. In an interview with Vinnie Wilhelm, Alarcón cites his admiration for the "quietly violent" short stories of Mexican writer Juan Rolfo, as well as the "fiercely intelligent" Argentine Jorge Luis Borges. He consciously rejects the magical realist style that, to his mind, has come to define the popular perception of Latin American fiction.

His writing hews closely to the reality of life in Lima because, he says, "The fact is there are more places in the world like Lima than there are like the pleasant, leafy suburb where I was raised. There are more people staking out a life on the peripheries of the global system than there are people like us—meaning anybody likely to be reading this interview—who bought in early, were raised in it, and who essentially have the world at our disposal. In my work, in my travels, I've been drawn to those places, to those people whose capacity for survival and hope overwhelms mine."

The majority of stories in *War by Candlelight* take place in the Lima in which people struggle to survive. The title story traces the progress of a revolutionary, Fernando, toward his untimely death, detailed in the story's opening sentence. Short

vignettes of Fernando's previous 20 years on earth offer flashes of his life, and like many of Alarcón's characters he seems resigned to his fate. He joins the revolution largely because, as another character tells him, "the side with the guns always wins." Alarcón's vision of Latin America as a continent indelibly marked by violence remains consistent throughout his work. Consequently, his stories focus on characters struggling to survive chronic fear and anxiety, along with an often acute sense of dislocation caused by living in a country that never seems to belong to them.

In "City of Clowns," the narrator remarks that, "In Lima, dying is the local sport." Against the greater absurdity of violent and inexplicable death surrounding them, some inhabitants choose to put on greasepaint. They hide behind brightly colored make-up and hustle for the money to survive. If Lima is a city of death, it is also, as the narrator puts it, "in fact and in spirit, a city of clowns." It is a city of migrants, few of whom feel they truly belong, and of wide class divisions: the narrator's father, a handyman, sends his son to a private school, where the other students mock him as *pirana*—a street thief. He repays one of them by robbing him, stealing a suit he will only later grow into. In this Lima, everyone is always moving somewhere else, dodging death, and putting on disguises in order to survive.

Alarcón's novel, *Lost City Radio,* portrays a similarly violence-wracked Latin American country, one whose troubled history recalls those of Peru, Chile, and Argentina. In the aftermath of a years-long war between guerrilla forces and a repressive government, a radio host begins trying to reunite those "lost" during the fighting. Norma, the host, becomes a hero to her listeners, a voice that can reconstruct their families and their lives. Her husband is among the missing, and she has never stopped searching for him. One morning, a young boy wanders into her studio, claiming to come from a jungle village of "the disappeared."

Within the novel, Alarcón pairs Norma's story with that of Victor, this young boy, and their individual stories become metaphors for the history of an entire continent riven by decades of violence, whose past has never entirely settled into an integral present. With only a violent past and no foreseeable future, the people live in resigned, inescapable ennui, "where another bomb hardly registered, where the Great Blackouts were now monthly occurrences, announced by vitriolic pamphlets slipped beneath windshield wipers like shopping circulars." Alarcón's vision is a dark one but always compassionate, and finely rendered in its attention to the countless anonymous souls seeking only to survive.

Bibliography

Alarcón, Daniel. *Lost City Radio.* New York: HarperCollins, 2007.
———. *War by Candlelight.* New York: HarperCollins, 2005.
Wilhelm, Vinnie. "Daniel Alarcón's Internal Migrations." Loggernaut Reading Series. Available online. URL: http://www.loggernaut.org/interviews/danielAlarcón/. Accessed February 10, 2008.

—Jesse Hicks

Alexie, Sherman (1966–) *American poet, novelist, short story writer*

Poet, novelist, short story author, comedian and screenwriter Sherman Alexie is arguably the most recognized, prolific, and critically acclaimed author in contemporary Native American literature. Known for his satirical voice and social criticism of both the modern tribal structure and contemporary American culture, Alexie is a weighty and frequently shocking voice of the Native American community. Alexie writes what he refers to as "Colonial literature," which tends to depict themes of displacement, subjectivity, and alienation (Weich 1). Quite often, the genesis of Alexie's characters involves the absence of one or both parents through death, poverty, or alcoholism because, as Alexie states: "Native Americans, [or] anybody who's been colonized, [a]re in the position of an orphan" (Weich 2).

Born in 1966, in Wellpinit, Washington, Alexie, a Spokane/Coeur d'Alene Indian, grew up on the Spokane Indian Reservation. He was born with hydrocephalus, a condition more commonly referred to as "water on the brain," and at six months endured a risky surgery that he was not expected to survive. After the surgery, Alexie showed no signs of

brain damage but suffered for years with debilitating seizures, was an outcast, and often endured the taunting of his peers because of his illness. He was an avid reader by the age of three.

In 1981, Alexie began attending his reservation high school but, after relentless bullying (his nose was broken six times), finally realized he needed to pursue his education at nearby and affluent Reardan High when he discovered that he and his mother shared the same school-issued textbook. At Reardan he faced other adversity, learning that, aside from the mascot, he was the only Indian in a school of rich white students. Some of Alexie's inspiration for cultural critiques stem from his experiences at Reardan. Referred to as an apple "red on the outside, white on the inside," by his peers on the reservation, Alexie became a tribal outcast at a young age (Weich 3). Nonetheless, having succeeded academically and played as a starter for the varsity basketball team, Alexie graduated from Reardan High in 1984.

After Reardan, Alexie attended Gonzaga University in Spokane, and eventually transferred to Washington State University. Initially, he enrolled in premedical courses with thoughts of being a doctor, but at the encouragement of his poetry teacher, he pursued writing instead, graduating from Washington State with a bachelor's degree in American studies. Within two years of graduation he was awarded both the National Endowment for the Arts Poetry Fellowship and the Washington State Arts Commission Poetry Fellowship.

A year after his graduation, two of Alexie's poetry collections, *The Business of Fancydancing* and *I Would Steal Horses,* were published. Having struggled for years with a drinking problem, Alexie quit as soon as he learned that he was to be published and has been sober ever since. *The Business of Fancydancing,* published by Hanging Loose Press, was named a New York Times notable book in 1992, and the poem "Distances" was nominated for the Bram Stoker Award in 1993. *I Would Steal Horses* was published in a limited edition chapbook by Slipstream Press. In poems such as "What the Orphan Inherits" and "Poverty of Mirrors," Alexie weaves the themes of alcoholism and alienation together to present a raw depiction of contemporary reservation life. In 1993, Alexie's poetry book, *Old Shirts and New Skins,* was published by the UCLA American Indian Studies Center and received rave reviews. Critic Kent Chadwick praised Alexie's poetry, stating: "Sherman Alexie . . . is the Jack Kerouac of reservation life, capturing its comedy, tragedy, and Crazy Horse dreams" (Chadwick 1). In 1994, his book of poetry and short prose, *First Indian on the Moon,* was runner-up for the William Carlos Williams Award.

In 1993, his short story collection *The Lone Ranger and Tonto Fistfight in Heaven* was published by Atlantic Monthly Press, and was subsequently published in Europe and Asia, becoming his first international publication and winning the PEN/Hemingway Award for Best First Book of Fiction. It explores themes of Native American representation in popular culture. "This Is What It Means to Say Phoenix, Arizona" was included in *The Best American Short Stories* in 1994, and was eventually adapted for film under the title *Smoke Signals.*

In 1995, Alexie's first novel, RESERVATION BLUES, was published by Atlantic Monthly Press and was reprinted by both Warner Brothers Press in 1996 and Grove/Atlantic in 2005. *Reservation Blues,* an exploration of oral and musical traditions, is the story of Thomas-Builds-the-Fire, a young musician on the Spokane Reservation who is given a guitar from the mysterious and eternally damned Robert Johnson. As Thomas-Builds-the-Fire meets Johnson, his mythical dance with the devil begins. Critics praised Alexie's first novel, stating that he had ". . . establish[ed] his place as one of America's most gifted writers, period" (Subblett 1). *Reservation Blues* was also published in Europe and Asia and won several awards including the Before Columbus Foundation's American Book Award in 1996 and the 1996 Murray Morgan Prize. In addition, Alexie and his longtime friend and collaborator, Jim Boyd, recorded a soundtrack that included music performed by Jim Boyd based on the novel's songs and readings by Alexie. "Small World," a song from the soundtrack, was also featured on the *Benefit for the Honor the Earth Campaign* album and was performed at the Honor the Earth Campaign Benefit Concert in 1996.

Also in 1996, Alexie published his second and most controversial novel, INDIAN KILLER. Set in Seattle, *Indian Killer* is the story of John Smith, an adopted Native American of unknown tribal origin, who struggles to find his place within the modern tribe. As John's story unfolds, a serial killer is haunting the streets of Seattle, murdering and ritually mutilating white men. As the search for the so-called Indian Killer begins, the central thematic question of the novel comes to the fore: Who is the "Indian Killer" truly harming? Though *Indian Killer* won the 1996 New York Times Notable Book of the Year prize, critics panned the novel as marred by excessive angst, one even referring to the author as "septic with his own unappeasable fury," a quote that Alexie later had printed on a T-shirt that he proudly wears while playing basketball (Weich 11). Despite such unfavorable reviews, not the least by Alexie himself—who called it "a pile of crap novel"—*Indian Killer* met with enormous commercial success and is arguably Alexie's best-known novel to date (Weich 7).

In 1998, *Smoke Signals,* the independent film based on Alexie's short story, "What It Means to Say Phoenix, Arizona," debuted. The moving story of two young men's journey to collect the ashes of one's estranged father in Phoenix, Arizona, *Smoke Signals* received much critical acclaim and marked Alexie's first foray into screenwriting. A collaboration with independent film director Chris Eyre, the film won several awards at the 1998 Sundance Film Festival, including the Filmmaker's Trophy and the Audience Award.

From 1996 to 2005, Alexie has published six books of poetry including: *Water Flowing Home, The Summer of Black Widows, The Man Who Loves Salmon, One Stick Song, Il Powwow Della Fine Del Mondo,* and *Dangerous Astronomy.* Though poetry remains Alexie's first love, he has also published two short story compilations, *The Toughest Indian in the World* and *Ten Little Indians,* and a screenplay for *The Business of Fancydancing.*

During the same time that the *Smoke Signals* project was gaining momentum, Alexie won his first World Heavyweight Poetry Bout competition in June 1998 in Taos, New Mexico, defeating then world champion Jimmy Santiago Baca. Alexie currently holds the record as the first and only poet to win for four consecutive years.

Alexie, known for his exceptional humor and candor during his live book readings, decided to try his hand at stand-up comedy in the late nineties. In April of 1999, Alexie made his comedic debut in Seattle at the Foolproof Northwest Comedy Festival, and was a featured entertainer at the Vancouver International Comedy Festival in July of 1999.

Flight, Alexie's first novel in a decade, is the story of an orphaned Indian named Zits who travels through time to search for his true identity, while coping with his cultural displacement and feelings of abandonment. Zits survives his abusive foster-care childhood—unwanted because of his dark complexion and acne-scarred skin—by acting out violently. Published in April of 2007, the novel is a sustained exploration of identity in the absence of culture. Though it received some negative reviews, it has also been dubbed "funny . . . self-mocking . . . and inassimilable" by Joyce Carol Oates, and "raw and vital, often raucously funny" by Tom Barbash.

Also in 2007, Little, Brown published *The Absolutely True Diary of a Part-time Indian*. Semi-autobiographical, the novel marks Alexie's first venture into young adult literature. The story of wise-cracking tribal outcast Arnold "Junior" Spirit relates Alexie's own experience of growing up on a poor reservation and leaving in order to pursue a better education at a nearby, all-white high school. Arnold copes with the loss of his father to alcoholism, as well as the deaths of several close relatives, while reconciling his own guilt for leaving his poor reservation in search of a more promising future. Told with Alexie's characteristic brand of often poignant sarcasm, *Absolutely True Diary* has been nominated for nearly 20 awards for outstanding young adult fiction, including the New York Times Notable Children's Book of the Year Award. In 2009, Alexie published a book of poetry titled *Face*, and his latest collection of short fiction, *War Dances*, which broadens both his geographical and thematic scope.

Sherman Alexie continues to write prolifically, and still pursues both stand-up comedy and screenwriting. He lives in Seattle with his wife and two sons.

Bibliography

Alexie, Sherman. "A Message from Sherman." Sherman-Alexie.com. Available online. URL: http://www.fallsapart.com/index.html. Accessed March 31, 2008.

Chadwick, Kent. "Sherman Alexie's Crazy Horse Poetry." Right Brain #2. Available online. URL: http://www.wafreepress.org/02/Books.html. Accessed May 10, 2009.

StarTribune.com. "Bio: Sherman Alexie." Available online. URL: http://www.startribune.com/entertainment/books/11435621.html. Accessed May 10, 2009.

Subblett, Jesse. "Native Son," AustinChronicle.com. Available online. URL: http://www.austinchronicle.com/issues/vol14/issue44/arts.books.html. Accessed May 12, 2009.

Weich, David. "Revising Sherman Alexie." Powell' Books. Available online. URL: http://www.powells.com/interviews/shermanalexie.html. Accessed May 12, 2009.

—Tealia DeBerry

Ali, Monica (1967–) *British novelist*

Monica Ali is a British writer with Bangladeshi roots, and the author of three novels, *BRICK LANE* (2003), which was nominated for the Man Booker Prize, *Alentejo Blue* (2006), and *In the Kitchen* (2009). In 2007, Ruby Films produced a controversial film version of *Brick Lane*.

Ali was born in Dhaka, Bangladesh, in 1967, to an English mother and Bangladeshi father, but the family moved to Bolton, England, in 1970, partly for Ali to obtain a better education. She gained entrance to Wadham College, Oxford, where she studied philosophy, politics, and economics (PPE). Ali has said of her early life that she seemed fixed on the periphery, not fitting in either her school or her Oxford college, and the pathos of the outsider pervades her first novel. However, she cautions against noting simplistic affinities: "I cannot draw any clear parallels with my family history. But I can feel the reverberations. It is not so much a question of what inspired me. The issue is one of resonance" ("Where I'm Coming From"). Among fictive models, *Brick Lane* has invited comparisons with the early work of ZADIE SMITH and JHUMPA LAHIRI.

The novel is set in the Bangladeshi community of Tower Hamlets in London (it is named after the central street in the community), and follows the life of Nazneen, a young Bangladeshi woman who moves to the area with her older (and arranged) husband. Her poor grasp of English prevents her from escaping the confines of the flat they share; in contrast, her elder sister Hasina defies all conventions and runs away from her family to embrace a life of poverty with the man she loves. Nazneen's arranged marriage to the much-older Chanu allows the major themes of the narrative to become apparent: identity, self-preservation and determination, and the weight of family expectations. Ali notes, "When people talk to me about my novel, the first question they ask is: 'What inspired you to write like this?' I cite a number of factors. My experience for instance of conflict between first and second-generation immigrants. The stories that my father used to tell me about village life . . . I tell the truth, but a truth so attenuated by the circumstances of the exchange that it casts as much light as a candle in a gale" ("Where I'm Coming From"). Nonetheless, it is a truth told so vividly, and with so little comment or judgment, that the tale is instinct with life and entirely convincing. It was this rich and exuberant novelistic life that earned the author of the yet unpublished manuscript Granta's Best of Young British Novelists award in 2003. The novel itself was short-listed for the 2003 Man Booker Prize.

Nonetheless, the work offended some members of the Bangladeshi community in Britain due to the supposedly negative portrayal of the indigenous peoples of the Sylhet region, whom they believed the novel and subsequent film (2007) caricatured as uneducated and insular. But Germaine Greer has commented that, "As British people know little and care less about the Bangladeshi people in their midst, their first appearance as characters in an English novel had the force of a defining caricature. . . . Some of the Sylhetis of Brick Lane did not recognise themselves. . . . Here was a proto-Bengali writer with a Muslim name, portraying them as all of that and more" (Lewis). Activists had told the *Guardian* that they would burn copies of *Brick Lane* as a protest on July 20, 2006, but this did not in fact happen.

In contrast to *Brick Lane*, Ali's follow-up novel, *Alentejo Blue*, received poor reviews; and

it has even been suggested that Ali has become a spent force, a "one-hit wonder." Liesl Schillinger in the *New York Times* commented that "the two [novels] seem to share no family resemblance, no authorial DNA. It's almost as if they were produced by different writers." *Alentejo Blue* consists of several intertwined stories set in and around a Portuguese village in the south of the country, narrated by different local inhabitants or passing tourists. Diffuse and inconclusive in structure, it nonetheless recalls a host of themes central to Ali's first work, among them the nature of place in the face of human and economic vicissitudes, the difficulties in communication between people of diverse backgrounds and beliefs, and the resultant tensions involved in any attempt at assimilation or even coexistence.

In 2009, Ali returned to her familiar geographical and thematic milieu, with the sprawling, almost Victorian *In the Kitchen*, which revisits some of the central questions of *Brick Lane*, but from the perspective of "native" British chef, Gabriel Lightfoot—head of a kitchen "staff of U.N. refugees"—whose dramatic and often humorous disintegration exposes fundamental tensions in 21st-century British life. Reviews of the novel were mixed, as critics alternately praised and condemned the same qualities of the work, most notably its dizzying and entropic fusion of vastly disparate characters and cultures and its ultimate lack of resolution.

Monica Ali lives in North London with her husband and two children.

Bibliography

Ali, Monica. "Where I'm Coming From." Powell' Books. Available online. URL: http://www.powells.com/fromtheauthor.ali.html. Accessed May 11, 2009.

Lewis, Paul. "'You sanctimonious philistine'—Rushdie v Greer, the sequel." Guardian Unlimited. Available online. URL: http://www.guardian.co.uk/uk/2006/jul/29/topstories3.books. Accessed May 11, 2009.

Schillinger, Liesl. "The Simple Life," New York Times (June 25, 2006). Available online. URL: http://www.nytimes.com/2006/06/25/books/review/25schillinger.html?pagewanted=print. Accessed May 11, 2009.

—Miles Leeson

Amazing Adventures of Kavalier & Clay, The
Michael Chabon (2000)

MICHAEL CHABON won the 2001 Pulitzer Prize in fiction for his fifth book, *The Amazing Adventures of Kavalier & Clay,* which tells the intertwined stories of Josef (Joe) Kavalier, a Czech refugee from Hitler's invasion, and his American cousin Sam Clay, who meet in 1939 Brooklyn and become comic-book artists in the golden age of Superman and Batman. Sam and Joe's contribution to the comic pantheon is "The Escapist": "Houdini, but mixed with Robin Hood and a little bit of Albert Schweitzer" (Chabon 153).

The novel itself is deeply concerned with escape, both thematically and structurally. Chabon's protagonists want to escape their pasts, their bodies, their memories, their families, and—most immediately—the horrors of the Holocaust. The text too "escapes" from what Lee Behlman calls the "tradition of realist narrative—the Jewish American immigrant novel tradition that combines blunt social critique with the story of a young man's economic struggle and advancement" (56), jumping freely between the experiences of Joe and Sam and those of their comic-book characters. Both in its form and content, *Kavalier & Clay* simultaneously critiques, questions, and celebrates escape. Ultimately, Chabon suggests that the escape offered by the comic books Sam and Joe create and love can be a valid method of dealing with the painful and confusing strictures of history.

Just before the moment Sam and Joe meet, Sam's mother, Ethel, "burst into his bedroom, applied the ring and iron knuckles of her left hand to the side of his cranium, and told him to move over and make room in the bed for his cousin from Prague" (Chabon 4). Significantly, though, Chabon actually commences the tale "in later years," with Sam spinning a "fabulation" about the genesis of the Escapist that nonetheless has a feeling of truth (3), and this opening sets the stage for the kind of narrative that is to come: a large and larger-than-life story, full of the fantastic, that will still ring true. Chabon introduces the idea of escape and connects it directly to transformation: in Sam's words, "'To me, Clark Kent in a phone booth and Houdini in a packing crate, they were one and the same thing. . . . You weren't the same person when you came out as when you went in'" (3). Despite the fact that the novel's narrator gently questions Sam's reliability from the very start, Chabon still uses this early moment to frame the narrative to come. By suggesting that there are metamorphic properties to escape, Chabon begins the process of reexamining and potentially redeeming "escapism," and emphasizes the importance of storytelling itself, the "fabulation" that is Sam's most reliable means of escape and transformation.

Alongside the voluble Sam is the much quieter Joe, who draws Sam's stories. After introducing his protagonists to each other, Chabon shifts back into Joe's recent past, describing his abortive training as an *"aufsbrecher,"* or escape artist, under the tutelage of magician Bernard Kornblum. By the time he meets Sam, Joe has already escaped from Czechoslovakia and the intensifying pressure of Nazi rule, though the rest of his immediate family is, he fears—and later confirms—lost. The Holocaust is, for Joe, immediate and personal; for Sam, it is distant; but both young men seem to understand that the cataclysmic scale of Hitler's all-too-real violence can be approached, even defeated, in the outsized world of the comics. The first cover of *The Escapist* features the hero punching Hitler in the face, an image that is "startling, beautiful, strange. It stirred mysterious feelings in the viewer, of hatred gratified, of cringing fear transmuted into smashing retribution" (150). It is, in short, a quintessentially escapist image, but one that enables Joe to fantasize about rescuing his family, to transform villain into victim and to create a hero.

The novel itself occasionally changes into a pictureless comic book, as Chabon shifts the reader's attention from the chronicles of Joe and Sam to tell the original stories of the Escapist and other characters, using pulp-style language and heightened description to turn Joe's art into narrative. Behlman explains that "the comic book story . . . is transmuted in the narrator's hands into a kind of literary hybrid," which "gives life to the pulpy energy, excitement, and crude imaginative power of superhero comics without a trace of condescension" (65). Even in the main story, Chabon's narrative is discursive and often nonchronological, jumping in a single page back and forth between past and present. Such ricochets through time, occurring throughout the novel, echo in literary form the broad spatial and temporal canvas of a comic book: Characters can break through the confines of individual panels, the superhero fantasy unbounded by realistic structure. Chabon lifts these characteristics from the comic to the novel in order to contain formally the outsize story he wants to tell.

Chabon emphasizes the debt that all-American comic books owe to their mostly Jewish creators. This link is made explicit in *Kavalier & Clay* through Joe's multiple personal and emotional connections with the Golem of Prague, a figure in Czech legend who plays a critical role in Chabon's novel. It is through an elaborate scheme to save the Golem, a clay giant created by rabbis to protect Prague's Jews from the invading Nazi army, that Joe is able to escape Czechoslovakia. And the Golem becomes a narrative touchstone, a symbol of incredible power, created by the powerless, that resonates in the superhero characters revered by comic books: as Joe says, "'To me, this Superman is . . . maybe . . . only an American Golem'" (86).

The Golem, however, is a figure of danger as well as protection, whose anger and violence cannot always be controlled once he has been called to life. And Joe's increasing frustration about his inability to rescue his brother or any members of his family from the hands of the Nazis develops into wildly dramatic Escapist stories; an artistic representation and repudiation of his own powerlessness. The death of Joe's brother Thomas—killed with hundreds of other refugee children by a German U-boat—leads Joe to enlist and abandon his cousin and pregnant girlfriend, Rosa Saks; another attempt at escape. During his absence, however, Joe's attention is turned to a wordless comic creation, *The Golem!*—a 2,256-page work that draws together his own story, that of the Escapist, and the golem legend.

As Joe reflects on his comic-book creations of the past, explicitly linking them to their golem predecessors, he thinks that

> the shaping of a golem . . . was a gesture of hope, offered against hope, in a time of desperation. It was the expression of a yearning that a few magic words and an artful hand

might produce something—one poor, dumb, powerful thing—exempt from the crushing strictures, from the ills, cruelties, and inevitable failures of the greater Creation. It was the voicing of a vain wish, when you got down to it, to escape. (582)

For Joe, and throughout the novel, human creativity is born of a desire to escape and to transform, here reimagining the birth of a vibrant form of popular culture, and transforming the superhero comic into a great American narrative.

Bibliography

Behlman, Lee. "The Escapist: Fantasy, Folklore, and the Pleasures of the Comic Book in Recent Jewish American Holocaust Fiction." *Shofar* 22, no. 3 (Spring 2004): 56–71.

Chabon, Michael. *The Amazing Adventures of Kavalier & Clay.* New York: Picador, 2000.

—Mary Wilson

America, America Ethan Canin (2008)

ETHAN CANIN's sixth novel is a lengthy and compelling exploration of the complex world of powerful political families in America. It chronicles the fictional story of Corey Sifter, a teenager working for the wealthy Metarey family, the most powerful family in his hometown of Saline, New York, during the 1971–72 election primaries. Liam, the head of the Metarey family, serves as campaign manager for Senator Henry Bonwiller in his bid to become the Democratic nominee for president, and the events that unfold during the campaign tell a complex and compelling tale of power, class, politics, wealth, and fatherhood.

A 50-year-old Corey narrates the story, his reminiscing prompted partly by Bonwiller's funeral in 2006. His principal audience is Trieste, a 17-year-old intern at the paper he publishes. Corey shuffles back and forth in time, describing his childhood with the Metareys, his time in preparatory school and college, and his present-day life as a husband, father, and newspaperman. In 1971, Corey's father works as a plumber at the Metarey estate, and through this connection, Liam Metarey asks Corey to help as a yard boy. The young man endears himself to the family, particularly one of Liam's daughters, and is gradually invited to join the family for dinners and outings. Corey's work ethic and reliability make him an obvious choice to assist Liam Metarey with the senator's campaign, which kicks off in late 1971 but abruptly ends in the spring of 1972. In the present day, the grown narrator recalls a flurry of campaign parties, conversations with Liam Metarey, and run-ins with reporters as he tries to piece together the events that so quickly unraveled the senator's campaign decades ago.

Corey is a quiet, contemplative narrator, returning to these events after his own daughters are grown, prompted by the realization that "all one's deeds—those of honor and those of duplicity and those of venality and those of ruin—that all one's deeds live doubly" (13). From his upbringing in a working-class family, Corey leaps classes as he enters the world of the Metarey family, attends a private preparatory school through a scholarship from the Metareys, and eventually marries into the family.

Corey is introduced to the world of wealth and power through the generosity of Liam Metarey, the son of capitalist Eoghan Metarey, a Scottish immigrant who built his controversial empire in New York from coal mines, timber yards, and usurped land in the early 1900s. The elder Metarey built the small town of Saline, and the majority of the town's men still work for the family's businesses. Despite his immense wealth, the second-generation Metarey is a down-to-earth, personable character, a man who fixes everything himself and wastes nothing. He becomes a father figure to Corey, teaching him new skills and exposing him to the world of powerful politicians.

Senator Bonwiller is presented as a political figure among the actual candidates who ran for the Democratic nomination during the 1972 primary, a man who serves as "the best friend the working men of this country have ever had" (416). He publicly vocalizes his disapproval of President Nixon and the Vietnam War, a cause that draws Liam Metarey to the campaign, as the latter's own son serves (and will eventually die) in the unpopular war. Bonwiller is a larger-than-life figure to Corey,

who is profoundly naive about the political process of the primaries and the machinations of politics in general. Liam works tirelessly to earn Bonwiller the nomination, driven both by his desire for his son to return from Vietnam and by his desire to compensate for his father's injustices to the community. However, as the campaign progresses, it is clear that like all politicians, Bonwiller is not without flaws; and finally, one cold winter night a drunken Bonwiller crashes his car, killing his passenger JoEllen Charney, the campaign aide with whom he has been having an extramarital affair. Impossible to miss are the parallels to *The Great Gatsby* and *East of Eden*, as well as to Senator Ted Kennedy's notorious 1969 Chappaquiddick car accident in which his secretary, Mary Jo Kopechne, died. Liam Metarey makes a similarly compromising moral decision when he joins in the attempt to cover up JoEllen's death, and Corey unknowingly assists him, only becoming aware of the magnitude of the situation as he contemplates it later, with the aid of age and experience: "But it wasn't until we had Andrea—she was our first—it wasn't until we had Andrea that it just broke over me. That I'd been involved with something—not that I *did* something, but that I was involved with something—something *unforgivably wrong*" (332). In the end, however, there is little understanding and no resolution for Corey.

Corey's reflections on these events with the Metareys are partly triggered by his own fatherhood; and fatherhood, in many guises, serves as an underlying theme in the book. Liam Metarey acts as a second father to Corey, and as Corey's own biological father ages he and Corey grow closer than before. Together they watch the old Metarey estate crumble and be replaced with big-box malls and gas stations, while the ancestral home becomes a diminished shadow of its former self. A related theme centers on questions of how to live morally in a corrupt world. Corey, for example, constantly reflects on whether he did the right thing for his daughters, or said the right thing to them, hoping that he has somehow provided them with the same kind of love and wisdom that he saw Liam Metarey provide for *his* daughters. Above all, almost like a morality tale in its singular vigilance, the novel warns of the dangers of unchecked power and ambition, from the exploitation in Eoghan Metarey's rags-to-riches past, to Corey's cynical scaling of the social ladder, to Bonwiller's relentless drive for success, which leads him to perform some real service to the people of New York, but ultimately, unrestrained, leads to his downfall.

Yet for all its overt morality, the multigenerational American epic offers few simple answers, instead inviting multiple readings and moral investigation on the reader's own part, while Canin's graceful touch and the tale's modest first-person narrative reveal quiet insights into human nature, and encourage both the reader's trust and her commitment to this dialogic process.

Bibliography

Canin, Ethan. *America, America.* New York: Random House, 2008.

—Meagan Kittle

American Psycho **Bret Easton Ellis** (1991)
BRET EASTON ELLIS's most famous (and infamous) novel has been praised as a masterpiece of postmodern angst and derided as misogynistic pornography. The tale centers on Patrick Bateman, a young, attractive, and wealthy financial executive living in New York City during the late 1980s, who occupies his nights away from Wall Street with gruesome murders and sex with prostitutes. Narrated in the first person and structured like a day planner, *American Psycho* satirizes the excesses and savagery latent in Reaganism and Yuppie culture.

Ellis's third novel recalls his favorite themes of youthful apathy and privileged discontent, while exploring the almost symbiotic relation between materialism and moral decay. Bateman, who first appears in Ellis's earlier novel, *The Rules of Attraction,* as a minor character, serves as a kind of cipher, an unnervingly blank symbol of white male privilege. Empty in himself, Bateman is obsessed with appearances and surfaces, emphasizing such exteriority throughout the novel by describing clothing, restaurant decor, and even business cards in excruciating detail. Despite such meticulous details, his descriptions lack any real knowledge or depth, and his flat, almost robotic narration gives the impression of simply regurgitating memorized product information from catalogues or his Zagat guide. He explains his skin regimen and exercise routine rather than his inner thoughts, while his sole, almost automatonic motivations all revolve around instant gratification and the unbridled pursuit of money, sex, and violence. Bateman's preoccupation with image and surface mirrors his own constructed facade; those around him constantly refer to him in the text as "the boy next door," and despite his role as a serial killer, he appears to be a pillar of culture, good taste, and etiquette.

Restaurants, nightclubs, and business meetings dominate the first part of the novel, but as the narrative continues Bateman becomes increasingly violent and erratic. In the end, his insatiable bloodlust offers a stinging critique of postmodern consumer society in which wealth and pleasure are valued over human life. The juxtaposition of Bateman's polite demeanor and murderous chaos aligns the novel with what literary critic Michael Silverblatt identifies as "transgressive writing," a genre concerned with the "violation" of both cultural norms and the human body. Anne H. Soukhanov enumerates its characteristic themes, including "aberrant sexual practices, mutilation, [. . .] urban violence and violence against women, drug use, and highly dysfunctional family relationships," all of which appear throughout Ellis's text. Bateman himself transgresses a myriad of cultural taboos, including rape, murder, child killing, dismemberment, necrophilia, and cannibalism. However, unlike Soukhanov's reading of transgressive literature, Bateman discovers no enlightenment "at the edge of experience" (128); yet according to Silverblatt, it is precisely this absence of enlightenment that makes Ellis's work more transgressive than other authors exploring similar themes of violence and sexuality.

The failure to acquire any awareness or understanding from his transgressions eventually identifies Bateman as a radical, and radically banal, nihilist. Toward the end of the novel he declares that "Reflection is useless, the world is senseless. Evil is its only permanence. God is not alive. Love cannot be trusted. Surface, surface, surface was all that anyone found meaning in . . . this was civilization as I saw it, colossal and jagged . . ." (375). His desensitization parallels his mental breakdown: as he loses his senses, his murders become intricately complex and increasingly gruesome.

Ellis consistently forgoes explanation of Bateman's crimes, but they appear at least partly connected to his desire for and horror of conformity. At one point he proclaims, "I . . . want . . . to . . . fit . . . in," but at the same time his transgressive behavior cries out for special recognition (237). In Bateman's murky world, however, identity is interchangeable. Throughout the novel, men are repeatedly mistaken for one another, and Bateman uses this to his advantage by impersonating numerous colleagues in order to perpetrate crimes. At the same time, he clearly calls for acknowledgment when he begins to insert violent comments into daily conversation and leaves a lengthy confession for his lawyer, but his confessions fall on deaf or indifferent ears. The anonymity and complacent conformity of postmodern urban society has transformed Bateman into a faceless monster, and his loss of identity hastens his descent into madness.

At this point both the narrative's structure and its prose become increasingly disjointed and fractured. Paragraphs commence with strange ellipses, mirroring the confusion experienced by Bateman as his sense of integral reality fades away. Absurd and surreal events are woven into his life; he watches a Cheerio being interviewed on his favorite daytime talk show and obeys an ATM that demands cat blood. As the novel progresses, Bateman refers to his daily interactions as performances and scenes; while watching television he confesses, "This is my reality. Everything outside of this is like some movie I once saw" (345). The most striking break with reality occurs when Bateman briefly slips from the first to third person: "I've been with Japanese clients . . . Patrick tries to put the cab into reverse but nothing happens" (349). Such psychotic breaks finally undermine the reliability of Bateman's own narration, and his mental instability creates ambiguity about whether he actually committed the crimes that he describes in such gory detail.

Ambiguity notwithstanding, its graphic scenes of sex and violence established *American Psycho* as a landmark of transgressive fiction and led to a controversial debate over its publication. The violence, and primarily the violence against women,

led Ellis's original publisher, Simon & Schuster, to drop the project at the last hour, and it remained without a publisher until Knopf issued it as part of its Vintage paperback series. During the debate over its publication, the National Organization for Women (NOW) led numerous protests against Ellis, his publishers, and bookstores stocking the book, while widespread animosity toward the published text led to a strong critical backlash and even death threats to its author. In one review, Roger Rosenblatt wrote, "*American Psycho* is the journal Dorian Gray would have written had he been a high school sophomore. But that is unfair to sophomores. So pointless, so themeless, so everythingless is this novel, except in stupefying details about expensive clothing, food and bath products, that were it not the most loathsome offering this season, it certainly would be the funniest."

However, much of the controversy surrounding the novel's publication night be seen as stemming from an inability or unwillingness to separate its author from its narrator. While Bateman is a misogynist, racist, and homophobe, *American Psycho* criticizes rather than praises his behavior. Ellis constructs the text as a scathing satire of masculinity in crisis, and Bateman's violence against women clearly issues from his own insecurities. Surrounded by powerful women like his fiancée, who is as successful as he, if not more so, and his mistress, who is engaged to Bateman's homosexual colleague, who in turn threatens Bateman's heterosexuality by making sexual advances, Bateman at last finds himself out of his (shallow) depth and out of control. Ellis even employs a daytime television episode entitled "Women Who Raped Men" to externalize Bateman's fears of emasculation. Bateman channels his insecurities into sadistic behavior directed at women he views as subordinates, such as his secretary and various prostitutes he picks up.

Despite, or because of such controversy surrounding its publication and representation of violence, *American Psycho* remains a prominent force in popular culture. In 2000, the debates arose again as Mary Harron released a film adaptation, which lacks the more gruesome details of Bateman's exploits but preserves the novel's inimitable tone and stinging social critique. Like Ellis, Harron experienced numerous setbacks as the studio attempted to push a new star, script, and even director onto the project. Additionally, the film survived its own censorship battle with the Motion Pictures Association of America through minor editing. Yet the result has only cemented the novel's place in popular culture. Indeed, during the film's release, Ellis published a series of e-mails written between Bateman and his psychiatrist, heightening the film's notoriety. Additionally, the novel and film inspired a loosely connected sequel, *American Psycho II: All American Girl,* in which a young survivor of Bateman's becomes a serial killer herself. The legacy of *American Psycho* remains strong today, as it is referenced constantly in popular culture's music, television, and film. Ellis extended his own connection to the story and character, featuring Bateman in his *Glamorama* (1998) and LUNAR PARK (2005).

Bibliography

Ellis, Bret Easton. *American Psycho.* New York: Vintage Books, 1991.

Rosenblatt, Roger. "Snuff This Book! Will Bret Easton Ellis Get Away with Murder?" *New York Times Book Review,* 16 December 1990, p. 3.

Silverblatt, Michael. "Shock Appeal—Who Are These Writers, and Why Do They Want to Hurt Us? The New Fiction of Transgression," *Los Angeles Times,* 1 August 1993, p. 7.

Soukhanov, Anne H. "Word Watch—Transgressive Fiction." *Atlantic Monthly* 278, no. 6 (1996): 128.

—Trae DeLellis

American Woman Susan Choi (2003)

SUSAN CHOI's second novel explores the psychology of Vietnam War–era radicalism, retelling the 1974 abduction of Patty Hearst by the Symbionese Liberation Army (SLA) through an allegory of the militant leftist cadre and its sympathizers. Rather than linearly follow Hearst's kidnapping, her conversion to her captors' ideology, and eventual participation in a bank robbery and police shootout, Choi's historical fiction details the mentality of revolutionaries already on the run from their crimes and the nation that pursues them.

American Woman begins as football player-turned-activist Rob Frazer scours upstate New York for his college friend, Jenny Shimada. Jenny has retreated to the East Coast to escape a federal investigation into her bombing of several government buildings in California. Once the two are reunited, Rob plays on Jenny's residual sympathy for antiestablishment movements and convinces her to lead three revolutionaries on the lam into hiding.

After a deadly showdown with the Los Angeles Police Department that left nine of their comrades dead, the three remaining members of The People's Liberation (TPL) go underground. Choi's fictional proxy of the SLA retains many attributes of its historical counterpart, most notable among them the resemblance the TPL's junior member, Pauline, bears to Patty Hearst. Like Hearst, Pauline is the 20-year-old daughter of a newspaper magnate, an unwitting representative of entrenched capitalist greed, when a squad of radicals abducts her from her San Francisco home. Similar to U.S. captivation with Hearst's disappearance in 1974, Pauline's abduction becomes a media event, with TPL leveraging Pauline against her wealthy family by demanding that her parents make food and financial donations to needy Californians. Following a series of ransom messages, the kidnappers record Pauline endorsing TPL's Marxist message of class revolution. For the radicals, there is no more poignant example of their righteousness than converting this upper-class "princess" to their cause. Pauline is soon fully inaugurated into TPL. However, the bulk of the group is killed in a storm of bullets and fire at a bank robbery, and only the male chauvinist Juan, his lover Yvonne, and Pauline escape with their lives.

Jenny Shimada, who like Pauline is modeled on an actual SLA constituent (Wendy Yoshimura), struggles with her own complicity in the novel's violence. Though she safeguards the trio at a bucolic (but spartan) farmhouse, mails their propaganda tapes to distant radio stations, and ultimately shuttles Pauline back to the West Coast, Jenny torturously debates the efficacy of TLP's violent methodology as well as her own legacy of destructive behavior. While *American Woman* is most certainly historical fiction, in that actual events are fictionalized in a narrative environment exclusive to the novel, Choi explodes the sequential or interlocking temporality of the genre. Instead, the narrative flow moves forward, backward, and sideways in time and space depending on the whims of Jenny or Rob (*AW*'s primary interlocutor narrators). Choi's intense, sustained examination of her characters' psyches, rather than their actions, suggests that her focus is attuned to how people understand the ramifications of violent protest rather than how they actualize it.

While many historical novelists privilege breadth over intimacy, populating their fiction with representatives of a seismic moment and allowing them to wander into significant stages, Choi resists such tendencies. All of the significant action of the novel occurs off-screen, as it were. National reaction to Pauline's exploits is mediated through newspaper and radio dispatches similar to John Dos Passos's *U.S.A. Trilogy* (though shorn of the modernist experimentation). In fact, Choi never lifts the narrative scope from its tight psychological confines, reminding readers at every turn that her novel ultimately measures American violence by its impact on consciousness and memory rather than materiality.

Perhaps because of its psychological register, *American Woman* is fraught with conflicted desires—at once a road and hideout novel. Characters are restless when stationary at the farmhouse, and static or numb when on the run, perpetually trapped in untenable tensions. Jenny's need to cloister the revolutionaries from the agencies that hunt them also atrophies The People's Liberation's subversive agenda. Not surprisingly, one of the novel's recurring themes is homelessness. Dogging police forces, nosy citizens, and the very real fear of exposure endlessly undermines Jenny's safe haven for Pauline and her cohort. After the cadre robs and murders a grocery store owner, even their corrupted continuation of their cause rouses them from their hideout and back into a nation that has no place for them.

The central interpretive issue in all accounts (fictional or historical) of Patty Hearst's abduction and subsequent absorption of radical Leftist politics is whether or not her sympathies were authentic. In other words, was Hearst's advocacy of armed revolt genuinely her own, or did the trauma of captivity prepare her to ventriloquize the doctrine of

her captors? Rather than settle on a narrow answer, Choi complicates this facile debate by extracting surprising integral features of post-1960s violent protest from Hearst/Pauline's unique situation. The result is a melancholic novel that dramatizes a nation that breeds violent revolt and yet is inured to its effects.

The first of these features is the reclamation of voice. Early in the novel, Jenny tells Rob that she will aid the troika of fugitives only if Pauline allies herself with the cause volitionally. Like much of the nation, Jenny suspects that Pauline may have been brainwashed into compliance. After the two women flee New York, Jenny implores the former socialite to "'say anything . . . as long as it's true'" (249). Juan, on the other hand, has continually belittled and silenced Pauline. Despite his egalitarian posturing, he hypocritically relegates Pauline to a subservient role in the farm community. Even after putting her through "ego reconstruction" to erase any bourgeois proclivities, Juan crudely edits Pauline's contributions to the group's archived history by omitting that he held her blindfolded in a closet. Duplicitous behavior is common to most of the men in Choi's work. Even Rob protects the trio mainly because he has arranged an exclusive book deal recounting their war on the American government.

In a fitting end to the novel, Jenny and her father visit the Japanese internment camp where he was held during World War II. Choi's departure point serves as a reminder of the United States's legacy of containing its dissidents. Jenny's epiphanic realization that perhaps the only way to protest the nation's inequities "was by simply removing oneself from the world" arrives as a wonderfully Pynchon-esque antidote to the disease of imprisonment afflicting the novel (351). Just as Pauline's abduction by TLP is a fallacious (and ultimately doomed) ideological conversion strategy, since it so closely resembles the institutional practices the group opposes in the first place, radical violence is also proven to be, at best, a dubious mechanism for remaking the nation. Fear, of revolt or retribution, Choi suggests, only engenders further suppression. At best, according to the novel's telos, revolution cannot easily rely on violent means "that might topple The System," but instead requires "a delicate process of changing individual minds" (295–296). Thus, Jenny's withdrawal from the world, and her denunciation of violence's "shock of the real," signifies a culture slowly relinquishing the gun and embracing escape as a viable dissent. Absolute disenchantment with the antiwar spirit of the Vietnam era ostensibly leaves one with few alternatives. The great irony of Choi's novel is not the singularity of Jenny's cynical, radical, yet reasoned response to the nation, but instead its typicality. She is, after all, the American woman.

Bibliography

Choi, Susan. *American Woman.* New York: HarperCollins, 2003.

—Kyle Wiggins

Ansay, A. Manette (1964–) *American novelist*

Award-winning author A. Manette Ansay was born in Michigan in 1964, and grew up in Wisconsin. She showed early promise on the piano and subsequently trained as a concert pianist, attending the Peabody Conservatory of Music. However, by the age of 21 she had to give up the pursuit because of recurring bouts of debilitating ill health, and by 23 she was in need of another outlet for her creative energies. She began writing and has since become a best-selling novelist. After her time at Peabody, she worked for awhile at the American Museum of Natural History before returning to school at the University of Maine to study anthropology. Since the 1990s, her crippling bouts of ill health have gradually stabilized, though there are still stretches in which even writing is challenging. Ansay went on to study and work at Cornell University, and then became writer in residence at Philips Exeter Academy and an assistant professor at Vanderbilt University. She has also been a Visiting Writer at Warren Wilson College and the University of the South, and spent a semester at Marquette University, Wisconsin, where she held the Women's Chair in Humanistic Studies. She has been awarded fellowships to Yaddo (1994) and to the MacDowell Colony (1991/95). She is currently a visiting professor at the University of Miami.

Ansay's novels focus on complex and even contradictory reactions to epochal events in the lives of people and communities, and to the emotions occasioned by them. She clearly draws inspiration from places, people, or experiences with which she is familiar—setting her novel RIVER ANGEL in Wisconsin, for example—and then weaves her vivid tales around them. Her narratives explore vagaries of the human condition—the need for faith, the possibility of miracles, the struggle to overcome disability, and the torment of debilitating rage, as well as the healing qualities of forgiveness and love.

Ansay's debut novel, VINEGAR HILL (1994), ostensibly concerns her grandparents and their relationship to each other as well as to Catholicism. The novel was named one of the Best Books of 1994 by the *Chicago Tribune,* and won a 1995 Friends of American Writers Prize (second place) for a book set in the Midwest. *Vinegar Hill* was also an Oprah Winfrey Book Club choice for 1999 and was made into a film for TV in 2008.

Her second novel, *Read This and Tell Me What It Says* is a collection of short stories written between 1988 and 1993. It won the Associated Writing Program's Short Fiction Series Prize for 1994, the Patterson Prize (1995), and the Great Lakes Book Award (1996), while one of its stories, "Sybil," also won the Pushcart Prize; the title story won the Nelson Algren Prize for 1992.

Anticipating the later and better known *River Angel,* Ansay's second novel, *Sister* (1996), explores profound tensions between faith and empirical experience. It won the Wisconsin Librarians' Association Banta Award and was named a Notable Book by the *New York Times.*

River Angel was published in 1998 and is set in a small town in Wisconsin where the arrival of a young boy one Christmas time and his subsequent death revive the legend of the town's apocryphal "river angel," forcing the townspeople to reconsider their complacent spirituality and uncritical assumptions. It too was a *Times* Notable Book.

Midnight Champagne (1999) is a poignant and delicately balanced study of two marriages, one beginning in hope, the other ending in despair. It became a National Book Critics Circle Award finalist.

Departing from the novel form, Ansay wrote *Limbo* (2001), a memoir covering 15 years of disability, which illustrates the capacity of the human spirit to overcome seemingly fatal obstacles. Yet it is ultimately a tale of acceptance rather than triumph, in contrast to stereotypical accounts of successful battles with disability—an attempt, as she puts it, "to write about what it was like not to triumph over anything" ("What's"). *Limbo* was a Book Sense and *Lifetime* choice.

More recently Ansay has written *Blue Water* (2006), which revolves around life on a boat, but is at the same time a searching study of the fallout when a child is killed by a drunken driver who until then had been the best friend of the child's mother.

Ansay's latest work, *Good Things I Wish You* (2009), is the story of two romantic friendships separated by time, one between Clara Schumann and Johannes Brahms, the other between Clara's present-day biographer and the man she meets during the course of her research. Throughout the narrative Ansay blends fiction with historical fact to deliver the timeless message that no matter what the period or place, love and lovers never really change.

Bibliography

Ansay, A. Manette. *River Angel.* London: Allison & Busby, 2008.

———. "What's going on with your health, anyway?" A. Manette Ansay. Available online. URL: http://www.amanetteansay.com/wordpress/limbo/what's-going-on-with-your-health-a nyway/. Accessed May 12, 2009.

—Linda Claridge Middup

Apex Hides the Hurt Colson Whitehead (2006)

COLSON WHITEHEAD's third novel is a farcical tale featuring an unnamed protagonist who ironically has the job of naming things. The novel begins as he enters Winthrop, a town he has been hired by the city council to rename. The three members on the council reflect three different viewpoints about this renaming process. Mayor Regina Goode wants the name to reflect the original one, "Freedom," which was given by former slaves who settled the area during Reconstruction. The name was changed to "Winthrop" after business magnate Sterling Winthrop started a barbed-wire factory there in the late 1800s; and Winthrop's grandson and member of the town council, Albie Winthrop, would like to keep the name as it is, even though the Winthrop barbed-wire dynasty has fallen on hard times. Lucky Aberdeen, the third council member, is a local millionaire who makes his money in computer software and wants the new name to reflect new capitalist sensibilities.

Apex Hides the Hurt satirizes contemporary America's personal and often parochial interests in linguistic choice, and does so with unflinching cynicism. The protagonist is introduced as an extreme example of a disinterested third party, a nomenclature consultant who is ultimately unknowable because he is so entrenched in the consumerist impulses of his job and the world that surrounds him. He arrives in the town with only the desire to give it a brand name that others will "buy." Increasingly, however, the reader learns that the protagonist is suffering both mentally and physically from the shallowness of this aim and of his existence in general. The backstory of the novel involves his greatest naming success: a bandage he named "Apex" that is available in a rainbow of "multicultural" colors. The bandage promises to match anyone's skin tone, or in other words, "hide the hurt." When the protagonist stubs his toe and puts one on, he is delighted that Apex does what it promises. It does not heal his hurt, however. In fact, because of his insistence on wearing the bandage, his stubbed toe becomes infected to the point where it interferes with his job of naming the town (a problem he has never had before). In this way, the name of something literally covers up a wound that needs to heal, and the bandage becomes a metaphor for the sort of easy fix that gives a temporary sense of relief and satisfaction, and then leaves things in a worse state than before.

The term "multicultural" is itself one of the prime linguistic targets of the *Apex* narrative. In general, the term connotes the achievement of social cohesion through recognizing and embracing many different cultures, and as such, it presents an alternative to America's metaphor of the melting pot, which is now generally thought to be a forced homogenization of culture where differences are melted down rather than remaining alive and distinct. While the theoretical meaning of "multicultural" describes an attempt to promote racial and social justice, critics like Jonathan Kozol believe words like "multicultural" and "diverse" are often used—like the Apex bandage—to mask harsher realities of racial segregation. Brian Barry's *Culture and Equality: An Egalitarian Critique of Multiculturalism* echoes this concern, arguing that in order to achieve social justice, people need to establish universal laws of social justice, rather than tacitly ignore problems through "a politics of difference," as multiculturalism tends to do. And as *Apex* progresses, the protagonist's seemingly depoliticized job becomes intertwined with racial concerns. As he looks through a book on the town's history, for example, he becomes uncomfortable with the writer's use of the word "colored," noting that he "kept stubbing his toe on it. As it were. Colored, Negro, Afro-American, African American . . . Every couple of years someone came up with something that got us an inch closer to the truth. Bit by bit we crept along. As if that thing we believed to be approaching actually existed" (192).

Such moments of trenchant cultural critique vie for space in the absurdist world of Whitehead's creation. Winthrop is both a caricature and an uncomfortably familiar portrait of small-town America. Whitehead himself describes the novel as concerned with "identity, history, and the adhesive bandage industry." Such a conceptual oxymoron, typical of the novel, forces readers to navigate a tricky tonal terrain, which, as is common in farce, veers widely from one exaggerated emotion to another. Even bandages are affected by this tonal shift. The protagonist learns that his bandage, first named after manufacturers Ogilvy and Myrtle, is no threat to the Johnson and Johnson brand for a host of quality-related reasons ("Ogilvy and Myrtle's Sterile Bandages," in its original form, failed to stick properly and the cotton swatch did not absorb). However, they offered the lowest prices and landed a lucrative contract with the military during World War I, which has

continued to the present day. Ogilvy and Myrtle, however, were not satisfied with these sales and wanted to break into the public sector. But instead of spending time fixing the inferior quality of their bandages, the company tried renaming them, first unsuccessfully as "Dr. Chickie's Strips," and then successfully as "Apex," the name suggested for the town by Whitehead's increasingly bewildered protagonist.

None of the characters in *Apex Hides the Hurt* is particularly likable, and the town of Winthrop is more pathetic than sympathetic. The novel resists any type of comfortable identification or easy resolution. In an *Esquire* review Anna Godbersen asserts that it "is not the most human kind of book," but concludes by noting that it is "so moving and worthwhile because it perfectly nails the tragic/comic nature of our smoothly packaged, hyper-verbal, and strangely stupid times." Though markedly different in tone from Whitehead's *The INTUITIONIST* and *John Henry Days*, there are similarities in the choice of subject matter. In a review for the *Boston Globe*, Saul Austerlitz notes that all three novels concern African-American protagonists who are "almost destroyed by an overwhelmingly white world that includes them, but never understands their history, or their pain." *Apex Hides the Hurt* is both laugh-out-loud funny and bitterly frustrated, with its protagonist representing the very corporate system that unifies the American capitalist society but never getting the chance to say anything of substance.

Though Whitehead's style is all his own, other contemporary American satires that draw attention to corporate America and racial tensions in a farcical way include Kurt Vonnegut's *Breakfast of Champions,* Ishmael Reed's *Japanese by Spring,* and Paul Beatty's *White Boy Shuffle;* while the advertising mantras near the beginning of the novel are delightfully reminiscent of Don DeLillo's *White Noise. Apex Hides the Hurt* is also available in an audio version read by the author.

Bibliography

Austerlitz, Saul. "Identity Crisis." Review of *Apex Hides the Hurt.* Boston.com. Boston Globe (February 19, 2006). Available online. URL: http://www.boston.

com/ae/books/articles/2006/03/19/identity_crisis/ ?page=2. Accessed April 30, 2008.

Barry, Brian. *Culture and Equality: An Egalitarian Critique of Multiculturalism.* Cambridge, Mass.: Harvard University Press, 2002.

Godbersen, Anna. "Smart Fiction about Stupid Times." Review of *Apex Hides the Hurt.* PowellsBooks.Blog. Available online. URL: http://www.powells.com/ review/2006_03_29. Accessed May 1, 2008.

Kozol, Jonathan. "Still Separate, Still Unequal." *Harper's* magazine, September 2005, pp. 41–55.

Whitehead, Colson. *Apex Hides the Hurt.* New York: Doubleday, 2006.

———. Biography. ColsonWhitehead.com. Available online. URL: http://www.colsonwhitehead.com/ biography.stml. Accessed April 30, 2008.

—Julie Babcock

B

Bad Haircut Tom Perrotta (1994)

Bad Haircut, TOM PERROTTA's first book, is a collection of 10 short stories told from the perspective of Buddy, a boy growing up in suburban New Jersey. The collection is subtitled "Stories of the Seventies," and it neatly spans that decade as it follows Buddy's formative experiences from the age of eight to 18 (like Perrotta, he was born in 1961). The stories' evolving portrait of Buddy presents him as both a part of and apart from his environs, as Perrotta deftly meshes the universals of the coming-of-age narrative tradition with the particulars of a specific time and place. While Buddy goes through some of the standard adolescent motions in the course of the book—he plays spin the bottle and high school football, endures driver's ed and the prom—the stories are told with a black-comic edge and preponderance of eccentric detail that elides the trappings of conventional bildungsroman. Perrotta seeks out some of the darker corners of suburbia and teenagerdom with an eye for how extraordinarily strange everyday life can be (though on occasion he makes this point a little too overtly; in one story, for example, Buddy's hometown is chosen as a "uniquely ordinary" American town to be featured on a national television morning talk show). According to the *New York Times Book Review,* we may locate the New Jersey of *Bad Haircut* "somewhere between Bruce Springsteen's 'Thunder Road' and Princeton's tennis courts;" and indeed, Buddy is bright, ostensibly from a loving family, and an outsider only by choice (he quits the football team to join a band), but the stories insist that the terrain he navigates is by no means easy, and the place he comes from has its share of casualties.

Adulthood is a sort of parallel universe of choice and regret that gradually settles into the background of the stories, which are populated with lonely uncles, cheating spouses, stepfathers, and lecherous gym teachers. In the first story, "The Wiener Man," Buddy and his Boy Scout troop (his mother is the "den mother") take a trip to a mini-mall parking lot to obtain the autograph of a company mascot dressed as a hot dog. While Buddy maneuvers within the social hierarchy of the Boy Scout ranks, assuming a middle ground between bullying boys and their nerdy target, the mascot deals with the taunts of some teenage loiterers. It turns out that the man in the costume, Mike, went to high school with Buddy's mother, and the two of them catch up in his trailer (the "Frankmobile"), where Mike tells the mother that her husband is "a lucky man" and he would like to get married but he does not "feel so young." Eight-year-old Buddy is oblivious to the wistful gravity that emerges from the grownup conversation, passing the time playing games and fantasizing about life on the road with the Wiener Man, yet his accruing empathy for the lonely adult souls that cross his path proves to be an integral part of his growth. In the final story, "Wild Kingdom," he serves at a pallbearer in the funeral for Mr. Norman, a neighborhood pariah with whom Buddy had cultivated a secret friendship despite the tacit disapproval of his parents.

The second story, "Thirteen," introduces another key theme—exploratory encounters with the opposite sex. Buddy's friend Kevin is infatuated with a pretty platinum blond named Angela, and Buddy's assistance with their courtship leads him to a playground with Angela's friend Sue, after the aforementioned game of spin the bottle turns into an exclusive make-out session between their respective friends. Outside "it was a beautiful night, the whole world at room temperature," but Buddy is not quite contented, passing time on the swings with Sue; he is still "chewing Angela's bland gum, thinking about her and Kevin." The following excerpt captures the story's mood of childhood lingering on the verge of adolescence:

> "I'm scared of going to high school," she said. "Aren't you?"
> "I'm not going yet."
> She seemed surprised. "How old are you?"
> "I'll be thirteen next week."
> "Huh," she said. "I thought you were older."
> She hopped off the swing and cartwheeled into a handstand. Her shirt came untucked, exposing a band of creamy skin.
> "Come on," she called out. "Let's go home."
> Sue walked effortlessly on her hands for an entire block, her palms slapping out a rubbery rhythm on the sidewalk. At the corner she arched forward like a Slinky and snapped into an upright position.

Although Buddy's romantic relationships become more serious in high school, they remain as baffling and unrequited. He loses his virginity to a girl in his driver's ed class who purports to have broken up with her steady boyfriend but flaunts an engagement ring the next time Buddy runs into her. In a motel room after the prom, Buddy and his date, Sharon, end up enjoying a platonic ride on the coin-operated vibrating bed; she has just confessed to him that she is a lesbian.

Throughout the stories, older working-class boys, acquaintances of Buddy's, highlight pubescent confusion's dangerous proximity to real violence, and the suggestive but generally morally upright Buddy wanders into some troubling sce-

narios. In "Race Riot," for example, he ends up in a makeshift gang gathered for a "rumble" in the parking lot of a Little League field, set to seek out the black kids who had encroached on their territory at a teen dance. Buddy has joined in under the sway of both curiosity and conformity, but soon finds himself among "psychos" to whom urban legend attributes such acts as the biting off of another boy's nipple in a fight and burying a cat to the neck and then running it over with a lawnmower. Though the full-scale riot never materializes, Buddy ends up tackling a lone black boy and stealing his basketball. In "Snowman," Buddy is sucker-punched by an older boy from a wealthier neighborhood, and then half-unwittingly becomes party to a manhunt for the boy organized by Andy Zirko, a former classmate who has grown angry and menacing since Buddy last saw him. The boys break into a house they mistakenly believe belongs to Buddy's attacker, and Zirko, brandishing a crowbar, proceeds to harass a woman they take for the enemy's mother. Buddy feels "like [he'd] stepped outside the boundaries of my own life and would never be allowed back in." But ultimately these regrettable excursions help Buddy define for himself where those boundaries should be.

Perrotta positions himself as an author in "the plain language American tradition," and his economical prose, marked by a preference for dialogue over protracted description, has garnered comparisons to Raymond Carver. Tobias Wolff, whom Perrotta studied under at Syracuse University, notes a kinship between *Bad Haircut* and Philip Roth's debut *Goodbye, Columbus*. Perrotta had difficulty finding a publisher for *Bad Haircut*, but he claims that "the timing was perfect" for his stories in 1994, amidst "the first wave of 70s anti-nostalgia" in popular culture, as exemplified by Richard Linklater's film *Dazed and Confused* of the previous year. Interest in Perrotta's work surged after a screenplay adapted from his then unpublished novel *Election*, which the author describes as "an allegorical version of the 1992 presidential election," was optioned by the director Alexander Payne in 1996. The attention helped to get the novel published, and the critical success of the film version, released by MTV Films in 1999 and starring Matthew Broderick and Reese Witherspoon, not only raised the profile of Perotta's fiction but led to an ongoing relationship with Hollywood. Perrotta was nominated for an Academy Award in 2007 for cowriting a screenplay adapted from his novel *Little Children* with director Todd Field.

Bibliography

Arrivistepress.com. "Q + A with Tom Perrotta: *Bad Haircut,* Making Movies, and American Literature Today." Available online. URL: http://www.arrivistepress.com/rmillerperrottainterview0703.shtml. Accessed May 10, 2009.

Perrotta, Tom. *Bad Haircut.* New York: Berkley Books, 1997.

—Chris Kamerbeek

Bag Men Mark Costello (John Flood) (1997)

Bag Men was the debut novel of East Coast law professor and novelist MARK COSTELLO. Published while Costello was employed as a federal prosecutor, *Bag Men*'s plot—official corruption in the world of a 1960s lawman—was deemed by the author to be in danger of being read as an exposé, as "a prosecutor blow[ing] the lid off" (Birnbaum). Costello thus released the novel under the pseudonym "John Flood," until the publication of his first novel after leaving federal employment (the award-nominated BIG IF, 2002) allowed him to acknowledge authorship of his earlier work.

There are three main narrative strands in *Bag Men,* set in Boston in early 1965 (although, Costello admits, "a few small liberties [are] taken with . . . certain dates in 1965. The rest is one big liberty" [title verso]). These involve, variously, orders from the Second Vatican Council of the Roman Catholic Church (1962–65) to hold mass in English rather than Latin, the emergence of a new drug among Bostonian junkies, and secret experiments at a military psychotherapy unit in New Hampshire. A series of unexplained murders and thefts link these three themes, and the narrative is presented from the perspective of three men, on both sides of the law: Ray Dunn, a Boston federal prosecutor from an Irish Catholic background; Manny Manning, a sergeant in the narcotics division of the Boston Police

Department (BPD); and Joe Mears, a survivor of the New Hampshire experiments.

It is not simply that the main characters link these narratives, however. There are connections drawn between the different aspects of the narrative—on both sides of the "law and order" divide—that provide a forceful sense of narrative unity. Manny Manning's thoughts on the subject of police patrol work are exemplary:

Patrol did to you what the dealers did to bags: diluted you and made you less, sold you after cutting you both ways. (47)

The "bags" in this instance are, of course, containers for drugs, and by suggesting a connection between illegal narcotics and their legal pursuers ("narcs"), Costello emphasises the thin line dividing different sides of the law. This is further illustrated by Manny's exchange with Ray Dunn, as Manning justifies his pursuit of narcotics offenders:

"Now I'm close, and I got to have it, whatever the cost."
"You sound like a junkie."
"Good narcs always do." (115)

An alternative meaning of "bag," however, reflected in the title of the work, is in the idea of a "bag man," a corrupt policeman who takes bribes and "run[s] bag from the local bookies" (41). Dominating the narrative of Ray Dunn is the fact that his father, Tim, a cop in the BPD, was arrested 10 years previously for his role as one of a group of "bag men." Ray's marriage—which a reader sees in 1965, as it grinds to a halt with the blossoming of an affair between Ray's wife, Mary-Pat, and the liberal entrepreneur Win Babcock—has been haunted by his fixation on the misdeeds of his father, something that Ray feels he cannot escape: "Your da [hangs] all over you, his good and his bad" (27). It is not just Ray who feels this way: when a friend discusses Ray's campaign for D.A., he is not particularly confident of success: "'[t]hey'll kill Ray with rumors. I mean, here's this guy talking about cleaning house, but his da was a bag man, and so's he'" (103).

Costello's work exhibits a contemporary development of the traditional detective story. Like James Ellroy, Costello uses a historical setting to consciously harken back to a different era, that of crime writers Dashiell Hammett (1894–1961) and Raymond Chandler (1888–1959). Ray Dunn's occupation links him with the straight-talking Philip Marlowe, Chandler's famous protagonist, who himself once worked for a district attorney (and was, significantly, "fired. For insubordination" [Chandler, 15]). Marlowe subsequently works as a private investigator, a position that blurs the boundaries between the legal, the extralegal and the illegal. Like Ellroy, however, Costello abandons the tale of the solo P.I., replacing it with a complex narrative involving Dunn, Manning, and Mears, who are, in addition, individually more complex than the Sam Spades and Philip Marlowes of the fictional detective world. Manning, for instance, used to be a "bag man" with Ray's father, Tim, and it was information provided by Manny in 1955—as an FBI informant, "spilling [his] guts to the Department of Justice" (43)—that led directly to Tim's arrest, breakdown, and death in a nursing home before he could be brought to trial. This troubled relationship between the Manning and Dunn families hangs over the tale, underlining Peter Messent's description of the crime genre as "a form that defends the established social system even as it reveals widespread corruption both in leading citizens and in public officialdom" (8).

Costello's subtle character development is indicated in his opening descriptions of Ray: like many a detective-story protagonist (from Arthur Conan Doyle's late-Victorian sleuth Sherlock Holmes to Sara Paretsky's contemporary private investigator V. I. Warshawski), Ray is a self-involved loner; and it is no surprise, then, that his marriage to Mary-Pat is disintegrating. What is interesting, however, is the perceptiveness shown by Ray, who understands that his marriage is over, knows why, and yet cannot voice his frustrations:

> Ray saw a second wineglass under the coffee table. "Company come?"
> "The Hunger Group was over. . . . Win stayed behind and helped clean up."

> *And sat on the carpet, because that's where his glass is, and you sat with him, because nobody sits on the carpet alone.* (19)

Later, linking his personal life to the narrative in which he becomes embroiled, Ray provides a sharp analysis of a lawyer, Whitaker, who takes a bribe to shut down a murder investigation and flees the state:

> Ray . . . was thinking about a prosecutor who sold out, and couldn't live it down. . . . He was thinking about Whitaker fleeing his self-disgust from Concord to Warsaw to here [a native reservation]. That was Whitaker's route and, later, Ray's. That was what happened to tainted lawmen. (151)

With his cynical attitude to the world around him, Ray's story presents a cautionary tale about the ease with which people from all walks of life—the church, the police, the caring professions—can get dragged into corruption. Ray's job, throughout the book, is summed up finally in the actions of his brother Biff—a beat cop left permanently mentally unstable by events involving the ex-patient Joe Mears—who passes the time filling secondhand photo albums with newspaper clippings: "Biff called the photo albums 'books,' a Narco term for surveillance files kept on long-term targets. . . . Ray figured Biff was carefully building a case against reality" (261).

Given his protagonist's attitude towards the legal world, it is perhaps no wonder that Costello decided to turn his back on prosecution. While his second novel, *Big If* (2002), was published after he had left his job, however, it is not far removed from *Bag Men*: *Big If* still focuses on the world of crime, largely through the eyes of secret service operatives guarding high-level politicians, in what one reviewer has described as "a novel about the folly of second-guessing the unexpected" (Miller). While the structure and content of the two novels are different, they present a unified attitude toward the contemporary legal world with which Costello—as a law professor—still deals; and this attitude toward issues of class and criminalization was established with his first published work, written before either novel, *Signifying Rappers: Rap and Race in the Urban Present* (1990), coauthored with DAVID FOSTER WALLACE.

Bibliography

Chandler, Raymond. *The Big Sleep.* New York: Knopf, 1939.

Costello, Mark (John Flood). *Bag Men.* New York: W. W. Norton, 1997.

———. "Interview with Mark Costello." By Robert Birnbaum. Identitytheory.com. Available online. URL: http://www.identitytheory.com/people/birnbaum56.html. Accessed May 10, 2009.

Messent, Peter. *Criminal Proceedings: The Contemporary American Crime Novel.* London and Chicago: Pluto Press, 1997.

Miller, Laura. Review of *Big If,* Salon.com. Available online. URL: http://dir.salon.com/story/books/review/2002/06/20/costello/index.html. Accessed May 10, 2009.

—Sam Knowles

Barker, Nicola (1966–) *British novelist, short story writer*

Nicola Barker is the author of an acclaimed and evolving body of literature, which includes seven novels and three collections of short stories. Barker's writing career was established in 1993 when she was awarded both the David Higham Prize and the PEN/Macmillan Silver Pen Award for the darkly humorous collection *Love Your Enemies.* In 1994 she published her first novel, *Reversed Forecast,* followed by *Small Holdings* (1995), both short and explosive narratives featuring quirky characters and off-kilter relationships in various corners of London. Barker's next novel was *Heading Inland* (1996), winner of the Mail on Sunday/John Llewellyn Rhys Prize. She was then awarded the International IMPAC Dublin Literary Award in 2000 for *Wide Open,* a touching and comical novel about the inhabitants of a small British seaside community attempting to come to terms with murky affairs from the past. She went on to publish *Five Miles from Outer Hope* (2000), *Behindlings* (2002), and a third collection of short stories, *The Three Button Trick* (2003), a volume that unites some of the author's more recent and earlier works. In 2003 Barker was nominated by *Granta* magazine as one of the 20 "best of the young British novelists." More recent works by Barker include *CLEAR: A TRANSPARENT NOVEL* (2004), set near London's Tower Bridge during illusion artist David Blaine's 44-day starvation stunt; and *Darkmans* (2007), a lengthy, anarchically constructed work featuring multiple characters and Edwardian historical resonances. *Darkmans* was short-listed for both the Man Booker and Ondaatje prizes. Two of Barker's short stories were adapted to film for British television: "Dual Balls" and "Symbiosis."

Nicola Barker was born in the city of Ely, Cambridgeshire, in 1966, although she lived in South Africa for part of her youth. She is a graduate of King's College, Cambridge, where she read English and philosophy, a course of study that she claims made her "socially useless" (Granta, 1). Following her studies she moved to London where she held positions in a bakery, a bookshop, and the Queen Elizabeth Hospital for Sick Children in Hackney, before dedicating her career entirely to writing. Today she shares her central London apartment with her two Boston terriers.

A comic and cynical writer, Barker paints a disconcerting yet convincing portrait of contemporary Britain. Each of her novels invites the reader into a peculiar pocket of British society, often nestled within dismal or mundane locations in London or in little-known provincial towns. *Darkmans,* Barker's most recent work, takes place in Ashford, Kent, whose sole claim to fame is the fact that its few heritage edifices were bulldozed to make room for the construction of the channel tunnel. As plain as such a location may appear on the surface, the novelist decorates this setting with plenty of colorful characters and absurd occurrences. She even gives Ashford a strange historical twist: the town is haunted by the ghost of John Scogin, Edward IV's court jester. Barker explains that the process of selecting locations for her novels is akin to that of a cancer invading a body: "I think: there's just enough going on here to be interesting but not enough to be overwhelming [. . .] I can re-inhabit this area, I can make things happen here, you feel a sense of possibility. And then I move all my characters in" (*Observer,* 1).

Barker's protagonists are often idiosyncratic antiheroes, dwelling on the margins of society. Daniel Beede from *Darkmans* is a hospital laundry supervisor, tortured by the threat of his hometown's erasure from history. *Reversed Forecast* features an eclectic assortment of down-and-out Londoners. Wesley, the "small-brained, big-jawed" (99) protagonist from *Behindlings,* is portrayed as a social outcast or misfit but is, in fact, pursued by a group of fans or "behindlings" after playing the role of the genius behind a nationwide treasure hunt organized by a confection company. Barker also tends to cast plentiful secondary characters who entertain knotty or ambiguous relationships with her protagonists. Rather than mothers, sisters, best friends, or lovers, she opts for ex-girlfriends, mistresses, ex-doctors, brothers-in-law, and these often display unexpected eccentricities. Sylvia, a friend of the protagonist from *Small Holdings,* is a magnet for all species of birds, despite being allergic to them. Aphra, the half-girlfriend of Adair from *Clear,* has an unusual obsession with footwear and owns over 200 pairs of vintage shoes. Although always intriguing, these individuals are often somewhat disagreeable. One example is Dina Broad, the mother of the ex-girlfriend of one of the protagonists from *Darkmans,* a crude and immensely overweight woman who is described as "Jabba the Hut with a womb, chronic asthma and a council flat" (107). These atypical personalities and imperfect relationships contribute to the absurdity of Barker's representation of intersubjective relations and contemporary life in Britain. Barker views her style of character development as an integral part of her approach to writing: "There are writers who exist to confirm people's feelings about themselves and to make them feel comforted or not alone [. . .] That's the opposite to what I do. I'm presenting people with unacceptable or hostile characters, and my desire is to make them understood" (*Observer* 1).

A lover of language, Nicola Barker often foregrounds her lexical imagination rather than concentrating on purely diegetic concerns. With *Darkmans* and *Behindlings* being the most noteworthy examples, many of Barker's novels contain minimal traces of a discernible plot. The narrative events are often subjugated to her more primary interest in decor and tone, and these atmospheric aspects are nourished by the novelist's heavy exploitation of syntactical strategies, punctuation, parentheses, italics, bold type, and formatting in order to enhance dialogue or emphasize intonation. For example, both *Darkmans* and *Clear* contain frequent italicized asides that convey the narrator's inner thoughts and impressions, and these phrases often function as appendices to the primary description and dialogue, expressing the true feelings and opinions of a given character, which often breach collective codes of communication. Another defining feature of Barker's writing style is her passion for adjectives and adverbs; without appearing wordy or long-winded, she often manages to squeeze a wealth of evocative information into a single sentence. She is also known for her outlandish metaphors and ribald sense of humor.

The lack of a linear plot in Barker's writing does not mean, however, that there are few narrative events. On the contrary, Barker's novels are bubbling with comical and chaotic occurrences that never seem to come to any resolution, thus presenting the reader with a vision of the contemporary world as rather opaque, tessellated, and disorienting. Instead of unraveling in a linear fashion, her plots tend to jolt back and forth, often veering off into dead ends.

Peppered with references to Nietzsche, Wittgenstein, and Kafka as well as historical events, Barker's writing has a scholarly quality. Yet she also lends an attentive ear to the messages that circulate in the media and popular culture. She does not hesitate to fully engage with mainstream trends, consumer society, political debates and scandals, youth fashion, media events. This tendency is exemplified by *Clear,* which contains numerous allusions to popular music, and deals directly with a current event in London. Barker wrote the novel as an enraged reaction to the denunciation in the British press of David Blaine's public self-starvation stunt, *Above the Below.*

Barker's digressive plotlines and the proliferation of absurd happenings and characters in her writing recall such postmodern epics as Thomas Pynchon's *Gravity's Rainbow,* while the depth of development in her characters gives her a style all her own. By dedicating her oeuvre to the exploration of relationships and the theme of marginality in the contemporary world, Nicola Barker is a strong narrative voice for modern society, but one that unsettles rather than reassures. In an entertaining and comical way, Barker presents the reader with a fictional world where identities, information, and symbolism thrive without anyone being sure what it all means.

Bibliography

Barker, Nicola. *Behindlings.* London: Flamingo, 2002.

———. *Clear: A Transparent Novel.* London: Fourth Estate, 2004.

———. *Darkmans.* London: Fourth Estate, 2007.

———. *Five Miles from Outer Hope.* London: Faber & Faber, 2000.

———. *Heading Inland.* London: Faber & Faber, 1996.

———. *Love Your Enemies.* London: Faber & Faber, 1993.

———. *Reversed Forecast.* London: Faber & Faber, 1994.

———. *Small Holdings.* London: Faber & Faber, 1995.

———. *The Three Button Trick.* London: Flamingo, 2003.

———. *Wide Open.* London: Faber & Faber, 1998.

Clark, Alex. "I won't make you feel better." Guardian Unlimited (29 April 2007). Available online. URL: http://www.guardian.co.uk/books/2007/apr/29/fiction.features3. Accessed May 12, 2009.

"Granta Magazine Contributors." Winter 2008. Granta Magazine. Available online. URL: http://www.granta.com/Contributors/Nicola-Barker. Accessed May 11, 2009.

—Daisy Connon

***Beasts of No Nation* Uzodinma Iweala** (2005)

UZODINMA IWEALA's *Beasts of No Nation* is the fictional memoir of Agu, a child soldier in an unidentified, war-torn African country. As the title implies, Agu's narrative chronicles both the intensely personal process of dehumanization engendered by civil war violence, and some of the larger-scale political fallout from national disunion. Thus, the novel's lack of geographic specificity underscores the literal and psychological no-man's-land Agu inhabits, contemplates, and articulates. Recounted primarily in the present progressive tense ("It is starting like this," he confides in the opening sentence), Agu's story unfolds with an intriguing series of nonlinear fits and starts.

The academically precocious son of a school-teacher, Agu begins life comfortably and auspiciously—scion of a respected family, teacher's pet, athletic standout, and aspiring doctor (or perhaps engineer). But his idyllic childhood ends abruptly with the onset of civil warfare, and prepubescent Agu can only watch in horror as his mother and sister are whisked away by UN aid workers, as his father and other men are murdered by marauding soldiers, and as his town goes up in flames. Agu either does not remember or chooses not to tell the story of his escape, but he picks up his tale at the point when he is discovered by and conscripted into a ragtag rebel militia led by a man known only as the "Commandant." Brutal, charismatic, and increasingly unhinged, the Commandant rules his corps with a capricious mixture of affection and cruelty, transforming them into ragged parodies of soldiers, initiating them into the arts of raping and pillaging, and sodomizing Agu and his only friend, Strika, by night. As his life becomes increasingly nightmarish, Agu attempts to preserve his humanity and justify his conduct by repeating childhood prayers and Sunday school stories. Recalling yarns about David's heroic, military violence and Job's noble suffering, Agu feverishly insists

> I am not bad boy. I am not bad boy. I am soldier and soldier is not bad if he is killing. I am telling this to myself because soldier is supposed to be killing, killing, killing. So if I am killing, then I am only doing what is right. I am singing song to myself because I am bad boy. . . . So I am singing,
>
> *Soldier Soldier*
> *Kill Kill Kill*
> *That is how you live.*
> *That is how you die.* (23)

Fueled by the Commandant's heady mixture of psychotropic drugs and gunpowder, Agu begins to take a bestial pleasure in killing, referring to himself, in these moments, as "a hungry dog," to whom each victim "is looking like one kind of animal, no more human . . . and smelling like chicken or goat, or cow" (44, 45). Nevertheless, by novel's end, Agu has recovered his sense of self sufficiently to tell his tale in all its complexity, confiding in a social worker that "if I am telling this to you, it will be making you to think that I am some sort of beast or devil . . . I am all of this thing, but I am also having mother once, and she is loving me" (142).

While dehumanization is the novel's most central concern, *Beasts* also plays fairly conspicuously with the politics of uniformity as they relate to both national (dis)union and to individual belonging/identity formation. In Agu's childlike consciousness, this issue emerges each time he rhapsodizes about sporting a uniform, first as a student, then as a soldier. From the moment he sets foot inside a schoolroom, Agu is acutely aware of the sense of belonging that uniforms confer, and longs for the day when he, too, can "[be] looking the same" (27). Once he joins the Commandant's regiment, malnutrition becomes its own kind of macabre uniform, mottling the boy soldiers' skin "just like camouflage dress everybody is wearing" (36). But when the Commandant harangues his troops for "not acting like real soldier," Agu rebels inwardly:

> We are not even looking like real soldier. There are almost one hundred and twenty of us standing at attention, but none of us is even wearing the same dress. Some of us is wearing green camouflage like real soldier are doing, but our own is just fulling with hole and having thread just blowing this way and that in the wind . . . Sometimes I am thinking, if army is always having one uniform for its soldier to wear, and we are not all wearing the same uniform, then how can we be army. And if army is made of soldier and we are not army, then how can we be real soldier. This is why I am not knowing why Commandant is always so angry with us. (34–35)

This visible slippage gives Agu the tools to begin questioning the Commandant's rhetoric of belonging, and to unmask homogeneity as a fragile con-struction. Thus, as his country falls to pieces around him, Agu's story exposes one final beast: the chimera of group identity.

While critics may be tempted to compare this work to other acts of novelistic African autobiography (Bessie Head's *A Question of Power* or Nega Mezlekia's *Notes from the Hyena's Belly*), and perhaps even to more straightforward memoirs by child soldiers (Ishmael Beah's *A Long Way Gone: Memoirs of a Boy Soldier* or China Keitetsi's *Child Soldier*), Iweala himself has taken pains to emphasize that his book is essentially well-researched fictional realism (Birnbaum). Thus, the novel might be more profitably compared to Emmanuel Dongala's *Johnny Mad Dog* (2002) or DAVE EGGERS'S WHAT IS THE WHAT: THE AUTOBIOGRAPHY OF VALENTINO ACHAK DENG (2006), works that are, like Agu's narrative, poetically rendered composites of multinational survivor stories and witness testimonies.

Bibliography

Birnbaum, Robert. "Uzodinma Iweala." The Morning News (9 March 2006). Available online. URL: http://www.themorningnews.org/archives/birnbaum_v/uzodinma_iweala.php. Accessed January 7, 2008.

Iweala, Uzodinma. *Beasts of No Nation*. New York: HarperCollins, 2005.

—Heidi LaVine

Bel Canto Ann Patchett (2001)

ANN PATCHETT's fourth novel is a self-consciously imaginative fictionalization of the December 1996 takeover of the Japanese ambassador's residence in Peru by members of the Túpac Amaru Revolutionary Movement. The event occurred during a gala celebration of Japanese emperor Akihito's 63rd birthday, causing a four-month standoff during which 72 guests were taken hostage. The standoff ended when government forces stormed the house in April 1997, causing the deaths of two government commandos, one hostage, and all 14 rebels. Unlike traditional historical fiction, Patchett's retelling does not derive its characterizations from biographical facts or the social-historical conditions of the actual event. Instead, her diverse and memorable characters are defined largely by elements of their natures that transcend the influences of their widely varied biographies. As months pass, acts of beauty, love, and understanding expose the superficiality of the characters' lives and concerns outside their captivity. As a result, Patchett fashions the hostage crisis as a process of liberation that affirms the transcendent value of art against the process of history, to which the captives are forced to return when they are violently freed at the novel's conclusion.

Like Patchett's first two novels, *The PATRON SAINT OF LIARS* (1992) and *Taft* (1994), *Bel Canto* creates a willfully imagined and fully realized world of its own. However, unlike her earlier novels, Patchett's narrative of the hostage crisis does not take place primarily in the mind of a protagonist contemplating a traumatic experience. Instead, Patchett focuses her attention on creatively retelling an actual historical event, thereby exploring the possibilities of imagination in historical circumstances dominated by insularity, violence, and global capitalism. *Bel Canto* begins as rebels from La Familia de Martin Suarez—three generals and a band of teenage soldiers—storm the house of the vice president during "a glowing birthday dinner, replete with an opera star," for Katsume Hosokawa, chairman of the Nansei Corporation (3). Though the takeover and subsequent release of all but the most strategically valuable hostages conforms closely to standards of novelistic verisimilitude, the seemingly magical extinguishment of the candles on the guests' tables, along with the room lights, at the onset of the takeover, hints that the events of the impending narrative will test the limits of realism.

The hostages' initial response to their situation is a mixture of anger and guilt. Both the vice president and Mr. Hosokawa obsessively contemplate their own complicity in arranging the party that resulted in the hostage takeover. Opera singer Roxane Coss expresses anger with herself and her manager for agreeing to perform outside of her typical venues in the United States and Western Europe. However, an initial and tragic act of love prefigures both the characters' and the novel's exploration of the variety of love and beauty in everyday life.

From the moment of the takeover, Roxane Coss's accompanist Christopf shields the body of the world's most famous soprano with his own. Despite an ever-worsening illness, Christopf, who professed his love during the flight to the concert, elects to stay in captivity with Roxane, even after the terrorists agree to release any sick hostages. It is only after his death in a diabetic coma that Roxane realizes, "He had chosen to stay with her rather than ask for the insulin that could save his life" (82).

In the wake of the accompanist's death, the events in the characters' daily lives establish relationships that transcend the boundaries of language and culture, and even the distinction between hostage and captor. Vice President Ruben Iglesias and French hostage Simon Thibault are united in their attempt to cook the raw food supplied by the government to feed the captives. Roxane's daily performances during her captivity lead to the emergence of a new accompanist, Tetsuya Kato, a lifelong pianist who had never displayed his remarkable talent in public before. Mr. Hosokawa plays seemingly interminable rounds of chess with General Benjamin, a rebel leader. Mr. Hosokawa's translator, Gen Watanabe, uses his vast knowledge of languages to translate tirelessly for each member of the group, and clergyman Father Arguedas performs religious services and gives spiritual counsel to both hostages and captors. The narrative also traces the ways in which these adult characters pass on the shape of these relationships to the teenagers in the rebel army, as the young soldiers themselves demonstrate aptitudes for cooking, singing, chess, languages, and prayer during the course of the occupation. Throughout the narrative, Patchett is careful to point out the ways in which each of these practices transcends the limitations of speech, allowing characters who are unable to communicate linguistically to share a set of common interests that lie more deeply in their natures.

This collapse of cultural and linguistic boundaries as the characters share personally meaningful experiences leads to the emergence of real love between numerous characters. Mr. Hosokawa, who "believed that life, true life, was stored in music," begins a relationship with Roxane Coss (5). Gen and Carmen, a young terrorist, fall in love during sessions in which Gen teaches her to read and write. Though these relationships begin surreptitiously, they eventually become obvious to both the captives and captors, who do little to constrain their development. It is important to note that Patchett does not restrict love to relationships between captives, as Simon Thibault's love for his wife, Edith—released from captivity early in the novel—persists as strongly as those between other characters. In addition to romantic love, Patchett explores the emergence of familial love as well. Roxane becomes a willing teacher of Cesar, a young rebel, when he demonstrates a remarkable facility for opera singing. Vice President Iglesias envisions himself adopting Ishmael, the youngest terrorist soldier, after the standoff ends. By far the most dramatic act of familial love occurs at the end of the novel when, as government forces storm the house to free the hostages, Mr. Hosokawa shields Carmen's body from gunfire with his own, an act that both fails to prevent her death and results in his own. At the conclusion of the novel, both Roxane and Vice President Iglesias are left cradling the bodies of the terrorist soldiers they imaginatively adopted during the course of their captivity.

In its breakdown of the seemingly insurmountable boundaries between political and economic leaders and country rebels, through the emergence of shared interests and experiences, *Bel Canto* stands as a stunning defense of the transformative power of art and the imagination. In an appendix to the novel, Patchett declares that "CNN is not enough to live on," and describes opera as "an enormous, passionate, melodramatic affair that puts the business of our lives into perspective." "While that world may be as fraught with heartache as our own," she says, "it is infinitely more gorgeous." In Patchett's novel, symbols of time are repeatedly destroyed as the aesthetic events that take place during the occupation free both captives and captors from the concerns of history that consumed their quotidian lives prior to the standoff. However, Patchett does not simply celebrate the aesthetic as an escape from the historical narrative told by CNN. She repeatedly emphasizes the potential for acts of real beauty and understanding to overcome all types of boundaries between individuals. As the novel's final juxtaposition of captives and

rebel soldiers suggests, playing together in the sun at the moment of the attack by government forces, cultivation of the aesthetic has the potential to serve as an antidote to the institutionalized violence that ends the standoff. In this way, Patchett's novel stands as a dramatic call for reflection on the remark made by General Benjamin near the end of the novel, "It makes you wonder. All the brilliant things we might have done with our lives if we'd only suspected we knew how" (300).

Bibliography
Patchett, Ann. *Bel Canto*. 2001. New York: Perennial, 2005.
———. *The Patron Saint of Liars*. 1992. New York: Perennial, 2003.
———. *Taft*. 1994. New York: Perennial, 2003.

—Ryan Wepler

Berne, Suzanne (1961–) *American novelist and short story writer*

Suzanne Berne has written three novels that explore familial relationships in middle-class America: A CRIME IN THE NEIGHBORHOOD (1997), A *Perfect Arrangement* (2001), and *The Ghost at the Table* (2006). She won the Orange Prize for fiction (U.K.) in 1997 for her debut, which was also selected as a *New York Times* Notable Book. Berne has published in *Ms.* magazine, and regularly contributes as a book reviewer to both the *New York Times* and *The New Yorker*.

She was born in Washington, D.C., and grew up in northern Virginia and the D.C. area. She graduated from Wesleyan University and attended the Iowa Writers' Workshop, then received a fellowship from the National Endowment for the Arts to complete her first novel. She has taught at Harvard University, Wellesley College and the Radcliffe Seminars, and currently teaches creative writing at Boston College, living outside Boston with her husband and two daughters.

In addition to being an Orange Prize winner and *New York Times* Notable Book, Berne's first novel—*A Crime in the Neighborhood*—was also a finalist for both the Edgar Allan Poe and *Los Angeles Times* awards for first fiction. The novel depicts what happens in 1972 to an idyllic middle-class neighborhood after a young boy is found molested and murdered. The narrator is precocious 10-year-old Marsha Eberhardt, whose parents are getting divorced because of her father's affair with her mother's younger sister. Marsha becomes obsessed with gathering evidence about both Boyd Ellison's murder and the Watergate scandal, another profoundly destabilizing event at the time. As an adult, Marsha reflects upon that pivotal summer, 25 years later. While the tale is compelling, the reader cannot help but question the veracity of Marsha's narration as she continually relates her fantasies as true events, and lies to herself, her family, neighbors, and police. The novel explores what happens when what was once the bedrock of one's life—a stable loving home, a safe neighborhood, and a trustworthy government—is shaken to the core by betrayal.

Berne's second novel, *A Perfect Arrangement*, again describes a supposedly idyllic suburban life, only to reveal its many faults and inconsistencies. Mirella Cook-Goldman and her husband, Howard, live in a quaint, middle-class New England town with their two children, Pearl and Jacob. While at first glance the family seems to be living the American dream, quickly and quietly cracks begin to show: Howard resents Mirella's long hours at the office, Mirella feels disconnected from her family, Pearl throws temper-tantrums, and Jacob may be developmentally disabled. The family hopes their problems will disappear with the hiring of their new nanny, Randi, who seems perfect, managing the family and home with boundless energy. But again, nothing is as it seems. Despite the characters sometimes feeling like stereotypes, Berne here continues her examination of familial life in suburban America with accuracy and authenticity; but the novel was not as well received as her first, partly owing, perhaps, to the host of other nanny stories published at the time.

The Ghost at the Table, Berne's latest novel, depicts a dysfunctional family holiday. The narrator, Cynthia Fiske, a San Francisco–based author, accepts her sister Frances's invitation to spend Thanksgiving with her in Concord, Massachusetts, where the sisters immediately resume their argument about the night their terminally ill mother

died, and whether their father in fact murdered her. The tension between them is heightened enormously by the presence of that father, who is now 82 years old and disabled after suffering a stroke. While they make a show of reconciliation, the shared trauma infuses their dialogue with deep resentment and passive-aggressive hostility. In addition, the novel is filled with concrete metaphors of dysfunctionality, including clear parallels between the sisters and the book Cynthia is writing about Mark Twain from his daughters' points of view. Berne's exploration of a familiar tale, told through an unreliable narrator, thus takes on new life. Her vivid characterization and well-articulated conflicts help the reader see through all pretense, into the real and disturbing heart of the tale, and the novel was well received by critics.

Suzanne Berne's work has been described as gothic by some, although it is admitted that the category does not truly reflect her style, as "there is no enthusiastic and deliberate sniffing of rot" (Carey) but instead "the tinny laughter of a sitcom" (Leone). Critics have also compared Berne to Joyce Carol Oates in her witty and compelling exploration of morally ambiguous characters (Leone), to Flannery O'Connor in her rather dark and intimate portraits of the American family (Carey, Pritchard), and to Shirley Jackson in her investigation of the often hidden conflicts in idyllic middle-class American life (Steinberg).

Berne is currently at work on her first collection of short stories.

Bibliography

Berne, Suzanne. *A Crime in the Neighborhood*. New York: Henry Holt, 1997.

———. *The Ghost at the Table*. Chapel Hill, N.C.: Algonquin Books, 2006.

———. *A Perfect Arrangement*. Chapel Hill, N.C.: Algonquin Books, 2001.

Carey, Jacqueline. Review of *A Crime in the Neighborhood*, New York Times Book Review (July 20, 1997). Available online. URL: http://www.nytimes.com/books/97/07/20/home/contents.html. Accessed July 30, 2008.

Leone, Michael. Review of *The Ghost at the Table*, SFGate Book Review (December 31, 2006). Available online. URL: http://www.sfgate.com/cgi-bin/

article/article?f=/c/a/2006/12/31/RVGJRN3U7R1.
DTL. Accessed July 30, 2008.

Pritchard, William. "Actual Fiction," *Hudson Review* 50
(Winter 1998): 656–664.

Steinberg, Sybil S. Review of *A Crime in the Neighborhood*, *Publishers Weekly* (March 31, 1997), p. 59.

—Amy Parziale

Big If Mark Costello (2002)

Nominated for the National Book Award in 2002,
MARK COSTELLO's second novel develops a complex and intensive portrait of a pre-9/11 America
anxiously bracing itself for an inevitable catastrophe at the hands of a maladjusted or insane terrorist from within, while trying desperately to prevent
such an attack. The novel examines the psyche of
a country living in fear of the future, while presenting the stories of the members of a Secret Service
detail that has been assigned to protect the vice
president as he runs for election to the nation's
highest office. While profiling each of the detail's
members both personally and professionally, the
novel offers us insight into the slow deterioration
of a late 20th-century America that seems on the
edge of implosion. As each character labors under
an increasingly intense sense of impending doom,
each hopes to salvage a damaged or progressively
deteriorating personal life.

The novel employs a hyper-visual narrative
style, interspersing traditional narrative description with short narrative bursts of simple sentences
or multiple phrases linked together with commas,
forcing the reader to form a visual image that glues
together small pieces of information. Such a technique mirrors the visual narrative of television
and film, in which quick-cut editing creates the
illusion of a collage of interrelated images, forcing the viewer to create a narrative by imagining
transitions and synthesizing complex patterns. In
the same way, Costello asks the reader to fill in the
gaps, often deploying this hyper-visual technique
when describing decision-making processes of the
characters, setting the stage for a scene, or providing insights into actions. The technique creates
a sense of fast-paced, at times almost hysterical
movement, effectively compressing time into mil-

liseconds that add to a feeling of obsessive anxiety
as the reader progresses through the narrative. The
harried characters, like the reader, feel unable to
examine their lives, to develop a moral underpin-
ning to guide their decisions, or to reason through
their actions. Locked into such a driven hyper-
reality, each is further haunted by a mentor from
the past who lived a life founded on beliefs that
the present appears to reject yet fails to replace. In
this way, Costello paints a portrait of a postmodern generation caught in a web of instability, disappointment, and disillusion, while at the mercy of
memory, the legacy of a historically accomplished
but personally dysfunctional past.

Through its piercing portrayal of the lives of
several members of the Secret Service detail, the
novel provides acute insight into the postmodern
condition, while its depiction of the lasting legacy
of the baby boom era provides a searching social
commentary on the lone remaining superpower.
America has here become a paranoid, morally
adrift society that finds itself paralyzed, merely
anticipating its own demise. Costello's fictional
intrigue thus reminds us of the work of postmodern writers such as William Gibson, DAVID FOSTER
WALLACE, Walker Percy, Joyce Carol Oates, Jonathan Franzen, and Nick Hornby, which typically
depict characters seemingly at the mercy of their
surroundings, vainly hoping to find meaning in who
they are and what they do. In Costello's examination of America adrift, multiple subplots focus on
the characters' failing personal lives and guarded,
mysteriously cold working relationships. The story
interweaves the characters' pasts with their present
to create a metaphorical examination of American life as it passed from the free-love 1960s to the
uncharted beginnings of the 21st century.

The novel begins with a visual pastiche of
the Asplund family, focusing on the growth of two
main characters, Jens and Vi, the son and daughter
of Walter Asplund. The Asplunds seem a typical
American family, but their eccentric father marks
them as the "Atheists" of their town, rigidly struc-
turing their lives according to his perceived principles of reason alone. An atheistic humanist and
Enlightenment thinker, Walter becomes a legend
in town for crossing out the word "God" in the
phrase "In God We Trust" on the bills of currency

that pass through his hands, symbolically pros-elytizing to and protesting against his culture. As an insurance claims adjuster, Walter coldly mea-sures the financial cost of tragedy and the loss of human life. He believes in "the dignity of human-kind, the Genius of Democracy, [and] the sanctity of the contract"; that is, "in almost everything but God." Walter's legacy seems to swell and harden in the lives of his children, who strive to fill a moral vacuum caused by his inflexible ideology. Vi lives according to aesthetic more than moral principles, while attempting to prevent the very tragedies her father coldly measured as a claims adjuster, while Jens turns to the empowering rush of computer programming in an effort to build and sustain a world of his own creation, a world his father calls amoral for its lack of ethical standards. Jens soon finds, however, that his world "grows beyond logic and sense," devolving into a postapocalyptic virtual war zone that lures its players into a never-ending game that cannot be won, controlled by the greed of the company that owns him.

Along with the Asplunds, the novel focuses on the struggles of the security detail's commander, Gretchen Williams, and its most experienced agent, Tashmo. A study in contrast, Gretchen, an African-American woman, represents the future of the Secret Service and America, while Tashmo symbolizes a romanticized past that has failed to guide its next generation. Gretchen quickly climbs the bureaucratic ladder, elevated into ever greater authority as the nation moves toward an ideal of diversity. But like Vi and Jens Asplund, Gretchen is painfully influenced by a violent past, having grown up in Watts, witnessing the riots of 1965 and the 1990s. These experiences shape within her a foreboding sense of Armageddon, and this para-noia leads to a workaholic lifestyle and neglect in the raising of her son. Her ambition is to raise a son "who would never see his city burn," but in so doing she ultimately abandons him to a crippling need to define who he is and what he means in a world that seems on the verge of destruction.

In contrast to Gretchen's angst-ridden activity, Tashmo pines for a past of romantic ideals while regretting personal failures produced by lust and indecision. As a member of the details that pro-tected Jimmy Carter and Ronald Reagan, Tashmo recalls his "best days," idolizing Reagan while liv-ing a life of deception. Confronted with having to choose between mistress and wife, Tashmo chooses to avoid both, thereby failing to live up to the Rea-ganite ideals of "America Regained" that he lived to protect. His life of sexual conquests and mari-tal affairs defines him even as he nears retirement, and his legacy results both in the tragic death of his best friend, Lloyd Felker, and in the aimlessness of a son that he has never known.

As Felker's suicide haunts their Secret Service detail, the two contrasting characters represent an America still haunted by the 1960s, one fearful of a return to the past, the other of its abandon-ment. Ultimately, the novel attempts to write large on a metaphorical canvas, depicting a microcosm of America, victorious in its cold war, yet adrift in an ether of paranoia and loss, its characters search-ing vainly for that which one of them sells, a home that "must begin in dreams."

Bibliography
Costello, Mark. *Big If.* New York: W.W. Norton, 2002.

—Christopher Wielgos

Bohjalian, Chris (1960–) *American novelist*

Chris Bohjalian is the author of 11 novels, includ-ing MIDWIVES, *Before You Know Kindness,* and *The Double Bind. Midwives* was selected for Oprah's Book Club in 1998, and subsequently reached number one on the *New York Times* Best Seller list. *Idyll Banter,* a collection of his newspaper col-umns of the same name, came out in 2003. His fiction and nonfiction have been published widely, appearing in *Reader's Digest, Cosmopolitan,* the *Boston Globe Magazine,* and the *New York Times.* Bohjalian's domestic dramas often play out as part of larger political controversies, and his novels have tackled social issues such as racism, midwifery, gun control, and animal rights. His intimate portraits of domestic life vividly depict the impact on cou-ples and families when personal tragedies become public spectacles. In his popular and critically acclaimed novels, significant historical forces com-bine and conflict with the most private of emotions in complex ways that shape the personal lives of his individual characters as well as the greater world of each novel. His unflinching portraits of people struggling to find their way in a range of extraordinary circumstances—from a snowed-in delivery room in the woods of Vermont to the Prussian front during World War II—are compelling illustrations of just how political the personal can be, and vice versa. His novels are among the most powerful contemporary depictions of the border wars surrounding the public and domestic spheres in modern life.

Bohjalian was born in 1960 in White Plains, New York. His father was an advertising executive, and after graduating from Amherst College in 1982, Bohjalian followed in his father's footsteps and became an account executive at J. Walter Thompson in Manhattan. Tired of the violence of 1980s New York City, however, he and his wife, Victoria Brewer, an artist and photographer, moved to Vermont in 1986, where they have lived and worked ever since. They have one daughter, Grace.

Bohjalian found his voice as a writer in Vermont, which he describes in an interview on his Web site as "a fascinating microcosm for issues that have relevance everywhere." *Water Witches* (1995) features a prototypical clash between the traditional Vermont values represented by dowsers—the titular "water witches"—and proponents of rural economic development who want to open a ski resort in a small town. Vermont has featured prominently in a significant majority of Bohjalian's works, with his novels frequently exposing a darker side of the country life he gushes over unabashedly in his newspaper columns. *Skeletons at the Feast* (2008), in which a group of refugees flees Prussia as the Third Reich collapses, was Bohjalian's first novel (since his disavowed debut, *A Killing in the Real World* (1988)) with no significant connection to New England life.

Midwives (1997), an account of the murder trial of Sybil Danforth as seen through the eyes of her teenage daughter, became an overnight bestseller when Oprah Winfrey selected it for her Book Club in 1998. Bohjalian described the selection in a newspaper interview as "the greatest professional blessing I could have." Bohjalian followed up *Midwives* with the *Law of Similars* (1999), which some

critics suggested was too similar to *Midwives* in its representation of a courtroom clash between practitioners of alternative and traditional medicine. *Trans-Sister Radio* (2000) tells of a college professor who falls in love with a man who is about to become a woman, while *The Buffalo Soldier* examines the friendship that develops between a young African-American foster child and an elderly neighbor in his new all-white neighborhood. In *Before You Know Kindness* (2004), a troubled but loving family is almost destroyed while an animal rights fanatic reconsiders what is most important to him after he is accidentally shot by his 12-year-old daughter with his brother-in-law's secret hunting rifle. *The Double Bind* (2007) portrays a young college student dealing with the aftermath of a brutal attack, who enters the world of Tom and Daisy Buchanan from *The Great Gatsby* in a work the *Library Journal* called "a complex exploration of the human psyche and its efforts to heal and survive in whatever manner possible." Bohjalian's second novel, *Past the Bleachers*, was adapted for a Hallmark television movie in 1995; *Midwives* was adapted for the stage in 2000 and for a 2001 Lifetime Original Movie starring Sissy Spacek and Peter Coyote.

Since his inclusion in Oprah's Book Club, Bohjalian has continued to embrace a book club model for engaging with his fiction, offering extensive discussion guides for his recent novels and frequently connecting with his readers online in special live chats as well as through his impressive Web site, www.chrisbohjalian.com. Bohjalian's remarkable engagement with his readers suggests that he agrees with his fellow Oprah author Toni Morrison that reading should not only be a solitary experience: "it should have," in Morrison's words, "a talking life, a discourse that follows" (Lamb, 256). Bohjalian follows Morrison's edict that "novels are for talking about and quarreling about and engaging in some powerful way," not simply through his selection of controversial subject matters but through his ongoing engagement with his readers. Bohjalian uses the Internet to "have an interaction with my readers I never thought I'd have," he told *Publishers Weekly* in December 2008, describing his Web presence as a way of "supporting readers in the digital ages." In her study of Winfrey's significant impact on contemporary reading practices among women, Mary Lamb argues that Oprah endeavored through her book club to show that electronic media might not thwart print literacy but instead be employed to emphasize the "social, rhetorical aspects of reading and its role in women's self-improvement" (256). Bohjalian's embrace of the Internet suggests that he is continuing Oprah's project and putting himself on the cutting edge of exploring not simply the tensions but the productive potential interplay between print and new media.

Bohjalian has said that he loves "novels that teach me something," and each of his own novels is painstakingly researched to ensure that it accurately and subtly captures its particular historical or social context. He researches his novels so carefully, he says, because he wants them to read as "fictional memoirs," which means avoiding any distracting false notes. He pays homage to his favorite authors in his fiction, and his novels feature elements of the "gloriously eccentric and idiosyncratic" characters he loves in John Irving, the page-turning courtroom thrills of John Grisham's best work, and the intensely personal dramas of Joyce Carol Oates. Although some critics have complained that Bohjalian's characters occasionally lack the complexity of his plots, his many readers embrace the vivid drama of his novels and the light-hearted personal reflections of his columns as enthusiastically as he, in turn, engages with them. Bohjalian's upcoming novel, *Secrets of Eden*, a suspenseful exploration of faith and sacrifice in the face of revelation—both sacred and profane—is slated for a 2010 release.

Bibliography
Boaz, Amy. "Chris Bohjalian: On the Fringes of Modern Life." *Publishers Weekly*, January 4, 1999.
Bohjalian, Chris. *Before You Know Kindness*. New York: Shaye Areheart Books, 2004.
———. *The Buffalo Soldier*. New York: Shaye Areheart Books, 2002.
Chris Bohjalian: His official Web site. Available online. URL: http://www.chrisbohjalian.com. Accessed May 12, 2009.
———. *The Double Bind*. New York: Shaye Areheart Books, 2007.
———. *Hangman*. New York: Carroll & Graf, 1991.
———. *Idyll Banter: Weekly Excursions to a Very Small Town*. New York: Harmony Books, 2003.
———. *A Killing in the Real World*. New York: St. Martin's Press, 1988.
———. *The Law of Similars*. New York: Harmony Books, 1999.
———. *Midwives*. New York: Harmony Books. 1997.
———. *Past the Bleachers*. New York: Caroll & Graf, 1992.
———. *Skeletons at the Feast*. New York: Shaye Areheart Books, 2008.
———. *Trans-Sister Radio*. New York: Harmony Books, 2000.
———. *Water Witches*. Hanover, N.H.: University Press of New England, 1992.
Humphrey, Joy. Review of *The Double Bind, Library Journal*, January 2007, p. 87.
Lamb, Mary. "Women Readers in Oprah's Book Club." *Reading Women*. Edited by Janet Badia and Jennifer Phegley. Toronto: University of Toronto Press, 2005, 255–281.
Rosen, Judith. "Finding Value in Author Web Sites." *Publishers Weekly*, December 15, 2008, Available online. URL: http://www.publishersweekly.com/article/CA6622225.html. Accessed October 16, 2009.

—Mary Lawless

Bombardiers **Po Bronson** (1995)
PO BRONSON's debut novel is a workplace farce set in the early 1990s, at the San Francisco high-rise bond-trading offices of the Atlantic Pacific Corporation. The story follows Sidney Greeder, a veteran trader known as the King of Mortgages, and Mark "Eggs" Igino, a trading wunderkind whose ambivalence toward the profession forces Greeder to reconsider his own life goals—mainly his decision to continue working at a job he hates until he can cash out his company stock. Greeder and Igino are at the center of a group of always-hustling bond salesmen and women who start work at 4 A.M., and have virtually no lives outside their work.

A novel very much of and about its time, *Bombardiers* relentlessly satirizes the hyper-capitalist mindset that came to prominence in 1980s America. Its sharp take on corporate greed and incompetence evokes nonfiction works such as Michael Lewis's *Liar's Poker* (1989), an account of 1980s Wall Street bond traders, and James B. Stewart's *Den of Thieves* (1992), which recounted the insider-trading scandals that marked that decade; as well as Tom Wolfe's *The Bonfire of the Vanities* (1987), a novel set partially in 1980s Wall Street. In his introduction to the 2003 reprint of *Bombardiers,* Bronson describes the novel as an angry work, an act of revenge for the people he saw brutalized by an increasingly inhumane corporate mentality.

In *Bombardiers* Bronson pushes that worldview to its absurd extreme, with the language and ideology of capitalism pervading every facet of life and making Atlantic Pacific's employees miserable. (Rather than marriage, one character proposes a "merger of his limited partnership and her corporation.") The story opens with Sidney Greeder explaining, "It was a filthy profession, but the money was addicting, and one addiction led to another, and they were all going to hell." Greeder then recalls the numerous ways in which their addiction has ruined—or will soon ruin—the lives of his fellow bond traders. He, meanwhile, assures himself that he truly hates the bonds he is asked to sell, a complex rationalization that allows him to believe he is subverting the system of which he is an integral part.

Yet it is that ostensible contempt for the financial system, his boss informs him, that makes Greeder such a great salesman. The boss, Coyote Jack, reminds Greeder to sell what he is told, including an upcoming offering that Greeder suspects will go bad, dooming the company. Sidney Greeder plans to ride out the chaos for the last few months until he has enough money to leave. But of course Coyote Jack has no plans to let him leave.

Into Atlantic Pacific Corporation's skyscraper of intrigue walks Mark Igino, a new recruit and Greeder's trading understudy. Igino arrives with a reputation as an iconoclast, having established a lucrative market for lecture notes during the company's mandatory training seminars. He watches the increasingly harried bond traders from a distance, amused but compassionate. As he watches, he formulates a series of Laws of Information Economics, which include the reminder that "Power is Temporary!!!"

As the only salesman willing to understand the accounting behind Atlantic Pacific's bonds, Igino quickly discovers a problem with the company's latest offering. The numbers add up to 110 percent, a mathematical impossibility. When Igino warns his bosses, they go ahead with the faulty math but promote him to senior vice president, telling the *Wall Street Journal* that he had discovered an extra 10 percent of collateral in their offering. "The corruption of language and the manipulation of time and the distortion of numbers," the novel states, "were all part of the art of selling."

Igino's blithe attitude toward this aspect of his job gives way to doubt about whether he should not return to Mexico and the woman who once loved him. In the world of *Bombardiers,* his lost love is one among many, as the bond-sellers continually defer their happiness to the future, living only to serve their addiction to making money. Bronson evokes the pathos of his characters' plights with subtle restraint, though as stand-ins for capitalist shortsightedness they remain fairly prototypical.

Igino's doubt about the company—not only about its accounting practices but about the moral defensibility of its business—spreads to Greeder. Still, the latter sees himself as invaluable to the company, and is only months from retiring with a hefty bonus. The five years he devoted to the company will give him the means to live the life he has always wanted, though he has no real idea what that life might look like. He confides all this to the company doctor, who soon after mysteriously disappears. Igino, too, effectively disappears, walking away in disgust, with no explanation.

Thus Greeder stands alone, as Bronson's satire culminates with the Atlantic Pacific Corporation managing a buyout not of another company, but of a sovereign nation, the Dominican Republic. This act of economic colonialism would effectively render the country a corporate state, but only Greeder has misgivings. His bosses think it a great innovation in business. The U.S. government assumes that the market can manage a democracy better than any government, and dispatches agents to help push through the deal. The United Nations sends a peacekeeping force to observe the transfer of power, with the Securities and Exchange Commission looking on. *Bombardiers* climaxes in a scene of frenetic financial farce as the bond sellers try to meet their quotas surrounded by U.S. military; the market and government have become merged completely, and the result is utterly dysfunctional.

To gain media exposure for the book's publication, Bronson chose to satirize both the financial and the publishing worlds by offering stocks in his book; a year later, shareholders would be allowed to cash in for $4 a share. Bronson and his publisher composed a prospectus touting *Bombardiers* as "*the* business novel of the 1990s, by one of the most exciting new authors we have had the privilege to publish." The strategy ensured a number of mentions in the business and mainstream press.

Bibliography
Bronson, Po. *Bombardiers*. New York: Random House, 1995.

—Jesse Hicks

Brick Lane Monica Ali (2003)

MONICA ALI's debut novel is a carefully constructed exploration of questions of cultural and personal identity. It tells the story of Nazneen, a teenage girl from Bangladesh, who enters into an arranged marriage with Chanu, a significantly older compatriot living in London. While the first part of the novel covers the initial years of Nazneen's time in London from 1985 to 1988, it is interspersed with occasional reminiscences of her childhood in her native village, and with letters from her younger sister Hasa. The second part of the novel bridges the years from 1988 to 2001, and is told exclusively by means of Hasa's letters; while the third and most substantial part of the book revolves around Nazneen's life as a wife to Chanu and a mother to her two daughters Shahana and Bibi from February 2001 to March 2002.

While there are many references to social and political events, such as the years of the Thatcher government in Britain, the race riots in English towns such as Oldham and Bradford, and the terrorist attacks of September 11, 2001, the focus of the novel clearly lies on the gradual development of Nazneen from a demure Bangladeshi country girl into a self-confident woman engaging in an illicit affair with a younger man. Radical as it may seem, Nazneen's personal transformation is never portrayed as a process of simple assimilation, of shedding one identity in favor of another, but rather as a complex negotiation between her mostly unarticulated desires and the expectations of those around her. Ultimately, the novel suggests that finding one's place in society depends more on a sense of self than on conformity with society's rules and expectations, although the significance of these is never wholly repudiated.

Nazneen's initial outlook on life is exemplified by the story, "How You Were Left to Your Fate," in which her mother desists from taking the newborn Nazneen to hospital even though the sickly baby refuses all nourishment for several days. Since the baby survived, Nazneen's mother concludes that the only way to deal with one's fate is to submit to it; a quiescence characteristic of Nazneen's initial years in London, as she enters into an arranged marriage, demurely occupies herself with household chores, and never ventures outside the boundaries of Tower Hamlets, a part of London traditionally considered the focal point of the city's Bangladeshi community. As a series of incidents in her life and in the lives of those around her gradually forces her to question the wisdom of her fatalistic outlook, Nazneen becomes increasingly active and vocal, just as her family faces the important decision whether or not to leave England and return to Bangladesh.

This development is paralleled by or contrasted with developments in many other characters surrounding Nazneen. Chanu, for instance, her significantly older and by no means attractive husband, is a man obsessed with the idea of self-improvement and education. In possession of a B.A. in English literature from Dhaka University, as well as several evening-class certificates, Chanu, who also provides much of the novel's comic relief, sees the world firmly divided into "ignorant types" and "respectable types," reckoning himself among the latter group. It is only toward the end of the book that he comes to realize that no such clear-cut dichotomy can reflect the true complexity of the world; and despite the fact that he persists in outwardly presenting himself as the head of his family, he gradually comes to rely on Nazneen's support and judgment. Hasa, Nazneen's younger sister, at first serves as a foil to her sibling's docile acceptance of fate. Refusing to enter into an arranged marriage, young Hasa elopes from her native village with the nephew of the local sawmill owner. As can be expected, however, in a novel that refuses to provide its readers with shallow truths, it remains highly arguable whether the path she chooses is a happier one than that of her less rebellious sister. Karim, the young man of Bangladeshi descent with whom Nazneen has an affair, was born in London, and thus belongs to a generation facing very different issues than do those older Bangladeshis who have a home that they hope to return to one day. Disaffected with his seniors' passivity in the face of growing hostility at the hands of English nationalists, Karim becomes the spokesman for the Bengal Tigers, a group of Muslims intent on defending the rights of their community. As their affair continues, however, Nazneen and Karim begin to realize that their mutual attraction is predominantly based on what they represent to each other rather than on who they truly are.

The various difficulties confronting people attempting to find a home away from home are further illustrated by a host of minor characters, none of whom seem at ease in their current situations. And the challenge of *Brick Lane,* as well as the controversy it has evoked, arises from its refusal to offer any blanket judgments or clear-cut recipes for personal happiness. With its focus on everyday life in multicultural London, *Brick Lane* is comparable to ZADIE SMITH's *WHITE TEETH* (2000); but just like Smith, Ali would abandon this setting entirely in her subsequent work, *Alentejo Blue* (2006), which is concerned with life in a Portuguese village. In 2007, Sarah Gavron turned *Brick Lane* into a film, which struggles to capture the psychological development of its heroine, and in so doing omits some of those scenes that are among the most poignant in the book.

Bibliography
Ali, Monica. *Alentejo Blue.* London: Doubleday, 2006.
———. *Brick Lane.* London: Doubleday, 2003.

—Patrick Gill

Brief History of the Dead, The Kevin Brockmeier (2006)

KEVIN BROCKMEIER's second novel stems from an evocative premise: The dead wind up in an afterlife limbo known only as The City, where they will remain as long as they are remembered by those still alive on Earth. The City "was not heaven, and it was not hell, and it certainly was not the world" (though it bears more than a little resemblance to the latter, with its office buildings, cafes, taxi cabs, all manner of churches, and even its own newspaper). The story pursues the possibilities of this concept through two alternating narrative threads. The odd chapters trace the quotidian travails of a handful of denizens of The City. The even ones follow Laura Byrd, an "environmental impact specialist" in her early 30s, in the employ of the Coca-Cola corporation, stranded in Antarctica on a mission to investigate the viability of using polar ice to make soft drinks. The novel is set in a near future in which gorillas, elephants, and whales are either extinct or very near to it, and the urban landscape is dotted with "terrorist warning beacons." We soon learn that a viral pandemic, referred to by the newly dead as "The Blinks," has decimated the population of Earth, thus flooding and subsequently draining the population of the City. Laura Byrd is the last living person, so those left in The City remain there only because their lives had intersected with hers at some point or another.

In an interview with powells.com, Brockmeier contends that *The Brief History of the Dead* "straddles the divide between literary fiction and fantasy. In some ways it's a survival narrative, in other ways a postapocalyptic character study, and in still other ways a sort of jigsaw story about the connections we forge with each other." Indeed, the novel is inventive enough to press at the limits of any particular genre, while still resonating with a number of venerable narrative and philosophic models. The speculative ore of what it means to be the last person on Earth has been well mined in literary circles, by works such as David Markson's *Wittgenstein's Mistress,* and in popular culture from *I Am Legend* to film's *Omega Man* and Pixar's current *Wall-E* (though the titular robot is not a person, strictly speaking). Though Brockmeier has cited

Apsley Cherry-Garrard's memoir *The Worst Journey in the World* as a resource for his Antarctic verisimilitude, the survivalist elements of the story also recall the work of Jack London, and iconic castaways from Robinson Crusoe to *Lost*. The novel's thematic exploration of death as a means to come to terms with life is akin to the film *After Life*, by the Japanese director Koreeda Hirokazu, as well as Alice Sebold's 2002 best seller *The Lovely Bones*.

The first chapter of *The Brief History of the Dead* was published years ahead of the rest (in the September 8, 2003, issue of *The New Yorker*), as a short story of the same title. It details the "crossings" of several of The City's inhabitants, their recollection of the journey from life to afterlife:

> The stories people told about the crossing were as varied and elaborate as their ten billion lives, so much more particular than those other stories, the ones they told about their deaths … Lev Paley said that he had watched his atoms break apart like marbles, roll across the universe, then gather themselves together again out of nothing at all. Hanbing Li said that he woke inside the body of an aphid and lived an entire life in the flesh of a single peach. Graciella Cavazos would say only that she began to snow—four words—and smile bashfully whenever anyone pressed her for details.

To some of the novel's detractors, Brockmeier's unfolding narrative fails to make good on the promise of the opening chapter's lyricism and imagination; to its champions, the interwoven narrative strands accumulate insightful musings on the nature of memory and the traffic of human relationships. Isolated and freezing to death, Laura Byrd sifts, Krapp-like, through the detritus of her short life, and Brockmeier emphasizes the degree to which ostensibly minor moments gain weight by retrospection. We feel the reverberations between inner and outer worlds. As Laura busies her troubled mind with the associative word-games she used to play as a child—"Ice. Frost. Frosting. Crossing. Railroad Crossing. Railroad Train. Fabric Train. Wedding dress."—one of her deceased coworkers, Nathaniel Puckett, endeavors to compile a list of

"the number of people [he's] capable of remembering when the right chain of associations occur": mailmen, people from the gym, his girlfriends, his softball team. Laura's journey across the polar ice to a radio station, in a last-ditch effort to make human contact, brings into relief the contacts she had made on Earth.

In The City, Laura's survival engenders a second chance for old relationships, as well as the forging of new ones. Her parents, Philip and Marion Byrd, achieve a closeness in death that escaped them in life, and her childhood best friend Minny Rings finds love with Laura's ex-boyfriend and journalism teacher, Luka Sims. Ultimately, the novel strives to balance its flashy and compelling sci-fi conceit with an earthy intimacy culled from finely observed personal detail. Brockmeier explored similar terrain of memory and loss in his first novel, *The Truth about Celia* (2004), which takes the form of a science-fiction writer's attempts to cope with the loss of his daughter through fictional reinterpretations of her life at different points in her brief past and imagined future.

After the publication of the opening chapter of the novel, Warner Brothers purchased the film rights to the story. *The Brief History of the Dead* has an interactive Web site, which includes a map of The City and lists "Kevin Brockmeier" as one of its inhabitants.

Bibliography

Brockmeier, Kevin. *The Brief History of the Dead*. New York: Random House, 2006.
Powells Books. "Ink Q & A: Kevin Brockmeier." Available online. URL: http://www.powells.com/ink/brockmeier.html. Accessed May 12, 2009.

—Chris Kamerbeek

Brief Interviews with Hideous Men David Foster Wallace (1999)

DAVID FOSTER WALLACE's second collection of stories revolves around a set of formal and thematic patterns that advance the concerns of his previous work: the alternately liberating and crippling nature of postmodern irony, self-consciousness, and critical distance; the frightening and potentially impossible transition from adolescence to adulthood; addiction in every possible guise; the omnipresence of corporate media, and its penetration into our private interior lives. Wallace himself suggested that its central preoccupation is "loneliness" (Silverblatt interview).

Thus, the challenging, broadly experimental, and resolutely impious *Brief Interviews* projects a greater sense of unity than many short story collections, including Wallace's own GIRL WITH CURIOUS HAIR (1989) and *Oblivion* (2004) but does so with only a minimal reliance on narrative and character continuity. Many of the book's pieces are presented as numbered fragments of larger cycles that may or may not exist—we are given only 16 of 72 "Brief Interviews with Hideous Men," for instance, along with three of the 24 parts of "Yet Another Example of the Porousness of Certain Borders." The book's centerpiece, "Octet," promises eight vignettes, but it appears that only five of these "Pop Quizzes" have made it out of the narrator's head, and one of them is obstinately entitled "Pop Quiz 9." This deliberate emphasis on the work's fragmentary nature recalls Wallace's most direct and obvious literary antecedents—Thomas Pynchon, William Gaddis, Julio Cortázar, John Barth—but also progenitors of romantic irony like Søren Kierkegaard, or Samuel Taylor Coleridge, who published the deliberately fragmentary "Dejection: An Ode" (1802), with two of its nine stanzas mysteriously omitted.

The collection's almost mathematical obsession with broken symmetries begins on page "[0]" with "A Radically Condensed History of Postindustrial Life." Using only 79 words, Wallace punches out the tale of an anonymous man and a woman who are introduced, don social facades in the hope of being liked, have dinner, and then drive "home alone, staring straight ahead, with the very same twist to their faces." Its monotonous final sentence—"One never knew, after all, now did one now did one now did one"—sets the tone for the rest of the collection, in which an isolated, iterated, and anonymous "one" is placed in opposition to dreams of a higher symmetry (e.g., eight vignettes, 72 "Brief Interviews," or 24 "Examples of Porousness"), or a clean slate, free from the corrosive effects of personal and collective trauma (e.g.,

the bracketed zero). Human beings, in Wallace's vision of contemporary America, are almost uniformly broken, uncertain, and alone.

As earlier Wallace works like INFINITE JEST (1996) and *The Broom of the System* (1986) implied, such isolation and uncertainty become a semipermanent aspect of lived experience with the onset of puberty. In "Laughing with Kafka," an essay from the *Consider the Lobster* collection (2005), Wallace concludes that "our present culture is, both developmentally and historically, 'adolescent'" (64n). "Forever Overhead," the first extended story in *Brief Interviews*, opens with a blunt "Happy Birthday," as a boy inaugurates his 13th year at an overchlorinated public swimming pool, accompanied by his nuclear family, despite wanting "to come alone" (6). A direct, almost naive juxtaposition of the childlike and the adult, "Forever Overhead" offers countless details of the boy's inner and outer life, including the recent growth of seven "hard dangerous spirals of brittle black hair" (5) in his left armpit and 12 in his right, and the resemblance of his towel to "one big face of Yogi Bear" (10). The protagonist's fear of the high dive is the central conflict. Summoning the will to climb it, he enters the region of pure thought that is suspended above the pool's frenetic "system of movement" (8). But thought is scarcely distinguishable from compulsive overthinking, which is, he realizes, the root of the fear and self-doubt that prevent him from diving. The boy wishes to remain "forever overhead," contemplating the dynamics of his family, the strange changes to his body, and the "movement" below; but a combination of his own shame and the complaints of the swimmers queued behind him finally pushes him to "step into the skin and disappear" (16). This skin is the disgusting accretion that the feet of generations of divers have left at the end of the board, but also the surface of the pool, which separates air from water, thought from action, and childhood from what two later stories will call the "Adult World."

The unusual second-person narration that runs through "Forever Overhead" addresses both the birthday boy and Wallace's reader. Its imperative to "step into the skin and disappear," followed only by the implied splash into the pool and a final hesitant "Hello," scarcely prepares us for the first of the "Brief Interviews with Hideous Men" on the following page, which plunges into the perverse and lonely realm of adulthood. The remainder of the book will invite us to "step into the skin" of characters with whom it is all but impossible to empathize. Yet this seems to be the collection's primary ethical imperative: to feel and understand that everyone—from adolescent boys to pornography addicts to fiction writers to sadomasochists who perform elaborate, vacuous self-analyses to snooker their victims—is driven by the same "loneliness" that drives each of us.

But the ethical project of *Brief Interviews* is transected by a critical project that seems to delight in its efforts to unravel the system of "needy and manipulative" tricks (62), which characters like "The Depressed Person" have adopted as postmodern coping strategies. The intermittent questions posed to Wallace's "hideous men" by their presumably female interlocutors make it clear that these dialogues are really extended monologues. Most of the conversation here takes place between the hideous men and themselves; the "Interviews" are an exhausting—and hardly brief— seesaw of revelations and concealments. Although some of their responses imply that they have been asked long and complex questions, Wallace transcribes these questions with one after another undifferentiated *"Q."* The defenses these men have built up over the course of their lives preemptively annul the possibility of productive conversation, much less personal growth. Stripped of empathy, their introspection becomes merely a tool for manipulating others, and for retroactive and proactive self-justification.

"Octet" translates this hideous psychology into the realm of fiction. The book's formal, thematic, and literal center asks whether an author can authentically communicate a story without sliding into either total uncertainty, which traps the reader in a web of manipulative solipsism, or total certainty, which traps her in a facile, melodramatic simulacrum of human experience. Wallace's answer in *Brief Interviews* (especially "Octet," "The Depressed Person," and "Adult World" [I] and [II]) is transparency. He attempts to expose the rhetorical trickery that fictional narrators, as well as real authors, use to conceal their personal flaws and ulterior motives. The problem with such an approach, which has

frustrated many readers and which Wallace was painfully aware of, is that it so closely resembles the calculating, ironic discourse utilized by the collection's cast of hideous characters. Perhaps Wallace's true intervention, in *Brief Interviews* and throughout his career, is not his trademark use of footnotes, but rather the way in which he posits irony as a visceral, actual problem that can never be completely resolved. It can only be temporarily circumvented in the hope of gesturing toward something more real— indeed, Wallace's next collection of stories, *Oblivion*, continues in the same vein.

If *Infinite Jest* gives at least some outline of what hope might look like in contemporary and near-future America (Pemulis's open endorsement of change, or Don Gately's strict adherence to AA's disciplinary ethics), *Brief Interviews* leaves us with nothing except the invitation to step into another's skin, an incomplete and insufficient "Pop Quiz" that leaves us with a blunt imperative: "So decide."

Bibliography

Coleridge, Samuel Taylor. *Coleridge's Poetry and Prose.* Edited by Nicholas Halmi, Paul Magnuson, and Raimonda Modiano. New York: Norton, 2004.

Kierkegaard, Søren. *The Concept of Irony with Continual Reference to Socrates / Schelling Lecture Notes, The Collected Writings of Kierkegaard Vol. II.* Princeton, N.J.: Princeton University Press, 1992.

Wallace, David Foster. *Brief Interviews with Hideous Men.* New York: Little, Brown, 1999.

———. "'Bookworm' 4/11/96." Available online. URL: http://web.archive.org/web/20040606041906/www.andbutso.com/rmark/bookworm96/ "Interview with David Foster Wallace." By Michael Silverblatt. KCRW 89.9 FM. Los Angeles, Calif., August 31, 2000.

———. *The Broom of the System.* New York: Penguin, 1987.

———. *Infinite Jest.* New York: Little, Brown, 1996.

———. *Oblivion.* New York: Little, Brown, 2004.

———. "Some Remarks on Kafka's Funniness from Which Probably Not Enough Has Been Removed." In *Consider the Lobster: Essays.* New York: Little, Brown, 2005.

—Andrew B. Warren

Brief Wondrous Life of Oscar Wao, The
Junot Díaz (2007)

JUNOT DÍAZ's Pulitzer Prize–winning novel, *The Brief Wondrous Life of Oscar Wao*, tells an intricate, multilayered, and compelling tale of a Dominican-American family and its origins in Santo Domingo. Through the voice of an unknown and omniscient narrator, we are first introduced to the novel's sheltered but sexually active protagonist, Oscar Wao, who lives with his mother and sister in Paterson, New Jersey. After he is rejected by one of his first loves, Oscar puts on weight, becoming indifferent to his appearance, and—not untypically—immerses himself in video games, role-playing, anime, and science fiction. In an SAT preparation course, however, he meets a young woman who wants to be his friend; but the budding romance becomes only another source of sexual frustration as he watches the young woman return to her much older (and thoroughly disreputable) boyfriend.

The novel's second section is narrated by Oscar's sister, Lola, a smart, rebellious punk aspirant, who tells the starkly contrasting tales of her mother's nascent cancer and her own sudden disappearance (along with her boyfriend) until discovered by Oscar and her mother and sent back to the old country for a time.

The third part of the first book tells the story of the mother Beli's tempestuous youth in Santo Domingo during the brutal rule of the dictator Rafael Trujillo. Beli, "a girl so tall your leg bones ached just looking at her" (77), is raised by her aunt, La Inca, and as a teenager twice falls in love with the "wrong kind" of man, the first a spoiled playboy at her school who does not love her and is whisked away to military school by his disapproving family, and the second a dangerous gangster who, the narrator notes, is "a flunky for the Trujillato, and not a minor one" (119). When Lola becomes pregnant with the gangster's child, his wife sends hit men after her and she is beaten very badly. Even after she is rescued by La Inca, the thugs continue to stalk her, and at last she must leave the country for New York.

The central narrator of *The Brief Wondrous Life of Oscar Wao* makes his appearance only in the fourth part of the first book, a weightlifting Rutgers

student and quasi-boyfriend of Lola, whom she has nursed after a bad beating and with whom she later lives. Yunior is a memorable and peculiarly omniscient narrator, possessed not merely of a wealth of knowledge of Dominican history and lore, but of intimate awareness both of the actions and the thoughts of the other characters. His voice displays a certain comic crudeness, but he makes astute observations about Dominican culture, Dominican-American issues, and the violence of Santo Domingo during this era (some in the novel's amusing colloquial footnotes, which are commensurate with his voice and style).

Yunior explains how his affection for Lola led him to live with Oscar in a dorm room at Rutgers University, in order to take care of the socially ill-adjusted boy. At this time, Yunior explains, Oscar was still obese and very much absorbed in his reclusive pastimes of role-playing, anime, and Tolkien. He describes how he tried to help Oscar lose weight and develop social skills, and how that effort failed when Oscar at last turned on him and the two fought. Yunior then narrates, in omniscient detail, how Oscar meets a goth girl who later abandons him, how Oscar throws a violent tantrum in the girl's dorm room, and how he later attempts suicide by jumping off the New Brunswick train bridge, a failure that results in two broken legs and a separated shoulder.

In addition to his narration of the lives of Oscar, Lola, and their mother, Yunior delivers a skillful account of Abelard, Lola and Oscar's grandfather, a clever doctor who shields his daughters from Trujillo, the notorious dictator. Shortly after Abelard fails to bring his two oldest daughters to a "Presidential Event," however, he is arrested by the secret police and imprisoned in appalling conditions. He is sentenced to 18 years in prison, soon after which his wife and two older daughters all die suddenly, leaving the youngest daughter, Beli, under the care of La Inca.

After his sister Lola's return to the United States, Oscar falls deeply in love with a prostitute, Ybón, with whom he starts a relationship. And at this point Oscar's life takes on the kind of resonance characteristic of tragedy, echoing salient features of his mother's otherwise dissimilar story—both engaging in mostly one-sided and highly dangerous love affairs that seem to outsiders to be mere folly. Oscar is nearly beaten to death by the men of the prostitute's jealous boyfriend, just as his mother was beaten by the men of her gangster boyfriend's jealous wife; and while he recovers from his injuries Oscar first reflects on the alleged *fuku*, or curse on his family. While he heals, he longs for the object of his affection, just as his mother had done before. Even when Ybón informs him that she is marrying the captain, the very man who had Oscar beaten, and even after Oscar's lonely return to Paterson, he still longs for her.

At last, his longing leads him to return to Santo Domingo in search of her, but he is soon captured and killed by the captain's men, after delivering a tragic monologue explaining the reasons for his act and musing on the pitiless fiats of love. Yunior then narrates how he accompanies Lola to reclaim Oscar's body, and she swears never to return to Santo Domingo. A year and a half later, Lola breaks up with him and they lose contact. But later, after she has married a Cuban man, had a child, and moved back to Paterson, they reestablish contact, and she introduces Yunior to her son as her brother's best friend.

The novel is freighted with literary references, even in its seemingly innocuous focus on Paterson, New Jersey, which was the subject of a long text by William Carlos Williams and a poem by Allen Ginsberg, and was the childhood home of both. Yunior describes the young Beli as "more Penelope than Whore of Babylon" (109), calls Oscar a "Caliban" (170), and refers to Salman Rushdie in his footnoted discussion of dictators (97). In one of the novel's later sections, in which Yunior narrates the story of Lola and Oscar's grandfather, Díaz has him identify himself as one of "us lit majors" (232). The intelligent and well-read Lola shares Yunior's literary sensibility, recalling in the course of her own narrative her pastime of reading Ayn Rand and her erstwhile ambition for Oscar to become "the Dominican Joyce" (62, 68). Yunior recalls seeing Lola reading "with such concentration I thought she might hurt herself" (198). Oscar himself nurses the ambition of becoming "the Dominican Stephen King" or "the Dominican Tolkien" (27, 192). Even according to "lit major" Yunior, Oscar spends an inordinate and even inappropriate amount of time

reading and writing; and in its intensity and lack of worldly success his devotion to writing reveals intellectual parallels to his own harmful romantic assymetries.

Throughout *Wao*, Díaz returns to the subject of Dominican superstition and belief in the supernatural. Very early in the novel, for example, Yunior explains the *fuku*, the bad luck or curse that is allegedly haunting Oscar and Lola's family. In telling Beli's history, Yunior remarks, "there are still many, on and off the Island, who offer Beli's near-fatal beating as irrefutable proof that the House of Cabral was indeed victim of a high-level fuku" (152). Alongside this spiritual concern, however, is a sustained, sensual, and subtle treatment of the body, from Diaz's vivid account of Oscar's ballooning weight, to the nubile bodies of teenage women and their dangerous allure for men; from the visceral details of Oscar's accident, to Beli's and Oscar's beatings, Lola's shaving of her head, and Beli's miscarriage and cancer. Politically, the novel offers a thorough and sensitive exploration of the roots and consequences of the "Dominican Diaspora" (Beli refers to Dominica as "this un-country"), and the social topography of this phenomenon is in many ways reflected psychologically in Oscar's status as a perpetual outsider.

Bibliography
Diaz, Junot. *The Brief Wondrous Life of Oscar Wao.* New York: Riverhead Books, 2007.
———. *Drown.* New York: Riverhead Books, 1997.

—Susan Kirby-Smith

Brockmeier, Kevin (1972–) *American short story writer, children's novelist*
Brockmeier is the author of two short story collections, *Things That Fall from the Sky* and *The View from the Seventh Layer,* and two novels, *The Truth about Celia* and *The BRIEF HISTORY OF THE DEAD.* He has also written two children's novels, *City of Names* and *Grooves: A Kind of Mystery.* His stories, both for children and adults, juxtapose the quotidian and the fantastic, while his adult work often addresses themes of memory and loss, using fantastic elements to illuminate the emotional lives of his

characters. His work is further known for its evocative and original figurative language.

Brockmeier was born in Hialeah, Florida, in 1972. His family moved to Little Rock, Arkansas, in 1976, where he showed an early aptitude for language and storytelling. He later developed an interest in theater, performing in plays and drama contests at the Parkview Arts and Science Magnet High School. After graduating in 1991 he enrolled in Southwest Missouri State University, where he pursued an interdisciplinary degree in creative writing, philosophy, and theater. He graduated in 1995 and next attended the Iowa Writers' Workshop, earning a master of fine arts degree in 1997.

He published his first work that year, and his stories have since appeared in numerous publications, including the *Georgia Review, McSweeney's,* and the *New Yorker,* as well as in anthologies such as *The Best American Short Stories* and *The Year's Best Fantasy and Horror.* Many reviewers describe his work as reminiscent of Italo Calvino and Jorge Luis Borges, as well as Milan Kundera and Donald Barthelme, all of whom combine realism and fantasy and show a strong inclination toward philosophical fiction. In an interview with Web Del Sol Literary Dialogues, Brockmeier himself mentions the Brothers Grimm as influences, and admits that Barthelme's stories "are all-or-nothing affairs for me: either I respond to them as wonderful, richly human flights of fancy or as sterile, wasted little language-experiments, though I'll admit that I might place a given story in one category and then the other during different readings."

Like Kelly Link (*Stranger Things Happen, Magic for Beginners*), Brockmeier often adapts figures from pop culture and folklore in his stories. His first published work, "A Day in the Life of Half of Rumpelstiltskin" (collected in *Things That Fall from the Sky*), offers a sequel to the fairy tale. In Brockmeier's story the title character, after tearing himself in half in a fit of rage, relocates to a contemporary, "realistic" America. "Half of Rumpelstiltskin," as he calls himself, lives a humdrum life dominated by an unforgiving boss and unsatisfying job, the drudgery of grocery shopping, and the salve of reality television. Giving a speech to the local women's auxiliary organization, he is repeatedly mistaken for another fairy-tale character, the

Big Bad Wolf. Half of Rumpelstiltskin stoically endures these small indignities but is haunted by his feelings of incompleteness. Meanwhile, the *other* Half of Rumpelstiltskin sends Mad-Libs letters, apologizing that "When the words don't come to me, I figure they must be yours." The story, which won the Italo Calvino Short Fiction Award, is marked by the offbeat humor and melancholic, yet unsentimental tone characterizing much of Brockmeier's work.

In "The Ceiling," from the same collection, the protagonist begins to be aware of the failure of his marriage, and to recognize his wife's increasing emotional distance. Simultaneously, a large black ceiling begins to descend on the town, and as with the sense of incompleteness felt by Half of Rumpelstiltskin, the protagonist's emotional life takes on a literal, yet fantastic meaning: for him, the sky is literally falling, albeit very slowly, and as the ceiling inexorably descends it flattens the entire life he has known.

Brockmeier describes the fantasy element in his work as "mainly practical" (McMyne). While his stories' themes seem congruent with much contemporary literary fiction, he notes that "When I try to write, say, strictly realistic domestic fiction—much of which I enjoy reading—a shade seems to descend inside my head, and I find it very difficult to see through to the other side." Thus, much of his writing involves fantastical elements strongly grounded in a realistic world, as in "The Ceiling," or fantastical characters treated realistically, as in "A Day in the Life of Half of Rumpelstiltskin."

The protagonist of Brockmeier's first novel, *The Truth about Celia,* shares the author's ambivalence toward distinctions between fantasy and reality. For Christopher Brooks, fantasy—the process of creating fiction—offers a powerful consolation. The novel, in stories, collects Brooks's fictions about his missing daughter, Celia, and he portrays his works as an extended act of mourning for failed rescue, beginning with the first story, "March 15, 1997." Titled for the date of Celia's disappearance, Brooks's story imagines her as radiant, then inexplicably gone; the following stories speculate on how she might have disappeared, and where she might have gone. In "The Green Children," Celia mysteriously appears outside a medieval town. In

"The Telephone," she calls her father, seemingly from beyond the grave. In the novel's most consistently realistic story, "Appearance, Disappearance, Levitation, Transformation, and the Divided Women" the abducted Celia has grown up in her own autonomous life, unaware of her real family. Revealing the story as his own coping mechanism, the author Brooks inserts within it a parenthetical "I want her to be happy." The novel, with its series of interconnected, multiple-genre stories, recalls the work of David Mitchell, particularly CLOUD ATLAS (2004).

Brockmeier's second novel, *The Brief History of the Dead*, more explicitly divides the realm of the fantastic from that of the ordinary. The principal link between the two, however, remains the theme of memory and storytelling. The novel's central conceit is The City, where people go after death, surviving there as long as they are remembered by the living. (Brockmeier bases this view of the afterlife on one attributed to "many African societies" and described in the novel's epigraph. The cited source for the story, however, is James Lowen's *Lies My Teacher Told* Me, further blurring the lines between fantasy and reality.) As an apocalyptic virus begins to ravage the real world, The City's residents themselves begin to vanish. Soon only a few are left, all of them remembered by humanity's lone survivor, Laura Byrd, a researcher in the Antarctic. Brockmeier alternates chapters between the search for an explanation among the characters of The City, and Byrd's struggle for survival; and the two worlds persist through mutually sustaining memory.

Brockmeier's second short story collection, *The View from the Seventh Layer*, sees him again adapting a well-known fantasy figure to a realistic world. This time, in "The Lady with the Pet Tribble," he recasts *Star Trek*'s Captain Kirk as "The Keptin," an adolescent adventurer irresistible to women but incapable of love. But while *Star Trek*'s Kirk remained so throughout the series, The Keptin finds himself confronting his own mortality. While addressing similar themes and employing similar techniques as his previous work, *The View from the Seventh Layer* shows a greater diversity of form than his earlier collection. Four "fables" run no more than eight pages each, shorter than any

of Brockmeier's fiction to that point. "The Human Soul as Rube Goldberg Device: A Choose-Your-Own-Adventure Story" enlists the reader in the storytelling process, asking him or her to make decisions that will affect the outcome. No matter what the reader's choices, however, the story concludes in the same place, with Brockmeier reasserting the ability of memory to bridge the often artificial separation between the living and the dead.

Bibliography
Brockmeier, Kevin. *The Brief History of the Dead.* New York: Pantheon Books, 2006.
———. *Things That Fall from the Sky.* New York: Pantheon Books, 2002.
———. *The Truth about Celia.* New York: Pantheon Books, 2003.
———. "Turning Inward: A Conversation with Kevin Brockmeier." By Mary McMyne. Web del Sol. Available online. URL: http://www.webdelsol.com/Literary_Dialogues/interview-wds-brockmeier.htm. Accessed December 12, 2008.
———. *The View from the Seventh Layer.* New York: Pantheon Books, 2008.

—Jesse Hicks

Bronson, Po (1964–) *American journalist and novelist*

Bronson is a journalist and the author of five books: two of fiction, three of nonfiction. Several have been national or international best sellers. Bronson is as well known for his journalism on technology and related culture as for his novels and nonfiction books, which he describes as "social documentaries."

Bronson was born in Seattle, Washington, and currently lives with his family in San Francisco. His given name is Philip, but Bronson has gone by the name "Po" since he was 14 months old. He attended the Lakeside School in Seattle and earned his bachelor of arts degree in economics from Stanford University in 1986, working as an assistant bond salesman in San Francisco after graduation. At the age of 22, he and his girlfriend founded a greeting card company, The Poettes, as a distraction from jobs they did not like, and sold 48 card designs. In 1989, Bronson began night classes at San Francisco State University, where he would earn his M.F.A. in creative writing in 1993. During this period, he focused on the short story form. From 1992 to 2006, he served on the board of directors of Consortium Book Sales and Distribution, and in 1994, alongside ETHAN CANIN and Ethan Watters, he founded The Writer's Grotto in San Francisco, a creative, cooperative workspace for artists (www.sfgrotto.org).

Bronson published his first novel, BOMBARDIERS, in 1995, and it has since been published in 15 languages. In a new introduction for the 2003 edition of the novel, Bronson wrote that his mother's experience as a stockbroker's assistant helped inspire him to write when he felt stuck, though *Bombardiers* is not based directly on his mother's experiences. The novel tells the story of two investment brokers—one almost ready to retire, the other new to the job—as they forge a bond and comically navigate the world of bond sales. Upon its initial publication, the *Kirkus Review* wrote that *Bombardiers* was a

> vicious, hilarious satire of bond traders and, by extension, the prevailing mindset of corporate America. This audacious first novel (by a former salesman for First Boston) echoes the biting tone of Catch-22. Rather than cogs in an absurd war machine, however, Bronson's protagonists are desk-bound hustlers trying to sell complicated and shady corporate bonds to the gullible or to those who know the government will bail them out when the bonds go belly-up.

Bombardiers was a number 1 best seller in the United Kingdom.

In order to make more money, Bronson began writing nonfiction for newspapers and magazines in 1996. He writes on his personal Web site that this is "harder to write, because you don't have the luxury of making stuff up," but that he might love writing nonfiction even more than fiction. It has also proven a valuable resource: he got the idea for his second novel, *The First $20 Million Is Always the Hardest* (1997), after doing research for an article

on the Silicon Valley in California for *Wired* magazine. The novel humorously explores the power struggles that its Stanford-educated main character, Andy Caspar, faces as he develops new computer technology during the early days of computers in Silicon Valley. Though it was never widely marketed or distributed, a film adaptation of *The First $20 Million Is Always the Hardest* was released in 2002, starring Adam Garcia and Rosario Dawson.

In addition to penning numerous pieces for publications such as *Time* magazine, the *Wall Street Journal*, the *New York Times*, *New York Magazine*, and the *Guardian*, Bronson has contributed to National Public Radio's *Morning Edition*. He has authored three books of nonfiction. The first, *The Nudist on the Late Shift* (1999), contains seven chapters that follow entrepreneurs, programmers, salespeople, and other key players in the development of the computer industry in the Silicon Valley during the relocation of 350,000 young people to the area in the late 1990s. The best-known chapter is entitled "The Newcomers," and features six individuals as they make their way around during their first year in California. Bronson cites Joan Didion, Upton Sinclair, and John Steinbeck as influences for the piece.

In 1999, Bronson began an 18-month stint in Hollywood, California, writing screenplays and television pilots, but three of his initial efforts—a television pilot for ABC called *South of Market*, which he cocreated, and two movies based on chapters from *Nudist on the Late Shift* entitled "Stick or Flip" and "Dotcomarama"—were never made. During the summer and fall of 2000, however, he wrote for the Fox show "The Street," starring Jennifer Connelly.

Bronson's next foray into nonfiction was *What Should I Do with My Life?* (2003), which contains 50 pieces on a host of diverse topics such as motherhood, coping with grief, and holding a day job. He was interviewed on *Oprah* along with people he featured in the book, and among its vast and varied audience, the work has been required reading in freshman courses at major universities as well as church Bible-study groups; even Nicole Kidman's Samantha is shown reading it in the 2005 remake of *Bewitched*. It was a number 1 *New York Times* best seller.

Continuing in the same successful vein, Bronson's Why *Do I Love These People?* (2005) is a collection of 19 family profiles, which *Publishers Weekly* described as:

> an unromantic view of family life; its foundations, [Bronson] believes, are not soul-mate bonding or dramatic emotional catharses, but steady habits of hard work and compromise, realistic expectations and the occasional willingness to sever a relationship that's beyond repair.

His latest nonfiction effort, the provocative *Nurture Shock: New Thinking about Children* (2009), is a wide-ranging and surprisingly rigorous discussion of modern parenting, written with his researcher from *Why Do I Love These People?* Ashley Merryman.

Bronson maintains an extensive Web site at www.pobronson.com that includes a blog and social commentary.

Bibliography

"Po Bronson." Barnesandnoble.com. Available online. URL: http://search.barnesandnoble.com/What-Should-I-Do-with-My-Life/Po-Bronson/e/978034548 5922/?itm=1. Accessed May 12, 2009.

—Kristina H. Zdravic Reardon

C

Canin, Ethan (1960–) *American novelist, short story writer, and screenwriter*

Ethan Canin is the author of four novels, three short story collections, and the screenplay for *Beautiful Ohio* (2006), directed by Chad Lowe. His novel *Blue River* (1992) was made into a film starring Jerry O'Connell in 1995, and the title story of his collection *The Palace Thief* (1994) was made into the film *The Emperor's Club* (2002), starring Academy Award winner Kevin Kline. Three of his other short stories were adapted into two other films (two were combined). He was named on *Granta*'s list of Best Young American Novelists in 1996.

Canin was born in Ann Arbor, Michigan, on a family vacation to the area from Iowa City, where his violinist father taught in the music department of the University of Iowa. Canin spent the majority of his childhood in San Francisco but also lived in Iowa City; Oberlin, Ohio; and Philadelphia. He attended Stanford University, where he initially majored in mechanical engineering before switching to English after reading *The Stories of John Cheever* during his junior year (Lane). After reading "Goodbye My Brother," he decided to be a writer (Barnes and Noble) and graduated with a masters of fine arts degree in creative writing from the Iowa Writers' Workshop in 1984, along with a medical degree from Harvard Medical School in 1991. He has taught at the Iowa Writers' Workshop since 1998 and lives with his wife and three children in Iowa City and northern Michigan.

Canin often describes how difficult it is for him to write, noting that he had only finished about 50 pages of writing when he left the Iowa Writers' Workshop in the mid-1980s. He entered medical school because he was discouraged and felt he needed a more practical job than writing (B&N). Ironically, he finished the manuscript for his first short story collection, EMPEROR OF THE AIR (1988), which won him the Houghton Mifflin Literary Fellowship, while he was still in medical school. Two of the stories in that collection—the title story and "Star Food"—were included in the *Best American Short Stories* anthologies from 1985 and 1986. Yet, as recently as the summer of 2008, while promoting his novel AMERICA, AMERICA (2008), Canin told interviewer Jill Owens that he still hates writing most of the time and is deathly afraid of it.

Canin's work often combines medical or scientific elements that can be traced back to his own medical career. The story "The Carnival Dog, the Buyer of Diamonds"—first published as "Abe, between Rounds" in *Redbook* magazine—is about a young Jewish medical student who announces to his father that he is quitting school. Throughout the narrative, the conflict between father and son parallels the conflict between the son and his medical career, and the focus, as in many of Canin's works, is on the complicated roles family members play in the narrator's life. Canin, also Jewish, wrote the story while a student at Harvard, and it was included in his award-winning debut collection.

"Batorsag and Szerelem," published in *The Palace Thief*, reveals a striking new layer in Canin's complex aesthetic (recalling his engineering background), as a teenager in 1973 grapples with two detailed and unsolved math problems. The critics Jack Slay, Jr., and Jack Slay, Sr., propose solutions to the word problems inscribed in the story and comment on their role in the narrative:

> Layering the story is a kaleidoscopic series of enigmas: the invented, gibberish language of Clive and his best friend Elliott; the virtually emotionless relationship between Clive and [girlfriend] Sandra; and the difficult word problems that Clive faces in the math competition. In the course of the story, however, every problem receives its solution. . . . In fact, all mysteries receive their due unraveling except for the two math problems that Canin presents as examples of the word enigmas that Clive must solve, both of which remain unsolved in the story. Demonstrating that these two word problems are, indeed, solvable helps to resolve the story of the unique and complicated Messerman clan. (27–28)

That these critics focus as much on mathematical and linguistic enigmas as on the family narrative, reveals the layered depth of Canin's art, but Slay and Slay correctly stress that the ultimate concern of the novel is the roles that the tale's protagonist eventually finds as son and brother.

After the publication of *The Palace Thief* in 1995 Canin left his medical career (he had completed residency at San Francisco General Hospital), but notes that his time as a doctor actually guided him toward and aided him in his writing career:

> In medicine you have the privilege of being tremendously exposed to the way that most of the world lives, at least I did during my residency at a big city hospital like San Francisco General. You see what prostitutes' lives are like, the homeless guys and all kinds of other people who tell you their secrets. . . . I can see why there have been a number of doctors who have also been interested in writing. It's the same interest in people and hearing other people's stories. (Lane)

Indeed, partly in order to mimic the day-to-day schedule and interactions of a doctor, Canin, PO BRONSON, and Ethan Watters founded The Writer's Grotto in San Francisco, a creative workspace for artists (Lane, www.sfgrotto.org).

While Canin is perhaps best known for his short stories—compiled in the two aforementioned collections as well as the recently published *The Bet* (2007)—his four novels have also garnered considerable attention. *Blue River* (1991) continues Canin's exploration of familial themes, here with medicine as a backdrop, as two estranged brothers (one an ophthalmologist) reunite and reflect on their past. *For Kings and Planets* (1998), which also deals with the complex relationship between two men, was a *New York Times* best seller and a *Publishers Weekly* Best Book of 1998. Canin's third novel, *Carry Me across the Water* (2001), features a 78-year-old Jewish-American protagonist, who escaped Nazi Germany as a child and then fought in World War II, ruminating on the life he has lived.

Canin's fourth novel, *America, America* (2008) inspires comparisons to Robert Penn Warren's Pulitzer Prize–winning *All the King's Men*, though Canin claims not to have begun reading Warren's book until after his was published (Owens). The novel takes place in the 1970s and features a young and ambitious protagonist caught up in the campaign of a New York senator running for president, and rapidly enmeshed in scandal, lies, and a struggle to salvage his own integrity. In his *New York Times* review of the novel, Geoffrey Wolff compares it to the works of F. Scott Fitzgerald, noting that "the explicit matter of *America, America* is social and economic class. The mighty squire plucks a townie from his fate and—literally—flies Corey to the clouds."

For his part, Canin cited the 10 pieces of literature most influential to his own writing in a Barnes and Noble interview in the summer of 2008. They were: *Mr. Bridge* by Evan Connell; *At Play in the Fields of the Lord* by Peter Matthiessen; *Libra* by Don DeLillo; *Open Secrets* by Alice Munro; *Ragtime* by E. L. Doctorow; *Henderson the Rain King* by Saul Bellow; *Sacred Hunger* by Barry Unsworth; *American Pastoral* by Philip Roth; *Notes from the Underground* by Fyodor Dostoyevsky; *The*

Deptford Trilogy by Robertson Davies; and *The Stories of John Cheever.*

Bibliography

Barnesandnoble.com. "Ethan Canin." Available online. URL: http://search.barnesandnoble.com/America-America/Ethan-Canin/e/9780679456803/?itm=1. Accessed May 12, 2009.

Canin, Ethan. "Interview with Barbara Lane." By Barbara Lane. Commonwealth Club. Available online. URL: http://www.commonwealthclub.org/archive/01/01-06canin-intro.html. Accessed May 12, 2009.

———. "Interview with Jill Owens." By Jill Owens. Powell's Books. Available online. URL: http://www.powells.com/authors/ethancanin.html. Accessed June 16, 2008.

Crawford, Andrea. "For Writers, the Doctor's Definitely In." *Poets and Writers* (January/February 2009): 16–20.

Redroom.com. "Ethan Canin Biography." Available online. URL: http://www.redroom.com/author/ethan-canin/bio. Accessed May 12, 2009.

Slay, Jack, Jr., and Jack Slay, Sr. "(Re)solving the (Math) Problems in Ethan Canin's 'Batorsag and Szerelem.'" *Critique* 46, no. 1 (Fall 2004): 27–30.

—Kristina H. Zdravic Reardon

Carter Beats the Devil Glen David Gold
(2001)

GLEN DAVID GOLD's impressive debut novel *Carter Beats the Devil* blurs the lines between history and fiction in an epic tale of magic, love, and political intrigue. Set during America's Golden Age, the tale spans the years 1888 to 1924 and chronicles the life of magician and native San Franciscan Charles J. Carter. Known to his public as Carter the Great—a name given him by Harry Houdini—Carter is in fact a historical figure, as are many of Gold's other characters here, including President Warren G. Harding, inventor Philo Farnsworth, and speculator "Borax" Smith. Although the novel primarily depicts Carter's struggle to gain professional credibility and find lasting love, it peripherally chronicles the astonishing ascension of American technology, from the first electrical out-

fitting of homes to the arrival of television; and the faithfully reproduced magic-show advertisements heading each major section contribute to the text's historicity. Despite the verisimilitude conjured by such techniques, the novel is best read as a fictionalized biography based upon factual core characters and events but interpreted with a liberal dose of artistic license.

Organized in three acts like a vaudeville magic show, book-ended by an "overture" and a "curtain," and introduced with a playbill, rather than a table of contents, *Carter Beats the Devil* emphatically challenges traditional notions of narrative structure. Although portions of the novel follow a clear timeline, much of the text is thematically, rather than linearly, arranged. This sense of disjunction is suggested by the overture's epigraph—a quotation by Albert Einstein reflecting upon the relationships among art, science, and mystery. Both the overture and the book's title set the dramatic stage for one of the novel's primary mysteries: Carter's role in the death of President Warren G. Harding. While on his "Voyage of Understanding" Harding participates in Carter's show, hoping to restore public trust in an administration damaged by sordid political and personal scandal. During preparations for the act entitled "Carter Beats the Devil," Harding repeatedly asks the magician what he would do if he knew a potentially world-changing secret. The show goes off without a hitch and culminates in an intense illusion in which Carter's lion appears to eat the president. However, things go awry when Harding dies a mere two hours after the performance. Carter is immediately implicated in Harding's "murder"—an event that leads to a number of unforeseeable consequences and mysterious situations that the reader must work to unravel over the course of the novel.

Although the overture appears to locate the narrative within a specific time and place (San Francisco, August 3, 1923) the expectation of continuity is quickly undermined by the shift to act 1. Act 1 covers the years 1888 to 1911 and, as the subtitle suggests, follows the arc of Carter's metamorphosis from a sheltered child of privilege in Pacific Heights to a struggling "kard and koin" man in a shabby traveling show. It is here that Gold introduces the reader to Carter's parents and younger brother James and reveals the series of traumas that impact young Carter's social and professional choices. Of these incidents, the "magical" theft of a valuable coin by sideshow act Joe Sullivan, and the Carter brothers' imprisonment (by the family gardener) in antique torture devices are most important, for they highlight the novel's trope of "lost innocence." While these experiences certainly shape Carter's life path, Carter is also strongly influenced by the unreliability of adult figures, from the aforementioned Joe Sullivan, "Tallest Man in the World," to Carter's mother, who leaves her family in order to follow her passion for psychotherapy. It is precisely this series of doubt-inducing episodes that leads Carter to the study of magic as a way of exercising methodical and deliberate control over his environment. As the novel progresses, however, we begin to see control itself as an illusion, and discover that even carefully planned situations can unravel with rapidity, leading to some surprising and occasionally tragic outcomes.

Like act 1, acts 2 and 3 focus on the consequences of situations gone awry. Although the novel's central portion explores Carter's maturation after his career-altering battle with professional rival Mysterioso, this is also where we see a major narrative shift. Secret Service agent Jack Griffin, who in the opening scenes appears as a bumbling, grumpy caricature of an early 20th-century flatfoot, is depicted in these sections as a character of great complexity and pathos. In many ways, we might read Griffin as Carter's negative parallel, for through him Gold induces a healthy dose of skepticism in the reader: Griffin, used to being the brunt of jokes, is always on the lookout for trickery. Ironically, in spite of his entrenched mistrust, Agent Griffin maintains an unshakable belief that hard work and loyalty are inevitably rewarded—a philosophy betrayed numerous times. Through these betrayals, Gold invites readers to empathize with both Griffin and Carter (who also experiences his share of disappointment), for their failures and weaknesses ultimately turn two professional *personas* into quirky, flawed, but humanized characters.

Ultimately, *Carter Beats the Devil* is as much a book about writing as it is about magic. The shifting focus and tone, and the tantalizing suggestion of mysterious puzzles (see page 342) indicates the presence of a behind-the-scenes puppeteer—an active author directing his readers through a maze of information. In fact, Gold suggests that he intentionally employs misdirection by submerging thematic elements within an inconsistent plotline. But we can also see the author's hand elsewhere, in the complex tension between historical accuracy and anachronism, and in Carter's own struggles to develop unique storylines and convincing illusions for his stage shows. Issues of authorship and authenticity also arise around the "ownership" of illusions, plagiarism of posters, and the development of new technologies. Regardless, the novel provides a fascinating study of the nature of truth within the context of historical (mis)representations. Ultimately, Gold constructs a world where fact and fiction converge, leaving the reader to ponder his or her own conceptions of reality.

Bibliography
Gold, Glen David. *Carter Beats the Devil.* New York: Hyperion, 2001.
———. *"Carter Beats the Devil* Reader's Guide." Carterbeatsthedevil.com. Available online. URL: http://www.carterbeatsthedevil.com/enter.html. Accessed March 8, 2009.

—Jennifer L. Powlette

Case of Curiosities, A Allen Kurzweil (1992)

Cabinets of curiosities (*Wunderkammers*) were personal collections of all things natural and artificial. Precursors to modern museums, they reached their height of popularity in the 18th century, symbolizing the expansive, exploratory spirit of the Renaissance. ALLEN KURZWEIL's *A Case of Curiosities* embraces this same zeitgeist, the fascination with display and documentation that obsessed scientists and amateurs in the 18th century; and as such, the first-time novelist's historical fiction joins other recent novels by Americans set in the 1700s, including Thomas Pynchon's *Mason & Dixon* (1997) and Susan Sontag's *The Volcano Lover* (1992). Set mainly in the French countryside and capital over 12 years beginning in 1780,

Kurzweil's well-reviewed, though critically over-looked, novel details the cultural crossroads of the late Renaissance, the late Enlightenment, and the early French Revolution.

Like many of his contemporaries, Kurzweil blurs the distinction between fact and fiction, and his principal focus on wonder, evoking the alliance between verity and invention, recalls the work of Lawrence Weschler, who has fashioned a career around the subject. As its title implies, the novel is concerned with narrative *and* with artifacts. A case can be an argument or situation, but also a box or container; and *A Case of Curiosities* is about a particular Wunderkammer, which is itself an arti-fact containing multiple artifacts. Moreover, each of these in turn represents a portion of a larger narrative: the story of inventor Claude Page as he progresses from pencil artist, to bawdy enamellist, to deft watchmaker, to peerless engineer, beginning with his recruitment for an informal apprenticeship by a defrocked abbé. Page's promising story, how-ever, ends in disgrace.

Like any worthwhile 18th-century narrative, as well as any model Wunderkammer, *A Case of Curi-osities* is monumental in its attempt to enclose the world in a smallish box—or book—and Kurzweil highlights the unfeasibility of this task by strictly limiting his narrative. The novel incorporates 10 chapters and two framing sections, and its 12 parts and 360 pages evoke the symmetry of timekeeping; heightening our sense of the constraints involved in encyclopedic representation. This is why Kurz-weil's narrator (an auction-house *habitué* who acquires Page's case of curiosities in 1983) frames the reconstruction of Page as his *own* version of the picaroon's development. Far from an empiri-cal chronicle, the story relies as much on invention as it does on research; and this may provide a clue to why Page's Wunderkammer has an empty com-partment: his case of curiosities is literally "unfin-ished" (358), his life extends beyond the contrived limits of representation. Page's incomplete Wun-derkammer likewise speaks to our sense of—and need for—wonder, our sense of things unseen, unreported, unrecorded, and unrecordable. Like Kurzweil's follow-up novel, *The Grand Complication* (2001), *A Case of Curiosities* illustrates how life is finally unlived without wonder.

Beginning at the age of 12, Page reads every-thing he can find in the abbé's voluminous library. Surrounded by a litany of books, he investigates the provenance of all things, from the popular to the forgotten, the lewd to the reverent. His "con-quest of man's capacities" (42) integrates Cicero, the laws of Muhammadan anecdote, Linnaean sound classification, Diderot, a Saxony prince's Wunderkammer, printed erotica, and the seven mechanical powers. Yet Page's study of "elegance and grime" and everything in between (185) is ultimately unfulfilling. Though he appreciates the range of the abbé's interests, he craves the tele-ology of the watchmaker: a design, a direction, a goal. Unlike Bouvard and Pécuchet, from Gustave Flaubert's eponymous novel (1881), Page realizes the futility of quests for all-inclusive knowledge, and finally leaves the abbé's Big House to settle in the anonymity—and imagined opportunity—of the city.

Deprived of documents, however, the prod-igy-turned-pauper cannot find employment. For more than a month he is even denied access to the guilds, where he had hoped to perfect things mechanical. He thus enlists as an apprentice to Lucien Livre, who traffics in pornographic tomes. Although Livre deals in books, of which he has a grand assortment, he is by no means a lover of culture, high or low. For him books are mere com-modities. After one of his tours and gastric cures, Livre counters the abbé's poetic "a book unread is like a cathedral glass that hides its beauty from all who do not enter" with the pragmatic "Books are bought less to be read than to be owned. . . . Read or unread doesn't much matter" (99). Indeed, the hard-nosed Livre appears to be a mindless accu-mulator of objects, determining value by means of commercial potential. The idealistic abbé on the other hand cherishes knowledge per se, but his intellectual acquisitions do not translate into profit, and Page is torn between the two extremes. With the abbé, he read too much, under Livre he does too little and is finally condemned to the mundane and uninspiring: dusting, deliveries.

Still, Page slowly gains neighborly notoriety, then a neighborhood name, first for modifications to his garret, and then for gadgets that at last he cannot produce apace with demand. Convinced that names are prophetic—Livre sells books, William Battie was weird, René Descartes played cards—the bookseller tries to stifle Page's technical gifts, deeming them incommensurate with destiny: a Livre, after all, needs its Pages. Offended by Page's refusal to embrace the trade his name implies, Livre takes pleasure in relaying news of a rural disaster involving the family of his now ex-apprentice.

Page at once returns to his boyhood home in the countryside with his Parisian comrade, a writer named Plumeaux ("Quills"), to learn of his family's demise in a fire. Somewhat offsetting this loss, however, is his reunion with the aged abbé, and with Plumeaux documenting their doings, the pair embarks on an ambitious project. Combining their artistic and mechanical resources, they aim to construct what the abbé sees as the culmination of his career: a talking automaton. They relocate to Paris, and despite numerous setbacks, complete the Miraculatorium, *une tête parlante*, also known as "The Talking Turk," which Page and his young family then travel the continent to exhibit.

But so entangled is Page in the wonders of the mechanical that he neglects life and the politics of culture. Returning to find the abbé dying and Paris consumed by the French Revolution, he is arrested at the city gates; his crime: treason against the republic; the reason: the Talking Turk's mantra— "*Vive le Roi.*"

Bibliography

Kurzweil, Allen. *A Case of Curiosities.* 1992. New York: Harvest, 2001.

—Jason Polley

Caucasia Danzy Senna (1998)

DANZY SENNA's debut novel narrates the coming of age of a mixed-race protagonist named Birdie Lee. The offspring of a civil-rights-movement union between a black intellectual father and white activist mother, Birdie appears white, but actively identifies with her dark-skinned sister, Cole. The sisters invent a secret language and imaginary world called Elemeno (after the middle letters of the alphabet), in order to express their sense of being caught between races. When Birdie and Cole

attend a black-power school amid the bussing crisis in 1970s Boston, fair-skinned Birdie has trouble fitting in, though she yearns to embrace her black heritage. By adopting certain brands of clothes, braiding her hair to disguise its straightness, and learning to speak Ebonics, Birdie finally passes for black and is accepted by a popular clique.

The first section of the book chronicles the effects of black power on Birdie's family, as the marriage of her parents suffers from the end of the integrationist politics that had brought them together. When the Lees divorce, they separate their daughters according to skin color: Cole disappears with their father, who goes in search of a racial utopia in Brazil, while Birdie and her paranoid mother go underground in order to elude the FBI, which the latter assumes to be on her trail for her involvement with militant radicals. To protect her from the authorities, Birdie's mother forces her to pass for white, and the women invent alternative identities for themselves. Renamed Jesse Goldman, Birdie becomes a half-Jewish girl. After spending time on the road and on a woman's commune, the two settle down to create new lives in small-town New Hampshire. Her mother becomes involved with a white man, while Birdie begins a relationship with the white boy next door, Nicholas Marsh, and must again find a place for herself in school, this time among white classmates. A series of incidents involving her new classmates—including the visibly mixed-race Samantha, the only other girl of color in town—leads Birdie to confront the racism of her peers, and her own passivity in the face of it. Rather than expose her identity, Birdie finally runs away from her mother, abandoning her white existence. In the final section, she embarks on a quest to find her lost sister and father, which takes her back to Boston, and then across the country to Berkeley, California, where the novel ends.

Caucasia recasts several prominent themes of African-American literature, most notably the tropes of *passing* (in which light-skinned black protagonists cross the color line to pass for white) and the *tragic mulatto* (in which mixed-race characters suffer ill fates due to their exclusion from both black and white worlds). While passing had been popular in African-American literature up until the civil-rights era, it eventually fell out of vogue because of its seeming idealization of white-ness. *Caucasia* explores the theme of passing, but maintains blackness as the desired identity: rather than choosing to pass because of the privileges conferred by a white identity, Birdie would rather retain strong ties to her black father and sister. Furthermore, like the protagonist of Philip Roth's *The Human Stain* (2000), Birdie passes for Jewish rather than simply white, thereby adopting another minority identity. Thus *Caucasia* employs the theme of passing to explore the social construc-tion of race itself. Birdie's assumed Jewish identity, for example, is described as a "performance" that she puts on in public (140). While the notion of passing owes its origins to the one-drop rule, which stipulated that any black ancestry made one black, *Caucasia* refuses biological definitions of race. Bird-ie's father proposes that "there's no such thing as passing. We're all just pretending. Race is a com-plete illusion, make-believe. It's a costume. We all wear one" (391). However, while *Caucasia* attests to the illusion of race, it also rejects color-blind-ness, insisting that race continues to matter. And while traditional tales of passing often ended with the literal or metaphorical death of characters who challenged the color line, Birdie resists the fate of the tragic mulatto, and the novel ends ambigu-ously, with its heroine on the verge of adolescence.

Caucasia is a significant contribution to the discourse on multiracialism that emerged in the 1990s. Described as a "post-soul" novel to indi-cate its temporal relationship to the civil-rights and black-arts movements whose writers claimed their blackness as a source of power, *Caucasia* also displays a "post-ethnic" sensibility. According to David Hollinger, post-ethnicity refers to the idea that identities are formed through processes more social than psychological: "the identities people assume are acquired largely through affiliation, however prescribed or chosen" (7). Throughout *Caucasia*, Birdie operates as a *tabula rasa* on which others inscribe various identities, but by the end of the novel, she moves toward defining herself entirely outside a black-white binary view.

Caucasia's self-consciousness about its liter-ary history is evident in numerous allusions to previous novels of racial passing, such as Nella Larsen's *Passing* (1929), Jessie Fauset's *Plum Bun*

(1929), and James Weldon Johnson's *Autobiogra-phy of an Ex-Colored Man* (1912). The novel also invites comparisons to Ralph Ellison's *Invisible Man* (1952), although here the protagonist's blackness is invisible beneath her white skin. Senna devel-ops several of these allusions further in her second novel, *Symptomatic* (2004), which, like Ellison's tale, employs the device of an unnamed narrator to tell the story of an obsessive relationship between two mixed-race women, a plot that clearly echoes Larsen's.

Caucasia participates in a tradition of passing novels that interrogate not only racial categories but also gender and sexuality. Birdie experiments sexually with members of both genders, and the novel refrains from defining her sexual iden-tity. Told from the first-person point of view of a young girl progressing into adulthood, *Caucasia* also belongs to the genre of the bildungsroman, or coming-of-age novel. Though it is structured in mostly linear fashion, the novel's unnumbered sec-tion- and chapter-titles float above the text in gray spaces that themselves suggest the visual ambiguity of its central character.

Bibliography
Hollinger, David. *Postethnic America*. New York: Basic Books, 1995.
Senna, Danzy. *Caucasia*. New York: Riverhead, 1998.
———. *Symptomatic*. New York: Riverhead, 2004.

—Lori Harrison-Kahan

Caught Up in the Rapture Sheneska Jackson (1996)

SHENESKA JACKSON's debut novel explores the nature of love and relationships in turbulent South-Central Los Angeles in the mid-1990s. A native of South-Central herself, Jackson centers the story on 26-year-old Jazmine Deems. Jazmine, known as Jazz to her friends, struggles to balance an increasing desire for independence against love for her often repressive, ultra-religious father. Although Jazz's dialogue opens the novel, we are later introduced to a large and varied cast of characters including her outspoken best friend Dakota, struggling gang members, and music industry heavy-hitters. The characters represent widely divergent backgrounds, and the addition of their voices allows for multiple perspectives, as well as emphasizing the ways in which circumstance affects cultural concepts such as community, family, and loyalty.

To illustrate Jackson's notions of community and family, the novel employs layered narratives, a technique in which more than one character narrates the same series of events, which establishes extended parallels between Jazmine and rapper Xavier Honor, two characters who initially seem worlds apart. Their alternating narratives build upon a series of commonalities and interconnected events, but also provide a critical lens through which to examine broader issues of social determinism and moral agency. We learn that while these pivotal characters share an important similarity—the death of one or both parents—they ultimately deal with this absence in very different ways; and Jackson here subtly challenges the popular assumption that such issues as poverty, geographic location, or household demographics inevitably impact children negatively. She underscores the importance of self-definition, and suggests that personal choices can and often do exert a profound influence on the success or failure one experiences in life. According to Carol Brennan, "Jackson was careful to draw upon her own experiences and those of her peers in depicting another side of life in places like South- Central, [and] [s]he cautions against stereotyping urban life as violent, dangerous, and a dead end by the entertainment industry" (Brennan). Although Jackson strives to undermine stereotypical notions of urban life in the novel—particularly as they affect African Americans—she nevertheless emphasizes the daily reality of violence and gang activity faced by many who live in South-Central. Just as Jazz might be seen as a reflection of the college-educated and working-class residents of South-Central, her love interest Xavier Honor speaks to the very real dangers of street life.

Xavier Honor, known on the street as X-Man, inhabits the misogynistic and drug-filled world of the Cross Street Gang. Like his best friends and fellow gang members, T-Bone and Rich, X-Man grew up on the streets without parents and without a sense of direction. Looking for protection,

support, and power, he joined the Cross Street Gang. As he matures, however, he begins to feel a sense of dissatisfaction with gang life, and wants something better for himself. Hoping to succeed in the music industry, he attends a party at Black Tie Records and crosses paths with Jazz. In an effort to impress Jazmine, whom he refers to as "Little Miss Redhead," X-Man jumps onstage and performs an impromptu rap. The crowd loves him, and he is immediately signed as a new Black Tie recording artist. But this very record deal and the success it represents creates a conflict between X-Man and his friends T-Bone and Rich, who feel that X's solo was a calculated maneuver to help him break away from the group and achieve fame without them, and his solo contract supports their suspicions. While Rich is ultimately pleased with X-Man's success, T-Bone sees it as yet another betrayal by a once-trusted friend. His violent reaction leads to a series of unexpected events, which permanently affect Xavier and Jazmine's lives, and redraw the boundaries of love, loyalty, and friendship.

If Xavier can be seen as the prototypical (ex)gangsta struggling to achieve legitimate success, Jazmine Deems functions not merely as a love interest but almost as a kind of alter ego. A UCLA masters degree candidate, Jazz dreams of becoming a successful R&B singer. Although Jazz and X share similar musical aspirations, their familial backgrounds are decidedly different; while X's world consists of an absent father, daily violence, and rampant drug use, Jazz grew up under the ever-watchful eye of her controlling and demanding father, Reverend Deems, the pastor of the local congregation. Unlike Xavier, whose attitude at first appears to be effectively amoral, Jazmine suffers the effects of oppressive and misdirected morality; the Reverend Deems's strict rules and manipulative, eccentric behavior stifle her freedom and personal development. Only through her outspoken feminist best friend, Dakota, is Jazz able to express her personality and her voice. With Dakota's encouragement, and through an invitation garnered by Dakota's parents, the two women attend the Black Tie Records party hoping to place Jazz's mix tape in the hands of an executive. As X-Man attempts to impress Jazz through his rap, Dakota gives Jazz's recording to manager

Bobby Strong—an action with far-reaching and irrevocable consequences.

For both Jazmine and Xavier, their chance first meeting at Black Tie Records marks the beginning of an intense romantic entanglement, which leaves both characters substantially changed. Through Xavier, the once submissive Jazmine embraces her sexuality, asserts her independence, and learns to balance filial loyalty with a newly awakened responsibility to herself. Because of Jazmine, Xavier begins to understand the importance of responsibility to one's community, and recognizes that blind loyalty is neither noble nor wise. Although the characters face a formidable array of obstacles, the novel ultimately suggests that when faced with faith, hope, and perseverance, even the direst circumstances are amenable to positive change. However, in its gritty, realistic look at life in South-Central, *Caught Up in the Rapture* holds out no promise of fairy-tale endings. Rather, as Jackson says, "the characters [in Rapture] have a definite dream and they go after it" (Brennan). In this way, the novel is as much about empowerment and the often painful process of achieving one's dreams, as it is about love and relationships.

Bibliography

Brennan, Carol. "Sheneska Jackson: Biography." Answers. com. Available online. URL: http://www.answers. com/topic/sheneska-jackson. Accessed March 5, 2009.

Jackson, Sheneska. *Caught Up in the Rapture*. New York: Simon & Schuster, 1996.

—Jennifer L. Powlette

Chabon, Michael (1963–) *American novelist, short story writer, and essayist*

Chabon is the author of six novels, *The Mysteries of Pittsburgh, Wonder Boys, The Amazing Adventures of Kavalier & Clay* (winner of the Pulitzer Prize), *Gentlemen of the Road, The Yiddish Policemen's Union,* and *Summerland,* a novel for young readers. He is also the author of two short story collections, *A Model World and Other Stories,* and *Werewolves in Their Youth.* His first essay collection, *Maps & Legends,* was published in 2008.

Wonder Boys and *The Mysteries of Pittsburgh* have been adapted to film.

Born in Washington, D.C., Chabon grew up primarily in Columbia, Maryland. He studied at Carnegie-Mellon University in Pittsburgh, Pennsylvania, which gave him some familiarity with the city that serves as the setting for his first published novel. He is married to the novelist Ayelet Waldman, and the two live in Berkeley, California, with their children.

Chabon received his M.F.A. from the University of California, Irvine, in 1987, although he began to write *The Mysteries of Pittsburgh* in 1985 (*Maps* 145). Inspired by *The Great Gatsby,* the novel was completed in 1987 and released in 1988, after its author received a six-figure advance. It went on to become a best seller.

It tells the story of three young people from the perspective of Art Bechstein, an outsider whose infatuation with Phlox Lombardi is partially displaced on his suave, wealthier friend, Arthur Lecomte. Taking place over the course of one eventful summer, the novel recalls the almost dreamlike intensity of the Truffaut film, *Jules & Jim.* A recently updated version of *The Mysteries of Pittsburgh* contains a postscript detailing some of the problems, literal (involving computers) and philosophical (involving plot), faced in composing the novel.

Although Chabon's next novel was eventually abandoned, he then published the acclaimed short story collection *A Model World and Other Stories* (1992).

His next novel, *Wonder Boys* (1995), describes a manic and bizarre weekend in the life of aging creative-writing professor Grady Tripp, who contends with a nubile 20-year-old student sharing his house, a disintegrating marriage to a Jewish woman of Korean descent, a literary festival that brings his raconteur gay agent, Terry Crabtree, to town, an unfinished novel more than 2,000 pages long, and a troubled but potentially talented student named James Leer.

These elements, and Tripp's reactions to them, finally wake him from a longstanding pot-induced torpor, and seem capable of ultimately grounding an intellectual rebirth and realigning of his values, although the comic novel takes care to skewer self-involved intellectuals and academic life along the way. In this respect, *Wonder Boys* is a precursor to Richard Russo's *Straight Man* (1997) and Francine Prose's *Blue Angel* (2000), both of which adopt a similarly comic tone and deal with the sexual frustrations and temptations mingling with the bureaucratic hassles facing academics.

Werewolves in Their Youth (1999) followed *Wonder Boys*, but it was *The Amazing Adventures of Kavalier & Clay* (2000) that established Chabon as a major literary force. He acknowledged the ambition behind it, quoting a reviewer in the *Washington Post* as saying, "'You've done well, but you haven't really tried much. Now's the time to set your sights higher.' I took that to heart. It chimed with my own thoughts" (Washington Post); the result was a Pulitzer Prize winner.

The Amazing Adventures of Kavalier & Clay revolves around the adventures of a pair of Jewish cousins, Joe Kavalier and Sammy Clay, both of whom are looking for work and find it by illustrating and writing comic books. Kavalier is an immigrant from Poland struggling to understand the United States (rather like a superhero struggling to understand his own powers), while Clay is an American forced into Kavalier's company by familial bonds. The heroes of the pair's comic books charmingly reflect their own strengths, weaknesses, and travails, most notably "The Escapist," whose powers recall Joe's training in Houdini-style magic.

The next several years saw the publication of *Summerland* (2002) and *The Final Solution: A Story of Detection* (2003), which features Sherlock Holmes during World War II, as Chabon appropriates a famous detective from another work while writing a mystery novel of his own.

After these Chabon began and discarded another novel before completing *The Yiddish Policemen's Union* (2007), the impetus for which was a phrasebook called "Say It in Yiddish" that Chabon found in a used bookstore. The author was intrigued by the pathos of the work, as it was published in 1958, after Yiddish had in effect been wiped out by the Holocaust, and Hebrew had been adopted as the national language for Israel.

The Yiddish Policemen's Union imagines a world in which a plan envisioned by a former secretary of state, to save European Jewry by creating a homeland for them in Alaska, has actually come to pass.

Chabon constructs a vivid and plausible alternate history in the tradition of H. G. Wells's *The Time Machine* (1895) and Philip K. Dick's *The Man in the High Castle* (1962). The novel represents his most significant foray into genre bending, for though he toyed with such themes in *The Amazing Adventures of Kavalier and Clay*, that novel still unfolded in a fundamentally realistic mode.

The Yiddish Policemen's Union follows police detective Meyer Landsman as he investigates a series of astonishing murders in the imagined Jewish enclave of Sitka, Alaska. In Yiddish, "Landsman" loosely means "someone from the same town," or more generically someone being Jewish in a non-Jewish setting. Landsman's characterization is firmly rooted in the Philip Marlowe tradition of a fundamentally good but marginalized detective at odds with the power structure and society in which he works. Other conventional elements include a steadfast partner who nevertheless doubts Landsman, and the protagonist's seemingly compulsive search for truth regardless of institutional authority and apparent good sense. This devotion ultimately leads Landsman to a conspiracy involving ultra-Orthodox Jews, derogatively referred to as "Black Hats." The novel won both Hugo and Nebula awards, the most prestigious prizes in science fiction.

Although *The Yiddish Policemen's Union* has a nebulous status in terms of traditional genres of literary, science, and detective fiction, it was not a major departure for Chabon in its fusion of disparate genres: *The Amazing Adventures of Kavalier & Clay* incorporates numerous allusions to comics and other forms of pop culture.

Having long been interested in genre crossing, hybridity, borders, and canonization, Chabon investigates such themes discursively in his essay collection *Maps and Legends* (2008), revealing a thoroughgoing skepticism toward the perceived divide between so-called genre fiction and its literary counterpart. In an essay titled "Trickster in a Suit of Lights," for example, he states that "From time to time some writer, through a canny shift in subject matter or focus, or through the coming to literary power of his or her lifelong fans, or through sheer, undeniable literary chops, manages to break out" (21). One thinks immediately of Raymond Chandler and Philip K. Dick, who have both been recently included in the prestigious Library of America series.

Chabon also praises graphic artists, stating that "Back when I was learning to love comic books, Will Eisner was God" (141). *The Amazing Adventures of Kavalier & Clay* consciously employs the themes, motifs, and dreams of the golden age of comics as a backdrop for a story about the often insecure men—and they were virtually all men—who invented superheroes. Many were themselves outsiders, especially the many Jews involved in producing comic books. Chabon himself has grappled with insider/outsider status throughout his career. Although he earned an M.F.A. and published *The Mysteries of Pittsburgh* and *Wonder Boys* in the traditional realist style of Flaubert (Wood 32), his own genre drift demonstrates that he is more than willing to experiment.

The first major film based on a Chabon novel, *Wonder Boys* (2000), directed by Curtis Hanson and starring Michael Douglas, received excellent reviews and achieved modest financial success. *The Mysteries of Pittsburgh* received indifferent reviews at its premiere in 2008 at the Sundance Film Festival and never received wide exposure. *The Yiddish Policemen's Union* has been optioned by the Coen brothers, but filming has not begun.

Bibliography

Chabon, Michael. *The Amazing Adventures of Kavalier & Clay.* New York: Picador, 2000.

———. "In Conversation with Michael Chabon." Washington Post.com (4 November 2007) Available online. URL: http://www.washingtonpost.com/wp-dyn/content/article/2007/11/01/AR2007110102327.html. Accessed September 28, 2008.

———. *Maps and Legends.* San Francisco: McSweeney's Books, 2008.

———. *The Mysteries of Pittsburgh.* New York: Harper Perennial, 2008.

———. *Wonder Boys.* New York: Random House Trade Paperbacks, 2008.

———. *The Yiddish Policemen's Union.* New York: HarperCollins Publishers, 2007.

Wood, James. *How Fiction Works.* London: Jonathan Cape, 2008.

—Jake Seliger

Chaon, Dan (1964–) *American novelist and short story writer*

Dan Chaon is an award-winning author of two collections of short stories, *Fitting Ends* (1995, 2003) and *Among the Missing* (2001), and two novels, YOU REMIND ME OF ME (2004) and *Await Your Reply* (2009). His fiction has appeared in *Best American Short Stories, The Pushcart Prize* anthology, *TriQuarterly, Ploughshares, American Short Fiction, Crazyhorse, Gettysburg Review, MSS, Story, Helicon,* and *Mid-American Review.*

Chaon was born in 1964 in rural Sidney, Nebraska, to a working-class family. In 1986 he moved to Chicago to pursue a bachelor of arts degree at Northwestern University, and in 1990 received a master of arts in English from Syracuse University. After graduate school, he was offered a visiting-writer position at Ohio University and then Oberlin College, where he was eventually hired as associate professor of humanities and creative writing. His wife, Sheila Schwartz, also a fiction writer, died of cancer in November of 2008. Chaon currently lives with his two teenage sons in Cleveland Heights, Ohio.

When Chaon was a child, he was drawn to science fiction, mostly because of its imaginative and intellectual ambiguity. Though *The Twilight Zone* had been canceled by then, Chaon subscribed to the magazine in high school and aspired to be published in it, often submitting but with no success. He also loved the work of Peter Straub, Shirley Jackson, and Ray Bradbury; in fact, he wrote Bradbury a letter when he was 13, and Bradbury responded, which was the encouragement he needed to pursue writing.

In an online interview with *The Believer,* Chaon says he started submitting "creepy little fiction stories" to powerhouse publications like *The New Yorker* at age 16, with little success until Reginald Gibbons of the *Triquarterly* realized his age and encouraged him to attend Northwestern (Believer). Under Gibbons's mentorship, Chaon published short stories in magazines like *Triquarterly, Ploughshares,* and *American Short Fiction.* His primary influences continued to be drawn from science fiction, but he also admired the genre-bending fiction of MICHAEL CHABON and Cormac McCarthy.

In 1996, Chaon published his debut short story collection, *Fitting Ends.* The book quietly entered literary circulation and was revised, reorganized, and re-released in 2004 after an encouraging reception of Chaon's second collection, *Among the Missing*. Unlike *Among the Missing*, *Fitting Ends* has no unifying theme beyond the age of the characters, mostly in their 20s. There is a recurring focus, however, on secrets and the private lives of people. "My Sister's Honeymoon: A Videotape" follows an isolated film-school dropout as he watches tape of his sister and her new husband in Colorado. With her husband taping, the footage is so unsteady that we only learn of the young man's sister through fragments of landscapes and body parts, and to the narrator the tape is a window on the eventual collapse of the marriage (Chaon 2003, 1–18). "Thirteen Windows" is another peek into private lives, a series of vignettes revolving around windows that expose characters as they are instead of as they often effortfully pretend to be (Chaon 2003, 89–98). "Transformations" is itself a kind of window, here on the thoughts of the brother of a transvestite in New York City as he grapples with his brother's lifestyle while snooping through a backpack that the latter has brought home on a visit.

Fitting Ends earned more acclaim on its second release in 2004, but not as much as *Among the Missing*, which, after its release in 2001, became a National Book Award finalist and was declared one of the 10 best books of the year by the *Chicago Tribune*, the *Boston Globe*, and *Entertainment Weekly*. In addition, *Publishers Weekly* and the *Washington Post* named it a Notable Book, and a review in the *New York Times* called the collection "unforgettable, if unnerving . . ." (Lowry). In this collection, whose stories are connected by a common and highly nuanced sense of loss, Chaon demonstrates an uncanny ability to disturb and delight at the same time. Particularly disturbing is "I Demand to Know Where You're Taking Me," the story of a family forced to care for a pet macaw when the owner, the lead character's brother-in-law, is imprisoned for rape. The bird, while delightful to the children of the lead character, Cheryl, haunts her with its crass, evocative catchphrases like "Smell my feet" and "Good God, baby" (Chaon 2001, 20). Cheryl grapples with profound unease toward Wendell, the bird's former owner, until she eventually confronts her feelings,

with perilous results (Chaon 2001, 18–49). "Safety Man," another upsetting but inventive story, is a tale of substitution for lost loved ones. When Sandi's husband dies she clings to an inflatable mannequin designed to deter intruders. Safety Man is life-size but anatomically incorrect, to the eventual dismay of the widow (Chaon 2001, 1–17). The stories are finally about replacement as much as loss, about how people often make bizarre but somehow understandable and always very human choices, when faced with emptiness, in order to feel whole again.

A sense of emptiness likewise affects characters in *You Remind Me of Me*, Chaon's first novel, praised by *Publisher's Weekly* as a "piercingly poignant tale of fate, chance, and search for redemption" (Maughan). The work initially resembles a short story collection, revealing defining but often disparate moments in the lives of its varied characters: there is Jonah, mauled by a Doberman as a boy; Troy, who long ago set out, seemingly inexorably, on a path toward dealing drugs; Norah, who gives up her first child for adoption but keeps the second; and a boy named Loomis, who wanders from his grandma's home in Nebraska on a summer day. But as the stories evolve, they begin to intertwine organically as Jonah searches for his biological half-brother, through a plot that ultimately spans three generations. Most of the pain comes through the filter of Jonah, a physically deformed, pathological liar whose awkward temperament frustrates any ultimate fulfillment (Chaon 2004, 1–356). Indeed, Jonah's introspection nearly removes him from reality altogether as, for example, he retreats into movies in his own mind about ideal outcomes of actual situations. But in the end, Chaon's unflinching exploration of the darkness in human existence serves, in the manner of Dickensian *chiaroscuro*, to throw into greater contrast otherwise trivial and easily unseen moments of radiance and redemption, when even a child scratching a dog behind the ears can seem glorious.

In 2009 Chaon published *Await Your Reply*, both structurally and thematically his most ambitious work to date. Ostensibly an intricate thriller revolving around identity theft, the novel reflects the same themes of attachment and loss and the same structure of interwoven narratives but is relentlessly bleak and disturbing in tone. Whereas Chaon's earlier work explores the complex and often poignant search for identity, *Await Your Reply* culminates in the chilling thought that, in the end, there may be nothing left to seek.

Bibliography

Ballantine Reader's Circle. *Fitting Ends.* By Dan Chaon New York: Ballantine, 2003.

Barbash, Tom. "Interview with Dan Chaon." *Believer.* Available online. URL: http://www.believermag.com/exclusives/?read=interview_chaon. Accessed May 15, 2009.

Chaon, Dan. *Among the Missing.* New York: Ballantine, 2001.

———. *Fitting Ends.* New York: Ballantine, 2003.

———. *You Remind Me of Me.* New York: Ballantine, 2004.

Lowry, Beverly. Review of *Among the Missing,* New York Times, 5 August 2001, sec. 7, p. 8.

Maughan, Shannon. Review of *You Remind Me of Me.* Publisher's Weekly (August 8, 2004). Available online. URL: http://www.publishersweekly.com/article/CA444652.html. Accessed October 17, 2009.

Straub, Peter. "Critical Praise." Reading Group Guides. Available online. URL: http://www.readinggroupguides.com/guides3/you_remind_me1.asp. Accessed May 16, 2009.

—Reed Stratton

Cheese Monkeys: A Novel in Two Semesters, The   Chip Kidd   (2001)

CHIP KIDD's debut novel follows its first-person narrator, Happy, through his first two semesters as a student at an unspecified state university. Kidd, who has attained a unique celebrity status in his career as a book-jacket designer for Knopf, has clearly written a semiautobiographical portrait of the graphic designer as a young man. The nameless university Happy attends is similar in setting to Penn State, from which Kidd graduated in 1986; and Winter Sorbeck, Happy's demagogical graphics design instructor, is recognizable as a parody of Lanny Sommese, Kidd's own favorite teacher from Penn State. Kidd, however, distances the protagonist by setting the novel in the 1957–58 aca-

demic year, more than 20 years before Kidd himself attended college.

Not surprisingly, the most immediately recognizable aspect of *The Cheese Monkeys* is its elaborate and playful book design, for which, Kidd has said, he utilized all the tricks he never got to use in his designs for other authors' books. The dust jacket slides off to reveal the title redesigned as a rebus, with illustrations of cheese and monkeys. Two of the novel's slogans, "Good is dead" and "Do you see?" are worked into the layout of the title on the spine of the book and also along the edge of the pages. Inside the soft-cover edition of the book, the acknowledgments are printed backwards, while the press blurbs disappear over the side of the page and are continued on the other side. Kidd wrote the book in Quark X-Press so that he could see the text as it appeared on the page as he composed the novel. The first half of the book, semester one, is set in Apollo typeface and the second half in Bodoni; and Himillsy Dodd's emotional collapse at the end of the book is represented by her dialogue fading typographically to gray. Such metafictional innovations are consistent with Kidd's statement that he thinks of writing as "designing with words."

The content of Kidd's book is also deeply engaged with the art of design. As the title anticipates, the novel is organized into two semesters, and each semester is further subdivided according to Happy's education as a graphic designer. The fall semester is divided into "Registration," two sections of "Art 101: Introduction to Drawing," and "Winter Break;" and the spring semester is divided by the four graphic design projects Sorbeck assigns, and concludes with Sorbeck's final exam. When we first meet Happy, his interest in art is ironic and indifferent: "Majoring in Art at the state university appealed to me because I have always hated Art, and I had a hunch if any school would treat the subject with the proper disdain, it would be one that was run by the government." Happy's drawing class under the tutelage of the uninspiring Dorothy Sprang seems to validate Happy's most cynical suppositions about art instruction at a state university. In the spring, however, Happy's enrollment in "Introduction to Graphic Design" challenges his complacency by putting him under the tyrannical thumb of Winter Sorbeck, the Ahab of graphic design.

Although he does not actually appear until the second half of the novel, the entire story is saturated by Sorbeck's influence. Sorbeck's lectures begin, conclude, and subdivide the narration, and the slogans, "Good is Dead" and "Do You See?" insinuated throughout the design of the book itself, are signature epigrams of Sorbeck. Throughout the novel, Sorbeck preaches the religion of graphic design, spouting formulations such as "Commercial Art tries to make you *buy* things. Graphic Design *gives* you ideas"; "The man-made world means exactly that. There isn't an inch of it that doesn't have to be dealt with, figured out, executed. And it's waiting for you to decide what it's going to look like"; and "Graphic Design, if you wield it effectively, is Power. Power to transmit ideas that change everything. Power that can destroy an entire race or save a nation from despair." He demands such a profound and uncompromised commitment to the rigorous discipline of design that he is ultimately fired from the university before the end of Happy's second semester as a result of the "Cookie cutter" administrators' adverse response to his scatological contribution to the art department faculty exhibition. Happy's emotional and even erotic fixation on Sorbeck transforms him from an indifferent doodler into a committed acolyte to the calling of Graphic Design.

In addition to Sorbeck, the other major influence on Happy is Himillsy Dodd, a cross between Holly Golightly and the Joker. She is an encyclopedia of iconoclastic opinions, and her sharp wit is almost equally matched against Sorbeck's. Happy's apprenticeship as an artist and his sexual maturation both circulate around Himillsy. Indeed, the title of Kidd's book is from one of Himillsy's sculptures, an empty pedestal that is the first work of art in the novel to captivate Happy; and Happy explores his emerging homosexuality through his friendship with Himillsy, which remains resolutely platonic. Winter Sorbeck and Himillsy ultimately constitute an alternative set of parents for Happy. If, at the beginning of the novel, Happy thinks of his uninspiring birth parents as "two loyal, ageless farm cows," by the end of the story he has come to think of himself as "the spawn of Winter and Himillsy." Through them, he is reborn into a new identity as a graphic designer.

The Cheese Monkeys was generally well-reviewed and received praise from notable authors whose books Kidd has designed, including James Ellroy, Bret Easton Ellis, and George Saunders. It was followed in 2008 by a sequel, *The Learners*, in which Happy lands a job in New Haven, Connecticut, at the same advertising agency that had previously employed Winter Sorbeck; briefly reunites with Himillsy; and takes part in the infamous social psychology experiments of Stanley Milgram. A considerably darker novel than its prequel, *The Learners* explores the human capacity for coercion and even sadism that is common to the Milgram experiments, Nazism, and corporate advertising.

Bibliography

Kidd, Chip. *The Cheese Monkeys: A Novel in Two Semesters.* New York: HarperCollins, 2001.
———. *The Learners.* New York: HarperCollins, 2008.

Randy Laist

Chess Garden: Or the Twilight Letters of Gustav Uyterhoeven, The   Brooks Hansen (1995)

BROOKS HANSEN's *The Chess Garden* is reminiscent of the Lewises—Lewis Carroll and C. S. Lewis—a fact immediately obvious to the reader, and one that several reviewers have noted. Hansen himself notes the influence of both Hans Christian Andersen and Roald Dahl. Hailed as a *New York Times* Notable Book, the aptly named novel merges the fantasy of discovering new lands with readable allegories of spirituality in a palimpsestic narrative.

Written in seven parts, the text includes a star-shaped map, with locations like "The Camp of the Limestone Totem" and "Macaroni" numbered for easy reference. Transnational and postcolonial, *The Chess Garden* explores with equal facility links between continents (Europe, America, and South Africa), husbands and wives, neighbors and friends, and a host of chess and game pieces. The novel chronicles events in dual universes: the physical space we inhabit, along with the fictional universe of the "Antipodes."

At times epistolary, the real-time story unfolds as a mystery, taking place during the morning of the "Great Flood" of Dayton, Ohio, in 1913, when Mrs. Uyterhoeven, the "Queen" of the Chess Garden has passed away and is lying in an upstairs bedroom. Her neighbor and nurse, Mrs. Conover, attempts to save the Uyterhoevens' belongings from the flood, and her concern about the backyard (the chess garden) piques the reader's interest, as well as her determination to save "sets," "pieces," and Dr. Uyterhoeven's cane that is suspended from a tree branch in the garden, treacherously close to the waters. Moreover, she spends considerable time saving the doctor's translations from the first floor library, and carrying armloads of books up to the attic. By evening, the attic holds Mrs. Conover, the Uyterhoevens' neighbors (the Tremonts), the dead body of Mrs. Uyterhoeven, and a cow, all having washed up from the swirling waters of destruction, waiting out the storm in the highest room of the house. As a treat, Mrs. Conover hands little Virginia Tremont the letters and pieces she has so carefully protected from nature's destruction. And thus in the attic of the Uyterhoevens, the mysteries of the chess garden, its treasured games and pieces, and the volumes of translations all unfold before the reader.

The enigmatic letters are written in Dr. Uyterhoeven's own hand, and detail his travels to the Antipodes. Mrs. Uyterhoeven acts as his voice, reading the epistles in the chess garden during the doctor's absence. It seems as if the entire Dayton community, one that has literally and figuratively grown up in and around the Uyterhoevens' chess garden over the past 30 years, turns out to hear them. Begun with a simple table or two and a few sets, the chess garden evolves into a central activity within the community for people of all ages, as they play not only chess, but games of all sorts over the years.

Parts of the novel are told through an omniscient narrator who explains the real purpose for the doctor's trip, how he "finds" a map to the "Antipodes" in his game shack and displays it in his library to cover up the real purpose behind his absence. Dr. Uyterhoeven "decides" that he must travel to this mysterious land to discover its secrets

and games. After two weeks of his absence, the readings of Dr. Uyterhoeven's letters by his wife begin, and thereafter occur regularly in the garden. Families flock to the garden to hear his adventures, young and old alike partaking in the fantastic accounts of his alternate world.

In this Antipodean world, varying types of game pieces exist and are fighting among themselves for "goods." There are effigies and totems who protect the goods, and vandals who attempt to destroy the goods. The doctor's travails both amuse and astound the listeners back home in his garden. The first tale describes his boat ride there, his meeting with a mercenary, and his later discovery of the mercenary's mother weeping for her lost son. The end of the doctor's letter instructs his listeners to look for a visitor, who may or may not have already arrived. As the entire cabal heads to the river with spotlights searching for their mysterious guest, only little Henry Gray is lucky enough to spot the tiny wooden mercenary in his boat, a carving that is floating in the river. The mercenary, then, like all the other pieces the doctor has previously given his wife, is placed on the Antipodes board in the library in anticipation of the next installment of fantastic encounters, the doctor's next adventure. Each reading in the chess garden is followed or preceded by friends and neighbors stumbling upon strategically placed pieces that fit on the game board, fulfilling the doctor's promises to write to them of games from the new world.

Along the way, through both narratives, more of the Uyterhoevens' personal lives unfold, including the story of their courtship in Amsterdam, Mrs. Uyterhoeven's early family life there, and Dr. Uyterhoeven's quest for knowledge and meaning in his professional life. The spiritual journey he undertakes in his determination to engage life as a vibrant participant, as evidenced in his conversation with a William James follower toward the end of the book, leads Jay Parini to call the book "ingenious," and adds a deeper tint to the colorful fantasy inscribed in the broader narrative. This journey requires considerable thought from the reader to decipher, as do the allegories of the game pieces themselves.

Eventually we discover that the benevolent doctor has traveled not to the Antipodes at all, but to South Africa, in order to help the communities and peoples displaced by the Boer War. But not until the very end of the novel do we discover more fully the reasons why he would choose to spend the last months of his life in a foreign country instead of at home, comfortable, with his friends and family around him.

The games and tales of the Antipodes are engaging, bizarre, even comical, and make for an easy and enjoyable read. In contrast, the tale of Dr. and Mrs. Uyterhoeven is realism at its finest, detailing marital troubles, career gains and losses, spiritual yearnings, and unexpected tragedy. Yet, the human will to make meaning, play games, and live after loss, connects the reader to these characters at a deep level, even as the early 20th-century American setting seems increasingly foreign to us in this postmodern age. Much like a rewinding chess game, each move that we take through the novel explains the moves that preceded it, until finally we comprehend the entire game up to the moment of the Queen's death, and with this comprehension comes a real and satisfying sense of checkmate.

Bibliography

Hansen, Brooks. *The Chess Garden: Or the Twilight Letters of Gustav Uyterhoeven.* New York: Riverhead Books, 1995.

Vandermeer, Jeff. "An Interview with Books Hansen." *The Newsletter for the Council of the Literature of the Fantastic* 1, no. 4 (December 4, 1997). Available online. URL: http://www.usi.edu/crtsci/english,clf/ n4_a2.html. Accessed October 17, 2009.

"Notable Books of the Year 1995." *New York Times,* 3 December 1995.

Parini, Jay. Review of *The Chess Garden: Or the Twilight Letters of Gustav Uyterhoeven, New York Times,* 24 September 1995, sec. 7, p. 14.

Willeford, Betsy. Review of *The Chess Garden: Or, the Twilight Letters of Gustav Uyterhoeven, Palm Beach Post,* 31 December 1995.

—Tatia Jacobson Jordan

Chevalier, Tracy (1962–) *American novelist*

Tracy Chevalier rose to international fame in 1999 with her best-selling novel GIRL WITH A PEARL-EARRING. She has had five historical novels published between 1997 and 2007, and is now writing another.

She was born in 1962, in Washington, D.C., and grew up there, attending Oberlin College in Ohio. During her studies there, she participated in a semester-abroad program in England and fell in love with the country. After graduating in 1984 with a B.A. in English, she returned to England, planning to stay for about six months, and still lives there today, having married an Englishman. She and her husband have one son.

She worked as a reference-book editor for several years, but became bored with the job and entered a creative-writing program at the University of East Anglia in Norwich, England, graduating with an M.A. in 1994. According to her Web site, although she had written some short stories when she was in her 20s, the year in this program was decisive, forcing her "to write all the time and take it seriously."

Chevalier began her first novel, *The Virgin Blue,* during her year in the creative-writing program. It was published in England in 1997 and was selected that year by W. H. Smith for its Fresh Talent promotion. The novel was not published in the United States, however, until 2003. The story alternates between the narratives of Ella, a 20th-century American midwife who moves with her husband to a small town in France, and Isabell, a midwife who lives in 16th-century France during the Reformation, and belongs to a Calvinist group opposing the cult of the Virgin. Haunted by dreams, Ella begins investigating her Huguenot ancestry, with her research leading her eventually into a romantic relationship with Jean-Paul, the local librarian, as well as to the discovery of interesting parallels between her life and that of her ancestor Isabell.

Chevalier's next novel, *Girl with a Pearl Earring,* was an instant success after its publication in 1999. Set in Holland in the 17th century, the novel, an extended meditation on the salutary force of art and its tension with worldly life, describes the relationship of Griet, a 16-year-old servant girl, and the famous 17th-century Dutch painter Johannes Vermeer. Conflicts arise in the household as Vermeer increasingly involves Griet in his work, first as an assistant preparing paints and ultimately as a model. Although Griet becomes romantically attracted to Vermeer, she knows her place as a servant, and finally must quit the Vermeer household when Catharina, the artist's possessive and jealous wife, discovers the portrait of Griet wearing Catharina's pearl earrings.

Falling Angels, Chevalier's third novel, appeared in 2001. Set in England in the first decade of the 20th century, the novel centers on two families who have adjoining cemetery lots, and employs an astonishing but deftly integrated assortment of 12 narrative voices. The Watermans, members of the lower middle class, cling to Victorian traditions, while the Colemans, members of the upper middle class, have modern views. Their two daughters meet when they are five years old and form a friendship that evolves over the 10-year period described in the novel, surviving their complex relationship with the gravedigger's son, and a sexual relationship between one of their mothers and the gravedigger himself.

The Lady and the Unicorn (2004), which also employs multiple narrators, was inspired by the famous unicorn tapestries now housed in the Musée de Cluny in Paris, and recalls a number of themes prominent in *Girl with a Pearl Earring.* The story takes place in 15th-century Paris, where lives the wealthy Le Viste family who commissions the tapestry, and Brussels, where live the weavers of the tapestry. A passionate love develops between Nicolas, the man who designs the tapestries, and Claude, the daughter in the Le Viste family, but the difference in their respective social classes prohibits a relationship between them, and so the artist incorporates Claude's image in the tapestries as an expression of his love for her.

Chevalier sets her fifth novel, *Burning Bright* (2007), in 18th-century London, and claims that the work, concerned with themes of innocence and experience, was inspired by a 2001 exhibit of Blake's works at the Tate Gallery there. (The title is taken from "The Tyger," a poem in Blake's *Songs of Innocence and Experience*). The Kellaway family moves to London and lives in a house next door to William Blake and his wife, who like to lie naked in their yard and read the poetry of Milton aloud. The two Kellaway children—Jem and Maisie—become friends with Maggie, who

leads them from childhood innocence to worldly experience.

Chevalier employs historical settings in all of her works, scrupulously researching each, and incorporating a wealth of historical detail and personalities in her fictional accounts. Such historical verisimilitude heightens her detailed explorations of social change and the relationships of people from different social classes, while her typical themes involves childhood friendships and the movement from innocence to experience, often in the shadow of sexual intrigue.

Chevalier's latest novel, *Remarkable Creatures* (2009), is set on the southern coast of England in the 19th century and tells the extraordinary true story of Mary Anning, an amateur and indigent fossil collector who discovered the first complete fossil of an ichthyosaurus (or fish-lizard).

Chevalier employs historical settings in all of her works, scrupulously researching each and incorporating a wealth of historical detail and personalities in her fictional accounts. Such historical verisimilitude enhances her detailed explorations of social change and the relationships of people from different social classes. Her typical subjects include childhood friendships and the movement from innocence to experience, often in the shadow of sexual intrigue.

Bibliography

Angell, Sue. "Talking Shop with Tracy Chevalier '84." Oberlin Online: News and Features. Available online. URL: http://www.oberlin.edu/news-info/03nov/tracy-Chevalier.html. Accessed October 23, 2007.

"Tracy Chevalier." September 2007. Available online. URL: www.tchevalier.com. Accessed October 23, 2007.

Charlotte Pfeiffer

Choi, Susan (1969–) *American novelist and essayist*

Susan Choi is an award-winning author of three novels, *The Foreign Student* (1998), AMERICAN WOMAN (2004), and A PERSON OF INTEREST (2008), and is the coeditor of the anthology, *Wonderful Town: New York Stories from The New Yorker.*

Her nonfiction work has been published in the *New York Times, Tin House, Vogue, Allure,* and *O,* as well as in anthologies including *Money Changes Everything* and *Brooklyn Was Mine. The Foreign Student* won the Asian-American Literary Award for fiction and was a finalist for the Barnes and Noble Discover Great New Writers Award, while *American Woman* was a finalist for the Pulitzer Prize in 2004. Choi is both a Guggenheim fellow and a fellow for the National Endowment for the Arts (www.SusanChoi.Com).

Choi was born in South Bend, Indiana, and lived there until her parents separated, when she moved to Houston, Texas, with her mother. Choi has been surrounded by writing and literature since she was very young. As Jessica Murphy notes, she sent stories to *Cricket* magazine, winning first and second prize in two different contests (38). She earned her B.A. in literature at Yale University, then pursued an M.F.A. and Ph.D. in literature at Cornell University. However, she did not finish her Ph.D. but instead became a writer. After she completed her M.F.A. she moved to New York City, where she has resided for more than 12 years (Murphy 38). She worked as a fact-checker for *The New Yorker* when she first arrived in New York, and there she met the editor David Remnick, with whom she edited the anthology *Wonderful Town: New York Stories from the New Yorker* (38). She and her husband, Pete Wells, have two children, Dexter and Eliot.

Choi's books incorporate mid- to late-20th century historical moments into psychologically complex and thematically gripping narratives. It is no surprise, then, that Jessica Murphy remarks:

> Research, obviously, is a big part of her writing process, and it's an activity that she says she enjoyed long before she took her job as a *New Yorker* fact-checker. To her, research, combined with writing, helps her feel like a perpetual student, to gather information that becomes grist for the mill. Eventually, she says, her research gives way to the story itself. (41)

Choi's novels recast historical events from the point of view of fictional characters of Asian or Asian-American descent, who typically and significantly erase ethnicity in their accounts. Therefore, the intersection of history and ethnicity is an important one in Choi's work, and one that she returns to time and again.

Choi's father is Korean, her mother's parents Russian-Jewish immigrants, and her mixed-race heritage has influenced both her writing and her refusal to identify herself as a Korean-American author (40). Her first book, *The Foreign Student,* is perhaps the closest to autobiographical, based as it is on her father's experiences working for America during the Korean War. It focuses on the experiences of Chang Ahn, who works as a translator during the Korean War, before the Americans accuse him of spying and torture him, after which ordeal, and with some irony, he then moves to Sewanee, Tennessee, to study at the University of the South (40). Choi's next two books are deeply rooted in historical moments in America: *American Woman* retells the story of the Patty Hearst kidnapping from the perspective of Jenny Shimada, a Japanese-American woman; while *A Person of Interest* is a fictionalized account of the Unabomber case, focused on the character of Professor Lee who is implicated in the death of his colleague and others.

In addition to such moments of historical tension (both global and local), Choi incorporates complex struggles associated with ethnicity, in particular those of her Asian and Asian-American protagonists. Yet there are complications and subtleties of ethnicity in her accounts that allow them to move beyond the traditional marginalization that is so often highlighted in ethnic fiction. In the tradition of CHANG-RAE LEE and Leonard Chang, the characters in Choi's novels steadily refuse to be categorized simply on the basis of their ethnicity. Professor Lee from *A Person of Interest* considers himself an American (he immigrated to the United States in his early 20's and has never returned to his home country), and his country of origin is never specified. Jenny Shimada of *American Women* is a second-generation Japanese-American who bristles (with good reason) when radicals call upon her to join their cause because her "[. . .] skin is a privilege. [Her] Third World perspective's a privilege" (40). And Chang Ahn in *The*

Foreign Student faces suspicion not merely from the Americans he works for, but from the students at his university and the people in his small southern town. Although ethnicity is not the driving force in her novels, it unquestionably plays a significant role in the overarching thematic exploration of Choi's oeuvre: the struggles of characters who are alienated, marginalized, and confused about their identity, for reasons *beyond* their Asian origins. Her narratives are politically charged, brutally real, and at the same time philosophically complex, redefining the boundaries as much of historical as ethnic fiction.

Bibliography

"About Susan Choi." Susanchoi.com Available online. URL: www.SusanChoi.Com. Accessed January 7, 2009.

Lee, Don. "The Foreign Student." Available online. URL:http://www.pshares.org/issues/article.cfm?prm ArticleID=4678. Accessed January 7, 2009.

Murphy, Jessica. "The Moment of Origin: A Profile of Susan Choi." *Poets and Writers* (January/February 2008). Available online by subscription. URL: www. pw.org/content/moment_of_origin-profile_susan_ choi. Accessed November 5, 2009.

—Genie Giaimo

Clear: A Transparent Novel Nicola Barker
(2004)

NICOLA BARKER's sixth novel is a fictionalized exploration of the atmosphere and events surrounding endurance artist David Blaine's 2003 self-starvation stunt, *Above the Below*. The central image of the novel is the transparent cube in which the American illusionist suspended himself above the Thames River at London's Tower Bridge, to endure a 44-day fast under the gaze of the public. Long-listed for the Man Booker Prize, *Clear* was written as an angry response to an article published in *Guardian* condemning Blaine's spectacle. Told from the point of view of a central male protagonist trying to come to terms with the event, Barker's story offers a more complex meaning for this act. By juggling a myriad of possible interpretations, both of the episode itself and of the public

and media's reactions to it, the novelist investigates its allegorical and cultural significance for both the microcosm of London and society as whole.

Barker divides her own fiction into two categories, the first being "very stylistically ornate but structurally simple—often written in the first person, very topical, full of jokes," and the second "much longer and more densely plotted" (Man Booker). *Clear* is a striking example of the former type. Ribald, comic, and sarcastic in tone, the novel displays certain stylistic liberties, such as frequent parenthetic asides directed at the reader, and fragments of italicized text to suggest the characters' intonation. Lending a self-conscious voice to the contemporary urban milieu, the text is punctuated with celebrity names, cultural icons and objects (the main character's IPod features prominently), and references to popular music. The novel was written in the space of three months, while Barker took time off from a more intensive project (her seventh novel, *Darkmans*, published in 2004, which, at 800 pages, falls into the second category); and its fluent, off-the-cuff style provides the reader with a strong sense of the spontaneity with which the work was created. However, the airy atmosphere of the work should not distract from the weighty themes that it considers. Anti-Semitism, death, starvation, and xenophobia are some of the prominent ideas that surface in the context of an event which, according to the author, brought out the worst in the people of London (HarperCollins).

The story is firmly grounded in a consistently deft and vivid depiction of the scene at Tower Bridge for the duration of Blaine's performance. The author conveys the broad range of reactions it sparked among onlookers, such as ogling, cheering, food-throwing, worship, hatred, mockery, and even violence. The happening provides her with a context in which to paint a somewhat cynical portrait of the British public, insightfully delineating the various sectors of society that have come together to take in the sight: hippies, art freaks, tramps, teenagers, grandmothers, matrons, crazy-angry types, intransitive haters, and so on.

Against this backdrop, the novelist foregrounds the quest of her fictional protagonist, Adair Graham MacKenny, a caustic, randy, and self-absorbed 28-year-old who is drawn into the event despite himself and is determined to attribute some sort of meaning to it. Adair is a clerical worker whose office in a London skyscraper, directly adjacent to Blaine's transparent prison, affords him a perfect view of the illusionist inside his Perspex box. A self-proclaimed "dispassionate observer of the human race" (2), Adair functions as a neutral figure, off of whom the author may reflect diverse opinions regarding the self-starvation act, which are offered up by the many colorful characters that inhabit Adair's everyday world. At first, lurking around the glass cube is simply a way for the protagonist to meet girls. But at the same time as his fascination with the magician takes hold, he finds himself engaged in a love affair with Aphra, an elusive and prickly Blaine-obsessed young woman with a colossal vintage-footwear collection, whose quasi-supernatural olfactory capabilities allow her to determine people's vices and eating habits by sniffing their shoes or skin. Early in the novel we are introduced to Soloman, Adair's sardonic flatmate from Ghana, who speaks Cockney and moves in celebrity circles, spreading his radical ideologies with his three Doberman pinschers always in tow; he is often accompanied by his bohemian girlfriend, Jalisa, a peppery African-American poetess who intellectualizes the Blain affair for Adair.

Amid the comings and goings of these various figures, the novelist raises questions concerning the politics of marginalization, the dynamics of scapegoating, and the role of the artist in society. Through Adair's acrimonious dialogue with various Londoners, the reader is presented with a variety of questions regarding Blaine's fast and its repercussions for local onlookers: Is this spectacle of self-starvation simply an exhibitionist or masochistic gesture, or is it an artistic statement of rebellion against mainstream culture? Do the often violent reactions of spectators reflect the public's need to blame "the other" for society's shortcomings?

Barker's heavy reliance on Kafkaesque intertext implies that she views David Blaine as a kind of "hunger artist." Parallels are evoked between Blaine and the fasting protagonist from Kafka's short story who, after emerging from his cage after 40 days without food, feels unappreciated by his spectators, who do not appear to acknowledge the "honour of his profession" (269). Critics have proposed various allegorical interpretations for "A Hunger Artist"; and the main character of both works may be viewed as a Christ figure (recalling Christ's 40 days in the desert), a suffering martyr, or an embodiment of the misunderstood artist; all of which seem at play in the novel's richly layered tale. Barker's insistence on the absurdity of the public's negative reaction to the illusionist's stunt is counterbalanced by an equally cynical portrayal of the behavior of the Blaine-worshipers. However, the complexity of the stances taken by the characters indicates the impossibility of assigning any stable meaning to the artist's gesture. As one of Adair's colleagues proposes, Blaine is a "blank canvas" (311) upon which the onlookers project their feelings, whether these be rage, hostility, sadness, or admiration—"a mirror in which people can see the very best and the very *worst* of themselves" (311). For Barker, as for many other contemporary writers, the literary text is thus a means of providing a nonreductive interpretation for societal phenomena which might be treated one-dimensionally in other discourses, such as that of media.

Bibliography

Barker, Nicola. *Clear: A Transparent Novel.* London: Ecco, 2004.

———. *Darkmans.* London: Fourth Estate, 2007.

———. "Nicola Barker on Clear." HarperCollins author interview. Available online. URL: http://www.harpercollins.com/author/authorExtra.aspx?authorID=15102&isbn13=978 0060797577&displayType=bookinterview. Accessed July 6, 2008.

Kafka, Franz. "A Hunger Artist." In *The Complete Stories*, edited by Nahum N. Glatzer. New York: Schocken, 1946, 268–277.

Man Booker Prize. "Nicola Barker: Messing with Our Minds in Ashford." Available online. URL: http://www.themanbookerprize.com/perspective/articles/102. Accessed July 5, 2008.

Sicher, Afraim. "The Semiotics of Hunger from 'Le Cygne' to 'Ein Hungerkünstler,'" *Applied Semiotics* 8 (1999): 449–455.

Daisy Connon

Clement, Jennifer (1960–) *Mexican-American novelist, short story writer, poet, and memoirist*

Jennifer Clement is the author of numerous short stories, two novels, four books of poetry, and a memoir. She is known for her skillful blending of the genres of fiction, poetry, and nonfiction. Her story "A Salamander-Child" was awarded the United Kingdom's Canongate Prize for New Writing in 2001, and her novel A TRUE STORY BASED ON LIES (2001) was a finalist for the United Kingdom's Orange Prize for Fiction in 2002. Her work has been anthologized in collections such as *The Best of the American Voice*, and has been translated into 10 languages, including Spanish, French, Italian, and Hebrew. Aside from her writing, she is best known for her work on San Miguel Poetry Week and her efforts to bridge the cultural divide between Mexico and the United States and other countries.

Clement was born in Greenwich, Connecticut, but moved with her family to Mexico in 1961 at age one. Her mother was a painter and her father a chemical engineer with a deep love of poetry. The *Jornada Semanal* reports that Clement and her older brother and younger sister listened to her father read the poetry of Shakespeare, W. B. Yeats, and Walt Whitman as young children. She wrote her first poems at the age of eight about Italy, influenced by the Italian food, culture, and language of girlfriends in Mexico. She attended Edron Academy, a British English-language school in Mexico City during her formative childhood years, and the academy served as the setting for her nonfiction short story "This Was When You Could Still Be Killed for Love," which was nominated for the Pushcart Prize in 2009. She returned to the United States for the final few years of high school, attending Cranbrook Kingswood School, a top-ranked boarding school in Bloomfield Hills, Michigan. She graduated with a bachelor of arts degree in English and anthropology from New York University in 1981, where she took a number of creative writing courses, and wrote her thesis on a women's prison in West Virginia. Clement says that her anthropology degree and work in the field has influenced her writing and cites Chaucer, Shakespeare, William Faulkner, and Latin American writers in general as major influences on her work. She has lived in Mexico on and off since 1981 and still calls Mexico City home. Clement primarily writes in English but also speaks Spanish and French and has written in both.

Alongside her sister (and fellow poet) Barbara Sibley, Clement cofounded the San Miguel Poetry Week in 1997, which is a yearly series of workshops over the course of one week each January in San Miguel, Mexico. Clement notes that the poetry week is perhaps the greatest manifestation of her effort to create bridges between Mexican writers and the writing communities in other countries. In pursuit of the same goal, in 1991 Clement founded the Tramontane Poets, a group of poets who translate Mexican poetry into English; and the group has published a comprehensive anthology of Mexican poetry, which includes the work of Mexico's most famous and most obscure contemporary poets.

In 2001, Clement was awarded the U.S.–Mexico Fund for Culture (FONCA, Fundación Cultural Bancomer, the Rockefeller Foundation) grant for the San Miguel Poetry Week. In addition, she was honored with Mexico's Sistema Nacional de Creadores de Arte grant. Primarily reserved for Mexican citizens, it is the highest literary award available in Mexico, and it admits recipients to an elite group of artists for life; as an American recipient Clement is a rare exception. She was also awarded a MacDowell Fellowship in 2007.

Surprisingly, Clement notes that in addition to being influenced by classic authors such as Chaucer and Shakespeare, her poetry has taken great inspiration from scientific writing, specifically citing the works of Louis Pasteur and Isaac Newton. Her books of poetry include *The Next Stranger* (1993), *Newton's Sailor* (1997), *Lady of the Broom* (2002), and *Jennifer Clement: New and Selected Poems* (2008).

Clement's first long work in prose, *The Widow Basquiat* (2000), details the life story of Suzanne Malouk and her relationship—as a lover and muse—to the artist Jean-Michel Basquiat, who died of a drug overdose in his 20s in 1988. It was praised upon publication for not sensationalizing their relationship or the events surrounding Basquiat's death, and it was named to the Booksellers' Choice list in the United Kingdom.

Clement's first novel, *A True Story Based on Lies* (2001), was named a finalist in the Orange Prize for fiction in the United Kingdom in 2002 and focuses on the struggles of a young Mexican peasant girl hired as a domestic for a rich Mexico City couple who (like Clement's own family) are distinguished by their English last name. The extraordinary emotional impact of the novel, written in a kind of prose poetry, has been justly compared to that of Toni Morrison's *The Bluest Eye.*

Clement's second novel, *The Poison That Fascinates* (2008), is a modern rendition of the founding myths of Mexico. In addition to its poetic prose style, it has been praised for its vivid and colorful descriptions of life in Mexico City, as well as the blending of mythical, Catholic, and secular presences in modern-day Mexico.

Clement's book of poetry *The Lady of the Broom* inspired Jan Gilbert to compose "Eleven Song Setting," a musical piece for soprano, flute, viola, and cello.

Bibliography

Clement, Jennifer. *Jennifer Clement: New and Selected Poems.* New York: Shearsman Books, 2008.
———. *The Poison That Fascinates.* New York: Canongate, 2008.
———. *A True Story Based on Lies.* New York: Canongate, 2001.
———. *Widow Basquiat.* New York: Canongate, 2003.

—Kristina H. Zdravic Reardon

Cloud Atlas **David Mitchell** (2004)

DAVID MITCHELL's genre-defying third book is an ambitiously assembled tour de force. Following the polyphonic *Ghostwritten* (1999) and multilayered *number9dream* (2001), Mitchell's "rollercoaster ride" (Byatt, 9) through history and literary pastiche challenges the reader with six interrelated novellas. The six novellas are designed like Russian dolls, with each section appearing as a literary artifact in the succeeding narrative, up to the central, post-apocalyptic section "Sloosha's Crossin' an' Ev'rythin' After," at which point the entire process is reversed. While each of the individual narratives has a distinct voice and story of its own, the plot

of the book as a whole comes from the strong thematic links between the sections.

In Mitchell's most political novel to date, the central theme of a society consuming itself commences with "The Pacific Journal of Adam Ewing." The genocide and enslavement of the Moriori people of the Chatham Islands serves as the background for a 19th-century historical pastiche that ends mid-sentence. The next section, "Letters from Zedelghem," leaps forward in time to 1931 and is told through the letters of the unscrupulous young composer Robert Frobisher to his friend Sixsmith, while the former is living a parasitic existence as amanuensis to his idol, Vyvyan Ayrs. Frobisher's comments on music introduce one of Mitchell's notable stylistic devices: a masked discussion on the theory and practice of the art of writing. In this, Mitchell is reminiscent of Haruki Murakami. After the eighth of Frobisher's letters, the narrative switches to "Half-Lives: The First Luisa Rey Mystery." The only section to be written in the third person, Mitchell's parody of the tone and content of a third-rate spy novel set in mid-1970s California brings the theme of predator vs. prey to a corporate level. Ending on a cliffhanger, the following narrative is "The Ghastly Ordeal of Timothy Cavendish," narrated by vanity publisher Timothy Cavendish, familiar to Mitchell fans from the "London" section of *Ghostwritten.*

Set in late 20th-century Britain, the Cavendish section challenges society's treatment of the defenseless by the powerful, showing how easily physical violence can replace reason. "An Orison of Somni~451" plunges the reader into a dystopian future of genetic engineering and consumerism gone mad. Using the form of a holographic interview with rebellious fabricant Somni~451, the nightmarish world of Nea So Copros—a fictional, corporate location in Korea—explores how extreme forms of capitalism can strip society of its humanity. The ensuing, central section is the only one to be presented as a whole piece. The post-apocalyptic Hawaiian setting of 'Sloosha's Crossin' an' Ev'rythin' After' shows the majority of humanity reduced to a primitive state, having lost the technological advances of civilization. The narrator, Zach'ry, tells the story of his tribe's genocide to strangers at a campfire, in a tale strongly reminiscent of the story of the Moriori tribe in the opening section. After the central section, Mitchell moves backward through the previous sections, completing them in turn.

Cloud Atlas owes a clear structural debt to Italo Calvino's postmodern novel *If on a winter's night a traveller* (1979), and in various interviews Mitchell comments on having read Calvino's masterpiece in his early 20s, and finding the lack of resolution both frustrating and compelling. *Cloud Atlas* reflects the structure of Calvino's book back upon itself, making a structural experimentation more accessible to readers less interested in postmodernity for its own sake. Mitchell ascribes his initial interest in the fate of the Moriori people to Jared Diamond's multidisciplinary *Guns, Germs, and Steel* (1999), leading to a travel scholarship from the Society of Authors that allowed him to visit the Chatham Islands and Hawaii when researching the opening and central sections of *Cloud Atlas*. The philosophical pathways between the six novellas are reminiscent of Jorge Luis Borges, as is Mitchell's interest in the transmission of the text in its changing forms as literary and social artifact.

Along with the thematic links, recurring characters and idiosyncrasies are used to create a sense of cohesion between the sections. For example, the 'Sixsmith' to whom Frobisher addresses his letters becomes Rufus Sixsmith in the Luisa Rey section, and each of the protagonists bears a "comet-shaped birthmark between his shoulder-blade and collar-bone" (122). In "Letters from Zedelghem," Vyvyan Ayrs dreams of the "nightmarish café, brilliantly lit, but underground, with no way out" (80) in which Somni~451 begins her ascendance; and in the concluding "Pacific Journal" section Ewing muses over the theological and social significance of "Civilization's Ladder" (512), and whether or not salvation lies in its ascent. Mitchell pokes self-conscious fun at his own postmodern literary experimentations through repeated references to the Russian doll structure of the novel itself, such as Vyvyan Ayr's *"Matruschyka Doll Variations"* (52), or Somni~451 hearing a circusman advertise "Madame Matryoshka and Her Pregnant Embryo." (353). Just as Frobisher's comments on music and composition can be seen as analogous to Mitchell's comments on literature and writing, the fate of Frobisher's best-known work, "*Cloud Atlas Sextet* must bring the kiss of death to all who take it on" (121), doubly comic in the light of the commercial and critical success of *Cloud Atlas*: short-listed for the 2004 Man Booker Prize and the Commonwealth Writers Prize (Eurasia Region, Best Book), winner of the 2005 British Book Awards Literary Fiction Award and the 2005 British Book Awards Richard & Judy Best Read of the Year.

The recurrence of characters in more than one section of the book is becoming one of Mitchell's trademarks, with characters, concepts, and settings echoed in all of his four books to date, following in the footsteps of writers such as Will Self and BRET EASTON ELLIS. For example, both Timothy Cavendish and Luisa Rey appear in *Ghostwritten*, and Frobisher's death is mentioned in Mitchell's fourth book, *Black Swan Green* (2006). However, Mitchell's most notable stylistic feature is his ability to present challenging social commentary and literary experimentation in an accessible, page-turning narrative.

Bibliography

Byatt, A. S. Review of *Cloud Atlas*, *Guardian*, 6 March 2004, Book Review. p. 9.

Mitchell, David. *Cloud Atlas*. London: Sceptre, 2004.

—V. S. Adams

Costello, Mark A. (1962–) *American novelist, critic, and lawyer*

A onetime former federal prosecutor, and now professor of criminal law at Fordham University, Costello is a frequent reviewer for the *New York Times*, and the author of three books, *Signifying Rappers: Rap and Race in the Urban Present* (1990), cowritten with DAVID FOSTER WALLACE, *BAG MEN* (1996), and *BIG IF* (2003). *Big If* was a *New York Times* Notable Book and a finalist for the National Book Award.

Mark A. Costello (not to be confused with the author of *The Murphy Stories*) was one of seven children born in Winchester, Massachusetts, to working-class Irish-Catholic parents. He attended

Amherst College, where he first roomed with Wallace in their sophomore year. Wallace, who wrote INFINITE JEST (1996)—a novel considered a late American classic—committed suicide in September of 2008, and Costello has spoken many times since then about Wallace's life, struggles, and genius. Harlan Coben, winner of the Edgar, Shamus, and Anthony Awards and author of 19 crime novels, was another dorm-mate of Costello's at Amherst. After graduating in 1984, Costello went on to law school at Yale, and received his degree in 1988. He was an associate corporate attorney for the firm of Testa, Hurwitz, and Thibeault from 1988 to 1990, district attorney for New York County from 1990 to 1995, and a U.S. attorney in the District of New Jersey from 1995 to 1998. Since 2001, he has been a professor of law at Fordham University in New York City.

Costello and Wallace played up their outsider status in order to gain admittance to a small recording studio in the North Dorchester area of Boston, and to the burgeoning world of rap music in the late 1980s. The result, Signifying Rappers, is a slim but ambitious volume dedicated to situating rap within the broader contexts of the African oral tradition, the conspicuous consumption of Reagan-era America, the perpetuation of racial boundaries in contemporary society, and the history of American poetry. The title of the book is borrowed from a 1988 gangsta rap single by Schoolly D, "Signifying Rapper," which was in turn a nod to the song, "Signifying Monkey," by Rudy Ray Moore. Henry Louis Gates's 1988 text, The Signifying Monkey: A Theory of African-American Literary Criticism, investigates the cultural practice of "signifying," a complicated rhetorical technique that can either express admiration for a work or alter it in order to criticize the original and showcase the signifier's talents. Costello and Wallace's Signifying Rappers locates early rappers within these diverse contexts and applauds their contributions to and advancement of many disparate genres.

Bag Men was published in 1996 under the pseudonym John Flood. Costello, a federal prosecutor at the time, explains that "Bag Men is about official corruption and corrupt prosecutors—all forms of corruption, both overt and sometimes more subtle. I didn't want the book read as a tell-all, as a prosecutor blows the lid off. So I felt there had to be some separation. And the nom de plume was the best mechanism I could come up with" (Birnbaum interview). The novel is set in Boston in 1965, and opens with the murder of a priest, George Sedgewick; after landing at Logan Airport Sedgewick is robbed of 4,000 communion hosts that were consecrated by Pope Paul VI, in advance of the first English-language mass to be held in America that year. The novel then traces the crime in the narratives of characters on both sides of the law, as the homicide investigation becomes intertwined with the contemporaneous introduction of LSD into mainstream America. Bag Men is a literary thriller whose plot is intricately woven out of a vast amalgam of details that seek to capture the essence of 1965.

Costello's novel—and the intensity of its prose—invited early comparisons with the work of Jonathan Franzen and Don DeLillo. In his 2002 review of Big If, Jay McInerney emphatically locates Costello "among the sons of Don" (7); and indeed, Costello claims DeLillo as one of his strongest influences, along with Joseph Conrad and Alice Munro. DeLillo's masculine style has proved to be highly influential on a new generation of authors producing literary prose with a kind of hyper-realism and Carver-esque economical phrasing.

Just as Bag Men is rooted in 1960s America, Costello's most recent novel, Big If, is linked to another epochal moment in the evolution of the nation's consciousness. America's post-9/11 anxieties are represented here through the overlapping narratives of computer programmers, Secret Service agents, and insurance adjusters. Programmer Jens Asplund has created a hugely popular video game called BigIf, set in a post-apocalyptic future, and the realism of the game's monsters underscores the fearful tension of the nation after the turn of this century. Jens's younger sister, Vi, is a burnt-out protection agent for the Secret Service. She and her colorful colleagues act in accordance with "The Certainties," a document created by consummate agent, Lloyd Felker, which consists of "fifty-seven seminal white papers" outlining possible-threat scenarios, and the steps necessary to prevent and counteract these threats. The novel works to destroy supposed certainties, however, challenging assumed facts and accepted truths. Felker, the ultimate protection agent and godlike figure to the younger operatives, is killed, leaving the agency in the hands of Gretchen Williams, a fallible woman whose uncertainty endangers the lives of both the vice president and the other agents. Walter Asplund, meanwhile, father and moral authority to both Jens and Vi, is described as replacing the word "God" on bank notes, so that the official motto of the United States now reads "In Us We Trust." Though "U.S." suggests a prioritization of country over God, Walter's "Us" is a manifest invocation to place our trust not in God, law, or country, but in ourselves—an understandable, if dangerous, move in times of such uncertainty.

With *Big If*, McInerney notes, Costello "enters the big leagues of American fiction," creating "a thoroughly original universe—which seems, in retrospect, to have been waiting for us all along" (7). If *Bag Men* critically reconsidered time-honored truths of a bygone era, *Big If* brings the same searching and uncompromising skepticism to the uncritical "certainties" of our own time.

Bibliography

Costello, Mark. "Author of *Big If* talks with Robert Birnbaum." By Robert Birnbaum. Available online. URL: http://www.identitytheory.com/people/birnbaum56.html. Accessed May 16, 2009.

———. [John Flood, pseud.] *Bag Men.* New York: W. W. Norton, 1996.

———. *Big If.* New York: W. W. Norton, 2003.

Costello, Mark, and David Foster Wallace. *Signifying Rappers: Rap and Race in the Urban Present.* New York: Ecco Press, 1990.

McInerney, Jay. Review of *Big If. New York Times Book Review,* 16 June 2002, 7.

—Katherine Edwards

Coupland, Douglas (1961–) *American novelist, playwright, and screenwriter*

Canadian visual artist, cultural critic, playwright, and screenwriter, Douglas Coupland is best known for his eclectic, postmodern novels: GENERATION X (1991), *Shampoo Planet* (1992), MICROSERFS (1995), *Girlfriend in a Coma* (1997), *Miss Wyoming*

(1999), *All Families Are Psychotic* (2001), *God Hates Japan* (2001, Japanese language only), *Hey Nostradamus!* (2003), *Eleanor Rigby* (2004), *JPOD* (2006), *The Gum Thief* (2007), and *Generation* (2009). Coupland also acted in his own first play, *September 10, 2001*, with Stratford-upon-Avon's Royal Shakespeare Company in 2004. His popular collection of short stories, *Life after God* (1993), was recently adapted for the stage by Michael Lewis MacLennan. And a film based on Coupland's first screenplay, *Everything's Gone Green*, premiered at the Vancouver Film Festival in 2007.

Coupland was born in 1961 on a Canadian air force base in Baden-Söllingen, Germany; his family relocated to Vancouver, Canada, in 1965, where Coupland has lived most of his life and where he currently resides. As a young adult, his foremost passion was for visual art, and he completed a degree in fine art at Vancouver's Emily Carr Institute of Art and Design, as well as traveling to Japan and Italy to devote time to his art.

Coupland has been labeled as a spokesperson, perhaps even a prophet, for his generation—a title he resents and repeatedly refutes. In 1989, he was offered a $22,500 advance to write a nonfiction account of Generation X, but the final product, a fictional exploration titled *Generation X: Tales for an Accelerated Culture*, was not at all what the editors had expected (Lohr). At the time, Coupland was a sculptor who frequently wrote witty articles of nonfiction cultural commentary for magazines such as *Wired*. He decided that fiction was the best way to approach the project; but his aim in *Generation X* (1991) was not to define his generation but to explore the tensions inherent in the lives of his privileged "slackers," protagonists Andy, Dag, and Claire, who move to the desert, away from the confines of a reality determined by antispiritual consumerism. And this search for a postsecular spirituality, the quest for what Coupland calls "epiphany and transcendence" (qtd. in Draper), is the defining feature of Coupland's fiction. But the pilgrimages that in Coupland's work seem to define the human condition are rarely enacted in traditional "sacred" spaces of worship; indeed, his characters begin their search in the most unlikely sacred spaces: the shopping mall (*Shampoo Planet*), a Greyhound bus (*Shampoo Planet*), a presidential inauguration *(Life after God)*. However, though Coupland rarely relies on dogmatic, theological terminology to depict depravity or revelation, he does frequently allude to both poetry and narratives from the Bible.

In a radio interview with Tom Ashbrook, Coupland claims that "What unites all people through time and history, regardless of place, is the need to make sense," a need evident in the desire of many of his characters to become part of a story, to have the isolated moments of their lives strung together, to progress toward something that will disclose ultimate truth and meaning. This theme, developed throughout his entire body of work, is strikingly articulated in *Generation X*, as his postmodern pilgrims gather in the desert to tell stories that will connect the dots of their lives, providing a narrative to make sense of reality for each of them. Claire, for example, admits that "it's not healthy to live life as a succession of isolated little cool moments. Either our lives become stories, or there's just no way to get through them" (8). Narrative implies direction and purpose for an individual life, but the individual must draw on the outside perspective of the community to legitimate her stories.

Coupland revisits similar themes in his next novel, *Shampoo Planet*, yet the novel's protagonist, Tyler, is a devout disciple of the modern religion of materialism that *Generation X*'s bohemians desperately try to reject. The story highlights Coupland's almost nostalgic love for the products and virtual spaces that we call home. Although these products provide young Reaganite Tyler with a sense of wellness and security, he longs to develop an identity around something more than his role as a member of a desired target market.

Life after God (1993) appears to be a turning point for Coupland, as it is the first book that has the "loss of God" in privileged middle-class culture as its most obvious premise. Its stories explore the interior world of a host of characters all coming to a crucial point of recognition of their own spiritual brokenness and need for change. It argues that, although popular culture may offer a surrogate paradigm to those who have been "raised without religion" (129), it is ultimately a false and inadequate one, pointing toward a deep need that it is not

equipped to meet. Although these glassy, thin, and ultimately artificial paradigms are initially common reference points, the collection intimates the presence of a deeper pool of reference, in the form of spiritual questions about the nature of life, death, and the possibility of afterlife that are common to all of humanity. These questions, and the act itself of relentlessly questioning, are at the heart of Coupland's novels, beginning with *Generation X*, but becoming more prominent as his oeuvre evolves, especially in *Life after God, Girlfriend in a Coma,* and *Hey Nostradamus!*

In *Life after God*'s "The Wrong Sun," Coupland provides us with a host of destructive fantasy visions of nuclear annihilation, reminding us that "technology does not always equal progress" (75). In the collection as a whole, and particularly in the story "1,000 Years: Life after God," we meet countless young, yet jaded protagonists, seemingly deadened, dazed, and confused by the abundance of artificial reality around them, a suburban inheritance that has provided them with a godless heaven on earth. Scout, the story's chief spiritual sojourner, flees from the city, abandoning the "evil empire" of the corporate world to find refuge in the lush Canadian forest, where he is finally forced to admit that he "needs God."

Coupland's interest in apocalypticism continues in 1997's *Girlfriend in a Coma*, the tale of a young woman named Karen who falls into a physical coma representative of her depthless culture's spiritual anesthesia. Here Coupland emphasizes the tension between the deadening and life-giving powers of technology, as Karen's friends experience the apocalypse fixated more on entertainment and addictions than the redemptive powers of divine revelation.

A frightening vision of the postmodern sublime, of technology created and nurtured by multinational capitalism, is the theme of both 1995's *Microserfs* and 2006's *jPod*. Both novels examine and humanize the self-proclaimed computer geek subculture, as Coupland ventures into the interior worlds of computer programmers and corporate-office veterans. Employing typically commodified language to describe the darkness of the human condition (another of Coupland's frequent themes), *jPod*'s Ethan admits, "I hoped that God would shake my Etch-a-Sketch clean overnight" (134).

The emphasis on human depravity and need for redemption is a central focus of 2003's *Hey Nostradamus!*, a novel told from the narrative perspectives of four individuals whose lives are devastated by the senseless violence of a suburban school massacre. Coupland's most theologically rich novel, it explores the problem of evil, the oppression of religious hypocrisy, and the tension between law and grace.

Coupland's *The Gum Thief* (2007) is a collection of fictive letters between Roger and Bethany, two Staples employees and highly unlikely friends. The focus on the written word, both in the letters themselves and in excerpts from Roger's novel, *Glove Pond*, again echo Coupland's concern with the role of narrative in the construction of identity and community, a concern developed and intensified in 2009's *Generation A*, which in the words of Coupland's Web site, "champions the act of reading and storytelling as one of the few defenses we still have against the constant bombardment of the senses in a digital world."

Because of his engaging, accessible, pop-culture-laden prose style, Coupland is often included in a list of "Blank Fiction" authors such as BRET EASTON ELLIS and Jay McInerney by such critics as Annesley, Caveney, and Young. However, blank fiction tends to depict the stylish urban scene, with all its technologies, glitz, and glamour, whereas Coupland frequently locates his novels in middle-class suburban settings. And unlike blank fiction, his focus is not on indulgence, excess, and extremes as much as the mundane and "normal" (though these may and often do encompass the eschatological). Moreover, though "blank" writers such as Ellis "resonate with the spirit of the age" (Annesley 5), Coupland seeks the hidden dimensions and possibilities of this spirit, questioning its roots and necessity, and implying, even in asserting its absence, the presence of some collective reference point that transcends our artificial constructions of meaning. He is simultaneously fascinated by and wary of popular culture, as evidenced by his *Girlfriend in a Coma*, which is named after a popular song yet decries our deadening reliance on popular culture as spiritual surrogate. Along with

Eleanor Rigby (2004), the novel muses on religious questions: prophecy, divine judgment, and the need for redemption; and such subjects, though alien to the contemporary, secular world represented *in* the novels, are persistently and impressively explored *by* them.

Bibliography

Annesley, James. *Blank Fictions: Consumerism, Culture and the Contemporary American Novel.* London: Pluto Press, 1998.

Caveney, Graham, and Elizabeth Young. *Shopping in Space: Essays on American "Blank Generation" Fiction.* London: Serpent's Tail, 1992.

Coupland, Douglas. *Generation X: Tales for an Accelerated Culture.* New York: St. Martin's Press, 1991.

———. "Hey Nostradamus." By Tom Ashbrook. On Point of WBUR.org. Available online. URL: http://www.onpointradio.org/shows/2003/09/20030909_b_main.asp. Accessed May 16, 2009.

———. *JPod.* London: Bloomsbury, 2006.

———. *Life after God.* London: Simon & Schuster, 1994.

———. "Engaging in Reflection." By Brian Draper. Damaris.org. Available online. URL: www.damaris.org/olr/features/1998/couplandinterview.htm. Accessed August 1, 2009.

Lohr, Steve. Review of *Generation X*, New York Times on the Web (May 29, 1994). Available online. URL: http://www.geocities.com/soHo/Gallery/5560/nyt6.html. Accessed May 16, 2009.

—Mary W. McCampbell

Crime in the Neighborhood, A Suzanne Berne (1997)

SUZANNE BERNE's well-received first novel explores a woman's recollections of a memorable summer in 1972 when narrator Marsha Eberhardt was 10. A 12-year-old boy from her neighborhood is murdered, her parents become divorced, and the Watergate scandal is breaking news; the majority of the novel focuses on the narrator's recollections of and fantasies surrounding this time in her life. The young Marsha's sense of stability is profoundly shaken both by her father's affair with her mother's younger sister and by Boyd Ellison's murder. She begins pasting news stories about the murder and current events into a notebook, in which she also keeps meticulous notes about the comings and goings in her neighborhood, especially those of her next-door neighbor Mr. Green.

More broadly, the narrative chronicles what happens to a quiet, affluent, white, suburban neighborhood outside Washington, D.C., when a child is found molested and murdered in a wooded area by the shopping mall. The neighborhood fathers form a night-watch group, the entire neighborhood is abuzz with rumor and speculation, and everyone hungers for an arrest that does not come. By the end of the novel, the neighborhood no longer feels as safe and secure as everyone once trusted it to be. People begin locking their doors and turning their suspicions on anyone who does not "belong," among them Marsha's family, now broken, and Mr. Green, a bachelor from "the country"; and in the end the title's "crime" seems to consist in nothing more than failing to fit into the idealized middle-class neighborhood of the country's collective imagination. In this way, the novel tells an almost fabular tale of the end of idyllic American suburbia and the beginning of a more cynical time in U.S. history.

The adult Marsha narrates the story, and is unreliable at best, often confusing memory with fantasy and the private events of her life with public events in the news. Her tale shifts between in-the-moment narration by her 10-year-old self, and the reflective, distanced recollection by her as an adult. It would seem that before that summer, Marsha and her family had largely fulfilled the American dream of living a quiet and contented life in the suburbs; but Marsha's teenaged siblings, Julie and Steven, are twins living in their own extended fantasy, in which they are British aristocrats Felicia and Rodney, even speaking with British accents, and callously excluding the younger Marsha, whom they call Swamp. Marsha was the closest to their father when he skipped town, leaving his family and career as a real estate agent behind, to have a relationship with his wife's sister (which ultimately fails). Ten-year-old Marsha watches helplessly as her mother deals with her devastating betrayal by both her husband and her sister by obsessively cleaning the house, and it will

take Marsha 25 years to gain courage enough to ask her father why he left them.

Marsha often imagines what may have happened when she was not present, and tells these imagined events as if they actually occurred, beginning with her mother's discovery of her father's affair. And when her relationship with her mother is tested by Mrs. Eberhardt's attraction to Mr. Green, Marsha lies to police, claiming he has been "watching" the neighborhood children and even striking her, causing him to be falsely arrested and finally forced to move out of the area. Marsha is morally ambiguous, as 10-year-olds frequently are, testing the boundaries of her narrow world, knowing the difference between fantasy and reality but allowing her often-told fantasies to rule.

Boyd Ellison was a neighborhood bully who stole other children's bikes and was accused of stealing from his Boy Scout troop by Marsha's brother. Marsha's only clear memory of the murdered boy is of the time he once asked to wear her glasses, and then both fascinated and appalled her as he slowly tortured a praying mantis. While Boyd Ellison's murder is never solved, Marsha gradually comes to terms with her own profoundly mixed feelings about him, using his memory as a kind of moral constant around which to cluster the novel elements of her evolving maturity.

Voyeurism, both literal and metaphorical, lies at the heart of the novel. Marsha intently watches her neighborhood "take place," believing that if she just pays enough attention she will be able to discover who murdered Boyd Ellison, and by extension make sense of the mysteries concomitant with his death. As an adult she reflects:

> In a confused manner, I think I'd begun to connect my father's leaving with Boyd Ellison's murder and even with whatever it was that had happened at Watergate. Although I couldn't explain it then, I believed my father's departure had deeply jarred the domestic order not just in our house, but in our neighborhood, and by extension the country, since in those days my neighborhood was my country. My father left to find himself, and a child got lost. That's how it struck me (129).

A Crime in the Neighborhood received the Orange Prize for Fiction, selected over Toni Morrison's *Paradise* and Barbara Kingsolver's *The Poisonwood Bible* among others. It was also a *New York Times* Notable Book and a finalist for the Edgar Allan Poe and *Los Angeles Times* awards for first fiction. Berne explores similar themes of troubled familial relationships and conflicts of middle-class American life in her follow-up novels, *A Perfect Arrangement* (2001) and *The Ghost at the Table* (2007).

Bibliography

Berne, Suzanne. *A Crime in the Neighborhood.* Chapel Hill, N.C.: Algonquin Books, 1997.

—Amy Parziale

Crooked River Burning Mark Winegardner
(2001)

MARK WINEGARDNER's second novel is "a love letter to Cleveland" (Hemley), a nostalgic tribute to the Ohio city whose political, economical, and cultural significance rapidly deteriorated in the decades after World War II.

Crooked River Burning is situated in the Cleveland of the late '40s to the '60s, but similarly to works such as Jonathan Franzen's *Twenty-Seventh City,* E. L. Doctorow's *City of God,* or Richard Ford's *Independence Day,* it explores broader issues relating to the 20th-century American city and its fate in rapidly changing capitalist society. At the novel's center is a romance between David Zielensky and Anne O'Connor, who though from the opposite sides of the Cuyahoga River, and therefore different social strata, share similar ambitions. Determined to overcome the limitations inscribed in their respective classes—David by becoming a councilor and Anne by becoming a reporter—they have the same passion for "racy" music, baseball and, above all, their hometown.

David is the son of a corrupt but charming Teamsters union leader who might or might not have killed David's mother. Although a constant in David's life, he is rarely present and David is brought up by Uncle Stan, a private detective with all-American mannerisms, and his Aunt Betty who shares her unconditional love between Stan and David. Anne, on the contrary, is the youngest child of an influential Democratic mayor and a Rockefeller descendant. Precocious and pretty, even as a little girl Anne is aware of her class benefits, as well as the marital problems of her parents and her mother's alcoholism. Anne and David's love story starts on one of the Lake Erie islands where David comes with his aunt and uncle to spend the weekend in a decrepit rented trailer; and where Anne's family finds a refuge from the city's heat in a posh villa. When the two meet, Anne lies about her young age, while David is already engaged to Irene Hrudka, "the real girl" with whom he grew up, and is on his way to the navy. In an episode that manifests the power of Anne's character and David's admiration for a girl of exceptional beauty and background, Anne wantonly destroys Uncle Stan's precious car that David borrowed for a night. Yet David takes the responsibility, and as a consequence of the incident the couple does not see each other for a number of years. Nonetheless, each of them is enthralled by the other and their contrasting background; David admires Anne's rich, gregarious Irish family, while Anne is impressed by the uncustomary warmth of David's relatives.

Focused on the protagonists' respective struggles to succeed, the narrative, which interweaves historical and fictional figures, is dominated by two typical Cleveland symbols: baseball and the river. Recalling Don DeLillo's *Underworld,* but also Winegardner's previous novel about the Mexican baseball league, *The Veracruz Blues, Crooked River* opens with a remarkable baseball scene. Fourteen-year-old David secretly takes a streetcar with his friends and goes to an Indians-Dodgers home game where he sees one of the first African-American professional baseball players, Satchel Paige. A minority in the predominantly African-American audience, David suddenly becomes aware of the racial segregation of his city, which causes him years later to describe the experience as the "day he become the man he was." Winegardner, a native of Ohio who lived in Cleveland from 1989 to 1997, said in an interview that the scene is based on the real experience of a friend who went to an exhibition Indians-Dodgers game as a 12-year-old and recalled it as life-changing. In addition, the historical decline of Cleveland is indicated by its team's own fate. Although expected to have a great future because of its progressive politics, the Indians' reputation steadily dissipates, while Cleveland, once America's sixth largest city, plummets to 12th position.

The Cuyahoga River, on the contrary, is a threatening constant of Cleveland's life and a focus of jokes about the city ("What's the difference between Cleveland and the Titanic? Cleveland has a better orchestra"). Because of its notorious pollution, the river actually burns twice, first in 1952, four years after the narrative begins, and then in 1969, when it ends. Nevertheless, it brings to its shores the craze about "black" music and the world's first rock concert, performed in the Cleveland Arena, a hockey venue (and now the location of the Rock and Roll Hall of Fame). Among other notable historical moments depicted in the novel, in 1967, Carl Stokes becomes the first African-American mayor in a predominantly white, major city; the newspaper mogul Louis Selzer manifests the power of mass media by influencing one of the most controversial trials in American history, openly blaming Dr. Sam Sheppard for the death of his wife; and Dorothy Fuldheim becomes the first female TV news anchor and first female TV show host. Yet Cleveland never matches the cosmopolitanism of New York, which both fictional and historical characters actually see as a merit of the "heartland" city.

Winegardner's postmodern style—ironic, playful, and encyclopedic—is typified by the novel's generous footnotes. Wry and penetrating, they not only function as a commentary on the events, and as the writer's interpretation of his own text, but as an annotation to post–World War II American culture in general. When Winegardner notes, for example, that "you weren't a bad person. It was a different time. The words *differently abled* had not yet crossed any human lips. It was a time, however, when no one found infantile paralysis shameful," he exposes the inscribed hypocrisy in the modus of political correctness. Even in—and through—its postmodernism, the text yearns for seemingly more sincere times, when language did not mask and distract from the often ennobling tribulations of our lives.

Although Winegardner is perhaps best known as the writer who successfully continued Mario Puzo's saga, *The Godfather,* his most accomplished work is unquestionably *Crooked River Burning.* The epic scope of the narrative, combined with its vivid and searching detail, manages to "transcend the very regionalism it celebrates" (Hemley), making *Crooked River Burning* a novel as much about its country as about the city at its heart.

Bibliography
Hemley, Robin. "Paean to Cleveland," *Chicago Tribune,* 4 February 2001.
Winegardner, Mark. "A Conversation with Mark Winegardner." By Angela Fasick. Available online. URL: www.markwinegardner.com. Accessed May 16, 2009.
———. *Crooked River Burning.* New York: Harcourt, 2001.
———. *The Veracruz Blues.* New York: Penguin, 1997.

—Damjana Mraović-O'Hare

Cruz, Ricardo Cortez (1964–) *American novelist and poet*

Ricardo Cortez Cruz has written two novels to date, STRAIGHT OUTTA COMPTON (1992) and *Five Days of Bleeding* (1995), both experimental and both produced by *Fiction Collective Two.* Cortez Cruz's fiction, nonfiction, and poetry have also appeared in several on-line and in-print magazines and periodicals, including *African American Review, Fiction International,* and *Flashpoint Magazine.* Cortez Cruz's work has received substantial critical comment and a host of awards, including a Nilson Award for Excellence in Minority Fiction (1991) and a Strand Diversity Achievement Award (2009). His unique contributions to the genre of experimental literature, and their focus on the underrepresented black and minority experience, have also resulted in Cortez Cruz's inclusion in several anthologies, including *A Norton Anthology of Postmodern American Fiction* (1997) and *Step into a World: A Global Anthology of the New Black Literature* (2000).

Cortez Cruz was born in 1964 in Decatur, Illinois, and would grew up "pretty poor" in a depressed, "ghettoized environment," which would provide transferable points of reference for his later works set in the urban centers of L.A. and New

York. He worked through his secondary and post-secondary education as a sports intern and news-room clerk for the *Decatur Herald & Review* and the *Bloomington Pentagraph,* and obtained his B.Sc., M.A., and Ph.D. from Illinois State University, where he currently teaches for the Department of English (Borgias 2004; Silverblatt 1993).

Cultural inheritances from the social move-ments of the 60's and 70's, especially civil rights and second-wave feminism, would echo through the 80's and 90's across all branches of the arts and academia, by lending a voice to those who had pre-viously been voiceless. In the era of Rodney King and NWA, authors like Cortez Cruz told the story of the marginalized inhabitants who occupied the "ghettoized" streets of urban America. Cortez Cruz describes his major works as: "Novels short 'n funky." Urban, experimental, avant-garde texts that empha-size language, slanguage, violence . . . the trappings of human life, which includes obscenity, tragically flawed characters, anti-heroes (Borgia 2004).

His graphic tales utilize a highly unconven-tional writing style, which defies easy categoriza-tion, deviating as it does from traditional literary convention in almost every respect, from syntax and word use/play, to narrative arc and temporal coherence. They present a virtual phantasmagoria of persons, places, and events, which invites the disoriented reader to wander unguided and pro-tected through the vital, inchoate experience of the streets (Silverblatt 1993).

Cortez Cruz freely samples and mixes from a vast cultural and literary repository, using visual and textual principles of collage, juxtaposition, and irony to challenge conventional attitudes and dra-matically extend the limits of conventional inner-city representation (Silverblatt; Polley). There is no accepted interpretation of Cortez Cruz's work because, as the author puts it, "not too many things operate on just a literary level . . . the sam-pling and repetition take on meaning, resulting in a collision of sights and sounds" (Silverblatt 1993). The musical and repetitive poetry of Sterling Club (*Always the Blues*) was a key influence on Cortez Cruz's style, and the result is frequently compared to the work of a disc jockey; deconstructing and reconstructing discrepant "bits and tricks" gained from widely varying sources to produce an entirely different finished product. Cortez Cruz states that "we are constantly getting language and informa-tion through other sources, whether we realize it or not," and his exercises in literary stereo-mixing offer an "open" read, encouraging us to consider why such "bits" functioned as they did in the first place (Silverblatt 1993).

The early Ishmael Reed *(Yellowback Radio Broke Down)* and Clarence Major *(My Amputations)* are also stylistic influences on Cortez Cruz's fiction, as well as the progressive and forceful work of writ-ers from the "hot aesthetic period" of the 1960s (Sonia Sanchez, later Gwendolyn Brooks). In addi-tion, Cortez Cruz was inspired by the socially driven trends that predominated in the dramatic and critical theory of the 1960s; but it was the work of French dramatic theorist, experimental artist, and interpretive Marxist Guy Debord (1931–94) that had the greatest single impact on his work. Debord felt that authentic social life had been replaced by "the spectacle," the commodified representations of the mass media. The best way to wake up the spec-tator drugged by such spectacular images, according to Debord, is to *detourn*/turn the spectacular images in on themselves, effectively disrupting the spec-tacle itself *(Society of the Spectacle).* "Detourning [is] putting things into a different perspective," says Cortez Cruz, "that forces us to rethink our reality . . . or parts of our reality" (Silverblatt).

Cortez Cruz himself has exerted a powerful influence on experimental and black and minority literature that appeared subsequent to his pioneer-ing works. Himself a product of a "ghettoized envi-ronment," he has striven to *detourn* the stereotypes representing his own background, ultimately writ-ing his own story (Borgia).

Bibliography

Cortez Cruz, Ricardo. *Five Days of Bleeding.* Boulder, Colo.: Fiction Collective Two, 1995.
———. *Straight Outta Compton.* Boulder, Colo.: Fiction Collective Two, 1992.
———. "Up." *African American Review* (Autumn 1997): 455–462.
Cortez Cruz, Ricardo, and Andrew Ervin. "Yin & Yang." *Fiction International,* no. 39 (November 2006).

—Stephanie Laine Hamilton

Cure for Dreams, A Kaye Gibbons (1991)

The third novel by KAYE GIBBONS tells the story of four generations in a southern family, from the late 1800s up to 1989. The novel's frame narrator is Marjorie Polly Randolph, of the fourth generation, but her tale is told mostly in the form of quoted recollections by her mother, Betty Davies Randolph. Betty's stories go back to the lives of her grandmother and mother, Bridget O'Caidhan and Lottie O'Caidhan Davies, respectively. She relates key events of their lives, from Bridget's Irish origins and life in Kentucky, through her mother's married life in North Carolina, and then turns to her own life and the raising of her daughter, Marjorie. Indeed, storytelling is at the heart of the novel, and binds each generation to the next. Each chapter heading, like a précis or brief overview, reflects a particular type of storytelling reminiscent of fiction from centuries past, for example, the heading for chapter 5: "An account of things which heretofore were unsaid, or a lesson for the tardy" (37). Still, they often have a familiarity of phrasing that sounds more like gentle reminders of stories already known to many, and the reader can imagine that they already have been told and retold. The novel in fact reads like a collection of oral histories, and is clearly inspired by the WPA Federal Writers Project of the 1930s, in which many such stories from southern families were collected.

Betty, as the main storyteller, begins her narrative with her mother Lottie's dream of courtship, followed by the reality as manifested in her suitor, Charles Randolph. The newlyweds move to North Carolina where Lottie informs Charles that she will not work for him on his farm or at his grist mill—that she has worked enough already—but will attend to the raising of their eventual offspring: "She promised to honor and cherish and obey and all the other, but she never saw the marriage as enrollment for torture. He didn't own her like a plow or a rake" (11). When daughter Betty is born, Lottie uses her power of storytelling to keep her daughter also away from a life devoted to working herself to exhaustion for the man in her life. A series of fabricated stories about Betty's fragile health serve the daughter in this aim, just as Lottie's flat refusals to work served her. In this episode, as in many others throughout the novel,

Gibbons presents strong women who refuse to be portrayed as victims of society. Though aware of the limited opportunities available to women in the early 20th century (and especially in the South at that time), the women are not social rebels out to challenge their culture's status quo, yet they show great strength of character in carving out their own spheres of existence within conventional society.

In fact, the reader becomes aware that it is men who are the outsiders here, who are not a primary part of the recounted histories. Two men meet violent ends, one by suicide and one by murder, after which their wives seem only to become stronger. The murder is actually committed by the victim's wife after years of abuse, and in a scene heavily reminiscent of Susan Glaspell's "Trifles," Lottie not only solves the murder but successfully covers it up, illustrating in an extreme form how the women of the novel form bonds of complicity for the sake of survival and prosperity on their own terms. While Lottie and her husband grow ever more distant from each other, Lottie's relationship with her daughter strengthens. Husband Charles is the one who becomes marginalized in the world that Lottie builds around her, for he is literally the odd man out at home; and at the women's social hours that Lottie organizes in the community, *all* men are unwelcome—at least all those who do not treat their women rightly. The women even find room in their community for a woman who would otherwise be an outcast, Trudy Woodlief. Intensely unconventional, Trudy hails from Louisiana (the first thing that distinguishes her from the other women in this small North Carolina community), and is the mother of several children, the first of whom she had at 14. Trudy scandalizes the town with her brazenness and relatively open sexuality. However, when her husband runs off, leaving a pregnant wife behind, the women's attitudes shift in Trudy's favor, even though she does not change her ways. Indeed, after her twins are born, the community women pitch in to help Trudy; and while most do it out of curiosity, some offer their help out of genuine concern, a sense of sisterhood.

Naming and language are integral to the structure of the novel as oral histories conjuring up the past, but the manipulation of language into story plays a part in the women's everyday lives and is inscribed in the narrative as a major theme. When several men in the community begin being unfaithful to their wives with a handful of "mill tarts" (37), Lottie employs storytelling (in the form of rumor) to set her friend's husband back on the straight path. In the concluding chapters of the novel, Betty tells the story of her own life beyond childhood, walking that same middle path between conventionality and unconventionality. The times (late 1930s to early 1940s) are allowing slightly more freedom of experience for women, and Betty does experience the faster pace of "big city" life; still, her highest aspiration is attending secretarial school while working at a five-and-dime store. A failed relationship with a "dope fiend" sends her back home, where she is courted by a local young man, and seems destined for what would appear to an outsider as a very traditional life. Yet she has inherited that strong, independent spark from her mother, and is able to dictate the terms of her married life.

A Cure for Dreams is thus a story of storytelling, women's storytelling, but in a subtle, southern manner. The result is an entertaining social history, not of great men in great events (indeed, "great events" of the period, like the two world wars, are peripheral subjects at most), but no less significant thereby. With a keen ear for dialogue, particularly in the local idioms and euphemistic parlance of the novel's women, Gibbons brings this history to life. Contemporary reviews of the novel were less enthusiastic than they had been for Gibbons's previous two works, but reviewer James Wilcox praised *A Cure for Dreams* for its greater maturity of craft, stating that "a much more satisfying sense of the real world abounds, an acknowledgment that good is always mixed up with, if not downright evil, at least a large dose of human folly" (14).

Bibliography

Gibbons, Kaye. *A Cure for Dreams*. Chapel Hill, N.C.: Algonquin Press, 1991.

Wilcox, James. Review of *A Cure for Dreams*, by Kaye Gibbons, *New York Times Book Review* 96 (May 12, 1991), 13–14.

—Joseph Schaub

Curious Incident of the Dog in the Night-Time, The Mark Haddon (2003)

The Curious Incident of the Dog in the Night-Time is the first novel by English writer MARK HADDON, who until 2003 had primarily written and illustrated books for children. Written from the perspective of an (apparently) autistic young man, the book won the 2004 Whitbread Book of the Year. It is an exemplary work of metafiction, as the book itself is shaped as a murder-mystery novel that the young narrator is writing, although it quickly transcends such genre classification to include elements of bildungsroman and comedy. The novel's narrative style, marked by frequent use of "and" and "then," as well as the incorporation of mathematical problems and philosophical meditations, intimates the protagonist's unusual sensibility. Haddon's sensitive rendering of Christopher and of his unique understanding of the world creates a novel imbued with humor, compassion, and poignancy, while offering rare insights into the mind of an autistic teenager.

The narrator, Christopher John Francis Boone, is a 15-year-old boy living in Swindon with his father. Although it is never explicitly stated in the text, Christopher appears to be autistic, as suggested by his regular one-on-one work with his teacher Siobhan, the use of only prime numbers in the novel's chaptering, the frustration expressed by his parents in dealing with him, his preference for not being touched, and his intense and otherwise unexplained interest in mathematics and logical order. As the novel opens, Christopher's life is disrupted when he discovers that his neighbor Mrs. Shears's poodle Wellington has been stabbed with a pitchfork. *The Curious Incident of the Dog in the Night-Time* is the book Christopher writes as he attempts to solve the murder, and the title obliquely references a story by Sir Arthur Conan Doyle; Christopher's favorite book is *The Hound of the Baskervilles* and he thinks that if he were a proper detective, he would be like Sherlock Holmes. The inquiry per se is frequently interrupted by his intriguing thoughts on a wide range of topics (such as God and animals) and especially mathematics (such as his meditation on the "Monty Hall problem"); indeed, his skill in the latter subject is so great that he successfully petitions to sit for the mathematics A-levels. The extraordinary eclecticism of Christopher's interests, however, disguises a deep-seated and sustained search for logical explanation in the world; he writes, "Lots of things are mysteries. But that doesn't mean there isn't an answer to them. It's just that scientists haven't found the answer yet" (100).

When his father, Ed, learns of Christopher's detective work, he insists his son stop, and a neighbor, Mrs. Alexander, attempting to explain his father's annoyance with the investigation, soon after informs Christopher that his mother (whom Christopher believes is dead) in fact left Christopher's father to marry Mr. Shears. When his father finds the book Christopher has been writing, he becomes furious, strikes Christopher, and hides the book. Christopher finds it, however, along with letters from his mother that his father has been hiding. And when his father realizes Christopher's discovery, he apologizes and confesses to murdering Wellington as retribution for Mrs. Shears rejecting his advances.

Fearing for his own safety, Christopher decides to go to London and live with his mother—a decision that proves daunting and even dangerous, as he struggles to buy a train ticket, must hide from the police, and narrowly misses being struck by a subway train. Although his mother is shocked by his sudden arrival, she is delighted to see her son again. Christopher's arrival, however, causes tension with Mr. Shears, especially when his mother says Christopher can stay. Christopher realizes he must return to Swindon to sit for his mathematics A-levels, but his mother says it is not possible and has the test canceled. Her relationship with Mr. Shears begins to crumble, and she and Christopher leave at last for Swindon.

Upon arriving back home, Christopher learns that he is able to take his mathematics A-levels after all. He remains afraid of his father, however, going so far as to barricade himself in his room; but Ed buys Christopher a golden retriever puppy, and the gesture regains his son's trust. Christopher learns that he has passed his A-levels with an A, and begins to prepare for the next level of testing, dreaming of going to university and

becoming a scientist. The novel ends with explanation and satisfaction: Christopher has solved the murder, passed his test, and written a book. For him, "that means I can do anything" (220).

The major theme of *The Curious Incident of the Dog in the Night-Time* is Christopher's desire for understanding—not necessarily to be understood but to understand the world around him. His mind searches for patterns because he believes, as a budding scientist, that patterns allow one both to understand and to predict surrounding events. Such a capability offers him a sense of order and control in an otherwise chaotic universe, and this longing endears Christopher to the reader, while deftly illustrating salient features of the working of an autistic mind. Another recurring theme is memory: both *what* one remembers and *how*, the matter and the mechanism of memory. Christopher's heightened self-awareness is both revealing and trustworthy, as he scrupulously informs the reader not merely of what he can clearly recall but also of the areas in which he is fuzzy or unsure. "My memory is like a film" (76), he writes, suggesting the cinematic quality of memory: seemingly connected and fluid, yet ultimately fractured and restricted. This fractured fluidity is highlighted by his repetitious use of "and" or "then" to begin sentences, suggesting that one's life is not intrinsically coherent, but rather a sheer succession of events, which are then subjected to selection, integration, and emphasis to create memory and identity.

Its deft exploration of autism aligns *The Curious Incident of the Dog in the Night-Time* with other works that explore such experience through first-person narration, especially with respect to our sense of time, identity, and language. The Benjy sections in William Faulkner's *The Sound and the Fury* (1929) and Daniel Keyes's *Flowers for Algernon* (1958) are perhaps the most obvious examples of this form of unreliable but profoundly illuminating narration. More specifically, both Christopher's age and sensibility qualify him as a "naive narrator," one who does not fully comprehend the ramifications of his or her observations. In contemporary fiction, this device has been successfully employed in Harper Lee's *To Kill a Mockingbird*

(1960) and Jamaica Kincaid's *Annie John* (1985). But the novel's nearest contemporary counterpart may be JONATHAN SAFRAN FOER's *Extremely Loud and Incredibly Close* (2005), in which Foer employs a nine-year-old narrator, Oskar Schell, to explore the trauma of 9/11. Like Haddon, Foer uses letters, lists, and pictures to show how the child attempts to make sense and bring order to the world around him. But though Oskar exhibits behavior similar to Christopher's, including a love of mathematics, rational order, and cataloging, the text suggests his unorthodox narration is more the result of precocity than autism.

The Curious Incident of the Dog in the Night-Time is thus exceptional not only in its plotting—an assemblage of action, mathematical problems, and philosophical musings—but in the sensibility and aspirations of its narrator. Having worked with autistic children years earlier, Haddon creates a world where a desire for a rational stability takes precedence over emotions and passion. At one point Christopher quotes Sherlock Holmes: "The world is full of obvious things which nobody by any chance ever observes." To this he adds, "But he notices them, like I do" (73). And in so doing, Christopher becomes one of the more unorthodox yet empathetic narrators in contemporary English fiction.

Bibliography

Haddon, Mark. *The Curious Incident of the Dog in the Night-Time.* New York: Doubleday, 2003.

—Peter C. Kunze

Cusk, Rachel (1967–) *British novelist and memoirist*

Rachel Cusk was born in Canada and lived in Los Angeles before returning, with her British parents, to live in England at the age of nine. She suffered from severe asthma throughout much of her childhood and teenage years and at 11 was sent to a Catholic boarding school in Cambridge, England, an experience that she described in an interview with the *Daily Mail* as "torture":

> I didn't make friends and was bullied. I saw the nuns who taught us as a symbol of fe-

> male powerlessness [. . .] They were passive, wore black habits and had given up their lives. Like lots of Catholic girls, I felt shame about my body and sexuality. It didn't help that I was rather weird-looking and slightly blue from not being able to breathe properly. ("Saving Rachel Cusk")

However, her health eventually improved and Cusk went on to study English at New College, Oxford. After the university, Cusk moved to North London, where she worked at an assortment of jobs and also began writing. In 1993, she published her first novel, SAVING AGNES, which won the Whitbread First Novel Award. The book focuses on Agnes Day, a woman in her 20s who struggles to find meaning in her life after the university. Shortly after the book came out, Cusk married a banker, Josh Hillman, but the marriage did not last, and the couple separated after only a year; a few months later, she ran into an old friend from her Oxford days, and the two eventually moved in together, with Cusk becoming stepmother to her partner's daughter from a previous relationship. In 1995, she published another novel, *The Temporary.* Christina Patterson, reviewing the novel in the *Independent,* noted that "At a time when most young writers seem to be opting for terse, Carveresque minimalism, [Cusk] flies the flag for the long word and the long sentence. . . . At its best there's something of the epigrammatic neatness of Jane Austen; at its worst the verbose pomposity of John Major" (Patterson). *The Temporary* was followed in 1997 by *The Country Life,* which won the Somerset Maugham Prize.

In 1999, Cusk gave birth to her first child, her daughter Albertine, who was born at eight months by Caesarian section; six months later, she became pregnant again with her second daughter, Jessye. The experience of birth and motherhood affected Cusk deeply, and she wrote her only nonfiction work to date: *A Life's Work: On Becoming a Mother.* Cusk reflected in a 2008 article published in the *Guardian,* on the controversy generated by the book: "First of all there was a letter, from a writer friend I had sent a copy to," wrote Cusk: "Be prepared, she said: your book is going to make people very angry" ("I Was Only Being Honest"). Cusk's portrait of motherhood is indeed brutally honest:

Looking after children is a low-status occupation. It is isolating, frequently boring, relentlessly demanding and exhausting. It erodes your self-esteem and your membership of the adult world. . . . Childbirth and motherhood are the anvil upon which sexual inequality was forged, and the women in our society whose responsibilities, expectations and experience are like those of men are right to approach it with trepidation. (*A Life's Work*, 8)

The book is a complex and thoughtful combination of analysis and memoir, and the controversy partially originated in Cusk's willingness to confront the conventional discourse and assumptions surrounding motherhood. An online article on the *Daily Mail* Web site, however, described it as "a coruscating attack on motherhood" and noted that the book "wasn't warts and all, . . . just warts" ("Saving Rachel Cusk"). Cusk herself recalls, "I was cited everywhere as having said the unsayable: that it is possible for a woman to dislike her children, even to regret having brought them into the world," and further, remembers:

Again and again people judged the book not as readers but as mothers, and it was judgment of a sanctimoniousness whose like I had never experienced. Yet I had experienced it, in a way: it was part of what I had found intolerable in the public culture of motherhood, the childcare manuals and the toddler groups, the discourse of domestic life, even the politics of birth itself. In motherhood the communal was permitted to prevail over the individual, and the result, to my mind, was a great deal of dishonesty. I had identified this dishonesty in *A Life's Work*: it seemed to me to be intrinsic to the psychical predicament of the new mother, that in having a child she should re-encounter the childhood mechanism of suppression. She would encounter the possibility of suppressing her true feelings in order to be "good" and to gain approval. My own struggle had been to resist this mechanism. I wanted to—I had to—remain "myself." ("I Was Only Being Honest")

She has also expressed disdain for the critics who vilified her as a mother after the publication of *A Life's Work*, saying, "I would have ripped it up if I'd had the approval of those alice-band-wearing mumsies who disapproved of it. I wanted to speak to intelligent women" ("Saving Rachel Cusk"), and also, "I'm not remotely afraid of what [her critics think] of me. I have no respect for them and I wouldn't have given them a second thought had not motherhood grouped us all together in the Venn diagram, which is very big and full of all kind of dimwits and numbskulls" (Merritt).

The struggle to retain an autonomous sense of identity as a woman as well as mother permeates Cusk's subsequent book, *The LUCKY ONES* (2003), a series of short stories arranged around the theme of emotional connection and understanding, here including a study of the experiences of a new father away from his family for the first time (in "The Way You Do It"). *The Lucky Ones* made the short list for the 2003 Whitbread Novel Award, and was followed in 2005 by *In the Fold*, which Anna Shapiro, reviewing the book in the *Guardian*, described as "a shaggy dog story of mismatched couples, disappointing parents, and defecting or defective children" ("Down on the Farm"); the book again deals with Cusk's principal themes of the minutiae of familial love, parenthood, childhood, and the past. She returns to these themes in her 2007 work, *Arlington Park*, which was short-listed for the Orange Prize for Fiction in that year.

In 2009, Cusk published both a striking account of a summer her family spent in Italy, in *The Last Supper*, and the novel *The Bradshaw Variations*, a tonal and thematic refinement of her fictional preoccupations.

Bibliography

Cusk, Rachel. "I Was Only Being Honest," Guardian Unlimited (March 1, 2008). Available online. URL: http://www.guardian.co.uk/books/2008/mar/21/biography.women. Accessed December 13, 2008.

———. *A Life's Work: On Becoming a Mother.* London: Fourth Estate, 2001.

Merritt, Stephanie. "Mum's the Word," Guardian Unlimited (March 30, 2003). Available online. URL: http://www.guardian.co.uk/books/2003/mar/30/fiction.stephaniemerritt. Accessed December 13, 2008.

Patterson, Christina. "Nothing Permanent," Independent.co.uk (13 August 1995). Available online. URL: http://findarticles.com/p/articles/mi_qn4158/is_/ai_n14000271. Accessed December 13, 2008.

"Saving Rachel Cusk," Mail Online (November 3, 2005). Available online. URL: http://www.dailymail.co.uk/home/books/article-367512/Saving-Rachel-Cusk.html. Accessed December 13, 2008.

Shapiro, Anna. "Down on the Farm," Guardian Unlimited (August 27, 2005). Available online. URL: http://www.guardian.co.uk/books/2005/aug/27/featuresreviews.guardianreview12. Accessed December 13, 2008.

—Claire Horsnell

D

Danielewski, Mark Z. (1966–) *American novelist*

Best known for his labyrinthine cult novel HOUSE OF LEAVES (2000), Danielewski is the son of Polish-born filmmaker Tad Danielewski. Active in the Polish resistance during World War II, the elder Danielewski was eventually captured and incarcerated by the Germans. He survived, however, and after the war made his way first to Britain, where he studied at the Royal Academy of Dramatic Art, and finally to the United States, where he founded the Professional Actors Workshop. Students in the Professional Actors Workshop included notable figures such as James Earl Jones, Martin Sheen, and Sigourney Weaver, while Tad Danielewski's filmic output ranged from feature films like *The Big Wave* (1961) to work on daytime soaps.

The Danielewski children—Mark, and his sister Annie—were raised in an artistic environment, and both received an elite education: Mark attended Yale as an undergraduate, where he studied English, and did graduate work at the prestigious School of Cinema-Television at the University of Southern California, while his sister, Annie, attended Princeton. Although Mark appeared in *Gettysburg* (1993) and had a role in the technical production of the documentary film *Derrida* (2002), it was Annie who first came to widespread national attention as a pop singer, performing under the moniker Poe. In the mid-1990s she signed to Atlantic Records, and her debut, *Hello* (1995), included the hit single "Angry Johnny." Poe's second release, *Haunted* (2000),

was created as a companion piece to her brother's novel *House of Leaves*, and the two appeared together on a kind of a rock-'n'-roll promotional tour, where they opened for Depeche Mode.

With the publication of *House of Leaves*, Mark Z. Danielewski established himself as a novelist with both popular and critical appeal. The novel itself is a vertiginous exercise in remediation. Its nominal subject is an impossible object, a shape-shifting house whose interior dimensions exceed those of the exterior, and the reader apprehends the whole through complexly layered narration. Photographer and filmmaker Will Navidson moves into the house, and begins a documentary of his family's life therein, including various explorations into the ever-expanding bowels of their new home. Navidson's film, meanwhile, is described and analyzed by a blind man named Zampanò, who compiles a treatise titled *The Navidson Record*. This account, in turn, is discovered and edited by a tattoo artist named Johnny Truant, who, in addition to providing an introduction, attaches a welter of footnotes detailing elements of his own life. Finally, the entire composite is mediated by "The Editors," whose comments appear throughout the novel.

This playfully postmodern narrative structure, in which the reliability of narrative authority is continuously being questioned and undercut, is clearly influenced by precursors ranging from Vladimir Nabokov to DAVID FOSTER WALLACE. The structure, moreover, is augmented by a host of virtuosic literary tricks and devices, some borrowed and recast, others wholly innovative. One of the most noticeable features of the novel is Danielewski's use of font and typesetting. Throughout the book, the various competing narrative voices receive their own individual fonts—the words of Johnny Truant, for example, are presented in Courier, while the Editors' remarks are rendered in Bookman. Moreover, whenever the word *house* (or a foreign-language equivalent) appears in the novel, it is either in blue (much like a hyperlink) or in grayscale, depending on the particular edition of *HoL*.

Danielewski's experimentation with textual layout throughout the novel has a profound effect on the readers' navigation. Borrowing from film technique, for example, he constructs a series of dense typographic tableaus that "intentionally slows the reader down, reorients the reader, [and] redresses that question of direction inside the book" ("Five Minutes"). Elsewhere, Danielewski explains, he "only has a few sentences per page so the reader will move [quickly] through a hundred pages" ("Five Minutes"). These techniques, together with a preponderance of other extra-narrative inclusions—anagrams, acrostics, and the like—render the novel a complex and intricately structured puzzle.

Danielewski does not shy away from discussions of his own virtuosity. One interviewer charitably describes him as "not by nature a modest person" (Brown), and for all the delights one can find in Danielewski's fiction, his public persona can be rather wearying. In interviews, he vacillates between supercilious dismissal and profound arrogance, and is particularly insistent on questions of authorial intent. "I have yet to hear an interpretation of *House of Leaves* that I had not anticipated," Danielewski tells Larry McCaffrey and Sinda Gregory in one interview (106). "I have yet to be surprised" (106). Indeed, Danielewski folds so much theory and self-reflexive criticism into *HoL* that readers might suspect he has, in fact, anticipated all critiques. When Danielewski announces, however, that his fiction is "written outside the present industry of academia" and that there does not exist "a vocabulary yet that can adequately address what's going on" in his work, his sheer hubris eclipses his genius (Brown).

Between *House of Leaves* and his second novel, *Only Revolutions* (2006), Danielewski published two minor works: *The Whalestoe Letters* (2000) and *The Fifty Year Sword* (2005). The former is a companion to *HoL*, an expanded version of one of the novel's appendices that collects a series of letters ostensibly written by Johnny Truant's mother. The latter, published in the Netherlands, is a limited-edition novella, which Danielewski has referred to as "a little bit of sorbet, between courses," something "[t]o cleanse the palate of *House of Leaves*, and get you ready for the next" (Knecht). In *The Fifty Year Sword*, five different narrative voices are distinguished by means of colored quotation marks.

Only Revolutions is similarly inventive, a formally experimental tour de force that labors under Oulipo-style constraints. The novel itself has a circular 360 pages, each containing 180 words of "primary" text. Properly speaking, the book has neither head nor tail, neither front nor back. The two narrators—perpetual 16-year-olds Sam and Hailey—begin at opposite ends of the book, their tales juxtaposed at 180 degrees (that is to say: Sam's first page is Hailey's 360th, and vice versa, as each page contains a block of text that is upside down when its counterpart is rightside up). Moreover, the size of the respective fonts changes throughout the book, with larger fonts employed at each narrator's beginning, and smaller ones at their respective ends. Complicating matters even further, the novel also includes a historical sidebar with entries that complement the primary narratives. The reader is thus forced to choose how s/he will navigate the text.

Only Revolutions was a finalist for the National Book Award in 2006, a clear indication of the critical respect Danielewski has garnered since his novelistic debut.

Bibliography
Brown, August. "An Outsider Novelist Goes, er, Traditional," Los Angeles Times (September 13, 2006). Available online. URL: http://www.calendarlive.com/books/cl-et-danielewski13sep13,0,5854593.story?coll=cl-books-t op-right. Accessed February 24, 2008.

Danielewski, Mark Z. *The Fifty Year Sword*. Amsterdam: De Bezige Bij, 2005.

———. "Haunted House—An Interview with Mark Z. Danielewski." By Larry McCaffery, and Sinda Gregory. *Critique: Studies in Contemporary Fiction* 44, no. 2 (2003): 99–135.

———. *House of Leaves*. New York: Pantheon, 2000.

———. "Interview Mark Z. Danielewski." By Stacey Knecht. *The Ledge* (October 31, 2005). Available online. URL: http://www.the-ledge.com/DOC/MarkZDanielewskiInterviewTextEng.doc. Accessed February 24, 2008.

———. *Only Revolutions*. New York: Pantheon, 2006.

———. *The Whalestoe Letters*. New York: Pantheon, 2000.

"Five Minutes with Mark Z. Danielewski," *Guardian Unlimited* (November 30, 2000). Available online. URL: http://books.guardian.co.uk/firstbook2000/story/0,6194,405144,00.html. Accessed February 24, 2008.

—Justin St. Clair

Danticat, Edwidge (1969–) *Haitian-American novelist, playwright, and biographer*
Winner of the Pushcart Prize for short fiction (1996), and nominated for the prestigious National Book Award (1995)—both for *KRIK? KRAK!*—Danticat was establishing herself as a literary force to be reckoned with well before her 30th birthday. Her popularity soared and was cemented when Oprah Winfrey added her *Breath, Eyes, Memory* to the talk-show host's popular book-club reading list in 1998. Debunking the problematic stereotypes of Haitian-Americans that became popular during the 1980s and 1990s, when so many misunderstood and impoverished refugees immigrated to the United States, Danticat develops stories that add realism and human faces to the plights that members of this immigrant group have surmounted in their efforts to escape discrimination and probable death in Haiti.

Pamela Shelton explains that ". . . Danticat writes from the point of view of a young woman of color who realizes all too quickly that the attributes she possesses are of little value in either culture" (25). In essence, Shelton calls attention to the irony of Danticat's success: Her writing would have been seen as futile in Haiti's disenfranchised economic infrastructure; and in America, her topic of choice should have been of little interest to readers more interested in conventional, native

reflections on the American dream. Despite these obstacles, however, Danticat has risen to the social, cultural, and professional challenges she faced as a young immigrant writer, and become a significant and enduring member of both American and international literary circles.

Born in Haiti in 1969, Danticat came to the United States in 1981 at the age of 12, joining her parents, André Miracin (a taxi driver) and Rose Souvenance (a textile worker), who arrived in America during the 1970s. Danticat was two when her father left Haiti for the United States, and four when her mother departed the island. She and a younger brother, Eliab, remained in the Caribbean, living with André's brother Joseph, an aunt, and Danticat's maternal grandmother. In New York the author enrolled in Clara Barton high school, and published her first work in a local newspaper. She continued writing privately in personal journals throughout high school, but ostensibly stifled her creative aspirations in an attempt to fulfill her parents' hopes, which were set on a career in nursing. Nonetheless, when she began her undergraduate studies at Barnard College, she decided to major in French literature and in 1991 matriculated in Brown University's creative writing program. Her M.F.A. thesis was an early draft of her first novel, *Breath, Eyes, Memory*, which she began penning as an immigrant adolescent in New York. In 1993, she returned to New York, working with Jonathan Demme at Clinica Estetico. She also conducted writing workshops with high school and college students. Briefly, she joined the faculty at New York University as a visiting professor (1996–97), and in 2002 moved to Miami, Florida, with her husband, Faidherbe Boyer.

Astonishingly prolific and eclectic in her tastes, Danticat has tried her hand at playwriting, with *The Creation of Adam* (1992), *Dreams Like Me* (1993), and *Children of the Sea* (1997); short fiction, with *Krik? Krak!* (1995) and *The DEW BREAKER* (2004); the novel, with *Breath, Eyes, Memory* (1994), *The Farming of Bones* (1998), and *Behind the Mountains* (2002); children's literature, in *Anacaona, Golden Flower: Haiti, 1490* (2005); anthology editing, in *The Beacon Best of 2000: Great Writing of Women and Men of All Colors and Cultures* (2000), and *The Butterfly's Way: Voices from the Haitian Dyaspora in the United States* (2001); literary translation, with Jackes Stephen Alexis's *In the Flicker of an Eyelid* (2002); nonfiction historiography, in *After the Dance: A Walk through Carnival in Haiti* (2002); and autobiography, in *Brother, I'm Dying* (2007).

The latter book documents her life in America, illuminating the time she spent with her Uncle Joseph between the ages of four and eight. When she turned nine, he lost his voice to throat cancer, and Danticat remembers herself being "his voice," ". . . an extension of his voice" in their Haitian community (Shea 386). Tragically, however, she was unable to speak for her uncle when he attempted to migrate to America. As recounted in *Brother, I'm Dying,* Joseph arrived in Miami illegally, fleeing death threats from local gangs in Haiti. However, upon his arrival in Florida, he was not given political amnesty because of stringent Homeland Security legislation. Denied medical attention and neglected during his detention at the U.S. Custom's holding facility, his family—Danticat and others legally living in Florida—learned of his untimely death at the very time they anticipated he would be released and granted political asylum to live with them.

Because of such personal and familial trials, along with the stories she has inevitably learned as a member of Haiti's American immigrant community, Danticat has become an advocate for Haitian affairs, lecturing about that country and its emigrant community while educating audiences about the obstacles and hardships so many Haitians have encountered in their efforts to gain amnesty in other countries. Typically, she exposes her readers to the desperation, poverty, and persecution that has caused so many to flee Haiti, and pushes the boundaries of her audience's literary expectations, integrating Haitian folk culture, religious rituals, and mythic or magic realism into her work, employing these aesthetic techniques not merely to enrich her tale but to invite her readers to hear the composite voices making up the collective consciousness of the Haitian diaspora. Hence, her work is important not only to global audiences wanting to better appreciate the diversity of contemporary literary voices and experience, but also to those wishing to correct fundamental American misperceptions of Haitian life and citizenry.

Recognition of her work includes a Lannan Foundation Fellowship in 2004; an American Book Award from the Before Columbus Foundation, for *The Farming of Bones;* the 2007 National Book Critics Circle Award for *Brother, I'm Dying;* PEN/Faulkner Award nominations for *The Dew Breaker;* and a series of awards and recognitions from periodicals, such as *Caribbean Writer, Seventeen,* and *Essence.* Included in *Granta's* 1996 list of best American novelists and the *New Yorker's* "Twenty Writers for the Twenty-first Century," Danticat is also one of few writers to be nominated for a National Book Award in both fiction and nonfiction.

Bibliography
Danticat, Edwidge. "The Dangerous Job of Edwidge Danticat: An Interview." By Renee H. Shea. *Callaloo: Emerging Women Writers: A Special Issue* 19, no. 2 (1996) 382–389.

———. "An Interview with Edwidge Danticat." By Bonnie Lyons. *Contemporary Literature* 44, no. 2 (2003) 183–198.

———. "Interview with Edwidge Danticat." By E. Ethebert Miller. Foreign Policy in Focus. Edited by John Feffer. October 16, 2007. Institute for Policy Studies. Available online. URL: www.fpif.org/fpiftxt/4642. Accessed May 16, 2009.

Figueredo, D. H., ed. *Encyclopedia of Caribbean Literature.* Vol. 1, A–L. Westport, Conn.: Greenwood Press, 2006.

Shelton, Pamela. "Edwidge Danticat." *Authors and Artists for Young Adults.* Vol. 29. Edited by Thomas McMahon. Detroit: Gale, 1999.

Telcher, Craig Morgan. "Diaz and Danticat among 2007 NBCC Winners." Publishers Weekly Online. Available online. URL: www.publishersweekly.com/index.asp?layout=articlePrint&arti. Accessed May 16, 2009.

Texas Public Radio. "Selected Shorts." May 30, 2008. Available online. URL: www.tpr.org/articles/2008/01/selected-shorts.htm. Accessed May 16, 2009.

"Two Blacks Named Among America's Most Promising Young Novelists." *Journal of Blacks in Higher Education* 12 (1996): 111.

Wilcox, Susan. *Edwidge Danticat Visits Her Haitian Roots.* Full Duck Productions, 2003.

—Karima K. Jeffrey

Dark Room, The Rachel Seiffert (2001)

RACHEL SEIFFERT's debut novel is split into three independent narratives connected only by theme. The events of the Third Reich and the Holocaust are seen through the eyes of Helmut, Lore, and Micha, whose names provide each section's title. While two-thirds of the book is set in prewar and wartime Germany, the final section takes place in the late 1990s, showing the continuing influence of the past on the present.

Helmut is born in Berlin, around 1920, with a missing pectoral muscle on the right side of his chest. As a boy, he helps out in a local photographer's workshop and shows great talent both in the dark room and with a camera. His growing up is linked closely with events in Germany: "Puberty and the Third Reich arrive simultaneously" (Seiffert 12). However, his disability and resulting shyness mean he never participates, only watches and photographs from a distance. He becomes obsessed with Berlin's railway station, where he catalogues the comings and goings, confirming his suspicion that the city is emptying itself of people. He also photographs crowds, once coming across a group of gypsies being brutally herded into trucks. He tries to record this event with his camera, but the developed pictures "convey none of the chaos and cruelty" (40), and even fail to clearly show what happened. This incident introduces Seiffert's ongoing theme of the unreliability of evidence.

The war starts, but Helmut's disability prevents him from enlisting. After his parents are killed in an air raid, Helmut remains in besieged Berlin, scavenging for food and recording the ruins with his camera. Later, refugees stream into the city bringing rumors of death camps and mass graves. Blindly patriotic, Helmut ignores these portents and enthusiastically joins the boys and old men of Berlin for the city's last stand.

Here Helmut's story abruptly ends, and Lore's begins. A German family are hiding out in the Bavarian countryside at the end of the war. Twelve-year-old Lore's Nazi father has been interned by American forces. When her mother too is taken away, Lore is left to lead her younger siblings to their grandmother's house in Hamburg. They travel on foot, sleeping rough and suffering great hardship. On the way they join forces with Thomas, a young man whose number tattoo and Jewish papers elicit sympathy and help them cross borders between the various Allied zones. In a village, they come across photographs of death camps and mass graves pasted up on trees, images that haunt Lore's dreams. These photographs are also the subject of overheard conversations, which once again suggests the ambiguous nature of documentary evidence. A young man on a train tells his friend:

> "It's all a set-up. The pictures are always out of focus, aren't they? Or dark, or grainy. Anything to make them unclear. And the people in those photos are actors. The Americans have staged it all, maybe the Russians helped them, who knows." (175)

In bombed-out Hamburg, Lore sees newspaper photographs of wanted Nazis, connecting their uniforms with memories of her father. But her grandmother tells her not to be ashamed: "Some of them went too far, child, but don't believe it was all bad" (188). When Thomas, too, is revealed to be not what he seems, Lore is left with a "sick feeling that Thomas was both right and wrong, good and bad; both at the same time" (210).

The final part of the novel develops the theme of moral ambiguity, this time from the perspective of later generations. In an unnamed German city in 1997, Michael ("Micha") is a young teacher who becomes obsessed with what his grandfather, Askan Boell, may have done during the war. Michael remembers his Opa as kind, attentive, and a gifted artist. However, Boell is known to have served in the Waffen SS in Belarus before being captured by the Russians and interned for nine years after the war. Michael cannot reconcile his personal memories with the possibility that his grandfather was a perpetrator of atrocities, and he obsessively researches the Holocaust, wrestling with the feelings of his generation: *"Stupid to feel guilty about things that were done before I was born"* (247). His investigations lead to tensions with family and friends, but despite his misgivings, Michael travels to Belarus to find out once and for all. The local museum's photographs of Nazis massacring Jews do not show Boell's face. However, Michael finds an old man who lived through the period, Jozef Kolesnik; and Kolesnik confirms Michael's fears, saying that he remembers the few who refused to participate in the killings, and Boell was not one of them. Here Seiffert seems to suggest that memory is more useful or reliable than photographic evidence. Though Kolesnik's recollections are tainted by his own dubious past, Michael, adding them to the accumulation of evidence produced by his researches, is fully convinced:

> Where is my proof? I have no reason not to believe it. There are no pictures of him holding a gun to someone's head, but I am sure that he did that, and pulled the trigger, too. The camera was pointing elsewhere, shutter opening and closing on another murder of another Jew, done by another man. But my Opa was no more than a few paces away. (370–371)

Seiffert's themes of guilt and responsibility are, as in Bernhard Schlink's *The Reader* (1997), represented from the perspective of perpetrators as well as victims. The novel could be considered "revisionist" in its emphasis on the sufferings of ordinary Germans, rather than on the past crimes of that nation, which are mostly only glimpsed in the background. However, definitive interpretations are discouraged by the style of the novel. By using straightforward prose, unadorned by metaphor or other imagery, and by writing in the present tense throughout, Seiffert focuses on the trajectory of individual lives. It is these human stories that emerge as the novel's main concern.

Bibliography
Seiffert, Rachel. *The Dark Room.* London: William Heinemann, 2001.

—Lewis Ward

Davies, Peter Ho (1966–) *British short story writer and novelist*

Davies is the author of two short story collections and one novel. In his fiction he explores cultural and familial gaps and fissures through a variety of lenses, while his multifaceted background, along with keen powers of observation and catholic sympathies, make for a richly nuanced and compelling style.

Davies was raised in England and spent his summers in Wales. His mother was Malay-Chinese and his father was Welsh, which caused him to stand out in his hometown of Coventry. His father was an engineer, and early on Davies followed in his footsteps, earning a degree in physics at Cambridge University. However, he shocked everyone by leaving the sciences to earn a second degree, in English, at Manchester University, and later an M.F.A. in creative writing at Boston University. He has received fellowships from the National Endowment for the Arts and the Fine Arts Work Center in Provincetown, Massachusetts, was named by *Granta* as one of 20 "Best of Young British Novelists" in 2003, and received a Guggenheim Award in 2004. He currently lives in the United States and directs the graduate creative writing program at the University of Michigan. Davies is married with one son.

The Ugliest House in the World, Davies's first collection, was published in 1998 and won the *H. L. Davis Oregon Book Award,* the *Mail on Sunday/ John Llewellyn Ryhs Prize,* and the *PEN/Macmillan Silver Pen Award.* The title story, which tells how a child's death affects a Welsh community, was first anthologized in *Best American Short Stories 1995* and has been compared to the work of preeminent short-fiction authors Katherine Mansfield and Raymond Carver (Hoggard, 1). The collection was critically acclaimed for its distinctive style, its sensitive observation of human nature, and its strong evocation of place.

Davies's second collection of stories, *EQUAL LOVE* (2000), was named a *New York Times* Notable Book of the Year in 2000, and short-listed for both the *Los Angeles Times* Book Prize (Fiction) and the Asian American Literary Award. Davies published the collection after moving to America, a move imagined in the amusing "How to Be an Expatriate," and which both informs the cross-cultural theme of "Everything You Can Remember in 30 Seconds Is Yours to Keep" and produces a broad, subtle shift to American perspectives in many of the stories. The stories are radically diverse in both form and content, but unified by the collection's complex exploration of the relationship between parents and children.

Davies's first novel, *The Welsh Girl* (2007), was short-listed for the British Book Awards Richard & Judy Best Read of the Year, and long-listed for the 2007 Man Booker Prize. It is set in 1944 and explores the intersection of three disparate lives in northern Wales, those of a young country girl, a German POW, and a German-Jewish captain. As in many of his short stories, the theme of multiple identities and pluralistic backgrounds drives the narrative. Davies was inspired to research and write about 1940s Britain by trinkets on his Welsh grandmother's mantelpiece that he played with as a child—a brass tobacco tin, an ashtray, a letter opener—which had been made by prisoners of war in Wales from old shell cases (Hoggard, 2). The novel's meticulous detail vividly evokes the period, yet its themes of identity and barriers between people transcend the time and speak eloquently to the modern reader.

Davies's style is notable for its seamless incorporation of a staggering range of voices and perspectives, with frequent displacements of time, place, emotion, and character. Davies himself expresses admiration for Flaubert's capacity to maintain stylistic continuity amid great narrative diversity: "He was a writer who never wrote the same book twice. I like that" (Chamberlin, 1). Anchored by a sure and straightforward style, Davies's work often explores raw relationships, deeply embedded in the chaos and ambiguities of ordinary life. "I think of both Vonnegut and Hemingway as early writing teachers," Davies notes, and the seemingly awkward combination is both illustrative of and a testament to his supple and complex style.

Davies's work invigorates age-old themes of identity, love, and belonging, reimagining them in contemporary contexts and challenging the reader to confront them anew. Much of his fiction is marked by a lingering sense of loss and melancholy, yet is peppered with unexpected touches of humor, and ultimately conveys an unmistakable if bittersweet hope in humanity.

Davies's background as a scientist also informs his work, and in intriguing ways. As a child he was an avid reader of "a lot of bad science fiction" and claims that the single most influential book in his life was *Who Writes Science Fiction?*" In an interview with Jeremiah Chamberlin, Davies explains how he discovered through this eminently pragmatic work that writing was a "do-able human endeavor. These writers weren't Gaulouise-smoking, beret-wearing intellectuals. Many of them were engineers and scientists like my father" (8). Moreover, the praxis of science itself is profoundly evident in his approach to fiction: "Working through a story is the extrapolation of possibilities," he notes, and these possibilities, imbued with compassion and hope, are ultimately what his fiction serves to evoke.

Bibliography
Davies, Peter Ho. *Equal Love.* Boston: Houghton Mifflin Company, 2000.

———. "Interview with Peter Ho Davies." By Jeremiah Chamberlin. May 2004. *VQR.* Available online. URL: http://www. vqronline.org/webexclusive/2004/06/15/davies-interview. Accessed May 4, 2008.

———. *The Ugliest House in the World.* New York: Houghton Mifflin Company, 1997.

———. *The Welsh Girl.* New York: Houghton Mifflin Company, 2007.

Hoggard, Liz. Review of *The Welsh Girl,* Guardian Unlimited (May 13, 2007). Available online. URL: http://www.guardian.co.uk/books/2007/may/13/fiction. Accessed May 16, 2009.

Holcombe, Garan. "Author Profile: Peter Ho Davies." ContemporaryWriters.com. Available online. URL: http://www.contemporary writers.com/authors/profile/ 2004. Accessed March 4, 2009.

Man Booker Prize. "The Welsh Girl." Available online. URL: http://www.themanbookerprize.com/prize/books/314. Accessed March 4, 2009.

Stainton, Leslie. "A Master Shape-Shifter of the Literary World: Peter Ho Davies once thought he was 'too strange' for fiction. Turns out he was wrong." Fall 2004. *Michigan Today,* 35, no. 1. Available online. URL: http://www.umich.edu/news/MT/04/Fall04/. Accessed February 9, 2009.

—Margaret Wade

Demonology Rick Moody (2001)

Nearly every story in Rick Moody's second collection of short fiction, *Demonology* (2001), has a deathly or calamitous trajectory. As the eponymous tale suggests, Moody's stories form a catalogue of monstrous possession. Though the (mostly) realist stories deal only with metaphorical demons, characters in Moody's fiction continually grapple with a vaguely defined sorrow until they are overtaken by rage and self-loathing, sometimes erupting with surprising violence. The short narratives, predominantly staged in modern suburbia, are studies in the disorientation grief provokes, and together they constitute a kind of anatomy of mourning in late 20th-century America, with each working as a "canto of loss" (110).

For much of his writing career, Moody has been wedged stylistically between postmodernism's brazen ironists (William Gass, John Barth) and the rejuvenated realists of whatever came after (Raymond Carver, Richard Stone, Bobbie Ann Mason). However, Moody's fiction has always bridged those two camps, striving for both estrangement and verisimilitude. His tales of upper-middle-class ennui often braid metafictional techniques with the kaleidoscopic surfaces of popular culture. Moody's prose scours away cheap nostalgia to reveal suburbanite psychologies utterly dependent on the institutions (marriage, religion, corporatism) that frustrate them. His characters are often cooled idealists or snapping malcontents, yet their disenchantment commonly plays out in the interior of the mind rather than in dialogic exchange. Moody depicts the migration beyond an initial (white) retreat from the city and into subdevelopments, but the men and women of his fiction flee even deeper, into the recesses of their minds, solipsistically sniping from the discomfort of tortured, first-person narration. It is not enough to say that Moody's work fictionalizes suburban unrest. THE ICE STORM, GARDEN STATE, and *Demonology* all explore the difficulty of vocalizing sorrow at the suburban interstice of the weird and the mundane.

Demonology's first story, "The Mansion on the Hill," lays the foundation for many themes that Moody returns to throughout the collection. Andy Wakefield recounts the early days of his employment at an event-planning agency, Mansion on the Hill. Armed with a name that has already prepared readers for mourning (*Wake*field), Andy confronts death's stalking reminder when the former fiancé of his recently deceased sister rents the Mansion for his upcoming wedding. Andy is wracked with guilt over his sister's fatal auto-accident, and the first-person narrative is an extended meditation on familial culpability. Moody deftly deconstructs the wedding as "the high watermark of your American life" by juxtaposing a ceremonial affirmation of life with the nagging reminder of death (11). In fact, Andy is so stunned that his former brother-in-law-to-be could remarry less than a year after his sister's accident that he vows to disrupt the wedding in the most sepulchral way possible. Dressed in a chicken costume and toting an urn, Andy flings his deceased sibling's ashes onto the newly married couple, the scene taking on a hallucinatory air such that Andy can no longer tell "what was wedding and what was funeral" (46). Phenomenological confusion of concepts, sounds, and even identities functions as one of Moody's most insistent diagnoses of the late century. Characters regularly misrecognize the meaning of words, until language itself becomes suspect. For example, in the compact story "Drawer," a jilted man lambastes his former lover for pretension. Their relationship disintegrates in large part because of her preference for complex diction (*armoire, demitasse, taffeta*) over utilitarian words. The furniture object itself becomes branded by so much ineffectual language that, like the relationship it symbolizes, it can no longer contain any meaning.

In "Ineluctable Modality of the Vaginal," theoretical jargon actually paralyzes one couple's relationship. Two academics grow so clinical in their expressions of passion toward one another (at one point sexual intimacy is replaced by a coffee table genital exam) that romance and even basic discourse alienates its speakers. Just like the confusion of death and life in "The Mansion on the Hill," language baffles the characters in this story such that words rip free of their referents and are "always something else" (247). The woman and man of the story speak through "hollow mouths," reciting rote intellectual positions in lieu of supposedly authentic somatic reactions (258). In this case, language is not an obfuscating symptom of some disease, but rather the disease itself. This is not the first time that Moody has treated language as a malady. In *The Ice Storm*, Ben Hood wonders if "language and its insidious step-relative, sentiment" ravaged his mouth with canker sores (9). In the titular story, "Demonology," as the narrator observes his sister suffering a horrific seizure on the floor, he laments that "figurative language isn't up to the task" of rendering such tragedy (302). The process of articulating anguish in Moody's collection is less about agents controlling their words, and more about being controlled by them, about how those agents are infected or taken over by speech. Moody's central metaphor in *Demonology* is a possessed griever afflicted by "the involuntary assemblage of [memories] into language" (305). In addition to "Demonology" and "The Mansion on the Hill," Moody revisits the atrophy of language in the wake of a sibling's death twice more in the book. In "Forecast from the Retail Desk," the narrator, gifted with an ability to forecast the future, wrestles with the implications of his prophecies. He questions whether articulating his visions of the future actually causes subsequent damage ("Did language, when you petitioned with it, cause such devastations. . . ?"), but his soothsaying is unable to save his brother's terminally ill son. In "Boys," two brothers are prematurely aged by their sister's battle with cancer, and left to drift as "ghostly images of younger selves . . . boys as an absence of boys" (244). The brothers fight bitterly as death surrounds them, and by the story's conclusion, they have lost their ability to converse with one another altogether. Interestingly, many of the stories in this collection were written shortly after Moody's own sister died. Moody's doubt that language can adequately contour grief suggests that while narrative (making words into temporal events) improves on the deficiencies of imperfect speech, the stories of *Demonology* are nevertheless imperfect dirges.

While Moody's examination of the vocabulary of grief is innovative, perhaps the most recognizable feature of *Demonology* is one it borrows from an early 20th-century realist. In a hilarious yet respectful parody of Sherwood Anderson's "The Egg," Moody invokes the "grotesque" in his story, "The Double Zero," a tale about an ostrich farmer's ruination, steeped in Anderson's contempt for homogenization and the disintegration of small-town industry. More important, the story relies on Anderson's penchant for depicting characters as

monstrous versions of their interiority. In Moody's version, pressures from chain restaurants and stingy customers have warped the young narrator's father into an angry man. When an ostrich egg demonstration goes awry, the literal yolk on the father's face is Moody's not-so-subtle reminder that ethnographic fiction like Anderson's often renders its subjects grotesque despite its sympathetic realism.

By the close of *Demonology*, Moody begins to lurk in the shadows of his stories as a metafictional participant, assembling variegated grief into a suburban composite. His first novel appears as a sale item in "Surplus Value Books: Catalogue Number 13." Later, the author also folds himself into the inclusive "We" voice of the catalogue peddling "Willie Fahnstock, *The Boxed Set*," a short story culled entirely from three decades of song titles. But despite overtures toward ironic distance in the more experimental pieces, Moody's narrators never settle on smirking detachment as a means for healing emotional distress. Rather, *Demonology*'s great lament is that language is so inadequate that it has left subjects without either an idiosyncratic means for expressing rage or a cohesive understanding of what was lost in the first place. All that remains is the questionable activity of cobbling together the fragments of personal history. Moody suggests that in the aftermath of postmodern irony, the author figure acts as an archivist fomenting traumatic narrative in the "convulsion of the imagination" (93).

Bibliography
Moody, Rick. *Demonology*. Boston: Back Bay Books, 2001.
———. *The Ice Storm*. Boston: Back Bay Books, 2002.

Kyle A. Wiggins

Desai, Kiran (1971–) *Indian novelist*
Kiran Desai is the author of two novels, *Hullabaloo in the Guava Orchard* (1998) and *The INHERITANCE OF LOSS* (2006). Her debut novel won her the Betty Trask award in 1998, while her second novel made her the youngest winner ever of the Man Booker Prize, in 2006. *The Inheritance of Loss* also won the National Book Critics Circle Fiction Award (2007), and was short-listed for the British

Book Awards Decibel Writer of the Year (2007), the Kiriyama Pacific Rim Book Prize (2007), and the Orange Prize for Fiction (2007).

Desai was born in 1971 in India, where she lived until the age of 14, before moving to England. She was educated in both England and the United States, and currently divides her time between the United States and India. She is the daughter of accomplished Indian novelist Anita Desai, a three-time Booker Prize nominee, who Desai claims to be her greatest influence.

Desai's first novel, *Hullabaloo in the Guava Orchard,* assembles a host of colorful characters from Shahkot, a small town of unspecified location, although the suffix—*kot* is typical of west-central India (Gujarat and Rajasthan). The main character, Sampath, is a young, exceedingly unmotivated post-office clerk who, after being fired for showing his behind at his boss's daughter's wedding, decides to abandon everything and everyone that keeps him in Shahkot, and retire to a forest in order to pursue his favorite pastime, day-dreaming. Against his hopes and expectations, however, he is eventually followed into the woods by his family and the rest of the town, who take him to be a wise seer for his knowledge of the intimate details of their lives, which he had gleaned from their correspondence while an employee at the post office. The novel has an unmistakably fabular quality, with no certain time indicators, exaggerated personality traits and behavior, and the most extraordinary events narrated with an almost child-like naiveté reminiscent of another Indian writer, R. K. Narayan.

Kiran Desai's second novel, *The Inheritance of Loss,* is as different from her first as could be imagined: if *Hullabaloo* is built on gentle humor and irony, it is a thoroughgoing skepticism that scaffolds the multiple locations and time frames constituting the narrative of *Inheritance.* Although set in the mid-1980s, pre- and postcolonial immigration are never out of sight in the tale, which revolves around a retired, Cambridge-educated and excessively Anglophilic judge who rejects—and is rejected by—all who surround him, be it in England or India: his orphaned granddaughter who must live with him in his chosen spot of reclusion at the foothills of the Himalayas; their cook; and his son, who works illegally in the restaurant kitch-

ens of Manhattan. Like most of the characters in the novel, each of these is voluntarily or involuntarily displaced, either due to parental fiat (the granddaughter), the exigencies of education and profession (the judge), or the need to find means of subsistence (the cook and his son).

The Inheritance of Loss is structured bitemporally, articulated as much around the precolonial desire for migration, spurred on by the lure of an English education, as around the post-Independence desire for the coveted green card and the lure of prosperity that America represents. In either case, departure represents the possibility of escape. The novel weaves together a host of narrative strands which take the reader back and forth in time and space, from Kalimpong and Manhattan in the present to Gujarat, Cambridge, and the judge's various postings in northern India in the past. Borders and border crossings are only two of the multiple dislocations in the novel, where the old—never completely left behind—is always discovered lurking in the recesses of memory, and the new—never achieving the wholeness of the past—is lived as a constant collision with barriers (class and generation, privilege and dispossession, defiance and subservience).

The Inheritance of Loss is a meditation on many aspects of contemporary life, including questions of (post-)imperialism and nationhood, race and ethnicity, multiculturalism, identity, class, modernization and globalization, immigration and the plight of illegal immigrants, the real and imagined boundaries around us and how we negotiate them, and the impossibility of return.

The novel was critically acclaimed in the West, but its reception in India was mixed: pride when the Booker Prize was declared, followed by anger and resentment at the depiction of locals. Indian critics seem to have taken Ms. Desai's skepticism literally, accusing her of drawing an "insensitive, one-dimensional, and racist" portrait of the people of the region (Anmole Prasad, a local lawyer) or of living in the colonial past (*Hindustan Times*). Thus, the novel, which stages spaces of encounter, itself becomes a space of encounter.

And here, for all their overt differences, suggestive similarities begin to emerge between Desai's two novels. In both there is a fascination with borders and the crossing of them; with what it means to be home and away from home; with identity, memory, and imagination in the face of such crossings; and with the unstable but creative tension between the individual and community in the construction of meaning.

Bibliography
Banerjee, Amitava. "'Inheritance' Bequeaths Bitterness," Hindustan Times, Kolkota edition (November 2, 2006). Available online. URL: www.kalimpong.info/2006/11/07/sorry-kiran-but-what-do-you-know-of-hills/. Accessed October 17, 2009.

Desai, Kiran. *Hullabaloo in the Guava Orchard.* New York: Anchor Books, 1998, 1999.

———. *The Inheritance of Loss.* New York: Grove Press, 2006.

Mishra, Pankaj. "Wounded by the West." New York Times (February 12, 2006). Available online. URL: www.nytimes.com/2006/10/11/arts/11iht-web.1011 bookerreview.3108156. htm/?scp=2&="wounded. Accessed October 17, 2009.

Ramesh, Randeep. "Book-Burning threat over town's portrayal in Booker-winning novel," *The Guardian,* November 2, 2006, p. 23.

Aparna Nayak-Guercio

Dew Breaker, The Edwidge Danticat (2004)

Writing about the Haitian-American experience, EDWIDGE DANTICAT was the youngest, and the first female, writer from the francophone country to write and publish in English. Born in Port-au-Prince, Haiti, in 1969, she immigrated to Brooklyn, New York, in 1981 at the age of 12. Her first novel, *Breath, Eyes, Memory* (1994), mesmerized literary audiences, quickly establishing the narrative merits and thematic significance of the young writer's voice; and she followed this with a collection of short fiction, *KRIK? KRAK!* (1995), and a second novel, *The Farming of Bones* (1998), broadening her scope to a pan-Caribbean perspective.

In *The Dew Breaker,* Danticat merges the narrative styles of these earlier works. As in *Krik?Krak!*, she shapes the novel out of a series of vignettes that here provide a sustained historical commentary on the nature and effect of the Duva-

lier regimes, especially between 1967 and 2004, when Haitian refugees underwent a painful oscillation between immigration to the United States in an effort to escape political oppression and poverty, and return to their homeland in an attempt to reconnect with lost familial roots.

Through vivid characters like Nadine (a registered nurse who cares for people who become mute as a result of laryngectomies), Claude (a two-time expatriate who returns to Haiti after being deported from the United States for criminal activity), Dany (an orphaned survivor whose parents were murdered by the eponymous dew breaker), Ka (the dew breaker's American-born sculptor daughter), and Aline Cajuste (an interning journalist for a Haitian community paper), Danticat explores with uncommon sensitivity and insight the private lives of second-generation Haitian-Americans, examining the hard-won, often fragile and unstable balance they achieve between their American identities and the tragic legacy of their Caribbean past.

Set against the complex and subtle struggle of this second generation is the almost euphoric liberation of Haitian emigrants who now enjoy economic success and comfort in their new lives in America; Mr. Bienaimé and his wife Anne own their businesses, as a barber and hair stylist, and rent rooms in their home to incoming transients from Haiti; Beatrice Saint Fort is a retired seamstress who owns her own home in a quaint Brooklyn neighborhood. Commensurate, however, with the exhilaration of their new found prosperity, is a more acute and visceral memory of that which no prosperity can assuage, the physical and emotional trauma of their Haitian experience.

Shifting between life in Haiti during the 1960s and life in the United States today, *The Dew Breaker* transports the reader into the freighted and resonant lives of this community of Haitian-Americans. All are connected by the "dew breaker," Mr. Bienaimé, who in Haiti would arrive just at dawn to set houses afire, arrest, torture, and kill innocent Haitian civilians (the haunting term is a Creole byword for such brutality). He has immigrated to New York with his wife, Anne, who tells their daughter Ka, "You and me, we save him. When I met him, it made him stop hurt the people" (25). His arrival in America appears to offer him not merely freedom from his past, but redemption for it. Adopting the name Bienaimé (from *bien aimé* or "well beloved"), he seeks both, through his daughter as well as a host of increasingly disillusioned relationships with other members of his American community, his tenants, and barbershop clients.

In a striking and beautiful inversion on Dandicat's part, he names his daughter Ka, in his Egyptian lexicon a word for the soul as "a double of the body . . . the body's companion through life and after life. It guides the body through the kingdom of the dead":

> ka is like soul. . . . In Haiti is what we call good angel, ti bon anj. When you born, I look at your face, I think, here is my ka, my good angel." (17)

In the novel's opening story, "The Book of the Dead," we learn that she is a promising sculptor, and her father, and especially her deluded belief in his victimization, is the source of her inspiration. He is her muse, her "single subject" (4), "the prisoner father" who somehow has survived the atrocities of the Tonton Macoute, the government-sanctioned militia. The pressure of this shameful disparity between his good angel's imagined father and the truth finally becomes intolerable, and the old torturer casts into a pond her prized sculpture, which, with the same brilliant inversion as appeared in her naming, depicts him, who caused so many scars, scarred and in prayer. At once a confession through denial, and a remembrance through forgetting, the act epitomizes the paradox of Haitian-American experience, locked into an almost dreamlike oscillation between unbearable memory and unconscionable forgetting; and the soul of Bienaimé, in being condemned to this perpetual purgatory, is finally an object of pity.

Rather than center on this single protagonist, however, for all his interest to us and symbolic force in the novel, Dandicat weaves a skillful tapestry of intergenerational stories bearing witness to a legacy of courage through suffering; and finally lends a proud, even noble voice to a people often thought of as mute victims.

In this novel, as in her other fiction, there is life after tragedy, and redemption for the sins of one's past. History can be rewritten, even if it should never be forgotten.

Bibliography

Danticat, Edwidge. *After the Dance: A Walk through Carnival in Jacmel, Haiti.* New York: Crown Journeys, 2002.
———. *Breath, Eyes, Memory.* New York: Vintage, 1994.
———. *The Dew Breaker.* New York: Vintage, 2004.
———. *The Farming of the Bones.* New York: Soho Press, 1998.
———. "An Interview with Edwidge Danticat." By Bonnie Lyons. *Contemporary Literature* 44, no. 2 (2003): 183–198.
———. *Krik?Krak!* New York: Vintage, 1996.
———. "Personalities: Birnbaum v. Edwidge Danticat." By Robert Birnbaum. The Morning News. 20 April 2004. Available online. URL: www.themorningnews.org/archives/personalities/birnbaum_v_edwidge_danticat.php. Accessed November 20, 2007.
———, ed. *The Beacon Best of 2000: Great Writing by Men and Women of All Colors and Cultures.* Boston: Beacon Press, 2000.
———, ed. *The Butterfly's Way: Voices from the Haitian Dyaspora in the United States.* New York: Soho Press, 2001.
Mardorossian, Carine M. "From Literature of Exile to Migrant Literature." *Modern Language Studies* 32, no. 2 (2002): 15–33.

Karima K. Jeffrey

Díaz, Junot (1968–) *Dominican-born American novelist and short story writer*

Díaz disappeared from the limelight for a decade after the publication of his 1996 debut *Drown*, an acclaimed 10-story collection that made "a huge mainstream literary splash" (Santiago, 70). The "beautifully crafted coming-of-age tales" (Jones, E1) earned the young Dominican American several notable accolades, including a Guggenheim fellowship and a six-figure, two-book contract. But Díaz's sudden success was not without attendant difficulty: In his introduction to *The Beacon Best of 2001*, which he guest-edited, he admits that "For the last couple of years I—a former five-pages-a-day type guy—have not been able to write with any consistency" (vii). "It's as if my writing has fallen off a cliff. I'm not rehabilitated yet," he lamented in 2003 (Jones, E1).

Writer's block notwithstanding, Díaz finally delivered, and his long-awaited first novel surpassed all expectations. Published in 2007, *The Brief Wondrous Life of Oscar Wao* captured the National Book Critics Circle Award, the Pulitzer Prize in fiction, and a host of other honors. In the words of *New York Times* book critic Michiko Kakutani, *Oscar Wao* is

> a wondrous, not-so-brief first novel that is so original it can only be described as Mario Vargas Llosa meets "Star Trek" meets David Foster Wallace meets Kanye West. It is funny, street-smart, and keenly observed, and it unfolds from a comic portrait of a second generation Dominican geek into a harrowing meditation on public and private history and the burdens of familial history. An extraordinarily vibrant book that's fueled by adrenaline-powered prose, it's confidently steered through several decades of history by a madcap, magpie voice that's equally at home talking about Tolkien and [notorious Dominican dictator Rafael] Trujillo, anime movies and ancient Dominican curses, sexual shenanigans at Rutgers University and secret police raids in Santo Domingo. (Kakutani, E1)

After immigrating to New Jersey at the age of six, Díaz divided his time between libraries and street corners (each complementing the other), and it is here that he began to cultivate the unselfconscious mélange of book smarts and street cred that would later distinguish his fiction. Following a B.A. in literature at Rutgers, he completed an M.F.A. in writing at Cornell, where the majority of *Drown*'s stories were composed. After obtaining a tenure-track position at Syracuse University he was induced to accept a professorship in creative writing at MIT by author Anita Desai and is currently employed there.

With a sensibility fashioned from often violently opposing worlds—*barrio calle* and academia, classic novel and space opera, magic realism and Dungeons & Dragons, boxing ring and Modern Language Association conferences, J. R. R. Tolkien and Toni Morrison—Díaz celebrates his hybridity: "[T]hat is the great multiplicity and diversity of life. We too often prefer our comfortable slices rather than the disorganized raucous pie. I am who I am because of those different parts" (Strauss, 14NJ6). This "polymorphous multiculturalism" (Scott, 9) is the most striking feature of Díaz's *Oscar Wao*, which incorporates several stories in different time frames, ranging from the old to the new New World and from academic to idiomatic English, as well as denotative Spanish and street Spanglish. In his first novel, Díaz "shows impressive high-low dexterity, flashing his geek credentials, his street wisdom and his literary learning with equal panache" (Scott, 9).

Though *Drown* concludes with a glossary of Spanish terms, *Oscar Wao* makes no such gesture toward comforting its primarily Anglo readership; indeed, like William Blake, Díaz makes a virtue of unintelligibility. If a reader cannot grasp all of the "fanboy stuff," he asks during his talk at the 26th Key West Literary Seminar, why should he or she deem it de rigueur to understand all of the Spanish usages? "Art as your friend," he makes clear, "is not art." Hence the intricate architecture of *Oscar Wao*, which at first appears to have three main narrators, integrating the first-person voice of literate womanizer Yunior, who narrated most of *Drown*; the second-person voice of Lola, obese and virginal sexy punk sister of Oscar; and the informed footnote writer, whose candor, anger, and Sandra Cisneros–inspired sense of social history seem to distinguish him from Yunior. But despite meticulous reports of Oscar's fantasy reading and fiction writing, we never hear the titular character's voice.

Indeed, Oscar Wao, whose name is a Latino version of Oscar Wilde, is gradually exiled from the text. Though ostensibly a portrait of Oscar as a not-so-young geek, the real focus of *Oscar Wao* shifts as the story develops. Like a great number of Dominicans, including some of his own forebears, who are "disappeared" during the 30-year Trujillo regime, Oscar's story begins, only to be silenced. In the Key West seminar, Díaz belabors the "dangerous" fact that "every story silences other stories," and Oscar's is silenced by Yunior. Likable (he tells it like it is) or insufferable (he *too often* tells it like it is), Yunior ultimately takes on shades of a grand manipulator. Yet, like many in his place, he can neither surrender his control, nor resolve, even to his own satisfaction, the threads of his narrative. For the last 20 pages he runs through a series of final titles, including: "The Final Voyage," "The Last Days of Oscar Wao," "The End of the Story," "On a Super Final Note," and "The Final Letter." But typically we are never shown this final letter. Instead, Oscar's last words are themselves filtered through Yunior. Nor are we shown the manuscript that the final letter promises; instead, Yunior informs us that "the fucking thing never arrived!" (334).

Díaz's ability to turn into narrative vast unreconciled disparities is perhaps his most distinctive trait as an author: he details how to capitalize on young lust in *Drown*'s "How to Date a Browngirl, Blackgirl, Whitegirl, or Halfie"; he describes "the ruthless brutality" of Dominican life under Trujillo "(also know as El Jefe, The Failed Cattle Thief, and Fuckface)" in the footnotes of *Oscar Wao* (2); he defends his inclusion of the proscribed "N-word," in both his crafted work and his casual conversation, in a Spanish-language interview ("Junot Díaz"); he liberally, at times extravagantly, intertwines street argot (man, chill, fuck, shit, y'all) and academic jargon (apparatchik, totality, praxis, unintelligibility) in his Key West talk.

Moreover, Díaz's uninflected authenticity encourages readers to challenge dominant authorial voices. Consider the problematic narration of *Oscar Wao*: because narrator Yunior is a version of author Junot, Díaz challenges his own authority as a writer; and in his broader oeuvre, Díaz consistently subverts the discourse of didactic pontificators. He never holds forth with clear cohesion, logic, or purpose. In the Key West talk, he stresses that since he grew up "in the shadow of a dictatorship," he is wary of providing "the simplified narrative of the dictator," and he links this sense of dictatorship to America's post-9/11 incursion in Iraq, extending the analogy even to the logic of discourse itself: "[E]very time we're in a story and we're not torn out of it, we'll like go to war based on a rumor."

Bibliography

Díaz, Junot. *The Brief Wondrous Life of Oscar Wao.* London: Faber and Faber, 2008.

———. *Drown.* London: Faber and Faber, 2008.

———. "Introduction." *The Beacon Best of 2001.* Edited by Junot Díaz, vii–xi. Boston: Beacon Press, 2001.

———. "Talk." 26th Key West Literary Seminar, January 18, 2008. Key West, Florida. Available online. URL: http://www.kwls.org/lit/podcasts/2008/01/junot_diaz_january_18_2008.cfm. Accessed May 20, 2009.

Jones, Vanessa E. "A Loss for Words: Junot Diaz Was Hailed as a Wunderkind When His First Book of Fiction Came Out. Seven Years Later, He's Still Working on a Follow-up." *Boston Globe,* 4 March 2003, E1.

Kakutani, Michiko. "A Dominican Comedy: Travails of an Outcast." *New York Times,* 4 September 2007, E1.

Santiago, Robert. "Books." *Hispanic* (December 1996): 70.

Scott, A. O. "Dreaming in Spanglish." *New York Times Book Review,* 30 September 2007, 9.

Strauss, Robert. "From Street to Scholar: A Writer Shows Off His Dexterity." *New York Times,* 25 November 2007, 14NJ,6.

Jason S. Polley

Dickey, Eric Jerome (1961–) *American novelist and screenwriter*

Eric Jerome Dickey is the author of more than 20 novels, of which 11 have been named to the *New York Times* best seller list. He also wrote the screenplay for the 1996 film *Cappuccino*. His most popular novels, SISTER SISTER, *Milk in My Coffee, Genevieve,* and *Sleeping with Strangers,* skillfully explore relationships mired in conflict, and his rich, diverse portrayal of African-American life has established him as a pioneer of contemporary African-American fiction.

Born in 1961, in Memphis, Tennessee, Dickey took an unconventional path to becoming a best-selling author. Evincing no interest in writing or the arts, he pursued a career as an engineer, enrolling at the University of Memphis (formerly Memphis State University) immediately after high school, and earned a degree in computer systems technology in 1983. In college, he took a variety of odd jobs ranging from an on-campus game-room attendant to a Fed Ex delivery man, and after graduating took a job with Rockwell (now Boeing) as a computer programmer and technical writer. After being released from Rockwell because of cutbacks, Dickey moved to California where he worked as an actor, comedian, and short story writer, and took creative writing classes at UCLA, his break coming in 1996 when his first novel, *Sister Sister,* appeared.

Its narrative offers a unique look at the experience of African-American women as it follows the lives, loves, and conflicts of its three protagonists Valerie, Inda, and Chiquita. The novel's sensitivity and veracity were rewarded with considerable popularity among African-American women, and Dickey built on this popularity with works like *Thieves' Paradise,* focusing on African-American men. The story of Dante, a 25-year-old ex-con who has recently lost his job in the collapse of the dot-com industry and is forced to return to a life of crime to support himself, helped to extend Dickey's audience to the hip-hop generation and men. As a contributing author to *Gumbo: A Celebration of African-American Writing,* released in 2002, his work was placed alongside literary giants such as Terry McMillan and E. Lynn Harris. Currently, Dickey is penning a six-part Marvel Comics book on Storm and Black Panther, two African-American X-Men (superheroes).

Although Dickey's novels have been perceived by some as little more than popular black erotica because of their vivid sex scenes and promiscuous characters, his work is in fact rich in social commentary, in-depth character development, and masterful use of location; and he remains true to his roots as a traditional African-American writer through his sensitive exploration of problems associated with African-American life, both past and present. A figure such as Genevieve in Dickey's eponymous novel—who flees her tumultuous upbringing and southern roots by changing her name from LaKeisha Shauna Smith to Genevieve (pronounced *zhawn-vee-ev*) Forbes (after the magazine), then moves to California and gets a Ph.D. from Pepperdine—is typical of his complex and nuanced characterization. Moreover, he deftly incorporates his urban settings as if they were themselves characters, both physically and emotionally tied to the lives of their inhabitants.

Given Dickey's straightforward first-person narratives, prolific output, and popularity, it is nat-ural to compare him to Donald Goines, who also wrote at an astonishing pace and remains widely read; and while Dickey's works lack the authentic, gritty feel of a Goines novel, there are a host of unmistakable affinities. Dickey has also been compared to African-American female writers such as Terry McMillan and Toni Morrison, and is credited with being one of few contemporary male writers to successfully write about women.

There can be no doubt that his move to Los Angeles inspired Dickey's writing, to the extent that one is tempted to categorize his work as traditional urban fiction; but if so, the very notion must be recast to include Dickey's lively, eclectic, and unstable fusion of gangster fiction, ghetto lore, black pulp-fiction, and hip-hop, which raises race and race culture above location.

Bibliography

"Meet the New York Times best selling author of gritty, sexy adventures," *Bakersfield Californian* (April 11, 2008). Available online. URL: www.bakersfield. com/entertainment/local/x261450265/Meet-the-New-York-Times-best-selling -author-of-gritty-sexy-adventures. Accessed October 19, 2009.

R. Alisa Robinson

Doerr, Anthony (1973–) *American novelist, short story writer, and memoirist*

Anthony Doerr has published three books, *The SHELL COLLECTOR* (2002), a short story collection; *About Grace* (2005), a novel; and *Four Seasons in Rome* (2007), a nonfictional account of a year in Italy. Doerr's fiction is notable for its fascination with nature, and for the author's exacting, artful portrayal of the natural world; his prose is particularly impressive when he is describing water in its many forms.

Themes of vision and visions dominate his writing, and protagonists frequently have professional interests in the observation of nature, as scientists, hunters, fishermen, gardeners or photographers. Many are on the run from their past, or are placed in unfamiliar surroundings and observed as they struggle to adapt. Doerr's female characters are often dreamy, distracted, depressed, or spiritually heightened; male characters are generally sensitive and vulnerable. His works demonstrate ambivalence toward the capturing of nature, even within the confines of writing: the imagery of shells and fossils, for example, suggests beautiful, petrified relics of something once alive. Doerr tends to present an unromantic vision of an uncaring world, albeit one embedded with the miraculous. Were it not for his forgiving, almost sentimental streak, Doerr's outlook might be compared with the bleak worldview of Thomas Hardy's later offerings; and Darwin and Copernicus would appear to be as influential in his work as the great fiction writers of the past and present.

Doerr was born in Cleveland, Ohio. As a child, he was inspired to study the environment by his family (his mother is a science teacher). On family trips, the Doerr siblings would fill tennis-ball cans with crustacea to examine at home, and finding one of these cans two decades later inspired Doerr to write his seminal story "The Shell Collector" (*Blogcritics Magazine*, 8 April 2007).

Doerr studied at Bowdoin College in Maine, majoring in history, then pursued an M.F.A. in writing at Bowling Green State University. He has lived in Alaska, New Zealand, Kenya, and the Windward Islands in the Caribbean. Preauthorial employment included working in a fish processing plant, as a grill cook, and as a farmhand. He now lives in Boise, Idaho, with his wife and two sons.

His first book, *The Shell Collector,* brought together the short stories Doerr had published separately in magazines including *Atlantic Monthly* and the *Paris Review.* Although each is idiosyncratic and separate, the eight stories can be divided into four broad thematic groups, with some fitting more than one category: those about unusual or unsettled women; those involving fishing, the sea and similar topics; stories partly set in Africa; and those that explore the inexplicable.

The reticent shell collector of the title story (one of three stand-outs in the collection), is blind. However, he understands the Kenyan coastal environment and culture far better than the interlopers, who swamp his solitude after he finds a deadly poisonous cone snail that is discovered to have curative powers. In "The Caretaker," a man who has fled atrocities in Liberia finds his way to Amer-

ica, where he is released from his mental suffering when a school of whales washes up on a nearby beach. Burying their hearts, and planting seeds in the soil above them, he finds a path toward some kind of redemption. The protagonist of "Mkondo" hails from Tanzania. She leads an American fossil expert through the jungle, thrilling him with her vitality. Once their courtship is over, however, he takes her to Ohio, where her life-force steadily deserts her. Only when she recognizes and develops her talent as a photographer can she feel alive again. "How to render three dimensions in two, the world in planar spaces," her instructor notes, is "the central challenge for every artist" (208). In these three stories, Doerr is at his best as an artist: like Naima, he can seem to capture life as it is; like Joseph the Libyan, he can create something beautiful from unpromising material; like the shell collector, he has both an instinctive and a learned grasp of small, perfectly formed objects like shells and, in Doerr's case, short stories.

Doerr's next work was the novel *About Grace.* Its protagonist, David Winkler, is a hydrologist, and his occupation allows Doerr to refract his natural observations through similarly expert eyes. However, the tale's drama arises from Winkler's supernatural gift, an ability to see the future. He becomes tormented by dreams that his daughter, Grace, will drown in the basement of their house during a flood. As the rain comes down and the river rises, Winkler wretchedly decides the only way to save his daughter's life is to flee alone. Somehow, and somewhat tenuously, he ends up in the Caribbean. Here he must build life anew, but (fortunately for the reader) surrounded by fresh panoramas for Doerr to examine beneath the lens of his prose. Eventually, Winkler can stand his uncertainty and guilt no longer, and returns to discover whether Grace survived the flood.

Three years in the making, *About Grace* was inspired by a series of snowflake photographs featured in Wilson Bentley's book, *Snow Crystals.* Most critics praised the novel—it was the *Washington Post*'s book of the year—but some deemed its narrative ponderous and overlong.

The American Academy of Arts and Letters was impressed enough to award Doerr a yearlong sabbatical in Rome with his wife and newborn twins. There Doerr intended to write a second novel, set in World War II France; but during his stay he kept a notebook and wrote letter-from-Rome-style articles for the online magazine www. themorningnews.org. Faced with insomnia, the demands of parenting, and the overwhelming nature of Italy's capital, Doerr finally only published revised drafts of these rather unoriginal observations instead of the unforthcoming novel: he notes that Rome is both exhausting and exhilarating; that Italians eat well and love children; that the pope's funeral was a major international event. His short story "Village 113," which he also wrote in Rome (published in *Tin House* and the O. Henry collection in 2008), was far superior to his travel notes.

Doerr is currently working on his World War II novel. His short story "Procreate, Generate," about a couple's attempts to conceive, was featured in *Granta 97: Best of Young American Novelists 2.* He also writes a column on science books for the *Boston Globe.*

Doerr's accolade-to-book ratio is impressive. He has won three O. Henry Prizes for his short stories, the 2002 Barnes & Noble Discover Prize, the Ohioana Book Award (twice), the New York Public Library Young Lions Fiction Award, and the Outstanding Book of 2003 Award from the American Library Foundation. He was awarded a grant from the National Endowment for the Arts, and the Hodder Fellowship from Princeton University. *Granta* named him one of the best young American novelists in 2007.

Bibliography

Doerr, Anthony. *About Grace.* New York: Penguin, 2005.
———. *Four Seasons in Rome: On Twins, Insomnia, and the Biggest Funeral in the History of the World.* New York: Scribner, 2007.
———. *The Shell Collector.* New York: Penguin, 2002.

Daniel Starza-Smith

Dress Lodger, The **Sheri Holman** (2000)

SHERI HOLMAN's second novel, *The Dress Lodger* illustrates Prime Minister Benjamin Disraeli's description of Victorian England as two nations, the rich and the poor, "between whom there is no intercourse and no sympathy; who are as ignorant of each other's habits, thoughts, and feelings, as if they were dwellers in different zones, or inhabitants of different planets." Holman, however, while showing their ignorance of one another, also depicts the social intercourse between the two social classes.

Set amid the intersecting worlds in the port city of Sunderland, the book weaves tales of the first cholera outbreak in Britain, the practice of "resurrecting" cadavers for anatomical study, and the plight of a cast of memorable characters as eccentric and grotesque as those in any Dickens novel. Both authors construct complicated plots full of chance occurrences, but Dickens underscores his works with a strong code of moral behavior and a sense that right will out. In Holman's world, as protagonist Gustine puts it, "Good and Evil are opposite points on a circle. . . . Greater Good is just halfway back to Bad."

Gustine, a 15-year-old mother and the "dress lodger," is exploited by both the poor and the wealthy in Sunderland. Wise beyond her years, and victim of the unjust social system, Gustine has worked by day as a potter's assistant since the age of nine, carrying heavy loads of clay to the potter at the wheel. She lives in a boardinghouse with the owner, his daughter Pink, and about 30 other boarders. It is her landlord, Whilky, who makes Gustine his "dress lodger," a prostitute who walks the streets at night in an expensive dress to attract a better-paying clientele. The "cool blinding blue" dress Gustine wears is too valuable for her to be trusted with it, so Whilky hires another boarder, an old woman with only one eye, to follow Gustine through the streets to protect his investment.

The struggle of the poor, and the willingness of the powerful to exploit them, is a central theme of the work. Holman ties Gustine's story into England's larger social history of class oppression and into the practice of "burking" or grave robbing to obtain cadavers for medical research. Gustine's unnamed child was born with the rare condition of *ectopia cordis,* the heart outside the chest cavity. Gustine chances upon the inebriated Dr. Henry Chiver one night, and he reveals his obsession with learning about the heart and his need for cadavers. She pledges to help him, thinking he will offer hope for her son.

Henry, however, is a member of the upper class; and although he will avail himself of Gustine's help in finding cadavers, and will himself use her body, he remains "ignorant of . . . [her] habits, thoughts, and feelings." When he takes Gustine on a picnic, for example, he thoughtlessly tosses out leftover food that "would have made soup for a week" for Gustine and her child. Henry has no compunction about asking Gustine to sell her child to him for study, but when she suggests that she might move into the house as a servant and be near her son, Henry is appalled. He cannot even consider "having her in the same house with Audrey," his fiancé. Henry's attitude toward women is typically Victorian. While he frequents prostitutes, he is acutely uncomfortable with what he sees as the impropriety of entering the pink and white bedroom of his fiancé. He has no qualms about placing Gustine in grave danger but is distressed when Audrey is exposed to vulgar words on the street. Henry does, however, expect both women to submit to his authority, becoming angry with Audrey because she "willfully disobeyed" him, and refusing to take no for an answer from Gustine.

Audrey herself represents another kind of exploitation of the poor. Although basically kind, and with the means to help others, she is deluded in her belief that her visits to the slums with gifts of blankets and darned stockings are actually making a difference in the lives of the poor. She enters the homes, sits with the sick, and asks Henry to help, but never grasps the vast divide between her life circumstances and those of the poor. When she sees Gustine's baby with his exposed heart, she sends him the gift of an expensive white christening gown. Ultimately, her largesse and charity only result in a heightened sense of her own complacency and goodness, and not in any material improvement in the plight of those she seeks to serve. Her attitude is exemplified in her description of Pink, Whilky's daughter, whom Audrey plans to rescue. Pink is the "little charity case" who has "been raised like a heathen, and lives among the lowest of the low; but . . . [I] hope to do a bit of good," Audrey says to Gustine, who lives in the same conditions as the child.

Like Dickens, Holman evokes a rich and varied cast of minor characters but with a peculiarly modern edge. Landlord Whilky is as much an abuser of the poor as are the wealthy. The lodging he provides is a windowless, cheerless room where 30 people sleep on straw, if they are willing to pay for it. He treats his rat-killing ferret with more love than he does his own daughter, and will do anything to increase his profits. Nevertheless, Whilky is a leader in the community and, ironically, one of the most outspoken critics of the oppression of the poor. His ferret has a human name, Mike, and his daughter is called Pink. Eye is the strange woman whose relationship with Gustine begins as jailer and protector, but evolves into something more. The matchstick painter Fos is so named because she "glows in the dark" as a result of her prolonged exposure to phosphorus.

Holman's choice of narrative viewpoint is one of the most intriguing aspects of the novel. The collective narrators move in and out of their tale, addressing characters, speaking directly to "Dear Reader," and even discussing the choices an author makes when writing a story. It is not until near the end that their identity becomes clear. Functioning much like a Greek chorus, these gathered dead, "those who have been stolen as long as doctors have been questioning," present part of the Grand Narration, and lead readers, and Dr. Henry Chiver, to look at "the human face of resurrection."

Bibliography
Holman, Sheri. *The Dress Lodger.* New York: Random House, 2001.

Jean Hamm

Drinking Coffee Elsewhere Z. Z. Packer (2003)

The final tale in Z. Z. PACKER's first short story collection ends with the protagonist admiring the sky: "the world was cold around her, moving toward dark, but not dark yet. . . . The sky had just turned her favorite shade of barely lit blue, the kind that came to windows when you couldn't get back to sleep but couldn't quite pry yourself awake" (265). Almost all of Packer's characters exist in a liminal space such as this, teetering between two worlds, not quite anywhere yet. Although all of the protagonists in the stories are black and most are female, they each straddle very separate worlds. Dina, the main character in the title story, is torn between a poor community in Baltimore, where reading is "antisocial" because "it meant you'd rather submit to the words of some white dude than shoot the breeze with your neighbors" (132), and Yale, where most of the black people are "from New York and tried hard to pretend they hadn't gone to prep schools" (121). Dina's superficial resentment of both worlds hides her dire longing to find a home in each. She quells this longing temporarily by entering a romantic friendship with a white, overweight, jazz-loving misfit named Heidi. Although the two bond over ramen, records, and cafeteria duty, their unlikely relationship is challenged when Heidi comes out publicly. Because Dina sees her world as polarized: black/white, gay/straight, rich/poor, educated/illiterate, she cannot, ultimately, identify as anything.

The worlds of "Speaking in Tongues" are equally polarized. Tia, the protagonist, is trapped in a world of evangelical clarity, a community that has no room for her jokes about Jesus or questions regarding her absent mother. So Tia, dressed in a long skirt and white blouse, and armed with her clarinet and 44 dollars, makes her way to Atlanta in search of her addict mother. When the search proves fruitless, Tia accepts the kindness, money, and affections of a hustler named Dezi. Although Dezi is seductive and manipulative, Tia is not easily swayed from her sense of moral correctness. Internal conflict arises for Tia when survival makes the "right" decisions impossible. When she first arrives in Atlanta, for instance, she searches for a place to spend the night. Finding the hotels and motels too expensive and the YMCA full, Tia walks to a wealthy neighborhood and breaks into an unlocked car—a decision she knows is wrong but also necessary. Ultimately, 14-year-old Tia and 30-something Dezi engage in a sufficiently awkward romantic interlude. Tia's morals get the best of her, however, and she pushes Dezi away before the moment reaches its crisis. Ironically, the real crisis comes for

Tia the following morning when, innocent of the workings of her own body, she mistakes signs of her own arousal (from the previous night) as evidence that Dezi has raped her. The symbolism here is clear: Tia is unable to distinguish between her desire and a man's ill intentions. The line demarcated in the worship services of her youth is clearly not so easily identified.

Although the tension in many of the stories is in a general way similar, the endings of the stories are vastly different. Viewed as a whole, the collection serves to illuminate a myriad of tenuous but possible solutions to the problem of polarized identity. In some instances, Packer's characters make a clear choice to return to the world they feel most comfortable inhabiting; either a choice of cowardice or an attempt to integrate new knowledge into old understandings. Other stories offer endings in which the protagonist makes the choice to immerse herself fully in a new world—be that a romantic relationship or prostitution. Typical of short stories, however, the success of these decisions is unknown. Some characters we feel will fare better than others; however, because Packer's protagonists are young, smart, and often wildly funny, there is generally the sense that these choices are not conclusive but rather points along a larger trajectory. As a result, the stories are imbued with an inalienable and infectious sense of hope, enriched and complicated by the weighty issues of identity, race, and familial tension that their protagonists face.

A critic from the *New York Times Book Review* claimed that Packer's writing is "the old-time religion of storytelling" (Thompson 7). Indeed, Packer's prose is clean and straightforward. Her humor is engaging and matter-of-fact, as in the opening line of "Brownies": "By our second day at Camp Crescendo, the girls in my Brownie troop had decided to kick the asses of each and every girl in Brownie Troop 909" (1). As reviewers have pointed out, Packer's attention to the effects of economic and racial claims on the lives of her characters is reminiscent of writers such as Zadie Smith, Toni Morrison, and Flannery O'Connor. More specifically, her focus tends to rest on young African-American women coming of age uneasily in a white-dominated world. However, although her tales confront issues of race in subtle and complex ways, to focus only on the racial tension in the stories is to misrepresent the scope of Packer's work. As Jean Thompson suggests in her *Times* review, this book is ultimately about the "struggle for the self to make its presence felt in the world. . . . Throughout the book, the obstacles to achieving identity are more complicated than the obvious ones, such as our grievous racial history. Characters are squeezed between competing assumptions and proscriptions, both societal and familial" (7). Indeed, the "elsewhere" these characters inhabit is not easily defined; Packer encourages us to reside, at least for a time, along with her protagonists in that shade of blue between waking and sleeping, "moving toward dark, but not dark yet."

Bibliography

Packer, Z. Z. *Drinking Coffee Elsewhere.* New York: Riverhead Books, 2003.

Thompson, Jean. Review of *Drinking Coffee Elsewhere. New York Times Book Review* (March 16, 2003): 7.

Kaethe Schwehn

Due, Tananarive (1966–) *American novelist and short story writer*

Tananarive Due is perhaps the most successful of the growing number of African-American women writing speculative fiction. She is the author of six novels and several short stories of "supernatural suspense" ("My Characters" 699), all of which are set in the context of a broad history and middle-class life that are distinctively African-American. She is best known for her "African Immortals" trilogy: *My Soul to Keep* (1997); *The* LIVING BLOOD (2001), winner of an American Book Award; and *Blood Colony* (2008). Other novels by the author include *The Between* (1995), in which a man discovers that his grandmother has granted him the ability to cheat death; *The Good House* (2003), in which a family is cursed by their grandmother's vengeful misuse of magic; and *Joplin's Ghost* (2005), in which a struggling musician's career is shaped by her relationship with the eponymous ghost.

In *My Soul to Keep,* Jessica Jacobs-Wolde discovers that her husband Dawit is part of an Ethi-opian brotherhood of immortals that possesses Christ's blood, and that he commits murder to protect their secret. He makes the pregnant Jessica immortal against her will. Parent-child relationships are central to *The Living Blood,* in which Jessica uses the blood to cure children in South Africa and Botswana of AIDS, cancer, and other diseases. She tries to teach her daughter Fana the appropriate use of her inherited supernatural powers before evil forces can corrupt her. In *Blood Colony,* the unique blood has appeared on the black market, and Fana is threatened by a group of Italian immortals.

The Black Rose (2000), a fictional biography of Madam C. J. Walker, was written using the research of *Roots* author, the late Alex Haley. The nonfiction memoir *Freedom in the Family: A Mother-Daughter Memoir of the Fight for Civil Rights* (2003), was written with Due's mother, Patricia Stephens Due. Due wrote the detective novels *Casanegra* (2007) and *In the Night of the Heat* (2009) in collaboration with her husband, the science-fiction writer Steven Barnes, and Blair Underwood. Due also contributed a chapter to *Naked Came the Manatee* (1996), a detective farce; and in 1999 she used the proceeds from that work to fund a $10,000 scholarship in honor of her parents at Florida A&M University.

Due was born in Tallahassee Florida, the daughter of two civil rights activists, who taught her "a long view of history" ("Immortals Rising"), and she grew up in suburbs that were predominantly white. Her mother spent seven weeks in jail in 1960 after participating in a sit-in at a Woolworth's lunch counter. In high school, Due won several awards for oratory, playwriting, and essay writing at the Afro-American Cultural, Technological and Scientific Olympics. She graduated from Northwestern University's Medill School of Journalism in 1987, where she also took several creative writing workshops. She then attended the University of Leeds as a Rotary Foundation Scholar, graduating in 1988 after writing her English master's thesis on African literary representations of the Nigerian civil war. After an internship, Due worked as a columnist and feature writer at the *Miami Herald* through the 1990s, covering such issues as the impact of Hurricane Andrew on children. She has taught seminars and workshops at the University of Miami, and at Cleveland State, Howard, and Michigan State Universities. She married Steven Barnes in 1998 and spent several years living in Longview, Washington. She now lives in Southern California, where she teaches creative writing in the Antioch University M.F.A. program in Los Angeles, and where she remains a diehard Miami Dolphins football fan.

Due played keyboards and sang backup vocals in Stephen King's band, the Rock Bottom Remainders, and cites King's influence as the most clearly evident in her work ("My Characters" 696). She also credits her 1992 *Miami Herald* interview with Anne Rice as inspiring her to pursue speculative fiction in spite of the lack of respect it receives ("My Characters" 701). Her other literary influences include Alice Walker, Gloria Naylor, Toni Morrison and, later in Due's career, Octavia E. Butler, with whom she is often compared. Due credits the success of Terry McMillan's novel *Waiting to Exhale* (1992) with proving the existence of a market for commercial black fiction such as her own (Interview, *CNN Sunday Morning*).

Due has often asserted that, like Butler and Rice, she writes about universal themes, albeit from a perspective particular to the black diaspora (Interview, Hood, 158), and that her consideration of black themes takes precedence over her interests in gender issues and in supernatural fiction. Her work is broadly comparable to King's in its treatment of the explosive intrusion of fear into middle-class comfort, and to Rice's in its treatment of the implications of immortality. It also bears comparison with fiction that blurs the boundaries between the white western gothic that firmly divides reason and superstition, and the folkloric, which does not, such as Morrison's *Beloved* (1987) and A. A. Carr's *Eye Killers* (1995). Due's insistence that seemingly remote family and cultural history has a direct bearing on the present is comparable to the treatment of histories in Butler's *The Kindred* (1979), Walker's *The Color Purple* (1970), and *Beloved*. Due's *The Living Blood* in particular has been likened to *Beloved*, as well as to the work of Nalo Hopkinson, in its suggestion that "racism, sexism, hierarchical oppression, and violence [can be] overthrown through parental and commu-nity love" (Wisker 85). Such love can also impose proper restraints on the use of power (Mohanraj).

Among the most consistent themes in Due's work is the responsibility that comes with significant power of any sort. Key territories for exploration in this area include responsibility to children and descendants, including, in the case of *The Living Blood*, very distant descendants (284–285); the importance of a sophisticated and far-reaching knowledge of black history—and of family history as well—to any understanding of contemporary African-American life; and the rejection of fear-driven uses of power in favor of humanitarian ones.

Bibliography

Due, Tananarive. *The Between.* New York: HarperCollins, 1995.

———. *The Black Rose.* New York: Ballantine, 2000.

———. *Blood Colony.* New York: Atria, 2008.

Due, Tananarive, and Patricia Stephens Due. *Freedom in the Family: A Mother-Daughter Memoir of the Fight for Civil Rights.* New York: Ballantine, 2003.

———. *The Good House.* New York: Atria, 2003.

———. "Immortals Rising." Tananarive Due's Reading Circle. Available online. URL: http://tananarive-due.blogspot.com/. Accessed June 10, 2008.

———. Interview. By Stacia Kane. The League of Reluctant Adults. February 16, 2008. Available online. URL: http://www.leagueofreluctantadults.com/2008/02/interview-tananarive-due-american-book.html. Accessed June 10, 2008.

———. Interview. By Yolanda Hood. *FEMSPEC* 6, no. 1 (2005): 155–164.

———. Interview. *CNN Sunday Morning.* 30 October 2005. Available online. URL: http://tananarivedue.com/Interviews.htm. Accessed June 10, 2008.

———. *In the Night of the Heat.* New York: Atria, 2008.

———. *Joplin's Ghost.* New York: Atria, 2005.

———. *The Living Blood.* New York: Simon & Schuster, 2001.

———. "My Characters Are Teaching Me to Be Strong." By Dianne Glave. *African American Review* 38 (2004): 695–705.

———. *My Soul to Keep.* New York: HarperCollins, 1997.

Due, Tananarive, et al. *Naked Came the Manatee.* New York: G.P. Putnam's Sons, 1996.

Due, Tananarive, Steven Barnes, and Blair Underwood. *Casanegra.* New York: Atria, 2007.

Mohanraj, Mary Anne. "Power Dynamics in the Novels of Tananarive Due." Strange Horizons. Available online. URL: http://www.strangehorizons.com/2002/20020520/tananarive.shtml. Accessed June 10, 2008.

Tananarive Due.com Edited by Tananarive Due. June 2008. Available online. URL: tananarivedue.com. Accessed June 10, 2008.

Wisker, Gina. "'Your Buried Ghosts Have a Way of Tripping You Up': Revisioning and Mothering in African-American and Afro-Caribbean Women's Speculative Horror." *FEMSPEC* 6, no. 1 (2005): 71–86.

—Alex Link

Eberstadt, Fernanda (1960–) *American novelist*

Fernanda Eberstadt is the critically acclaimed author of four works of fiction, *Low Tide*, ISAAC AND HIS DEVILS, *When the Sons of Heaven Meet the Daughters of the Earth*, *The Furies*, and one nonfiction volume, *Little Money Street*. Her prose is characterized by a highly articulated, almost baroque diction, and typically examines issues of class, education, religion, and art.

Eberstadt was born in 1960 in New York City to an artistic, high-society family. Her parents "threw parties which went down in social history, while her mother's dresses of feathers, vinyl and fur hang in the Museum of the City of New York" (Kaufman). Her mother, Isabel, a writer, and her father, Frederick, a photographer and psychotherapist, mingled in circles that allowed Fernanda to work for Andy Warhol's Factory at the age of 16. Fernanda's paternal grandfather is Ferdinand Eberstadt, a lawyer and policy adviser to the U.S. government, while her maternal grandfather is the poet Ogden Nash who, according to Eberstadt's account, encouraged her "fascination with words." However, Eberstadt remarked that "Growing up without parental guidance or boundaries of religion, sex or drugs was scary" (Kaufman).

A precocious child, Eberstadt wrote her first novel when she was 11, while spending a year in the Bahamas with her parents (the reason Eberstadt dropped out of the prestigious Brearley School); the novel is centered on the October Revolution. She also "read and read and read, everything, including the Bible" (Kaufman). At the age of 18, Eberstadt moved to the United Kingdom where she was one of the first women to graduate from Magdalen College, Oxford, earning a degree in English literature. Since 1998, Eberstadt has lived with her husband and two children in France but regularly contributes to the *New Yorker*, the *New York Times Magazine*, the *New York Times*, *Vogue*, *Vanity Fair*, and *Commentary*. Her only nonfiction book, *Little Money Street* (2003), discusses the culture and lifestyle of French gypsies, with whom she became fascinated after moving to France.

Eberstadt's literary career began in 1985, when she published *Low Tide* to such critical acclaim that she was invited to appear on William F. Buckley's *Firing Line* (1966–99). Although Buckley was staunchly conservative, the program was considered one of the nation's most prominent forums for intellectual debate, and almost exclusively featured notable politicians, writers, and scholars. *Low Tide* announces both a style and a set of themes that Eberstadt would inscribe in her future books: language rich in metaphors, a nonlinear plot, and an examination of class through art and education. The book also includes prominent autobiographical elements, including her characters' association with New York's Upper East Side life and high-society upbringing, as well as the protagonist's education at Brearley and Oxford.

Six years later, Eberstadt's next book, *Isaac and His Devils*, was an equal critical success. Unlike *Low Tide*, which has at its center a love relationship and the mores of class, *Isaac* explores the correlation between genius and environment. The narrative is focused on Isaac, a gifted but a socially inept child from rural New Hampshire who is certain that he is predestined for "bigger things"—escape from his provincial town and a great contribution to humanity. His social awkwardness is as much owing to his obesity and half-deafness as to his peculiar self-esteem, neither being welcomed in his oppressive surroundings. However, even when he flees to Harvard, presumably the center of intellectual life for which he longs, Isaac faces a series of crises that finally bring him back to his provincial hometown. His trials range from uncomfortable encounters with unsympathetic family members to hallucinatory dialogues with the devil. In Eberstadt's next novel, *When the Sons of Heaven Meet the Daughters of the Earth* (1997), Issac reaches New York, but instead of trying to become the literary voice of his generation, he recognizes painting as his new passion. Isaac becomes the protégé of a rich New York woman, and is exposed to the turbulent New York art scene of the 1980s, which Eberstadt had a chance to examine firsthand through her work at The Factory and the social life of her family. Whereas in the previous novel Eberstadt examined the personal trials of a contemporary genius, in its sequel she explores the broader struggles of the character within the art milieu, discussing questions of fame, originality, religious and political art, as well as the commodification of art and celebrity. Eberstadt explained that the novel "wasn't always set in the art world" but at a magazine, and that she decided to change the setting because she "found it too incestous, you know—a writer writing about writers" (Joyce).

Eberstadt writes with an exuberance and sophistication that evokes the literature of the 18th and 19th centuries; her long sentences are ornamented with abundant metaphors, similes, and images, while the vocabulary demands an educated and patient reader, capable of appreciating the intricacies of her highly stylized, almost Jamesian diction.

Bibliography

Joyce, Cynthia. "Fernanda Eberstadt: Subversion's Daughter." Salon.com. Available online. URL: www.salon.com/may97/interview970505.htm. Accessed October 19, 2009.

Kaufman, Marjorie. "Opening a Window to the Inner Souls of Artists, In a New Novel," *New York Times*. 4 May 1997.

—Damjana Mraović-O'Hare

Egan, Jennifer (1962–) *American novelist and short story writer*

Jennifer Egan has written three novels, each a dramatic departure from the one before, and a collection of short stories, *Emerald City* (1989). *The Invisible Circus* (1995), her first novel, earned immediate critical acclaim and was adapted into a movie of the same name; her follow-up, *Look at Me* (2001), was a finalist for the National Book Award; *The KEEP* (2006) became a national best seller.

Born in Chicago, Egan moved to San Francisco when she was seven, at the tail end of the '60s, an era whose hazy idealism figures prominently in her first novel. She majored in English literature at the University of Pennsylvania, and spent two years on a fellowship at St. John's College, Cambridge. Upon her return she moved to New York, where she still regularly contributes essays on contemporary culture to the *New York Times Magazine*. She currently lives in Brooklyn with her husband, theater director David Herskovits, and their sons.

Critics recognized Egan as a major new talent on the appearance of her first novel, but her intricately structured and ambitious narratives have defied easy description. In the *New York Times Book Review*, fiction writer Madison Smartt Bell calls her a "refreshingly unclassifiable novelist," contending that her work is at once dazzlingly postmodern and firmly grounded in more traditional realism. Other critics have adopted metaphors from game playing or architecture to describe Egan's work. Multilayered, multivocal stories-within-stories, elaborate narrative frames, shifting voices and fractured chronology are fused with convincing psychological portraits of complex and troubled characters.

The stories in *Emerald City* first sketch the fictional terrain Egan would go on to thoroughly explore in her novels. She constructs situations that quiver with tension and latent violence, characters unstably poised between hopelessness and volcanic self-discovery. As Donna Seaman notes, a "sort of mad, grand gesture is a leitmotif in many of Ms. Egan's stories. Intolerable, seemingly interminable situations are eradicated with one dangerous, dramatic act" (*New York Times*). A disgraced banker, a fashion photographer's assistant, young girls, a middle-aged couple, divorced women—for all of them the world suddenly opens up—however briefly—to reveal the possibility of meaningful human communication, escape, and even happiness.

Such "mad gestures" tend to structure Egan's novels as well. In *Invisible Circus* (1995) Phoebe O'Connor, haunted by the supposed suicide of her beautiful, reckless older sister Faith, leaves San Francisco after high school to trace Faith's earlier path across Europe, hoping to uncover the truth about her death. Armed with a single hit of LSD and a collection of old postcards that she uses to chart Faith's course, Phoebe pursues a relentless quest for her sister and the trippy idealism of the era Faith represents—an era Phoebe feels as if she missed out on but must have some kind of truth to offer. Phoebe's journey, which leads her to the doorstep of an old lover of her sister's, explores dark psychological, erotic, and even political realms. She does not find the answers she is looking for, but begins to forge an identity grounded more in present realities and less in a lost, half-imagined past.

Egan's next novel explores very different territory, but reveals her recurring interest in cultural excess and alienation, identity in a surface-oriented consumer culture, and the insistent presence of the past—what a character in *The Keep* describes as "history pushing up from underneath" (46). *Look at Me* was published in September 2001 and was described by critics as "eerily prescient" (Janet Maslin, *NYT Book Review*), in its treatment both of terrorism, and to a lesser extent, of Internet-based "reality" entertainment. One of the novel's many narrative threads involves a man living quietly and anonymously in Illinois, who is in fact a member of a Middle Eastern terrorist sleeper-cell, despising all he sees as "American" even as he learns to mimic it. For the most part, however, the novel is a tale of two Charlottes: Charlotte Swenson is a 35-year-old model whose face, entirely reconstructed after a car accident, is now unrecognizable, and who struggles to reconstruct a life and career founded on the beauty of a face she no longer possesses; Charlotte Hauser is an inscrutable young girl, the daughter of an old friend of Charlotte Swenson's, who lives in Rockford, Illinois. Desperate for some kind of love, the younger Charlotte embarks on a bizarre affair with the would-be terrorist. The final explosive convergence of the two Charlotte plots—in which Charlotte Swenson's car accident is reenacted (and falsified) for her Web page—suggests that even the most compromised and alienated selves can be reclaimed, perhaps even redeemed. Egan's reliance on the improbable intersections of multiple plotlines has not always met with critical praise. Structurally, however, such collisions generate a kind of epiphenomenal possibility—even magic—floating on top of and at odds with the bleak realism of the individual plots.

In *The Keep* (2006), Egan offers a postmodern spin on the gothic novel. Its dark, claustrophobic story of intrigue and imprisonment focuses on two cousins, Danny and Howie, reunited for the first time in many years at a crumbling eastern European castle. Despite its gothic trappings, the novel's concerns are strikingly contemporary. Danny is obsessed with and preternaturally attuned to modern communication technology, while Howie dreams of renovating the castle as a technology-free luxury hotel, disembodied forms of modern communication replacing the supernatural as a realm of mystery and fear. The uneasy power-dynamic that exists between Danny and Howie, suffused with jealousy, vengeance and a remembered act of violence, is juxtaposed with another narrative, set in a prison, in which a convicted murderer falls in love with his creative-writing instructor. After escaping from prison, he has his completed manuscript delivered to his teacher, and *this* manuscript is Danny and Howie's story, in which the prisoner's critical role does not become clear until its surreally explosive ending. As an imprisoned writer, the narrator's reaction to the experience of writing is a perfect instance of the kind of transcendent gestures that recur in Egan's fictions: "The door wasn't real," he tells us. "There was no actual door. . . . But I opened it up and walked out" (20).

Bibliography

Egan, Jennifer. *Emerald City.* 1989. New York: Random House/Anchor Books, 2007.

———. *The Invisible Circus.* 1995. New York: Anchor Books, 2007.

———. *The Keep.* 2006. New York: Anchor Books, 2007.

———. *Look at Me.* 2001. New York: Anchor Books, 2002.

Bell, Madison Smartt. Review of *The Keep.* New York Times Book Review (July 30, 2006). Available online. URL: http://www.nytimes.com/2006/07/30/books/review/30bell.html?scp=1&sq=jennifer%20egan%20the%20keep%20review&st=cse. Accessed June 9, 2008.

Maslin, Janet. Review of *The Keep.* New York Times Book Review (July 20, 2006). Available online. URL: http://www.nytimes.com/2006/07/20/books/20masl.html?scp=1&sq=jennifer%20egan%20the%20keep%20review%20janet%20maslin&st=cse. Accessed June 9, 2008.

Seaman, Donna. "Mad, Grand Gestures." New York Times on the Web. Available online. URL: http://www.nytimes.com/books/97/04/20/nnp/19281.html. Accessed June 9, 2008.

—Margaret E. Mitchell

Eggers, Dave (1970–) *American novelist, short story writer, journalist, and editor*

Dave Eggers grew up in the upper-middle-class Chicago suburb of Lake Forest, Illinois, and attended the University of Illinois in Urbana-Champaign. As a journalist he has been published in the *New Yorker,* the *New York Times, Esquire,* and the *Guardian* (U.K.), and was one of the founding editors of the now defunct *Might* magazine. In 1998, Eggers founded the independent publishing house, McSweeney's, which publishes emerging writers and experimental work that does not fit within mainstream commercial publications. McSweeney's, having repeatedly reinvented itself using unusual designs (boxes for example), recalls a cabinet of curiosities full of esoteric, untimely, and otherwise uncommercial pursuits and has expanded its publishing to include books and DVDs. McSweeney's also publishes *The Believer* magazine, an *almost* monthly publication of literary and social commentary, and *Wholpin,* a short-film DVD quarterly. In 2002, Eggers opened 826 Valencia, an educational center in San Francisco that gives one-on-one attention to students looking to improve their reading and writing, making use of writers and editors living in the community in which the center is located. Similar educational centers have been opened in Brooklyn, Michigan, Seattle, Los Angeles, Chicago, and Boston. Eggers is the author and editor of numerous fiction and nonfiction works, including *The Best American Nonrequired Reading Series,* and he cofounded *Voice of Witness,* a nonprofit series of books employing oral history to expose human rights violations and social injustice.

Eggers's first book, *A HEARTBREAKING WORK OF STAGGERING GENIUS* (2000) is a novelistic memoir that he wrote in his 20s. As a finalist for the Pulitzer Prize, *AHWOSG* ensured Eggers's instant recognition in America. As *New York Times* critic Michiko Kakutani put it: "Here was a virtuosic piece of writing: a big, daring, manic depressive stew of a book that noisily announces the debut of a talented—yes, staggeringly talented new writer." The book tells the moving story of the Eggers family as it was fractured and subsequently refashioned after the deaths of Eggers's parents within 32 days of each other. In the absence of parents, Eggers became the surrogate father of his eight-year-old brother Toph, and the two brothers move to Berkeley, California, to be closer to their sister Beth. The book's earnest sentiments are leavened—and at times rendered yet more poignant—by postmodern writing techniques and a self-reflexive style that is skillfully employed throughout. The prefatory material, for example, provides readers with "Rules and Suggestions for Enjoyment of this Book" and also playfully pre-empts reader criticisms by encouraging those who prefer pure fiction to exchange their copy for a digital document in which they can replace the names of characters and places so as to make the work appear more fictional. But as in the work of the late DAVID FOSTER WALLACE, such encompassing irony is ultimately repurposed here in the service of sincerity, suggesting that postmodern self-reflexivity can, in fact, serve as a kind of narrative protection permitting the expression of otherwise inexpressible tragedy.

In 2002, Eggers self-published *You Shall Know Our Velocity!* the travelogue of two young men, Will and Hand, who set about traveling the world over the course of one week in order to give away $32,000—money that Will made by happenstance and feels unjustified in holding onto. Unexpectedly the characters find it more difficult to get around the world than they had anticipated and "any thwarted movement was an affront." Their initial idea of "unmitigated movement, of serving any or maybe every impulse" is made untenable early on by the burden of visas, and flights that simply do not travel between Rwanda and Mongolia. They also find it surprisingly difficult to give away the money, and the simple philanthropic impulse at the heart of the journey is ultimately shown to be anything but simple, necessitating as it does the repeated and complicated choice of who exactly to unload the money on, and how to unload it on them. They try to give money to some young women, for example, only to find out these are prostitutes, and they find out that another target, a young, seemingly kind boy is in fact a con artist. Finally their attempts to get rid of the money become absurd, verging on performance art: They walk into a house and leave flowers randomly, tape pouches of money to the outer walls of a hut, and leave real treasure hunts for kids.

Hand's subsequent diaristic addition to the novel functions both to redress perceived errors in Will's narration and to suggest flaws in its own narrative retelling, extending their journey—and by extension the novel itself—to an "allegory for any sort of intervention, whether by governments or neighbors—but mostly the idea of humanitarian aid, on whatever scale, micro or macro—from NGOs to panhandlers and passersby." Throughout the journey Will and Hand also struggle with its secondary motivation, a cathartic attempt to deal with the death of their lifelong friend Jack in a car accident the year before; and the absurdity of the journey is in a sense ennobled by the realization that "the only infallible truth of our lives is that everything we love in life will be taken from us."

The collection of short stories *How We Are Hungry* was published in 2004 in Eggers' typically antiestablishment style: no reviewers' galleys, no back-cover blurbs, and no publicity. It met with largely negative reviews and assertions of unoriginality and self-indulgence. A wildly varied ménage of travel narratives in vastly different climes, the collection is replete with protagonists and plans flawed in ways that recall *You Shall Know Our Velocity!* Their attempts at reconciling past and present, or the ideal and real, reveal good and lofty intentions faltering and disintegrating in the very act of being realized. Peopled by young adults wanting to do good and act well, the collection explores the difficulty of doing just that, and suggests that human relations, no matter how simple they may seem on the surface, are profoundly fraught and vulnerable to sheer misfortune.

What Is the What (2006), or in its extended title WHAT IS THE WHAT: THE AUTOBIOGRAPHY OF VALENTINO ACHAK DENG, A *Novel,* combines Eggers's literary work with the worlds of philanthropy, advocacy, and education that have become a significant part of his contribution to literature beyond writing. Eggers met Valentino in 2003 and began recording the harrowing story of his having been forced to leave his village in Sudan at the age of seven and travel hundreds of miles on foot through the deserts of three countries, all while being pursued by various militias, a story typifying those of the "Lost Boys" of Sudan. At the beginning of the project, Eggers was uncertain whether it would result in a work of fiction or nonfiction. The initial impulse was to help Valentino write an autobiography, but as became apparent on a trip back to Sudan, his intimate and emotional engagement with the often nightmarish details of his own story made the demand for journalistic 'objectivity' constrictive and unrealistic. For this reason, the result operates as both a human document and a piece of literature, along the lines of Truman Capote's documentary novel, *In Cold Blood.* As a collaborative effort between Eggers and Valentino, all author fees and profits from its sales go to the Valentino Achek Deng Foundation, which works to build schools and community centers in war-torn southern Sudan.

Fall 2009 saw the release of three additional Eggers projects: *Zeitoun,* a well-received non-fictional account of a survivor of Hurricane Katrina, a film adaptation (screenplay by Eggers, director Spike Jonze) of Maurice Sendak's classic children's tale, *Where the Wild Things Are,* and a novelization of the screenplay. The film, which takes great liberties with the story, received mixed reviews, but the novelization, entitled *The Wild Things,* was more favorably received. The project had actually been recommended to Eggers by Sendak himself. The novel delves deeply into the mind of the child Max, who is here fatherless and neglected by his mother and teenage sister. Curiously recalling the protagonists of *They Shall Know Our Velocity!,* with their frustrated desire for "unmitigated movement, of serving any or maybe every impulse," the boy's behavior becomes increasingly violent and impulsive (including a biting attack on his mother), until, after a particularly nasty disturbance at home, he flees into the nearby woods and finds a boat. At this point, the novel takes up the main storyline of Sendak's tale, with Max eventually landing on an island of monsters and becoming their king. The most prominent difference between the two tales is that Sendak's Max maintains a wonderfully amoral equanimity (worthy of a king), while Eggers's Max passes through a familiar moral struggle, with the help of the "wild things."

Bibliography

Eggers, Dave. *A Heartbreaking Work of Staggering Genius.* Toronto: Vintage Canada, 2000.

———. *How We Are Hungry.* McSweeney's, 2004.

———. *What Is the What.* Toronto: Vintage Canada, 2006.

———. *You Shall Know Our Velocity!* Toronto: Vintage Canada, 2002.

———. *Zeitoun.* McSweeney's, 2009.

Kakutani, Michiko. Review of *A Heartbreaking Work of Staggering Genius.* New York Times on the Web. Available online. URL: http://partners.nytimes.com/library/books/020100eggers-book-review.html?scp=1&sq= michiko%20kakutani%20dave%20eggers&st=cse. Accessed May 16, 2009.

—Kate Morris

Eisenstadt, Jill (1963–) *American novelist, short story writer, and essayist*

Eisenstadt is the author of two novels, FROM ROCKAWAY (1987) and *Kiss Out* (1991), and gained critical prominence in the late 1980s after the publication of the former, which received favorable reviews and considerable media attention. Critics compared Eisenstadt to members of the literary "brat pack," a group of popular writers from the era that included BRETT EASTON ELLIS, Jay McInerny, Tama Janowitz, and Mark Lindquist. Eisenstadt's follow-up novel, *Kiss Out,* was also a critical success, although it is the last piece of long-form fiction she has published.

Eisenstadt was born in 1963 in New York City, and grew up in Rockaway, a working-class neighborhood in Queens. She studied English at Bennington College, a liberal arts college in rural Vermont, and received her M.F.A. in creative writing from Columbia University. She has not published a novel since 1991, but continues to write, contributing short stories, articles, and essays to a wide range of publications, including the *New York Times, Vogue, New York Magazine,* and *Glamour.* In recent years, she has collaborated with her sister, Debra Eisenstadt, on two screenplays, *Daydream Believers* (2001) and *The Limbo Room* (2006), serving as coproducer on both projects. She currently lives in Park Slope, Brooklyn, with her husband and fellow novelist, Michael Drinkard. Although she maintains a low public profile, Eisenstadt remains active in Park Slope's vibrant literary community.

Eisenstadt's first novel is the story of four friends, Alex, Timmy, Peg, and Chowderhead, who live in Rockaway, a beachfront community of blue-collar Irish Catholics in Queens, New York. After high school the group fractures when Alex leaves to attend a prestigious college in New Hampshire on a scholarship. Timmy, Peg and Chowderhead stick around the neighborhood, working dead-end jobs and partying continually. As Alex adapts to her new life at school, the rest confront the twin demons of boredom and desperation, and Eisenstadt contrasts Alex's challenging growth at Camden College with the dearth of opportunity that defines life in Rockaway. The novel culminates in a violent and explosive "death keg," a semi-barbaric ritual following the tragic death of a child on the beach. Eisenstadt, however, suggests that the real tragedy may be the needless and damaging waste of another generation of the neighborhood's youth.

Contrary to popular perception (itself a tribute to Eisenstadt's narrative skill), the novel is not autobiographical. Eisenstadt is of Jewish (not Irish) descent; she attended public school, and grew up in a different area of Rockaway than is depicted in the novel. Instead, stories she heard from other people growing up formed the backbone of the novel, and she fleshed these out with elements of her own experience. For example, her experiences at Bennington undoubtedly colored her creation of Camden, a fictional New England college that BRETT EASTON ELLIS, who also studied at Bennington, used as the setting for his second novel, *The Rules of Attraction.* The thematic overlap—as well as a joint appearance on the *Today* show—fueled comparisons between the two young writers and other members of the "brat pack." Eisenstadt, however, resisted the label, lamenting the fact that some critics rejected her work as insubstantial and faddish due to the association.

Kiss Out departs both in tone and in style from Eisenstadt's debut. Though also set in Queens, it chronicles the comic exploits of three Jewish friends from the fictional neighborhood of Sidehill. The convoluted plot revolves around Sam's engagement to Claire, a wealthy and directionless teenager from suburban New Jersey. Twin brothers Oscar and Fred, Sam's best friends since childhood, are dumbstruck by the impending marriage, and it turns out that Claire herself is less than thrilled at the prospect. Their relationship quickly unravels, and through a series of improbable events Claire ends up embroiled in an exotic-parrot smuggling scam with Oscar in the Yucatan Peninsula. Meanwhile Fred, a struggling street-performer and clown-college reject, attempts to learn the ropes at his family's beauty parlor business. The emotional centerpiece of the novel is Claire's gradual realization that Sam is wrong for her, until she finally calls off the wedding altogether. Though she does not know exactly what she wants, she at least knows what she does not want, and the subtle transformation born of this knowledge enables her to find something much nearer happiness by the novel's end.

Eisenstadt is known for her consistently vivid characterization and incisive humor, and although her two novels vary stylistically, there are notable thematic affinities between them. Eisenstadt is especially concerned about the deleterious effect of aimlessness on young adults. Many of the characters that populate her stories have no direction, and Eisenstadt suggests that such lack of opportunity and ambition is destructive, even dangerous: Sloane, a particularly brutal lifeguard and a fixture on *From Rockaway*'s dead-end beach, kills his dog, Schizo, in a drunken stupor; Claire agrees to marry Sam, even though she does not really like him or enjoy his company; Peg and Chowderhead are ostensibly young, but both already seem bored and weary of life. It is only when Eisenstadt's protagonists take risks that they prosper, and the most hopeful moments in her novels are when her characters recognize they are unsatisfied, recognize the somnolent grief in their dissatisfaction, and decide to do something about it: Timmy finally sends a letter to his long-absent father, and it suddenly seems possible that he will escape the drudgery of his life in Rockaway; Claire rejects a loveless marriage with Sam and runs off to Mexico, where she eventually ends up finding love with Fred. For Eisenstadt, hope—and with it the prospect of happiness—fundamentally depends on the individual's ability to reject enfeebling stasis, even for the mere possibility of change.

There is a cinematic quality to Eisenstadt's writing; the pacing of her novels is crisp and the dialogue snappy. It is no surprise, then, that Hollywood icon Sidney Pollack optioned *From Rockaway* for a film adaptation, and novelist J. P. Donleavy remarked that the novel "would make a great film." Currently, however, there are no concrete plans to produce film versions of either novel.

Bibliography

Eisenstadt, Jill. *From Rockaway.* New York: Knopf, 1987.
———. *Kiss Out.* New York: Knopf, 1991.
Silverman, Ethan. "Jill Eisenstadt." BOMB Magazine 36, no. 3 (1991). Available online. URL: http://www.bombsite.com/issues/36/articles/1453. Accessed May 12, 2009.
Wurtzel, Elizabeth. "The Bennington-Knopf Connection." October 19, 1987. The Harvard Crimson Online Edition. Available online. URL: http://www.thecrimson.com/article.aspx?ref=136524. Accessed May 16, 2009.

—Peter Farrell

Ellen Foster **Kaye Gibbons** (1987)

Ellen Foster, the first novel by KAYE GIBBONS, is the story of an 11-year-old southern girl's journey from an abusive family to an enduring and supportive love found in a foster home of her own choosing (a progress intimated by the novel's eponymous title). Ellen's opening words, "When I was little I would think of ways to kill my daddy" (Gibbons, 1), establish both the tone and circumstances of her early home, with its drunk, abusive father and a sickly mother whose marriage has alienated the rest of her family. In the midst of a household burdened by her mother's illness and her father's drunken anger, young Ellen takes care of the home as best she can, learning self-sufficiency early in life. After her mother dies, apparently of an overdose of heart medication, Ellen is left to fend for herself when her father goes away for days on end, and is forced to ward off his sexual advances as well. Her one source of support in this life is her black friend Starletta and her family, poor but loving farm workers who know Ellen's situation and gladly offer her a safe haven. Ellen's upbringing and milieu, however, have led her to consider them as inferior to whites, and she seeks shelter elsewhere, first with her mother's recently widowed sister, then with the school's bohemian art teacher and her husband. It is decided by the court, at last, that Ellen must be in the care of her blood relations, so she is sent to her maternal grandmother. But the grandmother despises Ellen, who to her serves as a reminder of the man who ruined her daughter's life, and ultimately drove the daughter to her death. Finally, after the grandmother dies, Ellen makes her way to a foster family sponsored by the local church, and here she finds the love and support she has missed all her life.

As a young protagonist forced to develop self-sufficiency in order to survive, Ellen recalls Twain's Huckleberry Finn. And like Huck, Ellen is a naive narrator who matures in her attitudes about race, moving from racial prejudice to acceptance and love with the help of her closest friend, who is black. But unlike *The Adventures of Huckleberry Finn*, *Ellen Foster* does not contain any significant picaresque elements, and each experience clearly contributes to her growth as a character. Also, Ellen's movement is not on the grand scale of Huck's Mississippi River adventures, but is rooted in quiet, unheroic shifts from one domestic sphere to another. Gibbons structures the narrative as an alternation of the present and past: in the present, Ellen is adjusting to life in her foster home, while a series of extended flashbacks shows us how she arrived there. Through this narrative pattern—and the humor that comes from Ellen's naive, first-person account—Gibbons avoids an overly sentimental approach. Nor does Ellen live happily ever after once she reaches the care of her foster mother, but instead must continue to adjust psychologically and emotionally to the radical change in lifestyle.

This adjustment reflects one of the major themes of the novel: While Ellen is highly self-sufficient, such independence is inseparably linked to her isolation and loneliness. The first evidence of this theme is Gibbons's epigraph, an inscription from Ralph Waldo Emerson's essay, "Self-Reliance":

> Cast the bantling on the rocks, Suckle him with the she-wolf's teat, Wintered with the hawk and fox, Power and speed be hands and feet.

Ellen, the "bantling," is thrown on the rocks of domestic hardship and develops strength from this adversity. Self-reliance is regarded, of course, as a preeminently positive American trait; yet a darker side of Emerson's passage emerges in the novel, too. Like the bantling child, "wintered with the hawk and fox," and thus isolated from human companionship, Ellen suffers from an intense loneliness. It seems that whenever she finds a warm relationship with another person, circumstances tear her away, and Ellen must increasingly turn inward if she is to survive. And thus, when finally arrived at her foster home, where there is love and companionship in plenty, it is very difficult for Ellen to adjust, because now she must relinquish much of the self-reliance that has been the very key to her survival. She must embrace sharing, cooperation, and dependence in her foster home; this is the price of the love and structure that she needs, her craving for which is evidenced, for example, in her need to set up Starletta's toy town according to the illustration on its box, and her taping together of Starletta's broken crayons (Gibbons 37).

A second theme, that of overcoming racial prejudice, is wound throughout the novel, and becomes its focus in the closing chapters, as Ellen grows to understand her flawed sense of superiority as a white person. The same love and dependence she witnesses in her new foster home were always there in Starletta's family, but Ellen could not see past their poverty and race. She will not drink after Starletta, or eat a "colored biscuit" (Gibbons 38), and prefers to pity the family for being black and poor, and having to supplement their diet by chewing nutrient-filled clay. This attitude slowly changes, and again through adversity, especially when Ellen is forced to work in the cotton fields owned by her grandmother. There, Mavis—a black field worker—looks out for Ellen and tells her more about her mother. Ellen steadily develops respect for African Americans, particularly Mavis, Starletta, and Starletta's family, and in the closing chapters of the novel, her greatest wish is to plan Starletta's visit to her new home, that she may express her love, appreciation, and change of heart.

Ellen's situation is in many respects Dickensian, but she evinces a rounder personality than the Victorian workhouse children of 19th-century fiction. Less dark in its vision than Dorothy Allison's *Bastard Out of Carolina*, *Ellen Foster* presents a protagonist with whom the reader can easily sympathize, and laugh along with. Ellen is precocious and smart, well-read for her age (despising children's books, she asks her school librarian to generate a list of books with some literary merit), and emotionally strong; at the same time she is infected by the racism that surrounds her, has streaks of impatience, pride, and selfishness, and is not above stealing and hoarding money (albeit money stolen from her worthless father and used mostly for her survival). Most of her faults, however, can be explained by her situation. Though she cheats to get her Girl Scout badges, quitting the Scouts after less than a year, and buys herself several Christmas presents while presenting Starletta's parents with a spoon rest, the reader can see these acts as part of her attempt to create a normal, stable family life. Ellen also struggles with her identity. Long after her travails, she says, "I still wonder sometimes if I am fine myself or if I have tricked myself into believing I am who I think I am" (Gibbons 80). She takes to calling herself "Old Ellen," the sign of a child forced too soon to grow up, and who is now longing to recapture all that she missed in her childhood. When Ellen notices Starletta maturing, her great desire is to keep Starletta all to herself, to become a maternal figure and treat Starletta as the child she herself was never allowed to be.

Ellen Foster was adapted as a television movie in 1997, starring Jena Malone as Ellen. In 2005, Gibbons published a sequel, entitled *The Life All around Me by Ellen Foster*.

Bibliography

Gibbons, Kaye. *Ellen Foster*. Chapel Hill, N.C.: Algonquin Press, 1987.

—Joseph Schaub

Ellis, Bret Easton (1964–) *American novelist and short story writer*

Ellis is the author of five novels: *Less than Zero*, *The Rules of Attraction*, AMERICAN PSYCHO, *Glamorama*, and LUNAR PARK. He has also written *The Informers*, a book of interconnected short stories. Often labeled a transgressive author, Ellis typically explores taboo subjects like drug use, rape, and murder, with a striking blend of humor and horror; and as a result has become as famous for the controversy his novels have created as for their content and artistry.

Ellis was born in Los Angeles in 1964, and grew up in Sherman Oaks, California. His father, Robert Martin Ellis, was a wealthy real estate developer, and his mother, Dale, was a homemaker. He graduated from the prestigious Buckley School in 1982, the same year his parents divorced. After graduation, Ellis left the West Coast to attend Bennington College in Vermont—thinly disguised as fictional Camden College in his novels. While at Bennington, Ellis played in several '80s bands before the publication of his first novel, *Less than Zero*, brought him significant literary attention in 1985. His literary success at such a young age led critics to hail Ellis as a leading author of the MTV generation and a member of the literary "brat pack," along with fellow '80s writers Jay McInerey and Tama Janowitz, whose works were, like Ellis's, aggressively marketed to readers under 30. After graduating from Bennington in 1986, Ellis moved to New York City where he continues to reside today. Though he has given extensive interviews during his literary career, Ellis rarely divulges details of his personal life, beyond his literary relationships with other writers. However, a year after the death of his best friend and lover, Michael Wade Kaplan, in 2004, Ellis revealed his bisexuality in a *New York Times* article. In addition to guarding his privacy, Ellis has routinely refused to provide insight into the meaning or significance of his novels.

Though his style and subject matter have evolved over time, Ellis's novels have maintained some structural consistencies. He always employs first-person narrators whose reliability is often in question. Typically they are complex but static characters who often reappear in subsequent novels (on the final page of *The Rules of Attraction*, protagonist Paul Denson muses, "I haven't changed" [283]). His character development usually takes the form of broader cultural exploration, tracing the ways in which unavoidable experiences have formed—and often malformed—his protagonists. For Ellis, the influence of culture often leads to self-deception, which leads the narrators of his novels to shape their worlds according to often perverse cultural fantasies.

Ellis's engagement with '80s culture in his early work was typically seen as an attempt to construct an evocative portrait of his generation, leading to comparisons with writers like Jack Kerouac and Ernest Hemingway, with whom Ellis also shares a propensity for vivid and unornamented prose. In *Less than Zero* (1985), the narrator and protagonist, Clay, returns to Los Angeles from Camden College in New Hampshire during Christmas break. While engaging in nearly constant drug use and numerous trysts—both heterosexual and homosexual—Clay encounters a snuff film featuring a 20-year-old girl whom his friends have kidnapped, drugged, and raped; and then witnesses his friend Julian's violent beating by a pimp to whom he has prostituted himself for drug money. Despite this portrait of the nihilistic consequences of a generation abandoned by its parents—and in many ways by itself as well—Clay's mildly sentimental attachment to a familial

past, transitory moral impulses, and a vague sense of duty suggest he could have turned out differently. His very name suggests his malleability, and the novel's portrait of his culture suggests why he has been molded into the disaffected hedonist he has become. Ellis continued to expand his exploration of the amorality and violence of '80s youth culture in *The Rules of Attraction* (1987) and *The Informers* (1994), both of which rely on multiple first-person narrators.

Though the release of *Less than Zero* sparked some moral backlash, *American Psycho* (1991) is Ellis's most contentious work, and likely the most controversial novel released in the United States since *Naked Lunch*. Narrated by a wealthy 26-year-old investment banker named Patrick Bateman, the novel explores the relationship between status and consumption during the Reagan era, and the violence that results from narcissistic self-deception. Bateman recounts, in a shockingly articulate and detailed fashion, his murders of homeless people and business rivals, as well as numerous acts of extreme sexual violence. But despite his lengthy and detailed account of murdering his associate Paul Owen, Owen turns out to be alive at the end of the narrative, suggesting that the novel's numerous acts of violence may simply be fantasies of Bateman's narcissistic and status-obsessed imagination. Before *American Psycho* was published, word of its shocking content spread and, faced with boycott threats by feminist leaders like Gloria Steinem and the National Organization for Women, Random House declined to publish it. Knopf soon bought the rights and released it in paperback. Defenders of the novel often note its satiric use of exaggeration—both Bateman's hyperbolic use of violence and Ellis's hyperbolization of Bateman—in order to suggest that its grotesque representations are not meant to be taken literally. However, it was the mere depiction of such excessive violence, particularly against women, to which feminist critics most vociferously objected.

American Psycho began a move away from the sparse prose style of Ellis's earlier novels, which culminated in *Glamorama* (1998). Perhaps his most ambitious novel, *Glamorama* also marks a shift in Ellis's cultural focus from the consumption-obsessed '80s to the celebrity-obsessed '90s.

Narrated by a male model, event planner, and B-list actor named Victor Ward, the novel traces the protagonist's movement from the New York fashion scene through an underworld of international terrorism in Europe. Ward's idiosyncratic narrative style leaves the reader uncertain whether the often horrific events he narrates are taking place in reality or on the set of a film, suggesting that the media and fashion industry have created a distorted sense of reality, which the novel portrays as, ultimately, an act of violence against the culture.

Ellis's critics—like some of his proponents—have often confused the voice of the first-person protagonists of his novels with the voice of the novelist himself, which has led to repeated characterizations of the author as a moral nihilist who has earned a living from the self-indulgent publication of his violent cultural fantasies. In *Lunar Park* (2005), Ellis satirizes these characterizations by creating a character named Bret Easton Ellis, a model of the disaffected, drug-addicted, misanthropic philanderer that his critics have accused him of celebrating in the form of his protagonists; and the ridicule of his detractors' portrayal is broadened when his fictional persona begins a suburban life by marrying an old lover with whom he had previously fathered a child. Developing into a complex and often terrifying ghost story in the tradition of Stephen King, the resulting narrative satirizes the very system of suburban values from which many of his detractors have launched their critiques. Though Ellis undermines critical characterizations of himself though the creation of a fictional mask, the reader of the mock memoir is finally offered little insight into the real author of the novel; and this predicament mirrors the reader's position when attempting to locate a positive value system in Ellis's broader oeuvre. Despite engaging in the moral project of satirizing American cultural values (or the absence of such values), Ellis's novels affirm no alternative value system, and thus would appear to offer little hope of moral revival.

All of Ellis's works have been, or are in the process of being, released as feature films. As a result of the novel's instant success, a film version of *Less than Zero* was released in 1987 and starred Andrew McCarthy as Clay. A highly successful adaptation of *American Psycho* starring Christian Bale as Patrick Bateman was released in 2000. *The Rules of Attraction* was released in 2002. *Glamorama* was filmed in 2004 but has yet to be released. Film versions of *The Informers* and *Lunar Park* are scheduled for release in 2008 and 2009, respectively. In addition to filmic adaptations of his novels, Ellis was the subject of the documentary film *This Is Not an Exit: The Fictional World of Bret Easton Ellis* (2000), and he has authored a screenplay, *The Frog King*, which is scheduled for release in 2009. Ellis has also begun work on his sixth novel, *Imperial Bedrooms*, a sequel to *Less than Zero* that examines the characters of his first novel as they approach middle age. It is scheduled for release in 2010.

Bibliography

Ellis, Bret Easton. *American Psycho.* New York: Vintage, 1991.
———. *Glamorama.* 1998. New York: Vintage, 2000.
———. *The Informers.* New York: Vintage, 1995.
———. *Less than Zero.* 1985. New York: Vintage, 1998.
———. *Lunar Park.* New York: Vintage, 2005.
———. *The Rules of Attraction.* 1987. New York: Vintage, 1998.
Wyatt, Edward. "The Man in the Mirror." *New York Times,* 7 August 2005, AR1(L).

—Ryan Wepler

Ellis, Trey (1962–) *American novelist and screenwriter*

Ellis is the author of four novels, *Platitudes* (1988), HOME REPAIRS (1993), RIGHT HERE, RIGHT NOW (1999), and *Bedtime Stories: Adventures in the Land of Single Fatherhood* (2008). He is also a successful screenwriter.

Ellis was born in 1962, and grew up in the mainly white, middle-class neighborhoods around Ann Arbor, Michigan, and New Haven, Connecticut, while his parents pursued degrees at the University of Michigan and Yale. He graduated from Philips Academy, Andover, Massachusetts, then from Stanford University where he majored in creative writing. Ellis has traveled extensively throughout Africa, and Central and South America. He speaks Italian, French, Spanish, and Portuguese, and has lived in Italy, France, and Japan.

Currently, he is an assistant professor of screenwriting in the Graduate School of Film at Columbia University. He lives in New York City with his two children.

Ellis began *Platitudes* (1988) in workshop classes at Stanford, and finished while living in Florence. As a piece of metafiction, the novel incorporates two distinct narratives. Dewayne Wellington, a failing postmodern black writer, begins writing a story following a geeky, black teenage boy bent on sex, school, and electronics instead of the typical depiction of dangerous black youth. Dewayne invites the help of a successful female black novelist who provides a strikingly different view of the protagonist. The novel was reissued to include Ellis's article, "The New Black Aesthetic," which he had begun at Stanford, where it was commissioned by the *New York Times Sunday Magazine*. When Ellis found that scope too limiting, it was published by *Callaloo*, an academic journal, in 1989. In the article, Ellis adopts the title term while envisaging an exciting intellectual community that finally brings together and celebrates "cultural mulattos," persons who can freely thrive in more than one race's culture.

In the structure of a diary novel, *Home Repairs* (1993) follows black adolescent narrator Austin McMillian's journey to adulthood through his experiences with women. He records every sexual exploit in his journal to determine his ineffective behavior and improve himself, hoping to become an urbane and confident young man. Austin has much in common with the protagonist in *Platitudes*'s novel-within-a-novel and with Ellis himself. Austin graduates from Andover and continues to Stanford University, all the while in hot pursuit of sex, a girlfriend, and recognition. Denzel Washington purchased the film rights, with Ellis to write the screenplay.

Right Here, Right Now (1999) won the American Book Award. The story follows another affluent male black narrator. A clever, charismatic motivational speaker and self-made millionaire, Ashton Robinson grows tired of fame and fortune. He renounces his success in the self-help industry and travels the world collecting disciples for a religion he engendered during a marijuana and expired-cough-syrup-induced high. Ultimately, a spiritual meltdown causes Ashton to publicly reveal the illness of the West and his hand in proliferating it.

Inspired by Dave Eggers's *A Heartbreaking Work of Staggering Genius*, Ellis most recently took on the project of a memoir, *Bedtime Stories: Adventures in the Land of Single Fatherhood* (2008). The first chapters recount a childhood freighted by the death of his parents, as well as the story of his marriage and its disintegration, but the heart of the memoir follows the abandoned single father as he rebuilds and reshapes his life.

Ellis's entire oeuvre is profoundly influenced by his early philosophical vision of the New Black Aesthetic, and his books make a point of not privileging the gravity of American race relations. Race is important in his work only as it affects his narrator's day-to-day existence, and Ellis's protagonists are all examples of cultural mulattos, as comfortable in the white community of their educational institutions as in the black communities of their families. Ellis makes clear that such hybrid existence is not easy—both communities are skeptical of outsiders—but he is emphatic in his endorsement of its merits.

Ellis's work vigorously investigates the contemporary notion of self-improvement. *Home Repairs* anatomizes the concept in action, as Austin writes constantly to gain awareness of his faults and celebrate his successes. *Right Here, Right Now* comments on the late 20th century's booming self-help industry with a protagonist that manipulates it to make millions. And self-improvement is the central theme of *Bedtime Stores*, as Ellis chronicles the story of his own self-recovery.

He typically employs a metafictional style of storytelling, whether narrating the tale of a novelist writing a novel or a diarist a diary; and such metafictional self-consciousness is most prominent in his searching memoir, where the narrator often pauses to explain how he has come to portray himself in a certain manner and why he wants that image for his image. No sooner has he done so, however, than he will present an opposite perspective, reminding us that in the realm of truth as well, *mulatto* may be the highest aspiration.

Bibliography

Chaney, Michael A. "Trey Ellis Biography." Brief Biographies. Available online. URL: *http://biography.jrank.org/pages/4297/Ellis-Trey.html*. Accessed February 23, 2009.

Ellis, Trey. *Bedtime Stories: Adventures in the Land of Single Fatherhood*. New York: Rodale, 2008.

———. *Home Repairs*. New York: Washington Square Press, 1993.

———. *Platitudes*. New York: Random House, 1988.

———. *Right Here, Right Now*. New York: Simon & Schuster, 1999.

—Kelin Loe

Emperor of the Air Ethan Canin (1988)

Emperor of the Air is ETHAN CANIN's debut short story collection, featuring nine short narratives that, the *Library Journal* notes, showcase "ordinary Americans [and] memorable individuals caught in situations leading to sudden, still moments of comprehension" (75). Published during Canin's final year at Harvard Medical School, eight of the stories were previously published in top magazines and journals, and two were included in *Best American Short Stories* in 1985 and 1986. The stories won Canin a Houghton Mifflin Literary Fellowship, and reviews were overwhelmingly favorable.

The eponymous first story features a 69-year-old astronomy teacher whose athletic wife, Vera, is away for several weeks, leaving him alone to deal with his neighbor, Mr. Pike. He does not want to cut down his 250-year-old elm tree, which is infested with insects, but Mr. Pike is insistent that the tree be leveled in order to preserve his own three saplings. The narrator's thoughts wander as he tries to save his tree: "I have taught the life of the simple hydra that is drawn, for no reasons it could ever understand, toward the bright surface of the water, and the spectacle of a thousand human beings organizing themselves into a single room to hear the quartets of Beethoven is as moving to me as birth or death" (7). The narrator then commences a plan to infect Mr. Pike's trees with insects as well, reasoning that Mr. Pike will not want to cut his own trees down and thus will be willing to spare his elm. The end of the story leads the narrator to witness, from an unexpected hiding spot, Mr. Pike's misidentification of the constellations Cygnus and Pegasus as the "Emperor of the Air," and suddenly his thoughts seem to crystallize into a paradoxical lucidity not possible before. The story was first published in *The Atlantic* and was chosen by Gail Godwin for inclusion in *The Best American Short Stories of 1985*.

Canin told *The Writer* in 2000 that after John Irving told him he disliked one of his stories while he was a student at the Iowa Writers' Workshop, he decided to go to medical school where, "my first year I wrote a book because I wasn't supposed to be doing it." Indeed, both this and Canin's time in medical school likely inspired the eighth story in the collection, "The Carnival Dog, The Buyer of Diamonds," first published in *Redbook* as "Abe, Between Rounds," in which the main character, Myron Lufkin, a medical student at Albert Einstein College of Medicine, announces to his father that he is quitting school. The story shifts between Myron's early morning jogs as a medical student and his childhood memories of living with his parents. Traditionally, if he and his father, Abe, disagreed, they would challenge each other to athletic competitions, most of which Abe won. It is clear from the second paragraph, where Canin describes Myron five years later as "a sometime Jew, member of the public gym where he plays basketball and swims in the steamy pool after rounds," that Myron is now a doctor. How he evolved from his shocking announcement to leave medical school to working at a hospital is illustrated through descriptions of Abe and Myron's challenges, though these point to more than physical events, much in the way that the drawing of the cathedral in Raymond Carver's classic story "Cathedral" represents far more than a place of worship.

This understated psychological complexity of character is a key to understanding Canin's stories. Only Myron's story is told in the third person; the rest present strong first-person narrators who are struggling bravely and resourcefully to make sense of complex familial relationships, often in the midst of epochal moments of self-discovery. The collection's final story, "Star Food," is emblematic. Here, Canin adopts a setting similar to John Updike's "A&P" but places the grocery store, called Star

Food, in a rural locale, intensifying the moral containment of the tale. The teenage narrator recalls the first time he disappointed his parents, when, one summer, he retreated frequently to the roof to escape stock work in his parents' store. His mother thinks he is on the brink of a great discovery and encourages him to continue daydreaming; his father asserts that he should be working harder in the store. Amid this conflict, a customer repeatedly steals small items, and the narrator fails to stop her. Yet the conclusion evinces authorial compassion in many ways absent from "A&P" and memorable enough to prompt Louise Rafkin, in a front-of-book blurb, to describe Canin's as "a voice of compassion rarely found in contemporary short fiction." The story was first published in *Chicago* magazine and selected by Raymond Carver for inclusion in *The Best American Short Stories of 1986.*

"Star Food" was combined with the second story in the collection, "The Year of Getting to Know Us," to create the 2008 film named after the latter tale, directed by Patrick Sisam and starring Jimmy Fallon, Sharon Stone, Lucy Liu, and Tom Arnold. The story is narrated by a middle-aged man who is sitting at his father's bedside at the hospital, recalling the year his parents divorced, which his mother had dubbed "the year of getting to know us." What he got to know about his father that year, however, left him in some ways wishing he had not got to know him so well, as illustrated in the story's final scene, a golf lesson on the beach, of which the narrator poignantly recalls: "I was sixteen years old and waiting for the next thing he would tell me" (43). The story was first published in *The Atlantic.*

"American Beauty," the only story in the collection not previously published, is a first-person exploration of the relationship between a young man, his older brother Lawrence, and his artistic but epileptic sister Darienne; it was hailed by the *New York Times* as "the collection's masterpiece."

In a sense, the tonic chord linking these nine stories is the resolution of near-transcendent compassion that resounds at the end of each, echoed in subtle revelations and epiphanies throughout. In "Where We Are Now," for example, Charlie agrees to lie for his wife but does not truly understand until the end of the story why he is doing it; a final

kiss in "We Are Nighttime Travelers" illuminates a forgotten and fragile love; petty theft is overshadowed by the salutary integrity of a unified family in "Pitch Memory"; and impulse and desire are (almost) happily redefined in the context of ultimate responsibility in "Lies." Images such as Katy in a red Cadillac on Fountain Lake in "Lies," or Darienne's rolled-up family portrait, are both tactile and moving, illustrating the process of self-discovery that ennobles each of the main characters in the collection.

In addition to the feature film incorporating "Star Food" and "The Year of Getting to Know Us," "The Emperor of the Air" was made into a 40-minute film in 1996 by Ali Selim.

Bibliography

Canin, Ethan. *Emperor of the Air.* 1988. New York: First Mariner Books, 1999.

"Canin, Ethan. Emperor of the Air." *Library Journal* 113, no. 2 (1988): 75.

Frumkes, Lewis Burke. "A Conversation with Ethan Canin." *The Writer* 113, no. 5 (2000): 19–21.

Lehmann-Haupt, Christopher. "Books of the Times." *New York Times,* 25 January 1988, sec. C, p. 24.

—Kristina H. Zdravic Reardon

Enger, Leif (1961–) *American novelist*
Leif Enger won the praise of critics and readers with his debut novel, PEACE LIKE A RIVER (2001), followed after seven years by *So Brave, Young and Handsome: A Novel.* Enger claims to truly enjoy writing, and his love of a good story and enthusiasm for the written word are clearly evident in his colorful and lyrical works.

Born in Sauk Center, Minnesota, in 1961, Enger was raised in Osakis, Minnesota, and began writing poetry at the age of eight. He reminisces, "There was no word I wouldn't misuse, no rhythm I wouldn't break for a rhyme." In his teen years he turned to fiction, and studied English literature at Moorehead State University, where he met his wife, Robin. He became a reporter and producer for Minnesota Public Radio in 1984, and worked for the company for 16 years. The job gave him the opportunity to meet "interesting and likable people," he says, and showed him the value of careful revision. In his spare time, he worked on a novel, which he put aside in the early 1990s when he and his brother Lin started writing a series of mysteries under the pen name L. L. Enger. These books, which center on a retired baseball player who has become a recluse, were never a financial success, but writing them, he says, offered him a "fabulous apprenticeship," and taught him to develop characters through action. He claims that his brother taught him the importance of "clean sentences, clear action, characters you can like and invest in."

A month after Enger finished writing the last mystery with his brother, he started making notes for what would become *Peace like a River,* a story about the adventures of Jeremiah, Reuben, and Swede Land as they try to find their son and brother, Davy, who is running from the law. Enger worked on the novel for five years, reading passages to his wife and two boys to get their reactions and suggestions. He did not expect to make a living writing fiction and did not anticipate that the novel would be published. Consequently he was in no hurry to complete the work. He explains, "I didn't think about the book commercially until I was over half done and I realized the book was going to have an end." Yet *Peace like a River* became a national best seller, named by *Time* magazine as one of its Top Five Books of the Year for 2001; and the *Christian Science Monitor, Denver Post,* and *Los Angeles Times* all selected it as Best Book of the Year.

Enger's family and life experience clearly influenced the novel. He grew up in Minnesota, one of the settings in *Peace like a River,* and continues to live there today on a 65-acre tract of land. When he was young, Enger often visited his grandparents, who lived in North Dakota, another setting in the novel. His eldest son, Ty, had asthma from the time he was four years old until he was almost 15. Enger witnessed his child's struggle and transferred the agony he felt for his own son to *Peace*'s Jeremiah, who witnesses his boy Reuben, an asthmatic, fight for breath. Enger's youngest son, John, suggested that his father include cowboys in the novel, and gave him the name Sunny Sundown, which became the name of the hero of the narrative poem about the West that Swede, the six-year-old daughter of Jeremiah Land, writes during the

course of the novel. Above all, living with two boys in the household provided Enger with the perspective of the 11-year-old narrator of his story. He explains: "It's fairly easy to write from a boy's point of view when you've got two of your own living in your pockets. Kids notice things in a different way—sometimes incompletely, but always differently. The way events occupy and grow inside a child's mind is easy to forget unless you've got one around; they're more interesting than adults."

After Enger sold *Peace like a River* to Grove/Atlantic Monthly Press, he was able to write full time, and he began working on his follow-up, *So Brave, Young and Handsome: A Novel.* The story takes place in 1915. Glendon Hale, a train robber hiding from the law, feels mounting guilt for having abandoned his wife 20 years before, and determines to go to California to ask her forgiveness; Monte Becket, a one-time novelist, leaves his wife and son and joins Hale on his journey.

Enger's two novels are written in the classic tradition of the western. Both concern outlaws attempting to evade arrest, and both center on westward journeys. But Enger augments their strong simple plots with vivid, nuanced, and entirely plausible characters, lovable in spite of their faults. And although he claims to be "terrible at thematic planning," the novels are notable for their fresh and sensitive take on time-honored values like family, faith, and friendship.

Enger readily confesses the influence of Robert Louis Stevenson on his writing, calling the latter "a great master." In an interview with Alden Mudge, he comments, "Mom read us *Treasure Island* every year for many years, starting before I was old enough to understand any of it. It was confusing to me, but I loved it. I loved the play of words. I loved the language. [Stevenson] was a strikingly contemporary writer for the time; he was ahead of his time. He's my favorite writer of all time. I just love his poems, his great adventure tales, his brand of moral fiction." And certainly, Enger's uncommon ability—and *willingness*—to simply tell a good story, with colorful and realistic characters, in clear, lyrical, and memorable prose, besides distinguishing him sharply from most of his contemporaries, make comparisons to that quintessential storyteller not entirely unjust.

Bibliography

Enger, Leif. *Peace like a River.* New York: Grove Press, 2001.

———. "Riding the Wave of Leif Enger's Dazzling Debut." By Alden Mudge. BookPage.com. Available online. URL: http://www.bookpage.com/0109bp/leif_enger.html. Accessed November 29, 2007.

———. *So Brave, Young and Handsome: A Novel.* New York: Grove Press, 2008.

"*So Brave, Young and Handsome: A Novel.*" Amazon.com. Available online. URL: http://www.amazon.com/So-Brave-Young-Handsome-Novel/dp/0871139855/ref=pd_bbs_sr_1?ie=UTF8&s=books&qid=1200946587&sr=1-1. Accessed January 21, 2008.

Writers and Books. "2004—If All of Rochester Read the Same Book." Available online. URL: http://www.wab.org/events/allofrochester/2004. Accessed January 21, 2008.

—Charlotte Pfeiffer

Englander, Nathan (1970–) *American short story writer and novelist*

Englander achieved recognition as a major literary voice with the publication of his first book, *For the Relief of Unbearable Urges* (1999), a collection of short stories that was acclaimed by critics, became a national best seller, and won the 2000 PEN/Faulkner Malamud Award and the American Academy of Arts and Letters Sue Kauffman Prize. He followed this, after seven years of painstaking work, with an equally well-received debut novel, THE MINISTRY OF SPECIAL CASES (2007).

Englander was born and grew up firmly ensconced in the intense, insular Orthodox Jewish community nestled in what he calls "hyper-suburban" West Hempstead, Long Island, New York; but he would later abandon this life: "I was in a closed world and I was suffocating in that world, and literature saved me—in the most pure form, where I had these ideas and thoughts and I found them in books. I really believe in the power of literature. I think there is no higher art form. I've always thought writing is the supreme form" (Bures). Along with the local yeshiva, he attended the Hebrew Academy of Nassau County, one of the oldest and largest Hebrew high schools in the world, then studied literature and Judaic studies at the State University of New York at Binghamton. He did graduate work at the famed Iowa Writers' Workshop and had his first story (the title story of the debut collection) published in the Spring 1996 edition of *Story*.

In 1989, during his junior year at Binghamton, Englander went abroad to Israel, and there heard the story that would form a centerpiece of *For the Relief of Unbearable Urges*, an account of Stalin's simultaneous execution in 1952 of 26 prominent Jewish citizens in the Soviet Union, most of them authors. In Englander's "The 27th Man," one of the men arrested (through a Kafkaesque clerical error) is the unknown and unpublished Pinchas Pelovits, who writes a story embraced and applauded by his 26 more famous fellow victims.

The collection is imbued with a deeply compassionate, tragicomic feeling reminiscent of the work of I. B. Singer, coupled with an almost eschatological focus on Jews in extreme circumstances, whether it be in the Soviet Union, Israel, or America. In addition to the pre-execution drama of "The 27th Man," for example, in "Reb Kringle" an Orthodox Jew confronts the margins of his faith when employed as a department store Santa Claus, and in "The Tumblers," a group of Polish Jews destined for Auschwitz and annihilation accidentally find themselves on the wrong train, and improvise an ersatz career as acrobats in a troupe of itinerant gymnasts, in order to survive. Thematically, the nine stories are unified by their searching exploration of what it means to be Jewish—or anything *like* Jewish (Englander fiercely resists ethnic labeling)—in modern secular society, and finally what it means to *be* (hence the *New York Times Book Review*'s praise of the work as "a revelation of the human condition").

Despite its often esoteric content and rigorous style, *For the Relief of Unbearable Urges* proved as popular with readers as critics, going through an astonishing 13 printings in hardcover alone, and being translated into 12 languages, with critical comparisons made not merely to canonical Jewish authors like Singer, Philip Roth, and Saul Bellow, but even Flannery O'Connor and James Joyce. It also firmly launched Englander's literary career, leading to a Guggenheim Fellowship, the Bard Fiction Prize, and a fellowship at the Dorothy and Lewis B. Cullman Center for Scholars and Writers at the New York Public Library.

With its seamless blend of compassionate irony, absurdist wit, and tragic pathos, Englander's debut novel, *The Ministry of Special Cases*, preserves much of the tone and style of his first work but on a far more ambitious scale. The novel's roots lie in much the same soil as Englander's debut, but here his thematic focus is sharpened: "I love Jerusalem," he notes in a Poets & Writers interview, "and more and more I identified myself as a Yerushalmi, a Jerusalemite. . . . I got really interested in the idea of loving a city and watching it crumble around you. That's how I got interested in the tragic love of city and of what's out of the individual's control. What is it to truly love a place?" (Bures). During his defining sojourn in Jerusalem, the 28-year-old Englander struck up an acquaintance with a number of expatriate Argentinian Jews, who, though in many ways disappointed and even betrayed by their homeland, remained devoted to it and its fate.

Once again the universal is firmly grounded in the particular and universal Jewishness in the experience of a single Jew: "It was 1976 in Argentina. They lived with uncertainty and looming chaos. In Buenos Aires they'd long suffered kidnap and ransom. There was terror from all quarters and murder on the rise. There was also then a growing sense of danger. It was no time to stand out, not for Gentile or Jew. And the Jews, almost to a person, felt that being Jewish was already plenty different enough" (2). Trapped in the midst of Argentina's "dirty war" and fettered equally by his past and present failings, Kaddish Posnan struggles to salvage both his disintegrating family and the dignity of a community that refuses even to acknowledge him; finally resorting to the last of all resorts, Argentina's notorious Ministry of Special Cases.

Englander is currently at work on an eclectic mix of fiction and nonfiction, including a second novel. He lives in New York City, and teaches Creative Writing at Hunter College, City University of New York.

Bibliography

Bures, Frank. "For the Relief of Unbearable Pressure: A Profile of Nathan Englander." Poets & Writers. Available online. URL: http://www.pw.org/content/mayjune_2007?was=/mag/0705/bures.htm. Accessed May 20, 2009.

Englander, Nathan. *The Ministry of Special Cases*. New York: Knopf. 2007.

—Douglas Melrose

Equal Love **Peter Ho Davies** (2000)

PETER HO DAVIES's collection of 12 short stories, *Equal Love*, explores themes of multigenerational love and family conflict with vivid characterization, sympathy, and real wisdom. The vast and varied spectrum of voices in the collection speaks both to Davies's keen ear for diverse experience and to his own multinational background: "He's writing what you might call World Literature," said his novelist friend Charles Baxter, "[t]he range is astonishing" (Stainton 2).

"The Hull Case" tells the story of a black man named Henry, who is confronted with questions of trust and belief when his white wife has an extraterrestrial experience. In "Brave Girl" a young girl studies her dentist father as she prepares to leave him in order to live with her mother. A young man prepares for his father's funeral in "The Next Life" and plays cards with the hired mourners. The protagonist in "Small World" has an affair with his childhood sweetheart in an oblique attempt to come to terms with his parents' divorce and his wife's pregnancy. "How to Be an Expatriate" describes in a staccato, "how-to book" style, its British narrator's journey across the pond. In "Frogmen," the friend of a 12-year-old boy drowns and the neighborhood children struggle to grasp the meaning and significance of the event. In "Equal Love," a man and the wife of his best friend toy with the possibility of an affair after they drink and smoke drugs together. "Sales" explores how a salesman's job ruins his marriage. "Everything You Can Remember in Thirty Seconds Is Yours to Keep" is the first-person narrative of a former drug addict who tries to turn her life around for her baby and her mother. In the somber "On the Terraces" a young man watches his gay brother die of AIDS. "Cakes of Baby" describes a stressful Thanksgiving gathering through the perspective of a young couple, Sam and Laura. A son and his father visit his grandmother who is suffering from Alzheimer's in "Today Is Sunday."

The voices are young and old, innocent and jaded, confident and insecure, and Davies masterfully employs close-to-character narration to place the reader in the scene and convey their most intimate emotions and aspirations. For all the disparate experience contained in the collection, it is unified by a tangible sense of compassion, and by an accumulated awareness—even celebration—of shared humanity.

Each story begins in medias res, as Davies engages the reader's sympathy before stepping back to reflect on the significance of what is described, or penetrating deeper into its causality. "The Next Life," for example, begins: "The mourners were playing poker around the rosewood table the night before his father's funeral, and Lim was winning" (35). Rapid transitions from action to characters' thoughts and memories create a blurring of time and space typical of dreams. Thus, though "The Hull Case" begins with dialogue, as Helen describes the extraterrestrial spaceship, the reader soon drifts with Henry into intimate memories of how the couple first met.

These qualities render the stories well suited to Davies's overarching exploration of the relationship between environment and identity, and how together they can—and can fail to—create a world, for protagonist and reader alike. The description of Somerville in "Small World" pivots on this sense of place in its treatment of the passage of time, when its protagonist returns after many years and "The Big Dig seems to have buried everything Wilson remembers" (50). "How to Be an Expatriate" vividly portrays differences between British and American culture—from the size of dinner portions to the character of sports crowds—like a kind of stream-of-consciousness

guide book. Davies's keen observation of sensory details heightens this sense of place: the "taste of steel tang" in "Brave Girl," the smell of the baby and of "static under the tires" in "Everything You Can Remember in Thirty Seconds Is Yours to Keep" (21, 133), the action of salt piling on Wilson's hand as "stray grains bounce and scatter on the bar" in "Small World" (49).

The considerable poignancy of the collection derives from bittersweet juxtapositions, as in Davies's exploration of the gap between parents and children through middle-aged reflections and childhood dreams. Both the comedy and the pathos of "How to Be an Expatriate" arise from the jarring differences between British and American culture.

The title of the collection, *Equal Love*, is revealing on a number of levels, both in its evocation of the constant thread of compassion that runs through love stories between brothers, couples, fathers and daughters, mothers and sons, grandmothers and sons, even countries; and in its evocation of the constant give and take of love between parents and children, as well as the inevitable conflicts that disrupt the balance of such reciprocity. Moreover, Davies's work, both here and in his first award-winning collection, *The Ugliest House in the World* (1997), has a musical quality, striking a delicate and moving balance between lightness and darkness, comedy and pathos, irony and sincerity. Even his recent novel, *The Welsh Girl* (2007), strikes this same balance, and in a similar exploration of parent-child relationships.

Bibliography

Davies, Peter Ho. *Equal Love*. Boston: Houghton Mifflin Company, 2000.
———. *The Ugliest House in the World*. New York: Houghton Mifflin Company, 1997.
———. *The Welsh Girl*. New York: Houghton Mifflin Company, 2007.
Stainton, Leslie. "A Master Shape-Shifter of the Literary World" Michigan Today. Available online. URL: http://www.umich.edu/news/MT/04/Fall04/story.html?literary. Accessed February 23, 2009.

—Margaret Wade

Eugenides, Jeffrey (1960–) *American novelist and short story writer*

Jeffrey Eugenides is the author of two critically acclaimed and best-selling novels, *The VIRGIN SUICIDES* (1993) and the Pulitzer Prize–winning *MIDDLESEX* (2002). He has also written a host of short stories, which have appeared in publications such as the *New Yorker,* the *Paris Review;* and the *Yale Review;* published a number of book reviews and literary essays; and edited and introduced an anthology of love stories entitled *My Mistress's Sparrow Is Dead: Great Love Stories from Chekhov to Munro* (2008).

Eugenides was born in Detroit, Michigan, the son of an Anglo-Irish mother and a father of Greek origin whose parents had immigrated to the United States from Asia Minor. He attended University Liggett School, a prestigious private school in the upper-middle-class suburb of Grosse Pointe. After graduating magna cum laude in English from Brown University, he received an M.A. in English and creative writing from Stanford University in 1986, and commenced a stellar literary career that has included awards from the Guggenheim Foundation and the National Endowment for the Arts, as well as the German Welt-Literaturpreis (2003) and the Ambassador Book Award. From 1999 to 2004, he held a fellowship in the Deutscher Akademisches Austausch Dienst's Artists-in-Berlin program and lived in the German capital for several years with his wife and daughter. He has subsequently returned to the United States and taken up a teaching position as professor of creative writing at Princeton University in 2007.

Eugenides' debut novel, *The Virgin Suicides* (1992), tells the story of the Lisbon sisters, five teenage girls who commit suicide one after the other. It takes place in the 1970s and is set in Grosse Pointe, Michigan, where Eugenides spent his youth. The tale is seen through the eyes of a group of adolescent boys who become infatuated and obsessed with the mysterious Lisbon sisters and are profoundly affected by their deaths. It is an extended retrospective, as the male narrator(s) struggle to reconstruct and make sense of the girls' enigmatic identities and their puzzling deaths. The use of an anonymous first-person-plural narrator is highly innovative, and adds to the air of mystery and uncertainty pervading the tale.

The novel was turned into a movie in 1999, written and directed by Sophia Coppola, and starring James Woods (Mr. Lisbon), Kathleen Turner (Mrs. Lisbon), Kirsten Dunst (Lux Lisbon), Josh Hartnett (Trip Fontaine), and Danny DeVito (Dr. Horniker). The film, which stays remarkably close to Eugenides' novel and succeeds in capturing the text's dark and subdued atmosphere, met with great critical acclaim and was nominated for a number of awards.

Almost a decade after the publication of his debut novel, Eugenides' immensely successful second novel *Middlesex* (2002) appeared, winning the Pulitzer Prize for fiction in 2003. On the surface, *Middlesex* resembles a traditional immigrant family epic, chronicling the history of the Stephanides clan but including an incestuous love affair between Desdemona and Lefty Stephanides, who are forced to escape from their war-ridden hometown in Asia Minor and settle in Detroit. However, woven into this tale is the remarkable coming-of-age story of Cal, the grandson of Desdemona and Lefty Stephanides. Both the protagonist and the narrator, Cal is born with an intersex condition known as 5-alpha-reductase syndrome (5-ARD). Because the family doctor fails to detect his enlarged clitoris or micropenis at birth, Cal is declared to be a girl, and grows up as Calliope despite being genetically male. During puberty, Calliope undergoes virilizing transformations, but it is not until her intersex condition is diagnosed accidentally at the age of 14 that she decides to adopt a male gender-identity. The story is told from the point of view of 41-year-old Cal, now living as a man in Berlin and reflecting both on his family's past and on his own life as he traces the story of the gene responsible for his intersex condition through time.

In writing *Middlesex*, Eugenides drew on his own family history, in particular his Greek ancestry; his childhood and adolescence in Detroit; and the years he spent in Berlin. However, as he has repeatedly stressed, the novel is far from autobiographical, and in fact required an extensive amount of research, not merely in the contemporary medical and sociological literature on intersex conditions, but also the rich literary and cultural tradition of hermaphroditism. The result is not only one of the few literary works to date to present an accurate and empathetic description of intersex as a real human condition but also a densely intertextual work of fiction, with repeated allusions to mythological figures such as Hermaphroditus or Tiresias.

At first glance, Eugenides' body of work can seem disparate in both subject matter and style. Despite their obvious differences, however, *The Virgin Suicides* and *Middlesex* show unmistakable similarities. Eugenides' tone, for instance, is often humorous, even when dealing with apparently tragic or traumatic events. He is justly renowned for his keen descriptive eye, and talent for witty, insightful, and critical social commentary. Thematically, he is drawn to characters struggling to construct an identity—whether their own or another's—and confronted with a thwarted or even impossible desire or love. The concepts of memory and temporality also play a significant role in both novels, as reflected in the employment of narrators trying to reconstruct a story retrospectively, and aware of their own unreliability. But if *The Virgin Suicides* and *Middlesex* correspond in their innovative and experimental construction of narrative voice, there is also an interesting point of divergence: whereas the "group narration" featured in *The Virgin Suicides* draws attention to the inherent limitations of the adolescent boys' perspective, which ultimately prevent them from uncovering the secrets surrounding the Lisbon sisters and their lives, *Middlesex* presents a narrator seemingly capable of crossing the gender divide, and thus presenting a more inclusive viewpoint.

Eugenides is one of the few contemporary authors who provokes equal interest in the academic world and the realm of popular culture. Both of his novels have been translated into more than 30 languages. Even his shorter fiction has appeared in translation, for instance in the German version of his short story collection, *Air Mail* (2003). And while Coppola's star-studded film adaptation of *The Virgin Suicides* succeeded in introducing Eugenides' work to a wider audience, *Middlesex* was both a literary and a commercial success upon initial publication, and its popularity was only augmented when it was featured on Oprah's Book Club in 2007 and Eugenides himself was interviewed on the *Oprah Winfrey Show.*

Bibliography
Eugenides, Jeffrey. *Air Mail.* Reinbek, Germany: Rowohlt, 2003.
———. *Middlesex.* New York: Farrar, Straus & Giroux, 2002.
———. *The Virgin Suicides.* New York: Farrar, Straus & Giroux, 1993.
———, ed. *My Mistress's Sparrow Is Dead: Great Love Stories from Chekhov to Munro.* New York: HarperCollins, 2008.

—Jana Funke

Everything Is Illuminated Jonathan Safran Foer (2002)

Jonathan Safran Foer's debut novel is a highly original and often hilarious (hence quite controversial) exploration of the reality and aftermath of the Holocaust. It tells the fictional story of a Jewish-American novelist, also named Jonathan Safran Foer, who travels to Ukraine in an attempt to find the woman who presumably saved his grandfather from the Nazis in a village called Trachimbrod. When he finally discovers Trachimbrod, nothing remains but a memorial stone to commemorate the destruction of this Jewish shtetl during World War II. Yet the past that finally becomes "illuminated" during the novelist's quest surpasses any discovery he could possibly have imagined.

The process of this illumination involves the reader in a subtle and far-reaching investigation into what Marianne Hirsch calls *postmemory:* "a powerful and very particular form of memory precisely because its connection to its object or source is mediated not through recollection but through an imaginative investment and creation" (22). This is a major concern of the second and third generation of Jews after the Holocaust: frustrated by the inaccessibility of a traumatic past that they can only witness in a highly mediated form (via written or visual documents) but which continues to haunt them, they have recourse to the imagination to fill in the missing pieces. One thinks of the imaginative representation of the Holocaust in

Art Spiegelman's *Maus: A Survivor's Tale* (1986), Michael Chabon's *The AMAZING ADVENTURES OF KAVALIER AND CLAY* (2000), Nicole Krauss's *The HISTORY OF LOVE* (2005), or Judy Budnitz's *If I Told You Once* (1999). This particular form of memory also lies at the heart of *Everything Is Illuminated,* which combines autobiographical detail with extraordinary feats of the mnemonic imagination. While still a student at Princeton, Foer actually visited Ukraine, armed with a picture of the woman who, according to family legend, had saved his grandfather. But when his quest came to a dead end at the Trachimbrod memorial stone, he decided to invent himself a family history, which became the basis of *Everything Is Illuminated.*

The fictional story of the hero's quest is told in two very distinct voices, that of Alexander Perchov, Jonathan's Ukrainian guide, also an aspiring novelist, who accompanies Foer on his quest along with Alex's anti-Semitic grandfather—the driver who claims to be blind—and Sammy Davis Jr. Jr., the grandfather's "seeing-eye bitch." Alex's writing—consisting of fragments from his novel about their journey, interlarded with the letters that he afterward sent to Jonathan—is rendered still more absurd by its bevy of English malapropisms gleaned from a thesaurus. And this exaggerated but fairly realistic account is itself repeatedly interrupted by the second narrative voice, Jonathan's own imagined, mythological history of Trachimbrod. This latter, an unchronological and fragmented novel-within-the-novel, tells the story of Jonathan's earliest ancestor who, not unlike Aphrodite in Greek mythology, is magically born from the river Brod. Named after the river, Brod becomes the object of every man's sexual fantasies in the village, and the sight of her beautiful body culminates in a collective orgy whose release of sexual energy illuminates the entire village to such an extent that, more than 150 years later, the light is still visible to the first man on the moon. Brod finally marries a man who survives an accident in a mill but who spends the remainder of his life with a saw blade lodged perpendicularly in his brain. As such, this prewar Jewish community achieves a supernatural, fairy-tale quality, until reality comes crashing in in the form of the Nazi *Einzatsgruppen.* Typical of the novel's mnemonic reality, the scene of the shtetl's bomb-

ing is in fact *missing;* Foer leaves out the traumatic moment, replacing it with empty pages filled with a series of dots. Thus, Foer typographically re-creates within his own writing the void, the absence he discovered at the Trachimbrod site.

While Jonathan's imaginative history is, in part, an obvious attempt to compensate for his absent family history, the protagonists' quest does unearth some unexpected secrets from the past. They find, for example, a woman whom they take to be the mysterious Augustine who rescued Jonathan's grandfather, but she is not. As the last remaining survivor of Trachimbrod, however, she has created her own archive, obsessively collecting all the material remnants from her vanished shtetl. Among the photographs she has managed to save from the inferno, Jonathan discovers a picture of Alex's grandfather in the company of a Jewish friend, Herschel. Only after the journey, when Jonathan has returned to the United States, can Alex reveal in a letter the confession made by his guilt-ridden grandfather just before he committed suicide: When the Nazis invaded the nearby village of Kolki, Alex's grandfather had been forced to betray his Jewish friend to the Nazis, for fear that harm would come to his own family. So the quest for the woman who rescued the Jew paradoxically reveals the man who betrayed the Jew. While they were companions and even friends during the quest, Alex and Jonathan now seem forever divided by the chasm between the Jewish victims and Ukrainian perpetrators. Yet the moral center of the novel becomes not Jonathan, who refuses a reconciliation, but Alex, who begs for forgiveness for the crimes committed by the preceding generations. As such, Foer (the novelist) not only displays an impressive openness to the radically Other—the anti-Semite—but also makes a powerful statement about the necessity for the third generation after the Holocaust to forgive. Such an empathic approach to the Other's suffering also characterizes Foer's second novel, *EXTREMELY LOUD AND INCREDIBLY CLOSE* (2005), which juxtaposes the trauma of 9/11 with the Allies' firebombing of Dresden and the destruction of Hiroshima.

One of the novel's most memorable features is the stunning complexity of its approach to history, presenting layers of different, often contradictory and mutually exclusive accounts of the past, which puts readers in precisely the same position as the third generation itself—here struggling (as with postmemory) to reconstruct or *imagine* what happened in the novel's fictional past—while the proliferation of witness testimonies makes this past only more opaque and inaccessible. In fact, the novel's title is, in the end, acutely ironic, as very few elements of Jonathan's past are truly illuminated.

In 2005, Liev Schreiber turned *Everything Is Illuminated* into a film featuring Elijah Wood, but the film completely omits the plot about Trachimbrod's imagined past. Instead, it focuses on the protagonists' contemporary journey through Ukraine, reduces the multiplicity of voices to a single account, and perhaps most strikingly, changes the story of Alex's grandfather's betrayal into one in which he is himself a Jewish victim. As such, it reduces Foer's dizzying construct of temporal layering, ethical ambiguity, multiple voices, and equivocal historical events to a univocal narrative seemingly bent on facile closure.

Bibliography

Foer, Jonathan Safran. *Everything Is Illuminated.* 2002. New York: Perennial, 2003.

———. *Extremely Loud and Incredibly Close.* London: Hamish Hamilton, 2005.

Hirsch, Marianne. *Family Frames: Photography, Narrative and Postmemory.* Cambridge, Mass.: Harvard University Press, 2002.

—Philippe Codde

Extremely Loud and Incredibly Close
Jonathan Safran Foer (2005)

JONATHAN SAFRAN FOER's first novel, EVERYTHING IS ILLUMINATED (2002), was centered on the Holocaust; and his second, *Extremely Loud and Incredibly Close*, again takes up weighty themes, juxtaposing the attacks on New York's World Trade Center on September 11, 2001, with the bombings of Dresden and Hiroshima during World War II. Nevertheless, Foer's approach in this novel is largely playful, experimental, and humorous.

The main narrator of *EL&IC* is nine-year-old Oskar Schell, who as the book begins is one

year on from the loss of his father, Thomas, on 9/11. Oskar's narrative is a mixture of dramatic irony—he is too young to fully understand his own story—and a highly precocious display of general knowledge. On his "business card" he describes himself as follows:

> INVENTOR, JEWELRY DESIGNER, JEWELRY FABRICATOR, AMATEUR ENTOMOLOGIST, FRANCOPHILE, VEGAN, ORIGAMIST, PACIFIST, PERCUSSIONIST, AMATEUR ASTRONOMER, COMPUTER CONSULTANT, AMATEUR ARCHAEOLOGIST, COLLECTOR OF: *rare coins, butterflies that died natural deaths, miniature cacti, Beatles memorabilia, semiprecious stones, and other things.* (Foer 99)

But these amusingly prodigious qualities are set against Oskar's profound and unresolved grief for his father. On 9/11, Oskar returns home from school to hear his father's calls from the stricken Twin Towers in a series of answerphone messages. Revealed one by one over the course of the novel, these begin with Thomas's confidence that he will be saved, and end with the plaintive repetition of "Are you there?" Oskar has hidden the telephone and its messages from his mother, thereby delaying the grieving process for both of them: "That secret was a hole in the middle of me that every happy thing fell into" (71).

Oskar's traumatized state also manifests itself in anxiety, obsessive behavior, minor self-harm (giving himself bruises), and an overactive imagination (constant "inventing") stemming from not knowing exactly how his father died. Did he jump from the window, get stuck in an elevator, or was he simply incinerated? The novel largely averts its gaze from such matters, unfolding instead as a detective or mystery story that also serves as an allegory for Oskar's psychological quest to complete the mourning process. Snooping in his father's closet, Oskar discovers a key in an envelope marked *Black*, and this provides him with a tangible if runic means to keep in touch with his father's memory, as he embarks on a seemingly futile mission to find the lock that fits the key. Deciding that Black must refer to a person, Oskar resolves to visit everyone with that name in New York. The portrayal of little Oskar criss-crossing the city shaking his ever-present tambourine recalls the dwarfish, drumming Oskar Matzerath and his wanderings around Europe in Günter Grass's novel *The Tin Drum* (1959). But whereas Matzerath's odyssey often reveals morbidity and enervation, Schell's serves to celebrate New York's diversity and vitality in the face of the tragedy; and the city is further mythologized in Oskar's father's bedtime story, "The Sixth Borough," whose whimsical, fairy-tale quality recalls the magical realism of Foer's first novel. The lock for Oskar's key is eventually found through an unlikely set of coincidences (again involving answerphone messages), though without revealing the longed-for details of his father's death.

Interspersed with Oskar's narrative are the ostensible writings of his German-born grandparents, which give contrasting perspectives on their shared memories. In prewar Dresden, Oskar's grandfather (also called Thomas) becomes engaged to Anna. After she is killed in the Allied firebombing raids of 1945, Thomas and Anna's (unnamed) younger sister emigrate separately to New York, where they meet again by chance and marry. In 1963, she becomes pregnant, their relationship fails, and he returns to Dresden. After their son, Oskar's father, dies in the events of 9/11, the grandfather comes back to New York and attempts to resume his relationship with his estranged wife.

These immigrants' lives are revealed as ruined by their traumatic past, thus developing the theme introduced by Oskar's own grief. As the grandfather says, "it wasn't the bombs and burning buildings, it was me, my thinking, the cancer of never letting go" (17). Moreover, the secondary narratives add a dimension of eyewitness testimony, with vivid descriptions of the horrific effects of firebombing in Dresden and the experience of watching 9/11 unfold in television reports. In a further instance of witnessing, Foer inserts an edited version of the real-life testimony of Hiroshima survivor Kinue Tomoyasu, in the context of a presentation given by Oskar to his class.

The astonishing and unsettling effect of these juxtaposed accounts is to set 9/11, an act of violence in which the United States is usually figured as a victim, against the historical backdrop of the bombings of Dresden and Hiroshima, in which America was the perpetrator of what some have called war crimes. Foer never makes this point explicitly, and indeed mostly ignores political, social, and military issues. However, the novel's unmistakable echoes of past and present—the way paper fuels the fires of both Dresden homes and the Twin Towers, for example—make parallels almost impossible to avoid. Foer's approach may be compared to that of more politically charged post-9/11 novels like Frédéric Beigbeder's *Windows on the World* (2003) and Don DeLillo's *Falling Man* (2007), while his exploration of the events in Dresden may be read in light of the debate over German literary responses to the air war that was reignited by W. G. Sebald's *On the Natural History of Destruction* (2003).

Indeed, writing is itself a major theme in the novel. Grandfather Schell, for example, writes thousands of unsent letters to his son, which in a symbolic moment, at the end of the book, are used to fill the latter's empty coffin. Foer also develops the theme through typographical experiments. Deprived of speech after his wartime experience, the grandfather must write on pads ("day-books") for basic communication. When he runs out of space, he has to write over what he has already written, and this is represented in the novel by the typeface getting more and more densely packed, eventually overlaying itself until it becomes an incomprehensible black mess. The account of Dresden bombings, meanwhile, is covered with circles in red pen, highlighting the mistakes; something Oskar's father is said to have enjoyed doing to the *New York Times*. In further experiments, a conversation is represented by the numbers of a telephone keypad, and the words an eavesdropper is unable to hear are removed from the page.

Foer's other main formal device is the inclusion of full-page images. Many of these represent items from Oskar's scrapbook, "Things That Happened to Me." However, the most striking instance is the final sequence of photographs, of a man falling from the World Trade Center. These are printed in reverse order, making the victim appear to fly upward and off the top of the page. This echoes the fantasies of the characters at the end of the novel, in which they imagine reversing time; as in Oskar's grandmother's dream, in which

> all the collapsed ceilings re-formed above us. The fire went back into the bombs, which rose up and into the bellies of planes whose propellers turned backward, like the second hands of the clocks across Dresden, only faster. (306–307)

Thus, while the novel ends with some hard-won progress in the characters' mourning, its final message appears to convey no more than a wistful longing for the impossible.

Bibliography

Foer, Jonathan Safran. *Extremely Loud and Incredibly Close*. London: Hamish Hamilton, 2005.

—Lewis Ward

Fight Club Chuck Palahniuk (1996)

CHUCK PALAHNIUK's *Fight Club* is a dark novel about an unnamed insomniac who tries to free himself from both his sleeplessness and his attachments to a repetitive job as a recall campaign coordinator. In a desperate search to cure his insomnia, he stumbles upon a network of support groups at his local church. Despite faking the requisite illness, he is still able to release his anxiety and sob uncontrollably on the chest of his nearest neighbor. In his own words: "This is the only place I ever really relax and give up. This is my vacation" (Palahniuk 18). His job consists of flying around the country calculating the costs of recalling a vehicle versus the cost of settling claims for fatal accidents, and he often daydreams about the endless ways his plane could crash so he could experience the "amazing miracle of death" (35). Into this life of repetition and isolation, where everything is "a copy of a copy of a copy" (21), enter Marla Singer and Tyler Burden. The three characters quickly form a complicated love triangle—"I want Tyler. Tyler wants Marla. Marla wants me" (14)—based more on desperation and animal need than any sort of conventional affection. The narrator's fragile stability is destroyed when his material possessions are lost in an explosion, and turning to Tyler Burden for help, he soon becomes enmeshed in a life of anarchy triggered by a simple request from the latter: "I want you to hit me as hard as you can" (46). From this simple statement, "fight club" is born, the first phase in an evolution of violence that ends in an anarchist army called Project Mayhem.

The novel centers on issues of masculinity, violence, and the American myth, deconstructing popular conceptions of "the American way of life" with its ruthless anatomization of working-class "space monkeys"—"You do the little job you're trained to do. Pull a lever. Push a button" (12). The narrator initially finds solace in the obsessive collection of material things, the commodity-driven culture manifested in the importance of the IKEA catalogue. However, when his apartment is destroyed, Burden helps him realize that commodities can be a type of confinement, where "the things you used to own, now they own you" (44); and the novel finally suggests that it is only through a stripping down to bare essentials that one can really learn to live. The removal of artificiality results in an instinctive approach to survival, synthesized through the violence of fighting: "you aren't alive anywhere like you're alive at fight club" (51). In questioning the value of "things," Palahniuk draws attention to his culture's pervasive and damaging lack of spirituality. For the narrator, Tyler Burden is a kind of surrogate both for his father and for God, and Palahniuk plays on the traditional father-son motif of Christianity; in the words of the narrator, "if you're male, and you're Christian and living in America, your father is your model for God" (186). One of the underlying goals of Project Mayhem is to draw attention to the working class, to make the invisible visible. But its members also wage a broader fight, against the metaphorical nation-as-father in the form of social law and order, radically reinventing a connection to God by perverting the classic father-son paradigm; Tyler argues, for example, that "getting God's attention for being bad was better than getting no attention at all" (141).

The stripping down to bare essentials is also a stripping away of civilization. Indeed, Tyler first appears to the narrator as a caveman-like creature, "naked and sweating, gritty with sand, his hair wet and stringy, hanging in his face" (32). He is a fascinating and charismatic character who lives according to his own anti-hegemonic code: "I see the strongest and the smartest men who have ever lived . . . and these men are pumping gas and waiting tables" (149). The narrator incorporates such observations into a simple credo:

> Maybe self-improvement isn't the answer.
> Tyler never knew his father.
> Maybe self-destruction is the answer. (49)

Tyler believes that, through the regenerative effects of violence, civilization can regain its strength. In essence, a limited case of Darwinian theory, and a brutally simple application of Nietzsche's dictum that "Whatever does not destroy me makes me stronger." Project Mayhem is envisioned as a path to this regeneration through the destruction of history, through wiping the slate clean and beginning again. Everything that civilization sees as beautiful must be destroyed, symbolized by numerous references to museums and classical art. The narrator sums up Project Mayhem's anarchy:

> I wanted to breathe smoke.
> Birds and deer are a silly luxury, and all the fish
>   should be floating.
> I wanted to burn the Louvre. I'd do the Elgin
>   Marbles with a sledgehammer and wipe my ass
>   with the *Mona Lisa.* This is my world, now.
> This is my world, my world, and those ancient
>   people are dead. (124)

This almost messianic compulsion to rewrite history is reinforced by the structure of the novel itself. Most chapters start in medias res, and Palahniuk spends the next pages filling in the details that led to a particular crisis point. In this way every important scene begins without historical context.

In particular, Project Mayhem seeks to rewrite American history from the beginning of frontier expansion, an aim emphasized by constant references to the gun, a symbol of the old West. The novel opens, for example, with the narrator clamping his teeth on the barrel of a gun held by Tyler, and the image of a gun held to someone's head is repeated throughout, even coming to symbolize the fatal lack of life in a civilization obsessed with the collection of things: "Everyone smiles with that invisible gun to their head" (19). Tyler and narrator both advance the thought that only through a brush with death can one appreciate the life they live; until Marla attempts suicide, for example, there was "no real sense of life because she had nothing to contrast it with" (38). In the end, the image of the gun both recalls the early frontier and heralds the apocalypse, and the novel explicitly conflates them: "Imagine hunting elk through the damp canyon forests around the ruins of Rockefeller Center" (150).

However, the novel as a whole in no way unequivocally subscribes to these radical ideas. *Fight Club*, in fact, is permeated with irony; for example, the very desire to destroy the social structure as a means of alleviating conformity finally *results* in conformity, with the same slur of *space monkey* being eventually employed by the narrator to describe his fellow members of Project Mayhem. The project even re-creates, in its context of anarchic violence, the corporate banalities of the cubicle—"Arson meets on Monday. Assault on Tuesday. Mischief meets on Wednesday" (119)—and the narrator's description of the project as a "Bureaucracy of Anarchy" (119) is an obvious oxymoron. Such irony is actually built into the structure of the novel itself. It begins and ends with the same scene, and redeploys large sections of text, in a satirical comment both on the cyclical nature of history and on the folly of those who for whatever reason fail to perceive it. In this sense, the novel is profoundly ambivalent, even pessimistic, condemning equally the culture of commodity and the project's manner of resisting it.

Fight Club was adapted for film in 1999, starring Edward Norton as the narrator, Brad Pitt as

Tyler Burden and Helena Bonham Carter as Marla Singer. Notably, the filmmakers change the goal of Project Mayhem from a messianic destruction of history to the narrower (and more bankable) destruction of financial buildings in an urban center—a seemingly fitting irony in itself.

Bibliography

Palahniuk, Chuck. *Fight Club*. New York: W. W. Norton, 2005.

—Jared Morrow

Foer, Jonathan Safran (1977–) *American novelist and short story writer*

Jonathan Safran Foer is the author of two novels EVERYTHING IS ILLUMINATED (2002) and EXTREMELY LOUD AND INCREDIBLY CLOSE (2005). He is also the editor of *A Convergence of Birds: Original Fiction and Poetry Inspired by the Work of Joseph Cornell* and coeditor of *The Future Dictionary of America*.

Foer was born in Washington, D.C., in 1977 to Esther Safran Foer, a Polish émigré who worked in public relations, and Albert Foer, a lawyer and the founder of the American Antitrust Institute, a nonprofit research and advocacy organization that lobbies to foster competition and prevent monopolies in the economic landscape. He attended the Georgetown Day School, and as a young student won a Bronfman Youth Fellowship to participate in a program of community service and intensive study in Israel. After high school Foer went on to study literature and philosophy at Princeton University, where he took courses taught by Joyce Carol Oates, Jeffrey Eugenides, and Russell Banks, and began drafting his first novel. During this time at Princeton, he was awarded the creative writing prize four times.

In 1999, the young writer traveled to Ukraine to search for a woman who had reportedly saved his grandfather from the Nazis during World War II. While Foer would not find this woman, the trip would serve as the inspiration for his first novel, *Everything Is Illuminated*, which was published by Houghton Mifflin in 2002. The storyline was, in fact, based on this very premise of a young man's

search for the woman who saved his grandfather's life when the Nazis invaded his shtetl, and the author went so far as to include a character named Jonathan Safran Foer. The book was highly acclaimed, praised by contemporaries such as Joyce Carol Oates, John Updike, Salman Rushdie, and Dale Peck. It was named in "best book" lists internationally, including the *New York Times*, the *Boston Globe*, *Newsweek*, *Esquire*, *GQ*, *Rolling Stone*, and many other venues. The book also won the National Jewish Book Award and the Guardian First Book Award, and was a finalist for the L.A. Times Book Award for First Fiction. In 2005, it was adapted for film under the direction of Liev Schreiber.

Foer's second novel, *Extremely Loud and Incredibly Close*, tells the story of a nine-year-old named Oskar Schell, a uniquely precocious boy struggling to make sense of the death of his father who perished on September 11, 2001. The book, published by Houghton Mifflin in 2005, won Foer the New York Public Library Young Lions Prize and was translated into more than 30 languages. Film rights were purchased by Paramount and Warner Brothers, and the adaptation is set to be produced by Scott Rudin.

The author's works of short fiction, including "A Primer for the Punctuation of Heart Disease," "Cravings," "Room after Room," and "About the Typefaces Not Used in This Edition" appeared in the *New Yorker*, *Conjunctions*, the *Guardian*, and *Granta*; while short works such as "The Very Rigid Search," "The Sixth Borough," and "If the Aging Magician Should Begin to Believe" became part of the composition of Foer's own books. Some of his short works were also anthologized in volumes such as *The Burned Children of America*, edited by ZADIE SMITH, *The Unabridged Pocketbook of Lightning* from the Pocket Penguin series, and *Lost Tribe: Jewish Fiction from the Edge*.

In addition to his composition of novels and short fiction, Foer has also submitted numerous op-ed pieces and reviews to newspapers such as the *New York Times*, the *L.A. Times*, and the *Washington Post*. Among these pieces are Foer's "A Beginner's Guide to Hanukkah," a tongue-in-cheek list of encyclopedic entries related to the Jewish holiday, and "My Life as a Dog," an exposition on the challenges of sharing space with other living beings. His operatic libretto, "Seven Attempted Escapes from Silence," premiered in Germany in 2005; and in 2006, the author narrated the film "If This Is Kosher," an examination of the kosher certification process in support of vegetarianism. Foer has also exhibited an interest in visual art and the potential of literature to embrace other mediums. His second novel contained a host of visual images, including a photographic flipbook. Foer has also worked on an art book entitled *Joe,* with sculptor Richard Serra and photographer Hiroshi Sugimoto, as well as various public art projects.

Despite a lengthy list of accolades and acknowledgments, which include international awards such as the BGN Book of the Year (Holland), Premio Letterario Adei Wizo (Italy), the Corine International Book Prize 2003 (Germany), and the Prix Amphi (France), as well as the Zoetrope: All-Story Fiction Prize, the William Saroyan International Prize for Writing, and placement on lists such as Granta's 2007 list of Best Young American Novelists, Rolling Stone's "People of the Year," and Esquire's "Best and Brightest," Foer has been a target for critics. Many believe his work is undeserving of the praise that has been lavished on it, citing his frequent use of postmodern devices such as multiple storylines, mock history, and invented language, as gimmicky, unoriginal, and insincere. However, Foer's novels, which take on cultural events of staggering proportion such as the Holocaust and 9/11, are also quite intimate, focusing on personal histories and the search for meaning and truth.

Foer has acknowledged that his work is largely autobiographical, and it is easy to find parallels between the author and his characters. However, there are also places where the lines of fact and fiction diverge. Although Foer was raised in a traditional Jewish household, he maintains that his work is ultimately secular. However, his writings continue to demonstrate a connection with Jewish culture and history, and as a member of the Holtzbrinck Fellow Class at the American Academy in Berlin during the spring of 2007, Foer reportedly began work on an English retelling of the Haggadah.

In the spring of 2008, the author took up a position as Visiting Professor at Yale University,

teaching writing to undergraduates. He resides in Brooklyn with his wife, the novelist Nicole Krauss, and their son, Sasha.

Bibliography

Eggers, Dave, Jonathan Safran Foer, Eli Horowitz, and Nicole Krauss, eds. *The Future Dictionary of America: A Book to Benefit Progressive Causes in the 2004 Elections Featuring over 170 of America's Best Writers and Artists.* San Francisco: McSweeney's Books, 2004.

Foer, Jonathan Safran. *Everything Is Illuminated.* Boston: Houghton Mifflin, 2002.

———. *Extremely Loud and Incredibly Close.* Boston: Houghton Mifflin, 2005.

———, ed. *A Convergence of Birds: Original Fiction and Poetry Inspired by the Work of Joseph Cornell.* New York: D.A.P./Distributed Art Publishers, 2001.

—Jennifer Banach Palladino

Fortress of Solitude, The Jonathan Lethem (2003)

At almost 600 pages, *The Fortress of Solitude* is more than twice as long as the longest of JONATHAN LETHEM's previous novels. It is also his most ambitious work to date, as well as his most unabashedly personal, presenting an intricately layered collage of personal and borrowed memories, social history, pop culture, and Lethem's own brand of mercurial, reality-bending imagination.

Divided into two parts connected by a brief interlude, *Fortress* tells the story of Dylan Ebdus, his uneasy coming of age in 1970s Brooklyn, and its reverberations throughout his early adulthood. The first half of the book ("Underberg") chronicles Dylan's childhood and adolescence as a white kid growing up in what was then a predominantly black Brooklyn neighborhood. Shy, cerebral, abandoned early by his headstrong mother, and largely ignored by his reclusive father, Dylan finds a friend in Mingus, the son of an equally absent white mother, and a declining black soul singer, Barrett Rude, Jr. Besides their similar familial fates, they share a love of comics and graffiti, early sexual experiences, and, in a twist of magical realism, a ring that endows its wearer with supernatural powers.

Toward the end of their teenage years, the friendship deteriorates as Dylan grows disenchanted with his neighborhood, and Mingus increasingly turns to drugs. Just as Dylan plots his escape from both Brooklyn and Mingus, a violent event that leaves the fates of several characters in the balance ends the first part of the narrative.

A 15-page "liner note" on the life and career of Barrett Rude, Jr., byline "D. Ebdus," serves as the fulcrum of the novel, tying up important loose ends and preparing for a switch in narrative point of view. While "Underberg" employs third-person narration that meanders between various focuses and degrees of limitation, part three (the aptly titled "Prisonaires") is narrated by Dylan himself, who is now a music journalist living on the West Coast. At 35, the damage and ill-suppressed memories of his childhood and adolescence have him living in a state of arrested development, unhappy with his life and relationships. A series of encounters, conversations, and epiphanies eventually lead him back to the East Coast, where he must face the friends, foes, and broken family ties of his youth, in an attempt to find closure.

Thematically and structurally, the novel is firmly rooted in the literary tradition of the bildungsroman, specifically sharing similarities with other accounts of growing up in New York City. The narrative of the first part distinctly evokes the dreamlike style of Henry Roth's *Call It Sleep* (1935); its complicated central friendship bears comparison to Chaim Potok's *The Chosen* (1967); and its slice-of-life descriptiveness recalls Betty Smith's classic *A Tree Grows in Brooklyn* (1943). Like many works of this genre, it is also based on personal experience. In this self-proclaimed "spiritual autobiography" (Sebela), Lethem draws a sprawling, lovingly detailed, and keenly observed portrait of the Brooklyn of his own memories. As in his previous novel, MOTHERLESS BROOKLYN (1999), both manifest and intangible aspects of the urban landscape are meticulously recorded and probed for meaning.

For Dylan, the world is divided into zones—his father's quiet studio, his mother's chaotic kitchen, Dean Street and the uncharted territories beyond, Mingus's room, Manhattan, and so on—each of them governed by their own obscure logic

and unwritten set of rules. The key to straddling these different realms is to decode their cultural practices. Like an anthropologist, Dylan detects systems of knowledge, or "hidden lore" (89), in the children's street games, in the rituals of abuse he suffers beyond the safe haven of Dean Street, in graffiti and comic books, in hip-hop and punk music. This preoccupation with popular culture spills into Dylan's adult life, but so does his inability to participate fully in life instead of merely observing and computing its particulars. At 35, he is "[r]eady to pass any and all litmus tests for self-partitioning" (279), but unable to feel at home anywhere or with anyone, least of all himself. When he learns of Mingus's downward spiral of drug abuse, crime, and imprisonment, Dylan's determination to set things right for his former friend mirrors his desire to mend his own life.

Although the novel is undeniably focused on Dylan and his growing pains, its considerable breadth and moral seriousness rescue it from any navel-gazing solipsism. The child's limited and sometimes naive vision in the first part is embedded in a more encompassing perspective that also illuminates the minds of other characters, and suggests a comprehensive vision of Brooklyn and its social and racial issues in the 1970s. The specter of gentrification is personified in gnarly landlady Isabel Vendle, whose vision of restoring the neighborhood to its former genteel glory prefigures the reign of yuppie coffee shops and remodeled brownstones in the novel's second half; while at the other end of the spectrum, Dylan's idealistic mother, Rachel, champions a well-meaning but largely misguided approach of integration, proud of the fact that Dylan is one of only three white children in his school. Dylan's childhood and adolescence are spent negotiating the complexities of racial tension, cultural appropriation, and political correctness. He is fascinated by whiteness, recurrently personified in a series of blonde girls, and at the same time deeply ashamed of his desire; but he also perceives his own whiteness as the cause for his constant victimization at the hands of black teenagers. On the other hand, he absorbs graffiti and black music as part of his identity, and in adulthood becomes obsessed with black culture, going even so far as confessing to his black girlfriend that her race is a defining factor in their relationship. Without offering morals or oversimplifications, the narrative grapples with the politics that are irrevocably tangled up with the lives of its characters.

Within this context of social and psychological realism, a subplot involving a magic ring may at first seem jarringly out of place—perhaps even a gimmicky vestige from Lethem's past works, which, with the exception of *Motherless Brooklyn,* all flirt with science fiction fantasy. The ring itself and its capricious powers weave in and out of the narrative, fueling various subplots dealing with Dylan's needs and desires—for empowerment, for revenge, for recognition, for compassion, or for merging his identity with Mingus in their composite hero "Aeroman." Yet neither the ability to fly that it grants in their youth, nor the invisibility it gives in adulthood, change anyone's life for the better, and only one life dramatically for the worse. On a thematic level, however, the superhero meme resonates deeply with the issues that lie at the heart of *Fortress.* Dylan's divided self and obsession with his past can be related to two integral aspects of the superhero figure: the concept of secret identity—the mask of ordinariness to show to the world; and the myth or story of origin. In its entirety, *The Fortress of Solitude,* whose title recalls Superman's arctic retreat of contemplation and memory, presents such a story of origin—not only of its protagonist, but also of a writer's consciousness, creating new worlds in the hidden chamber of memory and imagination.

Bibliography

Lethem, Jonathan. *The Fortress of Solitude.* 2003. London: Faber & Faber, 2003.

Sebela, Christopher. "A Novel Approach: Jonathan Lethem on his Novel *Fortress of Solitude.*" Comic Book Resources. Available online. URL: http://www.comicbookresources.com/news/newsitem.cgi?id=2834. Accessed March 14, 2008.

—Martina Sitling

Freudenberger, Nell (1975–) *American novelist*

Richard Ford's canon-defining 2007 anthology *The New Granta Book of the American Short Story* updates his selections of 16 years earlier (in *The Granta Book of the American Short Story*) by promoting a number of authors with only one book of stories to their credit. Displacing such promising younger authors of the previous generation as DAVID LEAVITT and Tim O'Brien, the new anthology presents stories by NATHAN ENGLANDER, Adam Haslett, Z. Z. PACKER, Julie Orringer, and—the youngest author in the collection—Nell Freudenberger.

Freudenberger was born in 1975, in New York City, but spent her formative years in Los Angeles, which provides the setting for her novel, *The Dissident* (2006). She began attending Harvard University in 1993 where she, along with future novelist Benjamin Kunkel, served on the staff of the *Harvard Advocate.* In its 130th anniversary issue, the *Advocate* published her short story "Real Life," which won the 1997 Dana Reed Prize for Distinguished Writing, judged that year by Nicholson Baker and the *New Yorker*'s music critic, Alex Ross. "Real Life" offers an image that recurs throughout Freudenberger's mature writings: a man walking away into the snow, engulfed by whiteness until he is nothing but a "speck" or "twig"—a wistful image of assimilation and identity loss, issues that would come to haunt her subsequent, geographically unstable characters.

After graduating from Harvard in 1997, Freudenberger traveled to teach English in Bangkok and New Delhi, locations that would figure prominently in her later fiction. Upon returning to the United States, she earned an M.F.A. in fiction writing at New York University. It was at this point that she began working at the *New Yorker* as an editorial assistant, checking facts and occasionally writing sidebar copy. Working in this capacity, as the *Sunday Times* (London) reported, Freudenberger was "discovered" by *New Yorker* fiction editor Bill Buford, who reputedly noticed a copy of Lorrie Moore's *Birds of America* on Freudenberger's desk, inquired about her literary ambition, and solicited a story from her.

This in-house discovery resulted in the appearance of Freudenberger's short story "Lucky Girls" in the *New Yorker*'s 2001 "Summer Fiction Issue." The editors devoted their annual special issue's considerable marketing power to "début fiction" by young writers. Along with Freudenberger, the issue featured JONATHAN SAFRAN FOER, Gabe Hudson, and Erika Krouse. "Lucky Girls" initiates what would become dominant motifs of dislocation and cross-cultural observation in Freudenberger's fiction. The unnamed narrator is an American artist in India, whose affair with Arun, an older, married Indian man who has just died as the story begins, prompts a confrontation with his mother, his widow, and his adult sons, as the characters all try to make sense of their connection with the departed.

On the merit of "Lucky Girls," Freudenberger was beset by publishers competing to offer her a contract for a book of stories that had not yet been written. She finally accepted a deal that, along with notice in *Vogue* and *Elle*, generated a great amount of controversy among those who felt that her marketing had come before her writing. *The Complete Review* offered a playlet titled "Whoa Nelly!" about characters who discussed what they felt was her easily won and all-too-predictable fame. CURTIS SITTENFELD, then an unknown Iowa Writers' Workshop graduate, authored an article on Freudenberger in Salon.com titled "Too Young, Too Pretty, Too Successful," discussing the phenomenon she called *schadenfreudenberger*: a compulsion to gossip about the young author, tinted by a playful "hatred" stemming largely from envy.

Freudenberger followed her *New Yorker* debut with stories in the *Paris Review* ("Letter from the Last Bastion") and *Granta* ("The Tutor"); and critics expecting a quick materialization of her already-contracted novel were largely silenced by the slow and steady quality of her work. "The Tutor"—which follows an American living in India being tutored by an Indian who has returned from a stay in America in the hope that his life will "fall back in place"—was later chosen by Lorrie Moore for *The Best American Short Stories of 2004*, and awarded a 2005 O. Henry Prize.

In 2003, Freudenberger's collection, LUCKY GIRLS, was released to great acclaim. It consists of her three already published stories, along with two entirely new ones: "Outside the Eastern Gate," the story of a depressive mother's abandonment of her family; and "The Orphan," which centers on the rape of an American expatriate in Bangkok and its aftermath. *Lucky Girls* won the 2004 Sue Kaufman Prize for First Fiction from the American Academy of Arts and Letters, a 2004 PEN/Malamud Award for Short Fiction, and a 2005 Whiting Writers' Award.

Describing her writing process to the *Washington Post*, Freudenberger cites the importance of being receptive to stories related by people she does not know well. Similarly, Miss Fish in "A Letter from the Last Bastion" believes that "A novel is a letter you write to someone you don't know." Such detached, interpersonal interaction dominates the way Freudenberger's strong-willed, introspective, and often self-consciously naive female characters attempt to make connections within unconventional or collapsing relationships. The narrator of "Lucky Girls" invites a young servant to watch her paint; Julia works closely with her hired tutor in order to get into UC Berkeley and "start over." These women wish to define themselves without recourse to the vagaries of context, often finding in the process that it is impossible to do.

The summer of 2006 brought Freudenberger's long-awaited first novel, *The Dissident*, which, like *Lucky Girls*, examines artistic creation as a means of creating identity. Yuan Zhao, a subversive artist "skilled at mimicry" with a questionable history, leaves Beijing's politically charged East Village to live with an American family, and take a visiting fellowship at St. Anselm's School for Girls, a fictionalized version of Freudenberger's own Los Angeles high school, in which she had the opportunity to briefly study with a visiting Chinese artist. The narrative focus shifts back and forth at irregular intervals, between first-person narration by Zhao and an omniscient voice suggesting the collective consciousness of the Americans who encounter Zhao, to whom the artist is known only as "the dissident." As Freudenberger states in a supplement to the paperback edition, "To me, the novel was about confusion—the way we Americans determine our own identities and the way we imagine foreignness (Chinese-ness in particular)" (10). On the merits of *The Dissident*, Freudenberger was named one of *Granta*'s "Best Young American Novelists."

Bibliography

Ford, Richard, ed. *The New Granta Book of the American Short Story*. New York: Grove, 2007.

Freudenberger, Nell. *The Dissident*. New York: Ecco, 2006 (supplemented paperback edition, 2007).

———. "Lucky Girls." *New Yorker*. 18 and 25 June 2001, pp. 68–80.

———. *Lucky Girls*. New York: Ecco, 2003.

———. "Real Life," *Harvard Advocate* 32, no. 4 (1997): 26–41.

Sittenfeld, Curtis. "Too Young, Too Pretty, Too Successful." Salon.com. Available online. URL: http://dir.salon.com/story/books/feature/2003/09/04/freudenberger. Accessed August 1, 2008.

—Nicholas D. Nace

From Rockaway Jill Eisenstadt (1987)

JILL EISENSTADT's debut novel is a colorful and often poignant coming-of-age story focusing on four teenagers from Rockaway, a blue-collar neighborhood in Queens, New York. Alex, Timmy, Peg, and Chowderhead grew up together. After graduating from high school, however, a chasm opens between college-bound Alex and her friends who remain in Rockaway. Eisenstadt (who was born and raised in Rockaway herself) deftly contrasts Alex's adjustment to life at a prestigious university in rural New Hampshire with the aimlessness of the young adults in Rockaway. Timmy, Alex's ex-boyfriend, particularly suffers from emotional inertia, longing to be reunited with his high-school sweetheart. The novel climaxes when a tragedy on the beach brings all four friends together to perform a grim ritual, and the uneasy reunion suggests that unless dramatic changes take place, a bleak future awaits Alex's old Rockaway pals.

From Rockaway opens on prom night, sometime in the early '80s. The Rockaway gang, speeding back to their home turf from Manhattan, share joints and take turns chugging whiskey. Alex and Timmy, already broken up, are enjoying one last fling of intimacy before summer—and before Alex leaves for college. Pam and Chowderhead, whose relationship occupies the ambiguous middle ground between lovers and best friends, are also there. The dance over, the four get dropped off at a raucous beach party. Despite the special occasion, however, the evening is pretty typical for Rockaway teenagers: there is dancing, a bonfire, skinny-dipping, sex, a few fights, abundant drugs, and alcohol. Everyone at the party knows each other, many work together as lifeguards. A few of the recent high-school graduates are planning to attend local colleges, but most are done with school. Alex is different: She is leaving to attend college in New Hampshire, where she has a full scholarship. Thus, though the beach party on prom night is not atypical, there is a charged symbolic significance to the celebration.

For most of Alex's friends in Rockaway, however, not much changes. Timmy, Peg, Chowderhead, as well as the other usual suspects, spend most of their time getting wasted, bar hopping, and sleeping around. Meanwhile, at the fictional Camden College, Alex's transition is slow and difficult. She does not particularly like her roommate or classes, and spends most of her time getting wasted, bar hopping, and sleeping around, with Eisenstadt skillfully sketching parallels between Alex's college exploits and the Rockaway gang's seemingly permanent intoxication. Both camps spend most of their time wasting time, but there is one critical difference: hope. Alex may smoke as many joints as Chowderhead, and drink almost as many beers as Timmy, but the dissipation is part of a more encompassing context of concentration, a rite of passage, not of stasis. Indeed, Camden College encourages its students to experiment and take risks, but Alex's friends in Rockaway are not rewarded for their "experimentation." Rather, they are quickly crossing the ambiguous middle ground between youthful excess and substance abuse.

Much of the excess in Rockaway, as in many adolescent tribes, is ritualistic, and Eisenstadt persistently explores the vapidity—and even violence—of Rockaway's rituals. One of the novel's most affecting episodes takes place when Peg runs over to build a snow fort with a group of young kids. Instead of welcoming her, the kids scatter to let the "lady" pass. Peg is in disbelief; she is much too young to be called a lady. In response, she quickly organizes a "hat party," an old Rockaway tradition where everyone dons a funky hat and takes a shot at each of Rockaway's numerous boardwalk bars. Peg had sworn off the event as juvenile the previous year, but after confronting her incipient loss of youth she is desperate to reclaim the juvenile. However, the distinction between young and old in Rockaway is ambiguous at best. Rockaway's older residents—beachfront drunks who had their own hat parties in the not too distant past—occupy the same bars as Peg and her friends, cheering them on, reminiscing about the past. In Rockaway, misery and ennui commingle past, present, and future generations. The contrast with Alex's initiation into the strange rituals of Camden College is revealing. Over the course of her first year, Alex gradually becomes accustomed to the foreign patterns of college life: theme parties, on-campus protests, and academic expectations; and Eisenstadt suggests that college rituals are ultimately just as meaningless, but less dangerous, and in some ways a necessary evil. Alex learns from her new experiences; Timmy, Peg, and Chowderhead are already reliving the past.

The gulf of opportunity between Alex and her friends in Rockaway only grows deeper and more poignant as the novel progresses. Peg is nervous and awkward when she visits Alex in New Hampshire. Alex, usually envious of Peg, is suddenly conscious of her lack of intellect and chastises her former best friend for having "been in Rockaway *too* long" (159). And while Alex immediately regrets the condescending comment, it is clear that she is right. Peg, Timmy, and Chowderhead *have* been "in Rockaway" too long, and the novel's tragic climax illustrates how hopeless—and even violent—Eisenstadt considers their situation. It begins with an accident: a sandbar breaks on the beach, and lifeguard Timmy loses a child in the wash. His failure earns him membership in the "Murderer's Club," a morbid distinction enjoyed by only a few

unlucky lifeguards. As a result of Timmy's failure, his coworkers throw him a "death keg," another Rockaway ritual. They beat him, burn him, and bury him in the sand; then they dump crabs and jelly fish on his head. Near the end of the night, Alex, who thinks the violence is getting out of hand, attacks one of the lifeguards and nearly gets raped. The depth of depravity is striking, and the episode serves as Eisenstadt's most pointed condemnation of the violent potential in Rockaway's seemingly complacent aimlessness, as if pointlessness itself had taken on a fine and fatal edge.

Published in 1987, *From Rockaway* garnered its author widespread attention and critical acclaim. Although she resisted the label, many critics classified her as one of the "brat pack," a group of young, hip writers that included BRETT EASTON ELLIS, Jay McInerny, and Tama Janowitz. The novel's vivid characterization and cinematic scope inspired acclaimed producer and director Sydney Pollack to option the novel for a film adaptation, though production of the film has yet to move beyond the planning stages.

Bibliography

Eisenstadt, Jill. *From Rockaway.* New York: Knopf, 1987.
———. *Kiss Out.* New York: Knopf, 1991.
Silverman, Ethan. "Jill Eisenstadt." *BOMB Magazine* 36, no. 3 (1991). Available online. URL: http://www.bombsite.com/issues/36/articles/1453. Accessed May 13, 2009.
Wurtzel, Elizabeth. "The Bennington-Knopf Connection." The Harvard Crimson online edition. Available online. URL: http://www.thecrimson.com/article.aspx?ref=136524. Accessed May 15, 2009.

—Peter Farrell

G

Gadol, Peter (1964–) *American novelist and short story writer*

Gadol is the author of six novels, none of which fits conveniently into generic categories, as they vary from a spoof of current literary trends to intense psychological studies to murder thrillers. His short stories have appeared in *Story* and *Tin House,* and his novels have been translated into several languages.

Gadol was born in Summit, New Jersey, and grew up in Westfield, the son of Norman and Sybil (Rickless) Gadol. After briefly considering architecture as a profession, Gadol attended Harvard where he discovered his love of writing while studying poetry with Nobel laureate Seamus Heaney. In 1986, he completed his B.A. in English and American literature, writing his thesis, "Man Carrying Thing: A Theory of Metaphor for Wallace Stevens," under Helen Vendler's supervision.

As a poet Gadol found his work dominated by narrative, and he at last turned his skills to fiction. While a student, he edited the literary magazine the *Harvard Advocate,* and later worked for two years as a fiction intern at the *Atlantic* magazine in Boston. After college, he began his first novel, *Coyote,* which was published—Gadol admits, with incredible luck—when he was just 24 years old.

In the 1990s, Gadol changed coasts, moving to California, where he first taught writing in the Extension program at UCLA, and then for nine years at the California Institute of the Arts. He is currently an associate professor in the graduate writing program at Otis College of Art and Design in Los Angeles.

Coyote (1990), Gadol's debut novel, was well received by critics, though reviewers puzzled over whether it was an adventure story, a sentimental romance, or the quirky creation of a writer who, according to the *Los Angeles Times,* is energetic and "seemingly unfettered by fashionable norms." Coyote Gato, the novel's loner protagonist, ekes out a living by giving directions to strangers in the New Mexico desert. Orphaned, and in his words "sexually ambidextrous," Gato guides investigative reporter Madeleine Nash in her search for a mysterious ashram headed by the reclusive Guru B. But when the community's secrets—including group sex, violence, misguided finances, and a purloined meteorite—are unearthed, the novel becomes suddenly complex, pitting spirituality against intellectualism, the Southwest against the mystical East, and personal ambition against unsettled love.

Gadol's second novel, MYSTERY ROAST (1993), is no easier to categorize than *Coyote* but far better written. It has been called a mystery, a romance, a work of philosophy, an adventure in magic realism, and a spoof of them all. The protagonist, a down-on-his-luck genXer, Eric Auden, has separated from his celebrity wife, and is nursing the wounds from his divorce by hiding in his mother's apartment. Eric wanders into the New York Museum of Art, which reawakens many of his youthful associations with art, his family, and his unsuccessful professional life. He also finds his childhood friend Timothy Rampling, a gay artist, using the men's room as a private art gallery. On a return trip to the museum, Eric becomes helplessly captivated by an ancient statue of the Goddess of Desire, and in a moment of improbable opportunity steals the statue without the slightest thought what to do with it. Andre, the owner of the Mystery Roast café and Tim's occasional lover, as well as Eric's own newly mysterious lover, gadget inventor Inca Dutton, team up with Tim and Eric to capitalize on both the resulting tabloid publicity blitz and the goddess's mysterious power, by selling replicas of the statue. An updated, fanciful version of a typical Horatio Alger story, the novel explores a host of 21st-century relationships: parent-child, lovers, business partners, friends, and even ex-spouses.

Gadol's next novel combines his study of architecture with his interest in intimate relationships, but without the whimsy characteristic of *Mystery Roast. Closer to the Sun* (1996) tells the tragic story of a young couple, Ethan and Helen Zayne, who, after having lost their home in a canyon wildfire, enlist the help of drifter Brad Gray to rebuild the house themselves; Gray himself is overcoming the loss of a lover to AIDS. Through traditional metaphors of carpentry and construction, the novel portrays how these three injured characters painstakingly restore themselves through their need to build and rebuild this Encantado Canyon home. Although more literary and much darker than *Coyote, Closer to the Sun* is replete with lively descriptions of the process of home building, and vivid pictures of the Southern California landscape near Malibu.

Closer to the Sun did not enjoy the critical success of *Mystery Roast;* however, Gadol's next novel did. In *Long Rain* he again focuses on West Coast culture, this time that of the wine country, in a literary thriller that explores relationships, guilt, and moral responsibility. Estranged from his wife and child, and denied a partnership in his law firm, San Francisco lawyer Jason Dark tries to put his life back together by returning to a family vineyard, and opening a small law practice in the rural town of Hollister, California. Basically a good man who makes some very bad decisions, over time he reunites with his family but still feels uneasy and insecure. Then one rainy night on a country road he accidentally runs over and kills high-school soccer star Craig Montoya. No one sees him, and nothing can bring the teenager back, so Dark decides to hide the body and lie about the crime. When officials charge a vagrant, Troy Frantz, with the hit-and-run, Dark takes the wrongly accused man's case as a public defender.

Raw and tersely written, *Long Rain* anatomizes deep-seated human flaws, and asks a host of unsettling questions. As Dark's anxiety grows, Gadol delves into visceral emotions and how they can shatter trust and twist relationships. Balanced against these themes are Gadol's disarmingly idyllic descriptions of California's wine country, and his earthy, engaging view of vineyard life. The novel has been translated into several languages and nominated for a prize from PEN West, and is currently under option by independent film producers.

Gadol takes more narrative chances in *Light at Dusk* (2000), set in a xenophobic and explosive future Paris. The French Front, a far right political faction, now rules. Bombs explode in the Metro, racist graffiti cover magnificent buildings, immigrant mobs overwhelm the city, and skinhead gangs freely roam the streets. Against this "Greeneland" setting, Gadol uses shifting, multiple viewpoints to tell an adventure-story nuanced with moral guilt, jealousy, damaged relationships, and profound self-discovery. For reasons never clearly disclosed, William (Will) Law abandons his diplomatic position in the U.S. Foreign Service in Mexico and drifts, finally to Paris to renew his heated affair with his elusive lover Pedro Douglas, a fellow American expatriate. Before Will and Pedro leave Paris, Will meets Jorie Cole, another American expatriate, who is trapped in a soulless relationship with Lebanese Luc Chamoun. Before Will's eyes, Jorie's supposed son Nico is kidnapped by a right-wing gang that has been terrorizing parents by snatching children in daylight and dropping them off on the opposite side of Paris. With the police unwilling to help, Will, Pedro, and Jorie band together to get Nico back, each seeing the search as a means of redemption for past mistakes. But Pedro will end up alone, and Jorie will reunite with Luc. Reluctantly, Will reenters the morally questionable world he had fled, and uses his abandoned diplomatic contacts to find the boy, perceiving the quest as a moral test, his chance to complete "one good act—one seed cast into a hard fallow field, from which a new good life would inevitably flower" (*Dusk* 110).

Like Gadol's other novels, *Light at Dusk* defies easy classification, recalling elements of John Rechy's neo-noirs, John le Carré's international intrigue, Graham Greene's suspenseful plotting, Ian McEwan's moral edge, and Joseph Conrad's mannered prose. But it lacks *Mystery Roast*'s humor and intriguing elements of magic realism, *Closer to the Sun*'s vivid descriptions and astute insight, and *Long Rain*'s suspense. In each case, however, Gadol grounds his tales on sympathetic portraits of otherwise despicable or morally conflicted characters who find themselves caught up in intricately plotted situations. The same is true of *Silver Lake* (2009), an intense study of trust, deceit, and hard-won redemption.

In March 2004, Gadol published "Modernhaus Projekt-H, 1933," a short story set at the Bauhaus on its last day, in 1933 Berlin. Appearing in the California Institute of the Arts journal *Black Clock*, "Modernhaus" is projected as a chapter in Gadol's forthcoming epic, currently titled *American Modern*.

Bibliography

Gadol, Peter. *Closer to the Sun.* New York: St. Martin's Press, 1997.
———. *Coyote.* New York: Crown Publishers, 1990.
———. *Light at Dusk.* New York: Macmillan, 2001.
———. *The Long Rain.* New York: Macmillan, 2000.
———. *The Mystery Roast.* New York: Picador, 1997.
Plunket, Robert. Review of "Light at Dusk." *Advocate,* 18 July 2000, p. 67.

—LynnDianne Beene

Garden State Rick Moody (1997)

Haunting and evocative, RICK MOODY's *Garden State* resembles a kind of prose poem, its peripatetic lens capturing a truly bizarre cast of characters: Alice, a funky 23-year-old for whom life is in perpetual stasis; Evelyn Smail, Alice's mother, who has suffered through a ruinous divorce; Lane, an intermittently recovering alcoholic and drug addict with a penchant for suicide; and Dennis, his brother, who uses sex and drugs as antidotes for his malaise; with six lesser characters no less memorable, and six more with colorful bit parts.

With consistent sympathy, but relentless candor, the novel explores its characters' wasted and tormented lives, with redemption only hinted at and never achieved. If any recovery is possible for the psychic invalids who populate the environmentally polluted world of the tale, it can only be assembled from the debris of the past; and of all the characters, only Alice and Lane seem remotely capable of that. Each shows a willingness to recapture the past and reconcile it with the present, essentially by reliving it through the mediation of children—Lane in his encounter with a newspaper girl, and Alice in her exchanges with delinquent schoolboys playing capture the flag near her mother's house on the Heights. Only by such vicarious animation can Alice and Lane realize the corrosive effect that their physical and social/domestic environments have had on who they are, and the fateful qualities of their deterioration.

The very structure of the novel frames the aimless, herky-jerky lives of its several protagonists and minor characters, revealing their vexing, inconclusive relationships with each other. Rather than focus on any one or two characters in depth, the novel restlessly shifts its gaze from one character or set of characters to another with kaleidoscopic rapidity, evoking its world—fragmented, chaotic, and unstable—both in the tale and in the telling of it. Made up of seven short sections of about 30 pages each, and with no less than 60 scene/character changes, the novel presents characters and events in an almost bewildering, rapid-fire style, resulting in an emphasis on plot and surface to the detriment of in-depth character development. But far from a flaw, this seems only fitting in a tale where none of the characters have much depth to explore. Alienated and suicidal, Lane yet pales in complexity when compared, for example, to one of Faulkner's young self-destructive isolationists, such as Quentin Compson of *The Sound and The Fury* and *Absalom, Absalom*.

Although some scenes in *Garden State* overlap, the movement of the story is basically linear, with occasional flashbacks, its action occurring over the two months of April and May. Springtime, but spring here brings with it little promise of growth, or with it hope, as nature itself is severely compromised in the smog-infested, toxic-waste dump of New Jersey's industrial cities and environs. The novel's first sentence is emblematic: "Drizzle coated Haledon, N.J., with a sad, ruinous sheen."

The narrative revolves around several young adults clinging to their disillusioned adolescence, and a number of mature adults, like Evelyn Smail and Ruthie, fitfully seeking to extricate themselves from their adult children's dependency upon them. Out-of-work or barely working, restlessly active but somehow profoundly static, most of the young people are "nesting" at their parents' homes, subsisting rather than living, in an almost parasitic stupor. Living at her mother's, Alice constantly violates house rules and is a rebel by nature. On and off the wagon, Lane lives with his mother, stepfather, and half-brother Dennis. He is manic-depressive, and after a probable suicide attempt is consigned for his own safety to a psychiatric hospital aptly named "The Motel" because of the short-term residency of its clientele and inefficacy of its cures.

The novel's principal themes are characteristic of Moody's other major works, The ICE STORM and The Diviners, and dominated by loneliness and alienation. Each of the characters is essentially alone, and repeatedly frustrated in efforts to communicate with or coalesce into a supportive and caring community. Sensing the inherent futility of their situation, Alice voices the resultant fatalism most succinctly when she tells the egotistic L. G., who has also defected from her band, Critical Ma$$: "Do whatever the fuck you want. Doesn't mean anything in the long run" (17).

As in The Ice Storm, sex is an inadequate surrogate for love. Far from an ecstatic experience, it has become robotic and banal, providing only temporary and unsatisfying release from the quiet desperation of daily existence. Overcome with rage at L. G.'s dismissive attitude, "Alice decided sex would help. She grabbed Dennis and held him to her. She grabbed the collar of his tee shirt, stretched it all out" (18). Sex has become adulterated and lost its ecstatic sense of togetherness. Whereas D. H. Lawrence in Lady Chatterley's Lover argued for the normalcy of sex in a loving relationship between a man and a woman, in a Rick Moody novel, sex is an exercise in autoerotic (non-)gratification.

Suicide also seems a banal, robotic alternative in a world without real choices, and in which individuals are already psychically dead; to put the body to rest seems merely the next logical step. One of the leitmotifs in the novel, then, involves the self-immolation of Mike Maas, a young man who takes his life before the action of the novel proper begins, and about whom the reader learns through casual asides. By his action of setting himself ablaze on the Garden State Parkway—and incidentally stalling traffic for hours—he becomes an icon for his peers and their successors, illustrating—pointlessly in the end—the extent to which one will go to escape such existential despair.

Its claustrophobic and noxious setting is integral to Garden State's tale, and the imperceptibly corrosive impact of this setting over time upon the lives and aspirations of Haledon's inhabitants, is as destructive as an earthquake. As a fictional device, moreover, setting helps to convey the theme of how industrial urban blight can impair and destroy human life. To the extent that one is what one sees, breathes, eats, touches, and smells, the consequences for Haledon's residents are dire, indeed.

However, even in the Garden State, where toxic fumes from auto and chemical factory emissions foul the air, the impacted skyline yields a decadent, lurid beauty: "The evening light of April seemed to detail the reveries of arsonists. The sunlight smoldered over the foothills" (12). Even the sleazy drug-dealer Max Crick perceives a latent beauty in his surroundings: "Now he was out on the piers looking over the goddamn Newark Bay, thinking how beautiful were the lights of all those factory spaces" (200).

Just as the skyline, for all the smog, augurs hope, so at least two of the main characters, Alice and Lane, have the potential to survive their respective pasts with a modicum of meaning and dignity. Moody intimates this in his description of their first date, a jaunt on a bus from Jersey to New York City. Arriving in the terminal in Manhattan, "at one of the newsstands, surrounded by hardcore pornography," Lane exults, "We made it" (212). While their ultimate success in escaping the wraiths of the past is left in doubt, the end of the novel offers a surprising moment of transcendence: "And Lane left off thinking about the past right then, when the doors opened./'Alice,' he said. / With all that in front of them, they looked up" (212).

While instances of love are predictably rare, there are fleeting moments of genuine tenderness in *Garden State,* moments that suggest that love may yet be possible, even in New Jersey. Ruthie's solicitude for Lane, and even for her ex-husband, Lane's father, who suffers from dementia, are cases in point. So too is the example of Alice, who apologizes to Lane for having, with Max, plied him with drinks, leading to his relapse. It is hard to write a novel without real conflict, where nothing has meaning or value, where everything is relative and commitment ultimately pointless, but Moody finds a way, in *Garden State,* to somehow float the hapless struggle against these things, like a Jersey oil-slick, shimmering on top of them.

Bibliography

Moody, Rick. *Garden State.* Little, Brown, 1992.

—Jerome L. Wyant

Generation X: Tales for an Accelerated Culture Douglas Coupland (1991)

DOUGLAS COUPLAND's first novel, *Generation X: Tales for an Accelerated Culture* (1991), is a social satire of mass culture that explores the crisis of "Generation X." Defining the spirit and mood of its time, the book explores the pathologies of apathy and the alienating effects of a consumerist society. While Coupland concentrates on "X generation" characters born in the late 1950s to the late 1960s, many scholars extend the generation to include those born as late as the '80s. The novel's three main characters—Andy (the narrator), Claire, and Dag—leave their stifling careers (what Coupland calls "Mcjobs") in order to escape their past and gain autonomy. Sharing a common dissociation from their past and families, they befriend each other in Palm Springs, California, which acts as their temporary hideout and the setting of the novel. Coupland's first description of this generation highlights their feelings of alienation and homelessness: the narrator's "group ... doesn't have a name—an X generation—purposely hiding itself" (56). With this novel, Coupland both

comments on and shapes this "X generation" as it enters the '90s.

The novel's style reinforces the three characters' isolation and aimless wandering, restlessly switching narratives and interrupting memory, which serves (as it indicts) the short attention span of the television-educated Generation X, and mimics its fast-paced consumer culture. As Dag explains, "the world has gotten too big—way beyond our capacity to tell stories about it, and so all we're stuck with are these blips and chunks and snippets on bumpers" (5). This embedded critique of the novel's own fractured style exemplifies Coupland's ironic and self-conscious narrative voice. Narrating in a conversational tone and colloquial style, the characters take turns telling fictional and autobiographical stories that punctuate their otherwise banal daily activities. They share the tales of their past life in metropolitan centers and memories of lost relationships, and ask each other probing questions such as, "what one moment for you defines what it's like to be alive on this planet. What's your takeaway?" (91). Despite the protagonists' plangent if not pathetic attempts to escape their history, however, most of their narratives are rooted in nostalgia and brief glimpses of something greater than themselves.

The novel exposes the moral and spiritual crises of Generation X, primarily targeting its commodity culture, obsession with pleasure, deification of the beautiful, and loss of subjectivity that accompanies the relentless accumulation of objects. For the characters in the novel, the crisis of their generation is not "just the failure of youth but also a failure of class and sex and the future and I still don't know what" (30). Using marketing techniques to convey the particular social context of Generation X, Coupland defines this cultural malaise by coining pop-culture terminology and by featuring small graphics in the margins of the text. His humorous definitions of cultural phenomena include "yuppie," "McJob," and "Dorian Graying."

As a postmodern novel, the book not only rejects elitism but comments on its own literary form. Packaged as a neon pink-and-yellow, marketable object, the book's cover aesthetics and the spattering of short comical blurbs in its margins make an explicit appeal to mass-culture tastes. Although the novel assails consumerism and argues that all facets of life—family, fame, pleasure, beauty—can be purchased, it also demonstrates an acute consciousness of its own role as product. In short, Coupland uses the unavoidable materialism of the novel to highlight the materiality of literature. This contradictory underlining and undermining of consumerist culture epitomizes the irony of *Generation X*.

The title *Generation X: Tales for an Accelerated Culture* further inscribes the ironic tone and major themes of the novel. Naming Generation X as "accelerated" seems to suggest a kind of superiority, yet the book reveals the inferior and underdeveloped nature of its fast-paced (or "accelerated") characters. Before he retreats to Palm Springs, for example, Dag lived in a metropolitan center (Toronto), and was thrilled to be the "most desirable target market" for advertisers (19); yet, in retrospect he describes this phase of his life as empty and meaningless. Claire's love-interest, Tobias, serves as another warning against the superficiality of an "accelerated culture" that privileges beauty over ethics and maintains a constant state of motion. Ultimately, "accelerated" merely signifies the sheer brute pace of the culture; any suggestion of an intellectual or moral superiority is ironic. In fact, in Coupland's fictional framework, the "accelerated culture" fosters a distancing from oneself from others, paradoxically resulting in regression rather than progression.

In addition to Coupland's satirical interrogation of the cultural environment of the 1990s, the novel features rich natural imagery. Evocative images of the sun, snow, and birds contrast with the sterile descriptions of city-living. Claire's most treasured moment on earth (her "takeaway") is her first sight of snow. During a trip to New York City, she was at first entranced by the big buildings, the "steel, stone, and cement" (93), but in the very act of reverently estimating the sheer mass of the city and the largeness of its structures, she experiences her first snowfall. Claire's "first snowflake ever" contrasts with the oppressive traffic that honks at her, and signifies the "*one* memory of earth" that she cherishes the most (94). Similarly, Andy's and Dag's takeaway memories are the smell of bacon

and gasoline respectively. It is important that these treasured memories are not purchased, "fake yuppie experiences that you had to spend money on," but are virtually "worthless" everyday occurrences (91). Taken as a whole, the natural imagery acts as a pervasive counterpoint to the city, with natural and simple experiences seeming to offer the only potential redemption and escape from that spiritually barren landscape.

Birds are associated with transformation, death, and rebirth throughout the novel. Claire tells a jarring tale about an American soldier (Arlo) who is surrounded by hummingbirds in the midst of a war. The birds are attracted to Arlo's bright blue eyes, seeking material for their nests. In waving away the hummingbirds, Arlo alerts the enemy. When the army retrieves his dead body the next day, his blue irises have been pecked out. And again, when a young heiress slowly kills herself, her soul flits up to heaven "like a small yellow bird that can sing all songs" (128). Finally, Andy fantasizes about lying on sharp rocks as a large pelican lands on his face. Birds thus signify the power of the natural sublime (a transcendent fusion of terror and beauty) that exists beyond the city.

Man's technological and economic triumphs contrast with the frightening tales of nature's sheer power. Dag explains that he needs to be expiated for his roguish behavior (vandalism) in order to be spiritually and morally cleansed, and this lesson arguably extends not only to the rest of the protagonists, but to all of Generation X. The novel ends with the realization of this punishment and of Andy's fantasy. In the last chapter, Andy travels south to meet Claire and Dag in Mexico, in order to start a hotel business. During his trip, he sees a mushroom cloud from an atomic bomb in the distance, and it is the sight (and reality) of the cloud that finally manages to slow the "accelerated culture" to a complete stop. The book concludes with the thematic coupling of urbanity and nature in a violent catharsis: in the midst of a traffic jam, a "cocaine white egret" flies overhead searching for prey (177). In a perfect realization of Andy's prophetic death fantasy, the large bird targets Andy's head and rips his scalp open.

Coupland's later works extend his first novel's exploration and critique of consumerism, alienation, and loss. In *Shampoo Planet* (1992), for example, the main character (Tyler) learns to distinguish between reality and the exploitive fantasy of advertisements. Coupland has written a host of other, highly acclaimed fictional works, such as the series of short sketches in *Life After God* (1993), the psychological thriller *Girlfriend in a Coma* (1997), and the compelling commentary on modern families in *All Families Are Psychotic* (2001). Fellow Canadian novelist Russell Smith, whose works include *How Insensitive* (1994) and *Noise* (1998), shares Coupland's satirical edge and concentrates on the drug-ridden lifestyle of the youth in Toronto. Coupland's debut has also sparked international interest in the X generation, exemplified by later works such as Chuck Klosterman's *Sex, Drugs, and Cocoa Puffs: A Low Culture Manifesto* (2004) and Jeff Gordinier's *X Saves the World: How Generation X Got the Shaft but Can Still Keep Everything from Sucking* (2008).

Bibliography

Coupland, Douglas. *Generation X: Tales for an Accelerated Culture.* New York: St. Martin's Press, 1991.

—Kailin Wright

Gesture Life, A Chang-rae Lee (2000)

A Gesture Life is CHANG-RAE LEE's story of Franklin, or "Doc," Hata, the determined "good citizen" of Bedley Run, a New York suburb. Hata is a Japanese man of Korean descent who has retired from running a medical supply store in Bedley Run, where he says he enjoys "an almost Oriental veneration as an elder" (1). He is respected and liked by his neighbors because of the way he has served and honored his community for many years. Yet his personal life seems empty; he has lost track of his adopted daughter, Sunny, and lost his most recent romantic partner to cancer without having been able to say good-bye. He has also suffered serious burns in a sudden house fire.

Much of the novel occurs as he is recovering in the hospital, when he recollects and reconsiders the seminal events of his life. At the hospital, Doc Hata strikes up a friendship with a candy-striper; and this relationship, along with a host of others deftly depicted in the novel, illustrates his calm and personable presence, which has charmed everyone except his daughter. His closest friend, Liv Crawford, a forceful real estate agent, respects Hata immensely, even going so far as to argue that "Doc Hata *is* Bedley Run," because of his benevolence and conformity to the interests of the community (136).

Through Doc Hata's memories, we learn that the disappearance of his daughter Sunny was both painful and inevitable. As he describes her, she was never given to warmth, toward her father or anyone else. She was intelligent and talented but utterly uninterested in personal attachment, and did not even seem to care about herself. As a teenager, she had taken up with the worst people in town and, as Doc Hata himself confirms, had become a more or less willing unpaid prostitute for them, something understandably devastating for her father.

While much of the early novel concerns Doc Hata's life with his adopted daughter, the middle section of the novel turns to his experience as a medic for the Japanese Imperial Army in Burma during World War II, when he came into contact and formed a relationship with Kkutaeh, or "K," a Korean "comfort woman" prisoner. The circumstances of that doomed relationship were intensely painful and difficult, and haunt Doc Hata even in his retirement.

The unresolved combination of vastly different elements in Doc Hata's life insistently demands the reader's attention and comparison. K was a sex prisoner who Doc Hata wanted desperately to rescue from her situation, his daughter a child he rescued from a Christian orphanage, but who from the time of her adoption has behaved as though held prisoner in her adopted father's house, and when she finally escapes, it is to a situation where in the eyes of her father, she is more or less a sex prisoner herself. Indeed, at times it seems as if K and Hata's adopted daughter led parallel lives, as if Sunny is a shadowy and haunting reminder of K.

Even as an adult, Sunny is determined not to accept her father's love, which, however calm and restrained, is constant and sincere. Hata reveals that after a violent incident at the dangerous house where she stayed in Bedley Run as a teenager,

Sunny disappeared and only returned once, to seek her father's help in getting an abortion. Afterward, she is gone again for many years. However, after the fire, Hata receives an unsigned get-well card, and eventually finds Sunny working in a clothing store in a mall. She is still extremely reluctant to have a relationship with him, but finally allows him to visit with her son. However, Hata knows that the situation is conditional and that he cannot depend on continuing to be able to see his grandson, who is himself imprisoned, in a sense, in the estrangement of his mother and grandfather.

Like Chang-rae Lee's previous award-winning novel, NATIVE SPEAKER, *A Gesture Life* is concerned with nationality and identity, or the lack thereof. The misfortune or emptiness in the life of Doc Hata subtly intimates that while having the best of intentions to serve his community, he is unwilling or unable to serve himself. He is reluctant to establish or maintain an identity that does *not* have to do with serving the community, one of his daughter's complaints about him. Early in the novel Hata recalls having once met a Japanese man who also ran a medical supply store, and who seemed very similar to himself. He explains how he felt conspicuous in the presence of someone so similar, almost as though seeing himself in this man had made his identity overly pronounced or too public. His outlook may in the end be *too* gentle and *too* accepting, but it governs his life with the firmness of tyranny. Early on he states:

> I think one person can hardly understand why another has conducted his life in such a way, how he came to commit certain actions and not others, whether he looks upon the past with mostly pleasure or equanimity or regret. (5)

Yet this mild philosophy issues in a troubling paradox: Hata seems to value fitting in as a useful part of his community far more than standing out as an individual, yet he is compelled to respect people like his daughter who sacrifice their involvement with a community or family to remain isolated individuals. And the stasis engendered by this paradox may well be a contributing factor in the unmonitored decline and eventual disappearance of his child. Occasion-

ally Hata states that perhaps he should not have been so lenient with her, but he never alters in his overly respectful treatment of her. It is as though he thinks that continuously showing his respect for her individuality will someday create in her the desire to reintegrate into their family and community, but unsurprisingly she never does. If Doc Hata were able to share some of his daughter's impertinence and individualism, and she were able to share some of his commitment to the community, they might understand one another better and develop a true bond instead of the static and unnourishing relationship they maintain.

Hata continually, even obsessively muses on the connections between environment and identity—that "one takes on the characteristics of the locality"—and affirms that "there is a gradual accruing recognition of one's face, of being, as far as anyone can recall, from around here"; but toward the end of the novel his musing is narrowed to baffled reflections on the fragility of identity, riddling who he is (1, 285). In contemplation of his time serving in the army, for example, he notes:

> All I wished for was to be part (if but a millionth) of the massing, and that I pass through with something more than a life of gestures. And yet, I see now I was in fact a critical part of events, as were K and the other girls, and the soldiers and the rest. Indeed the horror of it was how central we were, how ingenuously and not we comprised the larger processes, feeding ourselves and one another to the all-consuming engine of the war.

Despite his desire to live more than a "life of gestures," it is clear that Hata's good gestures in the community finally just *are* his life, his personality and contribution to the world, something his daughter seems only beginning to understand—and in the circumscribed confines of her own self-centeredness—toward the end of the novel.

Because of the prominence of Doc Hata's memories of the army camp, and his struggle to understand who he is in such circumstances, *A Gesture Life* recalls such emotionally fraught wartime novels as *The Remains of the Day* by Kazuo

Ishiguro, *The English Patient* by Michael Ondaatje, and *Doctor Zhivago* by Boris Pasternak. Thematically, it is similar to Lee's *Native Speaker*, and both novels, in their concern with the tenuous contingencies of identity, can be considered descendants of existential novels like Camus's *The Stranger*, as well as American works concerned with the voice of the minority individual, such as Ralph Ellison's *Invisible Man*.

Bibliography

Ellison, Ralph. *Invisible Man.* New York: Vintage, 1995.
Ishiguro, Kazuo. *The Remains of the Day.* New York: Vintage, 1990.
Lee, Chang-rae. *Aloft.* New York: Putnam. 2004.
———. *A Gesture Life.* New York: Riverhead. 2000.
———. *Native Speaker.* New York: Riverhead, 1996.
Ondaatje, Michael. *The English Patient.* New York: Vintage, 1993.
Pasternak, Boris. *Doctor Zhivago.* New York: Pantheon, 1997.

—Susan Kirby-Smith

Giant's House, The Elizabeth McCracken
(1996)

The subtitle of ELIZABETH MCCRACKEN's first novel is "A Romance," a phrase that evokes stories of love and of fantasy; and *The Giant's House* is both, drawing together the ordinary and the extraordinary. The story is told through the voice of Peggy Cort, a librarian on Cape Cod, who falls in love with James Carlson Sweatt, the tallest boy in the world. McCracken's previous work was a collection of short stories, *Here's Your Hat What's Your Hurry* (1993); in 2001 she published a second novel, NIAGARA FALLS ALL OVER AGAIN, which tells the story of a vaudeville comedy team. It is in *The Giant's House*, however, that McCracken's quirky and vivid characterizations are most memorably allied with a story at once disturbing, poignant, and lovely.

Peggy Cort's narration is one of the book's great strengths, from her arrestingly misanthropic opening declaration, "I do not love mankind" (1), to the novel's end, when she has become a kind of specter incarnate, perpetuating the memory of her great love. Additionally, Peggy's vocation as a small-town librarian provides her with a patient, trustworthy, and organizing sense of self. Indeed, her view of what it means to be a librarian informs her interactions with all of the novel's other characters, and with the reader. (Like her narrator, McCracken holds an M.S. in Library Science, and worked as a librarian.) Peggy both resists and revels in the antisocial, book-loving stereotype of the librarian, finding herself trapped by her own personality and the self-image she has created, until falling in love with James leads her out of herself. The unlikely pair first meet in Peggy's library, where James is visiting with his elementary school class. At the time, Peggy recalls, "I thought at first he was a second teacher, he was so much taller than the rest, tall even for a grown man" (3). James wants a book about magic tricks, which Peggy finds for him like many others over time. She sees her librarian's role as an opportunity to draw him out, and unconsciously strives in some small way to make him rely on her. Ultimately, James's interests turn to himself, looking for a cure for his gigantism; he grows to be more than eight feet tall by the time of his death.

Despite Peggy's insistence that the story she tells is about James and not about herself—"This is not my story. Let me start again" (3)—she is the novel's most compelling character. James remains somewhat inscrutable, wanting very much to be in the world but always aware of his distance—literal and figurative—from most other people. He turns to the librarian for her expertise and her knowledge, something Peggy claims all librarians secretly want from their patrons. But as their relationship progresses, what Peggy wants most is to know James—first to understand his interests, then to be drawn into his family and history. The connection between knowledge and love is McCracken's central theme, one that Peggy raises early on:

> I believe people fall in love based on knowledge. Either they are amazed by something a beloved knows that they themselves do not know; or they discover common rare knowledge; or they can supply knowledge to someone who's lacking. . . . Nowadays, trendy librarians, wanting to be important,

say, Knowledge is power. I know better. *Knowledge is love.* (6–7)

Peggy has an intimate knowledge of the contents of her library but finds herself fundamentally flawed when it comes to understanding other human beings. It may be, Peggy herself almost admits, that James's extraordinary qualities—including the fact that his gigantism fates him to an early death—are the source of her love: She is engaged in a giant project of accumulating knowledge about James.

Like most of the longings McCracken chronicles in *The Giant's House,* however, Peggy's is never completely fulfilled. What is, on one hand, a story about love is also a story about loneliness. The "giant's house" of the title refers to a cottage built in James's family's backyard when he outgrows the space inside. James's height literally removes him from the company of others, as does his growing fame and the inevitability of his early death. His end is apparent from the beginning; he is "doomed to be mostly enormous" (6), but also, ultimately and literally, doomed by that enormousness. As Tvrdi Terry notes, "Despite some fantastical aspects of the novel, we are presented with a situation to which almost anyone can relate: falling in love with someone you can never have, and realizing that we are all alone in some form or another" (207). *The Giant's House* raises questions about the nature of love, and of knowledge, through the multiple oddities of its central romance. McCracken clearly does not see Peggy's love for James as in any way predatory or pedophiliac, and yet this is a story told by a woman who repeatedly insists upon her love for a boy who—though already the size of a grown man—is only 11 years old when they meet.

McCracken accomplishes this by allowing Peggy to avow to the reader a love she knowingly enters into without the possibility of its being requited. She chooses to love James when she finds out he is going to die, "of himself," as a doctor puts it (76):

I would love him. It would be as easy as keeping his gaze, easy as saying, This is what to do. I would perfect my love for him, never care what others thought of me, or even what he was thinking of me. It was *this*

I'd waited for all my life: a love that would make me useful, a love that would occupy all my time. . . . I loved him because he was young and dying and needed me. . . . I loved him because I wanted to save him, and because I could not. I loved him because I wanted to be enough for him, and I was not. (77, 78)

Love, for Peggy Cort, becomes a calling in the same way that she is called to her books. *The Giant's House* implies that "librarian" is a profession that both creates and maintains an identity, so that on some level the self is fused with the work. In this way, Peggy's love for James is an extension of her librarian self, as she catalogs his injuries, records his height, and helps to maintain his clothes and shoes as she might the books in her library. For Peggy, these actions are not a diminishment of her love but the only and best way to show it. Perhaps most appropriately, then, when she does fulfill that love physically it is by proxy—an experience that is at once the ruin and scandal she alludes to as the novel begins, but also the consummation of that impossible love.

Bibliography

McCracken, Elizabeth. *The Giant's House.* New York: Bantam-Dial, 1996.

Terry, Tvrdi. Review of *The Giant's House, Prairie Schooner* 73, no. 2 (Summer 1999): 206–208.

—Mary Wilson

Gibbons, Kaye (1960–) *American novelist*

Kaye Gibbons was born on Bend of the River Road in Nash County, North Carolina, in 1960. She studied American and English literature at North Carolina State University and the University of North Carolina at Chapel Hill, where she took legendary critic Louis D. Rubin's southern literature course. With Rubin's encouragement, Gibbons completed a debut novel, *ELLEN FOSTER* (1987), which won her critical praise from such acclaimed writers as Eudora Welty, who said, "the honesty of thought and eye and feeling and word mark the work of this talented writer." *Ellen Foster* received numerous awards, including the Sue Kaufman Award for First Fiction from the Academy of Arts and Letters. Gibbons has also been honored with a Special Citation from the Ernest Hemingway Foundation, the PEN Revson Award for the best work of fiction published by a writer under 35, the *Chicago Tribune*'s Heartland Prize, and a knighthood from the French minister of culture for her contributions to French literature. In 1996, *Ellen Foster* and Gibbons's second novel, *A Virtuous Woman* (1989), were the featured selections in Oprah Winfrey's book club, which significantly broadened her national readership and reputation. Later that year, a *Hallmark Hall of Fame* adaptation of *Ellen Foster* was aired by the USA Network. Gibbons is now the author of eight novels, many of which have topped best-seller lists.

Ellen Foster is now taught alongside other American classics, and the protagonist, Ellen, has become an enduring character, in the tradition of Huck Finn and Scout Finch, for her intelligence, wit, and courage. Born into a dysfunctional family, Ellen endures her mother's suicide as well as her father's alcoholic abuse and premature death, to be welcomed at last into a loving foster family. A sequel to *Ellen Foster, The Life All around Me by Ellen Foster,* was published in 2005. Told by a now 15-year-old Ellen, this follow-up tale emphasizes the resourcefulness of the character, and the confidence that a maternal relationship (now possible through her adoptive mother, Laura) can provide for young women. Gibbons has admitted that she identifies closely with Ellen's character and has dealt with similar familial hardships, including her own mother's suicide when she was 10, her father's early death due to alcoholism, and her experience as an orphan raised by several relatives for brief periods.

Gibbons's rustic characters and rural settings are rooted in the tradition of writers such as William Faulkner and Flannery O'Connor, whose stylistic combination of local color and modernist technique helped to define 20th-century southern fiction. While Gibbons's characters often recall the alienated figures of Faulkner's creation, and the wit and humor of O'Connor's, her work departs from her predecessors in its feminist emphasis. Beginning with *Ellen Foster* her novels highlight the emotional impact of bonds forged and broken between her female characters, particularly between mothers and daughters.

Moreover, whereas southern literature is often characterized by the honor and valor of men, Gibbons's male characters, particularly her father figures, are often abusive, destructive men who cling to their patriarchal roles to justify their mistreatment of women. In *Divining Women* (2004), for example, Troop Oliver is a spiteful, uncaring husband, who terrorizes his pregnant wife, Mary, until she finally confronts him in a climax that leaves him defeated but provides her with a renewed sense of hope. Typical of Gibbons's emphasis on the strength of female companionship, *Divining Women* is also a story of two women, Mary and Troop's niece, Maureen, and their struggle to overcome the despair caused by Troop's abuse. In *A Virtuous Woman,* Gibbons departs from the unflattering portraits of southern men in her creation of Jack Ernest Stokes, a tenant farmer, who loses his wife, Ruby, to lung cancer. In Stokes, Gibbons develops a sympathetic character who embodies the warmth and charm of her most likable female protagonists. Most notably, *A Virtuous Woman* remains Gibbons's only published effort to be narrated from a male point of view.

Reflecting the southern tradition of oral history, *A CURE FOR DREAMS* (1991), Gibbons's third novel, traces the lives of four generations of women who pass down their stories of marital and economic hardships, as well as their defiant triumphs, in a male-dominated society. This theme continues in Gibbons's fourth novel, *Charms for the Easy Life* (1993), which focuses on the relationship among three generations of women living together in pre–World War II North Carolina. Both novels emphasize the salutary comforts of female companionship, and their southern women are characterized not only by homespun wisdom but also by their resourcefulness and courage in defying societal expectations. Similarly, the close familial ties between the characters engender questions of identity; and a tension between heredity and individuality dominates the mother-daughter relationships in both narratives.

In *Sights Unseen* (1995), Gibbons addresses the strain that mental illness places on families, and the difficulty of repairing damaged parent-child relationships. As in *Ellen Foster,* the narrator, Hattie Barnes, is a young girl who struggles to capture her mother's attention and affection, here amid the unpredictable mood swings produced by untreated manic depression. Set in a small North Carolina town, *Sights Unseen* returns to several familiar themes in *Ellen Foster*: the difficulty of growing up in an emotionally volatile environment, the importance of self-reliance in unstable family circumstances, and the pain caused by an estranged relationship between mother and daughter. Unlike Ellen's mother, Hattie's is able to finally receive the treatment she needs, and although the story, told in retrospect, begins and ends with her mother's death, the Barnes women have many years together to establish the loving relationship that Hattie craves. Diagnosed with manic depression in her early 20s, Gibbons admits that the character of Maggie Barnes is partially autobiographical. In a 1994 interview she discusses the benefits of manic episodes in her creative process, and the challenges of recovering from depression and hospitalizations. She has also published a nonfiction account, *Frost and Flower: My Life with Manic Depression So Far* (1995), which documents her struggle with mental illness.

Set in antebellum North Carolina, ON THE OCCASION OF MY LAST AFTERNOON (1998) explores the deep-seated regional and racial prejudices that divide an aristocratic southern family. The narrator, Emma Garnett, defies her southern-belle upbringing in both her support of the emancipation of African Americans and her marriage to a Bostonian, Quincy Lowell, whose family's abolitionist politics infuriate Emma's Confederate-leaning father. The South's troubling history of racism is suggested in other Gibbons novels (in Ellen's prejudiced relationship with her African-American friend Starletta, for example, or the role of black housekeepers in raising white children in *A Virtuous Woman* and *Sights Unseen*), but this historical novel confronts this legacy directly by deconstructing the myths of an idyllic antebellum South through the narrator's personal struggle against slavery and oppression. To some degree all southern writers must grapple with the history of the Civil War and Jim Crow, and Gibbons's work does its part to shed light on the social ramifications of racism and segregation, albeit through the perspective of white narrators.

Kaye Gibbons is an immensely popular author whose work reflects both historical traditions in American literature (as in her thematic emphasis on self-reliance) and contemporary trends (as exemplified in the independent perspective of her female protagonists). Formally, she narrates from a first-person point of view, typically a woman's, whose dialect and use of simple language strengthen the authenticity of her rural settings. In this regard, her characters' interior monologues demonstrate an often surprising depth of thought and emotion in these "rural folk," while Gibbons's female characters are memorable for their fierce independence and defiance of traditional roles for southern women.

Bibliography
Chandler, Marilyn. Review of *A Virtuous Woman*, *The Women's Review of Books* 6, no. 10 (1989): 21.
Cohen, Judith Beth. Review of *Charms for the Easy Life, The Laughing Place, Durable Goods, The Women's Review of Books* 11, no. 1 (1993): 24–25.
Gibbons, Kaye. 1993. *Charms for the Easy Life.* New York: G. P. Putnam's Sons, 1993.
———. 1991. *A Cure for Dreams.* Chapel Hill, N.C.: Algonquin Books, 1991.
———. 2004. *Divining Women.* New York: G. P. Putnam's Sons, 2004.
———. 1987. *Ellen Foster.* New York: Vintage Contemporaries, 1990.
———. 1995. *Frost and Flower: My Life with Manic Depression So Far.* Decatur, Ga. Wisteria Press, 1995.
———. "'In My Own Style': An Interview with Kaye Gibbons." By Jan Nordby Gretlund. *South Atlantic Review* 65, no. 4. (2000): 132–154.
———. 2005. *The Life All around Me by Ellen Foster.* New York: Harcourt, 2005.
———. 1998. *On the Occasion of My Last Afternoon.* New York: G. P. Putnam's Sons, 1998.
———. 1995. *Sights Unseen.* New York: G. P. Putnam's Sons, 1995.
———. 1989. *A Virtuous Woman.* Chapel Hill, N.C.: Algonquin Books, 1989.
Miller, Pamela. "Kaye Gibbons' Novel Draws from Her Life." StarTribune.com. Available online. URL: http://www.startribune.com/entertainment/books. Accessed May 15, 2009.

—Emily Rutter

Gilbert, Elizabeth (1969–) *American journalist, memoirist, and short story writer*

Born in Waterbury, Connecticut, in 1969 to John Gilbert, an engineer, and Carole Gilbert, a nurse, Elizabeth Gilbert is an acclaimed journalist and author of the No. 1 *New York Times* best-selling travel memoir *Eat, Pray, Love* (2006) and its follow-up *Committed* (2010). Once a fiction writer with no journalistic aspirations (Houpt), she has also published a collection of short stories, PILGRIMS (1997); a novel, *Stern Men* (2000); a biography, *The Last American Man* (2002); and *Eat, Pray, Love,* in addition to magazine articles that have earned her three National Magazine Award nominations.

Raised in a 19th-century farmhouse where she "washed [her] hair in a rain barrel," Gilbert skillfully draws from this uncustomary life in her work. In one of Connecticut's most opulent communities, Gilbert milked goats at home and played field hockey at school (*Last* 7), and this clash between modern affluence and old-fashioned tradition finds a prominent place in her narrative: "We were taught to disregard the values of the culture that surrounded us and to concentrate instead on this sacred and more ancient American tenet: Resourcefulness is Next to Godliness" (8).

The influence of E. Annie Proulx, Gilbert's favorite living American writer (B&N), is manifest in her first work, *Pilgrims.* Winner of the Ploughshares/Emerson College John C. Zacharis First Book Award (1999), *Pilgrims'* stories introduce the rugged terrain and characters typical of Gilbert's broader oeuvre, and encourage a distrust of the modern, the urban, and consequently—in Gilbert's rugged taxonomy—the pampered and effete. In the title story, Martha Knox from Pennsylvania is a newly hired hand at a Wyoming ranch, whose authenticity is called into question not only by her gender, but also by her eastern origins and "cowboy boots that anyone could see were new that week, the cheapest in the store and the first pair she'd ever owned" (2). Like Martha, Gilbert herself worked on a ranch in Wyoming. Upon graduation from New York University with a B.A. in political science, Gilbert found hard labor out West more attractive than the prospect of graduate school. With her signature wit, she relates her own lack of authenticity in her use of brand new rattlesnake

boots and her insistence that everyone call her "Blaze" (*Last* 8).

"At the Bronx Terminal Vegetable Market" depicts hard-working, hard-living men like those that inspire *Stern Men* and *The Last American Man.* In Gilbert's world, tough men are prominent, but shrewd, independent women drive both the fictive action and the narratives themselves, and their sexuality, of which they are in complete control, is a valuable commodity, as illustrated in many of *Pilgrims'* tales.

Independent, sexually resolved women dominate *Stern Men* as well, regardless of the title (a reference both to the character of the people in the tale and to the "sternmen" that work lobster boats on the rival lobstering islands of Courne Haven and Fort Niles, Maine). The protagonist, Ruth Thomas, a willful girl of 19, personifies the opposing forces of simplicity and decadence. Tied to the wealthy and powerful Ellis family of New Hampshire on her mother's side, Ruth is the daughter and granddaughter of two of the most steadfast fishermen on Fort Niles. While the Ellises attempt to shape Ruth's life with a prestigious boarding school education that exiles her to Delaware, upon graduation she obstinately flees to Fort Niles, though knowing there is no future there for an educated woman not married to the fishing industry. Principled as Gilbert herself, Ruth tells her mother that "Fort Niles [is] in her blood and soul; [home to] the only people who really [understand] her." She admits to herself, however, that her "passion for Fort Niles" is mostly on principle and "an expression of protest" (43).

Here, even more than in *Pilgrims,* tough women are highly visible, while weak ones, such as Ruth's mother, and austere laconic men are hardly seen. This balance contrasts with typical male-centered "cowboy" narratives, where the strong silence of the latter is finally illustrative of their *lack* of real power. Ruth's father, for example, repeatedly relinquishes his power over Ruth with the mantra, "I don't care who you spend your time with" (85).

In his emotional absence, and in the physical absence of a mother, Ruth is raised by Mrs. Pommeroy, who embodies the characteristics that fascinate Gilbert and to which Ruth herself aspires. Embracing her own sexuality while her husband was living, Mrs. Pommeroy now encourages Ruth's burgeoning sexuality. When her husband's death leaves the former with no means of support, the island men unite to insist that she leave. However, immune to their efforts and without notable hardship, Mrs. Pommeroy raises her eight sons by cutting hair; indeed, the island men themselves are at her mercy daily as she takes scissors to their heads and blades to their necks.

As self-sufficient as her guardian, 24-year-old Ruth is the first person capable of uniting Fort Niles and Courne Haven after 80 years of conflict. Principled and determined, Ruth parlays her sexuality into a marriage into the most powerful fishing family on rival Courne Haven. As a result, she convinces her father and her husband's uncle to join her nascent fishermen's cooperative and buy bait exclusively from her, ending the rivalry among the fishermen and turning a profit for all—a plan that no one had even conceived of before.

Gilbert's complex fascination with "men's men" inspired her first nonfiction book. *The Last American Man* (2002) was born of a story for *GQ*, where Gilbert was writer-at-large. Eustace Conway, a modern-day frontiersman who lives a primitive life in the woods near Boone, North Carolina, was one of many eccentric subjects that led the *New York Times* to call Gilbert "Queen of Quirk." Upon publication of the article, publishers fought for rights to a full-length work. After three years of research, which included weeks of physical labor on Conway's nature preserve and interviews with Conway's numerous lovers, Gilbert produced a draft after 30 days at a Wyoming writer's colony. Her telling of Conway's story woven into the context of American history and the frontier made her a finalist for both the National Book Award and the National Book Critics Circle Award.

Gilbert's memoir, *Eat, Pray, Love*, however, has garnered the most acclaim. On a solo trip through Italy, India, and Indonesia, Gilbert explored the arts of pleasure, devotion, and balance respectively. With more than 7 million copies in print in more than 30 languages, the work was named among the *New York Times*'s 100 most notable books of 2006 and *Entertainment Weekly*'s 10 best nonfiction books of the year. The memoir earned Gilbert a place among *Time* magazine's 100 Most Influential People in the World in 2008, and was optioned for a film starring Julia Roberts that began production in August 2009. Gilbert's follow-up memoir, *Committed*, published in 2010, has received good but less glowing reviews.

Bibliography
Barnes & Noble. "Eat, Pray, Love." Available online. URL: http://search.barnesandnoble.com/Eat-Pray-Love/Elizabeth-Gilbert/e/9780143038412/?itm=1. Accessed February 14, 2009.

Elizabeth Gilbert: Writer. Available online. URL: http://www.elizabethgilbert.com. Accessed February 14, 2009.

Gilbert, Elizabeth. *The Last American Man*. New York: Penguin, 2002.

———. *Pilgrims*. New York: Penguin, 1997.

———. *Stern Men*. New York: Mariner, 2000.

———. *Eat, Pray, Love*. New York: Penguin, 2006.

Houpt, Simon. "Queen of Quirk Meets Her Match." *Globe and Mail*, 8 June 2002, p. R7.

—Sonya Collins

Girl with a Pearl Earring Tracy Chevalier (1999)

Inspired by Johannes Vermeer's painting of the same name, TRACY CHEVALIER's second novel presents a fictional account of the relationship between the artist and the young girl who sat as a model for the painting. It achieved immediate success after its publication in 1999, and since then more than 2 million copies have been sold, the novel has been translated into 21 different languages, and, in 2003, it was made into a movie starring Colin Firth and Scarlett Johannson.

Set in 17th-century Holland, the novel opens with a visit by Johannes Vermeer and his wife, Catharina, to the home of a former tile painter who lost his sight when a kiln exploded. They have come to hire Griet, the 16-year-old daughter in the house, as their maid, with one of her responsibilities being the cleaning of the artist's studio. Griet's primary responsibilities in the large bourgeois household include cleaning the master's studio, going to the Meat Hall and fish stalls, and doing the laundry for 10: Vermeer; Catharina; their five children; Catharina's mother, Maria Thins; Maria Thins's servant, Tanneke; and herself.

She is also to help Tanneke with her duties. Griet enjoys her time in the studio, which "felt different from the rest of the house," and as she dusts, she is careful to measure the exact placement of objects set out for a painting and to return them to their original positions. She also devises a way to clean draped fabrics without disturbing their folds. And at last her artistic sensibility is noticed by the painter, who comments on the pleasing way the young girl has arranged the colors of vegetables she is chopping.

Trips to the Meat Hall and fish stalls provide a welcome diversion for Griet. Although she would prefer to use the butcher her family uses, she must get meat from one Pieter, whose stall and apron are not as clean as she would like. However, she soon becomes a favorite of the butcher and his son, also named Pieter, and consequently gets the best pieces of meat. Griet realizes that they consider her "obliged" for their special attentions, and she finds the younger Pieter attractive and kind. She cannot, however, overlook the blood under his fingernails.

Meanwhile, tension develops in the household: Tanneke grows jealous of Griet and is "often bad-tempered" with her; the seven-year-old daughter, Cornelia, challenges Griet's authority and, "determined to make mischief," stirs up trouble for her whenever she can; Catharina is moody during her repeated pregnancies. Griet sees her own family on Sundays but finds this "new life taking over the old." Moreover, a plague breaks out in the section of town where her family lives, and quarantine keeps Griet from visiting for a time, during which she learns through the younger Pieter that her sister Agnes has fallen victim to the outbreak. In the studio, however, Griet is always assured of order and serenity.

The novel speaks powerfully of this salutary force of art. Griet is mesmerized by Vermeer's paintings and, in her absorption, escapes the friction and pettiness of the household and world. She is never happier than when she is assisting her master, examining his pictures, or sitting for him as he paints. The artist himself goes to his studio to avoid his everyday cares, and he allows only Griet and Maria Thins, who share his love of art and appreciate his talent, to enter there without special permission, telling Catharina, "'You and the chil-

dren are not a part of this world. . . . You are not meant to be.'"

The master increasingly accepts Griet into this rarefied world of painting. At times, he has her purchase painting supplies and set out the paints he needs each morning. He teaches her to see the true colors of things and to grind and mix paints. Once, after seeing her master struggle with a painting, she dares to shift the position of a cloth and he approves of the change. On occasions the artist has Griet "stand in" for models.

Vermeer's lecherous patron van Raijvens, meanwhile, becomes fascinated with the "wide-eyed maid." Griet avoids his advances whenever possible, but inevitably, van Raijvens commissions a painting of her. Vermeer begins the work, which he attempts to keep a secret from Catharina in order to avoid her jealous anger, but as Griet sits for the portrait, her fondness for the artist grows: "It was the part of the week I liked best, with his eyes on only me for those hours."

The portrait of the girl progresses, but it does not satisfy the artist, and when he gives Griet permission to look at the painting, she knows what is missing: "that point of brightness he had used to catch the eye in other paintings." She remains silent, however, sensing both that the artist will eventually find the solution, and that it will bring her ruin. When Vermeer asks her to wear his wife's pearl earrings, Griet objects, saying that she does not have pierced ears; but he insists that she remedy this, and she does; the pearl earring, they both know, will make the painting complete. When the painting is later discovered by a furious Catharina, and neither Vermeer nor Maria Thins rise to the defense of the girl, Griet is forced to leave the household, and marries Pieter, the butcher's son, whom she had realized earlier "was my escape, my reminder that there was another world I could join."

Ten years pass, and Griet is comfortable in her new life. Her two children fill the emotional void left by her separation from Vermeer, and she and Pieter, working hard, provide an adequate life for their children and her mother. Then one day Griet receives a visit from Tanneke, who tells her to report to the Vermeer house that afternoon. Griet goes, assuming that she is to collect the 15 guilders owed to the butcher's shop, but learns there that Vermeer, who died two months earlier, has left a letter asking that Griet receive the pair of pearl earrings used for the portrait, which are grudgingly surrendered by Catharina. With no need for earrings, as she had pointed out once to the artist himself, Griet sells them for 20 guilders, gives 15 guilders to Pieter to settle the Vermeers' debt, and hides the other five, knowing that she will "never spend them," thereby striking a fragile but entirely human balance between the two worlds whose often destructive conflict has dominated the novel.

In addition to this over-arching tension, the work explores others that echo both its nature and deleterious effects, such as the rigid lines of demarcation drawn between Protestants and Catholics in 17th-century Holland. Coming from a strict Protestant family, Griet has never before ventured into the part of town where Catholics live, nor even known any Catholics until she becomes a maid for the Vermeers, whose paintings of the crucifixion scattered throughout the house make her acutely uncomfortable. Vermeer conclusively and unhelpfully explains, "There is a difference between Catholic and Protestant attitudes to painting."

The sharp and restrictive distinctions made by society between people of different social classes are also revealed in the novel. In posing for the painting, for example, Griet feels uneasy in Catharina's clothes, and reminds her master that "Maids do not wear pearls." Pieter warns Griet, "Theirs is not your world," and Griet tells Frans, her brother, that the wife of the owner of the company where he works is "not for the likes of you."

Kate Flatley, in her review of *Girl with a Pearl Earring* in the *Wall Street Journal*, writes that the book "mirrors the elegance of the painting that inspired it," and in the end, just as Vermeer's paintings captivate Griet and Maria Thins, Chevalier's novel charms the reader with a quiet and enduring beauty.

Bibliography

Angell, Sue. "Talking Shop with Tracy Chevalier '84." Oberlin Online: News and Features. Available online. URL: http://www.oberlin.edu/news-info/03nov/tracyChevalier.html. Accessed October 23, 2007.

Chevalier, Tracy. *Girl with a Pearl Earring.* London: HarperCollins, 1999.

Flatley, Kate. Review of *Girl with a Pearl Earring. Wall Street Journal,* 14 January 2000, p. 10.

Tracy Chevalier. Available online. URL: www.tchevalier.com. Accessed August 10, 2009.

—Charlotte Pfeiffer

Girl with Curious Hair David Foster Wallace (1989)

While perhaps neither as unconventional nor as experimental as his BRIEF INTERVIEWS WITH HIDEOUS MEN (1999), DAVID FOSTER WALLACE's first collection of stories does press firmly against the formal and thematic boundaries established by the genre: it is long (373 pages), ending with a 140-page novella entitled "Westward the Course of Empire Takes Its Way"; one of its stories, "Here and There," is dedicated to the logician Kurt Gödel, and is presented as the transcript of an extended session of "fictional therapy"; self-conscious metafictional asides creep into and out of the stories as though at will; and the collection as a whole openly embraces pop-culture even while criticizing it, reveling in descriptions of David Letterman's multilayered ironies and the sordid technicalities of McDonald's advertising culture. There is even a story, "Little Expressionless Animals," in which a demonic *Jeopardy!* host (Alex Trebek) regularly sneaks onto *Wheel of Fortune*'s stage to wreak all manner of game show havoc; and another, "Lyndon," in which an outrageous caricature of President Johnson conducts a prolonged affair with the narrator's (black, gay, male) lover. Yet, in spite of its wild experimentalism, intense intellectualism, and pervasive wackiness, the goals of *Girl with Curious Hair* remain fairly modest, almost classical: to entertain readers, to inform them about the world they inhabit, and to affect them on a basic emotional level.

This last goal—the one left out of Horace's description of literature as that writing which *delights* while it *instructs*—is what Wallace identifies as being the most difficult thing for a writer to accomplish in our postmodern, postindustrial, post-sentimental age: to make a reader feel that a piece of fiction is somehow both *real* and emotion-ally urgent. As Wallace argues in his 1993 essay "*E Unibus Pluram,*" we have become too distant from the fictions we create and populate: "irony tyrannizes us. The reason why our pervasive cul-tural irony is at once so powerful and so unsatisfy-ing is that an ironist is *impossible to pin down.* All U.S. irony is based on an implicit 'I don't really mean what I'm saying'" (67). As one of the char-acters in "Westward the Course of Empire Takes Its Way" sees it: "When he has emotions, it's like he's denied access to them. . . . I.e. he doesn't *feel* any-thing, or *he* doesn't feel anything" (303). Such is the problem with irony: either it prevents us from feeling, or we distrust what we feel, assume that we have been coerced into feeling it.

The collection's concluding novella goes to great lengths to address this problem of ironic distance, and thereby acts as something of a cul-mination and metafictional critique and summary of the collection's themes, preoccupations, and literary techniques. In its own way, "Westward" tries to summarize and culminate not simply *Girl with Curious Hair,* but also the so-called postmod-ern turn in American fiction that began in the cold war with writers such as Thomas Pynchon, Wil-liam Gaddis, and (especially) John Barth. Indeed, "Westward" would make a tough read without a knowledge of—and perhaps a deep and ambivalent emotional stake in—Barth's laboriously metafic-tional story collection *Lost in the Funhouse* (1968).

"Westward" opens with two epigraphs, the first by Anthony Burgess declaring, "we are all solipsists," and the second from Barth: "*For whom is the Funhouse fun?*" Barth himself offers a tenta-tive answer, "Perhaps for lovers" (69), before weav-ing a meandering, ironic, and—for Wallace and Mark, his fictional stand-in—ultimately cold and unsatisfying story. Dogged self-referentiality may have been an important tool for dismantling the conservative assumptions of the overly sentimen-tal 1950s, but in the Reagan era such metafictional tools had been hijacked by television and advertis-ing. In "Westward," the stand-in Barth character, Dr. C— Ambrose, is involved, for instance, in the construction of McDonald's franchise discotheques called "Funhouses." Perhaps this is why the Wal-lace-like Mark muses that the cool distance of

"postmodern" fiction no longer works: "A story, just maybe, should treat the reader like it wants to . . . well, fuck him. A story can, yes, Mark speculates, be made out of a Funhouse. But not by using the Funhouse as a symbol you can take or leave stand-ing there" (331). Rather, true fiction must carry with it an almost visceral punch strong enough to dislodge both writer and reader from their private, solipsistic worlds.

Writers should therefore model themselves on jealous lovers, not the cold architects of Fun-houses: "Please don't tell anybody, but Mark Nechtr desires, some distant hard-earned day, to write something that stabs you in the heart" (332). This late-coming revelation is surprising because up until that point Mark comes across as such a good, mild, ethical, and "healthy" character—pain-fully so. Thus when we learn of his secret desire to inflict violence—that is, to forge something resembling a true and real and present connection between himself and a reader—we are perhaps less horrified than relieved to discover that he is human and vulnerable.

Leading up to "Westward," *Girl with Curious Hair* is filled with a long genealogy of lonely, vul-nerable individuals who anticipate characters from Wallace's later fictions, such as Hal Incandenza of *INFINITE JEST* (1996), *Brief Interviews'* "hideous men," and the doubled Neal / "David Wallace" narrator of *Oblivion*'s "Good Old Neon" (2004). In *Girl with Curious Hair*'s "Say Never," for example, the perfect son Leonard Tagus becomes trapped within his objectively ideal life, and sabotages his family and happiness by sleeping with his brother's 20-year-old girlfriend. "Here and There" presents us with an "epic poet of technology" so enraptured by the precision of his own ideas that he cannot love or allow himself to be loved. And as children, a sister and her autistic brother in "Little Expres-sionless Animals" escape from their terrible home life by memorizing the encyclopedia. Later on, they become estranged when the brother's psychological problems become too severe and are then reunited as adults in a cruel media stunt on *Jeopardy!*

Perhaps the most bizarre and terrifying solipsist of all is the title story's sadistic Sick Puppy, a socio-pathic Young Republican who runs with a crew of nihilist punks (including a girl with a "curious" hairdo in the shape of a gigantic, erect penis), and whose greatest pleasure lies in burning people with lighters. Wallace suggests that these two wildly disparate groups—nihilist punks and Young Free Market Reaganite Republicans—are linked by a certain reactionary violence endemic to the alienating insincerity and irreality of their generation.

Aside from the sheer scope and richness of his ideas—impossible to summarize—what marks Wallace's style is the tenacious playfulness and varied texture of his prose. The Oklahoma-born narrator of "John Billy," for instance, employs phrases as ungrammatical as "was me supposed to tell Simple Ranger" or "a ambulance," while also, within the space of a few lines, delivering unbelievably complex locutions like "the vicissitudes of human relatings" (a phrase he is fond of), or "the moral coma and eye-and-T.-Rex-centered rage and *vengeancelüst*" (139), or even a list of "putative virtuous qualities headlined by charity-via-might, -main, altruism, Christian regard and duty, forgiveness, other-cheek-turning, *eudaimonia, sollen, devoir*" (140). The overall effect of this narration is to paint the picture of a bleak, but strangely rich world lying somewhere between Faulkner's Yoknapatawpha, Carson McCuller's Sad Café, and the carnivalesque polyphony of Joyce's Nighttown.

Girl with Curious Hair thus employs the very postmodern pyrotechnics (language play, varying screens of ironic distance, metafictional interruption) Wallace is so keen on criticizing. But rather than these fireworks being the point of the stories, they are simply tools—tools that all readers of modern fiction and watchers of TV know, and that Wallace uses to affect us as readers, "to stab us in the heart." Only the reader can decide whether he succeeds—or even whether he should.

Bibliography

Barth, John. *Lost in the Funhouse: Fiction for Print, Tape, Live Voice.* New York: Bantam, 1969.
Wallace, David Foster. *Brief Interviews with Hideous Men.* New York: Little, Brown, 1999.
———. "E Unibus Pluram: Television and U.S. Fiction." In *A Supposedly Fun Thing I'll Never Do Again.* New York: Little, Brown, 1997.
———. *Girl with Curious Hair.* New York: W. W. Norton, 1989.
———. *Infinite Jest.* New York: Little Brown, 1996.
———. *Oblivion.* New York: Little Brown, 2004.

—Andrew B. Warren

God of Small Things, The Arundhati Roy (1997)

The God of Small Things, winner of the 1997 Booker Prize, is the first and only novel to date by ARUNDHATI ROY, who is more widely known as a political activist and writer of nonfiction. The setting of the novel is Aymanam in Kerala, where Roy spent her childhood, known in the novel as Ayemenem. The novel casts a critical eye on the caste system in India, and after its publication, a lawsuit was launched against Roy to have the last chapter of the novel removed due to its depiction of sexual acts between individuals of different castes. The lawsuit was unsuccessful, but bore eloquent testament to how deeply affected contemporary Indian society still is by the caste system. The novel powerfully addresses the issues of transgression in the form of forbidden love, the inferior position of women in a patriarchal society, and the loss of childhood innocence.

The narrative shifts between two timeframes, the 1980s and, through flashbacks, the 1960s when communism was at the height of its development in Kerala. In spite of having as its objective the fall of the bourgeois class, the class struggle is unable to overcome the caste system, a lamentable fact attested to by the tragic events that unfold. While political struggle itself is not the novel's most immediate concern, the work is keenly interested in how such struggle adversely affects the everyday lives of people; and how, in the face of such struggle, "*personal* despair could never be desperate enough . . . That Big God howled like a hot wind, and demanded obeisance. Then Small God (cosy and contained, private and limited) came away cauterized, laughing numbly at his own temerity. Inured by the confirmation of his own inconsequence, he became resilient and truly indifferent" (Roy, 19). The conflict between personal desires and despair, and the need to suppress them for the interests of the larger community, are the driving forces of the narrative, which tells the story of one family in Ayemenem in the light of such conflict. While the main plot centers on Rahel and Estha and their mother Ammu, every individual in the family faces the same struggle of having to compromise their personal desires.

The novel opens with the return of Rahel to Ayemenem. After 23 years of estrangement from her twin brother Estha, who had been sent back to their father following the tragic events that mark a turning point in their childhood, Rahel gets news of his return to Ayemenem. She makes the journey to their childhood home to see him, and the unfolding of the narrative takes its cue from Rahel's return, in the form of a series of recollections leading up to the novel's tragic climax. The use of flashbacks that disrupt the development of the narrative, results in a nonlinearity characteristic of much postmodernist writing. Moreover, Roy largely employs stream of consciousness and third-person interior monologue, which heightens readers' awareness of the thoughts and feelings of the characters. There is, however, the sense of a darker, more secretive place, which readers are unable to access, further effectuated by the novel's highly poetic language. Another literary device recurrently employed by Roy is the use of setting to foreshadow the novel's tragic climax. The oppressiveness of returning to one's past is conveyed in the bleak introduction to Ayemenem:

> May in Ayemenem is a hot, brooding month. The days are long and humid. The river shrinks and black crows gorge on bright mangoes in still, dustgreen trees. Red bananas ripen. Jackfruits burst. Dissolute bluebottles hum vacuously in the fruity air. Then they stun themselves against clear windowpanes and die, fatly baffled in the sun. (Roy, 1)

The lush natural imagery here, as in other parts of the narrative, is rather ambiguous, contributing to its textual richness: on the one hand, it suggests paralysis and stagnation; but on the other, an excess that can be potentially dangerous. There are hints of change and overgrowth, of life that exceeds itself into death. This is further developed in themes of transgression:

> The countryside turns an immodest green. Boundaries blur as tapioca fences take root and bloom. Brick walls turn mossgreen. Pepper vines snake up electric poles. Wild creepers burst through laterite banks and spill across flooded roads. Boats ply in the bazaars. And small fish appear in the puddles that fill the PWD potholes on the highways. (Roy, 1)

Boats in bazaars and fish in potholes imply disorder, boundaries being crossed, and intimations of immorality. The steady encroachment of moss and pepper vines over walls and electric poles also suggests the implacable incursion of limits and boundaries in the form of manmade laws, especially "Love Laws," that "lay down who should be loved, and how. And how much" (Roy, 33). The theme of love, especially forbidden love, is explored through the transgression of Love Laws, and the widespread and extremely violent consequences that follow.

Another focus of the novel is gender, with a host of female characters portrayed as strong-willed and independent, yet unable to break out of the patriarchal system. Roy also describes a number of violent scenarios of domestic abuse. For example, the family-run business Paradise Pickles, had started out simply with Mamachi responding to requests for her banana jam and mango pickles for a bake sale organized by the Kottayam Bible Society. Her jam and pickles are received with such success, however, that Mamachi begins producing them commercially. Her husband, 17 years her senior and retired from government service, grows jealous of Mamachi's success and the attention she is getting as a woman in her prime. As a consequence, he begins beating her every night merely out of spite. When her son Chacko returns from his studies abroad, he takes over the business, and relegates Mamachi to the position of "sleeping partner." Mamachi's daughter, Ammu, also undergoes a similar fate in her own marriage. Her husband is "a full-blown alcoholic" (Roy, 40) and, when his job is threatened, is willing to offer Ammu to his boss sexually in exchange for keeping his job. Ammu finally leaves him and returns to Ayemenem, where she is looked down upon, not only because her marriage has failed, but also because it had been a love marriage, as opposed to an arranged one. As a result, Ammu's two children, Rahel and Estha, are themselves treated with disdain by other members of the family, innocently suffering the consequences of Ammu's mistakes. It is clear that there is a high price to pay for following one's desires, particularly for those who occupy an inferior position in society, as women do; and the novel also demonstrates how the consequences of the mistakes made by one generation are often borne by the next.

The extraordinary attention Roy devotes to description and detail illustrates her primary concern with *how* things happen, as opposed to simply what happens. Much of the plot is revealed to readers at the start of the novel, which suggests that Roy is less concerned with the unfolding of events, and more with the *way* things happen, crystallized in Vellya Paapan's observations of his son, Velutha, an untouchable who transgresses caste boundaries with calamitous consequences: "It was not *what* he said, but the *way* he said it. Not *what* he did, but the *way* he did it" (Roy, 76). As such, Roy masterfully conveys the childhood wonderment of Rahel and Estha, whose impressions, thoughts, and associations are largely the means by which the narrative unfolds. Conversely, when their happy childhood is disrupted by the onset of tragedy, of "Edges, Borders, Boundaries, Brinks and Limits [appearing] like a team of trolls on their separate horizons" (Roy, 3), readers are left with the haunting image of innocence lost, powerfully encapsulated in "the smell. Sicksweet. Like old roses on a breeze" (Roy, 6).

Bibliography

Roy, Arundathi. *The God of Small Things.* New York: HarperPerennial, 1998.

—Yong Wern Mei

Gold, Glen David (1964–) *American novelist, short story writer, and comic-book writer*

Glen David Gold is an eclectic and prolific American fiction and nonfiction writer. His debut novel, CARTER BEATS THE DEVIL (2001), received con-

siderable critical acclaim, and his follow-up novel, *Sunnyside,* appeared in 2009. Gold has also written a host of stories and articles that have appeared in such venues as *McSweeney's, Playboy,* the *Washington Post,* the *Los Angeles Times,* and the *New York Times.* He has also made recent contributions in the unexpected genre of comic-book writing for DC and *Dark Horse Comics.*

Gold was born in California in 1964 and spent his formative years in San Francisco, actually living for a time in the same neighborhood as the main character in *Carter Beats the Devil,* the historical magician known as Carter the Great (Charles Carter, 1874–1936; Rice, 2009). In 1995, Gold entered the M.F.A. program at the University of California, Irvine, where he met MICHAEL CHABON, and Gold's future wife, Alice Sebold (of *The Lovely Bones*). Prior to this, he had dabbled in a multitude of genres including fiction, nonfiction, and screenwriting for film and television (McCaw interview).

Described by his wife as "Mr. Research" (Scribner), Gold has immersed himself in all manner of subject matter and styles. He recollects magic, comic books, and the Marx Brothers as objects of childhood fascination (MacGraw), and claims to have had only a five-year love affair with comics in the mid-'70s, but that this was a formative influence in his writing career:

> When I was 13, I sent in a story to Marvel. Jim Shooter himself called me up to critique it. That turned me into a writer—it's pretty much that simple. He was of course humoring me, but also not. His attention made me take myself seriously. Which was good and bad. (Jensen interview)

In 1991, his object of fascination turned to Carter the Great after he received a vintage poster depicting Carter's notorious third act, known as "Carter Beats the Devil." Gold spent the next 10 years in city archives, researching every aspect of Carter's early 20th-century San Francisco. The result is a highly original novel of historical fiction depicting very real characters in generally plain language, all of which plunge the reader into Carter's peculiar and memorable world. While still engaged in researching *Carter*, Gold became intrigued by one of its tertiary characters, and this sideline would eventually result in the E.L. Doctorow-styled *Sunnyside*, which focuses on the character of Charlie Chaplin as a kind of heuristic portal on the rise of modernity itself, raising profound questions about the role of narrative in the face of ever-increasing contingency.

The tendency of genres like comic books to synthesize visual and textual elements in their storytelling also influences Gold's engaging style; indeed, he refers to himself as "a visual writer who can't draw." His work's extraordinary verisimilitude often prompts questions of where fact fades into fiction, but he notes that this "is, in part, verging on the old trade secret area" (Author/Profile 2001). He suggests that people take what they will from his writing, and if they question the historicity of any given detail, to seek out the answers for themselves, as the information is easily accessed. He feels that, if his writing creates blurring between fact and fiction, it is in the service of a "diagetic effect" among the members of his audience, absorption in the higher-order truth of good fiction.

Gold's *Carter* is an illustration of the current resurgence in historical persons, places, or events in popular entertainment. Sales of historical fiction titles have increased over the last decade and are now thought to comprise about 5 percent of all fiction sales worldwide (Asher 2007). This corresponds with the trend in television and film of combining accurate history dressed with story lines that reflect an alternative history, such as AMC's *Mad Men* and HBO's *Deadwood*. The textual and visual architects of the historical fiction produced today are increasingly combining fact and fiction with fewer obvious seams, resulting in increased mainstream popularity and instances of critical acclaim.

Bibliography

Asher, Levi. "Book Pricing for Literary Fiction: A Plea from Paperback Readers." Literary Kicks. Available online. URL: http://www.litkicks.com/BookPricing-Finale/. Accessed October 30, 2007.

"Author Profile: Glen David Gold." Book Reporter. Available online. URL: http://www.bookreporter.com/authors/au-gold-glen-david.asp. Accessed May 12, 2009.

Gold, Glen David. *Carter Beats the Devil.* New York: Hyperion, 2001.

———. "Exclusive Q & A: Glen David Gold (The Spirit #13)." By Van Jensen. Graphic Fiction. Available online. URL: http://graphicfiction.wordpress.com/2008/02/08/exclusive-qa-glen-david-gold-the-spirit-13/. Accessed February 8, 2008.

———. "From Master of Illusion to Master of Elusion: An Interview with Glen David Gold." By Derek McCaw. Fanboy Planet. Available online. URL: http://www.fanboyplanet.com/interviews/mc-glen-davidgold.php. Accessed May 12, 2009.

———. "Glen David Gold." By Gavin J. Grant. IndieBound. Available online. URL: http://www.indiebound.org/author-interviews/goldgd. Accessed May 12, 2009.

———. *Michael Chabon Presents The Amazing Adventures of the Escapist,* Vol. I. Milwaukie, Oreg.: Dark Horse Comics, 2004.

———. "Stacy Bierlein Talks with Glen David Gold." By Stacy Bierlein. Other Voices. Available online. URL: http://webdelsol.com/Other_Voices/GoldInt.htm. Accessed May 12, 2009.

———. *Sunnyside.* New York: Knopf, 2009.

———. *Wil Eisner's The Spirit # 13: The Holiday Issue.* DC Comics, 2008.

Schneider, Michael. "AMC conjures more dramas." *Variety,* 15 June 2008. Available online. URL: www.variety.com/article/VR1117987508.html?categoryid=1236&cs=/. Accessed October 20, 2009.

Scribner, Amy. "Dutybound: A daughter crosses the line in Alice Sebold's latest shocker." Book Pages. Available online. URL: http://www.bookpage.com/0710bp/alice_sebold.html. Accessed May 12, 2009.

———. "First Chapter of *Sunnyside* Reviewed: Interview with Glen David Gold." By Jason Rice. Three Guys, One Book. Available online. URL: http://threeguysonebook.blogspot.com/2009/01/first-chapter-of-sunnyside-reviewed-and.html. Accessed January 27, 2009.

—Stephanie Laine Hamilton

Goodman, Allegra (1967–) *American novelist and short story writer*

Having begun her publishing career at an unusually early age, Allegra Goodman is already the author of six works of fiction; two short story collections, *Total Immersion* (1989) and *The Family Markowitz* (1996); and four novels, *KAATERSKILL FALLS* (1998), *Paradise Park* (2001), *Intuition* (2006), and *The Other Side of the Island* (2008).

Goodman was born in 1967, in Brooklyn, New York, to Lenn and Madeline Goodman, college professors who two years later moved their family to Honolulu in order to assume academic posts at the University of Hawaii. Goodman's early life engendered an enthusiasm for reading literature that paralleled the "bobbing and swaying" of devout Judaism she witnessed in her local synagogue. Despite using the occasion of Shabbat services to imagine fictional stories, the Judaism of her upbringing nonetheless "rubbed off" on her ("Counting Pages"). Written in the context of her father's own intellectual sphere (he is a professor of religion), her work displays an interest in the conflicts inherent in religion, combined with those arising from the academic world. In a 1994 address to the Modern Language Association, she embraces her writing as distinctly "Jewish American" ("Writing Jewish Fiction" 268). However, Goodman's perspective on Jewishness is not static across her humorous and frequently satirical fiction. Through her characters, she often adopts different stances toward religious orthodoxy in order to reflect on the spiritual dimension of Judaism after the process of cultural assimilation described by earlier Jewish-American authors such as Saul Bellow and Philip Roth.

Goodman displayed a talent for writing very early on. Her picture-novel "Choo Choo," written at the age of seven for a school project, merited a 1975 profile of her as a child prodigy in the *Honolulu Star-Bulletin.* She continued with a precocious schedule of extracurricular reading; in fifth grade she was reading Jane Austen with a technician's eye, as her father reported to the *New York Times* in 1997. She was enrolled in Honolulu's Punahou School, where her remarkable success eventually earned her entrance to Harvard University in 1985. At the end of her first year at Harvard, she submitted a short story, "Variant Text," to the conservative Jewish magazine *Commentary,* which accepted it and published nine more stories over the following decade. "Variant Text" follows a

scholar attempting to negotiate the truth-seeking tactics of academic and religious study—a character who reappears, as many of Goodman's early characters do, in her later novels.

In 1988, Goodman received acclaim in an article on Jewish fiction in the *New York Times Book Review.* After this national recognition, a collection of stories titled *Total Immersion* was scheduled for release from Harper and Row the day of Goodman's graduation from Harvard in 1989. The "immersion" of the collection's title stems from Goodman's desire to "present the exotic as familiar," which she does even in linguistic terms by adopting the vocabulary and perspective of an "insider" in the stories, then supplementing her book with a "Glossary of Hebrew, Yiddish and Hawaiian Words." As she explains, "I write from the inside, taking . . . an idiom in which ritual and liturgy are a natural part of my fictional world, and not anthropological objects to be translated and constantly explained" (271). *Total Immersion* was later republished in 1998 with the addition of two new stories, "Onionskin" and "The Closet."

After entering the Ph.D. program in English at Stanford University in 1990, Goodman continued to publish stories in the *New Yorker* and *Commentary* throughout the early 1990s, resulting in a 1996 story cycle titled *The Family Markowitz.* In addition to already published stories, the collection presents only one entirely new story, "Fannie Mae," which reintroduces the Markowitzes, a family that first appeared in *Total Immersion* and serves as the connection between the collection's stories. "Fannie Mae" shows Rose, the matriarch of the Markowitz family, coping with the death of her second husband Maury, and attempting to reconnect with her two sons, Henry and Ed, a difficult process that plays out over the course of the collection.

In the year following the release of *The Family Markowitz,* Goodman finished her doctoral dissertation, a study of the marginalia John Keats inscribed into his pocket edition of Shakespeare, in which he reveals interpretative differences with Samuel Johnson, the volume's editor. While analyzing the divergent approaches of these two canonical figures in responding to a third, Goodman strikes a balanced "creative dynamic" in her view of an artwork as a "communicative catalyst between artist and audience" (2). Goodman's own creative concern with the material aspects of literary composition finds a natural subject of interest in the artifact of Keats's almost Talmudic marginalia. The ambiguous status of Keats's commentary hovers somewhere between critical dialogue with a deceased author (like that between the character Cecil Birnbaum and George Bernard Shaw in "Variant Text") and ruminative, self-revealing monologue (like that of Sharon Spiegelman, the disgruntled returning college student disillusioned by the lack of academic focus on life's "big questions" in "Onionskin").

Kaaterskill Falls, Goodman's long-awaited first full-length novel, was released in 1998, beginning her relationship with Dial Press. The novel has a relatively uneventful plot, but intrigues the reader with its subtle character development and personal interactions, while retaining a concern with religious heritage, generational distance, and strictness of devotion evident in the earlier stories. Continuing her interest in displacement, Goodman focuses on an upstate New York retreat for Orthodox Jewish families and followers of Rabbi Rav Elijah Kirshner over the course of two summers, as they react to one another and to the year-round local residents. The novel was a finalist for a 1998 National Book Award, and was followed in 2001 with a second novel, *Paradise Park.* Likewise drawing from her earlier stories, *Paradise Park* extends Goodman's layered satire on various modes of spiritual seeking by reworking material from her earlier story "Onionskin," a revised version of which constitutes a central chapter titled "Pilgrim."

After *Paradise Park,* Goodman slightly changes the direction of her fiction, away from matters of religion to broader issues of faith and integrity as they emerge in both science and science fiction. *Intuition,* her 2006 novel of biomedical intrigue, centers on an anxious research fellow named Cliff Bannaker, who apparently makes a momentous discovery in the field of oncology, which in the end may be a fabrication, but which, presented as a breakthrough, will certainly advance his career. The searching moral dilemmas engendered by contemporary science generate spiritual crises with no historical or scriptural precedents; and such dilemmas continue to occupy Goodman's characters

in her debut in young-adult fiction, a 2008 novel titled *The Other Side of the Island.* In the tradition of Aldous Huxley and Margaret Atwood, the novel creates a dystopia brought about by rampant industrialism and ensuing environmental disaster. The earth has been overtaken by water, and is strictly governed by a corporation called "Earth Mother"; continents have become archipelagos of institutionally numbered islands with citizens corralled into colonies; and "neighborhood watch" programs have become incorporated surveillance entities dedicated to seeking out and eliminating nonconformists, a group that increasingly includes the protagonist Honor Greenspoon's parents. The book's polemical edge is evident immediately in the nostalgic recollections of our present historical moment, a time before "the streets were air conditioned," only one generation prior to the disasters that reconfigure life on earth. While departing from the subtle analysis of the contradictions and consolations of Judaism, Goodman's writing thus retains its focus on the manifold ways in which humans interpret the world and their place in it.

Bibliography

Cronin, Gloria L. "Immersions in the Postmodern: The Fiction of Allegra Goodman." In *Daughters of Valor: Contemporary Jewish American Women Writers,* edited by Jay L. Halio and Ben Siegel, 247–267. Newark: University of Delaware Press, 1997.

Donnelly, Dave. "Novel Tale of Island Prodigy," *Honolulu Star-Bulletin,* 1 August 1997. Available online. URL: archives.starbulletin.com/97/08/01/features/donnelly.html. Accessed October 20, 2009.

Goodman, Allegra. "Counting Pages." *New Yorker,* 9 and 16 June 2008, p. 90.

———. *The Family Markowitz.* New York: Farrar, Straus & Giroux, 1996.

———. *Intuition.* New York: Dial Press, 2006.

———. *Kaaterskill Falls.* New York: Dial Press, 1998.

———. *The Other Side of the Island.* New York: Razor-Bill, 2008.

———. *Paradise Park.* New York: Dial Press, 2001.

———. *Total Immersion.* New York: Harper & Row, 1989; New York; Dell, 1998.

———. "Writing Jewish Fiction in and out of the Multicultural Context." In *Daughters of Valor: Contemporary Jewish American Women Writers,* edited by Jay L.

Halio and Ben Siegel, 268–274. Newark: University of Delaware Press, 1997.

Rimer, Sara. "A Writer without Neuroses?" *New York Times*, 26 June 1997, p. B28.

—Nicholas D. Nace

Grass Dancer, The Susan Power (1994)

Susan Power's first novel is a storytelling tour de force. A member of the Standing Rock Sioux, Power presents a tale of the force of the spirit world and the role of communal accountability. Encompassing a long period from 1864 to 1982, the novel depicts the interwoven lives of several generations of Standing Rock Sioux, and the complex patterns of interconnected events that ultimately impact the community as a whole. In common with much of contemporary Native American authorship, Power's story resists Western concepts of "*the* protagonist," opting instead for a more concentric storytelling arc, in which everyone within a community shares some role in affecting decisions, events, and outcomes—both positive and negative. Indeed, this communal, connected way of life ultimately embraces both the living and the dead, with the influence of ancestral spirits permeating, influencing, and often defining the lives of the living.

The novel tells a nonlinear story of several generations of Sioux. Some characters are introduced after their deaths, with shifting flashbacks subsequently painting in the details of their earthly lives and the persistent influence they continue to exert on the living. This is perhaps most evident in the Wind Soldier family, whose story bookends the novel. Harley Wind Soldier, a young man on the verge of adulthood, is haunted by the deaths of his father and brother four weeks before his birth, often dreaming of them crowned with broken glass and spotted with blood. Harley is further traumatized by the silence of his mother, who has not spoken a word since the day her husband died. Although he loves and honors his mother, Harley mistakenly believes that she silently grieves for a husband and son that she loves, even in death, more than her living son. However, readers discover by the novel's end that the roots of this vigilance are far more complex, as Lydia's vow of silence speaks to a cascade of events tying one generation to another. By the end of the story, Harley does not necessarily know all of the details surrounding his family history, but has learnt to accept his place in the world, both as a man and as part of the complex, inescapably connected web of human life in general, and his Sioux community in particular.

Various other thematic threads underscore the connective nature of Native American ways of considering life, death, and the spiritual. In particular, the novel deploys a storyline concerning the use of positive and negative powers of magic, and the often unintended consequences of spiritual power put to negative use. The character Red Dress and her female descendants, for example, struggle to appropriately invoke the power of magic that has been bestowed on the female line in their family. Although she herself attempts to use her power, however unwisely, to protect the people of her tribe from the destruction of the Sioux's traditional cultural existence, her grand-niece, Anna "Mercury" Thunder, turns from positive use of her magic to a life bent on manipulating, controlling, and terrorizing—even occasionally destroying—any person who interferes with her dark personal desires. However, the stories of Anna and Red Dress are as subtly complicated as that of the Wind Soldier family. Although each woman uses her power for what may seem at times indefensible purposes, the novel makes clear that the motives for such actions are often not as clear-cut as they may appear. In the case of Red Dress, for example, her intentions are to protect her people, despite the indefensibility of killing those entrapped by her magic. In Anna's case, the decision to embrace a selfish and destructive use of her power is the result of profoundly personal trauma beyond her control, lending to her actions a self-tormenting, almost Shakespearean quality.

This element of tribal magic must not be confused with modern literary devices like magical realism. As Power explains, "this is actual reality to me. It might not be another culture's reality but it is not a literary strategy for me. I'm really writing characters' reality. It never offends me when critics characterize it that way . . . it's their cultural interpretation. But I think it's a mislabeling" (Power

"Interview"). However, Power notes that neither should her novel be read as a literal representation of Indian people, cautioning, "Because my characters happen to be Indian, I worry that people read it and think, 'Oh, this is what it's like to be Sioux' or 'This is what it's like on a reservation.' This is just a human experience. If you have five different reservation Indians you are going to have five entirely different experiences . . . [the story] is really fiction. That is all it's meant to be" (Power and Oslos).

Disclaimers aside, *The Grass Dancer* offers a memorable glimpse into Sioux and Native American ideas of community, and the mutual influence of the individual and communal. Power cites her Sioux culture and her mother, as well as fellow Native American author Louise Erdrich and the plays of William Shakespeare, as major influences on her writing. Her love both of the written word and of Indian people and experience is evident in the evocative fictionalized rendering of her world; a world where Indian and non-Indian meet and negotiate meaning, where tradition and community still live in the pockets and crannies of personal experience, and where both, along with the individual, come together in a rich, constructive web of collective human experience.

Bibliography

Power, Susan. "Interview with Susan Power." By Shari Oslos. Voices from the Gap. Available online. URL: http://voices.cla.umn.edu/vg/interviews/vg_inter views/power_susan.html. Accessed October 2, 2008.
———. *The Grass Dancer.* 1994. New York: Berkley Books, 1995.

—Constance J. Bracewell

Graver, Elizabeth (1964–   ) *American novelist and short story writer*

Elizabeth Graver is the author of one short story collection and three novels. Her first book, *Have You Seen Me?* won the 1991 Drue Heinz Literature Prize for short fiction, while her novels, *Unravelling* and *The HONEY THIEF*, were named *New York Times* Notable Books of the Year in 1997 and 1999. Graver received fellowships from the National Endowment for the Arts and the Guggenheim Foundation, and her short pieces have been anthologized in, among many other publications, *Best American Short Stories, Best American Essays,* and *Prize Stories: The O. Henry Awards.*

Graver was born in 1964 and grew up in Williamstown, Massachusetts, where her parents taught English at Williams College. She attended Wesleyan University, majoring in English, and studied with the writer Annie Dillard, then went on to receive her M.F.A. from Washington University, where she worked with Stanley Elkin, Deborah Eisenberg, and Angela Carter. Graver completed several years of graduate study at Cornell before returning to Boston in 1991. She currently is a professor of literature and creative writing at Boston College. She lives near Boston with her husband and two daughters.

Critics praise Graver's work for its carefully researched settings, which vary widely from book to book. In an interview with Ben Birnbaum, she speaks of her research as integral to her writing process: rather than writing from biographical experience, she creates "new worlds . . . that speak to the one everybody lives in but also have their own shape, their own thickness and texture." Her short story collection *Have You Seen Me?* includes 10 stories that focus largely on incidents in the daily life of children and young people who are trying to come to terms with loss. Her second book and first novel, *Unravelling*, is about a young girl, Aimee Slater, who leaves her New Hampshire farm to work in the textile mills at Lowell, Massachusetts, in the mid-19th century. Graver's second novel, *The Honey Thief*, recounts how a reclusive beekeeper mediates the relationship between Miriam Baruch and her young daughter, Eva, during the summer in which they move from New York City to the country because Miriam wants to give her daughter "a safe and healthy" home (22). Graver's third and latest novel is *Awake* (2004), narrated by Anna Simon, a woman who discovers her own ambivalence about marriage and motherhood while attending a camp with her son, Max, who has a life-threatening light-sensitivity disorder.

Many of Graver's short stories, and all of her novels, revolve around mothers and children—their relationships to each other as well as their struggles to establish and maintain identities while making sense of shared and individual losses. She is consistently praised for careful and convincing depictions of childhood and adolescence; her children come to life with secret thoughts, desires, and hidden losses that are often misunderstood by the adults around them. In addition, all three novels explore the dynamic nature of parenthood, "the bewildering cycles of delight and frustration that . . . lie at the center of the nurturer's experience" (DeMott). The mothers in Graver's fiction confront but never quite solve the puzzle of how to keep their children safe while allowing individuality and imaginative exploration of the world. And *Awake* offers an unflinching view of the conflicts, mixed motives, and selfish desires that the job of nurturing both causes and conceals.

Driven more by character than plot, Graver's work focuses on interiority and emotion, and these focal points link her work to that of George Eliot and Virginia Woolf, whom she names as artistic influences. Suzanne LeFetra writes:

> Graver's books feature little dialogue between characters and are devoid of . . . zigzagging plot twists. The twists she explores are more internal: these are the intimate coils of personality, the often ambiguous convolutions of true human emotion.

One way Graver reveals her characters' interior lives is by examining the constant and minute processes by which they react and adjust to the circumstances that constrain them and the losses that haunt them. Her protagonists often react to such situations with imaginative acts that they alternately use as staging grounds for, escape from, or means of adjusting to reality. In the story "Around the World," for example, Hannah, who lives with a debilitating arm injury, imagines a life without pain: "In my farthest reaches I go where I have no weight, where weight means nothing—underwater, or on the moon, and I am not alone, but touching fingers with a ring of bundled astronauts" (19). Likewise, Anna of *Awake* imagines a world where a slight alteration in genetics would have given her a different, healthy son; Miriam of *The Honey Thief* ponders whether to continue to tell Eva romanticized stories of her father's life, or the truth about his mental illness and death; and Aimee of

Unravelling says of her estranged mother, "I go to see my mother in my mind" (272). All these acts of imagination—dreams, daydreams, lies, stories—give the reader a measure of a character's emotional response to the world, as well as sympathetic insight into their struggles both to make sense of past loss and to adjust to their present life.

Critics note that Graver avoids the easy, sentimental, or generic plots and resolutions that often plague contemporary affect-focused fiction; Demott's analysis of Aimee Slater's emotional progress is typical: "The movement forward . . . is humanly erratic, never sanctimonious, and is interrupted time and again by re-engagement with loss." Instead of sidestepping or trivializing the emotional struggles of her characters by neatly resolving conflicts, Graver's novels end by leaving characters in play, still struggling to make sense of themselves and their relationships with others and the world.

Bibliography

Burns, Carole. "Off the Page: Elizabeth Graver." WashingtonPost.com. Available online. URL: http://www.washingtonpost.com/wp-dyn/articles/A44485-2004Apr2.html. Accessed May 10, 2009.

DeMott, Benjamin. Review of *Unravelling*, New York Times on the Web (August 17, 1997). Available online. URL: www.newyorktimes.com/books/97/08/17/reviews/970817.17demott.html. Accessed October 20, 2009.

Graver, Elizabeth. *Awake*. New York: Henry Holt, 2004.

———. *Have You Seen Me?* Pittsburgh: University of Pennsylvania Press, 1991.

———. *The Honey Thief*. New York: Harcourt, 1999.

———. *Unravelling*. New York: Harcourt, Brace, 1997.

LaFetra, Suzanne. "Head Trip." Literary Mama. Available online. URL: http://www.literarymama.com/reviews/archives/000702.html. Accessed May 12, 2009.

—Maureen Benes

Gun, With Occasional Music Jonathan Lethem (1994)

In JONATHAN LETHEM's debut novel, the genres of science fiction and hard-boiled detective story are fused. But *Gun, With Occasional Music* goes beyond clever spoofing or homage paying. Its recombination of disparate genre elements, and the resulting depth of intertextual and thematic resonance, not only betray an intimate knowledge of its sources (most notably Raymond Chandler and Philip K. Dick) but also result in an intelligent and engaging experiment in hybridity. It was nominated for a Best Novel Nebula Award in 1994.

The story line follows protagonist and narrator Conrad Metcalf, a jaded, wisecracking gumshoe, through a cartoonishly dystopian near-future Oakland. He is hired by Orton Angwine, a hapless would-be blackmailer who is being framed for the murder of Maynard Stanhunt, a doctor and former client of Metcalf. In the course of his investigations, Metcalf encounters and trades barbs (and sometimes blows) with a cast of characters straight out of a Philip Marlowe case—dope doctors and dangerous dames, crooked cops and shadowy racketeers, as well as a talking kangaroo thug. The sprawling plot is also a direct Chandler transplant in that the original case provides merely the starting point, the occasion for a convoluted and confusing array of loosely related incidents that for the most part relegate the classic whodunit to the margins. And these collateral incidents are more violent, more grisly, and point to much deeper and more unpleasant aspects of society than the initial case. *Gun*'s fictional world reflects to some extent the model of Huxley's classic dystopia *Brave New World*, but its most distinctive elements (mind-altering drugs, an oppressive police machine, the devaluation of information and the media, a pervasive sense of entropy), as well as its focus on the underdog and the underbelly of society, recall the paranoid, drug-fueled worlds of Philip K. Dick. And like its predecessors, the novel explores the cumulative effect of these elements in the elimination of human autonomy and free will.

The society's penal system is based on karmic points, which are stored on a card and can be deducted and augmented by policemen called inquisitors. Once the karmic points run out, a person is considered karma-defunct and sent to the "freezer," which in this case is literal: jail time is spent in suspended animation. Information is hard to come by, as broadcast news is conveyed through instrumental music, and newspapers have to rely on pictures only. Evolution therapy takes care of genetic destiny, producing evolved animals that serve as menial workers and have legal subhuman status. Segregation is common (evolved animals are not allowed in many bars and other establishments), and killing an evolved animal is not considered murder. In humans, natural infant development is replaced by a process that speeds intellectual maturation but stunts growth. The products are "babyheads" (a term reminiscent of Dick's similarly evolved adult "bubbleheads" in *The Three Stigmata of Palmer Eldritch*): creatures with the intellect of adults, the bodies of infants, the emotional turmoil of adolescents, and a bloated and disfigured head—a combination that results, unsurprisingly, in highly neurotic and alienated individuals. "Make," the drug that nearly everyone in the novel habitually uses, is a powdered blend of various chemical agents that functions to repress or modify memories and their emotional impact. Their names—Avoidol, Forgettol, Acceptol, Regrettol, and the common base substance addictol—are self-explanatory.

Metcalf himself is clearly a fictive descendant of Philip Marlowe, not only in his wry, self-deprecating, and wisecracking narrative voice, but also in his unorthodox integrity and adherence to the professional code—he refuses to give up the case, for example, despite severe personal consequences—as well as in his volatile relationship to women and strong inclination toward substance abuse. Some of the science fiction elements effectively complement and emphasize these features. Asking questions is considered extremely rude, which puts a professional investigator like Metcalf automatically at odds with society, and highlights the traditional trope of the PI as troublemaker, a transgressive force in a deeply repressive society. Metcalf's tortured masculinity and misogyny is given a tangible basis in a neurological gender swap, which has left him with the sexual nerve endings of a woman. Finally, Marlowe's latent racism and classism are recalled in the deep unease and resentment Metcalf harbors toward evolved animals.

The juxtaposition of a surreal futuristic world with an anachronistic detective figure highlights the human drama of an individual deeply at odds with his society. When Metcalf returns from a six-year stint in the freezer, his world has deteriorated even further: it is now illegal to retain memories except in a highly edited tape-recorded version; a government-issued, particularly debilitating Forgettol-blend of Make is mandatory; and the profession of private inquisitor has now been outlawed. It is in this climate of total repression of individual autonomy that the incompatibility of Metcalf and his surroundings becomes absolute; and his dogged determination to solve the case and rehabilitate his client lead to a chain of decisions that, though outwardly defeatist, ultimately express a desperate, against-the-odds hope for a better future.

The novel's most notable stylistic feature, apart from its narrative voice, is the literalization of similes and metaphors, and their insertion into the fabric of the fictional world. The novel commences, for example, with an epigraph taken from Chandler's *Playback*—"the subject was as easy to spot as a kangaroo in a dinner jacket"—and then proceeds to introduce Joey the kangaroo thug. The "freezer" takes the hard-boiled cliché for a jail to its literal extreme of suspended animation, as well as recalling one of Lethem's own short stories, "The Hardened Criminals," in which calcified prisoners constitute the building blocks of their own prison. This emphasis on textuality finds its most vivid expression late in the book, when the titular gun that plays its own threatening "occasional music" orchestrates a climax of cheesy film noir. Besides intensifying the surreality and alienation of Metcalf's world, it highlights the artificiality of this world, its essential "madeness" out of genre components almost universally recognizable in a society with strong cultural roots in television and dime novels.

And it is mostly this textual foregrounding, along with the novel's affable humor and focus on the human drama of Conrad Metcalf, that sets *Gun, With Occasional Music* apart from cyberpunk, a genre that also mixes elements of science fiction with a noir atmosphere, but to largely different ends. In its literary ambition and textual density the novel is closer to the work of postmodern fabulists such as Vonnegut, Pynchon, or DeLillo, while its playful pop-culture sensibility prefigures more recent genre experiments, such as Max Brook's *World War Z: An Oral History of the Zombie Wars,* or Austin Grossman's superhero novel, *Soon I Will Be Invincible.*

Bibliography

Chandler, Raymond. *Playback.* 1958. Reprint, New York: Vintage, 1988.

Dick, Philip K. *The Three Stigmata of Palmer Eldritch.* 1965. Reprint, New York: Vintage, 1991.

Huxley, Aldous. *Brave New World.* 1932. Reprint, New York: Perennial, 2006.

Lethem, Jonathan. *Gun, With Occasional Music.* 1994. Reprint, New York: Tor, 1995.

———. "The Hardened Criminals." In *The Wall of the Eye, the Wall of the Sky,* 172–210. 1996. Reprint, New York: Faber & Faber, 2002.

—Martina Sitling

H

Haddon, Mark (1962–) *British novelist and children's book writer*

Mark Haddon is a British author and illustrator of children's books, novels, and poetry. His first book primarily for adults, *The CURIOUS INCIDENT OF THE DOG IN THE NIGHT-TIME*, was published in 2003 and won several awards, including the Whitbread Book of the Year and the Los Angeles Times's Art Seidenbaum Award for First Fiction. Told from the perspective of a teenager with Asperger's syndrome (a form of autism), the book fuses mystery and a coming-of-age tale to create a work rich in compassion, insight, and humor. He has since published another novel, *A Spot of Bother* (2006), and a collection of poetry entitled *The Talking Horse and the Sad Girl and the Village under the Sea* (2005).

Born in Northampton in 1962, Haddon studied English literature at Oxford University, graduating in 1981. He earned his master's degree at Edinburgh University, again studying English literature. In Scotland, he worked as a caregiver for disabled people at Mencap, inspiring his creation of Christopher John Francis Boone, the narrator of the best-selling *The Curious Incident of the Dog in the Night-Time*. Although this novel is called his debut, he had been writing and illustrating children's books for nearly two decades by the time of its publication. He remarked in the *Observer*, "I started writing books for children because I could illustrate them myself and because, in my innocence, I thought they'd be easier. I was wrong, of course" ("B is for bestseller"). His first book, a chil-

dren's book entitled *Gilbert's Gobbstopper*, was published in 1987. He is also the author of the popular *Agent Z* series about three boys—Ben, Barney, and Jenks—collectively known as The Crane Grove Crew. Books in the series include *Agent Z Meets the Masked Crusader* (1993), *Agent Z Goes Wild* (1994), *Agent Z and the Penguin from Mars* (1995), and *Agent Z and the Killer Bananas* (2001). In 1996, *Agent Z and the Penguin from Mars* was adapted for BBC1 television.

Haddon's work in children's literature has translated well to television, where he has written for several children's series, including *The Wild House, Microsoap,* and *Starstreet*. In addition, he adapted Raymond Briggs's *Fungus the Bogeyman* for the BBC in 2004. His efforts have won multiple awards, including two BAFTAs in 1999, one of which was a special award for his contribution to children's television.

Haddon gained widest acclaim with his first work of fiction for adults, yet even this admired book has the distinction of having two editions simultaneously published: one for children, one for adults (Holcombe). The narrator of *The Curious Incident of the Dog in the Night-Time* is Christopher John Francis Boone, a 15-year-old boy from Swindon who finds his neighbor Mrs. Shears's dog dead in her front yard and decides to find the murderer. Although he is never explicitly identified as autistic, it becomes clear through his behavior and idiosyncrasies that he is, and Haddon has said in interviews that the character has Asperger's syndrome ("B is for bestseller"). To realize Christopher's world, Haddon integrates mathematical problems, pictures, musings, and random thoughts into the overarching narrative of Christopher's search for the dog's killer. Christopher is endearing without being pathetic; he seems to be unable to understand emotions. The novel's representation of autism brought renewed attention to the disorder as well as a greater public understanding of its cognitive implications. The book was enormously popular in the United Kingdom and abroad, winning various prizes and staying atop the U.K. best-seller list for over a year.

In 2006, *A Spot of Bother* was published and short-listed for Costa Novel of the Year (the new name of the Whitbread, which Haddon had won for *The Curious Incident of the Dog in the Night-Time*). Here Haddon continued his interest in psychological drama with George, a 61-year-old recently retired hypochondriac. George fears he may have cancer and nearly bleeds to death removing an otherwise innocuous lesion. His wife, Jean, is having an affair with George's former coworker, while his daughter Katie announces plans to marry Ray, a man who does not meet the expectations of his future in-laws. Meanwhile, George's son Jamie, who has recently come out, quarrels with his lover, Tony. Anxiety plagues George, as the tension continues to rise in the darkly comic family drama. The novel received favorable reviews, but did not equal the success of Haddon's first novel.

Haddon is married to Sos Eltis, an English fellow at Brasnose College, and resides in Oxford with her and their two children. He occasionally teaches for the Arvon Foundation, a charity that encourages creative writing.

Throughout his work, Haddon's empathy for those who are frequently overlooked is clear; be it a child, an autistic teenager, or a lonely retiree. His meticulous portrayals help to re-envision the world from these characters' perspectives and undermine the social stereotypes that lead to their initial marginalization. Haddon exhibits great skill not only in illustrating characters' anxieties, but also in rendering them in a manner that is neither sentimental nor maudlin. Particularly in *The Curious Incident of the Dog in the Night-Time*, he deftly

suggests that those who are considered "normal" have just as many problems, if not more, than the "special" narrator; Christopher's rational approach highlights the ironies and hypocrisies that structure everyday existence, calling into question who is "normal," and even the very notion of objective "normalcy."

For his insightful depiction of an isolated, insular individual, Haddon has been compared to Kazuo Ishiguro, whose butler Mr. Stevens leads a memorable life of quiet desperation in *The Remains of the Day*. But Jay McInerney, in a back-handed compliment in his review of Haddon's first novel, remarks that Christopher's "range of emotional response is so limited he makes the repressed butler in Kazuo Ishiguro's *Remains of the Day*—a novel that this one resembles in its elegant economy of means—seem like Zorba the Greek" ("Remains of the Dog"). Haddon's exploration of developmental disorders draws further comparison to William Faulkner's *The Sound and the Fury* and Daniel Keyes's *Flowers for Algernon*, though it should be noted that as someone with Asperger's syndrome, Christopher neither has the typical verbal difficulties associated with autism, nor is he mentally disabled like Benjy Compson or Charlie Gordon. Haddon's skill and sensitivity in depicting the all-too-often silenced members of society, and his keen awareness, humor, and consideration, mark him as a distinctive, engaging voice in contemporary English fiction, epitomizing his own insight that "Reading is a conversation. All books talk. But a good book listens as well" ("B is for bestseller").

Bibliography

Haddon, Mark. "B is for bestseller." (April 11, 2004). *Observer.* Available online. URL: http://www.guardian.co.uk/books/2004/apr/11/booksforchildrenandteenagers.features3. Accessed April 29, 2009.

———. "Mark Haddon—CV." Mark Haddon. Available online. URL: http://www.markhaddon.com/cv.htm. Accessed April 29, 2009.

Holcombe, Garan. "Mark Haddon." Contemporary Writers in the UK. Available online. URL: http://www.contemporarywriters.com/authors/?p=auth3e38026813f8c194e5nnw1cf3087. Accessed April 29, 2009.

McInerney, Jay. Review of *The Curious Incident of the Dog in the Night-Time*. New York Times Online. Available online. URL:http://www.nytimes.com/2003/06/15/books/the-remains-of-the-dog.html. Accessed April 29, 2009.

—Peter Kunze

Hagy, Alyson (1960–) *American novelist and short story writer*

Alyson Hagy is the author of three collections of short fiction, *Madonna on Her Back* (1986), *Hardware River* (1991), and *Graveyard of the Atlantic* (2000), and two novels, KEENELAND (2000) and *Snow, Ashes* (2007). Her stories have appeared in venues such as *Shenandoah, Five Points,* and the *Virginia Quarterly Review* and on National Public Radio, and have been awarded a Nelson Algren Prize, a Syndicated Fiction Prize, and a Pushcart Prize, while "Search Bay" (included in *Graveyard of the Atlantic*) was selected for the *Best American Short Stories* of 1997. Hagy has been a fellow of the National Endowment for the Arts.

She was born in 1960, and raised on a farm in the Blue Ridge Mountains of Virginia, an upbringing later reflected in the rugged and deeply rooted heartland that forms a fictive backdrop for much of her oeuvre, against which the often complex and sophisticated emotional lives of her characters are played out. She was the child of country physician John Albert Hagy and homemaker Carol Elaine Lindsay, while her grandparents were ministers, blacksmiths, and schoolteachers, and this familial context is itself reflected in her frequent allusions to and explorations of vocational life.

By the age of eight, Hagy had already penned three detective tales in the style of the Nancy Drew mysteries she adored, and she was writing seriously before turning 20, opting for the vocation of a writer halfway through her undergraduate studies at Williams College in Massachusetts. During her time at college she read avidly and widely, and filled countless notebooks with journal writing, poetry, and fiction. After graduation, she entered the creative writing program in the University of Michigan, graduating with an M.F.A. Currently, she lives in Laramie, Wyoming, and teaches at the University of Wyoming.

Hagy's debut short story collection, *Madonna on Her Back* (1986), which won the Hopwood Award for Short Fiction, is made up of eight skillfully crafted and vivid tales of people, often women, and often isolated or at a loss, struggling to make sense of their own existence. Located for the most part in rural and southern settings, the deceptive passional simplicity of the narratives often masks subtle stylistic modulations, in voice (as in the internal dialogue between a mother and child in "Mr. Makes"), tone, or perspective. Similar formal and thematic concerns are apparent in Hagy's follow-up collection, *Hardware River* (1991), but here the focus—though remaining sharp as ever—widens to include a variety of male experience, and above all, the complex interplay of social relations, and the place of the individual within them. Though the voice is typically lyrical and first-person, the vividness and resonance of the described experience infuse the stories with universal relevance.

The year 2000 marked a banner year for Hagy, with the publication of both her third story collection, the haunting *Graveyard of the Atlantic,* and her first novel, *Keeneland.* The former is a brooding, evocative, and ultimately metaphorical exploration of life on and by the sea, with six of its seven tales located on the Outer Banks of North Carolina, and with its characters at times almost seeming human extensions of marine life, moving with that strange aquatic stoicism of fish, punctured by sudden flashes of emotion. With the critically acclaimed *Keeneland,* Hagy returns to her rural roots, chronicling the fall and double fall of 27-year-old Kerry Connolly, who retreats to her native rural Kentucky, bruised and broke (but for the $10,000 she has stashed in the trunk of her car) from a broken marriage to wealthy but abusive husband Eric Ballard, who has kept her beloved mare, Sunny. She descends on the familiar (and famed) Keeneland stables, recovering her old job as a stable girl. What then ensues reads in the abstract like a tragedy of folly and loss, but Kerry's indefatigable resilience and rugged, lively wit turn what could have been a tragedy into a comic voyage of self-exploration, and one that culminates, if not in any visible gain, yet in just the sort of hard-won wisdom that tends to prefigure one. And Hagy's tale leaves the reader similarly enriched, almost grateful for the lack of any straightforward narrative resolution.

With her latest and most ambitious work, *Snow, Ashes* (2007), Hagy dramatically extends her novelistic reach, telling a stark and compelling tale of traumatic memory, friendship, and healing. Having retired from his sheep business four years before, John Fremont Adams, 64, is snug but unfulfilled in his life on a 36,000-acre sheep ranch in Baggs, Wyoming, when childhood friend and Korean War buddy C.D. Hobbs suddenly appears and turns that life upside down. Both had returned damaged, physically and psychologically, by their traumatic experience in the war but reacted in opposite ways, Adams curling up defensively in his ranching life and Hobbs wandering restless as Cain, in and out of Adams's artificially stabilized existence. With searing flashbacks to the Korean conflict, and a penetrating and unflinching style, drawing in many ways from the best of Hagy's lyrical short story work, the narrative builds slowly but implacably, like a high-plains storm, until it breaks loose in an inevitable and disturbingly memorable conclusion.

Bibliography

Hagy, Alyson. *Graveyard of the Atlantic.* St. Paul, Minn.: Graywolf Press, 2000.
———. *Hardware River.* New York: Poseidon Press, 1991.
———. *Keeneland.* New York: Simon & Schuster, 2000.
———. *Madonna on Her Back.* Baltimore: Stuart Wright, 1986.
———. *Snow, Ashes.* St. Paul, Minn.: Graywolf Press, 2007.

—Doug Melrose

Half in Love **Maile Meloy** (2002)

MAILE MELOY's multiple award-winning first fiction collection offers 14 short but powerful stories whose unifying theme is the inner turmoil of their characters. Each of the stories in *Half in Love* captures its protagonist at a point in life when he or she is suffering a profound internal struggle, caught between moments of intense feeling and the routine events of quotidian life. This struggle for a sense of harmony, often amid commingled feelings of exhilaration and despair, situate the characters in similar circumstances, despite the different backgrounds, locations, and time periods in which their stories take place.

This conflict of emotion, and the struggle for balance between one's own wishes and the hard facts of reality, are particularly evident in stories like "Four Lean Hounds, ca.1976," whose protagonist, Hank, finds himself simultaneously dealing with acute sorrow brought on by the loss of his best friend, Duncan, and his own sexual attraction to Duncan's grieving wife, Kay. Adding to his despair is the realization of a possible affair that may have taken place between Duncan and Hank's own wife, Demeter. This unspoken possibility leaves Hank walking a fine line between the love he feels for his friends and his own wife, and anger at Duncan and Demeter's betrayal. But even as he struggles with the pain caused by this realization, he cannot ignore his own conflicted desire for Kay.

The characters in the collection's other stories are in a similar state of emotional flux, and as the collection's title suggests, typically discover that they are at least partially in love with someone, or some notion, while at the same time finding themselves at odds with the world around them. Often this revelation has its origins in deep grief, and many of the stories deal with either recent or impending death, and the confusing mixture of emotions that come into play when one is facing great loss.

In Meloy's stories, this profound sense of loss is not always limited to the death of a loved one or a friend; often the suffering or loss of an animal serves not only as a catalyst prompting characters' emotional conflicts, but also as a symbol of something deeper going on within them, such as tension in a close personal relationship. The latter is illustrated in stories like "Kite Whistler Aquamarine" and "A Stakes Horse," both of which are set on the horse ranches of Meloy's familiar childhood territory of Montana. The protagonists, in the business of breeding and racing horses (a frequent element in Meloy's stories), are deeply attached to their animals, which often function as metaphors for the tension between them and other characters in the stories. In "Kite Whistler Aquamarine," for example, the strained relationship between Cort and his wife is intimated in the conversations they have regarding the foal he is caring for. Similarly, in "A Stakes Horse," Addy's desperate actions concerning her promising racing filly, Rocky, reflects the desperate situation of her ailing father, which is further complicated by her feelings for Connell, her father's jockey, who also happens to be her ex-husband.

Another common element in the collection is the fear of losing those people and things that are most important, as illustrated in "Aqua Boulevard," which won Meloy the *Paris Review*'s Aga Khan Prize for Fiction in 2001. The tale takes place in Paris, and tells the story of a man who runs into a woman he used to know, who was once the wife of his dearest friend, Renard. The protagonist's sudden, unexpected meeting with Mia causes him to reflect on his own life—his child from his first marriage, his new wife who is almost as young as his first son, and their two small children, Alix and Gaétan. Even though he does not speak to Mia of Renard's death, the memory of his friend's drowning stays with him after their meeting and, while he does not seem to realize it, fills him with anxiety that finally compels him to seek out his young children (attending a party at Aqua Boulevard) to reassure himself that nothing has happened, and they are safe.

The stories that make up *Half in Love* examine intimate personal relationships, and the unspoken intricacies upon which they often unstably rest. While the writing is vivid and sure, and the focus often seems to be on some primary incident in the lives of the characters, it soon becomes apparent that there is much more going on beneath the surface: struggles against loss, bafflement before the seemingly inevitable changes taking place in their lives, and a haunting, almost ineffable sense of sadness and aloneness. But as the ambivalent title suggests, even such sadness is incomplete, always exceeded and somehow encompassed by fractions of hope and possibility.

Half in Love received the prestigious PEN/Malamud Award for Excellence in Short Fiction in 2003, the John C. Zacharis Award from *Ploughshares*, and the American Academy of Arts and Letters' Rosenthal Foundation Award. Meloy's other works include the novels *Liars and Saints* and *A Family Daughter*.

Bibliography

Meloy, Maile. *A Family Daughter: A Novel.* New York: Scribner, 2007.
———. *Half in Love.* New York: Scribner, 2002.
———. *Liars and Saints: A Novel.* New York: Scribner, 2004.

—Angela Craig

Half of a Yellow Sun Chimamanda Ngozi Adichie (2006)

Half of a Yellow Sun is a heart-wrenching account of the Biafran struggle for independence from Nigeria during the Nigeria-Biafra War of 1967–70. Effortlessly weaving historical realities together with her fictional narrative, CHIMAMANDA NGOZI ADICHIE brings the horrors and hopes of this war to life through her development of a memorable cast of characters, including twin sisters Olanna and Kainene, Olanna's "revolutionary" lover Odenigbo, Odenigbo's houseboy Ugwu, and Richard, a white British man who comes to Africa because he has fallen in love with Igbo art but stays because he falls in love with Kainene, and, ultimately, with the Biafran cause.

Adichie's debut novel, *PURPLE HIBISCUS* (2003), dealt with themes of familial strife, the oppression and abuse of women, and the widespread corruption found within politics, all of which are themes present also in *Half of a Yellow Sun.* However, *Purple Hibiscus* is primarily the coming-of-age story of a teenage girl; *Half of a Yellow Sun*, although still focusing closely on the personal lives of the characters in a style similar to *Purple Hibiscus,* is ultimately a much more ambitious project. This second novel tackles not only the violent coming apart of a nation, but also the irresponsibility and inaction of the rest of the world as Biafra is wracked by starvation, massacres, poverty, and deaths numbering in the millions.

Perhaps the most surprising aspect of the novel is the ease with which it weaves together the horrifying tragedies of war and the continuation of quotidian life. The story, which divides itself into four parts—moving back and forth between the prewar years of the early 1960s and the more tumultuous years of the late 1960s—devotes as much time to the personal traumas of the main characters as it does to the more widespread impacts of the war. At the heart of the novel, in fact, are the individual burdens and betrayals that these characters struggle with: Olanna's and Odenigbo's acts of infidelity; Richard's longing to "belong" to Biafra as a white British man and as Kainene's lover; Olanna's preoccupation with her family's fall from a comfortable, middle-class life of affluence to the humiliations of life in a refugee camp; Odenigbo's dreams of bringing about revolutionary freedom, which fail to materialize as he is haunted by the death of his mother and rendered virtually impotent by his bouts with alcohol. All of these suggest that even in the midst of war and genocide, the everyday concerns of people's private lives can continue to consume them.

Nevertheless, stunning tragedies abound throughout the novel, shattering any sense that the war is merely background. The tale is replete with the unforgettable: a woman on a train carrying her child's head in a calabash; the death of Kainene's servant Ikejide, whose head is cleanly sliced off by a piece of shrapnel as he runs to take cover during an air raid; the multiple rapings of a young bar maid by Biafran soldiers; the slitting open of pregnant women's stomachs before they are left to die; and the swollen bellies and yellowed skin of children dying from kwashiorkor (one such starving boy is playing "war" in the street with his friends one day, and is buried in a small grave dug by fellow refugees the next).

The ability of much of the rest of the world to ignore these tragedies, to "never *actively* remember death," is a major theme of Adichie's work (415). Included in the novel are eight sub-sections of a narrative work-in-progress, written by one of the characters and entitled *The World Was Silent When We Died*. Its author, whose identity remains unclear to us until the final page of the novel, undertakes the task of trying to write the political, economic, and social histories of Nigeria—both pre- and post-independence—and Biafra, as well as the ways in which the rest of the world ignores Biafra's suffering during the war. One section of the book asks, "there were photos displayed in gloss-filled pages of your *Life*. Did you see? Did you feel sorry briefly, Then turn round to hold your lover or wife?" (470).

> Yet, even as much of the work serves as an indictment of the inaction of other nations throughout the war (particularly Western powerhouses such as Britain and the United States), Adichie also subtly suggests that the lines between perpetrator and victim are not always so easily discerned. Ugwu, for example, learns that the "heroic" military life he was eager to become a part of is actually one of "casual cruelty," and that, in many ways, the Biafran soldiers—himself included—are no different than the Nigerians they fight against (450). Olanna, too, suggests that "we are all capable of doing the same things to one another, really"; indeed, *all* of the main characters are able to inflict violence or harm upon others with the same relative ease with which they dream of a new nation free of suffering and oppression. (222)

The structure of Adichie's novel is one that refuses to grant authority to any one voice. Rather than providing a linear historical account of the war, *Half of a Yellow Sun* is disjointed and fragmented, moving continuously between different time periods as well as between the very different narrative perspectives of Olanna, Ugwu, and Richard. These multiple perspectives, as well as the use of third-person narration, imply a hesitance to present any one "version" of the war as the complete "truth." Instead, the novel ultimately suggests that there are countless ways in which the experiences of war can be represented. The budding voice of Ugwu as a young writer struggling to capture the multiple realities of the "Life of a Country" reminds us of the difficulty of telling these stories in ways that will do them justice; and the questions of memory and representation that he tackles are two of the major themes shaping the novel itself (530).

Like other works such as John Alfred Williams's *Clifford's Blues* (1999) and Terry George's 2004 film *Hotel Rwanda*, *Half of a Yellow Sun* seeks to simultaneously recover and re-create memories of a mass genocide, whose victims have been forgotten by much of the world. Although recognized as a work of great literary worth, Adichie's novel ultimately serves the much larger political purpose of asking readers not only never to forget those killed in the Biafran war, but also never again to remain silent as others die.

Bibliography

Adichie, Chimamanda Ngozi. *Half of a Yellow Sun*. New York: Anchor Books, 2006.

———. *Purple Hibiscus*. New York: Anchor Books, 2003.

Hotel Rwanda. Directed by Terry George. Lions Gates Films and United Artists, 2004.

Williams, John A. *Clifford's Blues*. Minneapolis: Coffee House Press, 1999.

—Melissa Dennihy

Hansen, Brooks (UNKNOWN) *American novelist, screenwriter, and memoirist*

Raised in New York City and educated at Harvard University, where he met one-time co-author and friend Nick Davis, Brooks Hansen describes himself as an "author, screenwriter, and sometime illustrator" (Web site). Since the time of his first book-length publication, a coauthored novel in 1990, Hansen has written five novels, a memoir, and a book of fiction for children; the first four novels were all selected for the *New York Times* Notable Books list. The fifth, *John the Baptizer*, published by W.W. Norton in 2009, offers a fictional account of John the Baptist's life and history. Putting an original spin on an ancient and oft heard tale, Hansen writes Jesus as a secondary character and John as the focus of the narrative, while positing the two as greater rivals than many have believed. In so doing, he explores with great penetration the religious factions existing at the time of both men's ministries, and how these groups perceived one another. Hansen is quick to note that, rather than inventing the plot for his novel, he relied on often overlooked passages from the Bible itself, and then added his own fictive interpretations.

Hansen made his debut with the critically acclaimed *Boone* (1990), coauthored with Nick Davis, a lively account of the life and times of one Eton Arthur Boone, a fictional Greenwich Village comic with a colorful cult following. But it was the intricate and compelling fantasy, *The CHESS GARDEN: OR THE TWILIGHT LETTERS OF GUSTAV UYTERHOEVEN* (1995), that brought Hansen into critical and popular prominence, selected as a *New York Times* Notable Book for 1995. In an interview, Hansen mentions both Hans Christian Andersen and Roald Dahl as subtle influences on his work (Vandermeer), which shares with theirs a fascination not merely with the fantastic per se, but with its often profound aesthetic and moral relation to the "real." Here, the latter is represented by life in small-town Ohio, with the backyard "chess garden" of the Uyterhoevens a social and imaginative focal point for the community. In striking contrast, but linked to it by innumerable narrative and stylistic filaments, is Dr. Uyterhoeven's (ultimately imaginary) universe of "the Antipodes," scene of a host of the doctor's engaging, bizarre, and comical adventures. Against this already rich and nuanced backdrop, is a poignant treatment of the family life of Dr. and Mrs. Uyterhoeven, detailing marital troubles, career gains and losses, spiritual yearnings, and unexpected tragedy.

Hansen followed the extraordinary success of *The Chess Garden* with the modest but charming *Caesar's Antlers* (1997), a children's tale about the loyalties of love and friendship in the (all but fantastic) environment of wintry Norway, which includes illustrations by the author. *Pearlman's Ordeal* (2000) and *The Monster of St. Helena* (2003) are both extended works of historical fiction, the former attempting a full-blown re-creation of the lost city of Atlantis, the latter describing in compelling detail the exile of Napoleon Bonaparte on St. Helena in 1815.

Hansen released his first nonfiction work in 2008, a memoir entitled *The Brotherhood of Joseph*, which describes his and his wife's ongoing challenges with infertility. Since contemporary fertility memoirs are typically female-authored, Hansen's memoir fills a niche in the literary market, as it relates their struggles from the man's perspective. Although simultaneously exploring medical options, Hansen and his wife investigate adoption, a painstaking process that proves ultimately successful. The chronicle has been praised as offering the "heart-wrenching saga of parental desire and societal shame written, for once, from the perspective of a man" (Kettman).

Hansen's oeuvre often draws from a strong sense of spirituality that he describes on his Web site as rooted in Catholicism, but mingled and leavened with other, more liberal outlooks—his tastes as well as his skills being catholic in the widest sense. After having lived most of his life in New York City, Hansen recently relocated in 2007 to California with his wife, Elizabeth, whom he has known since childhood, and Theo and Ada, their two children and the focus of *The Brotherhood of Joseph*.

Bibliography

Hansen, Brooks. *The Brotherhood of Joseph*. Emmaus, Pa.: Modern Times, 2008.

———. *Caesar's Antlers*. New York: Farrar, Straus & Giroux, 1997.

———. *The Chess Garden: Or the Twilight Letters of Gustav Uyterhoeven*. New York: Douglas & Macintyre, 1995.

———. *John the Baptizer*. New York: W. W. Norton, 2009.

———. *The Monster of St. Helena*. New York: Farrar, Straus & Giroux, 2003.

———. *Perlman's Ordeal: A Novel*. New York: Farrar, Straus & Giroux, 2000.

Brooks, Hansen, and Nick Davis. *Boone*. New York: Simon & Schuster, 1990.

———. "An Interview with Brooks Hansen." By Jeff Vandermeer. *The Newsletter for the Council of the Literature of the Fantastic* 1, no. 4 (1997). Available online. URL: www.uri/edu/artsei/english/clf/n4_a2.html. Accessed October 20, 2009.

Kettman, Matt. "Brooks Hansen's New Book Reveals the Perilous Path to Parenting." Santa Barbara Independent. Available online. URL: http://www.independent.com/news/2008/jul/01/brooks-hansens-brotherhood-joseph-reveals-perilous/. Accessed March 15, 2009.

—Tatia Jacobson

Harrison, Kathryn (1961–) *American novelist and memoirist*

Kathryn Harrison is the author of six novels, each of which draws extensively on her family history, *Thicker than Water, Exposure, Poison, The Binding Chair, The Seal Wife,* and *Envy*. She has also written three memoirs (*The Kiss, Seeking Rapture,* and *The Mother Knot*), as well as a travelogue (*The Road to Santiago*), a biography (*Saint Thérèse of Lisieux*), and a book of true crime (*While They Slept: An Inquiry into the Murder of a Family*). Additionally, Harrison is a prolific essayist and regular contributor to the *New York Times Book Review*.

Harrison was born in Los Angeles, California, in 1961 to teenaged parents who divorced while the author was still an infant. Harrison then lived with her mother and maternal grandparents until the age of five, at which time her mother left the household to live in an apartment; and although Harrison saw her mother every day, neither she nor her grandparents knew where the mother lived. Harrison's mother had a variety of mental and emotional problems preventing her both from becoming independent and from being the principal caregiver to her daughter. After the divorce, Harrison's father returned to his home town on the border of Arizona and California, then earned two master's degrees and a doctorate from Garrett Theological Seminary in Evanston, Illinois. He saw his daughter only twice during her childhood, and his reentry into her life (when she was 20) created a destructive and traumatic relationship.

The Kiss, Harrison's first memoir, was published in 1997 and chronicles the author's incestuous affair with her father. The sexual relationship (initiated by a passionate kiss given to Harrison by her father) began while Harrison was a student at Stanford University in 1981, and continued until her mother's death in 1985. The memoir painstakingly explores the considerable power and influence her father was able to exert but is ultimately a lyrical documentation of her escape from that life and its damaging effects. Her three novels published prior to *The Kiss* (*Thicker than Water* [1992], *Exposure* [1993], and *Poison* [1995]) borrow heavily from this period of the author's life; *Thicker than Water* in particular reads like a more detailed version of *The Kiss*. What is "truth" in her first memoir is "fiction" in her early novels, and together the four books constitute a searching and far-reaching investigation of her own attempts to understand herself and her relationship with her father.

Harrison's relationship with her mother was less dramatic—though perhaps ultimately more traumatic—than that with her father. Indeed, the author contends that her father could not have gained such control over her if she had not already been weakened in childhood by her mother; she writes, "I'll never know how obviously needy and manipulable I appeared to him, but—given my history with my mother, my failure to win her love or even her approval—he managed to pressure me, eventually, into a sexual relationship" ("In Her Own Words"). The subtext of Harrison's earlier work—which focused on the trauma of her affair with her father—is elucidated in her second and third memoirs, *Seeking Rapture* (2003) and *The Mother Knot* (2004). In these later works she delves more deeply into the memories of her mother, and her attempts to exorcise the painful remnants of that relationship. She notes that at 18 she first "began to realize that [her] relationship with [her] emotionally distant, critical, and terribly unhappy young mother had been not only painful, but damaging—in some ways annihilating" ("In Her Own Words").

Harrison is remarkable for the frankness of her sexual expositions, and her willingness—even seeming compulsion—to reveal herself to an unknown audience. Moreover, she is a master of intertextuality, of weaving several narrative fabrics into a lyrical whole. The combination means that the disturbing revelations of her earlier works introduce her readers to characters whose progressive iterations in later novels are easily recognizable as Harrison or her family members.

The catharsis of Harrison's work during the 1990s gave her the freedom at last to explore other avenues. *The Binding Chair* (2000) borrows from her maternal grandmother's early experiences in Shanghai to create the backdrop for the story of May, a woman whose feet have been misshapen by the Chinese practice of binding. *The Binding Chair, Poison* (set in the late 17th century) and *The Seal Wife* (set during World War I and drawing upon Harrison's grandfather's fur-trapping days in the Northwest Territories) are all historical novels,

and their diverse settings provide fresh contexts and nuances for Harrison's continuing exploration of women's search for sexual and social power, and the perils of ubiquitous male desire. Her most recent novel, *Envy* (2005), reverses the incestuous relationship first introduced in *The Kiss;* here it is the daughter figure who knowingly and malevolently seduces the father, and this reversal adds yet another and very striking layer of complexity to Harrison's psychological topography.

The Road to Santiago (2003) recalls Harrison's three attempts to walk the Camino de Santiago, the 400-mile pilgrim route stretching from St.-Jean-Pied-de-Port in France to the Cathedral of Santiago de Compostela in northwest Spain. Her first trip occurred in 1992 when she was seven months pregnant, the last in 2002, accompanied by her 10-year-old daughter. That trip was abandoned after four days, and hardly resembled her 1999 solo voyage, which reached both Santiago and an acceptance of her painful past. Also published in 2003 was Harrison's biography of Therese, a tubercular nun who died in 1897 at the age of 24. *Saint Thérèse of Lisieux* chronicles the short and purportedly sexless life of a woman who—like Harrison—used writing as a means of catharsis and as a cure for crippling loneliness.

The author's most recent publication is a non-fictional variation on the central themes of her life and work: childhood abuse, and the trauma of being cast adrift as a result of that abuse. *While They Slept: An Inquiry into the Murder of a Family* (2008) investigates the murder of abusive parents by their 18-year-old son, Billy. After the murder, Billy declared himself and his younger sister to be "free," and Harrison's oeuvre itself, from *Thicker than Water* to *While They Slept,* may be seen as an effort, less violent and ultimately more demanding, to free herself from the devastation of her own dysfunctional parental relations.

Bibliography

Harrison, Katherine. *The Binding Chair.* New York: Random House, 2000.
———. *Envy.* New York: Random House, 2005.
———. *Exposure.* New York: Random House, 1993.
———. *The Kiss: A Memoir.* New York: Random House, 1997.

———. *The Mother Knot: A Memoir.* New York: Random House, 2004.

———. *Poison.* New York: Random House, 1995.

———. *Saint Therese of Lisieux: Penguin Lives Series.* New York: Penguin Books, 2003.

———. *The Seal Wife.* New York: Random House, 2002.

———. *Seeking Rapture: Scenes from a Life.* New York: Random House, 2003.

———. *The Road to Santiago.* Des Moines, Iowa: National Geographic, 2003.

———. *Thicker than Water.* New York: Random House, 1992.

———. *While They Slept: An Inquiry into the Murder of a Family.* New York: Random House, 2008.

———. "In Her Own Words." Kathrynharrison.com. Available online. URL: Kathrynharrison.com/own-words.htm. Accessed October 20, 2009.

—Katherine Edwards

Heartbreaking Work of Staggering Genius, A   Dave Eggers (2000)

Ostensibly a memoir, DAVE EGGERS's genre-bending debut is the unconventional account of a 20-something Gen-Xer as he attempts to raise his adolescent brother following the death of their parents. The Eggers family—father John, mother Heidi, and four children, Bill, Beth, Dave, and Toph—lives in the Chicago suburb of Lake Forest. At the outset of the book, John Eggers has just died, suddenly and unexpectedly, of cancer. His wife, Heidi, meanwhile, is bedridden, nearing the end after her own prolonged battle with cancer. While the eldest son, Bill, spends the majority of the narrative offstage (he works for the Heritage Foundation in Washington, D.C.), the other three children gather in the family home: Beth, who has deferred law school for a year to care for her ailing mother; Dave, home from college for Christmas; and eight-year-old Toph. In a matter of days, and barely a month after the passing of her husband, Heidi herself succumbs.

Following her death, Dave, Beth, and Toph relocate to California's Bay Area, and the balance of the book chronicles Dave's misadventures in "single parenting." Interspersed among his attempts to find housing, a school for Toph, and so

forth, is an engaging account of Eggers's own fledgling publishing venture, the short-lived indy magazine *Might* ("meaning," he proudly asserts, "both *power* and *possibility*") (202). While the magazine is clearly framed as an act of errant juvenilia, it nonetheless provides some of the book's most entertaining installments. Not only does Eggers upload gloriously awful snippets of prose from the magazine's back issues, but he also recounts a number of half-baked zine-related escapades (including his attempt to join the cast of the third season of MTV's *Real World* in San Francisco in 1994, and the hoax *Might* perpetrates concerning the purported death of former child star Adam Rich).

For all its humor, however, *AHWOSG* is shadowed by tragedy. The death of his parents hangs over the narrative like a pall, and Eggers reinforces this sense of loss with a host of minor tragic figures, including Shalini, a *Might* staff member who lapses into a coma following a fall from a fourth-story balcony; and Skye, an actress working part-time for the magazine who drops dead in NYC. "The only people who get speaking parts" complains one character self-referentially, "are those whose lives are grabbed by chaos" (424). Heartbreaking melodrama notwithstanding, the book's genius lies in its ability to channel the hopeful zeitgeist of the 1990s. Generation X may have been stigmatized as "the slacker generation," but a confluence of social, political, and economic factors led to everything from the ascendance of "alternative" to the dot-com revolution, and Eggers, in ebullient prose that might otherwise irritate if not so finely matched to the spirit of the era, captures it beautifully.

From a formal perspective, however, the most noteworthy aspect of *AHWOSG* is the way in which it repackages the devices and preoccupations of literary postmodernism in the trendy trappings of memoir, even while Eggers denies it: "I do not live in a postmodern time," he asserts in the afterword, "*Post* this, *meta* that. Here's a notion: These are the sorts of prefixes used by those without opinions" (*MWKWWM* 34). Yet the book (or, perhaps more appropriately, the novel) is insistently self-referential, employing a range of metafictional conceits à *la* John Barth: characters discuss their own characterization, the narrator repeatedly critiques his own tale, and both narrator and characters alike seem aware of their own fictional existence. "You're breaking out of character again," Eggers chides one personage (316); "Screw it, I'm not going to be a fucking anecdote in your stupid book," another objects (272).

Originally subtitled "A Memoir Based on a True Story," *AHWOSG* deconstructs the very notion of nonfiction's possibility. In part, this is accomplished through the aforementioned use of metafictional devices, which allow Eggers to reflect upon the difficulty of telling "True" stories. But further, much in the manner of his contemporary, David Foster Wallace, Eggers extends his exposition into the structural apparatus—footnotes, acknowledgments, the table of contents, and even the copyright page contain musings and meanderings. As the narrative bleeds into its apparatus, so too does fact into fiction, as Eggers admits to exaggerating, altering the chronology, fabricating conversations, and so on (and this in the sections that are ostensibly "true," for portions of the book are "narrated fantasies" set side-by-side with purported events). However, far from being a reason for indictment (as in the Oprah Winfrey/James Frey debacle), the unreliability of *AHWOSG*'s narration is yet another of the book's clever nods to literary postmodernism.

An enormous critical and commercial success, *AHWOSG* launched an Eggers media juggernaut. Following the book's publication, Eggers found himself something of a literary rock star, and his unconventional literary journal *McSweeney's*—which he had founded in 1998, following the demise of *Might*—suddenly vaulted to prominence. Spinoffs and side projects now include an internet version of the journal, mcsweeneys.net (also known as "McSweeney's Internet Tendency," and which soon gave rise to mcsweeneys.org, a dead-on spoof that may or may not have been engineered by Eggers himself); a publishing venture, McSweeney's Books; a monthly magazine, *The Believer*; and a quarterly short-film magazine issued on DVD, *Wholphin*.

Thanks to his sudden celebrity, Dave Eggers, his family, and compatriots were exposed to an increasing amount of scrutiny. In April 2000, *FoE!*, a blog reportedly run by a high-school student named Gary Baum, published e-mail correspon-dence with Beth Eggers, in which she objects to her characterization in *AHWOSG*:

> I am the sister who supposedly "helped out" while Dave "raised his little brother alone." Yeah right. I only picked him up from school every day, went to all the school events WITH Dave, although you'd never know it from reading all the reviews and the book. I took Toph to lacrosse practice, comic book stores, stayed overnight at Dave's all the time because he was up all night in San Francisco doing his magazine. (Baum)

What's more, Beth Eggers went on to suggest that her own journals had been the source material for parts of the book. Her comments caused a stir in the budding blogoshere, and were quickly picked up by *Harper's* ("Et tu, Beth?" August 2000). In response to the article in *Harper's,* Dave Eggers posted a piece on mcsweeneys.net, since removed, which included a lengthy apology from Beth. She refers to her earlier comments as "a really terrible LaToya Jackson moment," downplays the importance of her journals to *AHWOSG*, and says she's "just plain sorry" ("Ask"). As if this confusion were not enough, according to various sources, Beth Eggers committed suicide in 2001, overdosing on a mixture of antidepressants and acetaminophen (Adams). The unusual way in which the story was reported, however, coupled with Dave Eggers's history of spoofs, parodies, and media manipulation, has led to widespread speculation that the tale of Beth's demise may have been just another hoax.

In the years that have followed, the prolific Eggers has published *YOU SHALL KNOW OUR VELOCITY* (2002), (which he dedicated to Beth), *How We Are Hungry* (2004), and *WHAT IS THE WHAT: THE AUTOBIOGRAPHY OF VALENTINO ACHAK DENG* (2006). The latter, as it relates to *AHWOSG* is particularly noteworthy, as it represents a return to "fictionalized memoir." New Line Cinema purchased the film rights to *AHWOSG* for a reported $2 million, and after Nick Hornby and D. V. DeVincentis collaborated on the screenplay, offered the rights to the movie for sale (Saito). In an interview in October of 2007, Hornby referred to the project as "completely dead in the water" (Smith).

Bibliography

Adams, Lorraine. "The Write Stuff." February 1, 2003. The American Prospect. Available online. URL: http://www.prospect.org/cs/articles?article=the_write_stuff. Accessed December 30, 2007.

Baum, Gary. "FoE! Log #6: The Beth Eggers Exclusive (and Some Other Stuff)." Arphodigitaliac. Available online. URL: http://www.aphrodigitaliac.com/mm/archive/2000/04/17/. Accessed December 30, 2007.

Eggers, Beth. "Et Tu, Beth?" Harper's. August 2000, p. 23.

E[ggers], D[ave]. "A Very Special Episode of: Ask the McSweeney's Representative." Mcsweeneys. Available online. URL: http://web.archive.org/web/20020211214746/http://www.mcsweeneys.net/2000/07/31askmr. html. Accessed December 30, 2007.

Eggers, Dave. A Heartbreaking Work of Staggering Genius. New York: Vintage, 2001.

———. Mistakes We Knew We Were Making. New York: Vintage, 2001.

Saito, Steven. "20 Movies Not Coming to a Theatre Near You." Premier.com. Available online. URL: http://www.premiere.com/features/3861/20-movies-not-coming-soon-to-a-theater-near-you.html?print_page=y. Accessed December 30, 2007.

Smith, Kyle. "Nick Hornby on Success: 'If You're a Miserable Bastard, You'll Never Feel It.'" Kyle Smith Online. Available online. URL: http://kylesmithonline.com/?p=556. Accessed December 30, 2007.

—Justin St. Clair

Hemon, Alexandar (1964–   ) *Sarajevo-born American novelist and short story writer*

Having made a dramatic entrance on the literary scene with his critically lauded collection of short stories, *The Question of Bruno* (2000), Alexandar Hemon has since published two novels that have more than justified the early acclaim, as well as contributing pieces to journals on both sides of the Atlantic, from the *New Yorker* magazine to Sarajevo-based *BH Dani* (Bosnia-Herzegovina Days).

Even the circumstances of his birth speak tellingly of Hemon's later art: He was born in 1964 in Sarajevo, then Yugoslavia, now Bosnia and Herzegovina, to a father of Ukrainian descent and a Serbian mother. He graduated from the University of Sarajevo and enjoyed early success as a journalist, publishing in Serbo-Croatian magazines by the age of 26. His English literary career, though seeming inevitable in its brilliance (and reminiscent in some ways of that of Joseph Conrad, who is acknowledged by allusion in *The Question of Bruno*), was launched with the improbability of a Volm Kunderan fiction. Visiting America as a tourist in 1992, he found himself suddenly stranded in Chicago when his homeland descended into anarchy and civil war. On May 1, 1992, the very day he was scheduled to arrive home, Sarajevo itself came under siege, and Hemon, at 28, was an accidental refugee. Taking advantage of this fate with Kunderan élan, he plunged into the study of English as a graduate student at New York University and Loyola, and took any job that would pay, from a sandwich assembly-line worker and bike messenger, to a Greenpeace canvasser, bookstore salesman, and ESL teacher. In 1995, he began to write in English, and his work soon appeared in prestigious publications like the *New Yorker, Esquire,* and *The Paris Review.* He received a "genius grant" from the MacArthur Foundation in 2004, and his latest novel, *The Lazarus Project* (2008), was a finalist for the 2008 National Book Award and the 2008 National Book Critics Award.

In 2000, he published *The Question of Bruno,* composed of a novella and short stories, and introducing readers to the enigmatic Josef Pronek, who would later be the focus of Hemon's first novel, NOWHERE MAN (2002). Widely varying in style and tone, from ludic postmodernism to plangent realism, the stories are nonetheless unified in theme, revolving around the very experience that Hemon knew so well: the disintegration of one's homeland and the shocks of the accidental refugee. Images of loss, disorientation, two-edged memory, and incomplete recovery dominate the collection, with commonplace motifs like the starving cat of "Islands" accruing subtle layers of meaning and irony as they snake through the stories. The work's best-known tale, and the first published by Hemon in America, is "The Sorge Spy Ring," a typical blackly comic meditation on the last days of Tito and his repressive regime, told by means of a series of luminous cinematic details that invest the quotidian experience of a small family with the kind of universal significance we rightly associate with literary mastery.

Named after the John Lennon song, Hemon's episodic debut novel, *Nowhere Man,* shifts restlessly through scenes in Bosnia, Chicago, Ukraine, and even Shanghai, told through a series of disparate narrative voices but it constantly touches down, however lightly, on *The Question of Bruno*'s Josef Pronek, an itinerant Bosnian everyman with "the ability to respond and speak to the world." From his earliest infancy in the fragile stasis of the doomed Yugoslavia, through his youth spent negotiating its collapse, to his awkward maturation learning English in Chicago, Pronek acts as a kind of narrative window, unstable in shape and hue, but involuntarily revealing the truth of Hemon's rich imaginative world. Recalling Vladimir Nabokov's *The Search for Sebastian Knight* in its complex and nuanced style, and Milan Kundera's *Unbearable Lightness of Being* in its compellingly ambiguous tone, *Nowhere Man* established Hemon as an artist of the first rank, worthy of the most serious consideration.

Such consideration was amply rewarded with the recent publication of his follow-up, Kafkaesque tour de force, *The Lazarus Project.* Here the naiveté and superficial irony of Hemon's earlier protagonists is replaced with a mature, subtle, and finely nuanced portrait of the accidental refugee. Vladimir Brik has been stranded on a visit to Chicago when his Yugoslavian homeland descends into anarchy and civil war, but unlike Prozek, Brik, married now to a successful American neurosurgeon, muses thoughtfully and painfully on the postmodern "lightness" of his existence, his life a "permanent confusion." Each night before sleep he struggles to remember and make sense of the events of his day in what he calls his "nightly prayer, a contemplation of my presence in the world."

Into this diffuse but charged atmosphere, almost as a kind of hermeneutic lightning rod, the life and character of one Lazarus Averbuch appears. The real Averbuch was a young Jew who escaped the 1903 Kishinev pogrom in what is now Moldova and came to Chicago, where, on March 2, 1908, after a scuffle at the house of Chicago's chief of police, he was shot and killed. This seemingly trivial act, the semiaccidental killing of some anonymous Jew, nonetheless became part of a sudden outburst of xenophobic hysteria in Chicago (which Hemon skillfully parallels to post-9/11 America), and the frail corpse of Lazarus, photographs of which are included in the novel (recalling the work of W. G. Sebald), becomes a kind of heuristic focus for Brik's own attempt to make sense of his life. The "Lazarus Project," freighted with obvious biblical parallels, animates and clarifies the shapeless, undead "moral waddling" of Brik: he wins a grant to write a book on Averbuch, enlists the help of a fellow expatriate named Rora—a sort of postmodern Sancho Panza who provides much of the novel's Kunderan wit—and sets out on a nightmarish road trip through (what is left of) Eastern Europe.

Arriving at last in his native Sarajevo, Brik's own tale—and the life in which it is told—finally fuses metaphorically with those of the biblical and Chicagoan Lazarus, and he realizes—as accident meets providence—that the story he is writing is, and in the end can only be, his own.

Hemon currently lives in Chicago with his second wife, Teri Boyd, and their daughter, Ella.

Bibliography
Borger, Julian. "Brave New Words." Guardian Unlimited. Available online. URL: http://www.guardian.co.uk/books/2000/apr/08/fiction.features. Accessed May 21, 2009.

—Douglas Melrose

History of Love, The Nicole Krauss (2005)
NICOLE KRAUSS's second novel is a moving, sharply observant account of the grief and loves of human existence. At times a hard-hitting post-Holocaust narrative, *The History of Love* deftly interleaves the horrors of mid-20th-century Jewish experience with the commonplaces of contemporary American life.

The novel tells the story of an old man, Leo Gursky, who outlives a son he never met: Isaac was born and raised in America, after Leo's lover Alma fled their home country of Poland. Parallel to this is the contemporary narrative of a different Alma, a 14-year-old American named after the protagonist of her dead father's favorite book. This text-within-a-text, also called *The History of Love,* was written in homage to Leo's lover. Alongside these two stories runs that of Zvi Litvinoff, a friend of Leo's whose emigration to Chile during the war—and involvement in the composition of the text-within-a-text—both connect the stories of Alma and Leo, and divide them.

All three narrative strands are haunted by loss. Leo loses his parents on either side of the outbreak of war: his father to natural causes (168), and his mother in the Nazi invasion of their village (8). Alma loses her father to cancer at age seven and her mother to a lifetime of grief, as Charlotte "never fell out of love with [Alma's] father." (45) Litvinoff is a prematurely aging 32-year-old who has lost the ability to communicate meaningfully with anyone, and "liv[es] with an elephant"; he has lost everyone he once loved: "every morning he had to squeeze around the truth just to get to the bathroom" (156). It is a mark of Krauss's achievement, however, that no one of these losses, each traumatic, is foregrounded at the expense of another.

They are all linked by the character of Alma Mereminski, Leo's first and only love—protagonist of the text-within-a-text *History*—and the girl for whom Alma Singer was named. For all the centrality of Alma-the-elder, however, she is a remarkably intangible character. Existing only in the thoughts of others, she becomes a cipher for the love of anyone who reads the text-within-a-text. Like Brod, a quasi-mythical character in another post-Holocaust novel, JONATHAN SAFRAN FOER's EVERYTHING IS ILLUMINATED (2002), Alma is a focus for the desire of those around her, for the loves and losses of her friends—and in a metaphorical sense, perhaps, for those of the Jewish people.

The incompleteness of Krauss's characters can be read through Giorgio Agamben's concept of "bare life" (Agamben 182). Oppressed people(s) are denied the "humanity" of political and social autonomy, and are reduced to their bodily functions, "existing" in the barest form of the word, one of "pure being." (182) "Bare life" defines many

post-Holocaust works, in their search for meaning in the face of the Nazi annihilation: Art Spiegelman's graphical representations of people literally reduced to animals, in *Maus: A Survivor's Tale* (1986) and *Maus II: And Here My Troubles Began* (1991); or Anne Michaels's *Fugitive Pieces* (1997), in which a child is named "Ben," not as a diminutive of Benjamin, but from the Hebrew word for "son," in the hope that a lack of naming will fool the Angel of Death. Krauss captures this sense of an incomplete human identity in the octogenarian Leo, who loses 25 percent of his heart muscle to a heart attack, and who regularly makes a scene while shopping in an effort to combat invisibility: "all I want," he opens the novel by asserting, "is not to die on a day when I went unseen" (4).

The novel's two primary narrative voices—of Leo Gursky and Alma Singer—present very different approaches to this search for meaning. Leo's disjointed existence is reflected in the abrupt, free-standing conjunctions that puncture his narrative: "And yet. . . . But. . . . But" (5–6). When Alma enters into the story, she is a breath of fresh air, immediately drawing the reader into her life: "When I was born my mother named me after every girl in a book my father gave her called *The History of Love*" (34). Both stories, however, focus on frustrated quests. Leo obsesses over Isaac Moritz, the son he never knew, who becomes a famous writer. Alma starts by looking for someone to make her mother happy after her father's death but ends up following a whole trail of people: the mysterious Jacob Marcus, who commissions Alma's mother to translate the text-within-a-text, published in Chile by Zvi Litvinoff; Alma Mereminski, after whom Alma was named; and Isaac Moritz, who in turn leads her to Leo. This last connection is made with the help of Alma's brother, "Bird" (so named after a spectacular attempt to prove his capability for flight). Bird's response to their father's death is to retreat into religious fervor, believing that he is a "lamed vovnik," or chosen one of God; and it is this belief that leads Bird to intercede in Alma's search, in an attempt to do something for "someone who needs help" (207).

Krauss's novel can be read as a meditation on what it means to construct one's own narrative. Leo, for example, is a character who literally writes a history for himself, penning his own obituary, which appears both in Zvi Litvinoff's narrative (117) and in the text-within-a-text (189). This contested nature of personal histories and memories is a major concern for Krauss, and it was a prominent feature of her debut novel, MAN WALKS INTO A ROOM (2002), in which a brain tumor renders the protagonist unable to remember his life past the age of 12.

In offering her readers a reflection on the very idea of personal history, Krauss engages with Marianne Hirsch's idea of "postmemory," an important consideration for Jewish generations following the Holocaust, who had to construct histories of their own to cope with the experiences that were passed down to them. In contrast to "historical" memory, the very power of "postmemory" lies in the fact that "its connection to its object or source is mediated not through recollection but through an imaginative investment and creation" (Hirsch 23). Herein lies Krauss's achievement: from Bird the "lamed vovnik" to Leo the "invisible man," her characters build a "history of love" not founded on personal recollection, but on "imaginative investment"; and as Leo reaches the breaking point, addressing both his dead father and his dead son, Krauss concludes her searching exploration of the subjective nature of historical truth: *"The truth is the thing I invented so I could live"* (167).

The film version of *The History of Love* is scheduled for release in 2009, to be directed by Alfonso Cuarón (*Y Tu Mama Tambien* [2001], *Harry Potter and the Prisoner of Azkaban* [2004]) and produced by his *Azkaban* colleague, David Heyman. Fans of Krauss's work will hope that Heyman's assessment of Cuarón proves to be accurate: "[*The History of Love*] is a book that requires real tenderness without being overly sentimental, and that is something Alfonso does very well" (Murray).

Bibliography

Agamben, Giorgio. *Homo Sacer: Sovereign Power and Bare Life.* (*Homo sacer: il potere sovrano e la nuda vita,* 1995.) Translated by Daniel Heller-Roazen. Stanford, Calif.: Stanford University Press, 1998.

Hirsch, Marianne. *Family Frames: Photography, Narrative and Postmemory.* 1997. Cambridge, Mass., and London: Harvard University Press, 2002.

Krauss, Nicole. *The History of Love.* London: Viking, 2005.

Murray, Rebecca. "Alfonso Cuarón Takes on Directing Duties for 'The History of Love.'" About.com. Available online. URL: http://movies.about.com/od/moviesinproduction/a/historylv012105.htm. Accessed May 12, 2009.

—Sam Knowles

Holman, Sheri (1966–) *American novelist*

Sheri Holman is an acclaimed American novelist whose debut, *A Stolen Tongue* (1997), is a historical fiction centering on a 15th-century Friar's quest to capture a relic-thief while on religious pilgrimage. Holman followed up *A Stolen Tongue* with another historical thriller in 2000, *The DRESS LODGER.* Holman's only work to date that is not firmly set in past historical time, *The Mammoth Cheese,* was nominated for 2003's Orange Broadbent Prize for Best Fiction Novel. Holman has also written a historical fiction novel set in sixth-century Korea for young adults titled *Sondok: Princess of the Moon and Stars* (2002), and is currently working on a fifth novel, which is partially set in Depression-era America.

Born in 1966 in Richmond, Virginia, Holman was largely raised in its rural outskirts, escaping from some harsh realities in her adolescence—the divorce of her parents when she was 13 and being raised in a prejudiced environment—by delving into the worlds presented in the history books and biographies she found at her local library (Steinberg). Holman was the first member of her family to receive post-secondary education when she enrolled in theater at the College of William and Mary in Williamsburg. On graduating, she moved to New York City in 1988 with the intention of becoming an actress, but life in the city would ultimatcly engage Holman in literary pursuits. Holman found that she was suited to publishing and this, in her own words, was "how I learned to write" (Steinberg). But this learning had to be accomplished in the midst of some upheaval and hardship, including years of temporary work at Penguin, traveling through the Middle East, being swindled out of her life savings, working for literary agent Molly Friedrich, and the rejection of her first novel by 12 publishers. Yet the result, at last, was *A Stolen Tongue*, which appeared in print nine years after her arrival in New York. She has published three novels since. Holman currently lives in a character home in Brooklyn (c. 1809) with her three young children, husband, and multiple cats (Steinberg 2003).

Like many authors of historical fiction, Holman credits extensive research as the primary appeal of her work (Kobak). Layers of authenticity characterize Holman's oeuvre because she constantly engages relevant subject matter prior to and throughout her writing process; Holman notes, "you can't know too much about what you are writing about, the more you know the more you can forget [while writing]" (Kobak). Described by her husband, a trained classicist, as a "serious dilettante," Holman generally shifts her research and writing attentions to a new time and place every few years (Steinberg).

Holman's preferences in reading material actively inform her storylines. She lists *London Labor and the London Poor* (Mayhew 1850) as a favorite book, and it was here that she first became acquainted with the historical personage of the "dress lodger," among a host of other characters (Barnes and Noble). In *The Dress Lodger*, Holman tells the story of an uncustomarily well-dressed prostitute named Gustine who lived in Sunderland, England, during the cholera outbreaks of the 1830s. Gustine coexists with a rich cast of characters, including her physiologically unique son, an ever-intrigued medical doctor, and a one-eyed "protectioness" from the neighborhood.

Holman was profoundly influenced by D'Aulaire's *Book of Greek Myths*, which she read before the age of 10: "It was just gross enough to keep me going, Kronos swallows his children and vomits them out again, I loved it!" (Barnes and Noble). Holman draws on some of the deepest elements of religion and faith in her work, often including aspects of social mythologies and ritualized devotion, in order to induce the reader to explore otherwise daunting or off-putting concepts, such as acute displacement, death, and dismemberment—all of which are directly addressed through the theme of relic theft in *A Stolen Tongue* but are also apparent in Holman's other works, including

Sondok. When asked about the differences between writing for adult and young-adult audiences, Holman states:

> "Young readers are so sophisticated now, there is little difference. The main goal is to find themes that a smart adolescent will relate to—like the pressure kids [and adults] put on themselves to be perfect and to please everyone, the frustration they feel when not allowed to pursue their dreams because of something silly like prejudice or narrowly defined gender roles" (Scholastic).

The past, according to Holman, can provide a welcoming heuristic space within which to confront uncomfortable topics that may yield contemporary insight.

Sales of historical fiction titles have increased over the last decade and are thought to comprise about 5 percent of total fiction sales worldwide (Asher). The success of Holman's *The Dress Lodger*, *A Stolen Tongue*, and *Sondok* reflects this trend, and it is paralleled by a resurgence of historical persons, places, and events in popular entertainment. Young adult literature is also gaining momentum, both as a factor in total book sales worldwide and as a legitimate vehicle for literary contribution, as witnessed by the mass popularity and critical acclaim of series like Stephenie Meyer's *Twilight* and J. K. Rowling's *Harry Potter* franchise.

Bibliography

Asher, Levi. "Book Pricing for Literary Fiction: A Plea from Paperback Readers." Literary Kicks. Available online. URL: http://www.litkicks.com/BookPricing-Finale/. Accessed October 30, 2007.

Barnes and Noble. "Meet the Writers: Sheri Holman." Available online. URL: http://www.barnesandnoble.com/writers/writerdetails.asp?cid=1021669#interview. Accessed January 3, 2009.

D'Aulaire, Ingri, and Edgar Parin D'Aulaire. *Ingri and Edgar Parin D'Aulaire's Book of Greek Myths*. Garden City, N.Y.: Doubleday, 1962.

Holman, Sheri. *The Dress Lodger*. New York: Atlantic Monthly Press, 2000.

———. "An Interview with Sheri Holman." By Richard F. Abrahamson and Eleanore S. Tyson. Scholastic.

Available online. URL: http://www.scholastic.com/
dearamerica/parentteacher/guides/royaldiaries/son-
dok.htm. Accessed January 3, 2009.

———. *The Mammoth Cheese.* New York: Atlantic
Monthly Press, 2003.

———. *Sondok: Princess of the Moon and Stars.* New
York: Scholastic, 2002.

———. *A Stolen Tongue.* New York: Atlantic Monthly
Press, 1997.

Kobak, Annette. "Arrows of Desire." *New York Times,* 13
February 2000.

Mayhew, Henry. *London Labor and the London Poor* 1850.
Reprint, New York: A. M. Kelley, 1967.

Steinberg, Sybil. "Sheri Holman: Guarding Perfection,
Flaws and All." Publishers Weekly (28 July 2003).
Available online. URL: www.publisherweekly.com/
article/CA313545.html. Accessed October 20,
2009.

—Stephanie Laine Hamilton

Home Repairs Trey Ellis (1993)

TREY ELLIS's second novel is a humorous and
graphic coming-of-age story exploring the rapid
maturation of an upper-middle-class black teenager. Frustrated with his clumsy romantic interactions, Austin McMillan embarks on an accelerated
journey to adulthood in search of sexual experience, romantic stability, and smooth self-confidence. Bent on self-improvement, he begins
logging every female encounter in a notebook, and
this journal follows him from prep school at Andover, through his time at Stanford University, to a
mounting career as The Fix-it-Kid, the host for a
do-it-yourself home repair show.

Ellis employs an innovative diary-novel structure for *Home Repairs,* with Austin deciding to
mimic a Puritan spiritual diary, recording in detail
his every sexual exploit, and hoping the collection
will show a pattern revealing his flawed behavior,
which he can then correct. Yet, in one of the comic
ironies of the novel, this very diaristic mode of narration only intensifies his own youthful anxieties.
Whatever happens to him is highlighted (and often
magnified) immediately, generating a sustained and
convincing tone of teenage angst. The same structure also allows Ellis to highlight Austin's curiously

involuted maturation. Because Austin is his own
narrator, and because he narrates his story as he
lives it, there is no reflective or objective voice to
contextualize the events or make other connections for the reader. Moreover, Austin's ever-present tone of self-improvement engages both our
sympathy and our curiosity to analyze his analysis
and development. The diary form also simulates
the conversational, self-deprecating, and motivational tone one uses in conversation with oneself.
Helen Fielding brought this intimate and personable voice into popular culture in 1996 with her
wildly successful novel, *Bridget Jones's Dairy,* and
like that work, *Home Repairs* comprises the entries
of a humorous narrator bent on self-improvement
and finding love.

By crafting *Home Repairs* as a coming-of-age
story told by a self-critical narrator through the
lens of female interactions, Ellis further places
his second novel in conversation with works like
This Side of Paradise by F. Scott Fitzgerald and J.
D. Salinger's *The Catcher in the Rye.* In each, the
protagonist is occupied in a search for love and
confidence, but Austin spends far more (and more
awkward) time detailing his exploits. By chronicling his masturbatory, sexual, and romantic episodes, Austin meticulously charts his own rites of
passage into adulthood.

His first object of pursuit, Joie, instigates a
longstanding obsession with his physical appearance, as Austin struggles to maintain Joie's attention, but she repeatedly overlooks him for older,
bigger, and blacker young men. This motivates our
hero to shed his geeky appearance, brave his fears
of the gym's burly lacrosse players, and start building muscles of his own. Joie gives Austin his first
kiss, but is never a stable enough presence in his
life to become the girlfriend he so keenly seeks.

Many women whom Austin pursues com-
ment on his appearance. He now has the body of a
Greek god; his hands are beautiful. He even lands
work as a television host with a Playboy Bunny as
his cohost. Yet Ellis creates a sustained if oblique
tone of insecurity about Austin's appearance, even
as Austin constantly reminds himself of his own
attractions. Moreover, sexually appealing as he may
be, Austin still at times does not feel black enough.
He begins, for example, a stimulating adult rela-

tionship with Joanna, a white woman; however, Joanna still harbors feelings for her previous boyfriend. And when Austin learns that the man is a deep-voiced, black football player, his jealousy shatters both the relationship with Joanna and his own emotional stability.

The narrative deepens its exploration of race in its account of another of Austin's relationships. Jewelle is the first student Austin falls for as he begins his undergraduate years at Stanford University. She is from Grenada, and Austin is attracted by her Caribbean accent and darker skin, which remind him of his aunts. A marriage to her would root him in the historical tradition of his family, and thus he does not merely want her physically, but pictures the family legacy they would create. At Stanford she coddles him as a friend; but one night, he lets her read the ubiquitous journal, and they have sex. Yet after that, Austin looks on with venomous jealousy as Jewelle continues her relationship with an unattractive white man.

While sex might be the immediate goal of Austin's romantic endeavors, he is ultimately pursuing a monogamous relationship. Yet, in an intriguing inversion of the usual gender asymmetry, Joie, Johanna, and Jewelle are all hesitant to commit. Even before the tale properly begins, Austin meets Jenny in Martha's Vineyard (his parents choose Martha's Vineyard because other black families vacation there). Jenny sexually challenges him each summer, leading him on over the years with letters and steamy evenings, yet Austin can never tie her into that longed-for monogamous relationship, and ultimately gives up. She departs his life—and the narrative—a free spirit.

Didi, his first legitimate girlfriend, shares a number of characteristics with both Joanna and Jenny. Austin learns that Didi never officially left her boyfriend, a Cuban gangster pining for her in a jail cell in Florida. With Austin terrified of mob retribution and jealous of her other, macho boyfriend, Didi decides to leave the country to pursue her modeling career, and she drags the hearts of both men with her. Didi never returns, and Austin starts his first truly monogamous relationship with Monica, another model. Their relationship quickly blossoms into domestic ease, but with his long-

standing aim achieved at last, Austin actually gets bored and ends it after about a year.

In addition to this disappointing reversal, and for all his mature aspirations, Austin's keen and intransigent sexual drive ultimately destroys two promising friendships. Calista is a beautiful white student he meets at prep school. Acknowledging the oppressive male interest in her, Austin focuses on maintaining their friendship, though he hopelessly desires her physically. After he graduates, they take a trip to Mexico, and at last, hoping to relieve the sexual tension of their friendship, he pressures her to sleep with him. She finally relents, and their friendship never recovers. Then, working for Stanford's humor magazine, Austin meets Liz, who already has a boyfriend, so they become friends. They fall into a pattern of pleasuring each other, but Austin cannot persuade Liz to leave her boyfriend, and the friendship dissipates. But finally there is Michelle, whom he meets through work, and who listens patiently to the tedious synoptic narrative of his troubles. Surprisingly, but inevitably, he at last realizes her value, and through their mature relationship sheds the distracting and wasteful obsessions of his adolescence, along with the diary that both chronicled and nourished them.

Bibliography

Ellis, Trey. *Home Repairs.* New York: Washington Square Press, 1993.

—Kelin Loe

Homes, A. M. (1961–) *American novelist and journalist*

Homes is the prolific author of five novels (*Jack, In a Country of Mothers, The End of Alice, MUSIC FOR TORCHING,* and *THIS BOOK WILL SAVE YOUR LIFE*), two short story collections (*The Safety of Objects, Things You Should Know*), and two nonfiction books (*Los Angeles: People, Places, and the Castle on the Hill,* and the memoir *The Mistress's Daughter*). She has also worked as a journalist for publications such as *Artforum* and the *New Yorker.* Her thematic focus on almost unceasingly dark subject matter with an increasingly icy, postmodern flair made a sensational literary splash in the 1990s, and Homes herself became a subject of controversy in the media. After the 1989 publication of *Jack*, Homes released a book every three years, making her output a barometer of literary and cultural transformations in that decade. As a quintessential 1990s writer of transgressive fiction that reached a wide audience, Homes has continued to provoke great interest in the 21st century. Darcy Cosper, in his review of Homes's most recent and more optimistic novel, *This Book Will Save Your Life* (2006), provides a retrospective on the sardonic pessimism that made her famous: "After all, Homes' work isn't exactly what one would call uplifting. She's made her name with dark, often very disturbing fiction—ferociously intelligent, inky-black novels and stories rich in mordant humor that challenge convention, both literary and social" (Cosper 42).

Homes was born in Washington, D.C., and attended Sarah Lawrence College, where she studied under Grace Paley. She later attended the University of Iowa Writers' Workshop, where she earned her M.F.A. Before even enrolling at Iowa, however, she had written her first novel, *Jack* (1989), at age 19. This coming-of-age story of a young man whose father is revealed to be homosexual was written by Homes as a "homework assignment" (Lindner). While Homes's distinctive blend of grim humor, mordant social commentary, and heightened realist attention to detail (reminiscent of Don DeLillo) had not yet emerged in this novel, it is a winsome and engrossing text; and its sensitive treatment of a controversial social issue garnered it favorable reviews and an entry point into the literary canon for young readers.

With the short story collection *The Safety of Objects* (1990), Homes arrived as a talent worthy of widespread notice and acclaim. Arriving concurrently with the work of other exciting young writers like DAVID FOSTER WALLACE, the collection limned a seductive, startling world of dysfunctional families, suburban angst, and quirky yet vividly human characters. From an upwardly mobile couple who try crack on a whim (whom Homes would return to at the end of the decade) to a precocious kidnapped child, to a series of protagonists delivering stunning monologues on loss and regret, Homes's cast of characters is unforgettable. But most striking are the young narrator and tale of the notorious and often-

anthologized "A Real Doll," in which a young boy has an erotic obsession with his sister's Barbie, which Homes casts in the form of an intense dialogue between the two (and which naturally touches on the anatomically incorrect Ken). The boy's potentially ludicrous plight is made strangely believable and poignant, and it is perhaps for this reason that it remains Homes's most famous and widely read story, a compact text that allows her to work her particular magic with memorable force.

In a Country of Mothers (1993) deals with Homes's recurrent theme of family, estrangement, and surrogate attachment. The satiric tale of a young aspiring filmmaker's entanglement with her therapist, told in alternating chapters that focus on each protagonist, is shaped by thriller tropes. Dominated by sexuality and obsession, and probing into the darker corners of the psyche, it provides a larger canvas for Homes, on which to develop her incisive character portraits.

In a Country of Mothers seems, however, a relatively minor work compared to its follow-up, *The End of Alice* (1996). Here the narrator, a pedophile incarcerated for murder who is corresponding by mail with a college student he considers a kindred spirit, is easily Homes's most terrifying and precisely drawn creation. With a narrative that foregrounds its relation to dark literary psychological portraits of murderers past—Nabokov's erudite psychopaths are particularly flagged as a key intertext—the novel's effect on the reader is often startling. Wrote one-time Brit-lit enfant terrible Will Self, the novel "is properly exacting, while stiffly extracting a reader's uneasy, complicit" fascination; "If people are outraged, it's because they find it arousing" (Self). Others were quick to condemn the novel as socially irresponsible, their outrage already stirred by many of the 1990s' more lurid, even trashy pop-culture products (*The Silence of the Lambs, Twin Peaks*, gangsta rap and slasher films, the Michael Jackson scandals). In many ways, the controversy surrounding the novel echoed that surrounding another work with a tortured but compelling narrative voice: Bret Easton Ellis's yuppie serial-killer tale in AMERICAN PSYCHO. However, Homes treats the narrator, Chappy, with more sympathy, attempting to explain his existence in terms of familial trauma.

Appendix A: An Elaboration on the Novel the End of Alice (1996) is an unusual and enigmatic book, and not what many of its readers might expect. Rather than an extended essay explicating her artistic choices or engaging with her critics, the book is a 56-page collection of "supplementary material," including letters written by her characters and photographic "evidence."

Homes's next novel, *Music for Torching* (1999), revisits Paul and Elaine, the couple who first appear in *The Safety of Objects*. Given additional space to characterize both them and their antics, the narrative chronicles their casting off the yoke of suburban conformity circa the dot-com boom, which takes the form of a chaotic spree of infidelity, internet pornography, violence to each other and their neighbors, and the arson that gives the novel its title. With this novel Homes proved that she still possessed the ability to shock and entertain with a pitch-black sense of humor, while sustaining the same tone of heightened reality as Don DeLillo, an admitted influence (Weich). Her second story collection, *Things You Should Know* (2002), departed in a number of ways from her signature style but was still found by some to be a retread of previous works. In a lukewarm review in the *New York Times*, David Eder wrote that the collection's problems begin with its "archly didactic title[,] considering the things in it that you've no real need to know," while its stories illustrate a sustained effort to "display the grotesque very much for its own sake. The extremity is disproportionate to any human message; the transgressiveness is a sort of artistic complacency" (Eder). *This Book Will Save Your Life* (2006) was hailed by some as correcting these faults, but seen by others as a misfire. It does, however, boast a cover-jacket blurb by John Waters, which seems fitting given the novel's outré character.

In addition to *Los Angeles: People, Places, and the Castle on the Hill* (2002), a chronicle of the Chateau Marmont and its star-studded inhabitants, Homes published a second notable book-length piece of nonfiction, *The Mistress's Daughter* (2007), a memoir of her reunion with her birth parents. She also wrote an introduction to a compilation of Amy Arbus's 2006 compilation of her 1980s subcultural fashion photographs for the *Village Voice*. Outside of her strictly literary pursuits, Homes spent the 2000s working on two television projects for the cable Showtime network, serving as a writer/producer on a season of the flashy lesbian soap *The L Word* and writing Showtime's well-received 2004 TV-film adaptation of *Jack,* which won an Emmy for one of its stars, Stockard Channing. *The Safety of Objects* was also adapted for the screen in 2001 and starred Glenn Close and Dermot Mulroney.

Bibliography

Cosper, Darcy. "The End of Malice." *Bookforum* 13, no. 1 (May 2006): 42.

Eder, Richard. Review of *Things You Should Know,* New York Times on the Web. Available online. URL: http://query.nytimes.com/gst/fullpage.html?res= 9B0DE0DE1030F93AA1575AC0A9649C8B6 3&fta=y. Accessed December 27, 2008.

Lindner, Elizabeth. "A.M. Homes: Reasons to Be Cheerful." *Independent.co.uk.* Available online. URL: http://www.independent.co.uk/arts-entertainment/ books/features/a-m-homes-reasons-to-be-che erful-481559.html. Accessed January 5, 2008.

Self, Will. "The Killer as Aesthete." New Statesman. Available online. URL: http://www.amhomesbooks. com/index.php?mode=objectlist&section_id= 161&object_id=282. Accessed January 3, 2009.

Weich, Dave. "A.M. Homes Is a Big Fat Liar." Powells Books. Available online. URL: http://www.powells.com/authors/homes.html. Accessed January 2, 2009.

—Christopher Smith

Honey Thief, The Elizabeth Graver (1999)

ELIZABETH GRAVER's second novel is a subtle, imaginative, and lyrical examination of the relationship between a mother and daughter in the lonely years following the father's death. When 11-year-old Eva is repeatedly caught shoplifting, her mother Miriam impulsively decides to move them from Manhattan to a rural community upstate, where she hopes there will be fewer opportunities for Eva to get into trouble. Predictably, Eva is bored and resentful in their new home, but discovers an unlikely source of fascination in the beehives maintained by Burl, a middle-aged neighbor. Eva's relationship with Burl and his bees develops into a secret compound of sweetness, mystery, and danger, which resonates with the quality of her own adolescent anxiety.

Graver has said that the inspiration for the bee theme in *The Honey Thief* originated from a National Public Radio report on the devastation of the honeybee population by parasitic mites, and the pair of epigraphs at the beginning of the book juxtapose a verse from Emily Dickinson about the spiritual and generative characteristics of honey with a quotation from Rachel Carson about the ecological fallout that would result from any major disruption in honeybee activity. Graver's fictional beekeeper, Burl, also struggles with the problem of mites in his hives, and this struggle bears a close relationship to his personal attempts to cope with the disappointment in his love life. Eva is first drawn into Burl's world by a vision of a honey jar, which seems to represent in its rich hues the inner principle of life itself; honey is described as a "slow medicine" (56) to counteract the illness of contemporary dread. Graver's book peels back traditional clichés of bees and honey to reveal complex and rewarding parallels between the world of bees and the emotional worlds of her human characters. Eva's obsession with discovering the queen bee, for example, is a poignant expression of her own memories of being pampered by her effusive father when she was younger, and of her sense of rejection in the wake of her father's death. The beekeeper's veil fills her with the satisfaction of "an infant being swaddled in yards of sweet-smelling fabric" (74). The interior of the hive represents to Eva nothing less than "the secret heart of life" (86). More than anything else, however, Graver's bees ultimately represent the complexity of relationships, not only in nature but in the human world, as well as the connectivity between nature and humanity. Eva's fascination with the bees both symbolizes and reflects her growing desire for participation in the complex social interactions that characterize adulthood. Graver's use of bee imagery is inventive and intricate, and establishes a close connection between the ecological themes of her novel and the psychological dilemmas of its human characters.

Graver divides the telling of her story into three perspectives, each of which receives roughly equal treatment: those of Eva, Miriam, and Burl. Eva, who opens the novel with her eponymous theft of Burl's honey, appears motivated to steal by her desire to find anything she can to fill the void left by her dead father. Relocation to the country, where she is left alone all day with an elderly babysitter while Miriam works as a paralegal, exacerbates Eva's painful loneliness. But we discover through Miriam's story that Eva's mother has her own reasons for reacting dramatically to Eva's early signs of antisocial behavior. Although Miriam has told Eva that Francis, Eva's father, died of a heart attack, the truth is that he struggled with bipolar disorder and apparently committed suicide by overdosing on his medication; and much of Miriam's own behavior can be understood as the traumatic after-effects of having watched Francis descend into violent bouts of madness. The natural anxiety of motherhood is rendered more acute by Miriam's fear that Eva might have inherited Francis's disorder, and in trying to understand Eva's shoplifting Miriam is confronted with the daunting task of distinguishing normal adolescent behavior from incipient insanity. Her decision to move upstate is motivated by a sentimental ideal of the country as a bucolic remedy for the ills of civilization, but Graver's characterization of Burl (who has also dropped out of the urban rat race in search of the simple pleasures of rural life), suggests that relocation itself—what Francis had ridiculed as "the Geographic Cure" (22)—is an insufficient remedy for complex problems of grief and maturation. Burl is troubled by his own ambivalence about having cut himself off from his loved ones, and particularly from his lifelong occasional girlfriend, Alice. The crisis of the novel is set in motion when Eva surprises Burl while he is desperately masturbating to a photograph of his estranged love, an event that acutely disturbs her because of the manner in which it both corresponds to and violates her own sense of nascent sexuality.

The insinuation of an improper relationship between Eva and Burl, a possibility that both characters dimly recognize, lends a keen edge to their secret friendship. From the start, this danger is latent in the bees that bring them together, and it explodes in the climax of the novel. Disturbed by her encounter with Burl, feeling rejected on all sides, and desiring to explore the question of sexuality through the symbolic manipulation of bees, Eva takes it upon herself to "introduce" a queen bee into a hive. Her bungled attempt to do so causes the bees to attack her in a swarm. Burl arrives on the scene just in time to rescue her, but she is covered with stings and badly poisoned. As Eva recovers in a hospital, Miriam discovers what Eva has been doing with her days and takes the opportunity to reveal to Eva the truth about Francis's death. Graver laudably resists the temptation to reconstruct the nuclear family by having Miriam and Burl fall in love; Miriam remains suspicious of Burl, and Burl remains closed off in shame and solitude. The final chapter of the book suggests that Eva is starting to make friends of her own age and is developing along a healthy, normal trajectory, but there are no easy fixes in the beautiful but complex and dangerous world that Graver has imagined.

Bibliography

Graver, Elizabeth. *The Honey Thief*. San Diego: Harcourt 1999.

Sullivan, Mark. Review of *The Honey Thief*. *Boston College Chronicle*, 28 October 1999.

—Randy Laist

Hosseini, Khaled (1965–   ) *Afghan novelist*
Khaled Hosseini is the author of two international best sellers, *The KITE RUNNER* (2003) and *A Thousand Splendid Suns* (2007), both of which offer vivid accounts of life in Afghanistan, from the relative peace and prosperity prior to the Soviet invasion to the hardships associated with the Taliban. The international success of Hosseini's novels prompted a film adaptation of *The Kite Runner*, released in 2007 by DreamWorks, that was nominated for two Golden Globes and an Academy Award.

Hosseini was born in Kabul in 1965. His mother taught Farsi and history at a girl's high school, and his father was a diplomat. Because of his father's occupation, Hosseini's family traveled extensively, living in Tehran on the period 1970–73 and in Paris from 1976 to 1980. While the family was posted to Paris, the Soviet army invaded Afghanistan, and Hosseini's family sought and received political asylum in the United States, relocating to San Jose, California. Hosseini graduated with a bachelor of science degree from Santa Clara University in 1988, and completed his medical degree at the University of California, San Diego, in 1993, taking up practice in internal medicine in 1996. Despite initially pursuing a career in medicine, Hosseini, like Amir, the protagonist of *The Kite Runner*, had been passionate about storytelling since childhood, and in 2003 published his first novel, *The Kite Runner*, while still working as a doctor. The success of the novel enabled Hosseini to turn to writing fiction fulltime. He is currently a goodwill envoy for the United Nations High Commissioner for Refugees.

The Kite Runner is the story of Amir, a Pashtun boy, who grows up in pre-Soviet Kabul. Amir struggles to obtain the approval of his wealthy, masculine father, Baba, who cannot understand his son's bookish behavior and seems to prefer Amir's best friend Hassan, the son of Baba's servant. Hassan is Hazara, and the ethnic tensions in Afghanistan make him the target of the local bully, Assef. During a fateful kite-fighting tournament, Amir betrays Hassan, an event that eventually leads to their separation; and this separation becomes permanent when Baba and Amir flee Soviet-controlled Afghanistan and immigrate to California. Years later, having become a successful writer, Amir receives a summons from Baba's old friend, Rahim Khan, forcing Amir to confront his past and attempt to make amends.

Many elements of *The Kite Runner* are autobiographical. The nuanced, cosmopolitan world of pre-Soviet Kabul in which Amir grows up is based on Hosseini's own childhood memories. Indeed, Hosseini has stated that representing this world was one of the main motivations behind writing the novel:

> I wanted to write about Afghanistan before the Soviet war because that is largely a forgotten period in modern Afghan history. For many people in the west, Afghanistan is synonymous with the Soviet war and the

Taliban. I wanted to remind people that Afghans had managed to live in peaceful anonymity for decades, that the history of the Afghans in the 20th century has been largely pacific and harmonious. (Sethna)

Additional autobiographical aspects include the character of Hassan, who is a composite figure based on a neighborhood Hazara boy, Moussa, who was sexually abused, and a Hazara servant of Hosseini's family named Hossein Khan, whom Hosseini taught to read while living in Tehran. Baba's refusal to accept welfare in America reflects the commitment of Hosseini's father, who voluntarily removed his family from welfare as soon as he obtained a job. Hosseini and his father sold goods at the local flea market, surrounded by other Afghan refugees, as do Amir and Baba.

In *A Thousand Splendid Suns*, Hosseini eschews this autobiographical approach and focuses on the plight of two women, Mariam and Laila. Mariam is the illegitimate daughter of a wealthy businessman, Jalil, and his embittered former servant, Nana. After Nana commits suicide, Jalil quickly marries off the 15-year-old Mariam to a middle-aged shopkeeper, Rasheed. During the first few years of their marriage, Mariam miscarries several times, and Rasheed's indifference to her slowly turns into abusive behavior. Meanwhile, Laila is a happy child, growing up in Mariam and Rasheed's neighborhood. Her life becomes tragic, however, with the Soviet invasion of Afghanistan. Both of her brothers die fighting for the Mujahideen (the resistance movement), driving her mother into acute depression. In the civil war following the Soviet withdrawal, Laila loses both her parents in a mortar attack, and thinks she has lost her childhood friend turned lover, Tariq. In desperation, partly resulting from her unplanned pregnancy, Laila becomes Rasheed's second wife at the age of 14. Slowly, she and Mariam form a bond as they struggle together to raise a family, endure Rasheed's abusive behavior, and survive the hardships of Taliban rule in Afghanistan.

Hosseini explains that the story was inspired by his visit to Kabul in 2003, and the plight of women whom he encountered on the street: "I recall seeing these burqa-clad women sitting at street corners,

with four, five, six children, begging for change. I remember watching them walking in pairs up the street, trailed by their children in ragged clothes, and wondering how life had brought them to that point" (Penguin). According to Hosseini, the heartbreaking stories of destitution and struggle for survival that he heard from many of these women became the narrative pool out of which *A Thousand Splendid Suns* arose: "When I began writing *A Thousand Splendid Suns*, I found myself thinking about those resilient women over and over. Though no one woman that I met in Kabul inspired either Laila or Mariam, their voices, faces, and their incredible stories of survival were always with me, and a good part of my inspiration for this novel came from their collective spirit" (Penguin).

Both novels are multigenerational stories of characters whose personal lives are shaped by the violent upheavals in Afghanistan. Much of their emotional preoccupations center on parent-child relationships, whether biological or adoptive, and the complex and frequently flawed love between the generations deeply informs their respective motivations and decisions.

Hosseini's writing is a testament to the redemptive power of love, particularly in an environment where the comfortable routines of civil society have disappeared. *The Kite Runner* and *A Thousand Splendid Suns* vividly portray this breakdown of civil society in Kabul, through the contrast between evocative details of the music, customs, food, and street life that make up the city culture before the Soviet invasion, and the rubble-filled, war-plagued wasteland that follows it. Hosseini's novels are thematically linked to his charitable work on the immense Afghan refugee problem, with the latter stages of both works centering on a quest to find meaning and redemption by reconnecting with people who have been lost to the protagonists. As part of this quest, the characters must confront their own past, which reenters their lives in dramatic fashion. This aspect of Hosseini's narratives, along with their starkly contrasting good and evil characters and at times melodramatic plot twists, are reminiscent of the almost fabular tales of Charles Dickens; and despite the topicality of his stories on Afghanistan, Hosseini is a traditionalist in his style of storytelling. As he notes of his first novel, "Because the themes of friendship, betrayal, guilt, redemption, and the uneasy love between fathers and sons are universal and not specifically Afghan, the book has reached across cultural, racial, religious, and gender gaps to resonate with readers of various backgrounds. I think people respond to the emotions in this book" (Penguin).

Bibliography

Hosseini, Khaled. "Interview with Khaled Hosseini." Penguin Group (USA). Available online. URL: http://us.penguingroup.com/static/authors/popular/khaledhosseini.htm#top. Accessed April 30, 2008.

———. *A Thousand Splendid Suns*. New York: Penguin, 2007.

———. *The Kite Runner*. London: Bloomsbury, 2003.

———. "Interview—Khaled Hosseini." By Razeshta Sethna. Newsline. Available online. URL: http://www.newsline.com.pk/newsnov2003/newsbeat4nov.htm. Accessed April 30, 2008.

—Eugene Johnson

House of Leaves Mark Danielewski (2000)

House of Leaves is MARK DANIELEWSKI's highly experimental debut novel, employing copious footnoting, strange textual arrangements, colored text, an index and appendices, all to tell the story of a mysterious house in Virginia. The typographical devices, as well as the presence of multiple narrative voices, make any summary of the plot difficult, but the basic structure is that of a series of concentric narrative frames, each of which encloses and contextualizes those within. At the center is Will Navidson, who lives in the house and films his experiences. A man known only as Zampanò writes an analysis of this film, and beyond this is Johnny Truant, a young man who finds Zampanò's manuscript and edits it into a book.

Navidson is a Pulitzer Prize–winning photojournalist who promises his partner, Karen Green, that he will finally leave war zones and natural disasters behind, and the couple settle in suburbia with their two children, only to discover that their house is growing and changing shape. A closet becomes a hallway, which becomes a series of cold, windowless rooms and spiral staircases, all endlessly enlarging while the exterior of the home remains unchanged. Navidson decides to document this bizarre occurrence. At Karen's insistence, he distances himself from the danger, hiring professional spelunkers to investigate the enigmatic space. But when one explorer goes insane and the others become lost, Navidson and his brother Tom must venture on a rescue mission. Eventually, he edits this footage into a film, *The Navidson Record.*

Zampanò writes hundreds of pages analyzing the film, and thus much of *House of Leaves* is quasi-scholarly in tone. Some of Zampanò's writing describes the film, providing readers with Navidson's story, but this summary is augmented with a survey of criticism, reviews, interviews, and other materials supposedly written about the *Navidson Record*, as well as Zampanò's own interpretations. Little is revealed about Zampanò, but the authority of his account and analysis of the film is itself undermined when we discover that he is blind. Nor is the interpreter of *his* narrative able to be trusted very far, as Truant, though describing himself at length in his footnotes, turns out to be a drug-addled tattoo-parlor apprentice who has merely stumbled on Zampanò's output when breaking into his apartment after the old man's death. There he finds a massive and chaotic assortment of writings, "Endless snarls of words, sometimes twisting into meaning, sometimes into nothing at all, frequently breaking apart, always branching off into other pieces I'd come across later—on old napkins, the tattered edges of an envelope, once even on the back of a postage stamp" (xvii). As he attempts to pull the scraps of paper together into a cohesive document, strange things begin to happen. He hears growling noises, and believes his walls are moving, recalling the paranoia Navidson himself experienced in the house at the heart of the tale.

Much critical and scholarly attention to *House of Leaves* focuses on its textual arrangement, the frequent use of footnotes leading many to view the book as a satire of academic writing. More unusual than the number of footnotes, however, is their intrusive and whimsical deployment, with Danielewski placing them in boxes resembling windows or rooms all over the page (rather like the structural excrescence of Navidson's house). They are printed sideways, upside-down and backward, one citation followed by another, so that a reader must leaf back and forth through the same chapter several times to follow all the paths.

While this technique bears some resemblance to Talmudic typography, an inspiration the author readily admits, and while many critics recall the textual ironies of Laurence Sterne's *Tristram Shandy*, Danielewski cites film as his primary inspiration (his father, Tad Danielewski, was a film director). In a radio interview with Michael Silverblatt, he refers to his technique as "cinematic grammar." Just as a director controls the emotional response to a film through the length of shots and the pace of cuts, for example, Danielewski alternates very dense and spare pages to induce in his readers a sense of the frustration and invigoration felt by his own characters.

Another typological oddity is the printing of the word "house" (and its equivalents in other languages) in blue ink, prompting two main interpretations: one, that it is mimicking computer hypertext, and that *House of Leaves* invites readers (its "users") to choose links between sections rather than thinking of the narrative in a traditionally linear form; the other, that it means to evoke the blue-screen technology used in cinematic special effects, raising questions about reality and appearance in the text.

Unsurprisingly, then, a prominent theme of *House of Leaves* is literary interpretation itself, the novel being as concerned about how it is read as it is about what it describes. Danielewski displays considerable familiarity with literary theory, but also an impish irreverence. For example, when Zampanò includes a passage of Heidegger in German, Truant dutifully provides an English translation, but also adds, "Which only goes to prove the existence of crack in the early twentieth century" (25).

Moreover, Danielewski mixes the actual words of authors with invented contributions; prominent cultural figures such as Steven King, Harold Bloom, Ken Burns, Jacques Derrida, Hunter S. Thompson, and Stanley Kubrick each comment on *The Navidson Record,* though even within the narrative, Truant has difficulty confirming the film's existence: "no matter how long you search you will never find *The Navidson Record* in theaters or video stores" (xix–xx). He, like the reader, is never certain whether Zampanò was brilliant, mad, or merely a hoax-artist, and the line between truth and fiction, like that between conceptual and physical existence, is never clear.

Danielewski collaborated in the novel's creation with his sister, Annie, a rock musician who performs under the name "Poe"; and her second album, *Haunted,* reflects characters and themes from *House of Leaves,* with the two works being cross-promoted.

In 2006, Danielewski published *Only Revolutions,* a novel incorporating many of the same techniques as *House of Leaves,* such as colored text, marginalia, and multiple voices.

Bibliography

Danielewski, Mark Z. *House of Leaves.* New York: Pantheon, 2000.

———. "Mark Danielewski On Bookworm with Michael Silverblatt." Available online. URL: http://todgoldberg.typepad.com/tod_goldberg/2006/10/mask_danielewski.html. Accessed October 20, 2009.

———. *Only Revolutions.* New York: Pantheon, 2006.

Poe (Annie Danielewski). *Haunted.* Atlantic Records. 2000.

—Martin Brick

Ice Storm, The Rick Moody (1994)

The Ice Storm defies easy categorization, a curious composite of lugubrious humor, trenchant wit, and unresolved violence. Except for its final chapters, which contain faint but futile gestures toward warmth and tenderness, there is no thawing of the ice storm, no resolution to the exacting revenge of the elements on the meretricious world of the novel, the small, upscale boudoir town of New Canaan in Connecticut. Were it not for the novel's third and final section, which reckons the price of such vapid, meaningless existence, *The Ice Storm* might claim kinship with racy Restoration comedy, so replete is it with wife swapping, adultery, and other indiscriminate sexual romps that are all the more pathetic for being so conspicuously unsatisfying. In the end, the work may find its natural heirs in the deterministic novels of Theodore Dreiser and Frank Norris, as its characters are more automatons than people, their existence predestined to banality, and the engine that sparks their action, self-gratification, especially in the form of drugs and sexual release.

Though dominated more by pathos than tragedy, the novel observes the traditional unities, beginning on a Friday afternoon after Thanksgiving 1973, with its everyman protagonist, Benjamin Hood, looking for his mistress in her house—she has inexplicably disappeared after foreplay with him and prior to sexual consummation—and ending late on Saturday afternoon with Benjamin, his wife, Elena, and daughter Wendy picking up son Paul at the Stamford train station. Sandwiched between these incongruent scenes are roughly sequenced, overlapping scenes involving each of the four family members, sometimes conjointly, but more often than not with nonfamily; individuals suffering from an intoxicating mix of insecurity, inferiority, ennui, and isolation. Among the more memorable, in order of presentation, are daughter Wendy's nymphomaniacal tryst with Mikey Williams, the slightly older and much better endowed of the two Williams brothers; their discovery in flagrante delicto in the Williams's basement by Benjamin Hood, incomparably more deviant because more experienced and conscious of his turpitude; wife Elena's vituperative dressing down of Benjamin after his return home with the miscreant Wendy—this, prior to the couple's departure for the Halfords' house party; Paul Hood's trip to Manhattan to visit Libbetts Casey, another affluent cast-off preppy pubescent and his latest heart throb.

The house party at the Halfords dominates the second section of the novel, and epitomizes the depravity that festers in and consumes this suburbanite '70s world. The participating couples perfunctorily drop their house keys into a bowl upon entry to the party, and then each of the wives, upon exit, selects a set of keys other than her husband's to identify the man whom she will leave with and presumably bed. Although the feckless Benjamin Hood, out of self-recrimination, pledges nonparticipation, the reader gathers that his resolve will soon wilt in the face of temptation. Meanwhile, frustrated with her husband's previous infidelity,

Elena makes up her mind to overcome her inhibitions and habitual reserve, and to surprise even herself. While their parents are playing a sexual *spin the bottle* game at the Halfords, the Williams and Hood teenagers are riding roughshod on their own libidos, craving sexual release as an antidote to the existential isolation they already sense. From here, events inexorably mount to the climax of the third section, a freak accident outwardly attributable to the vehemence of the ice storm, but with its roots running deep into the culture and family buried beneath it.

Of the primary themes shaping the novel, and in spite of its almost hysterical socializing, perhaps the most prevalent is that of loneliness. None of the characters, particularly the husbands and wives, truly connect with, or even relate to each other—iced in, one might say. Benjamin Hood experiences insecurity and alienation everywhere: at work where he is becoming increasingly marginalized by upper management—and expects a pink slip in lieu of a bonus; at his mistress's where he is becoming more of an encumbrance than a handy tool; and at his home where his wife suspects him, rightly, of philandering. Hood's rejoinder to Elena's reprimands captures his sense of estrangement from her: "All I'm saying is that loneliness is the music of the spheres around here" (72).

At his expensive prep school, meanwhile, his son Paul Hood finds solace in the Kittredge Cult, a group of geeks and misfits: "The Cult is a tonic and a comfort" (87). Deprived and despairing of sexual gratification with girls like Carla Bear, who parry his awkward advances, Paul retreats further into fantasy, spending himself in bouts of unsatisfying autoeroticism.

Buried beneath this ubiquitous loneliness is systemic betrayal. "To be married," the narrator observes, "is to be both cuckolded and cuckolding." Janey Williams's infamous garter belt, into which Benjamin Hood masturbates after she goes missing, and which later resurfaces on his daughter Wendy, symbolizes the escapist sensuality in which the principal characters are enmeshed, and intimates the morbid urges that must ensue from such betrayals of trust. In the world of this novel, the sins of the fathers are assuredly visited upon their children.

As with their fabular experience of sexuality, the characters in the novel seem to flirt with caricature, almost devoid of subtlety or internal conflict. Benjamin Hood is as blithely disingenuous at the end of his New Canaan experience as he is at the beginning. Except for more promises of self-reformation, there is no evidence that he has learned anything material from his harrowing experience in the ice storm. The symbolism of the scapegoat evoked in the final episodes through the sacrificial offering of one of the teens for the sins of society is compelling and poignant, save for the fact that no social redemption ensues. "And right then there was a sign. An actual sign in the sky. . . . A flaming figure four" (278); yet even this portentous spectacle, for all its apparent significance, seems to result in nothing more than Benjamin's self-promising had done. The only redemptive trace that can be adduced from the sign is that Paul, Ben's drug-addicted teenage son, has learned to forgive his parents their fallibilities; in consequence, Paul can now embark on a life journey where fantasy need not be superimposed upon reality to make it palatable.

Bibliography

Moody, Rick. *The Ice Storm.* New York: Little, Brown, 1994. All quotes from the novel are taken from the First Back Bay paperback edition, August 2002, and page numbers of quotes are provided after the quote within parentheses in the text.

—Jerome L. Wyant

If You Lived Here, You'd Be Home by Now
Sandra Tsing Loh (1997)

Loh's novel captures the life of two young Los Angeles bohemians, living in their funky rental house and struggling to make ends meet, whose antiestablishment choices are set against the backdrop of the Los Angeles race riots and the booming real estate market of the early 1990s. The novel focuses on Bronwyn Peters, a Ph.D. dropout with fantasies of a perfect Cape Cod–style kitchen, her aspiring screenwriter boyfriend, Paul Hoffstead, and her formerly nerdy college friend Colin Martin (now a successful TV exec). *If You Lived Here, You'd*

Be Home by Now is a humorous love song to a generation trying to transcend their bohemian-college roots and attempt a more grown-up life.

When Bronwyn awakens to NPR playing on the radio in her rental house in the Tujunga neighborhood of Los Angeles, readers are immediately ushered into the weirdly familiar, ironic, and immensely amusing world of Loh's creation. Her lighthearted but penetrating exploration of the post-college experience brings to mind the work of other contemporary writers such as Aimee Bender (*The Girl in the Flammable Skirt*) and Miranda July (*No One Belongs Here More Than You*), while her lively style and sarcastic tone remind readers of satirist David Sedaris (*Naked; Me Talk Pretty One Day*). Like Sedaris, she is a successful commentator on NPR, and both use humor to highlight the moments in life when the melodramatic crosses over into the absurd.

As a chronicler of workaday life in the greater Los Angeles area, Loh brings her trademark daring wit to bear, portraying the young couple as leftie nonconformists, she a Ph.D. student in women's studies, he a struggling fiction- turned screenplaywriter. They listen to NPR, recycle, drive an old VW, and wait for "Paul's Talent" to be appreciated by the film industry. In fact, when he finally sells his first "real" script, they will marry and move fully into adulthood; until then, they cater their own parties with goods from Trader Joe's, vow to never go to the ocean because it's too cliché, and take in Paul's brother to help with the rent.

Although the novel focuses on both characters, its coming-of-age narrative belongs to Bronwyn. On the recommendation of an old college friend, she attends a housewarming party at the house of Colin Martin, a shy and awkward college acquaintance who has long had a crush on her. But she discovers there that her life-choices are not nearly as lucrative as the ones made by her peers. Colin's house is beautiful—a 1934 historic home with a kitchen that evokes all of Bronwyn's non-PC fantasies of material culture. Suddenly, the bargain-bin, faux-Thai brass elephant that Bronwyn brought as a housewarming gift seems not just out of style, but downright tacky and embarrassing; and for the first time Bronwyn begins to see her own bohemian style and life as less than charming.

A notable feature of Loh's narrative style is its skillful use of symbols, here illustrated by the Guatemalan doll earrings that Bronwyn purchases from a Pier 1 Imports–type store (Four Winds Emporium). Several minor characters in the novel admire the earrings, but the more attention they garner, the more Bronwyn begins to see them for what they really are: mass-produced "ethnic" kitsch. That they are dolls is significant, too, because they reflect Bronwyn's state of emotional immaturity.

Bronwyn's kitchen as fantasy object becomes a touchstone throughout the novel, representing her desire for adulthood, as well as her longing to participate in the world of successful young professionals. She invests her bourgeois fantasies into the perfect kitchen, and Colin's becomes "a sign, a totem, a set piece from another universe . . . another life entirely—*the life she should be living*" (52). It is significant and ironic that Bronwyn's fantasy room should be the kitchen, for as a traditionally feminine space, the kitchen represents gender-appropriate desires for this otherwise nontraditional female character. Indeed, considering that Bronwyn is a budding academic and her boyfriend an aspiring writer, it is important that Bronwyn does not dream of his-and-her offices or a library, or even a beautiful outdoor space (though they reside in Los Angeles). In Loh's novel, the kitchen signifies the promise both of heteronormative life and material abundance.

Eventually Paul's career gets a boost with a job writing for an "industrial"—a production tailored purely to the profit-making industry—here, a video on diversity training. The lure of a regular paycheck and health insurance pleases Paul and Bronwyn, especially since, as he begins work on "Diversity 2000 with Zibby Tanaka," Bronwyn discovers her funding in the women's studies department at UCLA has dried up. Nevertheless, with a little seed money from Paul's parents, the couple manages to buy a condo in downtown Los Angeles; and at their housewarming party they watch the unfolding Los Angeles riots on the streets below their high-rise building.

In the end, Bronwyn must confront the decidedly nontraditional choices she has made, and this theme is largely developed through her friendship with the successful Colin Martin. When Colin decides to leave Los Angeles to write his legal novel on a 25-acre farm outside Boulder, Colorado, Bronwyn is tempted to go with him; but she finally realizes that her fantasies have all been empty signs without real meaning, and that part of the process of growing into adulthood involves recognizing that these fantasies have retarded her growth and limited her happiness. The narrator notes, "in Bronwyn's life, for whatever reason, the only things that would ever be real were not the perfect things but the imperfect ones. The fearful, the ugly, the unmatched, the tattered, the battered, the worn" (216).

Bibliography

Loh, Sandra Tsing. *If You Lived Here, You'd Be Home by Now.* New York: Riverhead Books, 1997.

—Laura Gronewold

Impressionist, The Hari Kunzru (2002)

HARI KUNZRU's picaresque debut novel, *The Impressionist,* follows the transgressions and transformations of a mixed-race boy, first introduced as Pran Nath Razdan, who comes of age in the early decades of the 20th century. Throughout the novel, young Pran, a wealthy Kashmiri's randy (step-)son, dons and doffs multiple identities: Rukhsana, the sexually ambiguous hijra; Clive, the deferential British schoolboy; Pretty Bobby, the seductive neighborhood panderer; Chandra, the devoted native son; Robert, the studious pupil and apprentice; and Jonathan Bridgeman, the British lout and university don. Like Rudyard Kipling's Kim, who constantly wonders "Who am I?" against the backdrop of British colonialism's "Great Game," Pran must confront the unsettling possibility that identity (personal, national, racial, gendered, etc.) is fluid, changeable, and performed. Unlike Kipling's Irish urchin, Pran ultimately becomes a Homi Bhabha-esque colonial mimic, occupying a rebellious, hybrid space that defies colonialism's totalizing classifications (Bhabha).

Born of a capricious, monsoon-induced coupling between a British tree expert named Forrester and an Indian opium devotee named Amrita,

Pran's life is a study in the politics of colonial desire. Horrified by his "unnameable" and "potentially threatening" sexual transgression, Forrester flees the cave in which he is holed up with Amrita, and meets a watery end (13)—a curious echo of the annihilative Maribar cave experience described by E. M. Forster in *A Passage to India.*

Because Amrita's husband's family is Kashmiri, the boy's pale skin can be passed off within an Indian context, and his whiteness "is a source of pride to everyone . . . Kashmiris come from the mountains and are always fair, but Pran Nath's color is exceptional. It is proof, cluck the aunties, of the family's superior blood" (16). Yet once his true parentage is exposed, Pran's whiteness ceases to be a desirable attribute fetishized by multiple ethnic groups, and he is unceremoniously disavowed by Indians and British alike. Thus, Kunzru's text suggests young Pran simultaneously encapsulates the attraction, danger, threat, and rebellious potential of "miscegenation."

Forced by hunger and homelessness to take refuge in a brothel, Pran is forcibly refashioned into Rukhsana, a transvestite child prostitute. Here, Pran loses

> the pearl faculty . . . that secretes selfhood around some initial grain . . . leaving its residue dispersed in a sea of sensation, waiting to be reassembled from a primal soup of emotions and memories. Nothing so coherent as a personality. Some kind of Being still happening in there, but nothing you could take hold of. (53)

Now "a pile of Pran rubble, ready for the next chance event to put it back together in a new order," he is purchased by the Nawab of Fatehpur, offered to a pedophilic British major as part of an elaborate attempt to blackmail the empire, and thus used as a tool of anticolonial rebellion. While the major does rape Rukhsana (thereby neatly performing Edward Said's notion of an uber-masculine "West" that feminizes, infantilizes, and dominates the "East"), he is most aroused after having transformed the child into Clive, a traditional English schoolboy.

Once s/he realizes that s/he can pass for the real object of British desire—stereotypical, masculine Britishness itself—Pran/Rukhsana/Clive becomes a skilled, *intentional* mimic. In the midst of the turmoil following Dyer's 1913 Massacre, Clive begins a three-tiered existence as Robert/Chandra, an amanuensis and surrogate child to an estranged British missionary couple, and as Pretty Bobby, a flashy and desirable pimp in Bombay's seedier districts. After coming into possession of a murdered Englishman's passport and steamer ticket to London, Pretty Bobby sets sail, and becomes Jonathan Bridgeman, orphaned son of a British colonial officer. In 1920s London, and eventually as a student at Oxford, Jonathan strives mightily to perfect his impersonation of the quintessential English gentleman, although for years his massive gaps in knowledge and inability to play cricket mark him out as *"almost the same, but not quite"* (Bhabha 86, italics textual). Finally, Jonathan learns to obscure the "slippage," "excess," and "difference" that identify the colonial mimic, only to lose the object of his desire, an "English rose" who rejects him for being *"the most English person [she] know[s]"* (Bhabha 86, Kunzru 332, italics textual). Before embarking on a nihilistic journey to Africa, in which his rejection of Englishness and imperialism become complete, Jonathan visits a seedy Parisian cabaret in which he loses whatever faith he had left in the idea of an "essential" self. As he watches a professional impressionist transform himself into a succession of characters, he realizes that, like the weary performer, "[t]here is no escaping it. In between each impression, just at the moment when one person falls away and the next has yet to take possession, the impressionist is completely blank. There is nothing there at all" (333).

Kunzru's novel will inevitably draw comparison to ZADIE SMITH's *WHITE TEETH* (2000), and MONICA ALI's *BRICK LANE* (2003), works by and about people who challenge the definition of what it means to be "British" in the 20th and 21st centuries (Smith and Ali also joined Kunzru on *Granta*'s "Best Young British Novelists" list for 2003). However, Kunzru's exquisite, playful prose, and interrogation of the line between the personal and the political in Indian-British history also merits comparison to some of Salman Rushdie's work, including his Booker Prize–winning masterpiece, *Midnight's Children* (1980). Although not honored with Britain's top prize, *The Impressionist* was awarded the 2002 Betty Trask Prize for best first novel, the 2003 Somerset Maugham Award for best author of a novel under age 35, and the 2003 Jonathan Llewellyn Rhys Prize. Kunzru set the literary world aflutter by rejecting this final award on the grounds that its sponsor, the *Daily Mail,* maintained "an editorial policy of vilifying and demonising refugees and asylum-seekers." "As the child of an immigrant," Kunzru continued, "I am only too aware of the poisonous effect of the Mail's editorial line. The atmosphere of prejudice it fosters translates into violence, and I have no wish to profit from it" (Kunzru "Making Friends," Gibbons and Armitstead). Noted filmmaker Mira Nair (*Monsoon Wedding* [2001], *Vanity Fair* [2004], *The Namesake* [2006]) is also in no apparent rush to profit: although she purchased the film rights to Kunzru's novel, no imminent production schedule has been announced (Pais).

Bibliography

Bhabha, Homi. "Of Mimicry and Man: The Ambivalence of Colonial Discourse." In *The Location of Culture,* edited by Teresa Miller, 85–92. London: Routledge 1984.

Gibbons, Fiachra, and Claire Armitstead. "Author Rejects Prize from 'Anti-migrant' Newspaper." Guardian Unlimited. Available online. URL: http://www.guardian.co.uk/uk/2003/nov/21/pressandpublishing.books. Accessed March 12, 2007.

Kunzru, Hari. *The Impressionist.* New York: Dutton, 2002.

———. "Making Friends with the Mail." Hari Kunzru. Available online. URL: www.harikunzru.com/hari/jlr.htm. Accessed February 18, 2008.

Pais, Arthur. "Lost in Translation." Rediff.com. Available online. URL: http://in.rediff.com/movies/2008/feb/08lost.htm. Accessed March 13, 2008.

—Heidi LaVine

Indian Killer Sherman Alexie (1996)

Throughout the 19th century, the native population of North America was in steady decline. The indigenous peoples had been decimated by war and disease, or subjugated and imprisoned on government-sanctioned reservations, their lands effectively stolen from them and their culture forever changed by the "manifest destiny" of U.S. expansionism. From this oppression emerged a Native tradition referred to as the "Ghost Dance," which, beyond its mystical elements, was practiced as a means to organize resistance and demonstrate Native Americans' power as a nation on the brink of destruction.

Set in Seattle nearly 100 years after the Ghost Dance movement, *Indian Killer* is SHERMAN ALEXIE's treatment of a generation's struggle for Native authenticity in a starkly modern setting. As palpable anxiety becomes intertwined with the cool urban landscape of the novel, the morally ambiguous and ironically named figure of John Smith emerges. An adopted Native American of unknown tribal origin, Smith struggles to reconcile his adopted white heritage with the tribal collective he longs to be a part of. It remains uncertain whether Smith is in fact the true Indian killer, and Alexie leaves the ending open to interpretation. However, it is clear that the most violent possible manifestation of the spirit of the Ghost Dance is alive and haunting the streets of Seattle.

Though he is the physical embodiment of traditional Native masculinity, Smith struggles within the parameters of a "third-space" identity. As he helps construct what is rumored to be the last skyscraper in Seattle, and feeling a sense of impending extinction himself, Smith rebels against the increasingly oppressive whiteness that surrounds him. Meanwhile, in a startling new interpretation of the Ghost Dance, a killer haunts the streets of Seattle, scalping and ritually mutilating white men in an act of seemingly pointless rebellion. Told through an experimental fusion of stream of consciousness, interviews, radio transcripts, and traditional narrative, with severely repressed traces of Alexie's typical down-to-earth humor, *Indian Killer* is arguably the novelist's darkest work.

Smith's adoption has left him a cultural outsider in relation to the modern Native American collective, which relies heavily on family and community as a basis of social and cultural development. In his most recent novel, *The Absolutely True Diary of a Part-Time Indian*, a semiautobiographical work, Alexie's understanding of the tribal collective is explored in great detail. Deciding to leave his reservation after discovering that his class-assigned geometry textbook actually belonged to his mother nearly 30 years before, Arnold Spirit, the literary incarnation of Alexie, painfully comes to terms with being forever cast as an outsider in his own tribe. Through Arnold, Alexie recalls being referred to as an "apple": red on the outside, white on the inside; and this racially charged metaphor is directly related to the anxiety that Smith feels regarding his authenticity (Alexie, 132) in *Indian Killer.*

The complexities in Smith's character are as significant to present theories of collectivity as they are challenging to contemporary delineations of identity. While he is the physical embodiment of the imposing Indian warrior, he is fatally and unnaturally separated from the so-called tribal collective. Standing at 6'5", with long, traditionally braided hair, he leaves no doubt in the minds of passersby that he is of Native descent; the only questions about his identity come from Smith himself. His cultural anxiety principally stems from his inability to situate himself outside his adopted white lineage in any way *other* than by lying about his heritage—at various times claiming Navajo, Spokane, and Sioux descent when asked his tribal origin. He is mentally torn between the oppositional binaries of the so-called real Indian and the notorious "Wannabee."

Not generally considered a typical Native occupation, building skyscrapers is the profession that Smith has chosen for himself because it seems "The Indian thing to do" (22). He was first drawn to construction—most specifically to building skyscrapers—because of an article he read about the near-legendary Mohawk steel workers who built the Empire State Building. Reckless and daring, the Mohawk workers, described as walking across girders without safety harnesses like they were "Spiderman's bastard sons," are a compelling group of "real Indian" role models for Smith (Alexie, 132). Physically, and by all appearances emotionally removed from the reservation, tackling heavy construction in New York City, the Mohawks are as separated from their tribe as Smith is; and he is inspired by these freelance Indians, who are employing what he refers to as "real Indian instincts" to guide them through a life that is the opposite of "mundane"

(130)—so marginal, literally and figuratively, that they finally seem to transcend the racial distinctions that bedevil him.

The so-called Wannabee Indians, a common fixture in Alexie's work (most notably, *The Absolutely True Diary of a Part-Time Indian* and *Reservation Blues*), are ironically treated as a tribal collective in and of themselves. The Wannabees—exemplified in *Indian Killer* in the figures of American literature professor Dr. Mather, and author of Native American detective novels Jack Wilson—are a small "tribe" of turquoise-wearing whites who claim Indian heritage, but who in reality may or may not possess minuscule percentages of Native blood.

Over the course of several chapters, Smith fantasizes about his would-be life on his home reservation, complete with fry-bread, grass-dancing, and Scrabble in the tribal language, but his fantasies are the closest he comes to successful integration into tribal culture until he is haphazardly inducted into Marie Polatkin's urban tribe. Smith meets Marie during a student protest on the grounds of Washington State University; she is the confrontational and somewhat overzealous leader of the Native American student-union at Washington State. While doling out sandwiches to homeless Native Americans around downtown Seattle, Marie establishes relationships with the impoverished urban Indians, and becomes a militant supporter of Native traditionalism. Upon meeting Smith for the first time, she is puzzled by his shyness, and it is immediately obvious to her that he has, for whatever reason, been ostracized from his tribe. Ostracized from her own, Marie is coming to terms with her (successful) life outside the reservation. Though she is a "real Indian," Marie herself is suffering with a tribal disconnect stemming from the fact that she is one of the only members of her family to leave the reservation in order to pursue life in the "white world," much like Alexie himself.

The anxiety of authenticity felt by nearly every character is central to the novel's thematic progression, though the debate as to what a "real Indian" is remains ultimately inconclusive; and at the novel's rather abrupt climax, it is still uncertain whether the killer was the spirit of the Ghost Dance movement, a paranoid and confused John Smith, an enraged Reggie Polatkin, or an anonymous criminal with a desire for racial sabotage. However, it is certain that the Indian Killer has left the streets of Seattle in a state of desperate racial disrepair—or perhaps merely exposed it, and that the murders in Seattle may be only the beginning.

Bibliography

Alexie, Sherman. *Indian Killer.* New York: Warner Books, 1996.
———. *The Absolutely True Diary of a Part-Time Indian.* New York: Little, Brown Young, 2007.
———. *Reservation Blues.* New York: Grand Central Publishing, 1996.

—Tealia DeBerry

Infinite Jest David Foster Wallace (1996)

With its 1,079 pages of shuffled story lines, appended errata, and acronymic alphabet soup, DAVID FOSTER WALLACE's encyclopedic *Infinite Jest* at times resembles just that—although at whose expense remains undecided. In Wallace's comically critical vision of the near future, North America, Canada, and Mexico have been unified into one state called the Organization of North American Nations (O.N.A.N.), and a large part of the former northeastern United States and southeastern Canada has been transformed into a massive waste dump. Called "The Concavity," this toxic site spawns gooey unstructured babies, and even a legendary "giant Infant" that leaves house-high piles of its own waste while keenly searching for its lost parents. The monstrous scatology of both this setting and its by-products sets the stage for a cacophony of stories, narrated by a multitude of disparate voices, concerned with loss, neglected children, and infantile need.

For this is a novel about story-telling, and a novel of talking. As Thomas LeClair has pointed out (35), it thus invites comparison to *The Arabian Nights*, as characters tell their stories in desperate attempts to escape the deadly draw of solipsism that O.N.A.N. culture toxically manufactures. In its hyper-capitalistic world, corporations purchase naming rights to years, resulting in terms like "The Year of the Depend Adult Undergarment," under whose waste-invoking banner most of the novel's action occurs. Partially in response to a culture that promises an almost literal personal fulfillment through consumption, characters in the novel struggle, in ways alternately comic, tragic, and pathetic, with the emptiness and longing that remain despite even their most extreme attempts to fulfill themselves. Hal Incandenza provides a vivid example of such misguided attempts, submitting to torturous yet addictive training at the Enfield Tennis Academy (E.T.A.) while experimenting in increasingly dangerous ways with drugs. These he does primarily to avoid feeling the pain of the damage inflicted by his parents. His largely absent father, James, founder of the E.T.A., manages to engineer a way to explode his own head in a microwave oven—but not to keep young Hal from discovering the result; while his mother, Avril, locked in obsessive-compulsive disorders largely concerned with fear of filth, imposes her own apathy on Hal in the aftermath of this loss.

Hal's two older brothers exhibit their own scars from their relationships with their parents. The oldest, professional punter Orin, becomes a serial lover of young mothers, seemingly in an attempt to possess the love of the mother from whom he remains estranged. The middle brother, Mario, suffers debilitating physical deformations from birth, yet presents one of the few happy, earnest figures in the novel. Hal, devoted to the ironic hipness adopted by the culture at large, nurtures Mario like an older brother, while never understanding his sincerity and capacity for emotion. Failing to palliate himself through traditional means like talk therapy, as well as nontraditional ones like devotion to tennis, Hal ultimately finds himself (possibly as a result of taking the drug DMZ) stripped of the very powers of communication and athleticism that had previously defined him. And his story ends, as the novel begins, with an infantile regression so complete that his every attempt to express himself sounds only like animalistic screams.

Interwoven with Hal's story is that of Don Gately, a former Demerol addict turned counselor at the Ennet House drug rehabilitation facility. Plagued by his own memories (or fantasies) of being abandoned by his mother, Gately redeems himself after years of abusive drug use and accompanying selfish behavior by listening to the stories of newly recovering addicts. Among these is a veiled woman whose face has been maimed by acid thrown by her mother (and mixed by her father). Pre-acid, this woman, Joelle Van Dyne, had been a lover of Orin and assistant to his father James, and she appears as the central figure in James's most influential film series, *Infinite Jest,* providing one of many connections between the stories of Hal and Gately. Conceived as the ultimate cure for the pain of human incompleteness, *Infinite Jest* turns out to bring only the solace of death; and the final version shows Joelle looking into the camera—which has been blurred to suggest the gaze of a newborn babe—and repeatedly apologizing. Incandenza meant the film to salve the loss of completeness first experienced by the separating baby but felt most deeply and inescapably by the unfulfilled adult. And ironically, the film accomplishes just this magic, engrossing its viewers so completely that they become unable to break their gaze with the apologetic mother figure—dying where they are sitting. Hal's and Gately's story lines also link with a third, that of Quebecois separatists (Les Assassins des Fauteuils Rollants, or the A.F.R.), determined to kill off Americans by finding, replicating, and delivering to them copies of the film *Infinite Jest.* Known in English as "The Wheelchair Assassins," these maimed men, with deadly earnestness pose a question that remains unarticulated but crucial for both Hal and Gately: Do things exist worth acting and even dying for? How could we determine them, when our language is broken?

All of these attempted solutions (tennis, drugs, and film) to humanity's insatiable need lead only to regression to an infantile state, and the narcissistic solipsism that accompanies it. Shortly after publishing *Infinite Jest,* Wallace explored exactly this relationship between our inborn and culturally encouraged need, and narcissistic solipsism, in the essay "A Supposedly Fun Thing I'll Never Do Again," in a collection by the same name (1997). *Jest,* then, reads as a critique of the many ways our contemporary American culture creates and then tries to alleviate need through advertising, consumerism, media, and technology, as well as the "hip" ironic posture of disaffection that has come to characterize both high and low culture. In fact, Wallace explicitly positions his novel in opposition to this culture of apathetic irony in a 1993 interview with Larry McCaffery, and an essay on television entitled "E Unibus Pluram: Television and U.S. Fiction."

But as is typical of Wallace's writing, from his first novel *The Broom of the System* (1987) to his most recent collection of short stories, *Oblivion* (2004), *Jest* is above all comically clever, delineating its complex virtual world partly through its own jargon- and acronym-filled vocabulary, so extensive that it spawns a lengthy addendum of "Notes and Errata." Such linguistic playfulness produces in-jokes that pile up self-referentially as the novel moves along. But the linguistic complexity also points to one of the novel's main thematic concerns: the growing sense that, in this culture awash in technology, hip disaffection, and meaningless irony, language in the end may amount to nothing more than a meaningless trick. Linguistic tricks abound in the nearly 100 pages of notes that follow the novel proper, calling into question what we can know from the language that came before, whether yet more language can elucidate anything, and where if anywhere the novel truly ends. For the "Notes and Errata" prove integral to the novel, commenting on, adding to, and in some cases contradicting the storylines contained within the main text. In so doing, the section destabilizes novelistic elements like narrative and voice. This kind of end-noted self-referentiality has become a near staple in novels written since *Jest*, perhaps most famously in DAVE EGGERS's irony-busting *A HEARTBREAKING WORK OF STAGGERING GENIUS* (2001). Taken even further, such structural complexity becomes hypertextuality, in which one text or novel can seem to contain a host of texts that refer, without beginning or end, to each other, as in MARK DANIELEWSKI's groundbreaking hypertext *HOUSE OF LEAVES* (2000).

Bibliography

Danielewski, Mark Z. *House of Leaves.* New York: Pantheon Books, 2000.

Eggers, Dave. *A Heartbreaking Work of Staggering Genius.* New York: Vintage Books, 2001.

LeClair, Thomas. "The Prodigious Fiction of Richard Powers, William Vollmann, and David Foster Wallace." *Critique* 38, no. 1 (1996): 12–37.

Wallace, David Foster. *The Broom of the System.* New York: Avon, 1993.

———. "E Unibus Pluram: Television and U.S. Fiction." *Review of Contemporary Fiction* 13.2 (1993): 151–195.

———. *Infinite Jest.* Boston: Little, Brown, 1996.

———. "An Interview with David Foster Wallace." By Larry McCaffery. *Review of Contemporary Fiction* 13.2 (1993): 127–150.

———. *Oblivion.* Boston: Little, Brown, 2004.

———. *A Supposedly Fun Thing I'll Never Do Again: Essays and Arguments.* New York: Little, Brown, 1997.

—Mary Holland

Inheritance of Loss, The Kiran Desai (2006)

KIRAN DESAI's second novel garnered numerous critical accolades, winning the Man Booker Prize in 2006 and the U.K. National Book Critics' Award in 2007. Moving away from the magic realism of Desai's much shorter first book, *Hullaballo in the Guava Orchard*, the novel turns its attention to the larger themes of love and loss against a background of colonial and postcolonial politics.

Set in the town of Kalimpong, in the India-Nepal border state of Sikkim, the novel depicts an ethnic mix of Hindus, Indian-born Nepalis, and refugees from neighboring Chinese-occupied Tibet, and conveys a vivid sense of geography and politics:

> Here, where India blurred into Bhutan and Sikkim, and the army did pull-ups and pushups, maintaining their tanks with khaki paint in case the Chinese grew hungry for more territory than Tibet, it had always been a messy map. The papers sounded resigned. A great amount of warring, betraying, bartering had occurred; between Nepal, England, Tibet, India, Sikkim, Bhutan; Darjeeling stolen from here, Kalimpong plucked from there—despite, ah, despite the mist charging down like a dragon, dissolving, undoing, making ridiculous the drawing of borders. (9)

Set against this swirling backdrop of historical and political events, the novel is essentially a love story, the "loss" of the title describing an abortive love affair between Sai, the daughter of a retired Indian judge, and Gyan, a Nepalese-Indian mathematics tutor hired to educate her. The tale switches rapidly between the narrative present: "It was February of 1986. Sai was seventeen years old, and her romance with Gyan the mathematics tutor was just a year old" (8); and the history of the colonel, Sai's grandfather.

We follow the colonel through his preparation for service to the British colonial administration in the 1930s, to his experience of racism at Cambridge, and through his privileged legal career in India. Desai is intensely critical of the colonial system that bestowed privileges unequally on Indians, and we are introduced, through Judge Patel's memory, to the absurd logic of Anglophilia:

> He envied the English. He loathed Indians. He worked at being English, with the passion of hatred and for what he would become, he would be despised by absolutely everyone, English and Indians, both. (137)

It is out of this hatred that Patel later comes to regard his own wife as a liability, and sends her back to her parents, forgoing any relationship with his daughter. She in turn is alienated by her mother's family after marrying an Indian astronaut and giving birth to Sai. In a bizarre turn of events, both Sai's parents are run over by a bus in Moscow, and she is orphaned. Upon graduation from the Augustinian college where she is interned, Sai is returned to her grandfather.

Entwined with the twin-stories of the Patel family, the novel's other major narrative strand tells the story of Biju, the son of Patel's servant, an illegal migrant in the United States. Desai describes his movement from one exploitative job in the food industry to another, deftly narrating through his father's eyes the conditions faced by Indian diasporic communities the world over:

> "Terrible," he said. "My bones ache so badly, my joints hurt—I may as well be dead. If not for Biju. . . ." Biju was his son in America. He worked at Don Pollo—or was it The Hot Tomato? Or Ali Baba's Fried Chicken? His

father could not remember or understand or pronounce the names, and Biju changed jobs so often, like a fugitive on the run—no papers. (3)

Finally admitting defeat, Biju hears of the political strife in India and decides to return home to his father. Marshalling every penny he has, he makes his way to Kalimpong; but returns to find the regular means of transport blocked due to riots and takes a taxi ride, during which he is robbed of all his possessions. Limping home in the final pages of the novel, he has a joyful reunion with his father, witnessed through Sai's eyes:

> Sai looked out and saw two figures leaping at each other as the gate swung open. The five peaks of Kanchenjunga [Mt. Everest] turned golden with the kind of luminous light that made you feel, if briefly, that truth was apparent. All you needed to do was reach out and pluck it. (324)

This return to the epiphanic beauty of nature is another significant theme in the novel. Earlier in the narrative, Sai muses on Edmund Hilary and his guide Tenzing Norgay's "conquest" of the mountain, and wonders "Should humans conquer the mountain or should they wish for the mountain to possess them? . . . there were those who said it was sacred and shouldn't be sullied at all" (155). These descriptions of the natural world form a contrast to the political and personal tragedies in the novel, completing the sense of awe on the opening page as Desai describes the mist as "making ridiculous the drawing of borders" (9).

The Inheritance of Loss is thus as much about the *cultural* inheritance of tragedy as it is about the familial, dealing with love both at the level of individuals and families and at the level of world politics. Its interest in the increasingly globalized politics of love places it alongside other Indian novels of the era, such as ARUNDHATI ROY's *The GOD OF SMALL THINGS;* and Sai's portentous remark that "the simplicity of what she'd been taught wouldn't hold. Never again could she think there was but one narrative" (3) reads remarkably like Roy's declaration that "never again would a story be told as though it was the only one."

Bibliography

Desai, Kiran. *The Inheritance of Loss*. London: Hamish Hamilton, 2006.

George. Rosemary Marangoly. "At a Slight Angle to Reality: Reading Indian Diaspora Literature," MELUS, 21, no. 3 (Autumn 1996): 179–193.

Ondaatje, Michael. *In the Skin of a Lion*. New York: Knopf, 1987.

Roy, Arundhati. *The God of Small Things*. New York: Random House, 1997.

—David Nel

Interpreter of Maladies Jhumpa Lahiri

(1999)

Few literary debuts experience the immediate success that JHUMPA LAHIRI's *Interpreter of Maladies* enjoyed on its release in 1999. Winner of that year's Pulitzer Prize in literature, Lahiri's short story cycle about Indian and Indian-American life captured the attention of the international literary public, also winning the PEN/Hemingway Award and the *New Yorker*'s Best Debut of the Year Award. Though now a staple in literary anthologies and college classrooms, the book was distinguished by humble beginnings; Lahiri explains how, immediately after graduating from college, she had access to a personal computer for the first time, an opportunity that allowed her to come to work early and stay late in order to write (Lahiri "Interview"). She confesses her dissatisfaction with much of her early work but recalls her continued commitment to writing until her words pleased her, until they sounded good, often writing only a page or two at a time. Because writing lengthier text appeared a daunting task for the young writer, the short story became her primary vehicle, yet it is hard to imagine that these fitful starts could result in the artful and seamless prose of *Interpreter of Maladies*.

Lahiri deftly interweaves several recurring themes in the collection, including the value of individuals and families sharing a meal as an act of unity, or community. Similarly, the characters use food to reconnect with their homeland. Relation-

ships between Indian Americans in varying stages of assimilation, as well as the detailed struggles and silences that occur in and between both men and women are also explored, and skillfully exploited as tensions and motive forces in Lahiri's tight plotting.

The first story in the cycle, "A Temporary Matter," is emblematic. The narrator, Shukumar, modestly introduces us to himself and his wife. Recently married, the two are dealing with a fresh tragedy in their young lives together, in the form of a stillborn baby. Until now, Shoba has historically invested herself in shopping and preparing food: "the pantry was always stocked with extra bottles of olive and corn oil, depending on whether they were cooking Italian or Indian. There were endless boxes of pasta in all shapes and colors, zippered sacks of basmati rice, whole sides of lambs and goats from the Muslim butchers and Haymarket, chopped up and frozen in endless plastic bags. Every other Saturday they wound through the maze of stalls Shukumar eventually knew by heart" (7). They shop together and entertain together frequently: "When friends dropped by, Shoba would throw together meals that appeared to have taken half a day to prepare. . ." (7). After Shoba loses the baby, Shukumar takes over preparing the meals, and a temporary loss of electricity in their apartment provides the serendipitous opportunity for healing, as they are forced to eat Shukumar's hot meals by candlelight, whose flame helps to mend the frosty silences characterizing their now strained relationship.

Similarly, in the tale "When Mr. Pirzada Came to Dine," Lahiri dwells on the importance of the collective meals between Mr. Pirzada and 10-year-old Lilia's family; simple but evocative meals like "lentils with fried onions, green beans with coconut, fish cooked with raisins in yogurt sauce" (30). Lilia's family looks up Indian names in the local phone book, and subsequently invites one Mr. Pirzada over for "long leisurely meals" (34). Reviewer Charles Taylor writes that "food in these stories is a talisman, a reassuring bit of the homeland to cling to" (Taylor). The story of their evolving friendship with Mr. Pirzada, a temporary visitor to their American university during the war in Pakistan in 1971, takes place around the meals they share, and is told from Lilia's point of view, in a fresh perspective on the arbitrary idea of "nation."

In "Mrs. Sen's," the transplanted Mrs. Sen is committed to maintaining a meal of fresh fish once a day in America, as she had always done in India. Eleven-year-old Eliot, another child narrator in the collection, stays with Mrs. Sen daily after school and enjoys a snack while watching her chop vegetables and spices for her dinner: "With Eliot's help the newspapers were crushed with all the peels and seeds and skins inside them. Brimming bowls and colanders lined the countertop, spices and pastes were measured and blended, and eventually a collection of broths simmered over periwinkle flames on the stove" (117). As Mrs. Sen attempts to learn the customs of America, Mr. Sen presses on her the importance of her learning to drive, and frequently encourages her to try. Mrs. Sen resists, yet is motivated to drive once a day to obtain fresh fish, homesick for her native land: "In Calcutta people ate fish first thing in the morning, last thing before bed, as a snack after school if they were lucky. It was available in any market, at any hour, from dawn to midnight" (124). Mrs. Sen's reluctance to drive and to embrace American customs, as well as her dependence on Mr. Sen as her only relative and friend illuminates another of Lahiri's themes in this collection: the struggle for Indians to balance both Indian and American customs and cultures while living in America.

In "This Blessed House," Twinkle and Sanjeev argue over the religious objects found in their recently purchased New England home. As a Hindu, Sanjeev finds the statues of Christ irrelevant and even slightly offensive. Twinkle, on the other hand, appears more at home in American culture, and feels less threatened by the "biblical stickers"(145), "white porcelain effigy of Christ" (136), and the "larger-than-life-sized watercolor poster of Christ, weeping translucent tears the size of peanut shells and sporting a crown of thorns," tucked neatly behind the radiator in the guest bedroom (139). The story of their arranged marriage and ex post facto evolution as a couple is delicately interwoven with Twinkle's devotion to the religious artifacts and Sanjeev's quest to accept her idiosyncrasies as his wife and partner. And the delicate, luminous, almost Austenian architecture of the tale is a model both of Lahiri's thematic palette and of her great skill in its application.

Bibliography
Brada-Williams, Noelle. "Reading Jhumpa Lahiri's *Interpreter of Maladies* as a Short Story Cycle." *MELUS*, 29 (2004): 451–464.

Lahiri, Jhumpa. *Interpreter of Maladies*. New York: Houghton Mifflin, 1999.

———. "Interview with Jhumpa Lahiri." By Charlie Rose. Charlie Rose. Available online. URL: http://www.charlierose.com/view/interview/9106. Accessed May 20, 2009.

Taylor, Charles Review of *Interpreter of Maladies*. Salon.com. Available online. URL: http://www.salon.com/books/review/1999/07/27/lahiri/. Accessed May 20, 2009.

—Tatia Jacobson Jordan

Intuitionist, The Colson Whitehead (1999)

Like his subsequent novels, *John Henry Days* (2001) and *APEX HIDES THE HURT* (2006), COLSON WHITEHEAD's debut is allegorical, satirical, allusive, and set in a disarmingly idiosyncratic world. The novel's opening scene introduces an animated debate between two competing knowledge systems, "Intuitionism" and "Empiricism." Responding to a routine service call, city elevator inspector Lila Mae Watson stands in the car with her eyes closed, visualizing a series of variously colored geometric shapes as she travels between floors. As a highly trained Intuitionist, Watson does not require the visual observations and diagnostic tools favored by the Empiricist camp that dominates her field. When she cites the building supervisor for a violation, he notes two other differences that mark Lila Mae: "I haven't ever seen a woman elevator inspector before, let alone a colored one" (8). After the service call, Lila Mae discovers that an elevator at one of her buildings has gone into free fall and crashed, an unprecedented event that tarnishes her perfect accuracy rate. During the events that follow, the supposedly entrenched philosophical differences between Empiricists and Intuitionists become mere fodder for the broader political struggle between the two factions. Chancre, a leading Empiricist, uses the incident to exploit public doubts about Intuitionism and ensure his election as Chair of the Elevator Inspectors Guild. Assuming she has been framed by the Empiricists, Lila Mae goes into hiding, finding refuge with other Intuitionists before setting out to discover who might have engineered the collapse.

The first of *The Intuitionist*'s two roughly equal halves ("Down" and "Up") borrows extensively from the *noir* tradition of detective novels, popularized in the 1930s and '40s by writers like Dashiell Hammett and Raymond Chandler. We find a corrupt labor leader (Chancre) in league with a brutal mob boss (Johnny Shush), an investigative journalist (Ben Urich) determined to expose Chancre's misdeeds, the intrepid sleuthing of Lila Mae herself, and a Hitchcockian maguffin (secret plans for an elevator known only as the "black box") pursued by all of the novel's warring factions. While the narrative never specifies its historical setting, both its *noir* conventions and characters' casual use of antiquated racial epithets suggest an era pre-dating the civil-rights advances of the 1950s and '60s. Lila Mae is therefore both shocked and inspired when she discovers that James Fulton, the founder of Intuitionism and the creator of the black box, had an African-American mother. She learns the secret from Natchez, a nephew of Fulton's who wants to reclaim his birthright: "What he made, this elevator, colored people made that. It's ours. And I'm going to show that we ain't nothing" (140). Natchez makes clear his desire to elevate the black community as a whole, and the novel's central metaphor of verticality explicitly resonates with this hope of social advancement, especially for African Americans.

Fulton's passing narrative is but one of many instances in which the novel explores the performative nature of identity. Lila Mae assumes a number of disguises in the course of her investigation. More remarkable, however, are the role that disguise and concealment play in her everyday life, revealed through frequent flashbacks to her childhood, schooling, and early career. Whitehead frequently describes Lila Mae's everyday persona as a defensive construction, as in the scene in which she examines herself in the mirror at the Intuitionist House: "She puts her face on. In her case, not a

matter of cosmetics, but will. How to make such a sad face hard? It took practice" (57). The self-constructed nature of Lila Mae's "game face" contrasts with the skin lighteners and hair straighteners sold by salesman Freeport Jackson, a huckster she meets while trying to stake out a rival elevator worker. Of course, both are strategies for climbing the social ladder—in Lila Mae's case, from the segregated South to the quasi-integrated North, and from her father's occupation as an elevator operator in a whites-only department store to her middle-class civil-service position. Both her recognition of the tenuous nature of her position and her fervent desire to maintain it are key elements of Lila Mae's character, helping explain both the deliberately constructed nature of her public persona and her dogged attempt to clear her name of wrongdoing in the elevator collapse. She ultimately finds comfort in Fulton's long-missing third notebook, in which he writes of a "second elevation"—perhaps Whitehead's nod to the upcoming success of the civil-rights movement, or perhaps a more abstract transition from an emphasis on "the skin of things" to a deeper understanding of reality (255, 239).

A series of revelations in the novel's second half ("Up") disrupts the epistemological certainty promised by the preceding detective plot, demonstrating the folly of Lila Mae's attempt at empirical investigation in a world whose very terms are controlled by a power structure she is unable to see: not the warring guilds of Intuitionism and Empiricism she initially suspected, but the dueling industrial concerns of Arbo and United, elevator manufacturers driven not by philosophy or politics but by profit. By novel's end, Lila Mae has accepted the limits of both knowledge systems, abandoning the detective role she had played with such relish. As in Thomas Pynchon's *The Crying of Lot 49*, the search for knowledge is thus itself thematized, and what begins as a search for a hidden order ends with a tentative acceptance of the arbitrary: "What her discipline and Empiricism have in common: they cannot account for the catastrophic accident" (227). The elevator collapse reveals itself not as a product of conspiracy, but rather as an opportunity for multiple conspirators, each of whom hopes to use the incident for their own ends. Even the sincerity of Fulton's writings is drawn into question, and Lila Mae ultimately continues to believe in his work because she feels she has learned a new way to read that reveals far greater truths than those she lived by as an elevator inspector.

The Intuitionist's thematic concerns with identity, performance, and the social construction of knowledge ally it with a potent strain of postmodern literature and theory. While the narrative unfolds exclusively within the representative mode, the numerous plot shifts and revelations in the novel's second half frustrate any comprehensive and objectively verifiable reading. Whitehead's dense and often dazzling first novel earned overwhelmingly positive reviews from a wide variety of critics, and was a finalist for the PEN/Hemingway award for a distinguished first book of fiction. Along with *John Henry Days,* it led to a 2004 "genius grant" from the MacArthur Foundation. A frequent contributor to several journalistic outlets, Whitehead also published *Colossus of New York,* a 13-part essay cycle, in 2003.

Bibliography
Whitehead, Colson. *The Intuitionist.* Anchor: New York, 1999.

—Mark P. Bresnan

Isaac and His Devils **Fernanda Eberstadt**
(1991)
In her second, critically acclaimed novel, *Isaac and His Devils* (1991), FERNANDA EBERSTADT explores the correlation between genius and environment in a highly stylized language that recalls the premodernist traditions of American letters.

The narrative is centered on Isaac Hooker, a precocious, overweight, half-deaf, and socially awkward child from Gilboa, New Hampshire, who is certain that he is predestined for greater things: to escape the provincial New England town and join the select ones who "were composing symphonies and epics, designing fighter planes, staging plays, receiving prizes." He is unconditionally supported by his father, Sam, who gave up his own dream of becoming a poet when Isaac was born. In order to provide for the family and indulge the demands of his wife Mattie, Sam terminated his graduate stud-

ies and became a teacher at a local high school. Yet Mattie does not understand or sympathize with the child who on the day "he was born . . . had already spoiled his mother's evening." She is a typical anti-intellectual—beautiful, boastful, and a bully—who was not only repeatedly held back in school but is openly contemptuous of any unpractical knowledge. The marriage that Sam has come to view as a terrible mistake divides both parents and offspring. Isaac's younger brother Turner is his mother's son, eager to accumulate wealth. Despite his understanding of computer technology—still an exceptional gift in the 1980s—he accepts a job with a construction company and helps his mother run a taxi business. Given such an environment, it comes as no surprise that the first 22 years of Isaac's life are characterized by a struggle with demons, evoked equally by teachers who do not know as much as he does, girls who are terrified by his inappropriate small talk, and friends who ignore his verbose scholarly outbursts. Yet, when Isaac at last manages with the help of his math teacher and lover, Agnes Urquhart, to enter the alleged epicenter of intellectual life, Harvard University, he faces corresponding, if contrasting, challenges to those that were supposedly impeding his brilliant development in his provincial hometown. He cannot fit into what he perceives as the elitist, self-indulgent, and overly liberal environment, and finally drops out.

Isaac's spiritual and intellectual temptations are paralleled with the biblical story of Abraham, the father who is willing to sacrifice his son Isaac to prove his devotion to God. When the five-year-old Isaac learns the legend embodied in his name, he proclaims to his father: "Do you know what I would do if God told Abraham to sacrifice me? . . . I'd turn right around and sacrifice Abraham. Bind him and serve him up for Sunday dinner." Although years later Isaac apologizes for the statement, this scene hovers over the novel not only as a reminder of the poignant relationship between Isaac and Sam, but also as an indication of Isaac's failed attempt to successfully fight his own demons, a struggle that at times recalls the harrowing accounts in Fyodor Dostoyevsky (most notably *The Possessed*). At last, Isaac loses touch with reality altogether for a few months after his father's sudden death: He locks himself in a dark room, does not eat or bathe, and refuses any contact with his lover or his friends. Like Ivan in *The Brothers Karamazov* he has visions, all of them featuring the devil, who participates in long and cerebral discussions with Isaac. These hallucinatory dialogues, the most carefully reasoned—and least novelistic—passages in Eberstadt's book, further emphasize the protagonist's obsession with power and public acknowledgment.

It would be difficult to sympathize with such a character, despite his Faustian urge for knowledge, if Eberstadt did not explicate her hero's actions in the manner of older literary traditions. Her omniscient narrator rationalizes and contextualizes Isaac's sociopsychological struggles, evoking the 19th-century bildungsroman. More important, Eberstadt employs a baroque and exuberant diction that is almost old-fashioned in its appeal; contemporary authors are rarely found writing prose that is "rich as a fruitcake, plump with metaphors, images and illusions" (Kakutani). Such diction can even sustain a plot that is often reduced to the methodical anatomization of delusions of grandeur, whether intellectual or social.

Although Eberstadt suggests that her protagonist is based on historical prodigies such as Samuel Johnson, the famous 18th-century English author and lexicographer (Kaufman), Isaac lacks both the historical significance and public accomplishment commonly associated with a precocious child. In the opening paragraph of the novel, Eberstadt writes that "There is nothing sadder than the sight of a clever, nervy young man, agulp with ambitions enormous and vague as a headache . . . slowing down, retreating, and fizzling out like a planet still shining but dead"; while in a passage functioning as the essayistic summary of the novel, Eberstadt wonders "What fatal sequence of mistrusting led into this wilderness of compromise, silence, flitching mediocrity?" For attentive readers, then, Isaac's troublesome coming of age is not surprising, but rather illustrative of Eberstadt's almost clinical fascination with the socially inept and psychologically unstable genius. In the sequel, *When the Sons of Heaven Meet the Daughters of Earth* (1997), Eberstadt describes Isaac's attempts to become a renowned painter in New York, translating (rather than exorcising) his demons from his provincial home to the New York art scene of the 1980s.

Bibliography
Eberstadt, Fernanda. *Isaac and His Devils.* New York: Random House, 1991.

Kakutani, Michiko. Review of *Isaac and His Devils, New York Times,* 7 June 1991, Books of the Times, sec. C, p. 31.

Kaufman, Marjorie. "Opening a Window to the Inner Souls of Artists, In a New Novel," *New York Times,* 4 May 1997, sec. 13LI, p. 23.

—Damjana Mraović-O'Hare

I Was Amelia Earhart Jane Mendelsohn
(1996)

JANE MENDELSOHN's debut novel is the imagined firsthand account of what happened to aviation pioneer Amelia Earhart and her navigator Fred Noonan after they disappeared on their ill-fated round-the-world flight. Mendelsohn uses lyrical prose, liberal section breaks, and a fluid sense of time to create a sort of dream world that the two inhabit, while offering flashback insights into Earhart's "former life." These mnemonic flashbacks are interspersed in the main plot, in which Noonan and Earhart meet, prepare for the flight (when Earhart neglects many basic safety practices), begin their journey, and then crash-land in the Pacific.

The novel's language is perhaps its most interesting feature. Stylistically, Mendelsohn owes a debt to Stephen Crane's short story "The Open Boat," about four men attempting to land a lifeboat after their ship has gone down. Both works tend toward the surreal, making heavy use of color, image, and repeated text; but Mendelsohn's novel is brief—around 30,000 words in length—and intricately constructed. It progresses in alternating first-person and third-person sections, occasionally addressing the reader. Earhart explains this tactic early on: "Sometimes my thoughts are clearly mine," she says. "Other times I see myself from far away, and my thoughts are ghostly, aerial, in the third person" (10).

The novel opens with a brief prologue, which serves more to orient Earhart herself in the story of her life than it does to orient the reader. But when Earhart says, "What I know is that the life I've lived since I died feels more real to me than the one I lived before" (3), she is indicating what is to come. Part 1 introduces us to the younger Earhart, inspired by nickelodeon heroines Cleopatra and Joan of Arc. Her father takes her to air shows, buys her a .22 rifle; and we meet her husband, publishing magnate George Palmer Putnam, and learn of his aggressive marketing of Earhart. He bankrolls her flights but expects results; indeed, her disappearance has been partially blamed on Earhart being rushed to complete her flight so she could have a book in stores by that Christmas. Navigator Fred Noonan may be another wrench in the machine: highly qualified but a drunkard. He and Earhart do not take to each other, even as they take off on their perilous voyage.

Mendelsohn's Earhart is a flying contradiction: a tomboy with a silver powder compact always at the ready. She relates stories of earlier flights and media appearances, sometimes in successive first- and third-person descriptions of the same event. We see her as she sees herself, then as she sees others seeing her. As she and Noonan prepare for their flight, they both have forebodings of death; and the flight is arduous: "We spent our days feverish from the flaming sun or lost in the artillery of monsoon rains and almost always astonished by the unearthly architecture of the sky." Noonan drinks, and Earhart flies with "reckless, melodramatic abandon . . . wondering which of [them] was more forsaken: the navigator who didn't care where [they] were going, or the pilot who didn't care if [they] ever got there" (39).

He sees her as reckless, she finds him cowardly. They make stops along their way like episodes in a dream: Noonan plied by homemade rum into dominoes and a dalliance with "a Miss Montgomery"; finding himself the only private pilot in San Juan, Puerto Rico; accompanying Earhart to obligatory meetings with "local dignitaries, acting governors general or local"; always drinking. The flight itself is condensed into tiny vignettes, with equal space given to land and air. Just before their penultimate stop, in Lae, New Guinea, they discover that the wind is blowing in the wrong direction. They try to contact the Coast Guard cutter that is stand-ing by to listen for them and monitor the weather, but that fails, and soon after they realize they are lost. With fuel running low, the plane descends in a "soaring, howling fall," signaling the end of part 1 and of Earhart's "former life."

Miraculously they survive, and at this point the language of the novel takes an even sharper turn toward the poetic, as Mendelsohn describes Earhart's and Noonan's life on the island. A severe heat wave midway through the section further tests the bounds of surreality. That Earhart and Noonan begin a romantic relationship on the island should not come as a surprise, but throughout its narration are interspersed Earhart's conflicting thoughts on male/female relationships, culminating in a repeated insight on the similarity between rescue and capture. This section of the book has been criticized as being too much like a romance novel, but Mendelsohn does not dwell overmuch on the carnal aspects of the pair's life, presenting it instead in brief vignettes like the rest of the narrative. Most important, part 2 introduces Earhart the writer, as she lounges in her lean-to or the cabin of the Electra, inscribing the novel into her logbook. This adds to the surreal nature of Mendelsohn's tale, which continues in part 3 when, after spotting a potential rescue plane, Earhart and Noonan use the last of the Electra's fuel to send themselves skyward again.

The effectiveness of *I Was Amelia Earhart* as a fictional memoir, as well as its originality, was praised upon publication, but such admiration was later tempered by Mendelsohn's use of similar stylistic devices—multiple section breaks, poetic language, time as a permeable substance—in her follow-up novel, the less successful *Innocence* (2000). Moreover, the genre itself has come into some discredit, owing to scandals like the factual "errors" in James Frey's purported memoir, *A Million Little Pieces,* and the J. T. Leroy hoax, in which an author was invented out of whole cloth. Even the idea of a blatantly fictional memoir is a rather gray one, and can lead to reader dissatisfaction, since "the truth" is being bent to suit the author's fancy. However, in the case of *I Was Amelia Earhart,* since almost nothing is known about what happened to Earhart and Noonan after their plane disappeared, fictional memoir seems a valid tack to take with their compelling story.

Bibliography

Crane, Stephen. "The Open Boat." In *The Red Badge of Courage and Other Stories,* edited by Gary Scharnherst. New York: Penguin Books, 2005.

Mendelsohn, Jane. *Innocence.* New York: Riverhead Books, 2000.

———. *I Was Amelia Earhart.* New York: Knopf, 1996.

—Magdalen Powers

Iweala, Uzodinma (1982–) *American novelist*

Iweala published the acclaimed BEASTS OF NO NATION (2005) when he was just 23. The story of a child soldier in an unnamed civil war, it is one of several books to emerge at the beginning of the 21st century from a new wave of young Anglophone Nigerian writers engaging with the memory and experience of civil war.

Born to Nigerian parents, Iweala grew up in Washington, D.C., attending St. Albans boys' school and graduating in English from Harvard in 2004, where he was copresident of the African Students Association. His mother, Ngozi Okonjo-Iweala, was both foreign minister and finance minister between 2003 and 2006 under Nigeria's former president, Olusegun Obasanjo, and Iweala spent some of the time when his mother was in office living with her in Nigeria's capital, Abuja. In 2007, she was appointed managing director of the World Bank.

However, it was earlier, in his senior year of high school, that Iweala found the inspiration for his novel, when he read an article in *Newsweek* about child soldiers in Sierra Leone. Prompted by the article, Iweala made a start at the story before putting it aside for several years. In 2002, however, he heard China Keitetsi, author of *Child Soldier: Fighting for My Life* (2002), formerly a child soldier in Uganda, give a lecture at Harvard about her experiences. Iweala returned to his story once more, developing it into his senior thesis under the guidance of his creative writing professor, Jamaica Kincaid.

The novel describes, in first-person narration, the experiences of Agu, a young boy who loses his family, and is coerced into a military squad as a sol-dier. The squad includes boys and young men led by their brutal "Commandant," who governs them through fear and favors. Agu becomes friends with another young boy, Strika, who has been made dumb by all he has witnessed. The two support each other mentally and physically through their gruelling experiences of military combat, sexual abuse, and malnutrition. Agu struggles to come to terms with his sense of guilt about his actions, and to reconcile his life as a soldier with his former life as a studious and happy child in a stable home. Finally, following the death of Strika and "Luftenant's" murder of "Commandant," Agu breaks away from the squad, abandoning the gun which had been 'riding on my back like it is King and I am servant to be doing whatever it says' (128). In the final chapter Agu finds himself in a rehabilitation center where an American woman attempts to get him to talk about his experiences.

The novel refuses to locate itself through geographical or political reference to a specific country, although it is clear that its general location is intended to be sub-Saharan Africa. Likewise, although the narrative voice and reported speech employ a kind of Nigerian pidgin English, Iweala does not seek to reproduce a specific version of pidgin. Instead, he claims, "the language is a construct, it's an approximation of Pidgin English, but it's really its own thing, constructed purposely for the book" (Orbach). This construction is evident not only in sentence structure but also in occasional idiosyncratic spellings, such as "Luftenant," which draw attention both to the aural quality of the narration and to the young age of the narrator (who might not necessarily know how to spell *lieutenant*). In creating this compelling, yet unsituated narrative voice Iweala focuses the reader's attention on Agu's lived experience. Paradoxically, by limiting the focus in this way, Iweala is able to raise and universalize ethical questions that might otherwise be explained away as relating only to a specific time or place.

Another element of Agu's idiomatic narration is an insistent use of the present tense. On one level this simply creates an interior monologue: "Day is changing into night. Night is changing into day. How can I know what is happening?" (52). Yet there are further ramifications: memories come back to Agu in the present tense, throwing into relief his struggles to reconcile his former life with his present. Moreover, the interior monologue itself has an existential effect: "I am trying to be crying, but no tear is coming out from my eye, and I am trying not to be fearing" (131). These deeper implications of the insistent present tense open up the ethical themes of the novel once again, highlighting Agu's guilt, his attempts to rationalize his actions, and the depersonalizing effects of his experiences.

The novel takes its title, and its epigraph, from Fela Kuti's song of the same name, which incidentally also supplied the name for Bate Besong's play of 1990. Fela was a founder of the politically conscious Afrobeat movement, and his song, 'Beasts of No Nation' (1989), indicts the perpetuation of violence around the globe by governments bent on making animals of their citizens. In doing so, Fela points out, global leaders make animals of themselves. Iweala's book explores these two themes, the universality of war, and the depersonalization that is its result, through the small, strong voice of Agu. While some of Iweala's first readers have found the novel's ending surprisingly happy, it contains within it an acknowledgment of the immense and rarely bridged divide between those who have experienced at firsthand the horrors of war and those who have not. Iweala's attempt to communicate that divide places him alongside other Anglophone Nigerian writers such as Helon Habila, (*Waiting for an Angel*, 2002), and CHIMAMANDA NGOZI ADICHE (*HALF OF A YELLOW SUN*, 2006), but also engages with the longstanding American tradition of war writing, from Stephen Crane's *The Red Badge of Courage* (1895) to Tim O'Brien's *The Things They Carried* (1990).

Bibliography

Iweala, Uzodinma. *Beasts of No Nation*. New York: HarperCollins, 2005.

———. "Beasts of No Nation: A Conversation with Uzodinma Iweala." By Michael Orbach. The Knight News. Available online. URL: http://media.www.qcknightnews.com/media/storage/paper564/news/2006/04/27/Literary/Beasts.Of.No.Nation.A.Conversation.With.Uzodinma.Iweala-1881844.shtml. Accessed January 18, 2008.

—Katherine Isobel Baxter

J

Jackson, Sheneska (1970–) *American novelist*

Sheneska Jackson is the author of three novels, the critically acclaimed CAUGHT UP IN THE RAPTURE (1996), *Li'l Mama's Rules* (1997), and *Blessings* (1998). All three works center on the lives and loves of African-American women as they work toward professional success and personal fulfillment. Although her books fit neatly into the "chick lit" genre popularized in the last decade, Jackson's novels move well beyond entertainment to tackle serious issues such as H.I.V.-A.I.D.S., domestic violence, poverty, and drug abuse.

Jackson, who currently resides in Sherman Oaks, California, was born in 1970 in South-Central Los Angeles, an area often portrayed as crime-ridden and dangerous. However, the novelist questions this stereotype in her seminal *Caught Up in the Rapture*, which illustrates her belief that a person's upbringing and surroundings need not exercise a decisive or even restrictive influence on their life.

Like many of her characters, Jackson was raised in a single-parent household. Hoping for a better life, her mother Etna—a phone company supervisor—moved the family to a neighborhood outside embattled South-Central when Jackson turned 14. Ironically, this "better" location provided Jackson with her first experience of gang-related violence, a mugging in which her purse and money were stolen; and such ironies no doubt influenced Jackson's oeuvre. In fact, according to Carol Brennan, "Jackson was careful to draw upon her own experiences and those of her peers in depicting another side of life in places like South-Central" (Brennan). While her novels certainly contain autobiographical elements, they are best understood as a constructive exploration of romantic, familial, and socioeconomic issues affecting not merely her South-Central protagonists but by analogy us all.

After finishing high school, Jackson attended California State University at Northridge, where she graduated with a bachelor's degree in journalism in 1992. In spite of her degree, Jackson was unable to find employment as a journalist and finally accepted a job as a medical secretary from 1992 to 1995. During her secretarial stint, she attended a lecture by famed author Terry McMillan *(Waiting to Exhale)*, and was inspired to attempt a novel of her own. Jackson worked tirelessly on her writing, and submitted several short pieces to various magazines, including *Ebony*, all of which were rejected. Convinced of the importance of her artistic vision—in spite of the magazine editors' rejections—she continued to labor toward her goal of a completed manuscript, writing from 3:00 to 7:00 each morning before work, and after a month and a half she had completed the initial draft of her 1996 sensation, *Caught Up in the Rapture*. The semi-autobiographical novel focuses on the life of 26-year-old college student Jazmine Deems. Jazmine, also known as Jazz, dreams of achieving fame and escaping the confines of her life in South-Central LA. The book balances a realistic and gritty look at ghetto life with a strong message of hope that

211

underscores the importance of self-efficacy; Jackson says of its characters, "Some people think that their circumstances have to be bleak because their surroundings are bleak . . . but the characters have a definite dream and they go after it" (Brennan).

Upon completion of the manuscript, Jackson showed *Rapture* to her college writing instructor who immediately suggested she contact a literary agent. The agent—equally impressed with the text—submitted the drafts to the publishing house Simon & Schuster, and within days they had offered Jackson a $200,000 contract for *Rapture* and a follow-up novel. In 1996 *Caught Up in the Rapture* hit bookshelves and immediately garnered critical and popular praise for its witty, direct, and conversational tone, as well as its frank exploration of key issues in urban American communities. Jackson continued addressing serious social issues in her second novel *Li'l Mama's Rules,* which focuses on a 30-year old schoolteacher who discovers she has H.I.V.-A.I.D.S. as the result of an unsafe sexual encounter. Like *Rapture, Li'l Mama's Rules* proved popular with her readers; however, some—like one critic from the *Kirkus Review*—felt the novel, though strong overall, "succumbs to triteness in the form of safe-sex messages" toward the end ("From").

Jackson's third novel, *Blessings* (1998), reminiscent of the work of McMillan, follows the lives and loves of four women—Pat, Zuma, Faye, and Sandy—as they struggle with working-class existence in Los Angeles, and continues the exploration of her first two works, emphasizing the capability, generosity, and self-sufficiency of modern American women, even under trying circumstances.

Sheneska Jackson continues to write, and currently works as a contributor for *Ebony* magazine.

Bibliography

"From Kirkus Reviews." Available online. URL: www.amazon.com/Lil-Mamas-Rules-Sheneska-Jackson/dp/product-description10743218620. Accessed October 20, 2009.

"*Blessings*: Book Summary." Simon & Schuster. Available online. URL: http://books.simonandschuster.com/Blessings/Sheneska-Jackson/9780684853123. Accessed October 20, 2009.

Brennan, Carol. "Sheneska Jackson: Biography." Black Biographies. Ask.com. Available online. URL: http://www.answers.com/topic/sheneska-jackson. Accessed March 9, 2009.

—Jennifer L. Powlette

Jarhead: A Marine's Chronicle of the Gulf War and Other Battles Anthony Swofford (2003)

Jarhead is a memoir exploring the arcane and often brutal realities of life in the U.S. Marine Corps, while meditating on the author's experiences growing up in a military family and his subsequent deployment to the First Gulf War. Moving back and forth between different temporalities and locales around the globe (including Japan, Kuwait, and numerous towns and Marine Corps bases around the United States) the narrative focuses on significant moments in the childhood, military career, and postwar life of ANTHONY SWOFFORD, a former sniper with the Surveillance and Target Acquisition (STA) Platoon. *Jarhead* is Swofford's first published book.

At the outset Swofford explicitly informs the reader that the book is about remembering not merely the physical sensations of war and soldiering, but the "loneliness and poverty of spirit," "fits of rage and despondency," and "mutiny of the self" that pervade so many of the author's memories from his formative and prewar years (Swofford, 3). *Jarhead* is thus as much about the process of recalling an earlier version of the author's own self, an identity born of a military institution that prides itself on breaking down and then remaking the individual. The gap between Swofford the narrator (who used the GI Bill to attend the University of California, Davis, and the prestigious University of Iowa Writers' Workshop after leaving the Marine Corps), and the primary subject of this novel (Swofford the 20-year-old marine waiting for a war in the desert), leads to the most interesting if problematic questions posed in memoirs: How does one become who one is? In *Jarhead*, Swofford's remembering comes as a form of excavation, where a layer of selfhood—his experience as a marine, a "jarhead"—has been consciously buried. At the end of the book's first section, Swofford explicitly acknowledges the heuristic frame of his memoir: "I remember going in one end and coming out the other. I remember being told I must remember and then for many years forgetting" (3).

The narrative arc of *Jarhead* commences with Swofford attempting to put on his old uniform from the First Gulf War; he no longer fits into his gear, demonstrating both the passage of time since he served as an active-duty service member and the physical and psychological transition from young Marine to aspiring writer. In this first section, Swofford not only introduces the main thematic elements of the book (his own sense of detachment and loneliness, the camaraderie of the Marine Corps, deception in sexual and platonic relationships) but also the overarching character of his memoir project. While admitting that he saw more of the First Gulf War than the "average grunt," Swofford states that his "vision was blurred—by wind and sand and distance, by false signals, poor communication, and bad coordinates, by stupidity and fear and ignorance, by valor and false pride. By the mirage" (2).

Jarhead then shifts to the central focus of the narrative, the United States' imminent war with Saddam Hussein's forces, who have recently invaded Kuwait. But although the ever-present prospect of a full-scale war with Iraq underlies the majority of the narrative, Swofford uses particular images and interactions from the war to segue into his childhood. In one instance, after playing a game of football in the desert while wearing suits that are designed to keep the marines safe from chemical attacks, Swofford notes the strange, fish-scale-like dirt patterns on his skin, and this prompts an extended recollection of the childhood experience of running away from the military base in Japan where his father was stationed. After losing his way in the alleys in the merchant section of the city, the young Swofford comes upon a tattoo parlor where two locals are having their arms tattooed with the shape of fish scales. Such dramatic shifts, from the frontlines of war to bar conversations in Seattle, childhood memories or stateside funerals, and back again, define *Jarhead*'s restless, decentered narrative sensibility.

It is worth noting that the memoir was published the same year as James Frey's controversial account of drug and alcohol addiction, *A Million Little Pieces* (2003). While Frey encountered intense critical scrutiny regarding the veracity of his memoir, in *Jarhead* Swofford explicitly addresses the ambiguity involved in the production of a memoir: "what follows is neither true nor false but *what I know*" (2). The aftermath of the Frey affair, as well as legal action taken against fellow memoirist Augusten Burroughs, author of *Running with Scissors* (2002), has intensified the attention paid to both major and minor details of memoirs. While Swofford has been criticized for his depiction of the marines by other former soldiers turned writers, including sometime *Esquire* contributor Colby Buzzell, the author of *My War: Killing Time in Iraq* (2005), there has been no litigation involving *Jarhead*.

Jarhead clearly belongs to the tradition of memoirs, works of literary fiction, and films that have drawn both inspiration and subject matter from the wars fought by the United States over the course of the second half of the 20th century. Similar to Buzzell's own recollection of his time in the Iraq war as an army combat trooper, in *My War,* Swofford reflects on the role of the classic movies about the Vietnam War—*Apocalypse Now, Platoon,* and *Full Metal Jacket*—in preparing today's troops for battle.

In addition, the first few pages of *Jarhead* have Swofford, more than eight years after his discharge from the marines, going into the basement of his home to look at the material reminders of his time at war: field maps, his camouflage uniform, projectiles, and a brass bore punch for a sniper's rifle. As in Tim O'Brien's collection of stories about the Vietnam War, *The Things They Carried* (1990), the possessions of the soldier and the often luminous value they possess are a persistent motif throughout *Jarhead.*

However, in Swofford's memoir the soldiers' objects speak of a much more profane, visceral, and overtly violent contemporary military culture. For example, whereas in *The Things They Carried* the photograph of the high school sweetheart back in the United States functions as a romantic ideal, in *Jarhead* the photos of girlfriends are traded back and forth between soldiers or sold to the highest bidder. Yet, there are also a number of similarities between O'Brien's seminal meditation on the war in Vietnam and Swofford's *Jarhead;* the intimate and complex relationship between soldiers, for example, which shifts unpredictably from merciless bullying to loving camaraderie, is a central theme in both.

In 2005, Sam Mendes, of *American Beauty* (1999) and *Road to Perdition* (2002) fame, directed a film version of *Jarhead,* starring Jake Gyllenhaal in the role of Anthony Swofford, Peter Sarsgaard in the role of Troy (one of Swofford's platoon mates), and Jamie Foxx as Staff Sergeant Sykes (a relatively minor character in the book whose role was greatly expanded for the film). Typically, the movie omits many parts of the book and reworks a number of important sections. However, in addition to excluding a number of definitive scenes from Swofford's childhood and later years, which are integral to the book, the film alters a number of key "facts," including the demotion of Swofford from lance corporal to private (which never occurred), Troy's depiction as a drug dealer in the film, and the memoir's climactic scene in the sniper tower.

Bibliography

Burroughs, Augusten. *Running with Scissors.* New York: Picador, 2002.

Buzzell, Colby. *My War: Killing Time in Iraq.* New York: Penguin, 2005.

Frey, James. *A Million Little Pieces.* New York: Random House, 2003.

O'Brien, Tim. *The Things They Carried.* New York: Broadway Books, 1998.

Swofford, Anthony. *Jarhead: A Marine's Chronicle of the Gulf War and Other Battles.* New York: Scribner, 2003.

—Christopher Garland

Joe College Tom Perrotta (2000)

Published in 2000, *Joe College* is TOM PERROTTA's third novel, following *The Wishbones* (1997) and *Election* (1998). While *Election* was set in a high school, *Joe College* shifts the setting to Yale University in 1982, around the same time that Perrotta himself was a student there. The narrator Dante Roach, or Danny, is a New Jersey native majoring in English, working in the dining hall and attempting to balance his academic, economic, and social lives. Unlike his friends, Danny and his family are not wealthy; his father owns and operates a lunch truck that he drives around to local construction sites. The class tension between Danny's New Jersey roots and the upper-middle-class atmosphere at Yale provides one of the novel's major themes, and attentive readers will find a seemingly indiscriminate host of allusions stemming from high and low culture, including Wallace Stevens, Rick James, *Othello,* Bruce Springsteen, and Walter Benjamin. The accumulation of such references helps to create an atmosphere in which the characters seem to float in self-referential limbo between the reckless, transitory excitement of adolescence and the ever-growing responsibility of adulthood.

As the novel opens, Danny is returning to his dorm after a night of working in the dining hall, where he learns from his suitemate Max Friedlin that Cindy, a girl from home whom Danny has been avoiding, has called. A former high-school classmate, Cindy is now a secretary, and the two had reconnected while he was driving his father's lunch truck during summer break. From the beginning her insecurity over Danny's enrollment at Yale and her own self-worth trouble their relationship. She is reluctant to sleep with Danny, which frustrates him. She finally concedes on New Year's Eve, but he ignores her subsequent letters and calls. Back at Yale, a late night get-together between Danny and Polly, a friend from a campus literary magazine, shows promise of something more, despite her tempestuous relationship with their former Shakespeare professor, Peter Preston.

While grudgingly awaiting his parents' arrival, Max confronts Danny about avoiding Cindy, but Danny dismisses him. Angry, Max wanders off, frustrated by his wealthy parents and Danny's indifference. While Max's parents and suitemates anxiously await his return, Polly calls and tells Danny she wants to sleep with him after the party later that night. Max's parents take everyone to dinner without Max, where Mr. Friedlin buys expensive wine and Danny gets his first taste of filet mignon, Mr. Friedlin noting that "Reagan's been a great president for people like us" (100). Illustrating Perrotta's typical satire of 1980s class politics, Danny silently objects, questioning who, exactly, were "people like us." Later that night, Cindy's unexpected arrival thwarts Danny and Polly's plans and this tension is exacerbated when Polly, speaking to Danny, refers to Cindy as "your secretary" (129). Cindy also has news: She is pregnant.

While on spring break in New Jersey, Danny learns from his father that a new rival, Lunch Monsters, has been intimidating drivers. Danny spends his break driving the truck and reading Kerouac's *On the Road,* a wry illustration of the tension between what he has to do and what he wants to do. One morning, a Lunch Monsters driver tells Danny not to worry about his route anymore, and Danny responds by threatening to knock his teeth out, a move he soon regrets. Later, Danny hangs out with a friend from high school, Squidman, who takes him to a bar where a former classmate is a stripper, and then invites him to watch pornography in his basement. This uncomfortable encounter emphasizes the estrangement Danny feels from his high-school friends, and the class differences between Yale and his New Jersey neighborhood, a major theme of the novel.

On Sunday evening, he goes to Cindy's for dinner, where she reveals she is going to marry her boss, Kevin, who is leaving his family for her. The solution is obviously not what Cindy wants, but an uneasy Danny halfheartedly agrees it is best, and whispers to her, "You deserve to be happy" (214). Soon after, Danny has another incident with the Lunch Monsters, but is able to fend for himself by chance. The stress of the incident, however, haunts him, and he begins to see his life "as a car with no brakes careening down a dangerous mountain road" (256). He is awakened later that night by a phone call notifying him that his father's truck has been torched.

In the novel's final section, Danny returns to Yale with thoughts of rekindling his fractured relationship with Polly, only to find out she has gone back to Peter. The wounds of this rejection are exacerbated when Peter calls Danny into his office. Matt has plagiarized Danny's award-winning essay, which he found while rummaging through Danny's things during spring break. Danny confronts Matt, who not only admits he stole the paper, but that he has been lying: His father is actually a General Motors executive. Feeling betrayed, Danny

punches Matt, then runs into Cindy, who is there to visit Max. She admits to having had an abortion, telling Danny she now agrees with him that she needs to be happy; therefore, she is moving to Colorado to manage a store for Max's mother. At the party, Danny finds Lorelei, a coworker who is recently single after her boyfriend Eddie was beaten up by her brothers. They sneak off to a room to have sex, only to be disturbed by Matt, who insists they return for the entertainment. Just as the Whiffenpoofs are about to begin performing, the party is disturbed by two "scrawny and criminal-looking" townies (306), and the novel dissolves into picaresque non-conclusion—itself an eloquent counterpoint to the Reaganite obsession with articulated structures (and happy endings).

Perhaps the novel's greatest strength lies in its exploration of the contemporary anatomy and pathologies of class. Danny's sensibility and situation are clearly at odds with his background, particularly in his dealings with Cindy and Squidman; however, he is equally troubled by the bourgeois sensibilities of people like Mr. Friedlin. Additionally, his struggles reveal the tension between doing what one wants (here as a freewheeling college student), and what one should (as a maturing adult). As in all of Perrotta's work, however, humor helps relieve such tension, as Danny makes his awkward, often ignoble, but always richly human way through the transition.

Joe College thus joins the company of other campus novels focusing on moral dilemmas of student life, such as Donna Tartt's *The Secret History* (1992) and Tom Wolfe's *I Am Charlotte Simmons* (2004). Even closer affinities may be found with Bret Easton Ellis's *The Rules of Attraction* (1987), as both works explore college life, the trials of growing up (or failing to do so), and social anxieties in Ronald Reagan's America. Although differing in tone and in the conclusions they reach, both novels offer a revealing portrait of the moral crises facing youth coming of age in the 1980s, a decade often characterized by indifference and selfishness. Torn between independence and responsibility, Danny is among Perrotta's most sympathetic characters, and the novel adeptly depicts his protagonist's development, articulating with great sensitivity and nuance Danny's class consciousness and his moral dilemmas, as well as his difficulties in addressing both. As is the case with his other novels, Perrotta's *Joe College* satirizes suburban life with a skillful mixture of empathy and antipathy, celebration and condemnation, hilarity and sorrow.

Bibliography

Perrotta, Tom. *Joe College.* New York: St. Martin's Griffin, 2000.

—Peter C. Kunze

jPod Douglas Coupland (2006)

DOUGLAS COUPLAND's 11th novel centers on the lives of six cubicle-mates at a Vancouver-based video-game production company, thrust together simply because of their common "j-" last names (hence the "jPod"). The novel features Ethan, its narrator, in a series of strange, blackly comic scenarios that interrupt a primary narrative, which itself follows the development of *BoardX,* a skateboard video game under production: Ethan helps his mother bury a biker who threatened to extort money from his parent's basement marijuana grow-op; he harbors illegal Chinese immigrants in his apartment for his brother, Greg, and the human-smuggler, Kam Fong; he travels to China to retrieve Steve, his supervisor at work, who is held captive at a plastics factory and plied with heroin by Kam Fong for unwanted advances toward Ethan's mother; and he travels to the lesbian commune where his mother now lives with the mother of fellow jPoder, John Doe (birth name is crow well mountain juniper). Moreover, BoardX's development, which anchors the narrative, is itself shot through with odd and macabre events. Originally conceived as a skateboarding game geared for self-dispossessed teenage boys, BoardX is jigged by Steve to include Jeff, a cartoon turtle, to ingratiate himself with his estranged son; and when Steve goes missing, it is again repurposed as a fantasy game, into which the jPoders embed a secret character, Ronald McDonald, who initiates a murderous rampage within the game.

Such irreverent and comedic narrative structures are typical of Coupland's work, but *jPod* represents a significant departure, in a number of ways,

from his previous fiction. Coupland's other novels, *GENERATION X, Life after God,* and *Hey Nostradamus!* in particular, often operate as an exploration of life and morality in a generation whose primary orientation to the world is through mass-mediated images and mass-produced, synthetic commodities, with his protagonists typically finding themselves negotiating morally vacuous scenarios from nostalgic moral positions. In *Life after God,* for example, one of Coupland's characters confesses, "my secret is that I need God—that I am sick and can no longer make it alone" (359). jPod strikingly reframes this paradigm.

Amid the text art that precedes the opening of Ethan's narrative, Coupland posits a "Universal Goo" (5), seemingly dissolving the divine into an inarticulable, unsubstantiated mess. To invoke God in *jPod* is to refer to that goo on the floor—the mess that remains after God left the room. It is in this vestige of a moral framework that the reprehensible actions of *jPod,* like those of the XBoard game, are repurposed here as essentially amoral events: burying the biker interrupts Ethan's workday as easily as a routine doctor's appointment, and his mother is comforted simply knowing that Kam Fong did not *kill* Steve. Steve himself characterizes his time in China and new smack addiction in amoral terms:

> It [heroin] made being kidnapped seem like an in-flight movie.... They kept shooting me up. I wasn't sure if I was dead or alive, but the whole episode was great.... It wasn't heaven and it wasn't hell. It was interesting. (356–358)

What becomes "interesting," the novel asks, in those ambiguous spaces when events are no longer indexed according to good and bad, heaven and hell? Perhaps more important, what happens when we forget that this index ever mattered?

Complicating things considerably, and casting an almost solipsistic hue over the entire narrative, Coupland inserts himself as a fictional persona into the text. Early on, characters make frequent references to Coupland and his body of work:

> 'Oh God. I feel like a refugee from a Douglas Coupland novel.'
> '*That* asshole.' (15)

So begins Ethan's narrative, prefiguring both the thematic amorality that structures the text and the ambivalent role Coupland's persona will play within it. Later, on the flight to China to retrieve Steve, Ethan meets this Douglas Coupland, who agrees to write a story on Ethan's laptop while Ethan passes out, drunk. Ethan wakes up to find a Word file from Coupland eviscerating Ethan's life using information found on his own laptop. The file ends with the following invective from Coupland to Ethan:

> You live in a world that is amoral and fascinating—but I also know that your life is everyday fare for Vancouverites, so there's no judgement that way. But, for the love of God, grow up . . .
>
> This is weird diagnostic shit coming from a stranger, but, Ethan, you're on a one-way course to utter fuckedupedness. I'm not suggesting you stop—but I am saying *wake up.* (300–301)

Here Coupland's judgment, or non-judgment as it were, is not an intervention into Ethan's life, but a certain call to awareness about its amoral and aimless nature. The awareness Coupland advocates is ambivalent, however, its direct consequence clearly not change or action—Coupland himself acknowledges this—but merely a fascination with and interest in amorality itself; and for Coupland the author, Coupland the character is a means to explore the implications of emptying his own life of the vestiges of Judeo-Christian morality.

Coupland also experiments with how the text is presented. In a manner unseen in his fiction since *Generation X* and *Life after God,* but consistently present in his nonfiction (*Terry, Souvenirs of Canada, City of Glass,* etc.) and visual art, *jPod* is a mash up of textual forms. In addition to the standard text-based narrative, Coupland includes e-mails, lists of numbers, interviews, and text art to evoke the virtual, digitally mediated world of Ethan and his colleagues at the production company. Many of these are akin to computer-generated doodles: nearly two pages of nothing but dollar signs repeated over and over; 47 pages detailing the first 100,000 digits of pi with one intentionally incorrect digit, and a Magritte-like page with only two printed words—"intentionally blank" (473); all of them illustrations of Coupland's stated attempt to construct in *jPod* a record of what life was like in 2005, the age of the internet and Google (Anne Collins interview).

Such formal experiments, and the narrative exploration of amorality in which they occur, are clearly aspects of the same phenomenon. Coupland, a self-described futurist ("A Man with a Vision"), explores the moral implication of cultural change due to technological advances. In such an exploration, the amoral is not only understood in terms of an absurd narrative, and enlightened by laughable text art; *jPod* indicates that the amoral narrative experiment itself is akin to the comedic documents it includes. As a historical document for future generations, then, Coupland's text evokes both genuine, even urgent concern for contemporary moral ambiguities, and the possibility that this whole issue will end up just providing our grandchildren with a good laugh.

In May 2006, selections from *jPod* were presented as an installation at the Rooms Provincial Art Gallery in St. John's, Newfoundland, Canada. The Canadian Broadcasting Corporation debuted a television series based on *jPod* in January 2008; it was canceled in March of the same year.

Bibliography

Coupland, Douglas. *jPod.* Toronto: Random House Canada, 2006.

———. *Life after God.* 1994. New York: Washington Square Press, 2005.

———. "A Man with a Vision." Staff interview. Tiscali, England. 2002. Available online. URL: http://www.tiscali.co.uk/entertainment/film/interviews/douglas_coupland.html. Accessed November 8, 2007.

———. "jPod by Douglas Coupland." By Anne Collins. Random House. Available online. URL: www.randomhouse.ca/jpod. Accessed November 8, 2007.

—Matt Oakes

Julavits, Heidi (1968–   ) *American novelist*

Julavits was born and grew up in Portland, Maine, and currently divides her time between New York

City and Brooklin, Maine. Graduating from Dartmouth College, she went on to pursue an M.F.A. in creative writing from Columbia University, and in 2003, she cofounded the literary magazine *The Believer*. In the inaugural issue, Julavits exclaims, "Rejoice! Believe! Be Strong and Read Hard!" calling "for a new era of experimentation" and defining the shape of a new literary public sphere that eschews "consumer-reports" style reviews in favor of a more mature and dialogic intellectual criticism that emphasizes a service to culture over self-interestedness. As she writes, "reviews should be an occasion, not for tears or vendettas or shoe licking, but for dialogues."

Working as a waiter and English teacher in her early years, Julavits published her first novel, *The Mineral Palace* (2000), which chronicles the life of a young wife, mother, and journalist living in Depression-era Colorado. Meticulously detailing the novel's historical setting, Julavits provides a vivid and sensual narrative of a small town's survival during the early 1930s. Bena Jonssen, a recent émigré to Pueblo, Colorado, volunteers for the local newspaper at her husband's suggestion, and while reporting for her weekly women's column becomes acquainted with the dark underside of the neglected frontier mining town. Like their dust-ridden environment, characters are plagued by physical pain and amputation that symbolize a broader psychic suffering. The Mineral Palace itself is an arthritic relic of the hopeful prosperity that mining was to have brought to the community, and as a participant-observer, Bena bears eloquent witness to the slowly fading culture of Pueblo. Yet in its subjective depiction of this external desolation, the narrative reveals Bena's own internal and inspiring quest for self-understanding.

Following *The Mineral Palace*, Julavits published a collaborative photo-book with photographer Jenny Gage, entitled *Hotel Andromeda* (2003). Telling the story of five sisters born on the same day from the same mother but from different sperm donors, the short 2003 text chronicles their lackluster adventures in an anonymous hotel. The sisters' adolescence is isolated and surreal, the only parental figure present being "Dr. Gloria," with whom they have mandatory therapy sessions. Under surveillance, the sisters all attempt to

"lose" each other in order to get the attention of their absent mother, a game that has tragic consequences. Gage and Julavits illuminate the gaps and overlaps between genetics and personality, nature and nurture. In addition, Julavits begins to explore the literary themes of sisterhood, individuality, and imprisonment, which she would develop in her next two books.

Taking its title from a comment made by the Queen of Hearts in Lewis Carroll's *Alice in Wonderland*, *The Effect of Living Backwards* (2003) chronicles an often spiteful sibling rivalry wherein love and hate are at times indifferently intertwined in a relational battle for supremacy. Informing this struggle in a haunting and intriguing way is Julavit's telling depiction of the almost surreal atmosphere of post-9/11 America. In the topsy-turvy world of the novel, the September 11 attacks are referred to as the "Big Terrible," and as in Wonderland's house of mirrors, the plotline is difficult to decipher as the narrator/protagonist Alice meanders from one fragmentary persona to the next. On a flight bound for Morocco, Alice and her sister Edith become "victims" of a hijacking, staged by the "International Institute of Terrorist Studies." Alice's attempt to derail the hijacking is forestalled by her sister Edith, who does so in a characteristic attempt to win the affection of anonymous men, here the hijacker. As reviewer Art Winslow explains, one effect of "living backwards" is that life stories are often facetious—it is hard for Alice to tell a "true story" about herself since she is still uncovering her own identity; and Alice and Edith's relationship ultimately comprises what Winslow calls "representative anecdotes," illustrating a kinship that is, in the end, poignantly evanescent.

The Uses of Enchantment (2006) continues the themes of sisterhood and mother/daughter relationships, here in the historical context of 1980s suburbia. Mixing realist narrative with postmodern flashbacks, the novel tells of the disappearance and possible abduction of 16-year-old Mary Veal. Retrospectively narrated through the perspective of an adult Mary, the story questions the reliability of speech, highlighting how stable gender-identity is dependent upon set linear narratives originating in psychoanalytic discourse. Moreover, the novel's trenchant representation of the 1980s intellectual milieu demonstrates how feminism and antidomestic violence movements bled into psychiatric therapy and "politically correct" social legislation. Building on her exploration of the adult uses of children's literature in *The Effect of Living Backwards*, *The Uses of Enchantment* references stories such as "Little Red Riding Hood" and "The Girl Who Cried Wolf," questioning their capacity to instill a moral system of value or integrity.

The title of the novel refers to Bruno Bettleheim's psychoanalytic literary study that sees the reading of fairy tales as a way for children to better understand themselves and the world around them. The desire for "enchantment," for a belief in the power of fantasy, seems to counter the judgmental force of "disenchantment" in contemporary literature—the same disenchantment Julavits takes to task in the "Rejoice! Believe!" article. Ultimately, her oeuvre may be read as an extended, reflective meditation on the contemporary uses and abuses of telling stories about ourselves and others.

Bibliography

Gage, Jenny, and Heidi Julavits. *Hotel Andromeda.* Sebastopol, Calif.: Artspace Books, 2003.

Gates, Anita. Review of *The Mineral Palace, New York Times Book Review,* 24 September 2000, sec. 7, p. 19.

Julavits, Heidi. *The Effect of Living Backwards.* New York: G.P. Putnam's Sons, 2003.

———. *The Mineral Palace.* New York: G.P. Putnam's Sons, 2000.

———. "Rejoice! Believe! Be Strong and Read Hard!" *The Believer* 1, no. 1 (March 2003). Available online. URL: www.believemag.com/issues/200303/?read=article_julavits. Accessed October 20, 2009.

———. *The Uses of Enchantment.* New York: Doubleday, 2006.

Winslow, Art. "Curiouser and curiouser; An entertaining new novel brings together Alice in Wonderland, post-9/11 terrorism and questions about the nature of knowledge," *Chicago Tribune,* 20 July 2003, p. 1.

—Jenny James

K

Kaaterskill Falls Allegra Goodman (1998)

Kaaterskill Falls is ALLEGRA GOODMAN's third book and first novel. A 1998 National Book Award finalist, it traces the lives and traditions of several families in a community of orthodox Jews called the Kirshners, over the course of three years, beginning in 1976. This tight-knit enclave follows the teachings of Rav Elijah Kirshner. The Rav, who fled Germany in 1938, is well educated, steeped in tradition, and distanced from the secular world. Any follower who does not adhere to his word is looked down upon; and this is how the Kirshners retain a strong and unique group identity. Yet throughout the book, characters struggle to prevent their own individuality from being absorbed by the laws and customs of the community and religion. Goodman's story is as rich and moving as Chaim Potok's *The Chosen*, which also explores tensions between religious tradition and secular modernity faced by Jews living in America.

Each summer the Rav and his disciples move from New York City to tiny Kaaterskill Falls in upstate New York, and Elizabeth Shulman and her family are among this group. The Shulmans are devoted to their religious rituals, which come to them as naturally as breathing and eating. Privately, however, Elizabeth bears a romantic streak, "Poetry, universities, and paintings fill her with awe" (54). Thus Elizabeth is restless, and with her five girls no longer requiring all her attention, she discovers that she "is ravenously hungry. She needs something to do" (79). But Elizabeth's "religious life is not something she can cast off" (57); she loves her family and religion too much to leave them for a secular existence and so decides to open a store in Kaaterskill that sells kosher provisions. The store nourishes her desire for individual creative expression, as well as serving the Kirshner community, and it infuses Elizabeth's life with renewed meaning and energy.

The desire to lead a meaningful life not exclusively defined by Kirshner custom, however, plagues Andras Melish. A Holocaust survivor, Andras can no longer take religion seriously. He does not observe fasting days, and only goes to service on Shabbat because Nina, his devout wife, wants him to set a good example for their two children. Andras is disgusted by members of the Kirshner community, who he believes cringe "from the world in little enclaves" and "desire to keep the children from outside influences" (51). In his opinion, religion compromises true emotional and spiritual feeling. During his search for personal spirituality, he encounters Una, a woman who spurned society to live alone in the woods in communion with nature; but he is fettered by his felt ties with the Kirshners. Eventually Andras realizes that spirituality, for him, lies in the human spirit. Meaningful to him are his beloved elder sisters, Eva and Maja, who entertain him with lively conversation and bake mandelbrot every weekend; and his teen-aged daughter, Renee, needs his guidance in her search for her place in the secular and traditional worlds. His relationships with these people give his life spiritual and emotional significance.

The appeal of the secular world and its opportunities for unique individual expression even touches the Rav's family, proving that the most devout and cloistered families are not immune. The Rav's younger son, for example, Isaiah, faithfully fasts, prays, and dutifully studies the Torah every day; but his elder son, Jeremy, is a brilliant scholar and professor at Queens College, pursuing his love of classical literature and art rather than devoting his life to studying Jewish law. Jeremy's embrace of the secular world displeases his father and brother, and their relationship is strained.

When the Rav dies, he leaves nearly everything to Isaiah, but his vast library of precious volumes of theology and literature are inexplicably willed to Jeremy. Isaiah, the new Rav, wants Jeremy to donate the books to the yeshiva library, where they can be enjoyed by Kirshner students, but Jeremy refuses, dissenting from the new Rav as he had done from the old.

The gift of books is confusing. It is "[p]raise and rebuke at the same time. A blessing and a curse" (305). Sitting among the books overflowing in his apartment, Jeremy can barely look at or touch them; he knows he will not read them. Then Jeremy forces himself to open a volume of Plato, and discovers with a shock his long-deceased mother's signature on the inside of the cover. Half the volumes, in fact, bear her inscription. He was her favorite child, and to him she passed on her love of European literature and music. The Rav, then, has left the intellectual legacy—both religious and secular—of both parents to Jeremy to protect and carry on. But Jeremy

does not want to be, nor is he, the vessel of his mother's dreams. Nor can he be anymore his father's tragedy. His parents are gone, and his place between them is gone too. His father's objections have been silenced, as has his mother's praise. All his father's rebukes have not effaced the learning the Rav nurtured in him. And all his mother's books, all her poetry and German theology, cannot now shape him into her idea of a man. (308)

Jeremy decides to donate the books to the yeshiva.

Kaaterskill Falls dramatizes the struggle to balance individuality with tradition in a changing, increasingly secular world. Elizabeth Shulman finds creative expression in a way that adheres to religious beliefs. Andras discovers meaningful spirituality, not meaningless religious ritual, is possible in human relationships. Jeremy, however, must entirely give up his religious community to ensure stagnant religious belief and rituals do not consume him.

Goodman's earlier book of short stories, *Family Markowitz,* touched on similar themes of Jewish identity, ritual, fractured family life, and the tension between the secular and religious worlds; and *Paradise Park* (2001), her follow-up novel, portrays characters affected by the loss of cultural and spiritual traditions. Her oeuvre as a whole provides a searching contemporary account of the desire for tradition and community in conflict with the need—even necessity—of individuality for members of any group.

Bibliography
Goodman, Allegra. *Family Markowitz.* New York: Farrar, Straus & Giroux, 1996.
———. *Kaaterskill Falls.* 1998. New York: Dial, 2005.
———. *Paradise Park.* New York: Dial, 2001.
Potok, Chaim. *The Chosen.* New York: Simon & Schuster, 1967.

—Elizabeth Cornell

Keeneland Alyson Hagy (2000)

ALYSON HAGY's *Keeneland,* while ostensibly about horse racing's sordid backrooms and behind-the-scenes subterfuge, ultimately concerns itself with far more universal subjects: notions of identity, meaning, and self-worth. As Hagy follows her troubled and at times self-destructive protagonist, Kerry Connelly, she gives primacy to Kerry's evolution, and in so doing, invokes other coming-of-age identity crises, like those portrayed in J. D. Salinger's *The Catcher in the Rye* or Sylvia Plath's *The Bell Jar.*

Set in the famed Kentucky stables of the same name, *Keeneland* begins with Kerry's return from New York, where her marriage with fellow horse aficionado Eric Ballard has recently devolved into spousal abuse and desperation. Broke (excluding the $10,000 she has stolen from her husband) and unemployed, Kerry literally and figuratively limps back to a life predating marriage, loan sharks, and her mare, Sunny, which Eric has kept. And while she couches her return in self-deprecating language ("It was a low-rent, prodigal return. . . . I was just another saddle-sore working girl boomeranging back to where she came from"), it is clear that this retreat marks Kerry's 11th-hour investment in regrowth, perhaps even rebirth (13).

Yet the moral dissolution and iniquity that immediately follows suggests this renaissance may be unlikely; in its place, Kerry substitutes cheap imitation, a whitewashing of her fears and failures in place of meaningful, foundational change. Upon arrival, she summarily and unsuccessfully endeavors to avoid confrontation with her foreman and soon-to-be coworker, Reno; and while nothing remotely eventful transpires in their conversation, Kerry's interpretation of the exchange reveals basal, underlying cracks in her psychology. Not unlike Salinger's Holden Caulfield, Kerry finds in even typically banal conversation a deeper, sometimes devastating import. For instance, when Reno offers, "Found you a daddy up north, have you? Ain't that always the way," his tone is more conversational than caustic. Yet Kerry's internalized response, "He knew how to wrist-snap his punches," implies her ability (perhaps willingness) to perceive an otherwise inaudible bite to Reno's language, a sensitivity that suggests deeply rooted insecurities (15).

The conversations that follow also fit this pattern. Once past Reno, Kerry stumbles awkwardly through an impromptu job interview with her old boss, Alice Piersall, where she nearly talks herself out of the very job she presumably wants; and later, while seeking out her friend, colleague, and perhaps onetime lover, Billy T., she preempts any sort of amicable reunion with an egregious display of neo-adolescence concerning Billy T.'s current girlfriend, Louisa.

Such posturing again echoes Salinger's Holden, or Holden's imaginative archetype: the bereft, disconsolate adolescent spiraling toward hopelessness and catastrophe. However, Hagy's tale is far from derivative: While Kerry embodies certain qualities that connect her to a well-articulated tradition, her motivations and apprehensions are still profoundly nuanced and humbling in their complexity—her near phobic relation to happiness being a case in point. With an almost masochistic approach to misfortune, Kerry undermines with alarming efficacy every opportunity she faces; yet even as she diagnoses this tendency in herself, her inability to rectify it is never really in doubt. Once employed, she promptly loses her $10,000 (stolen by her quasi-lover, Danny, just after she had tripled her earnings at the racetrack); and, in the subsequent fall-out, Kerry loses her job as well, in a controversial firing to which she nonetheless capitulates: "[T]he results were the same as they'd always been. The Haves beating the Have-nots. The Have-nots beating themselves" (190). And while Hagy leaves little doubt that Kerry is one of the unfortunate "have-nots," Kerry's cognizance of this reality reveals a tendency toward salutary self-reflection that, for the first time, leaves the reader with a sense of optimism that she may in fact be larger than the problems she faces. Equally important, however, is the cognitive dissonance that manifests itself when Kerry's self-awareness collides with her habitually forward impulses, a deleterious reflex that suggests Kerry may in fact invite—even invent—the crises she navigates, in a backward effort to preempt any actual, substantive change, and instead lustrate her past with active, intentional struggle.

In this sense, Kerry's suffering is equal parts self-subversive and cathartic. After losing her lover (again applying the term loosely), her money, and her job, she confesses, "I wanted to get the hell away from my problems, [but] my problems followed me down here. So now I'm facing a shitload of music I don't like the sound of. I'm *facing* it" (218). In context, her tone rings false; however, 20 pages later, when the aforementioned Louisa violently acts out her vendetta in an altercation that leaves Kerry nearly incapacitated, Kerry simply absorbs her punishment, almost like a penance. The pain, while excruciating, is also baptismal; and literally reemerging from the river, Kerry is finally willing to confront her ex-husband and, still more important, herself.

Still, Hagy refuses to tidy up the novel's loose ends. Even after squaring with Eric and finessing her way back under Alice's aegis, Kerry is still without money, and almost certainly her beloved mare, Sunny. And yet, while Hagy deprives her reader of a happy ending, the denouement nonetheless allows for an aptly charged and perhaps fittingly partial closure: wounded but with her dignity intact, Kerry prepares to stumble home to her mother; Eric, having sold Sunny, now hopes for lenity from his debtees; and *Keeneland*'s other significant characters (more than a dozen) are free to continue their respective vices and virtues, for better or worse. Ostensibly, very little has changed from the novel's beginning, but when Kelly notes that "None of us knew what would happen. . . . Not the high hat trainers. Not the princes or the thieves," she invites the kind of speculation on the reader's part that makes for a good read, avoiding superficial closure in favor of a more expressive, convincing, and in the end insightful uncertainty (270).

Bibliography

Hagy, Alyson. *Keeneland.* New York: Simon & Schuster, 2000.

—Ben Staniforth

Keep, The Jennifer Egan (2006)

The keep of JENNIFER EGAN's third novel is a massive stone building, the oldest part of a central European castle that has been purchased by a wealthy American who plans to transform the whole into a high-priced spa-retreat. There is, however, a major obstacle to the American's ambitions in the form of one Baroness von Ausblinker, whose family formerly held the castle, and who still considers the structure and its surrounding lands her property. The baroness has locked herself inside the keep, and refuses to leave.

Such a summary makes the novel sound like a comic clash of cultures, new world affluence colliding with old world aristocracy, Henry James for the 21st century. But in fact the baroness herself takes second place, both in her role and in her significance, to the building that she keeps and in which she is kept; and as the narrative evolves, this keep emerges as a potent symbol both of memory and of isolation, for the way in which the past keeps us separate in the present.

The tale is woven out of two narratives, the first centering on Danny, a 30-something fleeing the complications of his life in New York City (among which are his involvement with men on the wrong side of the law, and his relationship with an older woman with whom he is more in love than he thinks he should be). Danny has accepted an invitation from his wealthy cousin, Howie, to join him at the central European castle ("the keep") he has recently purchased. In retreating to Howie's castle, however, Danny merely exchanges one set of complications for another. When he and Howie were children, Danny, together with Rafe, another cousin, played a harmless prank on Howie that went horribly wrong, leaving his cousin lost in a series of subterranean caves for days. Because of that trauma, Howie has spent a good portion of his life in and out of trouble, until finally settling down and making his fortune. Although Danny has labored under the weight of his mistake ever since, he has never discussed the episode with Howie, and in fact is optimistically unsure of how much Howie remembers of it. Despite the apparent generosity of his cousin's offer, then, Danny cannot escape the suspicion that Howie has brought him to this distant country in order to enjoy some long-delayed revenge. To make matters worse, Danny, whose life is defined by its connectedness via cell phone and internet, finds himself in a location where such technology functions intermittently, if at all.

This first narrative is contained within the second and is in fact a kind of product of it. This second strand focuses on Ray, a prison inmate who is taking a creative writing course in which he is working on Danny's story. Ray narrates both portions of the novel, Danny's in the third person, his in the first; and he is quite content to intervene in Danny's story, offering commentary and speculation, raising and answering questions. Asked by one of his fellow prisoners which of the novel's characters represents its author, Ray refuses to answer, reluctant to identify himself in his composition because of an infatuation with his creative writing instructor, Holly; but this refusal will come to haunt the narrative he creates.

The Keep deploys many of the tropes of gothic tradition: the decayed castle in a nameless country, the doubling of characters (Danny and Howie, Danny and Ray, Howie and Ray), crimes of the past reaching out and ensnaring the present. Moreover, there are moments in which the novel shades toward the supernatural, as when Danny encounters the Baroness von Ausblinker and her age appears to alter as he draws nearer. But such gothic inflections themselves shade toward extreme psychological states. Thus, later in the novel, for example, Danny flees the castle for a nearby town, only to become convinced of its unreality as he wanders its streets, in a scene uniting the visionary and the paranoid.

Nor are the novel's gothic elements confined to Danny's portion of its narrative. Sensitive, articulate, yet guilty of a terrible crime, Ray is himself a type of gothic hero; his cellmate attempts to communicate with the dead; his romance with Holly is freighted with the forbidden.

Yet if Egan makes free with gothic conventions, it is in the aid of more than a simple pastiche or parody. Ray's interventions in Danny's story, in fact, give the novel a metafictive flavor, heightened by the contrast between his voice, which is informal and contemporary, and the gothic machinery it employs, which is formal and historical. The novel exploits this tension to effect a broad and compelling inquiry into the uses and burdens of narrative itself. In the end, Danny merely flees one tangled plotline for another even more fraught, and there is a sense in which the complications of his present existence stem from his inability to bring the previous real-life narrative with his cousin to any meaningful close. Overwhelmed by this failure, Danny has to a large degree surrendered authority for the later narrative of his own life.

As a prison inmate, Ray too has lost control over his own story, his inscription of Danny's being an obvious effort to regain some measure of narrative control, however displaced. Yet his displaced storytelling holds out the possibility of resolving Danny's tale, and this helps explain why gothic elements figure so prominently in it. As a recognizable plot-type, the gothic offers clear precedents for composing a successful ending, a model for Ray to follow. The conclusion he reaches is powerful and striking.

While *The Keep* is in many ways distinct from the novels Jennifer Egan wrote before it (*The Invisible Circus* [1995] and *Look at Me* [2001]), all three works share a concern with secret histories, with what lies, literally and figuratively, beneath the surface of things.

Bibliography

Egan, Jennifer. *The Keep.* New York: Anchor, 2007.

—John Langan

Kennedy, Patricia "Pagan" (1965–   )
American novelist, short story writer, and artist

Pagan Kennedy has authored 10 books of widely varying styles and genres, created a zine series, and contributed regularly to newspapers and journals. Dubbed the "queen of zines," she has received a Massachusetts Book Award for Nonfiction, a National Endowment for the Arts Fellowship in fiction, and a Smithsonian Fellowship for science writing. Her autobiographical zine *Pagan's Head,* begun in 1988, is considered a pioneer in the zine movement. A native of Maryland, Kennedy graduated from Wesleyan University in 1984 and earned an M.A. in fiction at Johns Hopkins University. She is currently a visiting writer at Dartmouth College and has taught writing at Boston College. The prolific author currently lives in Somerville, Massachusetts.

Pagan's Head (1988–94) was a xeroxed zine created by Kennedy, in which she explored her own life and experiences. The zine had a large underground following despite the fact that Kennedy only gave copies to her friends in Boston. *Pagan's Head* was a multimedia collage incorporating cartoons, clip art, drawing, and stories, and has been compared to the work of Robert Crumb and Harvey Pekar.

STRIPPING + OTHER STORIES (1994) is Kennedy's collection of short stories, filled with dynamic female characters working through challenging life experiences and trying to become their most authentic selves. The stories are stripped of any pretense or facade, and anatomize the protagonists' struggles with great acumen, while never forsaking compassion or respect.

In *Platforms: A Microwaved Cultural Chronicle of the 1970s* (1994), Kennedy writes a personalized history of pop culture, exploring new ways to look at what has often been thought of as a silly and uninteresting decade in U.S. cultural history. In the book, she treats with wit and penetration a host of diverse icons, from Studio 54, the 8-track and television sitcoms, to the mass mediation of the Vietnam War and civil rights movements.

Spinsters (1995) is Kennedy's first novel and was on the short list for the 1996 Orange Prize (United Kingdom). The short text follows two spinster sisters, Frannie and Doris, as they travel from Virginia to Arizona in the late 1960s. The radical changes occurring in the United States, including the assassinations of Martin Luther King, Jr., and Robert Kennedy, as well as the 1968 Democratic convention and the Vietnam War, are skillfully juxtaposed with the sexualized metamorphosis of the sisters.

Zine: How I Spent Six Years of My Life in the Underground and Finally . . . Found Myself . . . I Think (1995) explores Kennedy's experiences publishing *Pagan's Head*, providing insight into the process and inspiration for her work in the zine, as well as including many examples of work from it. Kennedy describes how her identity as the "Pagan" of *Pagan's Head* became a "camped-up version" of herself, and how working on the zine was a refuge from difficult experiences, especially her father's illness.

Pagan Kennedy's Living: Handbook for Maturing Hipsters (1997) is written in a similar voice to *Zine* and *Platforms*, offering a tongue-in-cheek guide for Gen-Xers concerned about remaining cool in the 1990s. It is consciously and diametrically opposed to the handbooks of people like Martha Stewart, and includes bizarre but hilarious advice and social commentary.

Kennedy's second novel, *The Exes* (1998), chronicles the lives of four members of a Boston indie rock band named the Exes because its members are all ex-lovers. With a lively, he-says-she-says style, the novel's chapters tell the story of the band's formation from different band members' points of view.

Kennedy narrates the complex life and adventures of William Sheppard in *Black Livingstone: A True Tale of Adventure in the Nineteenth-Century Congo* (2002). Sheppard was an African-American Presbyterian missionary who traveled to the Congo in 1890 to convert Africans. Nicknamed "Black Livingstone," he fought to expose the atrocities in the Congo after King Leopold II sold the country to Belgium. Kennedy gives an unflinching account of religion, racism, and imperialism in this provocative work, which at times resembles fiction more than the true story that it is.

In her third novel, *Confessions of a Memory Eater* (2006), Kennedy explores the sci-fi premise of what would happen if people could relive the best moments of their lives, through the tale of Win Duncan, a history professor caught in an eroding marriage. It delves into the American obsession with an idealized past.

The First Man-Made Man: The Story of Two Sex Changes, One Love Affair, and a Twentieth-Century Medical Revolution (2007) is a nonfictional account of the life of Michael Dillon, born Laura Dillon to a wealthy British family. Dillon was the first recorded transsexual, and Kennedy traces his struggle with sexual and gender identity, as well as broader medical and cultural notions of gender, in a nonlinear narrative.

The Dangerous Joy of Dr. Sex and Other True Stories (2008) is a collection of literary essays previously published in the *New Yorker* magazine and the *Boston Globe Magazine*. The documentary-style stories follow a diverse group of visionaries as they attempt to change the world; some for the better, others for the worse. The title story concerns Alex Comfort's journey to become a self-made sex guru and author of *The Joy of Sex*, but each story evinces Kennedy's characteristic mixture of incisive clarity and black humor.

Pagan Kennedy's work is difficult to categorize because it spans such diverse topics and genres, but what binds it together is its always frank and searching exploration of the often ignored or hidden; there is no topic too difficult or forbidden, and each is tackled with stylistic resourcefulness, humor, and engaging honesty.

Bibliography

Kennedy, Pagan. *Black Livingstone: A True Tale of Adventure in the Nineteenth-Century Congo.* New York: Viking, 2002.

———. *Confessions of a Memory Eater.* Wellfleet, Mass.: Leapfrog Press, 2006.

———. *The Dangerous Joy of Dr. Sex and Other True Stories.* Santa Fe: Santa Fe Writer's Project, 2008.

———. *The Exes.* New York: Simon & Schuster, 1998.

———. *The First Man-Made Man: The Story of Two Sex Changes, One Love Affair, and a Twentieth-Century Medical Revolution.* New York: Bloomsbury, 2007.

———. "Homepage." Available online. URL: http://www.pagankennedy.net/. Accessed November 1, 2008.

———. "Pagan Kennedy: In conversation with Noel King." By Noel King. Jacket Homepage. Available online. URL: http://jacketmagazine.com/08/king-iv-kenn.html. Accessed November 1, 2008.

———. *Pagan Kennedy's Living: Handbook for Maturing Hipsters.* New York: St. Martin's Press, 1997.

———. *Pagan's Head.* Self-published zine, 1988–94.

———. *Platforms: A Microwaved Cultural Chronicle of the 1970s.* New York: St. Martin's Press, 1994.

———. *Spinsters.* New York: High Risk, 1995.

———. *Stripping + Other Stories.* New York: High Risk, 1994.

———. *Zine: How I Spent Six Years of My Life in the Underground and Finally . . . Found Myself . . . I Think.* New York: St. Martin's Griffin, 1995.

—Amy Parziale

Kidd, Chip (1964–   ) *American author, editor, and graphic designer*

Chip Kidd is best known for his book-jacket designs. Over the course of his career, he has designed book covers for such prominent writers as Bret Easton Ellis, Dean Koontz, Cormac McCarthy, Frank Miller, David Sedaris, and John Updike. James Ellroy has called him "the world's greatest book-jacket designer," and several authors, including Oliver Sacks, stipulate in their contracts that Kidd design their book covers.

Kidd was born in Shillington, Pennsylvania, and attended Penn State, where he majored in graphic design. After graduating in 1986, Kidd was hired by Sara Eisenman to the Alfred A. Knopf design team, and has worked there ever since. In addition to designing book covers for Knopf, Kidd has freelanced extensively and has designed books for Doubleday, Farrar, Straus & Giroux, Grove Press, HarperCollins, Penguin/Putnam, and Scribner. He is also an editor for Pantheon, supervising the creation of graphic novels and other projects. In 2001, Kidd published his first novel, *The CHEESE MONKEYS: A NOVEL IN TWO SEMESTERS,* and a sequel to this novel, *The Learners,* was released in 2008. Kidd currently lives in New York City and Stonington, Connecticut, with his partner, poet and Yale professor J. D. McClatchy.

In her monograph on Kidd, Veronique Vienne refers to him as "a pure product of pop culture," and speculates that the juxtaposition of images that is a characteristic feature of Kidd's book-jacket designs are a manifestation of the heavy influence that comics art has had on his sensibility. An avid collector of Batman memorabilia, Kidd calls himself "a sucker for the false promises of comic books." Another significant influence on Kidd's aesthetic was his favorite teacher at Penn State, Lanny Sommese, who impressed Kidd with the importance of the "verbal-visual connection," and on whom Winter Sorbeck, the demagogical graphic design professor in *Cheese Monkeys,* is loosely based.

Kidd's most famous book cover is his design for Michael Crichton's *Jurassic Park* (1990), which was incorporated by Steven Spielberg into the logo for the 1993 film adaptation. His designs for Cormac McCarthy's books, notably *All the Pretty Horses* (1992) and *The Road* (2007), have rapidly become iconic. Kidd's own favorite cover is his design for a 1996 translation of the New Testament for Farrar, Straus, and Giroux. The image on the cover is an extreme close-up photograph of a dead face covered in blood, by Andres Serrano, the controversial photographer of "Piss Christ."

His own debut novel, *The Cheese Monkeys,* is about a college student majoring in graphic design. Not surprisingly, the novel itself is elaborately designed, with the dust jacket sliding off to reveal the title redesigned as a rebus, with illustrations of cheese and monkeys. Two of the novel's slogans, "Good is dead" and "Do you see?" are worked into the layout of the title on the spine of the book and also along the edge of the pages. Inside the soft cover edition of the book, the acknowledgments are printed backward, while the press blurbs disappear over the side of the page and are continued on the other side. Kidd wrote the book in Quark X-Press so that he could see the text as it appeared on the page as he composed the novel. The first half of the book, Semester One, is set in Apollo typeface and the second half in Bodoni, while Himillsy Dodd's emotional collapse at the end of the book is represented by her dialogue fading typographically to gray. Such metafictional innovations are consistent with Kidd's statement that he thinks of writing as "designing with words."

The story of *The Cheese Monkeys* follows Happy, a freshman at a generic state university (a thinly disguised version of Kidd's own alma mater) in 1957. Withdrawn and naive, Happy quickly falls under the spell of the extroverted and ultra-sophisticated coed, Himillsy Dodd, as they both struggle through an uninspiring drawing class. In the second semester, Happy and Himillsy wind up in a class taught by Winter Sorbeck, who teaches art class as if it were boot camp, and whose eccentricities alternately terrify and inspire his students. Sorbeck's lessons are the heart of the novel, and Kidd intersperses the narrative with excerpts from his lectures on various elements of graphic design and their significance. Kidd's 2008 sequel, *The Learners*, follows Happy to New Haven, Connecticut, where he lands a graphic design job and reunites with Himillsy. Happy enrolls as a subject in the infamous psychological experiments of Stanley Milgram at Yale, and suffers an emotional strain reminiscent of his experiences as a student in Sorbeck's design class. A considerably darker novel than its prequel, *The Learners* explores the human capacity for coercion and sadism that is common to the Milgram experiments, Nazism, and corporate advertising.

In addition to his work as a book-jacket designer and author, Kidd is also an editor-at-large for Pantheon. In this capacity, he has drawn public attention to such artists as Dan Clowes, Alex Ross, and Chris Ware. Under the aegis of Pantheon, Kidd has collaborated with Art Spiegelman on a biography of Plasticman cartoonist Jack Cole, and with Geoff Spear on a coffee-table book about Peanuts creator Charles Schultz. He has also produced a series of books on Batman and Batman memorabilia: *Batman: The Complete History, Batman Collected,* and *Batman Animated.*

Bibliography

Kidd, Chip. *The Cheese Monkeys: A Novel in Two Semesters.* New York: HarperPerennial, 2001.
———— *Chip Kidd: Book One: Work 1986–2006.* New York: Rizzoli, 2005.
———— *The Learners.* New York: HarperPerennial, 2008.
Veronique Vienne. *Chip Kidd.* New Haven, Conn.: Yale University Press, 2003.

—Randy Laist

Kite Runner, The   Khaled Hosseini   (2003)

Khaled Hosseini's debut novel quickly gained international fame, spending two years on the *New York Times* best-seller list; it has been published in 48 countries and translated into 42 languages. Hosseini was born in 1965 in Kabul, Afghanistan, where the novel begins and much of the action takes place. Hosseini's father was a diplomat with the Afghan foreign ministry, while his mother was a teacher of Farsi and history at a high school. Due to political turmoil, Hosseini's entire family was relocated to Paris by the Afghan foreign ministry, and in 1980, they moved to San Jose, California, having been granted political asylum by the United States. After graduating from college, Hosseini earned his medical degree from the University of California, San Diego, and in 2001, his fifth year as a practicing internist at Cedars-Sinai Hospital in Los Angeles, he began writing his first novel, which became *The Kite Runner*. Although the novel is not autobiographical, many elements of the book echo aspects of Hosseini's life; its protagonist, for example, also ends up relocating to the San Francisco Bay Area due to political turmoil in Afghanistan.

The Kite Runner is the story of Amir, a privileged boy growing up in the new Wazir Akbar Khan district of Kabul. The novel is narrated in the first person from Amir's perspective and is conventional, personal, and confessional in nature, unfolding in chronological order with flashbacks that make the connections between the past and present vividly clear and resonant. It begins with Amir recounting his childhood, the memories of which center around his imposing father, whom he calls Baba. Early on we learn that Amir's mother died giving birth to him, and Amir's life is dominated by fear of and admiration for his father, who is a physically imposing, wealthy entrepreneur, and an extraordinarily generous philanthropist. Living with Amir and his father are Ali, his father's servant, and Ali's son Hassan, who reside in a hut behind the house. Amir's childhood is dominated by a sense of inadequacy as he strives to please his distant father, while Rahim Khan, Baba's business partner, shows the boy affection and support that he does not receive from his father.

Both Ali and Hassan are Hazara, an ethnic group long oppressed by the ruling Pashtuns in Afghanistan, and it is clear that Amir is confused by his relationship to Hassan. Hassan is obviously the closest friend that Amir has, and in many ways they seem brothers, cared for by the same wet nurse as infants and growing up in the same home. However, Amir ends up tormenting and teasing Hassan at several points in their childhood, and only plays with Hassan when there are no other children around. Early on, the novel takes on a confessional tone, and regret and repentance are rapidly established as central themes. One of the things Amir regrets most is teasing Hassan about being illiterate, especially as Amir later realizes that Hassan has been a major influence in his development as a writer.

When Amir was 12, there was an annual kite-fighting tournament in Kabul, which was and still is a major tradition in the culture. In the winter of 1975, Amir wins the competition, and Hassan, who has always been a gifted kite runner, goes after the prized last kite, which Amir has cut down. When Amir goes in search of the missing Hassan, he witnesses him being raped by a racist, sociopathic bully named Assef, who has threatened them before, and who has a bitter score to settle with Hassan. Driven by an ultimately unfathomable mixture of cowardice and longing (gaining the blue kite, at Hassan's expense, will impress his distant father), Amir flees instead of defending Hassan, who had always staunchly defended him.

Tormented as much by guilt as fear of discovery, Amir later compounds his shame by framing Hassan for theft, effectively driving away both him and his father (who had been the same kind of friend and servant to Baba since they themselves were children). Hassan admits to the theft, though he is innocent, and Amir recognizes, even as a child, that he does so solely out of loyalty to him. Ali and Hassan leave the household, and Amir never sees them again. This is an epochal moment for the boy, not only because his household changes forever, but because it fixes in the depths of his soul a syndrome of insomniacal self-loathing and regret that will continue for much of his life.

In 1981, political turmoil forces Amir and his father to flee Kabul for Pakistan, and they eventually end up in Fremont, California, where they make their home throughout the 1980s. Amir graduates from high school, goes to college, then courts and marries Soraya, the daughter of one of Baba's old friends from Afghanistan. In America, the relationship between Amir and Baba changes completely. Baba is no longer a successful businessman but a gas station attendant, who is eventually diagnosed with a terminal case of cancer. As Amir successfully pursues his path of becoming a published writer and Baba's health fails, Amir takes on the role of caring son and Baba a (more) affectionate father, proud of his son's accomplishments. After the death of Baba, Amir and Soraya make a home for themselves in San Francisco, where they are happy, though childless.

At this point, with his transition to America—and his escape from the worst of his past—seemingly complete, Amir is suddenly summoned back to Pakistan to see Rahim Khan, who is terminally ill. Khan reveals his knowledge about the secret past between Amir and Hassan, and that Hassan and his wife are dead, having been executed in the street in Kabul, leaving their 10-year-old son, Sohrab, an orphan. Amir hesitantly agrees to Khan's dying wish that he bring Sohrab back from Kabul, and in the course of his search there for the orphan, finds himself once again confronting Assef. History repeats itself, except this time Amir takes a beating from Assef, and Sohrab saves his life. Amir returns with Sohrab to the United States, and he and Soraya love and care for the boy, but he remains emotionally damaged and distant from them. Nevertheless, the novel ends with a sense of hope that love and time will allow him to heal and adjust to his new life in the United States. The major theme of the novel, developed with an almost poetic inevitability, is redemption, the attainment of inner peace by confronting one's past.

The Kite Runner is significant for its skillful depiction of the politics of modern-day Afghanistan, and was published in the wake of growing interest in that area after September 11. Its tale is closely intertwined with major events in the recent history of Afghanistan, especially the bloodless coup of Mohammed Daoud Khan in 1973 (the first time that Amir hears gunfire in Kabul), the Soviet invasion (which prompted Amir's flight from Kabul), and the Taliban's takeover in 1996 (which Amir confronts while going back to get Sohrab from Kabul).

The novel has nonfictional kin in Azar Nafisi's *Reading Lolita in Tehran* (2003), based on her experiences in neighboring Iran, and *The Bookseller of Kabul* (2004), by Norwegian journalist Asne Seierstad. These were published at the same time and served much the same purpose as *The Kite Runner* in educating the public about the real-life experience of living in politically charged areas of the Middle East.

The Kite Runner was made into a film by director Marc Forster, which follows its major story line but with some notable changes, among them the omission of Sohrab's suicide attempt toward the novel's end.

Bibliography
Hosseini, Khaled. *The Kite Runner.* New York: Riverhead, 2004.

—M. Marie Smart

Krauss, Nicole (1974–) *American novelist and short story writer*

Born in New York in 1974, Krauss grew up in Old Westbury, Long Island. A voracious reader as a child, she steeped herself in the literary lives and works of Henry Miller, Gabriel García Márquez,

Ayn Rand, and Philip Roth, and by 1996, at the age of 22, she had completed a B.A. and M.A. in English from Stanford University. As a Marshall Scholar she went on to complete a master of studies in English at Oxford (1997), and the following year received an M.A. in art history from the Courtauld Institute (1998). She currently lives in Brooklyn with her husband, acclaimed writer Jonathan Safran Foer.

Krauss is the author of two critically acclaimed novels, MAN WALKS INTO A ROOM (2002) and *The HISTORY OF LOVE* (2005), which was optioned by Warner Bros., directed by Alfonso Cuarón (*Y Tu Mamá También)*, and slated for a 2010 release. In 2004 she coedited *The Future Dictionary of America*, along with Jonathan Safran Foer, David Eggers, and the staff of McSweeney's, and 100 percent of its profits went to support progressive groups in the 2004 American election. Krauss has published short stories in *Harper's*, the *New Yorker*, and *Esquire*, and was included in *Granta's* Best American Novelists issue in 2007. Her poetry has appeared in the *Paris Review, Ploughshares, Double Take, Western Humanities Review*, and regularly in *PN Review*. She has also written countless reviews and essays for the *New York Times*, the *New Yorker*, the *Los Angeles Times*, the *Boston Review*, and the *Partisan Review*.

Nominated for the *Los Angeles Times* Book of the Year Award, *Man Walks into a Room* is the story of Samson Greene, a professor of English literature at Columbia University, who walks out of his office one day and is later found wandering the desert of Nevada. When discovered, he is suffering from amnesia as the result of a brain tumor. While the tumor is successfully removed, 24 years of his memory are taken with it, leaving behind his personal memories up until the age of 12 but eradicating all trace of what came afterward, particularly his adult life including his marriage to Anna. When the couple return to New York, Samson is unable to reintegrate into his life. And when attempts to revive their marriage and regain the love they evidently once had are consistently thwarted as a result of his memory loss, Samson increasingly retreats into "the blankness in the center of his mind. His memory had abandoned him, and though he had searched within himself all these weeks, he could find no desire to have it returned." While Krauss deftly explores the isolation Samson experiences, one is struck not only by the sudden power of the images of isolation ("a pay phone in the middle of nowhere, something against which to measure the desolation"), but also the potency of the novel's explicit articulations of it, which gesture beyond the particularity of Samson's condition to highlight a more general and morbid characteristic of loneliness, memory, and history: nostalgia.

Feeling that his "was a story he'd told countless times, now whittled down to a few phrases; a story that, like all true stories, lost something with each telling," Samson Greene returns to the desert, now as the subject of cutting-edge research on memory transplants. The scientific coordinator "spoke of human solitude, about the intrinsic loneliness of a sophisticated mind, one that is capable of reason and poetry but which grasps at straws when it comes to understanding another, a mind aware of the impossibility of absolute understanding." The obvious remedy to this solitude is love, but Krauss does not even approach this possibility without providing insight into its many and messy complications. The coordinator acknowledges that the young think love will solve the problem of loneliness, but "being close—as close as you can get—to another person only makes clear the impassable distance between you." While the theme of the novel centers on the philosophical question "how to be alone, to remain free, but not feel longing, not feel imprisoned in oneself," its narrative suggests that, in fact, solitude, freedom, longing, love, and memory are all intimately and intricately related.

This difficulty is more fully explored in Krauss's second novel, *The History of Love*, which was short-listed for the Orange Prize, Femina Prize, and Médicis Prize, while it won the Borders Original Voices award in 2006. The novel presents a colourful cast of distinctive characters, among them Leo Gursky, Alma Singer, and Zvi Litvinoff, whose lives are fundamentally secluded from those around them because of geography, age, and history. While their stories are presented separately, a fictional book, *The History of Love*, connects them. Written by Gursky in Poland, carried across the ocean by Litvinoff, and published under his name

in South America, then translated into English by Singer's mother, Krauss's internal novel sympathetically weaves the stories of each character, their family, their history and the multiple forms of their isolation, into a text whose structural experimentation mediates their differences, and enables poetic connections disavowed by their solitude. The fictional novel is excerpted throughout *The History of Love,* and these passages outline equations of love, loss, fragility, solitude, silence, and forgiveness with a stark poetic clarity that is muddled in the real lives of the main characters as they struggle with the same equations.

As is frequently the case with contemporary fiction, Krauss's work is difficult to categorize, but some of the more obvious influences include Bruno Schultz, Jorge Luis Borges, Grace Paley, and García Márquez. Similarities between her work and her husband's are frequently noted; yet this seems suspiciously common in cultural representations of literary couples, which also tend to favor the male writer. Krauss's second novel tacitly replies to this through a rather tongue-in-cheek question: "wasn't that what wives of artists were meant to do? Husband their husbands' work into the world, which, without them, would be lost to obscurity?" Yet, to quote from *The History of Love* again: "to call [her] a Jewish writer, or, worse, an experimental writer; is to miss entirely the point of [her] humanity, which resisted categorization," and this is what is most valuable in the writing.

Bibliography

Krauss, Nicole. *The History of Love.* New York: W. W. Norton, 2006.
———. *Man Walks into a Room.* New York: Anchor Books, 2002.
Kachka, Boris. Review of *The History of Love. The New York Magazine Book Review.* Available online. URL: http://nymag.com/nymetro/arts/books/reviews/11916/. Accessed May 12, 2009.
Wood, Gaby. "Have a heart." May, 2005. Guardian Unlimited. Available online. URL: http://books.guardian.co.uk/departments/generalfiction/story/0,6000,1484082,00.html?gusrc=rss. Accessed May 14, 2009.

—Kate Morris

Krik?Krak! Edwidge Danticat (1995)

EDWIDGE DANTICAT is one of the most important Caribbean-American writers of the late 20th and early 21st centuries. Similar to other authors from the region, she honors her formative roots, crafting texts that distinctly reveal the history, language, culture, and political concerns of her West Indian community. With *Krik?Krak!* she privileges these subjects, primarily documenting life in Haiti during the dictatorship of Jean-Claude Duvalier. She also includes emigrant stories about those who settled in the Crown Heights section of Brooklyn, New York, during the 1980s, while one story documents the massacre of Haitian refugees when they attempted to flee to the Dominican Republic in 1937.

In some way or other each story is connected to Ville Rose, "the city of painters and poets, the coffee city, with beaches where the sand is either black or white, but never mixed together, where the fields are endless and sometimes the cows are yellow like cornmeal" (34). A fictional composite of a prototypical Haitian town, Ville Rose represents a paradoxical community, struggling to sustain its familial infrastructure while its citizens are forced to defy, accept, or comply with a corrupt government. Some believe that their only recourse is to leave, as a narrator from "Children of the Sea" attempts to do, and many who successfully emigrate find themselves in the Brooklyn neighborhoods Danticat delineates in "New York Day Women" and "Caroline's Wedding." Those who remain strive to survive in the "poorest country in the Western Hemisphere [where] 80% of the population lives in abject poverty" (*CIA World Factbook*). All define themselves within the sociopolitical parameters of the times, whether finding their voice or remaining silent, and many use art as an outlet for their resistance.

Once such story displays Danticat's interest in using art, culture, history, politics, and even economic depravity itself as a means for addressing self-definition in the midst of Haiti's unstable political situation. In "The Missing Peace" she introduces Emilie Gallant and Lamort. Following a coup, Gallant visits Ville Rose. She fears that her mother, a missing journalist, has been buried in the town's mass graveyard (111–112). Having been told that Lamort is ". . . the only person who would take [her] to the yard," Gallant seeks Lamort out, booking a room at Lamort's grandmother's house. While there, she sews a quilt in order to honor her mother:

> Purple . . . was Mama's favorite color . . . and all her life, [she] wanted to sew some old things together onto that piece of purple cloth. (114)

By alluding to the quilt, Danticat suggests one way in which art can initiate one's own healing process. Not only is Gallant aspiring to remember her mother's life and trials, but in recognizing her mother's experiences, she aims to historicize the woman's life for posterity, linking it to her own. Gallant's love for her mother, especially her desire to preserve the woman's name and story, compels Lamort to acknowledge her own mother's name and history; and by the story's end, she demands that her grandmother—who named her "death" (la mort) because her mother died when giving birth to her (109)—call her "by another name . . . ," her mother's name (122).

Lamort and Gallant thus represent some hope for the future. Gallant is a Haitian-American emigrant whose artistic inclinations and rebellious curiosity force her to seek the truth about her family's history, especially her mother's disappearance. In aspiring to craft a quilt in memory of her mother, she seeks to define her own family history, and ultimately hopes to reveal to the world the atrocities that her mother experienced in Haiti. Lamort signifies the rebellious spirit of a generation of Haitian youth who increasingly resist subjugation in their homeland. Due to her interaction with Gallant, she realizes her cultural inheritance, especially the power of names and naming. In commanding her grandmother to call her by her mother's name, she establishes that her life is not a legacy of death, as suggested by the appellation Lamort. Rather, her very existence embodies the power, possibility, and promise epitomized in her survival, and in the act of not forgetting her mother's life.

"Missing Peace" not only addresses the violence that accompanied the Duvalier regimes, and two women's efforts to revive and sustain their mother's names—and in so doing recognize their own sense of identity—but also explores how many Haitians simply endure in one of the world's poorest countries. This latter fact is suggested by the grandmother who describes Raymond and Toto—Tonton Macoutes, a paramilitary force—as "vagabonds"; she secures her own income by opening her home to tourists (108).

The rampant poverty in Haiti, and its collateral damage, is a constant theme in other stories in *Krik?Krak!* "A Wall of Fire Rising" tells the moving tale of Guy, Lili, and their son. With Guy unable to procure steady employment, Lili is forced to scour the streets for litter, using it as barter to purchase food, with which she creates a humble meal for her family. In "Night Woman," readers encounter a prostitute, who dreads the night but "must depend on it . . . if [she is] to live . . ." (83). Marie, from "Between the Pool and the Gardenias," is a lonely, crazed, and impoverished housekeeper. Yet in telling her story, Danticat also ensconces Marie's solitary existence in a quiltwork of female relations:

> There was my great grandmother Eveline who was killed by Dominican soldiers at the Massacre River. My grandmother Défilé who died with a bald head in a prison. . . . My godmother Lili who killed herself in old age because her husband had jumped out of a flying balloon and her grown son left her to go to Miami. (94)

True to the oral tradition for which *Krik?Krak!* is titled, Danticat uses this cyclical collection of stories to define a larger narrative, the cooperative (and sometimes duplicitous) history of communities like Ville Rose. The concept of "Krik?Krak!" itself refers to a Caribbean folk tradition whereby storytellers invite their audience not only to warm up to the tale, but to be active participants in the telling of it. The griot, or West African bard, begins with the question, "Krik?" asking whether the hearers are ready and interested in the tale. When the storyteller solicits a cooperative "Krak!" from the audience, s/he begins (Abbott, Gates & McKay 2662, Davis 66–68). The ritual reinforces a sense of community among the teller and the listeners. Conversely, it conveys the idea that this oral tradition mirrors the collective consciousness of its participants. The tales are about them, especially their cultural underpinnings. Hence, Marie's story is Lamort's, or vice versa, and each person's story makes up a composite that can define the community.

With *Krik?Krak!*, then, Danticat patches the stories together, similar to the way in which Gallant historicizes her mother's life through the patches she sews into her purple quilt. In doing so, the author exhibits the ways in which each individual story is an intricate aspect of Ville Rose's larger community, of the island's history, and of the broader history of its expatriates. In so doing, she demonstrates the truth and significance of Caroline's claim, in "Caroline's Wedding," that people ". . . know [other] people by their stories" (185).

Bibliography

Abbott, Elizabeth. "Krik?Krak?" Krik?Krak? Available online. URL: www.wehaitians.com/krik%20krak.html. Accessed January 13, 2008.

CIA-The World Factbook. "Haiti." Available online. URL: https://www.cia.gov/library/publications/the-world-factbook/geos/ha.html. Accessed January 10, 2008.

Danticat, Edwidge. *Krik?Krak!* 1995. New York: Vintage, 1996.

Davis, Rocio G. "Oral Narratives as Short Story Cycle: Forging Community in Edwidge Danticat's "Krik?Krak!" *MELUS* 26, no. 2 (2001): 65–81.

Gates, Henry Louis, Jr., and Nellie Y. McKay, eds. *The Norton Anthology of African American Literature.* 2d ed. New York: W. W. Norton, 2004.

—Karima K. Jeffrey

Kunzru, Hari (1969–) *British novelist, short story writer, and essayist*

Hari Kunzru is the author of three novels, *The IMPRESSIONIST* (2002), *Transmission* (2004) and *My Revolutions* (2007), and a collection of short stories titled *Noise* (2005). Of Indian and British descent, Kunzru was named in 2003 as one of Granta's Best of Young British Novelists. *The Impressionist* garnered an impressive list of awards and nominations, including the 2002 Betty Trask Prize and the 2003 Somerset Maugham award (Contemporary Writers). Kunzru is a member of the editorial board of *Mute* magazine and the deputy president of English PEN; he has also established himself as a very public intellectual, contributing many articles to national and international publications like the *New York Times*, the *New Yorker*, the *Guardian*, and *Wired*. Kunzru created a furor in 2003 when he rejected the John Llewellyn Rhys award for *The Impressionist*, claiming that the two sponsors of the award—the British tabloids the *Daily Mail* and *Mail on Sunday*—pursued an "editorial policy of vilifying and demonising refugees and asylum-seekers ("Literary Critics"). He currently resides in London.

On the surface, Kunzru's three novels are strikingly different in theme and context, however, we can notice contiguities in certain narrative techniques and thematic elements. For instance, all deal with questions of multiple or disguised identities, while a common technique is the utilization of the narrative of the central protagonist as a node that opens out to a host of intersecting mini-narratives. In *The Impressionist* and *Transmission*, the frame narratives of the respective protagonists serve as structural bases that ground and connect a number of other narratives, some of which occur simultaneously with the frame narrative, while others make a foray into the past. *The Impressionist* and *Transmission* are also similar in their ambulatory plots, with settings in India, England, and West Africa in the case of the former, and North America, Europe, South and East Asia in the latter.

Salman Rushdie's *Midnight's Children* is an obvious influence on *The Impressionist*. Like Saleem Sinai in *Midnight's Children*, the protagonist of *The Impressionist*, initially named Pran Nath, is the product of a chance encounter between a British colonial official and an Indian mother; and his adventures, like those of Rushdie's Sinai, become a portal through which Kunzru explores issues such as the growth of national identity in pre-independence India, colonial and racist representations of each other, and questions of sexual identity. The novel begins in colonial India, and spans a period of roughly 25 years from 1903 to 1928, its basic premise being: "How easy it is to slough off one life and take up another! Easy when there is nothing

to anchor you" (Kunzru 2002, 227). While some critics find the lack of an "anchor" to be a weak point in the novel's own structure, Murat Aydemir argues that the avoidance of realistic *vraisemblance* by Kunzru is an effective narrative technique that allows the picaro-like protagonist to perform "nearly effortless impersonations of various ethnic, social and sexual identities" (Aydemir, 201). During the course of the narrative, Pran Nath assumes a host of different identities, including that of the *hijra* (eunuch), Rukhsana; the adopted son of a Scottish missionary couple in India, Robert; a streetsmart Bombay hustler, Pretty Bobby; and Jonathan Bridgeman, an impression of an heir to great wealth in England (the original Bridgeman having been killed by a rioting mob in the streets of Bombay).

The world of contemporary cybercrime provides the backdrop for *Transmission*. Arjun Mehta is a middle-class youth from the suburbs of New Delhi who gets an opportunity to join the burgeoning ranks of technical personnel from India who migrate to the United States in search of better economic prospects. However, when he arrives, he realizes that he has been hired as cheap unskilled labor, which his company feels free to dispose off as and when it wants. Eventually he finds a job in California as a lowly "ghostbuster" in a company specializing in computer viruses, but even this accomplishment proves specious when he is laid off in a company downsizing. Desperate to keep his job, he creates a virus named Leela1, named after his favorite Bollywood star, Leela Zahir. When his boss takes the credit for his solution to Leela1 and refuses to reinstate him in his job, he releases a more advanced virus, Leela2, and the release of the two viruses has a major global impact. *Transmission* can be read as a detective novel, a thriller, or a work of science fiction, and touches on important contemporary issues such as globalization, the exploitation of cheap third-world labor, and the dangers of cybercrime.

My Revolutions is narratively and thematically different from Kunzru's earlier endeavors. It does not traverse continents, for example, but limits itself largely to a specific locale and context—that of late 1960s Britain. However, there are certain contiguities in narrative technique with the earlier novels. For instance, like *Transmission, My Revolutions* can be read as a detective novel or a thriller, with the question of real and assumed identities at its thematic core. But *My Revolutions* is above all a compelling depiction of the mood and actions of the angry revolutionary generation of the late sixties. It is loosely based on the activities of the 1970s British ultra-leftist revolutionary party, the Angry Brigade, and follows the career of Chris Carver, a former revolutionary. At the novel's opening, Carver has reinvented himself as Michael Frame, and under this alias leads a comfortable, middle-class suburban life in mid-1990s Britain. However, the facade of normalcy breaks down when an acquaintance from his past arrives on his doorstep and begins to blackmail him. The narrative then shifts back to Carver's revolutionary past, and vividly re-creates the mood and ambience of that tumultuous period, whose ghosts still haunt the cultural structures of our conservative time.

Bibliography

Aydemir, Murat. "Impressions of Character: Hari Kunzru's *The Impressionist.*" In *Uncertain Territories: Boundaries in Cultural Analysis,* edited by Inge E. Boer et al., 199–217. Amsterdam, Netherlands: Rodopi, 2006.

Contemporary Writers. "Hari Kunzru." Available online. URL: http://www.contemporarywriters.com/authors/?p=auth03B5O073112634971. Accessed August 1, 2008.

Kunzru, Hari. *The Impressionist.* New York: Dutton, 2002.

———. *My Revolutions.* New York: Dutton, 2007.

———. *Noise.* New York: Penguin, 2005.

———. *Transmission.* London: Hamish Hamilton, 2004.

Rediff India Abroad. "Literary Critics Will Never Grow Up." Available online. URL: http://im.rediff.com/news/2007/sep/12inter.htm. Accessed October 20, 2009.

– Amit R. Baishya

Kurzweil, Allen (1960–) *Vienna-born American journalist and novelist*

Of Viennese origin, Allen Kurzweil was educated at Yale and the University of Rome, and worked as a free journalist in France, Italy, and Australia. He later moved to the United States, and now lives in Rhode Island with his wife and his son. The author of two novels, Kurzweil has won numerous awards for his fiction, and has been a fellow of the Center for Scholars and Writers at the New York Public Library, the Guggenheim Foundation and the Fulbright Foundation. In the mid-1990s he was on the list of *Granta*'s top 40 American writers under 40. Currently, he is a fellow at the John Nicholas Brown Center for the Study of American Civilization and a member of the board of the Rhode Island Council for the Humanities.

Kurweil's debut novel, A CASE OF CURIOSITIES (1992), was an international success, receiving literary honors in Italy, France, and England, and translated into 12 languages. It tells the story of an 18th-century mechanical genius named Claude Page, and is loosely constructed around nine seemingly arbitrary objects that give the titles to its individual chapters: a jar, nautilus, morel, lay figure, pearl, linnet, watch, bell, and button. The concept of an eclectic assortment of objects representing a person's life is epitomized by a "case of curiosities": a box, a life box, known more formally as a *memento hominem* (1992, 273). The box is divided into several compartments, with each containing one object that is often commonplace but valuable in the eyes of the owner, as it "indicates a decisive moment or relationship in the personal history of the compositor" (vii). At the beginning of the novel, the narrator describes having come into the possession of Claude Page's case of curiosities at an auction. Fascinated by the objects, he then spends six years researching and investigating Page's life. However, there is one empty compartment in Page's life box, and it is the mystery of this compartment that is investigated by the protagonists of Kurzweil's second novel, *The Grand Complication* (2001).

Although set in contemporary New York, the latter work, through its protagonist Henry James Jesson III—the nameless narrator of *A Case of Curiosities*—takes the reader back into the world of the late 18th century. Jesson's world opens up to readers through the eyes of Alexander Short, a reference librarian interested in list-making and shorthand writing who is hired by Jesson to help him in his (re)search for the lost object of Page's life box. The missing object turns out to be a precious Breguet watch commissioned for Marie Antoinette that was named the Grand Complication or the Queen and was stolen from a Jerusalem museum in 1983. Short's search does not lead to the recovery of the missing Queen—it remains eternally lost—but instead unfolds the secrets of Jesson's cloistered world; and this ultimately results in the dissolution of the partnership between Jesson and Short (compared with the fellowship of Johnson and Boswell in the formers pair's erudite imagination). Rather like his protagonists, Kurzweil himself spent almost five years traveling around Europe and the Middle East, "interviewing detectives, curators, horologists and watch dealers" ("Allen Kurzweil"). "[O]wing as much to *The Maltese Falcon* as to *The Name of the Rose*" (Caveney), the resulting narrative is a contemporary high-tech/literary thriller, recalling the work of Umberto Eco, Patrick Süskind, and Marguerite Yourcenar; Kurzweil himself cites two of the masters of "the metafictional or structurally innovative novel" (Hogan), Jorge Luis Borges and Italo Calvino.

Since 2002, Kurzweil has turned his literary attention to children's literature, publishing two novels in the "Leon" series: *Leon and the Spitting Image* (2003) and *Leon and the Champion Chip* (2005).

Bibliography

"Allen Kurzweil." Allen Kurzweil. Available online. URL: http://www.allenkurzweil.net/index.php?id=bio. Accessed March 27, 2009.

Caveney, Graham. Review of "*The Grand Complication* Independent.co.uk. Available online. URL: http://www.independent.co.uk/arts-entertainment/books/reviews/the-grand-complication-by-alle n-kurzweil-655024.html. Accessed March 27, 2009.

Hogan, Ron. "Allen Kurzweil." Beatrice.com. Available online. URL: http://www.beatrice.com/interviews/kurzweil/. Accessed March 27, 2009.

Kurzweil, Allen. *A Case of Curiosities.* New York: Harcourt, 1992.

———. *The Grand Complication* (2001). London: Arrow Books, 2003.

—Zita Farkas

L

Lahiri, Jhumpa (1967–) *English-born American novelist and short story writer*

Pulitzer Prize–winning author Jhumpa Lahiri has received exceptional praise from both critics and readers for her two collections of short stories, INTERPRETER OF MALADIES (1999) and *Unaccustomed Earth* (2008), and her novel, *Namesake* (2003). Her oeuvre sensitively explores the topography of human relationships, and her protagonists, many of whom are of Indian descent confronting Western culture, experience heightened, hybrid forms of the alienation, loneliness, misunderstanding, and disappointment—as well as love—characteristic of such "outsider" experience.

Lahiri was born in London, England, in 1967 to parents who had emigrated from India. Her family moved to the United States when she was three, and she grew up in South Kingstown, Rhode Island, where her father was a librarian and her mother a teacher. She began writing at the age of 10. After graduation from South Kingstown High School, Lahiri attended Barnard College, where she received a B.A. in English literature. At Boston University she obtained M.A. degrees in English, creative writing, and comparative studies in literature and the arts, and a Ph.D. in Renaissance studies. She taught creative writing at Boston University and the Rhode Island School of Design.

Interpreter of Maladies, a collection of nine short stories published in 1999, was named Best Debut of the Year by the *New Yorker.* The book also earned Lahiri an O. Henry Award and a PEN/Hemingway Award in 1999, and the Pulitzer Prize in fiction in 2000. The stories, six of which are set in the United States and three in India, focus on characters, many of Indian heritage, who struggle with issues of identity, loss, and personal relationships.

Lahiri's first novel, *The Namesake,* was a *New York Times* Notable Book and a *Los Angeles Times* Book Prize finalist and was chosen as one of the best books of the year by *USA Today* and *Entertainment Weekly.* Indian-born director Mira Nair made the novel into a film, released in 2007, starring Kal Penn and Bollywood stars Tabu and Irrfan Khan. In *The Namesake* Ashoke and Ashima Ganguli, immigrants to the United States from India, must name their newly born son before the hospital will dismiss him. Since the parents have not yet received the letter from the child's grandmother in India with the official name of the baby, they give him the nickname Gogol, the last name of the Russian author of a book of short stories that Ashoke believes saved his life when he was in a train wreck. Unsurprisingly, the son—born in the United States, with an Indian heritage, and possessing a Russian name—struggles to find his place in the world.

Unaccustomed Earth, Lahiri's second collection of short stories, reached number 1 on the *New York Times* best-seller list immediately after its publication in 2008, and made the *New York Times* 10 Best Books of 2008. The last three of the eight stories—"Once in a Lifetime," "Year's End," and "Going Ashore"—are grouped together under the heading "Hema and Kaushie" and recount the activities of the two characters at three different times in their lives. As in *Interpreter of Maladies,* the characters in *Unaccustomed Earth* attempt to understand who they are as they deal with cultural and personal conflicts. Lahiri has also had short works published in numerous eclectic and prestigious publications such as the *New Yorker, Agni, Epoch,* the *Louisville Review,* the *Harvard Review,* and *Story Quarterly.*

The author infuses her works with vivid and distinctive features of Indian culture ranging from curry and vermilion powder to saris and arranged marriages, and many of her characters are first- and second-generation immigrants to the United States from India, usually from Bengal, who attempt, with more or less success, to merge their two cultures. Some, like Twinkle in "This Blessed House," adapt with apparent ease, while others painstakingly adjust to their new country; the narrator of "The Third and Final Continent," for example, comments at the end of the story, "I have remained in this new world for nearly thirty years. I know that my achievement is quite ordinary. . . . As ordinary as it all appears, there are times when it is beyond my imagination." Some characters, for all their efforts, never feel comfortable in their new country. The protagonist of "Mrs. Sen's," for example, misses the family members she left behind in India, the fresh fish that was always readily available, and even the night noises; she tells Eliot, the young boy she keeps in the afternoons, "'Here, in this place where Mr. Sen has brought me, I cannot sometimes sleep in so much silence.'"

Lahiri's stories focus on relationships—husband and wife, lover and lover, child and parent, grandchild and grandparent, brother and sister, friend and friend. In "A Choice of Accommodations," Megan and Amit recognize and renew their love for each other when they attend a wedding of one of Amit's friends; Ruma's father and her three-year-old son fall in love with each other as they plant gardens in the back yard in "Unaccustomed Earth." More often, however, Lahiri reveals sterile, crumbling, or broken relationships. The tour guide/driver in "Interpreter of Maladies" wonders "if Mr. and Mrs. Das were a bad match, just as he and his wife were. . . . The signs he recognized from his own marriage were there—the bickering, the indifference, the protracted silences." In "A Temporary Matter" Shukumar and Shoba grow more and more apart after their baby is born dead, and at the end of the story, when Shukumar announces she will be moving out of the house, the two sit at the dinner table and cry together. Sudha in "Only Goodness" realizes, during a visit by the brother who had previously abandoned her family, that she is "waiting for him to walk out of her life all over again."

Loneliness and loss are prominent themes in Lahiri's writing. Mr. Pirzada in "When Mr. Pirzada Came to Dine" misses his wife and seven daughters who remain in Pakistan the year he is in the United States on a government grant. In "Sexy," Dev tells Miranda he knows "'what it's like to be lonely,'" and toward the end of the story, the seven-year-old boy who spends a Saturday with Miranda asks her to draw things in her living room so that he can "memorize" the day, explaining "'We're never going to see each other, ever again.'"

For all the richness of emotion, however, Lahiri's style is tight and controlled. In an interview with Isaac Chotiner the author claims, "I don't like excess," and comments, "When I rework things I try to get it as simple as I can." She has a masterful eye for telling detail and great sensitivity and compassion for her characters, while maintaining a well-tempered and restrained tone.

Lahiri currently lives in New York with her husband—also a writer—and her two children, and is working on a second novel.

Bibliography

"Jhumpa Lahiri." Voices from the Gaps. Available online. URL: http://voices.cla.umn.edu/vg/Bios/entries/lahiri_jhumpa.html. Accessed May 20, 2009.

Lahiri, Jhumpa. *Interpreter of Maladies: Stories.* Boston: Houghton Mifflin, 1999.

———. "Jhumpa Lahiri." By Isaac Chotiner. Atlantic Online. Available online. URL: www.theatlantic.com/doc/200802u/jhumpa-lahiri. Accessed May 20, 2009.

———. *The Namesake: A Novel.* Boston: Houghton Mifflin, 2003.

———. *Unaccustomed Earth: Stories.* New York: Knopf, 2008.

"The 10 Best Books of 2008." New York Times on the Web. Available online. URL: www.nytimes.com/2008/12/14/books/review/10Best-t.html. Accessed May 20, 2009.

—Charlotte Pfeiffer

Leavitt, David (1961–) *American novelist and short story writer*

David Leavitt is best known for his novels *The Lost Language of Cranes* (1986) and *While England Sleeps* (1994) and his short story collection *Family Dancing* (1984). Leavitt's work often deals with the troubled formation of homosexual identity, and he is sometimes pigeonholed as a writer of gay fiction. Though he has received awards from such prestigious organizations as the John Simon Guggenheim Foundation and the National Endowment for the Arts, his writing has generated significant controversy. The explicitness of Leavitt's descriptions of sexual acts has been a frequent source of complaint, and he has been criticized for inventing sexual scenes in his historical novels, as well as for promoting unsafe sex by writing supposed endorsements of "barebacking," or unprotected anal intercourse. In recent years, Leavitt has become a prolific nonfiction writer, covering such diverse topics as the city of Florence, the history of gay authorship, and the life and death of mathematician Alan Turing. Leavitt's editorial work includes *The Penguin Book of Gay Short Stories* and the literary magazine *Subtropics*.

Leavitt was born in Pittsburgh, Pennsylvania, the son of a university professor father and a mother who was very active in liberal politics. His two siblings were nearly a decade older than he, and he grew up as a de facto only child. Extremely precocious as a writer, Leavitt placed a story with the *New Yorker* when he was just 20 and published his first collection of short stories, *Family Dancing,* when he was 23. Leavitt attended Yale University, taking a B.A. in English literature. He now teaches creative writing at the University of Florida, while living part-time in Italy. Much of his recent writing, both fiction and nonfiction, has been concerned with Italian culture, particularly the experiences in Tuscany of ex-pat Americans like himself.

The emotional intricacies of several generations of family life, particularly as they relate to complicated sexual relationships, form a dominant theme in the bulk of Leavitt's fiction from the 1980s. Whether it is a young gay man's difficulties in coming out to his parents in *The Lost Language of Cranes,* or the various adulteries that torment an extended family in *Equal Affections,* Leavitt delicately explores the precariousness of human attachments and the uneasy relations of erotic and platonic love. Though he has been most celebrated as an author of urban gay fiction, his characterizations of middle-aged heterosexual women are often cited as especially perceptive. Attempts to limit Leavitt's concerns to "gay themes," as Edmund White explains, ignore the broader thematic interests of his work: "From the beginning he has been interested in the conflict and tenderness between generations of the same family, in sibling rivalry and love, in the gulf between immigrant grandparents, successful professional parents and neurotic, directionless children. His heritage as an American Jew—no matter how diluted that heritage might be—has always counted in his work at least as much as his homosexuality" (White).

A second collection of short stories, *A Place I've Never Been* (1990), chronicles the lives of Americans living in Italy. The work's focus on the collision of American ex-pats with European culture has prompted comparisons to Henry James, though Leavitt's style, sometimes called minimalist for its often fragmented and spare quality, is quite distinct from the serpentine complexities and dense psychological detail associated with James's writing. Indeed, Leavitt's work here, as in much of his writing in the 1980s, owes a good deal to the philosophy of literary pruning advocated and practiced by Gordon Lish, the influential American editor with whom he studied (Lish appears in partly disguised form in Leavitt's novel *Martin Bauman: Or, a Sure Thing* (2000)).

Leavitt's ambitious ventures into historical fiction have met with mixed reviews. His novel *While England Sleeps* is set in pre–World War II Spain and concerns the relationship between an upper-class author and the young subway worker with whom he falls in love. It reveals the author's increasing interest in class issues and their intersection with sexual desire. The book prompted a plagiarism scandal after the British poet Sir Stephen Spender filed a lawsuit alleging that Leavitt had copied passages of his memoir, while also attributing outrageous sexual fantasies to the fictional character based upon him. Among Spender's other accusations was that Leavitt's novel betrayed a striking ignorance of the historical realities of 1930s Barcelona and remained preoccupied with salacious representations of homosexuality. In his public response to Spender, Leavitt focused on his right to poetic license; he admitted to using Spender as one source among many, but insisted that he had refashioned the material into something unmistakably original. Viking Press, the publisher of *While England Sleeps*, eventually removed the offending passages from Leavitt's work.

In his second work of historical fiction, *The Indian Clerk* (2007), Leavitt explored the life of mathematician Srinivasa Ramanujan, an eccentric genius who left India for Cambridge University shortly before World War I. Leavitt chronicles Ramanujan's relationship with G. H. Hardy, a senior professor and closeted gay man who sponsored the young mathematician's career and collaborated with him on groundbreaking discoveries in number theory. The novel is meticulously researched, and has been praised for its insights into the sexual dynamics of Cambridge intellectual life. Several critics, however, have criticized the novel for its focus on scandalous detail and for its failure to transcend the historical documents on which it relies. Fellow novelist Nell Freudenberger summed up the novel in the *New York Times* this way: "Leavitt has a passion to inhabit the past, a particular novelistic impulse that goes beyond simple 'animation' of history. The research that went into 'The Indian Clerk' is impressive, but a good historical novelist has to do much more than get the facts right: he has to illuminate the relationship of his own time to the period he's writing about" (Freudenberger). *The Lost Language of Cranes* was adapted as a TV movie in 1991.

Bibliography

Freudenberger, Nell. Review of *The Indian Clerk*. New York Times on the Web. (16 September 2007). Available online. URL: www.nytimes.com/2007/09/16/books/review/Freudenberger-t.html?_r=l. Accessed October 20, 2009.

Leavitt, David. *Equal Affections.* New York: Weidenfeld & Nicholson, 1989.

———. *Family Dancing.* New York: Knopf, 1983.

———. *The Indian Clerk.* New York: Bloomsbury, 2007.

———. *The Lost Language of Cranes.* New York: Knopf, 1986.

———. *Martin Bauman: Or, a Sure Thing.* Boston: Houghton Mifflin, 2000.

———. *A Place I've Never Been.* New York: Viking, 1990.

———. *While England Sleeps.* New York: Viking, 1993.

White, Edmund. "Truth upon Truth." *Guardian,* 5 November 2005.

—Dale Brand

Lee, Chang-rae (1965–) *Korean-born American novelist*

Lee is the author of three critically and popularly successful novels: NATIVE SPEAKER, A GESTURE LIFE, and *Aloft.* While his work invokes a host of different types of storylines and genres, each novel reflects similar themes of the crossing of cultural divides, individual and ethnic-group identity, and the struggles experienced by ethnic Americans as they attempt to negotiate the contact zones where Euro-American and ethnic-American identities meet.

Lee was born in 1965 in Seoul, Korea, and immigrated to the United States with his family at the age of three. The family settled in Westchester, New York, where they remained throughout Lee's upbringing. He attended the prestigious Phillips Exeter Academy in Exeter, New Hampshire, and went on to graduate from Yale University with a degree in English. He then attended the University of Oregon on a fellowship, earning an M.F.A. in writing while working on his first novel. He also gained experience as a teacher while at Oregon, as his fellowship carried a teaching requirement.

Upon graduation, Lee briefly worked in the financial field, serving as a Wall Street financial analyst for a year. Thereafter, he turned his attention to writing and teaching, serving on the faculty at the University of Oregon and eventually landing at Princeton University, where he remains today. Lee lives in New Jersey with his wife and daughter and currently holds the positions of director of the Program in Creative Writing and professor of creative writing at Princeton. Lee says of his teaching career, "I kind of fell into it. Even though I had signed a book contract, I thought maybe I would try teaching. Then it just sort of kept on going" ("Chang-rae Lee," *Faculty Profiles*).

Lee has emerged as one of the most important and acclaimed writers of contemporary ethnic literature in America, and is the most successful Korean-American author to emerge on the American and world literary scenes. All three of his novels have enjoyed wide popular, critical, and academic success, and have earned him an impressive array of accolades, including the Anisfield-Wolf Prize, Myers Outstanding Book Award, NAIBA Book Award, Asian American Literary Award for Fiction, ALA Best Book of the Year Finalist, *New Yorker* Book Award in Fiction for *Native Speaker,* PEN/Hemingway Award, American Book Award, Barnes & Noble Discover Award, QPB New Voices Award, and the Oregon Book Award. Lee was also awarded a Guggenheim Foundation Fellowship in 2000.

Native Speaker, a pseudo-spy novel and Lee's first publication, details the experiences of Korean-American Henry Park, a man painfully caught in a state of semi-stasis between the Korean culture of his parents and the American culture of which he never quite feels a legitimate part. Lee's protagonist works as an industrial spy, stealing corporate intellectual property so that less-than-ethical clients can shortcut their own versions of competitor successes, a vocation that serves as a witty allegory for Henry Park's own cultural dilemma, in which he attempts to subvert both his Korean culture and his wider American culture in order to create a sort of postcultural identity—a process he never fully perfects or reconciles with his own conscience. Henry struggles with these competing frames of reference, fearing he will never completely belong to either and feeling it necessary at some point to choose one over the other. Eventually, Henry learns to accept identity in an amalgamated sense, in which the essences of his various cultural heritages are allowed to coexist, giving him new hope

for a future enriched by his complex cultural experiences and perspectives.

These themes of the outsider looking in and the difficulties confronting the Asian-American immigrant are further explored in Lee's second novel, *A Gesture Life.* The protagonist, Franklin Hata, is a Japanese man of Korean birth who experiences a life-changing reevaluation of his entire life as he contemplates his near retirement years, which loom in his imagination as a time of isolation and loneliness. Hata sets out to reconsider his life's course and the events that led him to lead "a gesture life," one bent less on inner fulfillment than on maintaining a seamless procession of accommodations to the type of Asian-American immigrant behavior that Hata felt was expected of someone like himself, a World War II Japanese military veteran who eventually settled in the United States. Similar to *Native Speaker, A Gesture Life* is a penetrating psychological study of how unusual life experiences, cultural conflicts of interest, and difficult individual human choices come to define the peculiar course of many immigrant Americans' lives.

Lee's 2004 novel, *Aloft,* steps back from the Asian-American immigrant experience to focus on the more general theme of the American dream itself, and the often false constructions of "the good life" that can obscure but not erase the struggle and heartbreak of dispossessed American life. Although something of a departure from Lee's earlier Asian-American narratives, *Aloft* retains an ethnic flavor with its Italian-American protagonist, the aptly named Jerry Battle, who must wrestle with the very real challenges lurking beneath the surface of his ideal American existence. Ultimately, the novel serves as a poignant analysis of nothing less than the American soul itself, and the varieties and nuances that define those things deemed American. In 2010, Lee published his fourth novel, *The Surrendered,* about a young refugee from the Korean War, an American soldier, and a missionary's wife.

Lee is best known for his keen analysis of the psychological makeup of individuals who find themselves living in what Mary Louise Pratt terms *contact zones,* which are "Social spaces where cultures meet, clash, and grapple with each other, often in contexts of highly asymmetrical relations of power, such as colonialism, slavery, or their aftermaths as they are lived out in many parts of the world today" (1). In particular, Lee explores the contact zones where the immigrant American experience is lived, illustrating the competing sources of cultural identity that are the hallmarks of a binary immigrant-American background. Lee's analysis of his own competing identities as author and teacher further illustrate the complexities of competing spheres of identity. He notes that, "When you're a teacher, you're thinking about your students' work and wondering about their concerns. When you're a writer, you're just completely focused on your own imagination. It is difficult sometimes to mix the two, as they are different activities entirely" ("Chang-rae Lee," *Faculty Profiles*). Similarly, Lee's novels depict the complications that can arise when two distinct aspects of identity must somehow be balanced and, to some extent, blended into a workable whole. His success in creating just such a balance within his own professional life bears witness to the potential of those who pursue fruitful avenues of cultural identity within the complicated, dynamic framework of contemporary American life.

Bibliography

"Chang-rae Lee." Princeton University. Faculty Profiles. Available online. URL: http://www.princeton.edu/admission/whatsdistinctive/facultyprofiles/lee/. Accessed October 5, 2008.

Lee, Chang-rae. *Aloft*. New York: Riverhead, 2004.
———. *A Gesture Life*. 1999. New York: Riverhead, 2000.
———. *Native Speaker*. 1995. New York: Riverhead, 1996.
———. *The Surrendered*. New York: Riverhead, 2010.

Pratt, Mary Louise. "Arts of the Contact Zone." *Reading the Lives of Others: A Sequence for Writers*, edited by David Bartholomae and Anthony Petrosky. Boston: Bedford St. Martin's, 1995.

—Constance J. Bracewell

Lethem, Jonathan (1964–   ) *American novelist and essayist*

Jonathan Allen Lethem is the author of several novels, as well as numerous works of short fiction. He also regularly pens essays, which have appeared in anthologies, Web sites, and magazines such as Salon.com, *Rolling Stone*, and *Harper's*. Additionally he has served as editor for various volumes of nonfiction, covering a variety of topics from memory to music. His novels, which combine elements of a multitude of genres such as science fiction, the detective story, the western, and autobiography, have helped Lethem gain a reputation for his unique ability to blend genres within a single work. His work has also been cited for its ability to function as both popular and literary fiction. In 2004, *Time* magazine book critic Lev Grossman linked Lethem to a movement of authors, including Michael Chabon and Margaret Atwood, whose work exhibited this same versatility and propensity for eluding traditional classification. Lethem deliberately eschews distinctions between the so-called high- and low-brow, and is candid and explicit about his eclectic influences, which include the work of Philip K. Dick and Raymond Chandler, art, western films, the music of Bob Dylan, comic books, and his own life experiences. He has attributed this openness and receptivity to the freedom he experienced during his bohemian childhood, to the influence of his father's artwork, and to his mother, who read freely without restrictions on genre or style. In fact, Lethem's childhood experiences and family background figure prominently in his work. His birthplace is the setting for many of his novels, and traces of his own life are featured throughout.

Lethem was born in Brooklyn, New York, in 1964, the first of three children; his father was a painter, his mother a political activist. The family resided in a commune in the Boerum Hill section of Brooklyn, and Lethem attended the High School of Music and Art, where he studied painting. His parents divorced when he was a boy, and his mother died of a brain tumor when he was just 13, an event which Lethem has described as a major factor in the formation of his unique style of writing. He attended Bennington College as an art student, but dropped out before completing his sophomore year, and hitchhiked to Berkeley, California. He lived in California for 12 years, working in used-book stores as a clerk and writing. In 1989, his first short story was published, and he continued to publish short stories throughout the 1990s.

Lethem's first novel, GUN, WITH OCCA-SIONAL MUSIC, was published by Doubleday in 1994 to critical acclaim. The work, which combines elements of the detective story and science fiction, was praised by *Newsweek*, and has become emblematic of Lethem's signature style of genre-bending literary collage, and pop-culture sampling. It was optioned by film producer and director Alan Pakula, allowing Lethem to spend more time on his writing. In 1995, the author published his second novel, *Amnesia Moon*, an apocalyptic tale inspired by Lethem's hitchhiking trip and the work of science-fiction writer Philip K. Dick. He subsequently released a short story collection called *The Wall of the Sky, The Wall of the Eye*, which also exhibited the influence of science fiction. *As She Climbed across the Table*, Lethem's third novel, was published in 1997, combining satire and science fiction with the campus novel. Lethem published *Girl in Landscape* in 1998, further augmenting his cross-genre style, here including elements of the American western, especially John Ford's 1956 film, *The Searchers*.

In 1999 Lethem returned to the detective story with MOTHERLESS BROOKLYN, which won the National Book Critics Circle Award, *Esquire's* Book of the Year, and numerous other awards, propelling the author into the mainstream consciousness. *This Shape We're In*, a novella, was published by McSweeney's Books in 2000. In 2003, Lethem published *The FORTRESS OF SOLITUDE*, which was chosen as an editor's choice book for the *New York Times*. Another short-fiction collection, *Men and Cartoons*, was published in 2004. One year later, the author published his first collection of essays, entitled *The Disappointment Artist*, an autobiographical work in which he discusses his propensity to utilize pop-culture references, and reveals the profound relationship between his childhood experiences and his writing. That same year Lethem was awarded a prestigious MacArthur Fellowship, otherwise known as a "genius grant," for the exceptional innovation and originality evident in his work. In 2006, Lethem published two short stories in a limited-edition volume entitled *How We Got Insipid*, followed by the novel *You Don't Love Me Yet* in 2007, in which the author returned to a California setting.

In 2009 Letter published *Chronic City*, a sprawling, offbeat tale of a disparate group of friends in Manhattan's Upper East Side.

Although each of Lethem's novels are unique in their content and source of inspiration, all are executed in what has become Lethem's signature style, with its tendency toward collage and propensity for nontraditional genre-bending, its employment of surreal plots, and complex character development that includes the use of nontraditional characters such as black holes and super-developed animals. Linguistically, he incorporates intense passages of dialogue into his narratives, using slang and musical references to create atmosphere and shape the characters. His major works are also linked thematically through their shared concern with alternative realities, including futuristic landscapes, dystopias, and postapocalyptic worlds. Within these surreal settings, Lethem explores universal themes like addiction and drug culture, gentrification, racial tension, love and friendship, and the timely theme of the interface of humanity and science.

In addition to novels, Lethem has continued to write short stories and contribute to anthologies and magazines. He has served as editor of *Da Capo Best Music Writing 2002: The Year's Finest Writing on Rock, Pop, Jazz, Country, & More; The Vintage Book of Amnesia: An Anthology of Writing on the Subject of Memory Loss*; and *Kafka Americana* with author and experimental composer Carter Scholz. Lethem has also begun publishing issues reviving the *Omega the Unknown* Marvel Comics character, and has recently contributed to DJ Spooky's book *Sound Unbound: Sampling Digital Music and Culture*, published by MIT Press. These essays, short stories, and projects echo the stylistic and thematic content of his novels, and are representative of the author's interest in facilitating collaboration in the arts. Lethem has acknowledged an interest in open source theory, the Free Culture movement, and the writings of Lewis Hyde and Lawrence Lessig. His essay, "The Ecstasy of Influence" in *Harper's Magazine*, allowed him to elaborate these concerns, offering insight into the value of collaboration, reuse, and appropriation in the arts, a defining quality of his oeuvre.

Bibliography

Lethem, Jonathan. *Amnesia Moon.* New York: Harcourt Brace, 1995.

———. *As She Climbed across the Table.* New York: Doubleday, 1997.

———. *The Disappointment Artist: Essays.* New York: Doubleday, 2005.

———. "The Ecstasy of Influence." *Harper's,* February 2007, pp. 59–71.

———. *The Fortress of Solitude.* New York: Doubleday, 2003.

———. *Girl in Landscape.* New York: Doubleday, 1998.

———. *Gun, with Occasional Music.* New York: Harcourt Brace, 1994.

———. *How We Got Insipid.* Burton, Mich.: Subterranean Press, 2006.

———. *Men and Cartoons: Stories.* New York: Doubleday, 2004.

———. *Motherless Brooklyn.* New York: Doubleday, 1999.

———. *This Shape We're In.* New York: McSweeney's, 2000.

———. *Wall of the Sky, Wall of the Eye.* New York: Harcourt Brace, 1996.

———. *You Don't Love Me Yet.* New York: Doubleday, 2007.

———, ed. *The Vintage Book of Amnesia: An Anthology of Writing on the Subject of Memory Loss.* New York: Vintage, 2000.

Lethem, Jonathan, and Carter Scholz, eds. *Kafka Americana.* Burton, Mich.: Subterranean Press, 1999.

Lethem, Jonathan, and Paul Bresnick, eds. *Da Capo Best Music Writing 2002: The Year's Finest Writing on Rock, Pop, Jazz, Country, & More.* Cambridge, Mass.: Da Capo, 2002.

—Jennifer Banach Palladino

Life of Pi Yann Martel (2001)

In its frame, Yann Martel's Booker Prize–winning novel is the story of an author's quest for success. At its center is the story of its protagonist's quest for land. On the level of metaphor, it is about the process of storytelling itself.

The extraordinary tale of the shipwrecked Piscine Molitor Patel, or Pi as he comes to be known, dominates the novel. It begins, however, with an italicized author's note that explains how the author—not exactly Martel, but the details are strikingly similar—came to write the novel. On his second trip to India for inspiration for his third novel, this meta-author meets a man who tells him that he knows a story that will "make him believe in God" (Martel viii). In order to hear the tale, the author is directed to return to his native Toronto to meet with Pi. What follows is Pi's story of his childhood growing up in the family's zoo, his religious conversions, the sinking of the ship carrying his family and the contents of their zoo to Canada, and most important, the 227 days he spends on a lifeboat with a Royal Bengal Tiger named Richard Parker. The story is mostly told by Pi in a straightforward manner, with interjections (always italicized) by the fictionalized author, who seems to spend a lot of time at Pi's house, recording the story, eating overly spicy food, and making cursory observations about Pi's unexceptional Toronto life.

Pi's early years were spent in relative contentment. We learn that he is named after his uncle's favorite French poodle, and that his name, Piscine, is a constant source of embarrassment for him, as it is so easily turned into *pissing* by classmates and teachers alike. On his first day of secondary school, with an authority that foreshadows what will be necessary to control Richard Parker, he renames himself Pi. The lessons he learns at his father's zoo also stand him in good stead later on in the lifeboat. In fact, the first third of the novel establishes, without explicitly claiming to do so, the reasons why Pi is able to survive so long in such treacherous conditions. Aside from the zoological knowledge he boasts, Pi maintains a wealth of spiritual insight gained from his simultaneous conversion and devotion to Catholicism, Hinduism, and Islam. The depth of reflection that necessarily accompanies such a varied spiritual life sustains Pi on the difficult days and nights on the raft, when his mood vacillates between boredom, fear, and despair. The pairing of the zoo narrative with the trinity of religions establishes for Pi an unconventional survival kit, which proves to be as valuable as the water stills, the fishing line, and the orange whistles stowed on the lifeboat. But nothing is as valuable to Pi's survival as his formidable feline shipmate Richard Parker. The tiger is at once a source of fear, a major distraction from the endless nothingness of the Pacific, and in the end a companion that Pi is sad to see go.

Before it is just Pi and Parker, however, there is a broken-legged zebra, a nervous and vicious hyena, and a maternal orangutan named Orange Juice. All succumb to the rules of nature. The hyena attacks both zebra and ape while the tiger bides his time, eventually taking out the lesser carnivore and enjoying the fruits of the hyena's labor. However, it is the rules of the zoo that Pi exploits. In his fear of Richard Parker, he constructs a raft out of oars, a buoy, and some lifejackets, and trails himself behind the lifeboat, which he has determined to be the tiger's turf. Eventually, however, he realizes that in order to survive rough seas he must be able to take up residency on the lifeboat, and, in preparation for this inevitability, he must show Richard Parker who is boss. He trains him as a ringmaster would, with Pavlovian negative association (seasickness + a shrill whistle = obedient tiger).

The outlandish story of a boy, a lifeboat, and three animals smacks of allegory. Like Jesus' 40 days in the desert, Rama's 14 years in the forest, or Muhammad's retreat to a cave, Pi's isolation and exile from humanity also suggests a parabolic search for meaning, heavy with metaphor. The sea here stands for the unknown, the lifeboat the confined safety of the known, while the animals are various virtues; the zebra is beauty and grace, the hyena instinct and savagery, and Orange Juice quiet reserve and dignity. Richard Parker, largely because he remains alive, fulfills a different metaphoric function. He is for the most part not anthropomorphized, but instead, in all his simple tiger-ness (reminiscent of Blake's "Tyger"), symbolizes a dark and seemingly intractable threat, one that exists beyond reason, that operates on pure instinct alone. In spite of having "trained" him, Pi is constantly expecting the tiger to attack him. As a threat that exceeds and cannot be checked by reason, the tiger speaks to a central theme in the novel; reason and rationalism have in fact very little power; both of them, arbitrary and fragile constructs in the end. That which exceeds reason is often more powerful, and far more significant than that which is governed by it. This notion is first evidenced earlier in the novel when Pi refuses to

choose between Islam, Catholicism, and Hinduism. The holy men attempt to force him into a choice, insisting that it is irrational and unreasonable to have three faiths. However, Pi's response—"I just want to love God" (76)—exceeds and finally baffles the reason of the clerics.

In spite of Pi's being able to catch fish, turtles, and the occasional seabird, and a fitful, yet constant supply of water, the exposure and deprivation begin to take their toll on tiger and boy. Both suddenly lose their eyesight; and it is at this point that Pi has an encounter with another shipwreck survivor, a blind French chef. Impossibly, but perfectly in the manner of allegorical fable, their two boats encounter each other in the vastness of the Pacific Ocean. They discuss their fantasies of glorious, sumptuous meals, and grope around, each in his private darkness, to come in contact with each other. The cannibalistic Frenchman attacks Pi, but Richard Parker comes to the rescue, easily disposing of their new foe. Pi's vision is restored as quickly and mysteriously as it disappeared, and a couple of days later he spies land. The island is curious, consisting of acres of freshwater algae. It appears to be free floating, as it absorbs the movement of the sea into itself. Waves do not break on its shores, but ripple through the algae plains. Its only inhabitants are hundreds of thousands of meerkats. The two survivors spend their days on the island, feasting on meerkats and algae, and their nights back on the lifeboat. For a while it seems ideal, until Pi discovers the island's sinister secret. With Richard Parker back on board, Pi regretfully takes off in the lifeboat, and the remainder of the story, until they reach Mexico, "is nothing but grief, ache and endurance" (314). Pi remarks to the reader that as low as he was, his thoughts naturally wanted to "soar." To him it seems "natural" that he "should turn to God" (315). And once again God is positioned as the ultimate term for what exceeds the rational: given the conditions Pi experiences, he should not have survived.

The novel concludes with a transcript, procured by the meta-author, of two Japanese representatives of the company that owned the sunken vessel, who arrive in Mexico to interview Pi, the freighter *Tsimtsum*'s sole survivor. Pi tells them his story, but they refuse to believe him; so he retells the story, substituting his mother for the orangutan, a Chinese sailor for the broken legged zebra, a barbarous French cook for the hyena, and himself for the tiger. The retelling suggests that the process of storytelling, particularly as it pertains to truth telling, is itself at the heart of the novel. Pi insists that he told the truth in the first story, but nonetheless yielded to the Japanese men's desire for a more believable story. He asks them, given both stories, which they think is "the better story" (352). They answer that the one with the animals is better; and this becomes a statement about the fiction that we ourselves are reading, encouraging us to privilege our sense of enjoyment, our sense of what makes a superior tale, above any yearning for rational truth. It is a final check on the impulse to cling to that which can be rationalized, and another call to value unreason, simply because it makes the "better story."

Some controversy surrounded Yann Martel when the novel achieved fame and captured the 2002 Man Booker Prize. Martel mentions a debt to Moacyr Scliar, the Brazilian author of a children's book called *Max and the Cats,* for the basic premise of the book (young boy, animals, raft), though he claims he never read the book, but only a review of it. Scliar reportedly considered suing Martel, but after the two met and discussed the matter, he decided not to proceed with the lawsuit. It has since been a nonissue.

Jean-Pierre Jeunet was signed on to direct a film version of the novel, but the production has since been delayed as a new director is sought out.

Bibliography
Martel, Yann. *Life of Pi.* Toronto: Vintage Canada, 2002.

—Aine McGlynn

Little Friend, The Donna Tartt (2002)

Donna Tartt shot to literary fame with her 1992 novel *The SECRET HISTORY,* and for a decade readers and critics keenly awaited a follow-up. Tartt delivered in 2002 with *The Little Friend,* a tragicomic coming-of-age story set in Alexandria, Mississippi, sometime in the 1970s. Like *The Secret History,* the novel opens with a prologue announcing a death,

this time eerily echoing a dark chapter in southern history: nine-year-old Robin Dufresnes is found hanging from a tree in his own front yard on Mother's Day. There are no witnesses, no suspects, and no resolution, but Robin's death marks the beginning of the unraveling of the Dufresnes family.

Twelve years later, Harriet Cleve Dufresnes, who was six months old when her brother was murdered, is bored. The summer stretches out endlessly before her, with nothing to do and nowhere to go save Camp Lake de Selby, a Baptist summer camp whose horrors Harriet had been subjected to the year before, and which she is determined to avoid. Her absentee and sometimes abusive father spends most of his time in Nashville, where he keeps a mistress who occasionally sends Harriet and her sister ill-fitting clothes. Harriet's mother, Charlotte, withdrew into tranquilized submission after losing her son, and emerges only occasionally to try, half-heartedly, to get to know Harriet and her older sister, Allison, a languid, almost narcoleptic 16-year-old who drifts aimlessly through the novel. In sharp contrast, Harriet is wide-awake, remarkably well read, and startlingly precocious; as Claire Zulkey wrote in her review of *The Little Friend,* the kind of heroine who is "so intelligent that [she] suffer[s] for it" (Zulkey). Indeed, her intelligence isolates her completely from her peers and her family, and is perhaps exacerbated by her age. Her intellectual maturity is juxtaposed with her (appropriately) adolescent and vehement reactions to disappointments and frustrations, which irritate Edie, her crusty grandmother, and bewilder her dithering spinster great-aunts, Libby, Adelaide, and Tat. This female quartet displays the most concern for Harriet's well-being, but even they seem mostly perplexed by her.

And so, left largely to her own devices, Harriet sets out to discover her brother's murderer. For a sidekick, she conscripts her best friend Hely, a younger boy who adores Harriet with a kind of terrified awe. Hely's house, full of boisterous sons, blaring radios, and convenience food, provides a comic mirror to Harriet's indolent, silent, all-female house. There, the long-suffering Ida Rhew, the family's underpaid African-American servant, prepares scanty meals and Charlotte refuses to let the newspapers be thrown out.

The more sinister doppelgangers for the Dufresnes family are the Ratliffs, a ragtag collection of brothers living on the wrong side of the tracks, held together by the wizened and decrepit grandmother Gum, and income from the crystal meth that the oldest brother, Farish, produces in a makeshift lab near the family's trailer. The hapless itinerant preacher Eugene, who was born again in prison and now consorts with snake handlers, and the speed-crazed Danny, complete a family as dysfunctional as any in Greek tragedy. When Harriet zeroes in on Danny as the murderer she seeks, she quickly finds herself in over her head—at one point literally fighting to stay above water when Danny tries to drown her in a water tower. (Fortunately, Harriet has been practicing holding her breath and swimming underwater in her quest to become like Harry Houdini.)

Unlike *The Secret History*, which reconstructs events whose outcome the reader knows from the start, *The Little Friend* revels in ambiguity. The identity of Robin's murderer seems ultimately less important than Harriet's quest. And so, as in *The Secret History*, the interest here is less about the *what* than the *how*—a distinction that applies equally to the style and pace of the book itself. Tartt's languorous, almost decadent prose, with its spiraling adjectives, is well suited to descriptions of a sleepy southern summer. You can almost hear the mosquitoes droning, and you can feel the sickly-sweet oppressiveness of magnolias and heliotrope. As Jane Schilling wrote, Tartt's specialty just might be "a kind of psychic suffocation" (Schilling). But Tartt has a gift for spinning out dramatic tension even in scenes where little is happening; for instance, Harriet and Hely at one point find themselves trapped in a dark apartment full of poisonous snakes, and Tartt captivates the reader with 24 pages of almost solid description. Likewise, she deftly flirts with dramatic catharsis: at one point, Harriet drops a king cobra off an overpass into what she thinks is Danny Ratliff's Trans Am convertible, but rather than relate the repercussions, Tartt switches gears and offers a flashback. Such strategies add to the novel's suspense, and compensate for an otherwise slow and overwrought narrative.

Harriet Dufresnes herself is probably the book's most notable feature. She is a superbly drawn character, full of life and personality, with a voice all her own; able to stand in the company of other memorable heroines of southern fiction, like Carson McCullers's Frankie in *A Member of the Wedding* or Scout in *To Kill a Mockingbird,* as well as of the eponymous heroine of Louise Fitzhugh's children's classic, *Harriet the Spy.* This Harriet, though, is the kind of child who views growing up as a "swift and inexplicable dwindling of character" (157) and so makes one envy that furious, often luminous energy of youth. But her troubles and frustrations also make one inclined to cluck along with her great-aunt Libby that "it's awful being a child," since one is so "at the mercy of other people" (363). While Harriet would never let us believe that anyone but she was in control of her destiny, her story is that of a prescient but troubled young girl, struggling to understand the anatomies of love and loss, with very few clear markers along the way.

Bibliography

Shilling, Jane. "Light in a Gothic Darkness." Review of *The Little Friend.* Telegraph (October 27, 2002). Available online. URL: www.telegraph.co.uk/culture/books/3584826/Light-in-a-Gothic-darkness.htm. Accessed October 20, 2009.

Tartt, Donna. *The Little Friend.* New York: Vintage, 2003.

Zulkey, Claire. Review of *The Little Friend.* Pop Matters (March 12, 2003). Available online. URL: www.popmatters.com/books/reviews/l/little-friend.shtml. Accessed November 6, 2009.

—Erin Branch

Living Blood, The Tananarive Due (2001)

In *The Living Blood*, speculative-fiction author Tananarive Due continues the story of Dawit/David Wolde and Jessica Jacobs-Wolde, who were first introduced to readers in *My Soul to Keep* (1997). While *The Living Blood* is sufficiently self-contained to be read as a stand-alone novel, the sequel picks up Jessica's story where *My Soul to Keep* leaves off, and tells of her attempt to confront the strange blood legacy her husband David has left her and her unborn daughter. In her determination to protect her daughter and make something positive of her extraordinary condition, Jessica leaves her home in Florida and travels to Africa where, along with the help of her sister, Dr. Alex Jacobs, she sets up a clinic for terminally ill children. Back in her hometown of Miami, Dr. Lucas Shepard, who, because of his beliefs in alternative healing methods, has been labeled Dr. Voodoo by his colleagues, hears of an African clinic where an American doctor uses a mysterious drug to effect seemingly miraculous cures on terminal patients. He sets out in search of Jessica and her clinic, in hopes that her cure can save his son, Jared, who is suffering from leukemia. He soon finds himself in great danger, however, as he discovers he is not the only one seeking Jessica and the secrets she keeps.

In many ways the characters of Jessica and Lucas, both deftly drawn by Due, parallel one another: both are healers, both have experienced recent and significant losses in their lives, and both are desperate to save their children. Jessica is dealing with the loss of her husband and Kira, her first child, while Lucas has lost his wife and is closer to losing his son Jared with each passing day. Their struggle with their grief, and their attempts to reconcile the pervasive sense of loss they feel, along with their refusal to give up hope, even when all possibilities seem to have been exhausted, demonstrate the sort of spiritual and moral strength typical of Due's protagonists. She often places her main and even secondary characters in situations that require them to deeply examine their philosophical and theological beliefs, and come to terms with fundamental questions of mortality, faith and spirituality, trust and betrayal, developing a strong sense of what is right and wrong and where that line becomes blurred.

Through their reaction to such situations, and their interaction with one another, *The Living Blood* examines the experience of the outsider/other. While not as overt as in *My Soul to Keep*, the novel's exploration provides telling glimpses into both African-American experience and subtle issues of gender and identity. The experience of the outsider/other extends beyond these traditional race/gender boundaries, however, as Due examines how parents, caregivers, and even the ill and the grieving often find themselves outsiders in the everyday world.

The focus on parenting and the role of the parent is extremely important in the novel, and several of the characters struggle both as parent *and* as child. A persistent question raised by the tale is how far one will—and should—go as a parent, to do what is best for one's child. Dr. Shepard is driven, seemingly beyond reason, to seek out a cure for his son's leukemia, and must decide between staying at the bedside of his dying son or leaving Jared in an effort to chase down his only remaining hope; a dilemma heightened by his knowledge that he might not only fail in his search, but also discover the miracle to be nothing more than rumor or superstition. And even if he is successful in finding Jessica, and the cure is real, time may run out before he is able to return to his child. Jessica, too, is faced with a terrible decision, forced to choose between protecting her young daughter Fana, whose special and often frightening powers are growing beyond her control, and putting herself and the child in danger by seeking out the colony of immortals (and the origins of Fana's gift), in an effort to help the child gain control over these powers. In confronting these painful decisions, Lucas and Jessica must each, in their way, ask what is truly right for their children, what a parent can live with, what sacrifices they are willing to make, and how far they are willing to go in their attempt to save their children, despite the dangers and possibility of death.

Conversely, in the case of Justin O'Neal, Due explores the boundaries children, and particularly grown children, are willing to cross in order to please a parent, or out of simple deference to the parent's authoritative role. This two-sided exploration is broadened and enhanced by the novel's subplots, in which Due examines potentially negative aspects of the parent-child relationship; in the choices made by one such as Khaldun, for example, who serves as a figurative parent to the Life Brothers; or in the consequences of Teferi's son's sense of betrayal by his father.

Due's work has been compared to that of pioneering speculative-fiction writer, Octavia E. Butler, as well as to Pauline Hopkins's *Of One Blood*, which also explores issues surrounding an advanced underground African colony.

The Living Blood received the American Book Award in 2002. The third book in the series, *Blood Colony*, was released in summer 2008.

Bibliography

Due, Tananarive. *Blood Colony.* New York: Atria, 2008.
———. *The Living Blood.* New York: Pocket Books, 2001.
———. *My Soul to Keep.* New York: HarperCollins, 1997.

—Angela Craig

Loh, Sandra Tsing (1962–) *American novelist, journalist, and essayist*

Sandra Tsing Loh is a popular contemporary author, journalist, performance artist, and radio commentator. She is the author of five books: *Depth Takes a Holiday: Essays from Lesser Los Angeles* (1996), the monologue *Aliens in America* (1997), IF YOU LIVED HERE, YOU'D BE HOME BY NOW (1997), *A Year in Van Nuys* (2001), and the recently published *Mother on Fire: A True Motherf%#$@ Story about Parenting!* (2008). Her essays have been selected for *The Best American Magazine Writing 2007* and *Writing Los Angeles: A Literary Anthology,* and she regularly contributes articles and book reviews to the *Atlantic Monthly.*

Loh was born in Los Angeles, California, the daughter of Gisela, a German immigrant, and Eugene, a Chinese immigrant who was formerly an aerospace engineer. She has one sister and one brother. Loh majored in physics at the California Institute of Technology, and after graduating in 1983 went on to pursue graduate work at the University of Southern California from 1983 to 1989, where she shifted her focus to the study of English and writing. In the early 1990s, Loh wrote a weekly column for L.A.'s *Buzz* magazine; and later in that decade, her essays and fiction began to appear. She also became a regular commentator on a Santa Monica, California, radio station, as well as a contributor to National Public Radio programming. In 1995, she married the musician Mike Miller; they have two daughters.

Prior to embarking on a career as an author and commentator for public radio, Loh did performance art at various locations in Southern California, in one instance performing her own piano compositions on top of a parking garage next to a busy freeway in rush hour; in another, scattering one-dollar bills out a window. However, Dinitia Smith reports in the *New York Times,* Loh could not successfully obtain an artist's grant to support her performances ("A Family 'Disaster'"), so she turned her sharp eye and sense of humor to social observation and critique in her "Valley" column for *Buzz* magazine. Currently, Loh is a commentator for 89.3 KPCC-FM, Southern California Public Radio in Pasadena, where she reflects on the ordinary events that nonetheless shape and make meaningful our lives, from parenting issues (dealing with her family's lice problem), to personal trials (negotiating school traffic), to cultural critiques (assessing the cultural phenomenon of the "Burning Man" festival). Loh has also served as a contributor to NPR's *Marketplace,* where her commentaries in "The Loh Down" focused on the ways that money—and its attendant woes—impact aspects of daily life.

Unsurprisingly, Loh's books vary widely in theme, but all share a similar approach, employing irony and sarcasm—framed by a generous humanism—to point out the absurdities of daily life. Loh's first major work, *Depth Takes a Holiday: Essays from Lesser Los Angeles* emerged from her observations in the "Valley" column for *Buzz* magazine. It chronicles the workaday lives of the young and unwealthy denizens of Southern California, and highlights the struggles of 20-somethings to find a place within the sprawling, often dizzying L.A. culture—from the guilty delight of *Baywatch* to her generation's uncritical love of IKEA, to the struggles of young artists, as she had once been. Her next work, *Aliens in America,* was a performance piece that features three vignettes of family life, commenting wryly on what it means to be an outsider. The first piece, "My Father's Chinese Wives" is based on her award-winning short story, and depicts a miserly father who rejects the commercialism of family gift-giving at Christmas, rejecting an expensive briefcase for an empty cereal box. Loh's novel, *If You Lived Here, You'd Be Home by Now,* is a vivid account of the life of young, bohemian Los Angeles writers. Set against the race riots and booming real estate market of the early 1990s, the novel focuses on Bronwyn, a Ph.D. dropout with fantasies of a perfect Cape Cod–style kitchen, and her aspiring screenwriter boyfriend, Paul. It is a humorous love song to a generation trying to transcend their bohemian-college roots and achieve a more responsible mode of life.

Coping with the jealousy that comes from observing the successes of others is also a theme in Loh's *A Year in Van Nuys.* Loh returns here to nonfiction essays, on topics such as dealing with writer's block, or surviving an existence saturated with media representations of every aspect of life. Over the course of the collection, Loh plays freely with style and genre, interspersing her often-cutting commentaries with charts, e-mail messages, and drawings, which lampoon the intellectuals whose indignant reactions to popular culture provide fodder for her broader critique of the absurdities and hypocrisies of contemporary life. In the recently published *Mother on Fire: A True Motherf%#$@ Story about Parenting!,* Loh turns her attention to the woes of marriage and parenting, and the pitfalls of negotiating the public education system.

Commenting on her performance in *Aliens in America,* T. E. Foreman writes, "Anyone who has read one of Sandra Tsing Loh's books . . . is already aware that she is a wonderfully witty writer with an amusing perspective on the incongruities of everyday life. Specifically that would be everyday life in the Los Angeles area, but in a more general way it would be life anywhere on this planet" (Foreman).

At Loh's active and personable Web site (http://www.sandratsingloh.com/), readers can keep track of her latest publishing efforts and upcoming public events.

Bibliography

Athitakis, Mark. Review of *A Year in Van Nuys. New York Times,* 2 September 2001, sec. 7, p. 19.

Foreman, T. E. "Loh's One-Woman Presentation a Comedic Singular Sensation." A07.PE.com—The Press-Enterprise (Riverside, Calif.). Available online. URL: http://www.press-enterprise.com/newsarchive/1999/08/24/935459605.html. Accessed October 20, 2009.

Loh, Sandra Tsing. *Aliens in America* (monologue). New York: Riverhead Books, 1997.

———. *A Year in Van Nuys.* New York: Crown Publishers, 2001.

———. *Depth Takes a Holiday: Essays from Lesser Los Angeles.* New York: Riverhead Books, 1996.

———. *If You Lived Here, You'd Be Home by Now.* New York: Riverhead Books, 1997.

———. *Mother on Fire: A True Motherf%#$@ Story About Parenting!* New York: Crown Publishers, 2008.

Sandra Tsing Loh. Sandra Tsing Loh's Official Web site. Available online. URL: http://www.sandratsingloh.com/. Accessed August 15, 2008.

Smith, Dinitia. "A Family 'Disaster' As One-Woman Theater." July 24, 1996. New York Times Online. Available online. URL: http://www.nytimes.com/1996/07/24/theater/a-family-disaster-as-one-woman-theater.html. Accessed August 15, 2008.

—Laura Gronewold

Lucky Girls Nell Freudenberger (2003)

Each of the five stories in *Lucky Girls* fits the classic short story paradigm typified by the lyrical, multilayered, extended short fiction practiced by William Trevor or Alice Munro. Beyond this, however, Freudenberger often muses on the nature of storytelling itself, either by invoking memory as text ("Outside the Eastern Gate") or by addressing the writing process ("Letter from the Last Bastion"). Her characters roam between continents, nomadic young women with shifting identities: "She was an American girl, but one who apparently kept Bombay time"; "I was supposed to be born in Delhi, but . . .". In the title story, the narrator is a painter becalmed in Delhi for three years through an improbable affair with a married Indian man twice her age—an affair ending in his sudden death, and mourning that only seems to prolong her dreamy half-life. "The Orphan" shifts the perspective from the younger generation to the mother of an American volunteer at a Bangkok orphanage. When Alice receives a distraught phone call from her daughter, the whole family rushes to Thailand; but by the time they arrive, Mandy's story has changed, and it soon emerges that both parents and children have been concealing critical elements of their lives from each other. "Outside the Eastern Gate" moves fluidly between past and present, reconstructing a childhood trip across the Khyber Pass instigated by the narrator's melodramatic mother. Set in Bombay, "The Tutor" explores the relationship between Julia, a manipulative teenage expatriate, and 29-year-old Zubin, who has been hired to improve her chances of getting into Berkeley. The final story, "Letter from the Last Bastion," recounts a version of the past given to one of his students by a writer-in-residence and author of a fictive Vietnam novel called *The Birder.*

Freudenberger is fully aware of the privilege behind these drifting Bohemian lifestyles. When, in "The Tutor," Julia's father tells Zubin that he first came to India on the toss of a coin, Zubin contrasts the ease with which Americans can move around and still preserve their own lifestyle with his own experiences as a student at Harvard. Julia's father was drawn back to India by the exotic—Hindu funeral rites along the Ganges in Benares. But such orientalism is frequently subverted by references to a more heterogeneous and fragmented global culture. Zubin has never been to Benares; in the poems he is writing there are no picturesque references. On the other hand, he is sufficiently acquainted with the world of an American teenager to forge a convincing essay for the Berkeley application. Frequent intertextual references—Ray Bradbury in this story; *The Secret Garden* and Greek tragedy in "Outside the Eastern Gate"—subvert the notion of insurmountable cultural divisions. The encounters between West and East confound expectations of the kind of irreconcilable Other found in earlier fiction from the perspective of white Americans abroad, as in the Morocco stories of Paul Bowles, or of the British in E. M. Forster's *A Passage to India.* While there are culture clashes, these are concurrent with more fundamental acultural deceptions and misconceptions circulating among Freudenberger's characters.

Inauthenticity, even outright fraudulence, is a central theme in the collection, as in "The Tutor"'s corrupt business practices and Julia's pretense that she is not a virgin. Ironically, Freudenberger was herself at the center of a debate over questions of authenticity and marketability when *Lucky Girls* was first published. A Harvard graduate, she was an editorial assistant at the *New Yorker* when "Lucky Girls" was picked for its 2001 Summer Fiction issue. On the strength of this single published story, she was given a reputedly large advance and was featured in several glossy magazines. The fall-

out is documented in "Too Young, Too Pretty, Too Successful," an article for the online journal Salon.com by another young female writer, Curtis Sittenfeld, who argues that the subtlety and maturity of Freudenberger's fiction confute accusations of insider privilege and the exploitation of the author's sex appeal. Like Munro, whose influence she has acknowledged (along with, more surprisingly, Grace Paley), Freudenberger patterns her stories elliptically, using abrupt time shifts to juxtapose her characters' immediate perceptions with memories from the past. Her stories are also marked by a fondness for epiphany (a term made famous by Joyce, connoting a fleeting instant of intense, transformational insight), which has become an important structural device in many short stories. The epiphany at the close of the title story is especially daring. On her first visit to India, to stay with her old roommate Gita, the narrator is persuaded to go on an excursion to see the Taj Mahal at sunrise. The girls set off, accompanied by Gita's uncle, Arun. Arun and Gita are so determined to stage her first perfect vision of the landmark that they spend the day of their arrival averting her gaze, then arrive the next morning to find the Taj closed. However, the abortive tourist trip results in a parallel initiation: a sexual consummation of the narrator's love affair with Arun.

The super-charged simulacrum that is the Taj Mahal is contrasted with the mundane setting in which the real-life sexual encounter is played out, marked by trivial details like the noisy fan that drives the narrator from her bed. As Arun points out, reality is shaped by the accidental; indeed, his own fate is decided by a simple mosquito bite. Afterward, the narrator is haunted by fractured pieces of the past, although, tellingly, she cannot summon up his face. In the story's last sentence, the image of the Taj is again evoked, in "what had been blotted out . . . a white slice of dome, like an eye behind a half-closed lid—the unexpected view of something everyone in the world has seen a thousand times" (27). The epiphany integrates subject and object, spectator and thing half-seen, and affirms transcendence, transfiguring the over-familiar.

Since winning the PEN/Malamud prize for *Lucky Girls*, Freudenberger has published *The Dis-*

sident (2006), a novel set partially in Beijing; thus far, however, the short story would appear to be her native element.

Bibliography
Freudenberger, Nell. *The Dissident.* New York: Harper-Collins, 2006.
———. *Lucky Girls.* New York: HarperCollins, 2003.
Sittenfeld, Curtis. "Too Young, Too Pretty, Too Success-ful." Salon.com Available online. URL: http://dir.salon.com/story/books/feature/2003/09/04/freuden-berger/index.html. Accessed March 12, 2008.

—Ailsa Cox

Lucky Ones, The   Rachel Cusk (2003)

The Lucky Ones is Rachel Cusk's fifth major work. Although subtitled "A Novel," structurally it bears more resemblance to a short story cycle, as it consists of an interconnected series of five stories that deal with tangentially interwoven networks of characters. "Confinement" deals with a young pregnant woman, Kirsty, who is serving a life sentence for a crime she did not commit (burning down the house of her lover's ex-girlfriend, which kills both her and her children). The story commences strikingly with Kirsty going into labor in the knowledge that her child will be taken into foster care. "The Way You Do It" focuses on a group of young London professionals—Martin, Lucy, Christine, Thomas, and Josephine—on a skiing trip (one of whom, Lucy, works at the law firm dealing with Kirsty's case), and especially on the concerns of Martin, a new father who has just left his children for the first time. "The Sacrifices" is narrated by an unnamed woman (the sister of one of the women on the ski trip) who reminisces about a broken relationship as she visits the house where she grew up. "Mrs. Daley's Daughter" is the story of a mother's insensitive and overbearing mishandling of her daughter Josephine's independence and post-natal depression. The final story in the collection, "Matters of Life and Death" is set in the same village as "Mrs. Daley's Daughter" (in which the main partner of the law firm dealing with Kirsty's case also lives) and details the struggle of a young mother, Vanessa, to cope with two young children and the discovery that her husband is having an affair.

Like Cusk's other books, *The Lucky Ones* is concerned with the complexity of the relationships binding people together, especially familial ties. The narratives primarily deal with women's experience of the mother-daughter relationship, and their own experiences of parenthood (although "The Way You Do It" is unusual in its focus on a new father). In this sense, Cusk's work belongs to the tradition of contemporary women writers who have striven to document and center female experience in literature, such as Alice Munro, Fay Weldon, and Margaret Atwood. However, while this has frequently been viewed as a political act—and Cusk's memoir, *A Life's Work,* has been read as an extremely political book, detailing as it does the author's frustrations with the contradictions between the myths and reality of motherhood—her characters often suffer from a self-enforced passivity (highlighted by the literal prison in Kirsty's case) that is constructed from their own and others' expectations of them. For example, in "Matters of Life and Death," Vanessa reflects upon her frustrations with her husband as if she herself is not an active participant in maintaining their marriage:

> No one, Vanessa included, had ever believed that Vanessa would be alone, but she had worried enough to make her unsentimental. She knew herself well and she knew her enemy.
>
> Her enemy was not her husband; it was the capacity in herself, of which she was aware, for finding her husband unsatisfactory. Vanessa had no intention of letting this capacity have its head, nor any fear that it might one day just bolt without her permission and carry her away with it. What she stood on her guard against was a degree of private pain that this dissatisfaction, and its public suppression, could cause. (Cusk 159)

This dissatisfaction is common to Cusk's young and middle-aged female protagonists. However, characters such as Vanessa, Josephine, and the unnamed protagonist of "The Sacrifices"—like the protagonist in Cusk's *SAVING AGNES*—also seem entirely unaware of their own potential for agency; nor do they try to address this dissatisfaction by seeking the root cause of it, but like the age-old figure of the *mater dolerosa*, bear it uncritically. Thus Vanessa's frustrations with her husband, we are told, "furnished her inner world with beautiful forms, silent sculptures of lamentation and suffering. She walked among them, and by no word or gesture let Colin or anyone else know that they were there" (Cusk 159). Cusk creates a romanticized version of the interiority of female suffering, in stark contrast to the harsh mother figures (such as Mrs. Daley) and husbands (Colin in "Matters of Life and Death," the mostly absent Shane from "Confinement," Robert in "The Sacrifices") that surround and often oppress them. Mrs. Daley, for instance, not only refuses to believe that her daughter is experiencing post-natal depression, but refuses to admit even that it exists:

> You don't go to the doctor for being unhappy," she said, with a little laugh that felt as though it might spark a deeper, louder laughter but didn't. "Can you imagine?"
>
> "Depression is a recognized medical condition," her husband replied. . . .
>
> "I think I'd know if Josephine was depressed," she said. "She just wants attention—that's all there is to it. It's perfectly normal after having a baby, and I should know. You've spent your whole life being the centre of attention and then suddenly there's this little scrap that everyone's taking more notice of than you—it sounds silly, but believe me, it can be very difficult!"
> (Cusk 143)

Indeed, at times, the older female characters such as Mrs. Daley seem to exist in the novel primarily in order to exacerbate the frustration of those younger and less secure than themselves; while the peers of the latter, such as the glamorous newspaper columnist Serena Porter, only exacerbate their sense of inadequacy and inability to cope. Christina Patterson, reviewing the book in the *Independent*, goes so far as to claim that "[Cusk's] tendency to over-state can . . . push her characters towards caricature," although she also notes that "[i]n her perception and precision . . . Cusk remains a very good writer indeed" (Patterson, "The Lucky Ones").

The Lucky Ones is reminiscent of the work of Virginia Woolf not merely in its preoccupation with the interior state of its central characters and in its poetic tone, but also in the homogeneity of the society it depicts. With the exception of Kirsty (and "Confinement" is probably the weakest story in the collection), all the characters are white, English, and upper middle class. The title itself is an ironic commentary on the status of women who are able to stay at home with their children, since Cusk depicts domestic life as tedious and isolating, and children—particularly infants—as monstrous and quasi-parasitic. The protagonists are also "lucky" in that any shift in their situation occurs as a result of outside influence or others' decisions, rather than their own deliberate agency. However, Cusk does not really address the questions, especially those surrounding privilege, that such an ironic designation necessarily provokes. Even the novel's final revelation, that Vanessa begins writing to Kirsty—which closes the circle of connections running through the tale—carries overtones of paternalism, since Cusk's relentless interrogation of women's community leaves little room for her to plausibly portray a genuine connection between the two characters.

While effective in increasing our sense of the isolation surrounding her protagonists, Cusk's vigorously negative critique of the idea of women's community, and the self-enforced passivity of her characters make it problematic, therefore, to categorize her as a feminist writer. Nevertheless, *The Lucky Ones* centralizes female experience, albeit in a highly privileged form, and is provocative in its challenge to many of the myths of motherhood intrinsic to that stratum of English society.

Bibliography

Cusk, Rachel. *The Lucky Ones*. London: Fourth Estate, 2003.

Patterson, Christina. Review of *The Lucky Ones*. Independent.co.uk. Available online. URL: http://www.independent.co.uk/arts-entertainment/books/reviews/the-lucky-ones-by-rachel-cusk-593807.html. Accessed September 28, 2008.

—Claire Horsnell

Ludmila's Broken English   DBC Pierre
(2006)

Ludmila's Broken English is the second novel from DBC PIERRE, winner of the coveted Man Booker Prize for his debut, *VERNON GOD LITTLE* (2003). Its narrative is built of two initially separate stories that eventually, through alternating chapters in three sections, come to both a literal and a metaphorical clash/union of characters and cultures. Considering Pierre's propensity for social commentary, it would not be at all surprising if this complex move toward narrative integration mirrored his own feelings about global integration.

The first narrative centers on the recently separated 33-year-old conjoined twins, Blair and Gordon-Marie ("Bunny") Heath, who are fending for themselves in the London of a not so distant future after their release from Albion House, an institution for those born with birth defects and disabilities. In this London, the National Health System has been privatized, and Albion House has at last succumbed to financial pressure to tighten resources and rehabilitate its inhabitants. Thus Blair and Bunny, once bound together at the lower chest, are ". . . cut free[,] [q]uickly, and in secret" (3).

The other story is that of young, beautiful, and impoverished Ludmila Derev. Originally planning to escape from her mountain home in fictional Ublilsk (part of the war-torn Caucasus) with her soldier boyfriend, her plans change radically when she accidentally kills her abusive grandfather, and must leave her home to secure a job in a munitions factory. On arriving in Kuzhnisk, however, she faces a series of unfortunate events that land her on a Russian-brides Web site, where, under the influence of a gin high, Blair Heath finds her among the virtual masses and is soon dragging his brother to Heathrow airport on a mission to find her.

Before the characters' lives intersect, Pierre places a host of impediments in their way. In Ludmila's case, she must contend with the unceasing threat of war and invasion by the ever-looming Gnez troops; miles from the nearest town, she and her family teeter on the verge of starvation. For Blair and Bunny, once shielded from the world, the impediments are both personal and social. First they must learn to live together (in separate bodies) in a London that has raced forward during their years in Albion House. The result is constant bickering, binge drinking, illegal drug use, and physical conflict, despite supervision and visits from a care worker. But whenever it appears that the men are broken and defeated, they seek comfort in each other and in their old ways. Just as Bunny did when they were conjoined, he places a gentle hand on Blair's back, tracing circles and repeating "Who's a silly sausage?" comforting them both.

Blair and Bunny must also learn to survive as individuals. Blair is obsessed with escaping his past. He craves sex and independence; he gets a job at Global Liberty Solutions, and tries to mesh, often unsuccessfully, into a variety of social situations. Bunny, on the other hand, is just trying to cope. The city unnerves him and he seems constantly scared, "mindful of the violent tangle around him, the city of lurid reflections on fetid tarmac, the hamster-wheel of never-quites" (46). Their vastly different approaches to modern life represent conflicting points of view in rapidly evolving British society. Blair adopts a progressive Anglo-American approach to life, while Bunny prefers more traditional ways; Blair is willing to take risks, while Bunny gravitates toward the comfortable and well-known. Bunny, according to Blair, is "like a medieval gnome in post-modern times" (84).

Pierre was in his satiric element in *Vernon God Little*, his criticism focused on America and its eccentricities, its myriad stereotypes, and the role of the media. In *Ludmila's Broken English* the focus broadens and turns to Europe, post-globalization, national health care, and British politics. Among the political nuances are the twins' names—Blair and Gordon—which naturally recall the once-conjoined political twins, Tony Blair and Gordon Brown. Others have commented that Truman (the driving force behind Global Liberty Solutions) is a reference to former American president Harry Truman. The Truman of this story provides munitions to foreign wars, sends his employees into war zones to sort out problems, and makes additional money through various "dirty" and corrupt business ventures such as nightclubs, suspicious consciousness altering cocktails, and foreign brides. American business meets British opportunity.

London too, along with its inhabitants, comes under attack: the streets are "asquirm with floaty-type people so contorted by casualness that they seemed driven by internal gusts of wind"; London itself is "[a] lurid juggernaut in its gran's old bloomers. Somewhere in London's gizzard stood a lever that drove it, but with no setting for fast or slow, no notch forward or back. Its welded lever read, 'Gone. Mind the fucking gap'" (107, 60). When Bunny cannot get through to anyone when he phones an emergency service, his careworker instructs him to dial a new system and use a PIN number, because "it's all private now, you have to ring a main number" (65). Nothing is straightforward or easy, nothing makes human sense. More than once, Bunny refers to himself and Blair as care files, alluding to the impersonal, callous nature of the health care system.

Like Pierre's previous work, *Ludmila's Broken English* relies heavily on graphic violence, humor that often borders on slapstick, and brilliant, sometimes vulgar dialogue. Pierre is known for his candid and visceral storytelling, and again the novel does not disappoint, with the stories of the Heath twins and Ludmila Derev coming to a frantic, catastrophic collision at the end of the novel. Someone is raped; someone is sodomized; many die (including a twin); a child is conceived; someone escapes poverty; someone returns to the past. And it is in the final section of the novel, years after the narrative returns to England, that the title of the tale is truly illuminated: its "English" is a man more than a language, and Ludmila's inability to speak unbroken English is eclipsed by her touching relationship with Bunny, and *his* inability to "find his own feet" (318).

Bibliography

Pierre, DBC. *Ludmila's Broken English*. London: Faber & Faber, 2006.

—Sherri Foster

Lullaby Chuck Palahniuk (2002)

CHUCK PALAHNIUK has described how the murder of his father, and his experience of being asked by a court to make a statement about the crime's impact—including whether he would advocate the death penalty for the guilty man—influenced the writing of his fifth published novel, *Lullaby*. He explains, "This is the story behind the story in *Lullaby*. The months I talked to people and read and wrote, trying to decide where I stood on capital punishment." ("The Story behind *Lullaby*").

But Palahniuk has also provided a different account of *Lullaby*'s creation, situating it in a more global context. In an interview with Adam Dunn he claims,

> It's my attempt to reinvent the horror novel . . . I've gotta make the transition to something else . . . since 9/11, transgressional novels really have lost favor. People don't see *The Monkey Wrench Gang* in the same light that they saw it before 9/11. They don't see any form of pranking or terrorism in the same light. So you just can't hit that note again and get the same response. (Dunn)

The term "transgressional" presumably refers to such things as the account in his FIGHT CLUB (1996) of the blowing up of the headquarters of financial institutions, or in his *Survivor* (1999) of a hijacked airplane, while *Invisible Monsters* (1999), a tale of reinvention and revenge, is scarcely less deserving of the title. If we accept such a claim, *Lullaby* would then emerge as a pivotal shift from Palahniuk's early novels to a "post-transgressional" phase in his career; and *Lullaby* was indeed the first of a trilogy of "horror" novels, followed by *Diary* (2003) and *Haunted* (2005).

Palahniuk's accounts of the novel's origin should not be ignored, but his insights only partially explain the tale's shape, for *Lullaby* is not merely a novel about death or about Nietzschean-Foucauldian power struggles. It is about themes that recur in Palahniuk's fiction both before and after September 11, 2001: memory, the past, and coming to terms with heart-wrenching loss; obsessive-compulsive thought processes; and love and reconciliation.

The lullaby of the title is a "culling song," an ancient rhyme that kills others when someone speaks or even thinks its words, even if such should occur involuntarily. The protagonist, Carl Streator, is a reporter researching Sudden Infant Death

Syndrome (or *crib death*), who discovers that victims were read the rhyme on the evening before their deaths, from an anthology entitled *Poems and Rhymes around the World*. Realizing that he himself unwittingly killed his own wife and child 20 years earlier by reading the rhyme, Streator resolves to control the poem's murderous potential. He is aided by Helen Hoover Boyle—a realtor who also discovered the rhyme's potent threat through painful personal experience—in traveling America in a quest to destroy all known copies. They are joined by Helen's assistant, Mona Sabbat (a white witch) and Mona's eco-anarchist boyfriend Oyster (whose habit of sarcastically referring to Streator as "Dad" while enacting an antagonism suggestive of an unresolved oedipal complex provides one of the novel's many sources of humor). Out of the spiralling body count, and the power games involved in trying to gain control of the culling song and its power, emerges "an utterly Palahniukian resolution, sure to revolt his critics and thrill his growing legion of fans" (Dunn).

Like so many of Palahniuk's works, *Lullaby* is an exploration of destruction that ultimately redeems, and of the rehabilitation of an alienated (male) protagonist; and it too is obsessed with existential questions of individual and collective human agency. It is also arguably Palahniuk's most far-reaching examination of the contagious, invasive nature of ideas, language, and noise: We encounter a society overpowered and subdued by distraction, where the individual's ability to think independently has been fundamentally undermined:

Old George Orwell got it backward.

Big Brother isn't watching. He's singing and dancing . . . Big Brother's busy holding your attention every moment you're awake. He's making sure you're always distracted. He's making sure you're fully absorbed.

He's making sure your imagination withers . . . He's making sure your attention is always filled.

And this being fed, it's worse than being watched. With the world always filling you, no one has to worry about what's in your mind. With everyone's imagination at-

rophied, no one will ever be a threat to the world . . .

Anymore, no one's mind is their own. You can't concentrate. You can't think. (18–19)

The novel displays Palahniuk's characteristic satire, featuring some of contemporary literature's most humorous murder scenes, as when an overbearing, moralizing radio talk-show host makes the mistake of broadcasting while Streator is near a radio and the culling song is running through his mind. More chillingly, however, when Streator reflects that people will give up culture to protect themselves from the culling song, Palahniuk creates a parallel of the surrender of civil liberties in Western societies after 9/11 in the name of protection from terrorism:

The kind of security they now have at airports, imagine that kind of crackdown at all libraries, schools, theaters, bookstores, after the culling song leaks out. Anywhere information might be disseminated, you'll find armed guards . . .

People will be happy to give up most of their culture for the assurance that the tiny bit that comes through is safe and clean. (43)

There will be one redeeming consequence: "Maybe without Big Brother filling us, people could think . . . maybe our minds would become our own" (60).

Despite an intermittent focus on this mass panic, however, the novel never strays far from its searching exploration of the effects on its protagonists of the natural and supernatural phenomena it describes. As Jesse Kavadlo observes, one of Palahniuk's themes is "obsessive compulsion" (Kavadlo, 18), and the novel vividly dramatizes the obsessive thought processes of the millions worldwide who suffer from the strain of obsessive compulsive disorder (OCD) that subjects them to incessant involuntary thoughts of doing harm to strangers; thoughts that terrify them. Tormented by his involuntary capacity to kill, Streator even illustrates behavior that psychologists call "thought blocking": the attempt to repress unwanted thoughts of harming others by conspicuous counting, to try to keep the mind otherwise occupied.

Lullaby's ultimate hopefulness lies in Streator and Helen's overcoming of the horror of their own existence: haunted by what they have unintentionally done to their loved ones, they nonetheless learn to accept that, in one of the novel's choral refrains, "There are worse things you can do to the people you love than kill them." Moreover, even in the face of his appalling fate, Streator is in a sense redeemed through his renewed ability to experience human connection, albeit in a extra-human form; as Palahniuk himself puts it:

> That's what all my books have been about, bringing people who are not in community back into a form of community and giving them a cause that keeps them together. . . . If nothing else, this is just another romance. It puts Helen and Streator together. (Dunn)

Bibliography

Dunn, Adam. "Chuck Palahniuk: Road Trips and Romance." *Publisher's Weekly,* 2 September 2002, p. 49.

Palahniuk, Chuck. "Freak Speak: The Story Behind *Lullaby*." Random House. Available online. URL: http://www.randomhouse.com/features/lullaby/story.html. Accessed March 25, 2008.

Palahniuk, Chuck. *Lullaby.* London: Jonathan Cape, 2002.

—Steve VanHagen

Lunar Park Bret Easton Ellis (2005)

Lunar Park, the fifth novel by BRET EASTON ELLIS, is a quasi-fictional account of an author's attempt to come to terms with some of his own ghosts. Set in an "anonymous suburbia" (27) near New York City, the novel's blend of fact, fiction, and the supernatural creates a house-of-mirrors effect, suggested by its title, an allusion to the amusement park that operated on Coney Island during the early part of the 20th century. The narrator, however, denies this connection, claiming that the novel's title is actually a private message from a father to his son. The novel's narrator, Bret Easton Ellis, is a famous—some would say infamous—author who has decided to give up his dissolute, drug-fueled life for the relative normalcy of marriage (albeit to a famous actress) and family life in the suburbs, with a teaching job at the local college. However, this attempt to lead a so-called normal life is disrupted when, only several months after moving in with his new wife, their 11-year-old son, and her six-year-old daughter, Sarah, bizarre events begin to occur in their McMansion on Elsinore Lane. References to Hamlet are plentiful in a novel concerned with the havoc wreaked by a father's ghost, and a son's attempt to put things right.

The first chapter of *Lunar Park* takes the reader on a darkly funny and semifactual tour of Ellis's career, a look at the high- and low-lights of the young writer's meteoric rise to fame in the mid-1980s and his subsequent notoriety as part of the literary "Brat Pack" and author of the controversial novel AMERICAN PSYCHO (1991). While the basic facts of the real-life Ellis's career are recounted truthfully—the publication of his first novel, *Less than Zero;* the furor caused by the publication of *American Psycho;* the celebrity and substance-heavy lifestyle—details are altered or invented (most notably the narrator's relationship with the fictional model-turned-actress Jayne Dennis that produces a son named Robby), making it clear that this novel is not a true account. Though the narrator notes that "this is, ostensibly, a true story" (29), an interested reader would have no trouble discerning fact from fiction by conducting a minimal amount of research into the very public record of Ellis's life and career, though Ellis has gone to some lengths in real life to contribute to the confusion, setting up a Web site for Jayne Dennis complete with photographs, for example. This blend of fantasy and reality is exacerbated by the introduction, in chapter 2, of bizarre and possibly supernatural events in the narrative. The narrator's reliability is also compromised by his use of drugs and alcohol, substances he had ostensibly forsworn as a condition of marriage to Jayne.

At first it seems, given Ellis's intoxicated state at the wild Halloween party he hosts on the night of October 30, that the events—the arrival of an unknown young partygoer dressed as the serial-killer protagonist of *American Psycho*, lights coming on inexplicably, the appearance of scratches on the ceiling, Sarah's Terby doll seemingly moving of its own accord—are simply the hallucinations of a man under the influence of alcohol and cocaine. However, the supernatural occurrences increase over the course of the next several days, and it is increasingly clear that the house on Elsinore Lane is actually physically transforming—though other characters do not seem to notice—into the California house in which Ellis grew up, green shag carpet, pink stucco exterior and all. In addition, e-mails have been arriving on Ellis's computer at 2:40 A.M. from the Sherman Oaks branch of a bank in California where his father's ashes have been stored in a safe deposit box since his death in 1992, and a Mercedes the same color and model as Ellis's father's begins to appear on the roads of Midland County. The father-son theme expands over the next few chapters, which detail Ellis's inept efforts to connect with his own son, his father's namesake, even as the supernatural occurrences become increasingly impossible to ignore. He finally realizes that he is being sent a message—a warning—from his own dead father, at a time when local boys Robby's age are mysteriously disappearing.

The presence of the metaphorical (and eventually literal) ghost of Ellis's father in this novel is furthered by the narrator's complex relationship with his literary progeny, particularly the character of Patrick Bateman from *American Psycho*, who Ellis claims was based on his own real-life father. The appearance of the student dressed as Bateman at the Halloween party is merely the first manifestation of this imaginary character in Ellis's "real" life. Several days after the Halloween party, Ellis is visited by a police detective named Donald Kimball, who informs him that he is investigating a copycat killer re-creating Bateman's fictional crimes. The specter of his own literary production thus becomes another ghost haunting Ellis; yet it is just another supernatural development to which his wife, children, and others around him seem oblivious, further complicating the question of what is real and what merely the fevered fantasy of a writer. In fact, the narrator will introduce a figure he calls "the writer" as the supernatural events begin to reach a fever pitch, and the exter-

nal transformation of the house on Elsinore Lane appears as a kind of objective correlative of the troubled state of the family dwelling within it—a family that, as the narrator notes, is "not a family yet . . . simply a group of survivors in a nameless world" (225). It is this not-yet-family that Ellis fights to protect in a hair-raising penultimate set piece in which Ellis, Robby, and Sarah are terrorized by a bizarre creature that Ellis himself imagined as a child, in an early piece of writing still stored at his mother's home in California along with other manuscripts—including the original first draft of *American Psycho*.

Similar to other postmodern writers like Philip Roth and Martin Amis, who have deployed themselves as characters in their own fiction, the author of *Lunar Park* is clearly placing himself in a tradition of metafiction concerned with the act of writing itself, and the role of art in the construction of reality. A fictional serial killer can become real when a disturbed fan of a novel decides to begin acting it out, a fear that the fictional Ellis claims to be plagued by and that comes true in *Lunar Park*. But the creation of art also allows a writer to change the reality of the present and future. In writing his fictional son Robby into existence, Ellis the author is able to exorcise the demons of his own past, and create a present in which a father can reach from beyond the grave—and the page—to make up for what was missing or lost in reality. The last pages of *Lunar Park* are perhaps the most emotionally affecting of any in Bret Easton Ellis's work, marking a departure from the aloof and ironic tone of his previous writing. However, *Lunar Park* continues the author's long-running indictment, begun with *Less than Zero*, of contemporary American culture's spiritual emptiness, rampant consumerism, parental indifference, and disaffected youth.

Bibliography
Ellis, Bret Easton. *American Psycho*. New York: Vintage, 1991.
———. *Less than Zero*. 1985. New York: Vintage Contemporaries, 1998.
———. *Lunar Park*. New York: Alfred A. Knopf, 2005.

—Elizabeth Davis

M

Man Walks into a Room Nicole Krauss
(2002)

NICOLE KRAUSS's debut novel tells the story of Samson Greene, who at 36 has lost all memory beyond the age of 12. Following a fragmentary prologue set in the 1940s and describing an unnamed character, Greene is found wandering in Mercury Valley in the Mojave Desert, Nevada, in 2000. It is discovered that he has been listed as missing for eight days by his wife Anna, medical examinations subsequently showing that he has a brain tumor obliterating most of his memory. Before this, Greene was an English professor at Columbia University in New York; but one day his tumor "finally gained enough mass that its gradual exertion of pressure became too much. Between two words in a book Samson's memory had vanished" (16). He simply leaves the university and disappears, until found in Nevada. After he is found, the removal of the tumor does not recover his lost memories, and the subsequent action of the novel provides an extended meditation on searching philosophical questions about the role of memory in the formation of identity, with Greene attempting to negotiate his experience as a married man who has lost more than half of his life's experiences. Able to create and retain new memories, Greene can understand the breadth of what he has lost, yet has no hope of its recovery.

The first section of the novel explores his growing understanding of his condition and its profound implications to his life. His marriage fails, for example, as he no longer remembers anything of his relationship with his wife, only now and then faintly sensing why he might have fallen in love with her in the first place. Returning home with her after the removal of his brain tumor, he realizes the shockingly reduced state of their relations: "He trusted her because she cared for him and there was no one else" (16). Greene's extreme vulnerability emerges as he negotiates encounters and experiences in New York City, his adulthood home, but a home no more, devoid of all meaning and purpose. He attempts to navigate the minutiae of everyday life: No longer comfortable wearing the tailored clothes of his former self, he buys sneakers. Anna advises him they look ridiculous, yet Greene believes "they were the only ones in the whole store . . . that weren't ugly" (49), raising, even in this banal context, subtle questions about the role of accumulated memory in aesthetic judgment. Visiting the Museum of Natural History with Anna, he comes across a special exhibition of time-capsule designs, and in attempting to decipher their captions-without-context, Greene confronts a problem perfectly analogous to his own. Through such physicalizing of the abstract notion of memory, Krauss is able to explore the ramifications of Greene's amnesia.

As Greene negotiates his post-tumor life, he forges new connections that exist on the margins or even entirely outside the life he previously led, finding his first post-amnesiac friend in former student Lana Porter, and discussing his new interest in scientific ideas during his appointments with neurologist Dr. Lavell. Lavell both raises and offers a possible answer to the question that remains one of the mysteries of the book:

> "Why Nevada?" he asked, pacing like a detective along the circumference of a crime. He answered himself: "Because it's perfect." Because the desert is where you go when you find your brain scorched, blown-out, uninhabited. You go there for camouflage. Like a wild animal, you follow your instinct. (71)

Following this exchange, Greene stops seeing Lavell, feeling there is nothing left to say. There are no answers to his condition: The memories he has lost are irrecoverable, and the task of forging a life with the gap these lost memories leave in his mind is something he recognizes he must face alone. He leaves the home he has shared with his wife, and tries to shape a future alone and anew.

After receiving a call from neuroscientist Dr. Ray Malcolm, Greene travels first to Los Angeles and then once more to the Nevada desert, where he participates as an "Output" in an experimental research project run by Malcolm at Malcolm's research institute, Clearwater. Here he meets and becomes friends with Donald Selwyn, an "Input" in the same project. Greene's peculiar condition makes him the perfect candidate to be a test subject in Dr. Malcolm's research, receiving the memories of an "Input," here those of Donald himself, who has become a kind of father-figure to him. Finding the implantation of this memory intrusive after the fact, Greene is forced to confront feelings about the 24 years of memories he has lost; and this experience prompts him to leave the research facility and try anew to make sense both of his existence and of the sheer emptiness that has replaced his former life. The project at Clearwater raises serious ethical questions, as Malcolm describes his research as the ultimate empathetic tool, allowing people to understand truly each other's point of view; and he has difficulty empathizing with Greene's trauma following the implantation of memory. The backdrop of scientific research allows Krauss to unfold the implications of Malcolm's research. And while its subject matter resembles that of speculative fiction, Krauss's novel is ultimately rooted in the philosophical questions surrounding memory and the individual experience of Samson Greene.

While at Clearwater, Greene assimilates Donald's stories about Las Vegas, and as a result he travels to the city in the novel's third section. Here he tells his story to a teenager he meets, and makes an extraordinary attempt to retrieve his memory in the physical form of the tumor that was removed from his brain. When this proves impossible he leaves Las Vegas for California, encountering on the bus Pip, a seeker of spiritual knowledge. Arriving in the California of his childhood, he finds the one family member of his who is still alive; and through his conversations with this Uncle Max in a nursing home—albeit with the latter in a deteriorating mental state—he is at least able to learn what happened to his mother as she died.

All these encounters emerge, at last, as aspects of Greene's overarching search for physical and spiritual understanding of what has happened and who he is, in light of the realization that he is to "begin again with nothing, or almost nothing, and still one must begin" (157). Each phase of his journey, in this light, for all its apparent futility, serves both as discipline and accrual, as moral strengthening and accumulation of a new, hard-won, and entirely personal identity.

An epilogue to the work shifts to first-person narrative in Anna Greene's voice, as she describes her experience more than a year after Greene was first found in the desert. Still grieving for what she has lost, she attempts to reconcile Greene after his brain tumor has been removed with the man she had married.

Bibliography

Krauss, Nicole. *Man Walks into a Room:* New York: Anchor Books, 2003.

—Kate Middleton

Martel, Yann (1963–) *Spanish-born novelist and short story writer*

Born in Salamanca, Spain, in 1963, Yann Martel is the award-winning author of the novel LIFE OF PI, the fictive autobiography *Self*, the novel A

20th-Century Shirt, and *The Facts behind the Hel-sinki Roccamatios,* a collection of short stories.

As the son of two Canadian diplomats, Mar-tel spent much of his youth traveling. He lived in a host of countries growing up, including Mexico, Spain, France, Costa Rica, and finally Canada, where he pursued his undergraduate studies in philosophy. After receiving his degree from Trent University in 1981, Martel continued his travels, visiting Iran, India, and Turkey. He worked at a host of odd jobs before becoming a full-time writer at the age of 27, and publishing his first book, *The Facts behind the Helsinki Roccamatios,* in 1993, at the age of 30. He currently lives in Saskatoon with girlfriend and fellow novelist Alice Kuipers, and is a visiting scholar at the University of Saskatchewan.

Although much of Martel's work is marked by religious content or overtones, Martel admits to having grown up in a "reasonable" agnostic household. By the time he began researching what would become *Life of Pi,* however, he "was just fed up with being reasonable. It's a waste of life to be nothing but reasonable. If you do that, you strip away everything marvelous in life. . . . To me faith is the better story" (Posner).

The Facts behind the Helsinki Roccamatios (1989) is a collection of short stories concerned with youth, death, storytelling, and memory. The title story focuses on two friends, one of whom is dying of AIDS. In order to pass the time and help deal with their grief, the friends write a story using articles from the Encyclopedia Britannica as meta-phors in each chapter. The eponymous short story won the 1991 Journey Prize. There was some con-fusion over the collection during the 2004 Orange Word Festival in London, where Martel was to open the festivities. The *Guardian* newspaper had printed the title of Martel's reading as "We Ate the Children Last," whereas Canongate—Martel's pub-lisher in the United Kingdom—listed "The Facts behind the Helsinki Roccamatios" (Grainger). In fact, the short story "We Ate the Children Last" is not included in many editions of *The Facts* but can be read on the *Guardian* Web site under the "Origi-nal Fiction" subsection.

Self (1996), Martel's fictional autobiography, follows the life of a young man who morphs into a woman. As a woman, the protagonist struggles

with his identity and gender and is eventually raped by a neighbor. Exploring themes of sexuality and social constraint, *Self* confronts the question of what ultimately makes people who they are. It was short-listed for the 1996 Books in Canada First Novel Award.

Martel claims that the inspiration for his most famous work, *Life of Pi* (2001), came "on top of a big boulder" (Powell's) at Matheran, near Bom-bay. In the book, Pi Patel, an Indian boy interested in both zoology and religion, finds himself in the middle of the ocean with a zebra, an orangutan, a hyena, and a full-grown male Bengal tiger. Though the other animals die, Pi must learn to live with Richard Parker, the tiger. As Martel cogently dis-cusses in its introduction, the novel is ultimately about finding "the better story." Having traveled to India to complete a different book but frustrated by its lack of progress, Martel took a break from his work and visited Matheran. While taking in the sights, he remembered a book review he had read on Moacyr Scliar's 1981 publication, *Max and the Cats,* and the premise of Scliar's book functioned as "the spark of life" for Martel's novel, which rap-idly evolved into *Life of Pi.* Even Martel cannot fully explain the inspiration that struck him on top of Matheran:

> Where did that moment of inspiration come from? Why did I think that religion and zo-ology would make a good mix? How did I think up the theme that reality is a story and we can choose our story and so why not pick "the better story" (the novel's key words)? I could give approximate answers. That India, where there are so many animals and religions, lent itself to such a story. That tensions simmering just below my level of consciousness were probably feverishly push-ing me to come up with a story. But in truth I don't know. It just happened. (Powell's)

The supposed plagiarism of Moacyr Scliar's *Max and the Cats* caused a minor scandal after Mar-tel received $75,000 for *Life of Pi* from the Man Booker Prize in 2002 (*Life of Pi* had already won the Hugh MacLennan Prize for Fiction in 2001). Martel claims that he had not read Scliar's novel before writing his novel, but only Herbert Mitgang's review of the book in the *New York Times*. Scliar reported to the *New York Times* that he was upset Martel had not contacted him to gain permission before using his premise, but having read the book he noted that "writers should be able to share ideas," claiming that *Life of Pi* was "very good," and that "he was proud Martel paid homage to his book" ("Martel Accused of 'Borrowing' Novel Idea").

A film adaptation of *Life of Pi* is scheduled for release in 2011. It is being produced by Fox 2000 Pictures, with Jean-Pierre Jeunet as director.

In Martel's next work, the fabular *A 20th-Century Shirt* (2008), a donkey and monkey travel across the shirt of a Jew during the Holocaust. Although Martel again employs animals to tell his story, he claims that these will be "used for a completely different purpose than in *Pi*. Here, they're anthropomorphized; they do speak. It's more traditionally a fable" (Posner). Martel has expressed dissatisfaction with the way contemporary authors approach subjects like the Holocaust. With a few notable exceptions (Art Spiegelman's *Maus*, David Grossman's *See Under: Love*, and W. G. Sebald's *The Emigrants*), texts about the Holocaust sit squarely in the tradition of historical realism. Although he finds no fault with historical realism per se, Martel feels that the genre has acquired a kind of representational monopoly on the subject; and the problem with such monopolies, says Martel, is that, "If anything happens to that representation, it negates the entire event" (Posner). Such negation often appears as sanitation, another wrong that Martel hopes to set right in his novel.

Currently, Martel is planning a tale based on three chimpanzees (one a statue, one deceased, and one alive), which will explore how people react when their "guru" dies (Posner); its working title is *The High Mountains of Portugal*.

Besides his literary work, Martel has masterminded a project called "What is Stephen Harper Reading?" According to the Web site, "For as long as Stephen Harper is Prime Minister of Canada, I [Martel] vow to send him every two weeks, mailed on a Monday, a book that has been known to expand stillness." (For Martel, moments of still-ness are necessary to life, self-contemplation, and appreciating art.) Martel recognizes that Harper is a busy man, and so this project is an endeavor "to make suggestions to his stillness." Every text that Martel sends to Harper is posted on the Web site, as well as the text of the letter that accompanies it, with the Web site updated roughly once a month. To date, none of the books have elicited a response from the P.M. other than a form letter thanking Martel for the first text, *The Death of Ivan Ilych* by Leo Tolstoy, sent in April 2007.

Bibliography

Grainger, James. "Martel Tops Orange Word Festival." *Quill and Quire*. Available online. URL: http://www.quillandquire.com/blog/index.php/2004/09/. Accessed June 17, 2008.

Martel, Yann. *The Facts behind the Helsinki Roccamatios*. New York: Knopf Canada, 1993.

———. "How I Wrote *Life of Pi*." Powell's Books. Available online. URL: http://www.powells.com/fromthe-author/martel.html. Accessed June 17, 2008.

———. *Life of Pi*. New York: Knopf Canada, 2001.

———. *Self*. New York: Knopf Canada, 1996.

———. "We Ate the Children Last." July 17, 2004. The Guardian. Available online. URL: http://books.guardian.co.uk/originalfiction/story/0,13773,1262253,00.html. Accessed June 17, 2008.

———. "What is Stephen Harper Reading." June 9, 2008. What is Stephen Harper Reading? Available online. URL: http://www.whatisstephenharperreading.ca/. Accessed June 17, 2008.

"Yann Martel Accused of Plagiarism." November 6, 2002. CBC.ca. Available online. URL: http://www.cbc.ca/arts/story/2002/11/06/martelNY061102.html. Accessed January 20, 2010.

McMurtrie, John. "French Director Swept Away by 'Life of Pi.'" SF Gate. Available online. URL: http://www.sfgate.com/cgi-bin/article.cgi?f=/c/a/2005/10/13/DDGVAF6PQ733.DTL& type=movies. Accessed June 17, 2008.

Posner, Michael. "When the Tough Act to Follow Is Yours: The Author of Life of Pi Muses on Spirituality, His (Distant) Relationship with Stephen Harper, and What the Next Chapter Holds." Globe and Mail. LexisNexis Academic. Available online. URL: http://www.lexisnexis.com /us/lnacademic/. Accessed June 17, 2008.

Rohter, Larry. "Tiger in a Lifeboat, Panther in a Lifeboat: A Furor over a Novel." *New York Times on the Web.* Available online. URL: http://query.nytimes. com/gst/fullpage.html?res=9802EEDA133EF935A 35752C1A9649C8B63 &scp=1&sq=Tiger+in+a +Lifeboat%2C+ Panther+in+a+Lifeboat&st=ny t. Accessed June 17, 2008.

—Cari Keebaugh

Martin and John Dale Peck (1993)

If there is such a thing as a "high postmodern novel," in the sense that *Mrs. Dalloway* or *Ulysses* are high modern novels, then DALE PECK's *Martin and John* would seem to qualify as a model instance. It is frequently cited as one of the most poignant and compelling treatments of the AIDS crises that ripped through the gay community in the 1980s and '90s. The shock and absence that it registers evokes an "after the worst has happened" atmosphere, which often delimits the postmodern novelistic paradigm. Its playful and shifting narrative style, self-consciousness about the creative process, unstable characterization, challenge to authorial convention, comfort with profanity, and unashamed treatment of taboo also mark *Martin and John* as emblematic of the novels of its era.

There are many Martins and Johns in the novel; there are also several Beatrices and Henrys, and a couple of Susans as well. The novel is composed of a number of different narratives, all of them featuring a pair of lovers named Martin and John. John delivers the first-person narration while Martin typically plays the role of his lover. Though the names are the same, and the positions they occupy in relation to each other are fairly consistent (Beatrice is the mother, Henry the father), it is obvious from elements like setting, ages, characteristics and timelines that these characters are not the same from one chapter to the next. For instance, the first chapter introduces John's troubled home life: He delivers his stillborn sibling in the goriest fashion, and for the rest of the story is a helpless observer of his mother's paralysis and his father's neglect of her. In the chapter that follows, Bea and Henry are both alive and well, taking care of their son somewhere in Kansas.

In spite of the shifting of time, place, and characteristics, there is an identifiable trajectory to the novel. Its overarching storyline is distinguished by brief chapters written in italics: John is born, struggles with his parents, faces alienation from them when he comes out, moves to the city, falls in love, grieves the loss of his lover; the straightforward narrative behaving like an autobiographical roadmap to guide the reader through the longer "fictionalized" chapters. In these, John appears to be writing a series of stories that seek to express the depth of his love for Martin, and consequently the anguish he feels after Martin's death. In both the italicized and nonitalicized chapters there is a consistency to John's voice, registering a threat from his father, a suspicious sense that his mother might disappear, and a consistent fascination with whichever Martin arrives on the scene (sometimes he is a drifter, sometimes a stepfather, sometimes a sophisticated Manhattanite).

These experiments with form complicate the traditional relationship between storytelling and memory. Even in a narrative that gestures toward autobiography, the reader must, by virtue of the fact that she is reading fiction, be suspicious of any truth-claims the novel might make. By constantly shifting the characters to whom the names refer, *Martin and John* reveals a keen self-consciousness about the novelistic form and the process of writing, deliberately refusing to participate in straightforward realism, and undercutting any attempt to construct a true story. Indeed, the line between truth and fiction becomes almost indiscernible toward the conclusion of the novel, when the experiment in form and voice reaches a climax. The antepenultimate chapter, called "Lee," should, following the sequence of the rest of the book, be italicized, but instead italics are woven freely into nonitalicized passages. It is a particularly brutal chapter, in which John asks the man he is with to penetrate him with a gun, and eventually to pull the trigger. Unsurprisingly disturbed by the request, the man leaves, and John weeps for the "hundreds of men" he remembers "by a common name, a name that remains unconnected to any identity no matter how many times it is assumed"(197). He reminds himself that "that name . . . is my own: John." The chapter that follows sees John and Susan, two years after Martin's death, about to have sex in order to get Susan pregnant. Susan, seeing John's tears, says "Dale?"(219), and immediately the narration switches from first- to third-person, as though in invoking the name of the novel's author, a kind of spell is broken. John no longer has a voice. He is now an object of observation, and the *I* is disembodied from the John that the reader has come to know. It is suddenly unclear, then, who is speaking in the conclusion of the chapter. What is clear, however, is that the voice has a kind of authority that entitles it to comment on John's narration. It remarks that "the sum of life . . . isn't something that can be captured in words," and that none of the details, be they accurate or not, really matter (220). This profound instability of names and authorial identity reveals a subtle and desperate, but deeply convincing strategy for representing loss on a scale such as the AIDS crisis presents us with.

Aharon Appelfeld's *Beyond Despair* is a collection of lectures delivered in the early 1990s about literary responses to loss. In it, Appelfeld refers specifically to the Holocaust, but the ideas are translatable to any massive grief. Appelfeld remarks that realism, statistical recall, or public commemorations are inadequate means of representation. Rather, a mode must be employed that attempts to represent the experience with a kind of sensitivity, complexity, and even narrative instability that reflects the turmoil of enduring trauma and loss on the largest of scales. This mode must be able to "rescue the suffering from huge numbers, from dreadful anonymity" (Appelfeld 39). *Martin and John* performs such a rescue, personalizing without sentimentalizing the horrific experience of succumbing to AIDS. And while it personalizes, it universalizes, giving the names Martin and John to a number of different men, allowing their stories to blend together just enough to evoke a sense of solidarity, but not enough to obliterate difference. Dale Peck has published several other novels since this debut. Among them, *The Law of Enclosures* features a married couple named Henry and Beatrice, the parents' names in *Martin and John*, and the names of Peck's own parents.

At the age of 26, when *Martin and John* was released, Peck was courted as the darling of the gay literary scene. He has since tarnished that reputation somewhat by writing a number of vicious reviews for the *New Republic*, including the infamous RICK MOODY review in which he called Moody "the worst writer of his generation." However, in these prickly but exquisitely written reviews, he proves himself to be a writer who cares deeply about crafting literature as art, a fact that will not be lost on any reader of *Martin and John*.

Bibliography

Appelfeld, Aharon. *Beyond Despair: Three Lectures and a Conversation with Philip Roth*. New York: Fromm International, 1994.

Peck, Dale. *Martin and John*. New York: Farrar, Straus & Giroux, 1993.

—Aine McGlynn

McCracken, Elizabeth (1966–) *American novelist, short story writer, and memoirist*

Although she began her professional life as a public librarian, Elizabeth McCracken is now an award-winning novelist and writer of short stories and memoir. Born in Boston, she was raised in nearby Newton, Massachusetts, and studied at Boston University where she earned both a B.A. and an M.A. in English literature. While she holds an M.S. in library science from Drexel University, it is her M.F.A. from the prestigious program at the University of Iowa that facilitated her relatively early literary fame.

In addition to being a finalist for the National Book Award with The GIANT'S HOUSE (1996), McCracken has received grants from the John Simon Guggenheim Memorial Foundation, the National Endowment for the Arts, the American Academy of Arts and Letters, the American Academy in Berlin, the Fine Arts Work Center in Provincetown, and the Michener-Copernicus Society of America. Among her awards are the L.L. Winship/ PEN New England Award, the Barnes & Noble Discover Great New Writers Award, a *Salon* Book Award, and a Pushcart Prize.

McCracken's first short story collection, *Here's Your Hat What's Your Hurry: Stories* (1993) was selected for the American Library Association's

Notable Books for 1994, and "It's Bad Luck to Die" is typical of the offbeat but affecting stories in the collection, telling the tale of a six-foot middle-class Jewish girl from Iowa who, after getting a small tattoo, falls in love with the older man and tattoo artist Tiny. Although her soul mate eventually dies, he leaves her tattooed to the neck so that she remains, after his death, a kind of "canvas to their love," a "living love letter" to her dead love *(Bold Type).*

Although she worked as a librarian before full-time work as a writer, McCracken's path to success as an author was relatively short. After literary agent Henry Dunow discovered McCracken's collection of short stories at the Iowa Writers' Workshop, he forwarded them to Random House editor Susan Kamil who, like Dunow, recognized McCracken's unique talent immediately. Kamil describes McCracken as being "like a tuning fork. The editorial process with Elizabeth is very simple; she really knows what she wants. She's the very best kind of an author to edit, because she doesn't look to me to be a tuning fork for her. She's very clear about what she wants to achieve."

At the young age of 30, McCracken published her first novel, *The Giant's House* (1996), an excerpt of which ("The Giant of Cape Cod") was included in Granta Books' *Granta 54: Best of Young American Novelists.* A finalist for a National Book Award, *Giant's House* tells the intensely romantic but never saccharine story of a Cape Cod librarian's platonic love for an adolescent patron 14 years younger, who suffers from gigantism. As in "It's Bad Luck to Die," the giant does not live long, but is memorialized with aching poignancy by the bereft spinster. As with many of the stories in *Here's Your Hat, Giant's House* is peppered with bittersweet, often humorous, and unforgettable imagery told in a sure and affecting style.

McCracken's second novel, *Niagara Falls All Over Again* (2002), won the L.L. Winship / PEN New England award, and tells a different kind of love story, that of vaudeville comic partners, Carter and Sharpe. The plangent simplicity and sincerity of their travails, and of the relationship that survives them, is set in stark contrast to the grotesque, wearying shtick of their profession. Describing the novel as "exquisite," a *New York Times Book Review*

is typical in its assertion that "McCracken unpacks her metaphors with the intensity of a poet."

McCracken followed her first two novels with the nonfictional *An Exact Replica of a Figment of My Imagination* (2008), a frankly written, beautifully expressed reflection on the stillbirth of her first child, Pudding. When describing the book to an interviewer, McCracken explained part of the initial motivation behind the effort: "I want[ed] a book that acknowledges that life goes on but that death goes on, too, that a person who is dead is a long, long story" *(Exhale).* Especially given its heartaching subject matter, *An Exact Replica,* which McCracken wrote in three weeks and then revised only minimally, epitomizes the author's unique blend of often black humor and pathos, firmly controlled by her skillful prose.

Having taught creative writing at institutions such as Skidmore College and the Iowa Writers' Workshop, McCracken is currently the 2008–09 Frieda L. Miller Fellow at the Radcliffe Institute for Advanced Study at Harvard University. There she is completing work on her third novel, tentatively titled *Thunderstruck Not Lightning-Struck,* a fictional memoir narrated in the first person by a female athlete named Christian Wrede, who trains as a weight-lifting prodigy under the tutelage of her dentist father, also named Christian. She is also at work on a second short story collection, entitled *The House of Two Three-Legged Dogs.*

McCracken's writing is known for its intimacy, its quiet, often poignant humor, and its stunning command of language, expressed in a deceptively clear prose style. While Random House editor Susan Kamil describes McCracken as a "fierce romantic" *(Bold Type),* author of *Geek Love* Katherine Dunn puts a slightly finer point on it, describing her as a "true romantic, not the sloppy, gushy kind that lie to themselves, but the robust, ferocious romantic who sees reality with all its chinks, twitches, and zits, and finds it beautiful." Both in her fiction and nonfiction, McCracken's voice, though at times quirky and often humorous, appears to spring from a sensibility familiar with pain, isolation, a need for compassion, and an awareness of what it is like to live the life of an outsider. In a review for the *New Yorker,* Daphne Merkin compares McCracken's to other unusual "outsider" voices in modern American fiction, such as that of Harper Lee, Marjorie Keller, and Carson McCullers, the latter of whom is McCracken's favorite writer. On a similar note, Kamil argues that McCracken occupies "a certain gothic tradition, except for the fact that she turns it on its head, with the kind of no-nonsense, straightforward literary voice that is romantic and at the same time extremely clear" (*Bold Type*).

Elizabeth McCracken currently lives in Cambridge, Massachusetts, with her husband, playwright, novelist, and artist Edward Carey, with whom she has one son, August "Gus" George Carey Harvey, and a daughter, Matilda Libby Mary Harvey.

Bibliography

"Elizabeth McCracken." Radcliffe Institute for Advanced Study at Harvard University. Available online. URL: http://www.radcliffe.edu/research/fellows_2009 emccracken.aspx. Accessed March 24, 2009.

Elizabeth McCracken. "Elizabeth McCracken Homepage." Available online. URL: http://www.elizabethmccracken.com/. Accessed March 24, 2009.

"*Exhale's* Cara Tyrrell Taps Highly Acclaimed Author Elizabeth McCracken for Insight into Loss." Exhale. Available online. URL: http://www.exhalezine.com/ISSUE4March/mccrack   eninterviewissue4.html. Accessed March 24, 2009.

"An Interview with Elizabeth McCracken's Editor Susan Kamil." Random House. Available online. URL: http://www.randomhouse.com/boldtype/0397/mccracken/. Accessed March 24, 2009.

McCracken, Elizabeth. *An Exact Replica of a Figment of My Imagination.* New York: Little Brown, 2008.

———. *The Giant's House.* New York: Avon, 1996.

———. *Here's Your Hat What's Your Hurry: Stories.* New York: Random House, 1993.

———. *Niagara Falls All Over Again.* New York: Dial Press, 2001.

—L. Bailey McDaniel

Meloy, Maile (1972–) *American novelist and short story writer*

Meloy has published two collections of short stories, HALF IN LOVE (2002) and *Both Ways Is the Only Way I Want It* (2009), and two novels, *Liars and Saints* (2003) and *A Family Daughter* (2006).

She was born and raised in Helena, Montana, and attended Harvard College; she also holds an M.F.A. in fiction from the University of California, Irvine. Her short stories have appeared in the *New Yorker* and the *Paris Review,* and *Half in Love* won the Rosenthal Foundation Award from the American Academy of Arts and Letters, the John C. Zacharis Award from *Ploughshares,* and the PEN/Malamud Award, while *Liars and Saints* was short-listed for the 2005 Orange Prize. Critics have praised her work for its grace, clarity, and confidence, all in a minimalist style. In an interview with the *Telegraph,* Meloy describes her writing process as "digging for oil. You dig a lot of holes and sometimes you find something down there, and other times it's just rocks and water." In the end, she discards a "depressingly huge" amount of her work before the final product is published.

The short stories in *Half in Love* are set in such diverse locales as Montana, Paris, wartime London, and Greece, but the protagonists are all caught in the middle of a significant transition, and are seen dealing with situations they were neither expecting nor equipped for by their lives. For example, in "Ranch Girl" a young woman is torn between staying in her native Montana after returning from college or leaving and discovering what the world has to offer. When tarot-card reader Suzy moves to the town, she tells the young woman to "be interesting in your twenties . . . otherwise you'll want to do it in your thirties or forties, when it wreaks all kinds of havoc." The young woman, however, only knows how to be a ranch girl and is daunted by the prospect of abandoning the known and secure. Suzy's tarot cards, on the other hand, tell her to leave and see the world. Like many of the short stories in the collection, the reader is left not knowing what decision the character will ultimately make, causing Meloy's stories to be filled with the same kind of tension and uncertainty that life itself often provides. In her 2009 collection, *Both Ways Is the Only Way I Want It,* Meloy intensifies this uncertainty, yet frames it with understanding, as the extraordinary restraint and balance of her prose stands in creative, complex, and always revealing contrast to the often self-damaging irrationality of her characters.

Liars and Saints and *A Family Daughter* both depict the Catholic Santerre family in California. Although the novels can be read separately, the latter is really a companion novel to the former, which begins in Santa Barbara during World War II with the marriage of Teddy and Yvette, and then follows the family for the next four generations. Jealousy, betrayal, and damaging secrets are interwoven with the family's fate for 50 years, eventually bringing the family itself to its breaking point. The two novels are strikingly and skillfully linked by the character and story of Abby, Teddy, and Yvette's granddaughter. In *Liars and Saints*, Abby has a one-night stand with her uncle and becomes pregnant but in the end dies of cancer. In *Family Daughter*, she sleeps with her uncle several times but does not become pregnant or die of cancer, instead becoming a novelist; and the latter work is in many ways Abby's interpretation of the events in *Liars and Saints*. Abby writes the novel to explore the secrets and lies within her family, and to cope with the death of her father. In this way, Meloy anatomizes how reality and fiction can be fused and warped, and generations affected; while in depicting Abby's later vocation she reveals the anatomy of novel-writing itself, noting in the *Telegraph* that *A Family Daughter* "would be a book about writing a book. But the best candidate was the one that was dead, so I decided to bring Abby back to life."

Meloy's style is similar to that of Alice Munro, with the addition of strong shades of Catholicism and its far-reaching moral and social taxonomy; while her measured prose and skillful thematic balance between novels has been described as Canadian, evoking as they do the style of Atwood and Ondaatje. Her writing influences include Vladimir Nabokov, Flannery O'Connor, Raymond Carver, Richard Ford, Evelyn Waugh, and Richard Hugo. One of her favorite books is *The Collected Short Stories of John Cheever*, of which she notes in a *Meet the Writers* interview that she is still "overcome with the memory of them. Not really specific scenes or lines but the feel of reading those stories."

Meloy currently lives in Los Angeles.

Bibliography

Barnes&Noble.com. "Meet the Writers: Maile Meloy." Available online. URL: http://www.barnesandnoble.com/writers/writerdetails.asp?cid=1077319. Accessed September 14, 2008.

Hagestadt, Emma. Review of *A Family Daughter*. Independent.co.uk. Available online. URL: http://www.independent.co.uk/arts-entertainment/books/reviews/a-family-daughter-by-maile-m eloy-471925.html. Accessed September 14, 2008.

Mailemeloy.com. "Maile Meloy." Available online. URL: mailemeloy.com. Accessed September 14, 2008.

Meloy, Maile, *A Family Daughter*. New York: Simon & Schuster, 2007.

———. *Half in Love*. New York: Simon & Schuster, 2003.

———. *Liars and Saints*. New York: Simon & Schuster, 2004.

"A Writer"s Life: Maile Meloy" (March 12, 2006). Telegraph. Available online. URL: http://www.telegraph.co.uk/arts/main.jhtml?xml=/arts/2006/03/05/bomeloy.xml&sShee t=/arts/2006/03/05/bomain.html. Accessed September 14, 2008.

—Elizabeth Rust

Mendelsohn, Jane (1965–) *American novelist*

JANE MENDELSOHN is the author of two novels, *I WAS AMELIA EARHART* (1996) and *Innocence* (2000). Emily Schirner narrated her last novel *Innocence* in an audio book format that was released in 2005. Mendelsohn also works as a journalist, with her reviews and articles appearing in the *Village Voice*, the *Guardian*, *Yale Review*, and the *London Review of Books*. She was an assistant to the literary editor of the *Village Voice* and worked as a tutor at Yale University.

Mendelsohn was born in 1965 in New York. Her father is a psychiatrist and her mother a professor of art history at the State University College at New Paltz, New York. She graduated summa cum laude from Yale University in 1987 and had legal aspirations, but after a year at the Yale Law School she decided to become a writer. Her wedding to Nicholas Davis, a writer and filmmaker, was announced in the *New York Times* on February 23, 2009.

Her first novel, *I was Amelia Earhart*, is inspired by the life of the famous aviator, Amelia Earhart (1897–1937), who went missing over the central Pacific Ocean while attempting to fly around the world in 1937. An article in the *New York Times* that discussed the possibility of a piece of Earhart's plane being discovered sparked Mendelsohn's interest in Earhart's life. The novel was an instant success and was short-listed for the Orange Prize for Fiction in 1997; it has since been translated into 15 languages. It is shaped as an autobiography of Earhart, however, the first-person voice is juxtaposed with a third-person narration, and Mendelsohn explains her choice of the two narratives by telling the story of how the novel developed. The first version of the tale was exclusively in the third person, but after completing the book Mendelsohn confesses that "I felt that I didn't like it in the third person, but I also felt that I finally understood the story enough to know how to tell it in the first person" (Hoggan, 1997). Due to its quasi-autobiographical character the novel has a shared genealogy with Virginia Woolf's *Orlando* or Gertrude Stein's *The Autobiography of Alice B. Toklas;* and considering the thematic focus of the novel, John H. Lienhard (2003) includes it among those works that discuss the mystery of flying, such as Antoine de Saint-Exupéry's *The Little Prince* and Beryl Markham's *West with the Night.*

Beckett, the main character of Mendelsohn's second novel, *Innocence* (2000), recalls J. D. Salinger's now classic protagonist, Holden Caulfield, as she struggles with the emptiness and shallowness of the world around her. After her mother's death, Beckett is transferred to an upscale school in Manhattan. As a newcomer she would like to belong to the elite club of the beautiful girls, Sunday, Morgan, and Myrrh, but remains an outsider as she is seen as "the ugly girl, the smart girl, the boyish, the loser" (9). The beautiful girls, however, are suddenly found dead in an alley, covered in blood, and are said to have committed group suicide. The scene suddenly imbues Beckett's story with shades of a slasher/vampire tale, and she identifies herself with the "Final Girl" (13) of horror movies who survives everybody and finally kills the killer. The novel now shifts its focus to a coven of women-vampires, led by Beckett's stepmother, who kill beautiful virgin girls to remain alive and beautiful. As Beckett blossoms into a beautiful virgin, she is alone in her struggle with the evil forces, as no one believes her. In the end she confronts and destroys her stepmother, the head of the vampires, and at that moment the artifice of this inner narrative and its world begins to dissolve. However, the reality of her story is defined by Beckett herself as she affirms that "What matters isn't whether something is real. What matters is if it is true" (168). She has discovered the effect that an unreliable narrator can have on the reader in her literary class and employs this persona "for creating ironic distance" (38) in her own narrative. Her horror story that "is not a dream" and ". . . is not based on a true story" (vii) can perhaps best be read as a complex coming-of-age narrative, in an age when narration itself is becoming increasingly unreliable, and influenced by cinematic fluidity and the "hyper-reality" of its special effects; or as Beckett herself describes it, "the video of the movie of my life" (181).

Bibliography

Lienhard, John H. *Inventing Modern: Growing Up with X-rays, Skyscrapers and Tailfins.* Oxford: Oxford University Press, 2003.

Mendelsohn, Jane. *Innocence.* New York: Riverhead Books, 2000.

———. *I Was Amelia Earhart.* London: Vintage, 1997.

———. "Jane Mendelsohn: Flying High with Debut Novel on Earhart." By Ron Hogan. Available online. URL: http://www.beatrice.com/interviews/mendelsohn/. Accessed February 23, 2009.

—Zita Farkas

Microserfs Douglas Coupland (1995)

DOUGLAS COUPLAND's *Microserfs* has rapidly emerged as one of the era-defining novels of the 1990s. Set in the booming world of software development (the title combines a reference to its characters' initial employment at Microsoft with an allusion to serfdom, the most subservient class in medieval feudal society), it is a satirical exploration of the impact of computer interaction on human relationships, and the contemporary search for meaning within the flow of virtual contact and information overload that constitutes life after the Internet revolution (the ultimate microsurf). Like much of Coupland's work, *Microserfs* stands as both an exploration of and an ironic commentary on contemporary popular culture. Its format, that of an electronic diary kept by Dan, the main protagonist, challenged traditional literary structure, questioning the boundaries of narrative and meaning through the inclusion of seemingly randomized "computer subconscious" sections, and self-conscious computerized manipulation of the text itself. Prefiguring the rise of the "blog culture" it immediately preceded, its speculations were both timely and prescient, and its 2006 sequel, JPOD, developed the same themes, reflecting the increasing disintegration of traditional communication structures.

Dan's diary chronicles the lives of his 20-something friends over the course of roughly a year. As the novel opens, he and his five housemates (Michael, Todd, Susan, Abe, and Bug, collectively referred to as the Channel Three News Team) all work for Microsoft, and this work defines their lives: 14-hour working days are standard, stock vesting and arbitrary shipping dates provide the landmarks by which they measure the passage of time, their cars are "personality-free gray Microsoftmobiles," they check WinQuote compulsively, and Bill Gates represents the apex of authority and achievement. Their characters are sketched through lists of *Jeopardy!* dream categories, demonstrating Coupland's habitually ironic use of popculture references in unconventional and distinctly postmodernist ways, as a supposedly "deeper" inner reality is inscribed in and presented as apparently trivial surface detail. This becomes a recurring theme in the novel: Lists scattered throughout *Microserfs* juxtapose or combine the traditionally significant (psychological problems or developing relationships) with the insignificant (taste in multimedia products or snack food). "Computer subconscious files," constructed from miscellaneous words or sentences alongside proper nouns and brand names, create implied links between the human subconscious and the virtual world of computers.

Early in the narrative Dan develops a relationship with fellow Microserf Karla, shiatsu masseur, recovering anorexic, and extemporizing philosopher. If anyone can, Karla represents the book's

spiritual authority; talking "like an episode of Star Trek made flesh" (17), her functionality hinging on acceptance of the multifarious and growing connections between human and machine, which is physically realized at the book's climax. For Karla, human beings "remember everything" (92) by using the body like a computer hard drive; computers are "where humanity dreams."

The narrative is episodic and picaresque, recalling the epistolary novels of the 18th century. Significant incidents, such as Dan's cohabitation with Karla or his father's redundancy, are interspersed with the minutiae of daily life and the consumer realities that dominate it. Karla, in particular, is expert at manipulating these intersections, and Dan's simultaneous awareness of this and susceptibility to it represents an ironic commentary on a seemingly universal human state. Similarly, as Dan and Karla's intimacy grows, the novel's relatively traditional narrative format is interspersed with increasingly disjunctive typographical and structural reiterations or extensions: a section in what has become "txt spk," for example, or chunks of seemingly random symbols. "After a certain point," Dan tells us, "real language decomposes into encryption code" (19), and it is possible to see the novel itself as an extended and timely investigation of precisely when this point is reached.

When Michael has an inspirational encounter with Bill and comes up with "Oop!," a kind of virtual Lego (and an acronym of "object orientated programming," a programming methodology), all the housemates with the exception of Abe (whose e-mails are interpolated into the text) decide to leave Microsoft and work for him in Silicon Valley, calling their fledgling company Interiority. Initially they live with Dan's parents, and provide them both with a new lease on life. Revitalized, Dan's father takes up mysterious "work" for Michael, prompting Dan to address his own insecurities about his long-dead elder brother Jed; and his mother joins a swimming group and expands her social circle. Within the group, too, things begin to change. Ethan reveals his brush with cancer and bonds emotionally with the others; Bug comes out as gay; Todd hooks up with fellow bodybuilding champion Dusty, who subsequently joins Interiority, and under their influence, Dan and Karla decide to get fit. Susan continues to search for meaning through a string of failed liaisons.

The formation of idiosyncratic but functional human relationships is a major theme in the novel. Like Dan, Karla, Todd, and Dusty, Bug abandons his lifelong celibate isolation and meets lovers; Susan becomes involved with fellow programmer Emmett; and even arch-geek Michael sends Dan to confess his love for online entity BarCode. Suitably enough, the latter is revealed as a 20-year-old, super-tough computing student who also joins the team. Susan, meanwhile, forms the other women into "Chyx," a support network for women who code, and becomes increasingly famous. Todd and Dusty have a daughter, Lyndsey Rose. During a trip to Vegas for a computing-industry meet that enables the characters (and readers) to reflect on their development since their days as Microserfs, Dan receives bad news: His mother has had an accident and is in a coma. At the novel's climax, Karla's theories about the fusions of human body, soul, and machine are tested and eventually proved correct, as the combination of massage, human contact, and the provision of a keyboard finally enable his mother to communicate once more. Such symbolic and optimistic conclusions are typical of Coupland; *Girlfriend in a Coma* follows a similar pattern.

Microserfs searchingly explores the relationship between computer and human identity in the late 20th century. Alongside Karla's philosophies and Dan's questioning, Todd and Dusty are initially obsessed with making their bodies "'post-human' ... like the Bionic Woman's and the Six Million Dollar Man's" (241). Dusty, however, abandons this as soon as her pregnancy is confirmed, implying a more traditional set of values underlying the novel's highly contemporary zeitgeist. This is also evident in Coupland's repackaging of the American dream: The characters swap corporate security for the risky independent enterprise of Michael's vision, expressed here as the search for being "one-point-oh," "the first to do something cool or new" (87). Life as a Microserf—an "interchangeable bloodless PlaySkool figurine" (135) to be hired and fired at will, and regarded with utilitarian contempt by an inaccessible and arbitrary managerial aristocracy—is contrasted to the risky freedom of small-scale enterprise dependent on human relations ("all of us staying together," 199). "This time," comments Dan, "we're killing ourselves for our*selves* . . ." (135), which is portrayed as an unequivocally good thing.

The novel also explores the changing nature of communication, and the construction of meaning in an increasingly virtual world. Unexplained messages are concealed in the text: An adaptation of the Rifleman's Creed in an encoded binary message (104–105), and a letter from Patty Hearst to her parents (308–309) confront the reader with apparently incomprehensible texts, and thus fundamental questions about the construction of narrative itself. (It is perhaps telling that awareness of these sections was initially heightened by means of the internet). Above all, however, *Microserfs* emphasizes the importance of communication and human connections (both physical and emotional) amid rapidly changing media and environments; and offers a guardedly optimistic perspective on the potential of such change.

Bibliography

Coupland, Douglas. *Girlfriend in a Coma.* Toronto: HarperCollins, 1998.
———. *JPod.* London: Bloomsbury, 2006.
———. *Microserfs.* London: Flamingo, 1995.

—Sasha Garwood

Middlesex Jeffrey Eugenides (2002)

When *Middlesex* was first published in 2002, it quickly became a best seller, meeting with great critical acclaim and winning the Pulitzer Prize in fiction in 2003. JEFFREY EUGENIDES' second novel is both an immigrant family epic and a coming-of-age story focusing on the novel's intersexed narrator and protagonist, Cal Stephanides. At the age of 41, Cal sets out to recount the story of the recessive gene responsible for his intersex condition, 5-alpha-reductase deficiency. As a result of 5-ARD, chromosomal and gonadal males appear externally female before undergoing "masculinizing" transformations during puberty due to hormonal changes. In the first half of the novel, Cal recounts the story of the Stephanides family, beginning with the incestuous love affair of his grandparents, Desdemona and Lefty. The siblings grow up in Smyrna, in Asia Minor, where they fall in love and are confronted with the horrors of civil war. By emigrating to America, they leave behind not only their war-ridden home, but also their past identities as brother and sister. Desdemona and Lefty get married and move to Detroit, Michigan, where they have a son, Milton. Milton marries his second cousin, Tessie, and the couple has two children, Cal and his older brother, who is only referred to as Chapter Eleven.

The second half of the novel focuses on Cal's coming of age. Calliope grows up as a seemingly normal girl before she is hospitalized after an accident at the age of 14, and her intersex condition is discovered by chance. After this decisive turning point, Calliope decides to live as a boy and calls herself Cal. In order to avoid surgical genital alteration, Cal runs away from home and hitchhikes to San Francisco, where he joins a freak show. He moves in with another intersexed individual, Zora, who teaches him about the difference between sex and gender, sexual dissidence and the necessity for resistance and activism. Though this is an empowering experience for Cal, he ultimately feels unable to identify with Zora and her cause, and decides to return to Detroit, just in time for his father's funeral. His family ultimately comes to terms with the fact that Cal does not want to undergo normalizing surgery, and accepts his male identity.

Though the novel can thus roughly be divided into two separate halves, the story is not told in a strictly linear fashion as it repeatedly jumps from the time before Cal's birth, or the time of Cal's childhood and adolescence, to the present day in which Cal is writing the story at the age of 41. By piecing together the fragmentary bits of narrative dealing with Cal's present situation, the reader learns that Cal's gender identity is not straightforward and unequivocal but highly complex and often unstable. It is no coincidence that Cal is living in Berlin, the once divided city that continues to carry the traces of its past despite its unification. Even though Cal has no problems when it comes to passing as a man in society, he is painfully aware of the fact that he is "[n]ot a real man at all" (492).

He even experiences several moments in which his former female self reappears spontaneously and destabilizes his male identity:

> I've lived more than half my life as a male, and by now everything comes naturally. When Calliope resurfaces, she does so like a childhood speech impediment. Suddenly there she is again, doing a hair flip or checking her nails. It's a little like being possessed. Callie rises up inside me, wearing my skin like a loose robe. (42)

The very instability of Cal's adult identity links up with the novel's often contradictory and ultimately inconclusive treatment of the question whether nature is more influential than nurture. If *Middlesex* presents itself as the story of the "roller-coaster ride of a single gene through time," and Cal repeatedly refers to his genetic status to justify his gender identity, it is important to note that the novel does not affirm any essential or natural "truth" of sex (4). On the contrary, Cal often mocks simplistic naturalistic explanations, for example, when he apologizes for his mock-Homeric style by jokingly pointing to his Greek heritage, saying it is "genetic too" (4). Similarly, the alleged inevitability of his being a man is questioned when acting like a man does not come naturally to Cal—or any other biological male for that matter: "My swagger wasn't that different from what lots of adolescent boys put on, trying to be manly. For that reason it was convincing. Its very falseness made it credible" (449).

This seems to imply that the fragmentation and fundamental uncertainty of the self are not linked to Cal's intersex condition, but should rather be seen as universal aspects of human life. As Cal puts it, "[w]e're all made up of many parts, other halves. Not just me" (440). In fact, the quest for and transformation of identity, and the corresponding struggle to come to terms with a fragmented self that often comprises opposing elements, run through both halves of the novel, often in a threatening way. Like his grandparents, who remake their identities in order to live as a married couple despite being brother and sister, and struggle to assimilate to American society while maintaining their Greek roots, Cal lacks a secure place in society, and feels displaced and ostracized due to his physical difference and complex gender identity. Thus, the novel suggests that Cal is not fundamentally different from other individuals whose identities are equally fragmented and contradictory, be it on the level of gender and/or sexuality, ethnic or racial origin, etc.

The construction of narrative voice in *Middlesex* underlines this destabilization of certainties, and has a disorienting effect on the reader, which mirrors the feelings of the novel's main characters. The fact that Cal is often writing about events that took place before he was born emphasizes his unreliability, to which he himself openly admits when he writes that "a narrator in my position (prefetal at the time) can't be entirely sure about any of this" (9). Furthermore, Cal's writing as or about the previous female self that contrasts with his present male gender has not only a comic but often an extremely ironic and unsettling effect.

With its treatment of intersex (or hermaphroditism, to use an older term that has recently been exposed to strong criticism due to its mythological connotations), *Middlesex* stands in a long tradition of cultural and literary representations of sexual ambivalence that goes back to Greco-Roman times. Eugenides makes good use of this backdrop, interspersing his tale with intertextual references ranging from the mythological figure of Tiresias, to the story of Hermaphroditus as presented in Ovid's *Metamorphoses,* to the 19th-century memoirs of Herculine Barbin.

This second novel of Eugenides is remarkably different from his first publication, *The VIRGIN SUICIDES* (1993), both in content and in scope. Nevertheless, some similarities can be noted, for instance in the nuanced treatment of identity, the often humorous and ironic depiction of serious or tragic events, and above all the construction of a narrative voice that is difficult if not impossible to locate, with *The Virgin Suicides'* collective narrative echoed in the sexually ambivalent narrator of *Middlesex*.

Bibliography
Eugenides, Jeffrey. *Middlesex*. London: Bloomsbury, 2002.

—Jana Funke

Midwives Chris Bohjalian (1997)

In Vermont-based novelist and newspaper columnist CHRIS BOHJALIAN's fifth work of fiction, midwife Sybil Danforth is arrested after a laboring mother dies in her care, and her trial exposes deep cultural divides in the small Vermont town where she lives with her husband and teenage daughter. The novel was selected for Oprah's Book Club in 1998, catapulting Bohjalian to overnight literary celebrity and the novel onto the *New York Times* Best Seller List, where it stayed for 20 weeks and peaked at number 1. *Publishers Weekly* selected the novel as a "best book," and many critics shared the publication's enthusiasm for the "gripping" and "insightful" novel. It was adapted for the stage in 2000, and in 2001 was made into a Lifetime Original Movie starring Sissy Spacek and Peter Coyote.

Told from the point of view of Danforth's daughter Connie, who refers back to her mother's diaries many years later (when she herself is in medical school to become an obstetric gynecologist) in an attempt to understand the extraordinary events that transpired when she was 14. *Midwives* is frequently compared to Harper Lee's *To Kill a Mockingbird,* as both novels place a coming-of-age narrative in the context of a socially and ethically charged courtroom drama, allowing readers to experience dramatic legal battles through the eyes of an appealing young female narrator. Bohjalian writes on his Web site that Lee's novel is one of his personal favorites because of its "father-daughter love story," and said in a 1998 interview that he sees *Midwives* as a "mother-daughter love story."

This love story develops after Danforth, who is passionate about her practice and devoted to her client families, is arrested and charged with involuntary manslaughter and practicing medicine without a license following the death of Charlotte Fugett Bedford, a minister's wife and conservative Christian transplant from the southern United States to the tiny Vermont town. The fateful events of the night Bedford goes into labor are recounted from a number of different points of view over the course of Sybil's trial, but the characters generally agree that Charlotte fell into grave distress at some point during her labor and that, by the time Sybil, Charlotte's husband Asa, and Sybil's assistant Anne realized how serious her condition had become, a winter storm had made it impossible for them to get to a hospital. With Charlotte unconscious and not breathing, Sybil makes a snap decision and asks Asa to bring her a knife. She uses the knife to cut open Charlotte, saving the baby that the widowed Asa will go on to name Veil. At issue in Sybil's trial—and in her psyche—is Anne's contention that Charlotte was not already dead when Sybil decided to perform the emergency caesarean section. The question is hotly debated in the courtroom and in the town, with Sybil's story becoming a flashpoint for tensions between doctors and homeopaths, and between the traditional and alternative lifestyles that flourish in rural Vermont. Connie grows up as the dramatic trial unfolds, viewing events with increasing social and sexual sophistication and eventually making a desperate and dramatic snap decision of her own. The mother-daughter love story is driven forward by a page-turning courtroom drama. "The world is filled with grey but the legal system will have nothing to do with that," Bohjalian said in a 1998 interview with a Durham, N.C., newspaper, explaining that he finds this inherent tension "compelling to explore."

Midwives presents a rich portrait of what Bohjalian calls "wondrous small-town paranoia," a phenomenon he confronted in his own life when he moved to Vermont from Manhattan in 1986. The novel profoundly illustrates his observation to a Massachusetts newspaper that "there is no such thing as anonymity in Vermont." Like the upstate New York novels of Russell Banks and Joyce Carol Oates, the latter author a favorite of Bohjalian's, *Midwives* revels in the complex and intimate details of small-town life, celebrating the community that exists between the midwives while exploring the complicated interconnections that develop among the very different people and families who live their lives in isolated villages.

In the opening lines of the novel, Connie tells her readers that she likes to use the word *vulva* to "stop adults cold in their tracks" because it is a word that has an edge to it in every household except her own; in her own home, sex and reproduction are spoken of without shame, indeed with something bordering on reverence (9). Her mother's celebration of birth as beautiful and natural

places her outside the cultural mainstream of her small town and at odds with most of the local medical establishment. In her diaries Danforth objects to the medical profession's use of harsh scientific words like *contraction, zygote,* and especially the charged *penetration* to describe the processes of birth and conception (44, 33, 19). Although she is not generally hostile to doctors and even enjoys the respect of the more open-minded among them before Charlotte's death, the trial propels her into a cultural debate over medical professionalization and control of women's reproductive bodies that reaches back to the 18th century. In *A Midwife's Tale,* based on the diary of early American midwife Martha Ballard (and a source for Bohjalian's novel), Laurel Thatcher Ulrich writes that, during Ballard's lifetime, newly professionalized male doctors fought against the centuries-old practice of women gathering together to assist each other in giving birth. Medical professionalization required the merging of "ordinary" and "emergency" care in birthing, Ulrich writes—a distinction that Danforth insists on, writing in her diary that birth is fundamentally spiritual and "beautiful. Incredibly, incredibly beautiful," and not inherently a medical emergency, despite the potentially intimidating amount of blood that can be involved (100, 45, 99). For Danforth, as for Ballard, midwifery is a "mechanism of social control, a strategy for family support, and a deeply personal calling," and one that potentially threatens male-dominated medical hierarchies (33). Despite the passage of several centuries, the practice of midwifery that brings both the fictional hippie Sybil Danforth and her historical predecessor to the centers of the families they help grow, also places them in a culturally fraught position on the margin of both society and science. Thanks to the "great blessing" bestowed by Oprah's Book Club, millions of readers have explored this profoundly significant tension on an intimate level, through what many consider the most powerful of Bohjalian's acclaimed "fictional memoirs."

Bibliography

Bohjalian, Chris. *Before You Know Kindness.* New York: Shaye Areheart Books, 2004.
———. *Midwives.* New York: Harmony Books, 1997.

Chris Bohjalian. "Chris Bohjalian: The Official Web site." Available online. URL: http://www.chrisbohjalian.com. Accessed May 13, 2009.

Hodges, Betty. "Novelist Falls in Love with Character in Book," *Durham (North Carolina), Herald-Sun,* 18 October 1998, sec. G, p. 4.

Seymour, Susanna. "Call from Oprah Gives Vermont Author New Notoriety," *Worcester (Massachusetts) Telegram & Gazette,* 12 February 1999.

Ulrich, Lauren Thatcher. *A Midwife's Tale.* New York: Vintage Books, 1990.

—Mary Lawless

Ministry of Special Cases, The   Nathan Englander (2007)

The Ministry of Special Cases is NATHAN ENGLANDER's first novel, following his acclaimed collection of short stories, *For the Relief of Unbearable Urges.* The tale is centered in Buenos Aires, Argentina, in 1976 during the beginnings of the "Dirty War," and follows the exploits of a family of Jewish outcasts (father Kaddish, mother Lillian, and son Pato) after the son is "disappeared" by the military government.

The novel begins strikingly, with Kaddish and Pato Poznan in a graveyard where Kaddish makes his living chiseling names from Jewish headstones for clients who wish not to be associated with the "embarrassments." Kaddish is immediately and memorably established as an outsider, a *"hijo de puta"* or son of a whore, a role (and theme) that dominates the novel and complicates its already complex Jewishness. The novel's early chapters skillfully depict the mounting hysteria in advance of a threatened coup of the current government, paralleled by Lillian's overwhelming private fear that "they" may come and take her son away (a fear exacerbated by mounting tensions between son and father, which result in Pato spending ever more time away from home). Amid the hysteria, a plastic surgeon, Dr. Mazurzky, is unable to pay Kaddish for a job and instead proposes to perform plastic surgery on the family's Jewish noses. Pato refuses, but Kaddish and Lillian proceed with the surgery, adding a physical distance to the mounting familial tension. Kaddish and Lillian finally insist

that Pato burn his political books to keep the government from investigating him, and when Pato refuses, Kaddish burns the books in the bathtub. Incensed, Pato runs away but forgets his identification card at home, and is rounded up after a rock concert with his friends Rafa and Flavia (who are released with their proper identification). He is imprisoned for the night, and is bailed out harshly by his father, but in the midst of the ensuing verbal confrontation at home, mysterious men in suits knock on the door and are unknowingly let into the house by Kaddish. They take Pato out the front door, and he is never seen again.

The novel's second part commences with Lillian coming home from work to find her son "disappeared," and Kaddish locked in the bathroom unable to face her. They begin their search for Pato with a photo, but—in a blackly comic touch characteristic of Englander's style—because of the drastic difference in their noses the police do not believe Pato is their son. They then turn to the parents of Pato's friends but are shut out by justifiable fears that the parents' own children will suffer the same fate. They succeed in tracking down Rafa and Flavia, who have themselves run away from home, but this too proves a dead end. In desperation, Lillian steals the phone number of a powerful general, a client of her insurance company, and lies to set up an audience with him, but the general is not sympathetic to their cause and laughs them off. At last, Lillian turns to the notorious Ministry of Special Cases, where she is given a heartbreaking, Kafkaesque run-around, waiting in a hopeless line every day. And when she and Kaddish finally get some results (learning that the owner of the bakery across the street from their apartment will testify to Pato's apprehension) and the necessary paperwork is completed, instead of Pato, a tortured young woman is released to Lillian. She takes the girl home to her parents.

The third and last section of the novel explores the seemingly inevitable disintegration of the Poznan family. Despite protests from Kaddish, Lillian turns fruitlessly to the Jewish community leader Feigenblum, and Kaddish, upset that Lillian would ask for help from the same Jewish community that ostracized him, leaves Lillian and goes to his friend Dr. Mazurzky to find out if his son is alive or dead. Mazurzky sets up an appointment with a man who may have information on Pato. Lillian, on the other hand, returns to the Ministry of Special Cases, where she befriends a military chaplain who offers to help find Pato for a hefty price. Meanwhile Kaddish meets "the navigator," a man who drops drugged victims out of a plane into a lake where they will never be found. Kaddish, now at last believing Pato to be dead, returns home to tell Lillian, but she steadfastly refuses to accept it, investing an increasingly hysterical faith in her expensive chaplain. She finally kicks Kaddish out of the house, and Kaddish goes to the rabbi who named him, asking how he can bury his son. The rabbi tells Kaddish he must have at least a part of a body. When Kaddish returns to Lillian, she tells him he can only return to her if he has money to pay for Pato's return. Mazurzky tells him to ransom some bones, so he desecrates the grave of the general's wife's father and demands ransom. When this plan too proves unsuccessful, he at last decides to use the same bones to give Pato a proper burial.

Despite the important role that politics play in the story, Englander skillfully spares his tale any cumbersome political weight, remaining focused on the lives of the Poznan family as they struggle with the worlds outside and within their troubled home. The stunning brutality of the totalitarian government is deftly funneled into the domestic setting; Lillian, for example, observes how her neighbor Cacho constantly scratches his eye until it bleeds, and notes the increased number of clients taking out policies at her insurance agency. The true narrative and thematic center of the novel, framed and informed by extraordinary events, but always familiar and utterly convincing, is the family. The Poznans bicker, eat dinner, love, suffer, struggle, and somehow survive as any family would. Father and son never see eye to eye, and the mother will stop at nothing to protect the life of her son. The disappearance of Pato tears the lives of Kaddish and Lillian apart, and Kaddish, named for the most important Jewish prayer of mourning, must bear the burden of burying his son despite never really knowing what happened to him. Yet in his very hardship, as in the motherly suffering through which Lillian must pass, the two are

tested, strengthened, and finally ennobled in a way few families ever are.

Fused with the drama of the political catastrophe is Englander's sensitive exploration of the life of an outsider in a community of outsiders—Jewish in name but universal in its fate. Considered a vandal by most of the rabbis in Buenos Aires, Kaddish struggles with his place in Jewish society. Although he accepts his role as a chiseler of graves, it is apparent that his wife believes she and Pato deserve better. And only when, near the end of the novel, Lillian banishes Kaddish from their home, does he truly find his place *within* it, properly burying their son according to immemorial Jewish custom, becoming what he always was, "saying Kaddish."

Bibliography

Blythe, Will. "Innocents Lost," New York Times on the Web, 3 June 2007. Available online. URL: http://www.nytimes.com/2007/06/03/books/review/Blythe-t.html. Accessed May 10, 2009.

Englander, Nathan. *The Ministry of Special Cases*. New York: Knopf, 2007.

Mitchell, David (1969–) *British novelist*

Mitchell is the author of several critically acclaimed works of fiction: *Ghostwritten* (1999), *number9dream* (2001), CLOUD ATLAS (2004) and *Black Swan Green* (2006). His newest novel is *The Thousand Autumns of Jacob de Zoet*. Named one of 20 "Best of Young British Novelists" by *Granta* magazine in 2003, Mitchell's rapid rise to literary fame has established him as one of the most prominent contemporary British fiction writers today.

Born in Southport in 1969, Mitchell grew up in Malvern, Worcestershire, where his father was a designer for Worcester porcelain. He studied English and American literature at the University of Kent, followed by an M.A. in comparative literature. After living in Sicily for a year, he moved to Hiroshima, Japan, in 1994, where he taught English for eight years. He currently lives in Ireland with his wife and daughter.

Shifting perspectives of time and viewpoint characterize Mitchell's first three novels, reflecting the dissolving boundaries of a globalized society, and questioning preconceptions of identity and genre. Mitchell's M.A. concentrated on the postmodern novel, and his interest in experimental narrative structures is a key feature of his work to date. *Ghostwritten*, for example, is a collection of nine interlocking stories, set in nine temporally and geographically diverse locations, with nine separate narrators. *number9dream* is also in nine sections, which are further split into parallel plot lines and have a tendency to segue into other stories. *Cloud Atlas* is created from six nested novellas, moving from the 19th century to a postapocalyptic dystopia and back again.

While Mitchell's fourth book, *Black Swan Green*, is seen as a departure from his trademark style due to its linear chronological progression, univocal narrator, and single setting, it continues his exploration of literary architectural possibilities. Following 13 months in the life of the narrator, 13-year-old Jason Taylor, each of the 13 chapters of this bildungsroman also serves as an autonomous short story. *Black Swan Green* is a semiautobiographical novel, containing many details from Mitchell's experiences as an adolescent, most notably his struggle with a debilitating stammer, personified in the book as "hangman."

Winner of the 1999 John Llewellyn Rhys Prize, Mitchell's first novel, *Ghostwritten*, impressed critics with its scope and technical achievement. The stories of the narrator-characters are linked through a variety of apparent coincidences, and are brought together into a coherent whole by Mitchell's trademark attention to significant detail. Continuing many of the themes introduced by its predecessor, *number9dream* follows the narrator, Eiji Miyake, in his attempts to track down the father who abandoned him at birth, through a collection of quasi-hallucinatory experiences in contemporary Japan. Short-listed for the 2002 Man Booker Prize, *number9dream* explores contemporary perceptions of reality, nationhood, and isolation. The majority of Mitchell's narrators are characterized by their inability to fit in with the world around them, creating a sense of isolation heightened by his repeated use of first-person inner monologues.

Cloud Atlas, Mitchell's third book, was a huge commercial success, winning both the British Book Awards Literary Fiction Award and the British Book Awards Richard and Judy Best Read

of the Year in 2005. It was also short-listed for the Man Booker Prize in 2004. Developing the style of "connection through juxtaposition" first employed in *Ghostwritten*, each of the six novellas of which *Cloud Atlas* is composed appears as an artifact in the subsequent section. Like Mitchell's previous two books, *Cloud Atlas* contains many references to the theory, composition, and enjoyment of music, a technique Mitchell uses in order to comment indirectly on the process of reading and writing literature; one of the narrators in *Cloud Atlas*, Robert Frobisher, even composes a piece of music called *The Cloud Atlas Sextet*. Frobisher is also one of Mitchell's recurring characters, and his death is mentioned in *Black Swan Green*. Likewise, both Timothy Cavendish and Luisa Rey appear in *Ghostwritten* and *Cloud Atlas*, and one of Jason Taylor's classmates, Neal Brose, appears in both *Black Swan Green* and *Ghostwritten*. The many recurring characters, settings, and themes that characterize Mitchell's four books to date suggest a confident belief in the alternative fictional reality that they share, and in which the reader becomes instantly caught up.

Although generally classified as literary fiction, Mitchell's narratives flirt with all prose genres, especially science fiction. His narratives are fast-paced and packed with energetic encounters with the sort of criminals, underworld gangs, prostitutes, and fraudsters one would expect from an airport thriller. It is, therefore, perhaps ironic that the only one of his books currently being adapted for film is the slower paced, more reflective *Black Swan Green*. The inter-cut nature of his books reflects the digital generation's brief and overstimulated attention span, reminiscent of television channel hopping.

Drawing strongly on literary predecessors for inspiration (for example the obvious relationship between Italo Calvino's *If On A Winter's Night a Traveller* [1979] and *Cloud Atlas*), Mitchell's narratives have reinterpreted them for a contemporary audience, in an accessible, enjoyable way. The influence of Mitchell's time in Japan has led to an exciting cross-cultural fusion, mixing influences such as Jorge Luis Borges with Haruki Murakami, Muriel Spark with Junichiro Tanizaki, and Nabokov with Mishima. His writing is continually self-commenting through its playful reinterpretation of classical literary structures and genres. Mitchell's next book, *Deshima,* slated for a 2010 release, is rumored to be a return to pure fiction and his interest in juxtaposing East and West throughout the centuries.

Bibliography

Mitchell, David. *Black Swan Green.* London: Sceptre, 2006.
———. *Cloud Atlas.* London: Sceptre, 2004.
———. *Ghostwritten.* London: Sceptre, 1999.
———. *number9dream.* London: Sceptre, 2001.

—V. S. Adams

Model World and Other Stories, A Michael Chabon (1992)

A Model World and Other Stories was MICHAEL CHABON's second book, following his first novel, *The Mysteries of Pittsburgh* (1988), and the collection brings together 11 short stories that appeared between 1987 and 1990 in the *New Yorker, Gentleman's Quarterly,* and *Mademoiselle,* grouped into two sections: "A Model World," featuring stories loosely linked by theme and tone, and "The Lost World," a cycle of five stories about a boy named Nathan Shapiro during and after his parents' separation and divorce.

The tone of Chabon's stories is wistful, and his characters tend to be disappointed or damaged individuals for whom happiness seems just out of reach—either in a nostalgically recalled lost world of the past or in an imagined ideal world that will never be attained. Ira, the central character of "S ANGEL," is a lonely man in search of "the woman with whom he had been destined to fall in love" (17). The story's setting, a wedding reception, might seem conducive to such idealized notions, but Ira's search for romance is thwarted. The wedding guest who attracts his attention proves more interested in a flashy real estate agent, and the story ends with Ira and the bride acknowledging their mutual, but futile, desire. The central character in "Smoke" is Matt Magee, a once promising pitcher now "five years past his best season," divorced, broke, and about to begin

the long slide down through the minor leagues, a situation he greets by drinking "with care and a method to poison himself" (92). Brought back to Pittsburgh by the sudden death of his former teammate, Magee finds himself examining the unpromising trajectory of his own life; indicating his next destination, a Triple-A franchise in Buffalo, Magee inadvertently gestures toward the dead man's coffin. Brian Blumenthal, the narrator of "Blumenthal on the Air" is a self-described fool, tormented by his love for his Iranian bride, who has married him, candidly, so that she may gain American citizenship. Having "breached our contract by actually falling in love" with her, Blumenthal has relocated them both to the lovers' city, Paris, where they now wait "for her heart, or mine, to undertake a change" (76), a resolution that appears certain not to come.

Thwarted lovers like Ira and Blumenthal recur throughout the collection. "Ocean Avenue" describes the passionate but poisonous relationship of architect Bobby Lazar and his ex-wife, Suzette, whose marriage ended in bitterness and hostility, with each taking revenge on the other by disposing of the other's most treasured objects. Their mutual, fatal attraction is rekindled during a chance meeting in a coffee shop, but the circumstances do not promise happiness for either: Their passionate kiss on the street is preceded by a tense rehearsal of their destructive history, which culminates in Suzette throwing a cup of coffee at her ex-husband. The assessment of Lazar's friend as he watches him plunge back into the maelstrom—"You're sick" (46)—appears equally applicable to both partners in the relationship. "Millionaires" centers on a male friendship that comes under pressure within a love triangle. The unnamed narrator and his friend Harry both fall in love with Harry's newest girlfriend, Kim Trilby, and the tangled relationships lead only to estrangement for all.

The title of "Millionaires" refers to Harry's "treasure," a box full of gold-painted cardboard doubloons. Despite Harry's claim that "it's supposedly real gold dust in the paint," the narrator's closing assertion, "we're rich" (127), is heavy with irony in the face of the "large, whistling hole that was torn in the fabric of our lives by my marriage to and then divorce from Kim" (123). This pattern, too, recurs throughout *A Model World:* the sudden appearance of a "large whistling hole" in the fabric of a life, followed by an attempt to repair the damage or find some form of consolation, which inevitably fails; explored most fully in the five-story cycle, "The Lost World," which chronicles the life of a young boy struggling to cope with his family's dissolution.

The first story in this haunting cycle, "The Little Knife," depicts Nathan Shapiro's traumatic fall from childhood innocence "in the last interminable summer before his parents separated and the Washington Senators baseball team was expunged forever from the face of the earth" (131). An annual family holiday in Nags Head is a comforting ritual until Nathan begins to see the cracks in his family's foundations. Suddenly, his childish play takes on a new and darker meaning for him: A trick of making strange footprints in the sand and ascribing them to some unknown creature becomes associated in his own mind with his parents' conflict, and he feels a terrible sense of responsibility for their marital problems. The eponymous "little knife" title is a memento he steals as the family makes its early departure, an emblem for Nathan of "all the discord for which . . . he was and always would be responsible" (141).

The title of the second story is borrowed from Theodore Sturgeon's 1953 science fiction novel, *More than Human*—an ironic allusion, since Sturgeon's novel details the difficult process of integrating several individuals into *homo gestalt,* a new form of humanity, while in Chabon's story, Nathan's father prepares to move out of the family home. As the boy matures, we see him gradually developing a more adult view of his father, adding another level of irony to the story's title, since his father, too, is all too human. The elder Shapiro realizes that "the boy was cognizant, however dimly, of the fear and shame and failure his father could not bring himself to express" (147). Nathan, in turn, becomes aware of this recognition on his father's part, which he comes to believe is the reason for his leaving. Heartbreakingly, Nathan's attempted healing gesture—his acknowledgment over the phone that "You were a good father"—fails utterly to convey its message with the significance he intends. Dr. Shapiro's unheroic stature

becomes even more apparent to Nathan in the third story, "Admirals," which is set a year and a half after the divorce. Their father is humbled in the eyes of Nathan and his younger brother, Ricky, during a casual encounter on the street with a wealthy poseur, whom the boys identify as a "playboy" and "millionaire," while recognizing that their father is a lesser being, "a man whom a playboy would shun" (164).

As the sequence continues, "the inevitable outward expansion, as of an empire or a galaxy, of what had once been his family" (188) becomes ever more pronounced. At the time of "The Halloween Party," Nathan's younger brother has moved to Boston with his father and his new stepmother. And the final story, "The Lost World," takes place two weeks after Nathan's mother's second marriage, and on the very night that Nathan has learned that his father and Anne are going to have their first child together. In his confusion, Nathan, now 16, has turned to alcohol, bingeing on malt liquor with three friends. The alcohol inspires an ill-considered midnight excursion to the home of Chaya Feldman, reputed to be a "skeezer," although only Nathan actually knows the girl (188). Their acquaintance dates back 10 years, but the two children played together only on one occasion, which Nathan has retained in his memory: when they imagined themselves on a planet of Chaya's creation, Jadis, the Planet of the Birds. When Nathan gains entrance to Chaya's bedroom, he is surprised by the news that this second brief encounter is likely to be their last: She is to leave in the morning for Jerusalem and is unlikely to return. In the context of this story of retrospection and separation, the name of Chaya's imagined world, *Jadis,* has a particular resonance: a French adverb meaning "long ago," it is perhaps most familiar from the poet François Villon's 15th-century lament, *"Ballade des dames de temps jadis"* ("Ballad of the women of long ago"), whose famous refrain is *"Mais, où sont les neiges d'antan?"* ("But where are the snows of yesteryear?"). The cold comfort Nathan's father offers his son—"I know that everything seems different now but you have to get used to it" (207)—answers Villon's rhetorical question, but falls dismally short of consolation.

Bibliography

Chabon, Michael. *A Model World and Other Stories.* 1992. New York: HarperPerennial, 2005.

Sturgeon, Theodore. *More Than Human.* 1953. New York: Vintage, 1981.

Villon, François. *Complete Poems.* Edited by Barbara Sargent-Baur. Toronto: University of Toronto Press, 1994.

—Brian Patton

Moody, Rick (1961–) *American novelist, short story writer, memoirist, editor, and musician*

Hiram Frederick [Rick] Moody's fiction, essays, and poetry have appeared in the *New York Times*, the *New Yorker, Conjunctions, Esquire, Harper's, Details, Paris Review*, and Salon.com. His lyrics are featured on the 2004 CD *Rick Moody & One Ring Zero*, and he is a member of the Wingdale Community Singers, a "woebegone and slightly modernist folk music" group that Moody says sounds like "Peter, Paul, and Mary on bad acid." He has received a Pushcart Prize, the Addison Metcalf Award, the *Paris Review* Aga Khan Prize, and a Guggenheim Fellowship. His writing matches the experimental, playful spirit of his music, skewing genres and upsetting conventions; his prose is typically daring, darkly comic, and impressionistic.

Moody was born in 1961 in New York City. After his parents' divorce in 1970 he lived with his mother and older sister Meredith in several affluent Connecticut suburbs, including New Canaan and Darien, settings for several of his works. His ancestry is replete with poets, academics, theologians, and published essayists. His grandfather delighted in telling family legends and Yankee folklore; his family collected books; his father, a banker who studied American literature in college, read aloud the Bulkington chapter from *Moby-Dick* every Thanksgiving Day. Moody credits both his lineage—a "singular collection of murderers, eccentrics, mesmerists" *(Black Veil)*—and his immediate personal history as factors drawing him naturally to writing as a profession.

As a child, Moody's broken family caused him to withdraw further into his created worlds. In the sixth grade he attempted to write a techno-futuristic novel centering on a teenager seeking to define the self, but abandoned this and another juvenile novel after a few pages. At age 13, Moody was enrolled in St. Paul's Boarding School, New Hampshire, where loneliness prompted him to drink, a habit that increased at college, and in 1987 landed him in a psychiatric hospital to dry out. After briefly considering seminary school, Moody opted to study creative writing at Brown University, where his teachers included Angela Carter, Stanley Elkin, and John Hawkes; he completed his M.F.A. at Columbia University in 1986. Sober and back in New York City, he first worked as an editorial assistant at Simon & Schuster, and then for a short time as an assistant editor at Farrar, Straus & Giroux.

Moody's first published piece, "Gambit Declined," appeared in the 1987 edition of *Antioch Review*. He saw himself as primarily a short story writer until his first novel, GARDEN STATE (1992), won the 1991 Pushcart Press Editors' Award. Set in a New Jersey suburb during the 1980s, the novel introduces several thematic elements that Moody would explore throughout his work: youthful insecurity, popular culture influences, disaffection, Christian imagery and metaphors, change, and complex—often flawed or fragmented—families. *Garden State*'s protagonists, dead-end New Jersey post-teens, struggle through drugs, sex, alternative music, psychiatric hospitals, and disillusion, searching for their own stable place between childhood and maturity.

Moody sets his next novel, ICE STORM (1994), in New Canaan, limits the action to a single night in 1973, just after Thanksgiving, and uses an unidentified narrator to tell a "comedy about a family I knew when I was growing up." Yet humor hardly softens the searing depiction of the dysfunctional neighboring families, the Hoods and Williamses. Ben Hood, who thinks love is "close to indebtedness," has married Elena to pay off that debt. Their older son Paul is a "garbage head . . . a loser," their daughter Wendy "a sylph" experimenting with drugs, sex, and the neighbors' sons. Jim Williams refuses to acknowledge his wife Janey's affair with Ben, and his sons Mike and Sandy are both dallying with Wendy. Mike's accidental death both divides and unites the families as it reveals to them "the spectacle of a lost future." Praised for its perceptive exploration of and oblique tribute to the American family, *Ice Storm* became an acclaimed 1997 Ang Lee film starring Kevin Kline and Joan Allen. The novel drew favorable comparisons to the work of John Updike, John Cheever, Don DeLillo, and other urban/suburban authors.

Moody next published a collection of stories, *The Ring of Brightest Angels around Heaven* (1996), which critics applauded for its experimentation, style, and black humor. The title novella, told in grim yet expressive language, chronicles three young people whose lives connect and crash in a dystopian Lower East Side New York. "Preliminary Notes" is a journal, by a techno-savvy paranoid husband, of his wife's phone calls. "Pip Adrift" continues Melville's *Moby-Dick*, but this time the narrator is Melville's African-American cabin boy, who here recounts the real story of how he fell overboard. A variation of Nabokov's *Pale Fire*, "The Apocalypse Commentary of Bob Paisner" is shaped as a term paper written by a college misfit who sees his life in the Book of Revelations. "Primary Sources" correlates Moody's commentary on various theorists, including Angela Carter, Roland Barthes, Jacques Derrida, and Umberto Eco, with significant events in his own life, underscoring the continual intersections between Moody's fiction and life.

Described by one critic as Moody's "John Cheever-meets-*The China Syndrome* novel" (Leonard 9), *Purple America* (1997) is a melodramatic account of another dysfunctional family. Dexter "Hex" Raitliffe, a stuttering alcoholic and perpetual loser, returns to care for his terminally ill mother, Billie Raitliffe, after his stepfather Lou Sloane leaves her. Lou's note on Billie's computer laments, "I can't watch you retreat from life this way. Your poverty has tired me out." Told with irritating lists and nonstandard punctuation, the tale explores the threesome's destructive manipulations, attempting to humanize them and reflect on how their interactions illustrate the morality of a postmodern family.

While Moody was writing *Purple America*, his sister died after suffering an unexpected seizure, and her death deeply affected the author, who wrestles with this grief in DEMONOLOGY (2000),

whose 14 experimental stories set in the urban and suburban Northeast and narrated by variously possessed speakers, thematically dissect fragmentation itself. In "The Mansion on the Hill," the unbalanced narrator talks to his deceased sister. "The Ineluctable Morality of the Vaginal" is a 17-page, single-sentence story. The protagonist in "Forecast from the Retail Desk" believes he can tell the future, though he is typically wrong. The title story, awarded both the Pushcart and O. Henry prizes, remembers a dead sister through snapshots, lists, and extemporaneous dialogue, with the narrator eulogizing his sister even as he questions his methods: ". . . I should make Meredith's death shapely and persuasive, not blunt and disjunctive, I shouldn't have to think the unthinkable."

While at Yaddo Artists Community in 1997, Moody began his family memoir, *The Black Veil* (2002), whose title refers directly to Hawthorne's "The Minister's Black Veil," which it reprints and analyzes, and to Joseph "Handkerchief" Moody, a possible inspiration for Hawthorne's story. *Black Veil* recounts Moody's sense of desertion, his depression, alcoholism, and voluntary psychiatric stay, while discussing Marx, Freud, and deconstruction. Yet ultimately Moody is less concerned with chronicling his life than in probing what stays hidden in the past, in the present, and in the human soul. Nonsequential and alternately comic and coldly depressing, *Veil* is a kind of literary jazz improvisation that struggles to understand depression and addictions of all kinds.

Much less pitiless than his memoir but equally inventive, *The Diviners* (2005) comically blends several implicitly connected stories and a host of characters in the tale of Vanessa Meandro and her efforts to produce a television miniseries about water dowsers or diviners. She has no script, but a colorful assortment of egomaniacs, prostitutes, alcoholics, and inept clergymen to support her. The extravagant parody here mimics those of T. C. Boyle, but without Boyle's more controlled absurdist satire.

Between his music and many public appearances, Moody recently published *Right Livelihoods* (2007, British title *The Omega Force* 2008), three unrelated novellas that draw on America's post 9/11 paranoia. The title novella centers on buffoonish Dr. Jamie Van Deusen in a magic realism comedy cum sci-fi adventure in which his use of language makes him utterly outlandish. Ellie Knight-Cameron narrates the second novella, "K&K," reconstructing the strange notes she finds in her insurance company's suggestion box. The third novella, "The Albertine Notes," takes place in a post-apocalyptic New York. Its narrator, Chinese-American journalist Kevin Lee, investigates the story of the "Zero" user of Albertine, the street name for "the buzz of a lifetime," which offers a mind-altering experience but regrettable memories. The story folds back on itself several times, displaying both Moody's penchant for experimentation and a relentlessly bleak, contemporary world vision.

Moody is a "writer of the nineties . . . who beats a sentence to death, ten or twenty or thirty or even forty times on occasion, and then maybe cuts the sentence just the same" (*Beat Writers* x). At times taxing, his writing probes the struggle to define the self and is often parable-like, unconventional, darkly comic, and pointedly metafictional. He is a writer's writer, not a common storyteller, who continues to refine his talent and expand the genres in which he writes.

Rick Moody writes full time, and teaches occasionally at State University of New York at Purchase and at Bennington College. In 2003 he married Amy Osborn, a specialist in decorative arts history. They divide their time between Brooklyn and Fishers Island off the coast of Connecticut. His new novel, to be released in 2010, is *The Four Fingers of Death*.

Bibliography

Dewey, Joseph. "Rick Moody." *Review of Contemporary Fiction* 23, no. 2 (Summer 2003): 7–50.

Leonard, John. "Get Out Your Handkerchief," *New York Times*, 7 July 2002, p. 9.

Moody, Rick. "The Art of Fiction CLXVI." *Paris Review* 42, no. 158 (Spring/Summer 2001): 203–230.

———. *The Black Veil: A Memoir with Digressions*. New York: Faber & Faber, 2002.

———. *Demonology*. New York: Little, Brown, 2001.

———. *The Diviners*. New York: Little, Brown, 2005.

———. "Flirting with Disaster." By Bill Goldstein. *New York Times*, 25 February 2001, p. 13.

———. *Garden State*. New York: Little Brown, 1992.

———. *The Ice Storm: A Novel*. New York: Little, Brown, 1994.

———. "Introduction." *Beat Writers at Work*. Edited by George Plimpton. New York: Modern Library, 1999.

———. *Purple America*. New York: Little, Brown, 1997.

———. *Right Livelihoods: Three Novellas*. New York: Little, Brown, 2007. (British title *The Omega Force*. London: Faber & Faber, 2008.)

———. *The Ring of Brightest Angels around Heaven*. New York: Little, Brown, 1995.

———. "The Wingdales." November 2, 2006. Rick Moody's Amazon Webblog. Available online. URL: http://www.amazon.com/gp/blog/A3RJX2-DOJ1N6Y5. Accessed February 9, 2009.

Moody, Rick, and Darcey Steinke, eds. *Joyful Noise: The New Testament Revisited*. New York: Little, Brown, 1997.

—LynnDianne Beene

Motherless Brooklyn Jonathan Lethem (1999)

Living up to his reputation as an inspired genre-bender, JONATHAN LETHEM takes on the hard-boiled detective formula in his 1999 novel *Motherless Brooklyn*, both expanding and transcending the boundaries of the genre. Part murder mystery, part bildungsroman, the novel is a moving (and often hilarious) investigation into the mechanisms and mysteries of the mind, tackling themes like normality and aberration, belonging and exile, guilt and revenge, and the restorative power of really good sandwiches; all related by one of the most unusual narrator-protagonists in this or any genre.

Lionel Essrog announces his peculiar condition right away: "I'm a carnival barker, an auctioneer, a downtown performance artist, a speaker in tongues, a Senator drunk on filibuster. *I've got Tourette's*" (1). His disorder results in a myriad of verbal and physical tics that rule and often disrupt his everyday life and interaction with others. When under stress, for example, Lionel may get the irrepressible urge to "to deliver small taps on [the doctor's] shoulder[s], in a pattern that was absolutely symmetrical" (34); and a word like *alibi* can spontaneously evolve into "*alibi hullabaloo gullible bellyflop smellafish*" (109). Lionel works for local hood Frank Minna, whose limousine service is ostensibly a front for a detective agency, but for the most part runs errands for an aging pair of Jersey mobsters. Years ago, Minna recruited Lionel and three other orphans from St. Vincent's Home for Boys in Brooklyn, and has since become their mentor and beloved father figure. When Frank is fatally stabbed, Lionel embarks on a quest to find his killer and possibly avenge his death.

As the proverbial plot thickens, Lionel comes to question almost everyone's loyalties and motives. Why did Julia, Frank's sulking, sultry wife, skip town right after Minna's murder—and how did she hear about it in the first place? Why does Tony, his fellow Minna Man, want Lionel to stop his investigations? And why do the two mobsters want him to go after Julia? Who controls the terrifying "Polish giant" that has sent Frank off to his demise? And how do you pronounce the symbol of The Artist Formerly Known As Prince anyway? His rambling, bumbling, but tenacious investigations take Lionel beyond the borders of his familiar and beloved Brooklyn, first to Manhattan, where Zen monks turn into unlikely goons, and later to rural Maine, where he must confront not only Minna's killer, but also come to terms with the implications and consequences of asserting his own role in the world.

A large part of Lionel's quest is the search for valid expression itself, a goal that converges with his role as the novel's storyteller (it is important to note that the narrative voice itself is free from verbal tics). Through Lionel's frequent musing on his condition and its implications ("Have you noticed yet how I relate everything to my Tourette's? Yup, you guessed it, it's a tic" 92), the theme of language as both signifier and arbitrary symbol emerges. This duality particularly vexes Lionel, whose compulsions tend to make him overinterpret signs, to look for and assign meaning where others can see none. Brooklyn, for example, to him is a verbal (and nonverbal) construct full of hidden meanings and conspiracies, "a placid ageless surface alive underneath with talk, with deals and casual insults, a neighborhood political machine with pizzeria and butchershop bosses and unwritten rules everywhere. All was talk except for what mattered most, which were unspoken understandings" (55).

Then there is the white noise of his own verbal tics, which in subverting the sense-making function of language often stands between him and successful communication. And the question persists, whether these tics actually signify anything or are just the sound and fury of tonal nonsense. While the novel refrains from assigning any mysterious or supernatural properties to a neurological disorder, the resonances found in the assorted Essrog Variations often add a layer of meaning or comment to the straight narrative. Lionel's own name in particular produces linguistic offshoots that pertain to the character's self-image or to the situation at hand: *"Liable Guesscog. Final Escrow. Ironic Pissclam."* (7), *"Unreliable Chessgrub"* (229), *"Lionel Arrestme!"* (109).

Like its protagonist, the novel delights in raising and razing forms of meaning, playing with genre clichés and undermining conventional structures. Perhaps exacerbated by the absence of family to provide identity, Lionel's self-image is suffused with pop culture. He spends most of his youth with books and movies, searching for "signs of my odd dawning self" (37), and finding kinship with comic underdogs like Daffy Duck, Art Carney, Charlie Chaplin, and Buster Keaton. But his main influence, besides Frank Minna's verbal flourishes, is the noir genre. Whether he is being inexpertly roughed up by amateur thugs or matching wits with the ominous "black homicide detective," Lionel often remarks on the similarities and disparities of his own situation to the conventions of the hardboiled genre: "So many detectives have been knocked out and fallen into such strange swirling darknesses, such manifold surrealist voids ('something red wriggled like a germ under a microscope'—Philip Marlowe, *The Big Sleep*), and yet I have nothing to contribute to this painful tradition" (205).

At first glance, his affliction may seem to make Lionel an ill-qualified hardboiled detective, as both his stealth and wisecracking skills are severely impaired by his tics. But surprisingly, they more often work in his favor, causing his opponents to underestimate or even ignore him, and leaving them baffled and confounded. However, the one aspect of Tourette's that truly makes him a born investigator is his compulsiveness. Life, for Lionel, is "laced with structures of meaning" (67) that he obsessively plucks at, trying to decode the mystery underneath. The duality of his Tourette's impulses—to disrupt smooth surfaces on the one hand and restore order to disruption on the other—perfectly mirrors the role of the detective in hardboiled fiction as a figure of both transgression and integration.

Although the scope of the book transcends its professed genre, it is never just a vehicle to dress up postmodernist abstractions. Just as Lionel's Tourette's never turns into a gimmick or lessens his humanity, the author's affection for and understanding of the noir genre is felt on every page. The novel, of course, is Lethem's second excursion into the genre after his debut novel, GUN, WITH OCCASIONAL MUSIC (1994), pitted a noir detective against a science fiction world to great comic effect. Although there are some similarities between the two novels, comparison tends to highlight the shift in Lethem's poetics, away from science fictional surrealism and intertextual play, and toward a style of gently skewed realism that emphasizes characterization, sensuality, and linguistic density. Thematically, *Motherless Brooklyn* is closer to its immediate predecessor, *Girl in Landscape* (1998), and successor, *The FORTRESS OF SOLITUDE* (2003), as both of these novels present coming-of-age stories that deal with growing up motherless, with loss and nostalgia, and with the mysterious layers and structures that inform everyday existence.

The critical and popular success of *Motherless Brooklyn* marked Lethem's introduction to a wider audience. The book won the National Book Critics Circle Award for best novel in 1999 and the Gold Dagger award for crime fiction in 2000. A film adaptation directed by and starring Edward Norton has been in the works since 2005, with a projected release in 2010.

Bibliography

Lethem, Jonathan. *Motherless Brooklyn.* New York: Vintage, 1999.

—Martina Sitling

Music for Torching A. M. Homes (1999)

A. M. HOMES's *Music for Torching* opens with an act of wild liberation from the soul-killing tedium of middle-class suburban life: Elaine and Paul, parents of two young boys, set their house on fire. They initiate the act with disbelief at their own angry aggression, but then stand back to watch with undisguised glee as flames consume this sym-

bol of their consuming lives. Later, in the smoking aftermath of the fire, Elaine will take an ax to the damaged dining room table with similarly unapologetic joy. But while the burned house liberates the parents, it exiles the children: Asthmatic Sammy must live with a friend's family until the house no longer threatens his health, and Daniel all but disappears in the chaos unleashed by his parents' self-indulgent act. Thus Homes marks the house, and the domestic sphere it contains, as the novel's relentless source of trauma, wounding, and threat. The rest of the novel follows the dissolution of the family as mother and father indulge separately in increasingly transgressive attempts to overcome their apathy: "I'm so bored," Elaine cries, while Paul "humps" her from behind; "I'm unbelievably unhappy," he responds (15). Ultimately, no amount of risky sex, self-induced pain, or domicile dismemberment can shock them out of their solipsistic suffering and turn their attention back to their children, or to each other. So the novel finally relies on a traditional act of sacrifice—the death of nine-year-old Sammy—to convert this seemingly postmodern novel of meaningless, unconnected acts into a morality tale that has been pushing toward meaningful narrative resolution all along.

Such unnamed domestic affliction lies at the troubled heart of all of Homes's work. An almost unspeakable sense of terror at what family life does to the individual psyche, this horror permeating every Homes story seems a direct descendant of the nameless terror in Edward Albee's *A Delicate Balance* (1966), whose influence on *Music* Homes has acknowledged ("Conversation"). In Albee's play, neighbors invade the main characters' house, bleating, "We were frightened . . . and there was nothing" (49). Homes invokes a similar existential terror when Paul realizes "anyone else would think it's a perfectly lovely Saturday but . . . he's scared, absolutely petrified, and he doesn't know why" (273). Earlier works by Homes tend more simply to expose the ugly underbelly of the mythical happy American family that results from this terror, much like David Lynch's *Blue Velvet* (1986) or the more recent *American Beauty* (1999). Similarly, Homes's "Adults Alone," from the short story collection *The Safety of Objects* (1990), first introduces us to Elaine and Paul's childish escapades, and culminates in their smoking crack cocaine while the kids are away. But her most recent novel, THIS BOOK WILL SAVE YOUR LIFE (2006), follows one lost man as he meditates on the unnamable fear itself and seeks ways to escape his closed-off, selfish life, joining communities to break free from his suffocating amorphous suffering.

Elaine and Paul, however, simply flail, acting out like the children who have become too much for them to bear. Paul, already sexually involved with the mother of Sammy's friend Nate, begins another affair with a younger, unattached, more dangerously provocative woman. At her behest, he gets a groin tattoo, hoping it will "wake [him] up, like electroshock therapy" (243)—but then finds it so painful that he becomes unable to make his way home or, once delivered there by a kind neighbor, to take care of himself. Elaine hires a babysitter to watch after him. Meanwhile, Elaine begins a half-hearted sexual affair with the wife and mother of the creepily perfect family next door, the Nielsens. Indeed, this family, whose name recalls the media research group that for decades has discovered and shaped the likes and dislikes of the American family, provides the novel's only example of American familial "normalcy," in which Father dutifully works, Mother stays happily home, and children smilingly obey. But the extremity of these characters' devotion to their roles, and their occasional startling departures from them—the kids presenting self-authored plays on Wednesday nights; the mother introducing Elaine to a studded leather strap-on in the laundry room while the dryer rumbles alongside—mark their normalcy in the world of this novel as monstrous. Elaine and Paul call the Nielsens "shapeshifters."

Unable to participate in the Nielsens' brand of domestic happiness, Elaine, like Paul, attempts alternately to shock herself awake or numb herself from her own apathy. Even before tipping over the lighted grill with her toe to begin the house fire, Elaine aggressively attacks her domesticating life: (half) playfully she draws across Paul's neck the knife she has used to prepare a meal for a dinner party. When he winces at the long thick slash she says, "Don't be a baby." She drinks; she sits; she has mean sex with a cop who wanders into her burned kitchen. She says to her mother, "I want to be the child" (261), while Paul cries in Daniel's room, not for his neglected little boy but for his inability to

be that little boy. Together the parents take pills and repeatedly fail to notice the accumulating signs that their own children are in trouble. When finally Sammy's friend Nate, with whom he has been staying since the fire, shoots him at school, we need only flip back through the pages to register the warnings that Elaine and Paul remained too self-focused to see: Sammy begging to leave Nate's house, crying at the sight of Nate, pretending that Nate is moving away. Amid all of these signs of Sammy's persistent misery, Elaine notices only that Sammy seems "a little strange," while Paul remains too preoccupied by fantasies of Nate's mom to register anything amiss. But to the reader attuned to the morality play Homes has set up, it is no surprise that just before shooting Sammy in the head, Nate commands him, "Get out of my house."

These are the words of a man protecting his house, and in a novel in which the parents have so noticeably ceded their positions of authority to wrest from the children their positions of helplessness, they announce the novel's central critique: Sammy's death is the price paid for his parents'—and for Nate's parents'—selfish response to yuppie suffering. Children in this world pay dearly for their parents' inability to keep their houses in order. In this way, the novel's final 20 pages convert what has been a dryly ironic collection of disconnected and meaningless incidents—much like Don DeLillo's endlessly ambiguous *White Noise* (1985) and David Foster Wallace's wry INFINITE JEST (1996)—into a purposeful narrative arc whose moral echoes that of the conservative social critic Christopher Lasch. Lasch's *The Culture of Narcissism* (1979) argues that, in a consumer culture whose media and advertising produce a "longing to be free from longing" (241), and construct the individual as a centerless conglomeration of infantile need, parents wind up devoid of stable identities, and so are unable to bond with or care for their children.

Mark Danielewski's HOUSE OF LEAVES (2000) proceeds from a similar anxiety, imagining an impossibly centerless house that swallows up self-absorbed parents whose children drift farther and farther away. But whereas Danielewski's groundbreaking hypertext recuperates parents, children, and relationships through the very acts of mediation that endangered them, *Music for Torching* implies quite clearly that what we have lost is unrecoverable: while Elaine, Paul, and all other present adults remain fixated on the TV screen that broadcasts via police robot the shooting of their younger son, it is their older boy, Daniel, who attacks the gun-toting Nate with all his big brother's rage and carries out a wounded Sammy. "Did they find the eye?" someone says (354), and to this, as to Paul's beeping watch alarm, reminding him of his date with his mistress, and to her cop and the pills and the dildo in the laundry room, all Elaine can say is, "It's over" (358).

Bibliography

Albee, Edward. *A Delicate Balance.* 1966. New York: Penguin Books, 1997.

American Beauty. Directed by Sam Mendes. Performers: Kevin Spacey, Annette Bening, and Thora Birch. Dreamworks, 1999.

Blue Velvet. Directed by David Lynch. Performers: Dennis Hopper, Isabella Rossellini, and Laura Dern. MGM / United Artists, 1986.

Danielewski, Mark Z. *House of Leaves.* New York: Pantheon Books, 2000.

DeLillo, Don. *White Noise.* New York: Penguin Books, 1985.

Homes, A. M. "Adults Alone." In *The Safety of Objects.* New York: William Morrow and Company, 1990.

———. "A Conversation with Amy Adler and A. M. Homes." Hammer Museum. Los Angeles, California. July 24, 2002.

———. *Music for Torching.* New York: HarperCollins, 1999.

———. *This Book Will Save Your Life.* New York: Viking, 2006.

Lasch, Christopher. *The Culture of Narcissism: American Life in an Age of Diminishing Expectations.* New York: W. W. Norton, 1979.

Wallace, David Foster. *Infinite Jest.* Boston: Little, Brown, 1996.

—Mary Holland

Mystery Roast, The Peter Gadol (1993)

PETER GADOL's second novel opens with a polar bear escaping the New York City Zoo on a mystifyingly warm winter day. Trapped, tranquilized, and unceremoniously lifted by helicopter high above the city's buildings, the bear is returned quietly to her safe seclusion, none the worse for her adventure. Shortly thereafter, as a winter storm blankets the city, the novel's protagonist Eric Auden leaves the seclusion of his mother's apartment. For the last week, Eric has indulged his depression over his pending divorce from newscaster Margot Brandon by eating his mother's groceries and sleeping late in his childhood bedroom. Having achieved little, and being even less motivated, he is a stereotypical slacker, date-stamped as belonging to Gen-X. On this day he is breaking out much as the polar bear did. The question is whether he will numbly return to his hiding place or will follow through with his resolve to get on with his life.

Eric's immediate destination is New York's prestigious Museum of Art, a place filled with nostalgia for him. As a young child, he took art appreciation classes there; as an adolescent, he went on numerous field trips, dates, and luncheon meetings with his now estranged father, Jack Auden; his high school graduation was held in the museum's grand medieval courtyard. On today's trip Eric finds his childhood best friend, Timothy Rampling, amazingly holding his own art show—Ten Drawings of My Friends Andre and Inca—in the museum's upstairs men's room. Eric had lost touch with Tim more than 10 years ago, and his surprise at finding his friend mingles with nostalgia, disbelief, and an awkward sense of disengagement.

Uncomfortable with one another and the setting, they awkwardly relate details of their decade of separation. When Eric mentions he needs a place to live, Tim suggests a loft in his building; Eric, uneasy, agrees to look at the place. Though attractive, it is far too expensive and Eric retreats to his mother's apartment without committing himself.

Eric's mother, Lydia Auden Maldemer Bruckner *née* Carver, is amused to hear about Tim's business venture and agrees that the loft is too expensive; however, Lydia chides her son about his need for a job, his forgotten ambitions and, without direct allusion, his adult failures. Eric reacts somewhat childishly and retreats to his room and his collection of adolescent memories.

The next day Eric packs his belongings and returns to the NYMA. On his way to find Tim in the bathroom he impulsively slips into a wing under renovation. And there, with the same lack of self-reflection as Albert Camus's Meursault *(The Stranger)*, and a similar indifference to standards or mores, he impulsively walks away with a priceless artifact, a 4,500-year-old Cycladic statue called the Goddess of Desire. But where Meursault becomes incapable of feeling anything, Eric begins, in this improbable manner, a process of rediscovering and healing his own traumatized feelings.

Eric is now guided by the goddess statue who, he imagines, speaks to him. The theft is soon discovered, and the media—including Eric's ex-wife—speculates, sometimes wildly, about the bold thief's identity. Eric meanwhile finds himself at Tim's building, agreeing to sublet it and stunned at how his life is changing. Tim tries to make Eric feel more welcome by introducing Eric to Andre Orso, Tim's sporadic lover and owner of the café The Mystery Roast. He also introduces Eric to Melior Earhart the cat, and Inca Dutton, an architect and sometime gadget inventor. Andre has an approach to coffee making that is a metaphor for how the goddess's spell blends together the characters' lives. Andre creates his intricate coffee blends daily by shoveling "the raw beans into several different bins. He roasts the mixed beans in a special oven in the kitchen. And when it comes time to make the coffee, he has no idea what he'll turn up with" (49). The game for his customers is to guess the individual coffees, a diversion that most thoroughly enjoy. Melior, the café cat, named after the French coffee press and the aviator, instinctively recognizes customers who are alone and, purring steadily, keeps the visitors company. Inca, the gadget inventor qua architect, is tall and angular, chic and beautiful to Eric's eyes; but she is convinced that relationships do not last, that monotony curbs passion, and that safety evolves from coldness. Eric falls in love with her nonetheless, and despite her misgivings she begins to have feelings in return.

With the goddess hidden in his sparsely furnished loft, Eric's life becomes a whirlwind of dreams that are mysteriously fulfilled. Eric admits the theft to Tim, telling him that he was "drawn to the idol. Seduced. I fell into a trance. It was like I was having some sort of revelation, a dream that I can't really remember now . . . I just scooped her up . . . and ran" (61). Although he fears being apprehended, Eric eventually comes up with the insane idea that other loners like him "could own idols. Maybe they would have bizarre daydreams or talk out what they want in life or simply feel a little less lonesome. Like me. Everyone would have his own personal goddess—" (84).

Driven by such salvational enthusiasm, Eric gets Tim to abandon painting and sculpt copies of the statuette, and capitalizing on the tabloid publicity blitz caused by the theft and the goddess's mysterious power, they place replicas of the idol in the café and rake in enormous profits as the copies sell out. Tim's stone carvings of the Goddess of Desire become first a downtown art happening—"artifactualism"—and then a fad that sweeps the city, making celebrities of Eric and Tim. The museum, meanwhile, hires an investigator, Maret Vanetti (Eric's mother's lover), to try to locate the goddess.

The novel is notable for its skillful blend of urban mystery, humor, romance, magic realism, and characters' own vivid and detailed anxieties about their relationships. Gadol imagines turbulent romances that are convincing and unmistakably modern, and sets them against the lively, often crass background of contemporary New York. The goddess inspires each character to seek (and ultimately find) fulfillment and intimacy, though the journey is at times bumpy and deflected by comic turns. The intricate and satirical plot results in an unexpected but welcome conclusion wherein each character finds security, love, and self-confidence; and Gadol himself proves not just a clever and skilled craftsman, but an inspired storyteller, capable of creating a narrative so realistic that even its overtones of magic realism seem perfectly at home.

Bibliography

Cassada, Jackie. Review of *The Mystery Roast. Library Journal* 117 (November 15, 1992): 104.

Gadol, Peter. *The Mystery Roast.* New York: Picador, 1993.

O'Connell, Patty. "A Tasty Cup of Literary Espresso," *Washington Post,* 29 January 1993, p. C2.

Steinberg, Sybil. "Forecasts: Fiction." *Publishers Weekly* 239 (October 26, 1992): 54.

—LynnDianne Beene

N

Names of the Dead, The Stewart O'Nan
(1996)

"The war lived within ... like an extra organ, pumping out love and terror and pity for the world," writes STEWART O'NAN in *The Names of the Dead* (175), which explores protagonist Larry Markham's suburban existence after serving as a medic in the Vietnam War. His life in Albany is consumed by nightmares of being in the war and flashbacks to the jungle. Writing for the *New York Times*, Rand Richards Cooper describes Larry's life as occurring in "a bleak American dystopia that Mr. O'Nan has inherited from writers like Raymond Carver and Russell Banks." While his father is a doctor and his sister a lawyer, Larry is a Wonder Bread delivery driver, and his wife, Vicki, processes film at the mall, while their son Scott is developmentally disabled, adding stress to an already fragile marriage.

The disintegration of this marriage is what begins the book: "Larry Markham's wife left him while he was asleep" (1). Vicki takes both Scott and the family car, leaving Larry abandoned in his own home—not for the first time. Faced nonetheless with the demands of the workday, Larry finally gets a ride from their neighbor, Donna, but is late for work, in one of those depressing banalities that in a sufficiently malignant context take on symbolic significance.

Excepting the latest loss of his wife and child, Larry's days proceed with a numbing sameness: He goes to work, eats the crumb cake he is supposed to be delivering, dreams about the war. Interrupting the monotony—for the reader at least—and

characteristic of O'Nan's subtle style, flashbacks comprise a large part of the layered narrative. The trauma in Larry's marriage is juxtaposed with his hellish experience in Southeast Asia, with this striking difference, that there Larry was responsible for taking care of his injured comrades, while here he can barely guarantee on-time delivery of his company's pastries.

One of his duties in Vietnam was to mail the belongings of his dead friends back to their families, and Larry still possesses some of their things, having brought them back with him to New York. Especially given the gray, almost cipherlike quality of his own existence, these charged relics, and the multiple identities they invoke, lend a complex, layered quality to Larry's own identity.

What holds him together, though he often fails to *function* integrally, is a group of Vietnam veterans that he councils in a VA hospital. The men all suffer from major physical impairments and are inpatients in the hospital. Larry himself shares half their fate, having suffered physical trauma as well, with the loss of his foot in the war. O'Nan implies that when these men are together, they are individually more whole that when apart. Because of their shared experience of war, they know each other better and can palliate if not heal each other better than anyone else. Larry's wife, for example, cannot understand or sympathize with his unceasing and crippling preoccupation with the war, and this is a major source of their disconnection.

Larry's father, however, understands. Dr. Markham served in Korea, yet has never told his son about the experience, and, like his son, slowly unravels, declining from a once skilled and respected doctor to an invalid needing chronic care.

In the middle of the narrative, O'Nan introduces a critical complication into Larry's peculiarly static existence, in the form of a former Vietnam prisoner of war who stalks Larry, threatening him with a series of elaborate traps, and forcing him at last, in a sense, to become a soldier once more, merely to defend against this subtle but relentless aggression.

In common with O'Nan's other work, author Stephen King makes a cameo appearance in the novel: Vicki is reading a Stephen King book when she returns to Larry, picking it up when she does not want to talk to him. In real life, Stephen King and Stewart O'Nan are friends, and they cowrote a book about the Boston Red Sox called *Faithful* (2004).

A persistent theme in O'Nan's oeuvre, and one that dominates the novel, is the anatomy, effects, and treatment of deep psychological trauma. In *The Names of the Dead*, the central action is framed and instigated by the trauma of the war. *The Night Country* tells the story of a horrific car crash that killed a group of teenagers, and follows the living—and the dead—after the fact. *The SPEED QUEEN* tells the story of a woman on death row for serial murders, who has sold her story to Stephen King; hours away from her execution, she completes the tapes that will enable him to write the book.

The Names of the Dead gets its title from the celebrated Vietnam memorial in Washington, D.C., where names of all the American servicemen killed in the war are engraved. Larry's support group wants him to go to the wall in honor of their friends, and at the end of the story he finally does. He has kept the belongings of the dead with him, transporting them from Vietnam much as he accompanied the bodies of the dead on route to America, and when he is at last able to visit the wall, he deposits them there. He has always only referred to these men by their nicknames, but now he finds them by their real names and restores their belongings, allowing them, like himself, to attain a measure of wholeness once again.

Bibliography

Cooper, Rand Richards. "Flashbacks," Review of *The Names of the Dead*. New York Times on the Web (7 April 1996). Available online. URL: http://query.nytimes.com/gst/fullpage.html?res=9E06E4D91339F934A35757C0A960958260&sec=&spon=&pagewanted=all. Accessed May 12, 2009.

O'Nan, Stewart. *The Names of the Dead*. New York: Penguin Books, 1996.

Rich, Motoko. "Requiem for a Red Lobster: A Novel of Downsizing." New York Times on the Web (3 December 2009). Available online. URL: http://www.nytimes.com/2007/12/03/books/03stewart.html. Accessed May 12, 2009.

—Katie Watson

Native Speaker   Chang-rae Lee (1995)

Henry Park, the primary character and narrator of CHANG-RAE LEE's *Native Speaker*, is a private investigator who has been hired to follow and take notes on John Kwang, a Korean-American city councilman who aspires to become the mayor of New York City. Henry works for Glimmer & Company, a firm that hires detectives to infiltrate powerful groups within immigrant communities. Spying on Kwang proves to be a difficult assignment for Park because he too is Korean-American and finds that he sympathizes with Kwang's mission to represent ignored or powerless citizens. Park's assignment coincides with his American wife Lelia's leaving him for an uncertain length of time as they both grieve for their deceased young son. Although *Native Speaker* is an exciting political-spy drama, it serves also as an exploration of immigrant culture and identity, its primary tale that of Park's confrontation with himself.

Early in the narrative, Park finds a biting note Lelia has left him, a brutal list of the narrator's failings, many of which concern his lack of a real identity. She writes that he is a "surreptitious, B+ student of life, illegal alien, emotional alien, Yellow peril: neo-American, stranger, follower, traitor, spy . . ." (5). Although Park muses on her message, he does not seem emotionally affected by it or by his wife's disappearance; or if he is, he does not reveal it to the reader. But following the separation, a gaping hole has opened in the identity of Henry Park. He is withdrawn, almost half-present, diminishing. His grief appears to be swallowed up in mere contemplation, his activities, including his job, only pastimes, and his goals abandoned. What does stand out in him still is an acute consciousness of his race and ethnicity, and of how his life is affected by them.

Throughout *Native Speaker*, Park portrays himself as an outsider, accepting of his otherness. He is an outsider as a Korean in a white world, but also because he feels alienated from his own Korean culture. Park recalls that when he and his wife first met, she commented on his self-conscious manner of speech and pegged him as "not a native speaker" minutes after first meeting him, noting that he looked "like someone listening to himself" (12). He describes his parents' household as rigid and dedicated to preserving conservative Korean culture, and he reveals that he is and always has been alienated from his grocery store-owning father. He describes his father's hard path toward economic success, and the distance of their relationship, as well as his father's lack of warmth, impatience, and constant state of frustration, much of which seems caused by being a Korean immigrant. Park also explains the ways in which his mother, and later, his widowed father's hired housekeeper lived cloistered lives; how they were extremely reserved and suspicious of non-Korean people and practices. He admits that as a child he wished he were from another race or culture, one more prone to outward expression. As an adult he wished that his son could grow up white, although he tags that impulse as his own "assimilist sentiment, part of [his] own ugly and half-blind romance with the land" (267). He also speaks of his discomfort upon entering Korean businesses, which caused him to feel as though he was "an audience member asked to stand up and sing with the diva"—he knows "every pitch and note but can no longer call them forth" (167). Park would seem to have lost a greater portion of his identity than his family, because his job as a spy requires that he be changeable and forever assimilating, that he be a listener, an observer, a man without a real face.

Park's subject, John Kwang, presents an acute challenge to him, partly because his very identity is intensely puzzling. As a New York mayoral candidate, Kwang wants to be in the limelight, speaking publicly, recognized by the media, negotiating in the public sphere, and attaining power in America's largest city. He is unafraid of shame and mistreatment and desires to work within a much greater world than that of his own family and small community; all of which is, Park notes, completely contrary to traditional Korean cultural values. Although he attempts to follow the rules that should govern his professional behavior as a detective, Park develops a very close friendship with Kwang, to a point that seems dangerous for both. During this period, Park's wife half-heartedly returns to their marriage, and they become reengaged in their relationship and life together.

Much of *Native Speaker* is devoted to Park's meditations on Korean-American behavior, and the role of the outsider or foreigner. Working with Kwang gives Park an opportunity to consider many issues that seem obstacles to his own self-actualization. He often compares the behavior of Korean-Americans with that of native Koreans, and finds that the former have combined aspects of both lands to formulate their successful behavior as immigrants. For example, as Kwang attempts to assuage a conflict between Koreans and blacks, Park is reminded of the racial tension in his own father's stores, and the way that his father treated black customers. Park's identification with Kwang makes him unable to produce the "damning" reports that his job requires, but even without them a series of violent events propels Kwang's campaign toward ruin. As Park ponders the situation, he hears his mother's voice, imagining what she would have thought about Kwang:

> She would have called John Kwang a fool long before any scandal ever arose. She would have never understood why he needed more than the money he made selling dry-cleaning equipment. He had a good wife and strong boys. What did he want from this country? Didn't he know he could only get so far with his face so different and broad? He would have had ambition for only his little family. In turn, she'd proudly hold up my father as the best example of our people: how he was able to discard his excellent

Korean education and training, which were once his greatest pride, the very markings by which he had known himself, before he was able to set straight his mind and spirit and make a life for his family. This, she reminded me almost nightly, was his true courage and sacrifice. (333)

Throughout *Native Speaker*, Park analyzes and reanalyzes such memories of his upbringing and his parents, as well as his situation as an immigrant. With great difficulty, it seems, he embraces the values of his parents and the opinions of his wife. He also still treasures the voice and intention of John Kwang, which he hears as "the ancient untold music of a newcomer's heart, sonorous with longing and hope" (304). Toward the end of the novel, after Kwang's campaign has disintegrated, Park seems to find a kind of separate peace, working with his wife to teach foreign children to speak English. He notes that his wife knows he "was raised by language experts, saved from the wild," and he enjoys his job playing the "Speech Monster" who is vanquished by the children's correct pronunciation of the day's secret phrase (232, 349). Along with relinquishing his former job, and beginning to take daily walks in the city, especially to visit Korean concerns, Park's participation in Lelia's private language-classes helps him to unearth his long-suppressed identity, and finally embrace his heritage.

Despite the novel's obvious affinities to the spy-suspense genre, recalling as it does stories like *Vertigo* and *The Big Sleep*, Henry Park's voice is as much a Korean-American echo of Ralph Ellison's African-American narrator in *Invisible Man*, as well as that of Albert Camus's outsider protagonist in *The Stranger*.

Native Speaker won the Hemingway Foundation/PEN award, and was a *New York Times* Notable Book of the Year and *Publishers Weekly* Best Book of the Year.

Bibliography

The Big Sleep. Directed by Howard Hawks. Warner Bros., 1946.
Camus, Albert. *The Stranger.* New York: Vintage, 1989.
Ellison, Ralph. *Invisible Man.* New York: Vintage, 1995.
Lee, Chang-rae. *Aloft.* New York: Putnam. 2004.
———. *A Gesture Life.* New York: Riverhead. 2000.
———. *Native Speaker.* New York: Riverhead, 1996.
Vertigo. Directed by Alfred Hitchcock. Hitchcock, 1958.

—Susan Kirby-Smith

Nowhere Man Alexandar Hemon (2004)

Nowhere Man tells the story of Jozef Pronek, a peripheral figure from ALEXANDAR HEMON's debut short story collection *The Question of Bruno* (2000), here given center-stage for an extended character study. Not so much a sequel as a parallel text, *Nowhere Man* chronicles the life of Pronek from his youth in Sarajevo, through a period in Ukraine in his 20s, to his arrival and subsequent residency in Chicago during the disintegration of his homeland, the former Yugoslavia, in the early 1990s. In this sense, Pronek bears more than a passing resemblance to his creator; indeed, the autobiographical aspects of the novel are conspicuous, blurring the lines between fact and fiction and disrupting the reader's sense of security, orientation, and understanding in the process.

Pronek, the Nowhere Man of the title, is a character for whom a stable identity is always an elusive ideal. When asked whether he is Serb or Muslim (a question he quickly tires of during his time in the United States), his response is "I am complicated" (146), a telling moment of self-recognition from a character whose life is a patchwork of disparate events held together by the loosest of threads. For readers seeking a logical, linear narrative with a satisfying resolution, *Nowhere Man* will come as a frustrating disappointment; instead, the novel is a literary mimicking of the collaged, fragmentary existence of the outsider, told by a variety of narrators, only some of whom are named, and not all of whom are assuredly human. Hemon has been compared to Joseph Conrad and Vladimir Nabokov, and from a biographical perspective this may be valid. Stylistically, however, he is arguably more adventurous than either; in structural terms, *Nowhere Man* is complex, innovative, beguiling, and at times infuriating, recounting Pronek's story from multiple perspectives, a technique that has been likened by Terry Egan to the cubism of

Picasso. This often disorientating method is offset, however, by a lightness of touch that renders the text both endearing and highly accessible. It is an approach reminiscent at times of Kurt Vonnegut's *Slaughterhouse-Five* or Joseph Heller's *Catch-22*, in which polemic and hard-edged satire are refracted through a lens of innocence and naiveté, their problematic narrative strategies counterbalanced by the buoyancy of the author's prose. Hemon is a stylist of considerable ability, his precise, deceptively blunt sentences at times enveloping a wealth of unwritten meanings, symbols, and allusions, at others threatening to reveal themselves as confidence tricks, red herrings, and blind alleyways. Nowhere is this more apparent than in the final chapter, an account of Evgenij Pick, a Russian spy born at the turn of the 20th century, who has no obvious bearing on the story, but whose persistent autobiographical exaggerations, half-truths, and delusions of grandeur cause the reader to reflect on the intersection of the genres of autobiography and fiction, and thus on the relationships between Hemon and Pronek, reality and fantasy.

The bildungsroman feel of the earlier sections affords Hemon the scope to exercise his comic talents, exploring Pronek's growing obsession with the West, pop music, and the opposite sex. Enrolled in English and accordion classes by his father when he is six (in order to temper his unruly behavior), Pronek becomes smitten with music (though he quickly abandons the accordion in favor of the guitar) and Western culture. With an almost clockwork inevitability, he forms a Beatles cover band, adopts the John Lennon role, and becomes a minor local celebrity. The band's first performance (in their music class) is met with "tepid applause," an indisputable sign of triumph; the second is canceled out of respect for Comrade Tito, whose "selfish mortality" has conspired to end his life on the very night they were scheduled to play the school dance, where "eighth-grade girls would be in the audience, in abundance, deep enough into puberty to create a shapely landscape" (44). Yet the charm with which this period is recounted masks a deeper concern with the growing tension of a region on the brink of one of history's bloodiest and most controversial conflicts; we come to know, for example, long before he does, that Pronek's first girl-

friend, Sabina, will lose her legs in a bomb attack, a violence that is offset against Pronek's stint in the army, most of which is spent peeling potatoes and discussing *sevdah*, Bosnia's traditional folk music, and its similarity to the blues of John Lee Hooker.

Hemon is an author for whom the juxtaposition of the mundane and the catastrophic is an endlessly rich seam of material. It is during a spell in Eastern Europe that Victor Plavchuk, an American national of Ukrainian descent and the narrator of the substantial third chapter, learns "to appreciate unremarkable things" (80), which might well be Hemon's own literary motto. The reader, too, is confronted with a carefully constructed catalogue of the everyday, the minutiae of inconsequential existences interspersed with occasional heartbreaking or catastrophic incidents, often occurring at a remove from the narrative itself, as in the fourth chapter, which takes the form of a letter to Pronek in America from a friend in Sarajevo, and which tells of the death of a grotesquely wounded soldier and the (surreal yet deeply moving) suicide of his horse. Chronologically, this letter coincides with Pronek's work for Greenpeace, which finds him campaigning door to door with his future girlfriend (and perhaps future wife) Rachel, an idealistic Sonic Youth fan. Through their doorstep encounters, Hemon paints a portrait of a dysfunctional, misguided North America, where wolves are kept in cages in garages to protect them from Wyoming hunters, where lonely, confused women keep won-ton soup prepared in case of visits from people who may no longer exist, and where respectable businessmen succumb, in the moonlight, to insanity and paranoia.

This is an America of intense isolation, a long way removed from the utopian Western vision of Pronek's youth. The tensions of Eastern Europe, he finds, are replicated on a small, almost petty scale in the United States; when Pronek takes a job to track down and serve papers on a Serbian immigrant who has deserted his wife and is wanted by the courts for not paying child support, he finds himself enveloped in a cultural simulacrum, a miniature of the situation in his native land. For Hemon, the cultural and political difference between the impoverished disillusionment of the American underbelly and the war-torn brutality of Eastern Europe are presented in jarring terms;

traveling to meet the errant Serb, for example, Pronek is confronted with the chilling *Chicago Tribune* headline, "Thousands killed in Srebrenica," a possible reference to the bombings in which Sabina loses her legs. Yet it is the micro-event that, for Hemon, always comes to stand for the bigger picture. When he finally meets the gun-wielding Serb, Pronek identifies himself as a Ukrainian, rather than a Bosnian, an act of self-preservation that serves to highlight not only the fragility of his identity, but also the myth of American freedom, the value he was sent to Chicago to learn.

Somehow the glamour of Sinatra and the Beatles, which informed so much of Pronek's youthful understanding of the inclusivity of Western culture, seem incongruous in this landscape of impotence, banality, and desperation; and it is this sense of disappointment and futility, the sense of being lost and exploited in a world that promised much and failed to deliver, that lies at the heart of the novel. It is this sense, too, which percolates beneath the surface for much of the narrative before bursting forth in a wave of rage and destruction that undoes Pronek's seemingly unshakable acceptance of life, its absurdities, and its shortcomings.

Bibliography

Egan, Terry. *Ink19.* Available online. URL: http://www.ink19.com/issues/march2003/printReviews/nowhereMan.html. Accessed May 20, 2009.

Hemon, Alexandar, *Nowhere Man.* London: Picador, 2004.

—Jim Byatt

Obedient Father, An Akhil Sharma (2000)

An Obedient Father is AKHIL SHARMA's debut novel and the winner of the PEN/ Hemingway Award in 2000. The story takes place in the early 1990s in New Delhi, India, and focuses on the lives of corrupt government official Ram Karan and his family. Akhil Sharma is part of a younger generation of Indo-American writers, including JHUMPA LAHIRI, Vikram Seth, and KIRAN DESAI, whose work centers on contemporary cultural themes within the Indian diaspora and subcontinent. Sharma was born in New Delhi, and moved to the United States with his family when he was a child. He attended Princeton University where he took creative writing classes with Toni Morrison and Joyce Carol Oates, later receiving a Stegner Fellowship at Stanford University. Sharma now works as an investment banker in New York City and continues to publish stories in major literary magazines. The idea for *The Obedient Father* came to him when visiting India in the early 1990s. While Sharma was in New Delhi, Rajiv Gandhi was assassinated, and this epochal event functions as a structural focus for *The Obedient Father,* in which the political landscape of modern India is recast alongside the personal misfortunes of the Karan family.

A searching dialogue between the personal and political structures the narrative. Ram Karan works for the Delhi municipal education department where his job involves bribing and being bribed by school administrators, local politicians, and businessmen. As the novel progresses, Sharma reveals how little loyalty exists in contemporary Indian politics; Ram Karan and those around him are motivated purely by self-interest and the drive for economic and political profit. Within this volatile landscape, allies and enemies switch roles, political parties are formed based on profit rather than principle, and those who are weak are sacrificed for the sake of personal gain. Karan is mostly a pawn in this system, although he attempts to negotiate power using the limited tools in his control; and Sharma demonstrates how the corruption and insecurity that characterize Karan's professional life reflects his failed personal life as well. The novel begins just as his wife has passed away, and his recently widowed daughter, Anita, and her child Asha have moved in with him. The father and daughter's relationship is deeply fraught with painful memories of Ram's abuse of Anita when she was young. The details of this abuse are revealed early in the novel, a shocking series of events that indicate the depth of Karan's self-loathing and the trauma endured by his daughter. What follows is a narrative in which the shifting power structures in Delhi politics are echoed in the Karan household, as Anita becomes increasingly hysterical in her efforts to exact revenge on her father.

Sharma is not the first Indian author writing in English to juxtapose the personal and political. In novels like *Storm in Chandigarh,* written during the 1960s, Nayantara Sahgal explored the relationship between a newly independent India, major political events like the partition that followed, and a shifting drama of personal relations. More recently, Salman Rushdie has employed magical realism to incorporate the political and personal realms of Indian life in narratives of memory and conflict. This structural approach to literary themes is particularly suited to novels about contemporary Indian society, because it reflects how postcolonial politics in India impacts social norms and cultural values. Indian authors who focus on these dynamics are keen to examine and expose the residual inequalities of gender, class, and caste that make problematic the modernization of India.

Power and isolation are the two central motifs that run through *The Obedient Father*, and Sharma employs them to correlate the personal and political vectors of the book. The power relations between Ram Karan and his immediate superiors, those he bribes in the public school system and other satellite political figures, reflect the shifting power relations at home between him and his daughter. While the characters in the novel seem inextricably bound to one another in a tense, almost claustrophobic social structure, they all suffer a paradoxical loneliness, each one alienated from the other. Not only are Anita and Karan isolated from those around them, but all the characters in the novel, from political powers to mere pawns, fail to make meaningful connections with others. And the moments when they *are* able to communicate their own pain and conflict are themselves distinguished by extremes of emotion and violence. Moreover, Sharma demonstrates how corruption, both on personal and political levels, gnaws at the soul of India—so much the norm that it hovers constantly about the surface of characters' dialogue and interactions.

The Obedient Father's narrative point of view is especially well suited to convey the extreme alienation and cruelty these characters suffer. Told from a first-person perspective, the novel primarily expresses the thoughts of its protagonist, Karan; and the voice Sharma grants this figure is at once matter-of-fact and horrified by the atrocities he himself has committed, and that he sees committed by those around him. Sharma is able to develop a highly complex and nuanced character by gradually revealing the conflicting motives that drive Karan: at times he exhibits a moral conscience, a sense of guilt and clarity about his corruption, while at others he seems so convinced by his own self-deception that he gleefully revels in his own exploitive power plays. These opposing traits result in jittery, ambivalent, and spontaneous acts that expose how Karan deals with his own alienation, by identifying at once as victim and predator. The novel is also told, at times, from the point of view of Karan's two daughters, Anita and Kusum, and these perspectives are illuminating not only because they provide another view of the actions and mind of the protagonist, but because they emphasize the intense relationships between people in the family. Whether it be leaving the family at a young age to live in America as Kusum does, or remaining in the household all her life like Anita, the actions of the family members are intimately tied to the desires, weaknesses, and fears of one another, and Sharma explores their loneliness as part and parcel of these inescapable relationships.

As in his short story "Cosmopolitan," Sharma seeks to portray the humanity of his characters by sympathetically revealing their inadequacies and loneliness, and he digs beneath such pathos to understand the fears and insecurities that motivate individuals' desire for power rather than companionship. As in JHUMPA LAHIRI's fiction and Paul Theroux's *The Elephanta Suite*, Sharma is not afraid to cast a critical eye on the complicated and often hypocritical culture that has developed in India over the past 50 years. His characters are flawed and even self-contradicting, but these very weaknesses, like the structural limitations of their lives, ultimately shed light on how India itself must develop, both economically and culturally, while Sharma's firm but flexible prose gives voice to those who are denied or suppressed in the world his characters inhabit.

Bibliography

Akhil Sharma. *The Obedient Father.* New York: Harvest Books, 2001.

—Monika Gehlawat

O'Nan, Stewart (1961–) *American novelist, short story writer, and screenwriter*

Stewart O'Nan is the award-winning author of more than 15 major works, including novels, short stories, nonfiction, and screenplays. He has also edited two nonfiction collections. While his writing varies widely in setting and subject matter, his work is consistently grounded in understated explorations of violence and loss seething beneath the surface of quotidian American experience.

O'Nan was born in 1961, and grew up in Pittsburgh, Pennsylvania. He graduated from Boston University with a B.S. in 1983, and worked as a structural test engineer until the age of 28, when he left his job to become a writer. He received his M.F.A. from Cornell University in 1992, and in 1993 published his first and only collection of short stories, *In the Walled City*, for which he won the Drue Heinz Literature Prize. He has taught writing at Trinity College in Hartford, Connecticut, the University of New Mexico, and the University of Central Oklahoma, and he was named one of Granta's Best Young Novelists in 1996.

SNOW ANGELS (1994), O'Nan's first novel, won the Pirate's Alley Faulkner Prize for the Novel, and was adapted into a 2007 film of the same name, directed by David Gordon Green and starring Kate Beckinsale as Annie, Sam Rockwell as Glenn, and Amy Sedaris as Barb. O'Nan cowrote the screenplay for the film, which was nominated for a Grand Jury Prize at the 2007 Sundance Film Festival. O'Nan's debut novel reveals many of the qualities and trademarks of his later work. Its first-person, past-tense narrative of teenager Arthur Parkinson experiencing his parents' divorce and his own budding sexuality alternates with a third-person present-tense story of Annie and Glenn Marchand, a separated couple. These storylines overlap at a few crucial points, but more significantly O'Nan's juxtaposition of the two families' experiences illuminates universal themes of alienation, (mis)communication, changing relationships between parents and children, and the sometimes destabilizing persistence of memory. Also characteristic is the novel's grayscale suburban landscape, with its ubiquitous fast-food restaurants, American car culture, and often minute but always telling details of middle- and working-class homes (the contents of refrigerators, the placement of furniture, how people treat their pets). Like Raymond Carver (whom O'Nan

cites as an influence), the revelatory tension in O'Nan's writing often resides in its luminous depiction of such seemingly minor details.

O'Nan cites influences as varied as George Romero's horror films, punk music, and writers Tim O'Brien, Flannery O'Connor, and Stephen King, whose presence dominates O'Nan's *The SPEED QUEEN*, which was initially entitled *Dear Stephen King*. The novel is narrated from the perspective of death-row inmate Marjorie Standiford, recording tapes for a famous thriller writer who plans to chronicle her part in a drug-fueled murder spree in his upcoming novel. O'Nan's publisher, editor, and agent refused to support his original title in the face of King's objections, a situation that actually led to O'Nan finding new representation. Curiously, however, O'Nan ended up working with the horror-fiction icon in 2005, when they coauthored *Faithful, Two Diehard Boston Red Sox Fans Chronicle the Historic 2004 Season*. The book is currently in production for a television series.

While eclectic in setting and narrative structure, O'Nan's writing is consistently distinguished by his tendency to focus on "ordinary" 20th- and 21st-century Americans, and what is strange, unstable, or extraordinary in them and in their lives. The often palpable sense of tragedy that troubles O'Nan's literary world stems sometimes from explicitly violent events (epidemics, murders, accidents), and sometimes from the gradual, even imperceptible, but devastating collapse of relationships, or the burden of depression. He employs colloquial language, not only in characters' dialogue, but also in the voices of his narrators, lending an air of familiarity to his prose, regardless of whether he writes in an omniscient third-person voice, or an unreliable first- or second-person (all of which O'Nan employs at some point in his oeuvre). His careful rendering of domestic spaces, working-class lifestyles, and relationship dynamics underscores the sense of familiarity in his work. His settings are the seemingly generic but uniquely American suburban landscapes of water towers, snowbanks, and highways, punctuated by neon signs, brand names, and the taillights of automobiles. He throws into sharp relief the details of the ordinary, but his novels go beyond simply rendering the everyday, to expose the dangerous and violent tendencies, lingering memories, alienation, and presence of death and human frailty that exist within and beneath the commonplace. In a sense his work is an eschatology of normal life, often focusing on the moments just before personal tragedy strikes, or lives spiral out of control.

O'Nan addresses the unspeakable—the death of a child, suicide, war, addiction—with frank and humanizing prose. He also gives voice to, and makes somehow familiar, characters that society marginalizes: veterans, substance abusers, convicted criminals, teenagers, the disabled, even the dead from beyond the grave (in 2004's *The Night Country*). The frankness and readability of his style is complicated but not impaired by his use of alinearity, and tense- and person-shifts that disorient the reader in a way consistent with the unnerving quality of his subject matter.

His novels are distinguished by an eerie and vivid sense of America-as-place. Even in *The NAMES OF THE DEAD*, with its striking account of the war memories of Vietnam veteran Larry Markham, the essential focus is ultimately on Larry's stateside life and the crumbling family relationships back home in Ithaca, New York. Like his literary, cinematic, and musical influences, O'Nan's own experiences of life in America figure prominently in his work, from the time he spent teaching in Oklahoma (the prime setting for *Speed Queen*), to the bleak winters of his childhood in the Northeast that color so much of his fiction.

Bibliography

Debord, Matthew. "Stewart O'Nan: American Pastorals," *Publishers Weekly*, May 25, 1998, pp. 57–58.

Fleming, Michael. "HBO goes to bat for the Red Sox mini." Variety.com. Available online. URL: http://www.variety.com/article/VR1117964174.html. Accessed August 8, 2009.

O'Nan, Stewart. *The Names of the Dead*. New York: Penguin, 1996.

———. *The Night Country: A Novel*. New York: Picador, 2004.

———. *Snow Angels*. New York: Picador, 1994.

———. *The Speed Queen*. New York: Doubleday, 1997.

Scott, A. O. "*Snow Angels*: Gunshots underneath a Gray Sky," *New York Times*, 7 March 2008, p. E10.

The Works of Stewart O'Nan. "Timeline: How I Became a Writer When I Used to Be an Engineer." Available online. URL: stewart-onan.com/timeline. Accessed August 2, 2008.

—Kristen M. Haven

On Beauty Zadie Smith (2005)

On Beauty is ZADIE SMITH's third novel, her follow-up to the relatively downbeat *The Autograph Man* (2002), which—as was nearly inevitable—met with a much cooler reception than her enormously successful debut, *WHITE TEETH* (2000). However, *On Beauty* was generally greeted as another substantial and successful novel from Smith, and was awarded the 2006 Orange Prize for Fiction and short-listed for the 2005 Man Booker prize.

On Beauty is set primarily in the imaginary Boston suburb of Wellington, with brief forays into Smith's own home territory of northwest London. Wellington is an enclave of privileged middle-class families that also houses Wellington College, an elite liberal-arts school where art historian Howard Belsey teaches, and continues work on a long-delayed book debunking the supposed genius of the painter Rembrandt. Howard Belsey is an expatriate white Briton who has traveled far from his humble, working-class roots in London's East End; while his wife of 30 years, the African-American Kiki, traces her own American roots back to the days of slavery. Their three children—Jerome, Zora, and Levi—have all grown up in the sheltered environs of Wellington and are all now discovering, in various ways, the greater world beyond. Despite their considerable differences, Howard and Kiki's marriage has been a good one, but it has recently been threatened by Howard's affair with another woman, a Wellington colleague—although he has somewhat placated Kiki with a lie about a one-night stand with a woman she does not know. With his marriage threatened by his infidelity and untruthfulness, Howard's professional failings are also thrown into relief with the arrival at Wellington of his chief rival, Sir Monty Kipps. Kipps is a conservative Christian, an opponent of the liberal policies that Belsey promotes, and a highly regarded academic whose achievements include a successful book on Belsey's chosen subject, Rembrandt. The sudden entry into Belsey's small world of Kipps, his wife, Carlene, and his daughter, Victoria, heralds a series of disruptions in the lives of both families.

While a novel set in a liberal-arts college is unsurprisingly rich in allusions, Smith acknowledges her particular indebtedness to two key works: *Howards End,* a 1910 novel by E. M. Forster, and *On Beauty and Being Just,* a 1999 treatise by the American literary scholar Elaine Scarry, whose home institution, Harvard University, hosted Smith during a fellowship year in 2002–03 and almost certainly informs her portrait of Wellington College. Forster's novel deals with the unlikely convergence of three English families in the early years of the 20th century, each inhabiting a different stratum of the middle class: the commercially minded upper-middle-class Wilcoxes; the struggling lower-middle-class Basts; and, occupying the ground between these two extremes, the mildly bohemian Schlegel sisters, the novel's principal characters. *On Beauty* is replete with echoes of Forster's book, which also begins with a series of letters (updated to e-mail messages in Smith's novel) detailing a hasty engagement that ends quickly, an awkward preface to the subsequent union between the Schlegels and Wilcoxes. That union is forged first by Margaret Schlegel and the ethereal Ruth Wilcox—a friendship that finds its parallel in *On Beauty* in the bond that forms between Kiki Belsey and the ailing Carlene Kipps. Forster's Leonard Bast, the struggling London clerk whose love of music and literature brings him to the margins of the Schlegels' social circle, has his latter-day American equivalent in Carl Thomas, the gifted but not formally educated spoken-word poet whose cause is championed by the well-meaning Zora Belsey. Like Forster, Smith is keenly aware of the material necessities that precede cultural endeavors—that Howard Belsey's contemplations of Rembrandt are underwritten by the labor of his Haitian maid and driver, just as the university's spectacles of privilege are supported by the underpaid temporary employees who don rented uniforms to serve food and drink to students and faculty who know nothing of their servers' lives and worlds. Smith also shares with Forster an alertness to the limitations

and potential hazards of the liberal impulse that leads the more socially conscious among the privileged—Zora Belsey, for instance, or the poet Claire Malcolm—to seek to help others who are less so, such as Carl Thomas and Chantelle Williams, nonregistered students whom Claire takes into her poetry class. However, Smith is also alert to the generosity informing such gestures. Like Forster's novel, *On Beauty* celebrates humane connections that defy the many mundane social obstacles separating people. To *Howards End*'s famous summons, "Only connect!" (134), Zadie Smith adds a line from a poem by her husband, Nick Laird, "There is such a shelter in each other" (93). In both novels, such human connections are rich and profound, if hard won and fleeting.

The title of Smith's novel, and of one of its three major sections ("on beauty and being wrong"), as well as one of the book's epigraphs, all allude to Elaine Scarry's defense and celebration of the beautiful, *On Beauty and Being Just.* Scarry notes with concern that, while humanities departments within universities continue to devote their attention to various art objects, "conversation about the beauty of these things has been banished, so that we coinhabit the space of these objects . . . yet speak about their beauty only in whispers" (57). The result, she argues, is an impoverishment of the university, which, in a line Smith quotes, is "among the precious things that can be destroyed" (8). This circumstance, Scarry contends, arises from dubious arguments against beauty, one of which is that beauty makes us political dupes—"that beauty, by preoccupying our attention, distracts attention from wrong social arrangements" (58). This, in essence, is the position of Howard Belsey, whose long-delayed study is to be entitled "Against Rembrandt: Interrogating a Master." As one of his students notes, Howard's class on the Dutch painter is all about never admitting a liking for the work: "prettiness" is merely "the mask that power wears," and "Rembrandt . . . was neither a rule breaker nor an original but rather a conformist . . . a merely competent artisan who painted whatever his wealthy patrons asked" (155). Against this notion that beauty in art must always be interrogated, its manipulations exposed, *On Beauty* offers an apparently simple, humane alternative. During a performance of Mozart's Requiem, while Howard contemptuously dismisses "the Christian sublime" (71), and Zora listens to an explanatory lecture on her Discman, the young poet Carl Thomas simply listens and weeps. Carlene Kipps experiences beauty in similar terms, locating her love of poetry in its ability to convey "everything I cannot say and I never hear said. The bit I cannot touch?" (94). And the bond that forms between her and Kiki Belsey begins with a shared experience of two paintings that is barely articulated by either woman. Indeed, Carlene is able to acknowledge that bond only through a sharing of art—through her intended gift to Kiki of a Haitian painting, and the accompanying note, which bears a beloved poetic line, "There is such a shelter in each other" (430).

Ironically, *On Beauty* follows the humane education of the art historian, Howard Belsey. Despite his earlier railing against the notion of Mozart's "genius" (71), he finds himself powerfully affected by a choir's performance of another Mozart piece during Carlene Kipps's funeral, suddenly forced to confront his own mortal bond with the dead woman and with humanity in general. And, in the end, despite his career-long struggle "against Rembrandt," he ultimately finds himself speechless in the face of one of that painter's portraits of his beloved wife, a painting in which Howard finally sees for the first time the enormous worth of his own beloved Kiki.

Bibliography

Forster, E. M. *Howards End.* 1910. New York and London: W. W. Norton, 1998.

Scarry, Elaine. *On Beauty and Being Just.* Princeton, N.J., and Oxford: Princeton University Press, 1999.

Smith, Zadie. *On Beauty.* 2005. Toronto: Penguin, 2006.

—Brian Patton

On the Occasion of My Last Afternoon
Kaye Gibbons (1998)

North Carolina author Kaye Gibbons's sixth novel, *On the Occasion of My Last Afternoon,* presents the life story of slavery-era plantation daughter and bipartisan Civil War wife, Emma Garnet Tate Lowell, narrated by Garnet herself on what she deems will be the last day of her life, a day that evolves into what she describes as "such a glorious afternoon [that] my heart would not weep if I did not live to see another" (273). Garnet's words can, in a sense, be seen as a summation of her life itself, one that is bookended by deaths and tragedies, small and large, yet imbued with stretches of sweetness, love, and peace in its middle. Through the course of a lifetime marked by emotional and physical conflict, Garnet attempts to hold firm to her sense of what is honorable, right, and fair—at some times more successfully than at others. She worries about her ability to succeed in this difficult process, about whether she could "control who [she] was to be by taking this or that from the array of inherited offerings" (28). Ultimately her story is an exploration of the universal capacity of individuals, through hard work, self-knowledge, determination, and love, to overcome sometimes terrible forces threatening to misshape their future and themselves.

Emma is the daughter of nouveau riche Virginia plantation owner Samuel P. Tate, a man of domineering, repressive, and cruelly disdainful temperament, who holds clues to the brutal circumstances of his own upbringing, and painful secrets from his commoner past. Growing up in Samuel's oppressive household, Emma nonetheless finds sane (if sometimes tragic) outlets for love, and positive lessons in life, in the persons of Alice, her ladylike mother; Clarice, the household servant who tends her for most of her life; and Whately, the older brother who awakens her to the joys of reading and the idea of life beyond the repressive walls of her father's household. Throughout her formative years, Emma idolizes her gentle, harried mother and fears for her health on the many occasions when she becomes ill after being subjected to her husband's diatribes. When she realizes that running interference often serves only to postpone and even worsen her father's damaging tirades, Emma skillfully devises subtle intercessions between her parents in order to shield and protect her mother from the worst of Samuel's temper.

However, Emma finds herself unable to protect her brother Whately, who falls victim to Samuel's disdainful neglect in particularly horrifying fashion.

Similarly, Emma's desire to permanently protect her mother by removing her from Samuel's household after her own marriage, at age 17, is gently thwarted by her mother, who tells her, "He loves me, Emma Garnet. I have to stay" (48). In writing her life's narrative, years after her mother's death, Emma is characteristically honest and unflinching in her self-assessment: "I left her there. I left my mother with a fiend, went to Paris, strolled down the Champs-Élysées and ate *petits fours*. I am ashamed" (52).

In contrast, Emma Garnet *is* successful in taking both herself and Clarice away from the Seven Oaks plantation. Clarice leaves with Emma upon her marriage to prominent northern doctor Quincy Lowell, settling with the young couple in their new home in Raleigh, North Carolina. For the next two decades Clarice provides incalculable support and guidance to Emma as the latter raises her own children and encounters the brutal realities of a war she denounces as "a conflict perpetuated by rich men and fought by poor boys against hungry women and babies" (164). Strengthened in clarity and purpose from her years on the plantation, Emma faces these realities head-on throughout four years of nursing in her husband's hospital, where the dead, dying, and wounded line the rooms and halls in claustrophobic numbers. However, the love between Emma and Quincy, the extension of that love in their three young daughters, and the mothering care of faithful and practical Clarice, provide a stabilizing counterpoint to the harsh realities of the War Between the States, and the privations and horrors it brings. Although her life is marked by numerous tragedies, Emma realizes a rich, satisfying life in which she successfully denies her tragic upbringing the power to define her character and choices, electing instead to forge a life based on her own, hard-won wisdom, integrity, and love.

Published in 1998, *On The Occasion of My Last Afternoon* represents a portion of a lengthier Civil War manuscript originally intended to be published as a single novel. In the broader work Gibbons centered her story on a mother-son relationship; and speaking of the larger novel in a 1996 interview with Jan Nordby Gretlund, she states that the mother character "is very close to her son, but he turns out to be the one who ruins her during the War, because he is a never-do-well" (136). If published, the novel would have represented a marked departure from the well-tried pattern of mother-daughter relationships in the South that typically serves as a formulary for virtually all of Gibbons's work. However, the portion of the manuscript that did find its way to publication as the well-received *On the Occasion of My Last Afternoon* held true to the mother-daughter thematic formula, delivering a clearly recognizable Gibbons character arc. Although not departing from the usual thematic found in her other published works to date, the novel does succeed in breaking new ground for Gibbons in the story's expansive depth and emotional complexity.

If Gibbons's immensely popular *ELLEN FOSTER* saga had a weakness, it lay in its somewhat thin narrative construction. *On the Occasion of My Last Afternoon* suffers no such lack of complexity, instead offering a tightly layered, psychologically driven story of suffering and redemption in the Civil War–era American South, in which one woman's struggle is filtered through elements from her traumatized childhood that are reflected in the wider social traumas—both literal and metaphorical—of that devastating event. As such, it deserves a place beside the dark yet hopeful narratives of Charles Frazier's *Cold Mountain* and Margaret Mitchell's timeless masterpiece, *Gone with the Wind*.

Bibliography
Gibbons, Kaye. "'In My Own Style': An Interview with Kaye Gibbons." By Jan Nordby Gretlund. *South Atlantic Review* 65, no. 4 (2000): 132–154.
———. *On the Occasion of My Last Afternoon*. 1998. New York: Perennial, 2005.

—Constance J. Bracewell

P

Packer, Z. Z. (1973–) *American novelist and short story writer*

Z. Z. Packer is the author of DRINKING COFFEE ELSEWHERE, a collection of short stories published in 2003 to considerable critical acclaim. On the strength of this debut, Packer was named a finalist for the PEN/Faulkner Award (the award ultimately went to John Updike, who had chosen her book as a *Today Show* book club selection). She is the recipient of a Whiting Writers' Award, a Rona Jaffe Foundation Writers' Award, and a Guggenheim Fellowship for fiction. Although she had been publishing stories for years, she truly rose to prominence when her story "Drinking Coffee Elsewhere" was selected for the 2000 *New Yorker* debut fiction issue. Her work has since been widely anthologized, and she has served as editor for the 2008 edition of *New Stories from the South.*

Packer was born in Chicago and raised in Atlanta and Louisville, Kentucky. After receiving a B.A. from Yale, she attended Johns Hopkins University's graduate writing seminar and the University of Iowa's acclaimed writers' workshop, earning an M.A. and M.F.A. respectively, and was a Stegner Fellow at Stanford University. Packer believes that African-American writers of her generation benefit from a freedom not afforded their predecessors, who frequently felt the "obligation to ditch their dream for something more practical" (Southgate). It is not surprising, then, that she should cast what some may view as a personal career decision in political terms, as her writing (including a piece addressing Geraldine Ferraro's remarks about Barack Obama) engages actively with politics, particularly the politics of race. Francine Prose calls "Brownies," the first story of *Drinking Coffee Elsewhere,* a "great political story," asserting that "[t]here has rarely been a more incisive picture of how power gets tossed around in a group. . . . Race reveals itself as an issue, as a social hierarchy with a remarkably subtle and complicated architecture that is only revealed to us as the plot keeps turning" (90).

Drinking Coffee Elsewhere consists of eight stories, most written from the perspectives of children or young adults. In "Brownies," the narrator's troop decides to challenge an all-white troop to a fight. The ostensible reason for the challenge is that one of the girls is called a "nigger," but a deeper motivation, according to the narrator, lies in the fact that unlike the common abstract images of whiteness these white girls "were instantly real and memorable" (5). When the girls finally confront the other troop, they are surprised to find that they are mentally disabled and were unlikely to have committed (or, at least, intended) the offense.

Innocence and guilt feature prominently in Packer's stories, particularly as most take place in a world shaped by the church. Of her fascination with the experiences of those raised in religious households, Packer notes "their tendency to have a split self: a self that cannot help remaining faithful to religion even while rebelling against it, rebelling against it even while ostensibly remaining faithful" (Grimes 674). This internalized conflict describes the psychology of the naive girl in "Speaking in

Tongues," who is raised by her religious aunt but tries to reunite with her drug-addict mother in Atlanta; instead, she meets an unsavory man who exploits her helplessness. Perhaps the most moving of the stories, "Doris Is Coming," takes place on New Year's Eve 1961, when the title character's Pentecostal church predicts the Rapture will occur. The story is set in the South, against the backdrop of the civil rights movement, and Doris, eager to assert her place in her world, stages a one-person sit-in at a local whites-only drugstore counter.

Packer describes her approach to writing as fundamentally social or worldly: "I do think that one aspect of being a writer, probably the biggest aspect of being a writer, is being a fully developed human being" and "being a person who is in the world and engaging in the world" (Janssens and Wexler). Contrary to the image of the hermitlike author, her view insists upon productive encounter and experience; and this desire to expand her scope beyond the knowable self may have led her to inhabit the male narrator of her story "The Ant of the Self." Yet despite Packer's stated need for community—or perhaps ultimately because of it— her characters often suffer from deeply felt loneliness. In "Our Lady of Peace" a novice high school teacher is unable to manage her classroom until a troubled girl arrives with whom she forms a strange alliance; when that alliance collapses, the teacher's frustrations overwhelm her and erupt in destructive ways. In the collection's title story a misanthropic, wounded Yale student befriends a girl for whom she feels a homoerotic attraction, but when her narcissistic behavior eventually leads to the dissolution of the friendship, she is left trapped in her isolation and fantasizing about a reunion. And in "Geese," a woman who moves to Tokyo ends up living a life of starvation and degradation in a tiny apartment with a motley crew of other foreigners, all alone though yoked together.

"Geese" ends abruptly with the protagonist recalling a book about kamikaze pilots, with the clear implication that she herself is on a kind of suicide mission; and the reader's disquiet here is typical of the experience of witnessing the troubled lives of Packer's characters. More than one finds him- or herself vulnerable or abandoned in a bus or train station; several are victims or perpetrators of unexpected violence; characters struggle to come to terms with disordered families, attempting to resolve relationships with parents who are absent, negligent, or exist only as shadowy presences in the lives of their children.

Packer is currently writing her first novel, tentatively titled *The Thousands*, a portion of which was published in 2007 as "Buffalo Soldiers" in *Granta 97: Best of Young American Novelists 2*. The novel is an account of "the forgotten masses of blacks who went West" during the postbellum period, with three characters' perspectives assumed in the novel: "a white officer commanding a black cavalry regiment in the Indian Wars, a young black soldier and a woman who joins the Army disguised as a man" (Decarlo).

Bibliography

Decarlo, Tessa. "Comedienne of Manners." *Smithsonian Magazine*. Available online. URL: http://www.smithsonianmag.com/specialsections/innovators/packer.html. Accessed December 1, 2009.

Grimes, Tom. *The Workshop: Seven Decades of the Iowa Writers' Workshop—43 Stories, Recollections, & Essays on Iowa's Place in Twentieth-Century American Literature*. New York: Hyperion, 1999.

Janssens, Jeff, and S. Zoe Wexler. "Being Part of the World: An Interview with ZZ Packer." Nidus 9. Available online. URL: http://www.pitt.edu/~nidus/current/packer.html. Accessed November 14, 2008.

Packer, Z. Z. *Drinking Coffee Elsewhere*. New York: Riverhead Books, 2003.

Prose, Francine. "Out from under the Cloud of Unknowing." *Tin House* 10, no. 1 (Fall 2008): 87–91.

Southgate, Martha. "Writers like Me." New York Times Book Review. Available online. URL: http://www.nytimes.com/2007/07/01/books/review/Southgate-t.html. Accessed November 14, 2008.

—Nadia Nurhussein

Palahniuk, Chuck (1962–) *American novelist*

Chuck (Charles Michael) Palahniuk (pronounced 'paul-ah-nik') was born in 1962, in Pasco, Washington. He is the author of eight published novels and is one of America's most successful and controversial writers, catapulted to fame initially not just by his first published novel, *FIGHT CLUB* (1996), but by its iconic Hollywood film adaptation.

Palahniuk is of French, Russian and Ukrainian ancestry, his father a railroad brakeman, his mother an office manager at a nuclear power plant. He studied at the University of Oregon's School of Journalism, and during his student years worked as an intern for National Public Radio's KLCC in Eugene, Oregon. He graduated in 1986 and moved between jobs, including movie projectionist, bicycle messenger, dishwasher, diesel mechanic, and newspaper journalist, also spending time as a volunteer hospice escort.

Palahniuk began writing after attending workshops run by the novelist Tom Spanbauer, whom Palahniuk has credited with inspiring his minimal prose style. He has also been influenced by Gordon Lish and Amy Hempel, and his essay "She Breaks Your Heart," published in *L.A. Weekly* (2002), praises Hempel for her mastery of the minimalist credo. Palahniuk's earliest published work dates back to 1990 when two short stories, "Negative Reinforcement" (in the August 1990 issue), and "The Love Theme of Sybil and William" (in the October edition) appeared in the now discontinued journal *Modern Short Stories.*

Palahniuk's first attempted novel, *Insomnia: If You Lived Here, You'd Be Home Already,* was rejected by all of the agents who saw it. Its 700 manuscript pages remain unpublished. His next effort, *Manifesto,* was also unsuccessful, although it was later retitled and published as *Invisible Monsters.* Having been turned down for writing fiction that was considered too disturbing, Palahniuk only redoubled his efforts in this regard, and *Fight Club* (part of which was published in short story form in 1995) was the result. Initially the book was only a modest success, but David Fincher's cinematic version starring Edward Norton and Brad Pitt topped the U.K. box-office chart, and was even more successful when it went on subsequent DVD release. An inevitable surge in sales of the novel followed, and it was reissued three times in the six years after the film's release.

Fight Club is a dark, ingenious tale about an unnamed, insomniac protagonist with multiple dissociative personality disorder. His alter ego, Tyler Durden, carries out the bold, aggressive actions for which the unnamed narrator lacks the courage, founding an anarchistic underground movement, the "fight club" of the book's title. It sees men in blue-collar and low-grade white-collar jobs in cities across America enacting the violent, testosterone-fueled tendencies suppressed by a politically correct, post-feminist society. The fight clubs, however, prove to be only a means to the end of establishing the anarchistic, nihilistic Project Mayhem (allegedly based partly on Oregon's Cacophony Society, of which Palahniuk is a member) that aims to strike at the heart of corporate America. The novel both begins and ends explosively, atop the 191-floor Parker-Morris Building, supposedly the world's tallest. By its end the narrator has been forced to confront the horrifying truth that he and Tyler, who he had believed to be a coconspirator (albeit a dominant one), are the same person. The novel also showcases Palahniuk's minimalist technique, with its spare, aphoristic style and occasional refrains (which Palahniuk calls "choruses"). Both the novel and the film generated controversy on either side of the Atlantic, as charges of nihilism, misanthropy, and misogyny were leveled against them. It was not the last time that Palahniuk would face such criticism.

In his relatively short career, Palahniuk has been almost as prolific as controversial. His 10 other published novels are *Survivor* (1999), *Invisible Monsters* (1999), *Choke* (2001; the first to make the *New York Times* best-seller list), *LULLABY* (2002), *Diary* (2003), *Haunted* (2005), *Rant* (2007), *Snuff* (2008), *Pygmy* (2009), and the forthcoming *Tell All* (2010), a fictional account of the life and work of the playwright Lillian Hellman. Palahniuk has also published numerous short stories and two works of nonfiction, *Fugitives and Refugees: A Walk in Portland, Oregon* (2003) and *Stranger Than Fiction: True Stories* (2004). As a journalist, too, he has contributed to a range of publications including *Gear, Playboy,* the *Portland Mercury,* the *Independent, L.A. Weekly,* and *Black Book.*

The events of September 11, 2001, when Al-Qaeda hijacked and crashed American passenger planes into the World Trade Center in New York, might be seen as providing a dividing line between Palahniuk's earlier and later fictional output. The ultimate significance of 9/11 for Palahniuk's work can, however, be overstated. Palahniuk has called his novels that predate this period "transgressional fiction" (Dunn), featuring acts of wanton resistance and rebellion. They invariably anticipate 9/11, sometimes presciently: apart from *Fight Club*'s destruction of the world's tallest building, *Survivor* depicts the last remaining member of a religious cult relating his story to the black-box recorder of a hijacked airplane, while *Invisible Monsters* describes two women (one of them formerly a man) pursuing and exacting violent revenge.

Arguing that the American public will not tolerate such work after 9/11 (rumors persist that a film of *Survivor* was shelved in the post-9/11 period), Palahniuk has diversified into the horror genre with his post-2001 offerings, beginning with *Lullaby*. Nonetheless, to draw clear distinctions between his pre- and post-9/11 fiction would be misleading, since his core themes have remained essentially intact, as have Palahniuk's characteristic formal and stylistic traits, and his favorite plot devices (such as the road trip). The novels typically feature an alienated male protagonist (*Invisible Monsters* and *Diary* are the exceptions) who is reconciled to society during the narrative; and although the action is told from this character's perspective, Palahniuk prefers to "submerge the I" (as he puts it), limiting actual first-person narration. His other major themes—those of destruction for the ultimate purpose of reassembly (which rather refutes the claims of nihilism), and of beliefs and ideas as contagious viruses—continue to permeate his later novels. Similarly, the influence of Palahniuk's favorite philosophers continues unabated. These include existentialists such as Kierkegaard, Sartre, and Nietzsche, as well as Marx and Michel Foucault, whose ideas about identity, Palahniuk has stated, influenced *Invisible Monsters*.

As Palahniuk's fame has grown, his extraordinary personal history has aroused public interest. His family background is scarred by tragedy: his paternal grandfather murdered his grandmother with an axe while Palahniuk's future father hid under the bed. Then, in 1999 Palahniuk's father, Fred Palahniuk, was himself murdered. Divorced from Palahniuk's mother, his father answered a personal ad from a woman named Donna Fon-

taine, and the two began dating. At this time Fontaine's ex-boyfriend, a far-right activist named Dale Shackleford, was in jail for abusing her and had vowed to kill her, a threat he carried out when released. Both Fontaine and Fred Palahniuk were shot dead as they returned from a date to Fontaine's home in Kendrick, Idaho. Shackleford was convicted of two counts of first-degree murder in December 2000.

Palahniuk's private life was laid open a second time in a peculiar sequence of events in September 2003. At a point when some journalists had erroneously reported that he was married to a woman, Palahniuk (seemingly) inadvertently outed himself as a homosexual on his Web site, The Cult, accusing the journalist Karen Valby of being set to reveal his sexuality in her write-up of an interview conducted for *Entertainment Weekly*. Palahniuk posted an audio recording on the Web site criticizing Valby, alleging that she was about to publish information told to her in confidence. After confirming that he is gay, he went on to make derogatory comments about Valby and one of her relatives (see Kavadlo, 5). When Valby's article appeared, it contained no such revelations. Palahniuk apologized and removed the online recording.

Despite such events, Palahniuk's place as one of America's most talented and contentious novelists seems secure, with his profile likely only to rise. He has intermittently spoken of working with Tom Spanbauer on a third nonfiction book concerned with minimalist writing. Palahniuk's novels have been the subject of increasing critical interest, and in 2005, *Stirrings Still: The International Journal of Existential Literature* devoted a special issue to articles about his works. Several collections of academic essays about his fiction are currently in preparation. While a number of Web sites are devoted to Palahniuk's works, his official site, The Cult, also offers writers' workshops and advice, complete with essays on style and technique by Palahniuk himself. He has been the subject of a documentary film—*Postcards from the Future* (2003, directed by Dennis Widmyer, Kevin Kolsch, and Josh Chaplinsky), and other Palahniuk novels have been optioned by Hollywood. A film adaptation of *Choke*, directed by Clark Gregg, was released in 2008, and *Invisible Monsters* is set for 2010, while rumors are lively concerning the adaptation of other works.

Bibliography

Dunn, Adam. "Chuck Palahniuk: Road Trips and Romance," *Publisher's Weekly*, September 2, 2002, p. 49.

Kavadlo, Jesse. "The Fiction of Self-destruction: Chuck Palahniuk, Closet Moralist," *Stirrings Still: The International Journal of Existential Literature* 2 (Fall/Winter 2005): 3–24.

Palahniuk, Chuck. *Diary.* New York: Doubleday, 2003.

———. *Fight Club.* New York: W. W. Norton, 1996; London: Vintage, 1997.

———. *Fugitives and Refugees: A Walk in Portland, Oregon.* New York: Crown, 2003.

———. *Haunted.* New York: Doubleday, 2005.

———. *Invisible Monsters.* New York: W. W. Norton, 1999.

———. *Lullaby.* New York: Doubleday, 2002; London: Jonathan Cape, 2002.

———. *Rant.* New York: Doubleday, 2007.

———. "She Breaks Your Heart: Chuck Palahniuk on Amy Hempel." LA Weekly. Available online. URL: http://www.laweekly.com/art+books/books/she-breaks-your-heart/3590. Accessed March 25, 2008.

———. *Stranger than Fiction.* New York: Doubleday, 2004.

———. *Survivor.* New York: W. W. Norton, 1999.

Widmyer, Dennis, ed. *The Cult: The Official Chuck Palahniuk Site.* Available online. URL: http://www.chuckpalahniuk.net. Accessed March 25, 2008.

—Steve VanHagen

Parks, Suzan-Lori (1964–) *American playwright and novelist*

Suzan-Lori Parks is best known for her Pulitzer Prize–winning play *Topdog/Underdog* (2001) and her debut novel *Getting Mother's Body* (2004). Her first play, *The Sinners Place*, was rejected by the theater department she was involved with at the time, because of its unconventional style and controversial themes (Armstrong). Later, during Parks's commencement address at Mount Holyoke College, she shared with the crowd another instance when she was discouraged in her pursuit of writing, having been advised not to study English by a high school teacher who told her, "You haven't got the talent for it." However, far from extinguishing her aspiration, she relates that "It forced me to think for myself" (Mount Holyoke College). Despite such early discouragements, Parks's ability to create vivid characters, thought-provoking plotlines, and captivating dialogue proved impossible to ignore. She creates a distinctive voice, not merely for each of her characters, but for passages and scenes and acts in which they play.

Born in Fort Knox, Kentucky, in 1964, Parks's childhood was spent, like those in many military families, on the go, with her father's career finally taking her to Germany. There, instead of attending English-speaking military schools, Parks entered the German public system, and the experience forced her to step out of her native language and into an environment completely unfamiliar to her. Later she would describe the experience as a decisively positive influence on her writing (Armstrong).

After high school Parks attended Mount Holyoke College in South Hadley, Massachusetts, and studied fiction writing under the guidance of James Baldwin. It was with Baldwin's suggestions and encouragement that Parks began to focus on playwriting (Armstrong), and very early on she began experimenting with both style and content, deviating from traditional approaches to drama. In 1985, she graduated cum laude from Mount Holyoke and in 2001 received an honorary doctorate from the college.

From the late '80s onward her plays increasingly began to make it into production. In 1987 *Betting on the Dust Commander* opened in New York City, and two years later *Imperceptible Mutabilities in the Third Kingdom* opened in downtown Brooklyn, and received an Obie Award for Best New American Play. In the fall of 1990, *The Death of the Last Black Man in the Whole Entire World* opened at the same location in downtown Brooklyn. Premiering shortly after were *The America Play* (1994), *Venus* (1996), and *In the Blood* (1999). *Venus* received an Obie award in 1996, while *In the Blood* was nominated for the 2000 Pulitzer Prize.

Parks also penned several screenplays. In 1996 she wrote *Girl 6*, her first feature film, which was directed by Spike Lee. In 2001, she received a MacArthur "Genius" grant, and in 2002 became the first African-American woman to receive a Pulitzer Prize, for *Topdog/Underdog*.

Topdog/Underdog delves into the lives of Booth and Lincoln, brothers who in desperate straits find themselves sharing Booth's small apartment. Confined in close quarters, they struggle to deal with a myriad of difficulties; and as they reflect on their shared past, while confronting a bleak future, their complex relationship unfolds. Parks's talent with language turns the simple apartment in *Topdog/Underdog* into a rich microcosm of contemporary realities, and the love story that unfolds there is poignant and richly nuanced.

The play partly sprang from an earlier work, *The America Play,* which opens with an Abraham Lincoln impersonator working in an arcade. In her introduction to *Topdog/Underdog,* Parks writes, "I was thinking about my old play [*The America Play*] when another black Lincoln impersonator, unrelated to the first guy, came to mind: a new character for a new play" (Parks).

Another influence for the Pulitzer Prize–winning play was Parks's recent interest in the time-honored three-card monte scam, which, she relates, "began one day when my husband Paul and I were walking along Canal Street." As they watched the scam pulling unsuspecting customers in, Parks's husband, Paul Oscher, a blues musician, explained how it worked, and later taught her how to "throw the cards" (Topdog/Underdog). In a stylistic tour de force, the scam develops into the dynamic linchpin in the play's inexorably tragic progress.

Parks's novelistic debut, *Getting Mother's Body,* focuses on Billy, a pregnant adolescent trying to ameliorate the vagaries of her current situation. Rumor has it that Billy's mother, Willy Mae, buried years ago, was placed in the ground with her expensive jewels. Prompted by this rumor, a long and complicated road trip from Texas to Arizona ensues, involving not merely Billy but a rogue's gallery of fellow aspirants, and culminating in a host of stunning revelations at the graveside.

Parks's prolific theatrical output continued with 2006's compilation of her play-a-day experiment, *365 plays/365 days,* then *Ray Charles Live!*

(2007) and *Father Comes Home from the Wars (Parts 1, 8 & 9)* (2009); she also wrote a screenplay for Toni Morrison's *Paradise.*

Bibliography

Armstrong Jenkins, Rhonda. "Suzan-Lori Parks." Voices from the Gaps. Available online. URL: http://voices.cla.umn.edu/vg/Bios/entries/parks_suzanlori.html. Accessed February 1, 2007.

Parks, Suzan-Lori. *Getting Mother's Body.* New York: Random House, 2004.

———. *Topdog/Underdog.* New York: Theatre Communications Group, 2001.

Mount Holyoke College. "Pulitzer Prize-Winning Playwright." Available online. URL: http://www.mtholyoke.edu/cic/about/reasons.shtml?num=5. Accessed March 3, 2009.

—Rylan Morton

Patchett, Ann (1963–) *American novelist*

Ann Patchett's career as a literary novelist has been exemplary. Her talent was nurtured in the best writing programs in the United States; her work has been accepted by major publishers and praised by critics. Her fourth novel, *BEL CANTO* (2001), brought popular success, selling more than a million copies in the United States, in addition to earning the Pen/Faulkner and National Book Critics Circle Awards.

Born in California, Patchett was raised in Nashville, where she currently resides. She frequently refers to the influence of 12 years of Catholic school, explaining in her memoir *Truth and Beauty* that "we were not in the business of discovering our individuality . . . when we prayed, it was together and aloud. It was impossible to distinguish your voice from the crowd" (4). Nevertheless, she discovered in Eudora Welty an individual voice that spoke to her and decided by age 12 to become a writer. Since then Patchett has articulated a clear voice of her own in a body of distinguished novels, whose characters develop humanly flawed but supportive, essentially moral communities.

With uncommon dedication, Patchett pursued her vocation from fiction-writing courses at Sarah Lawrence to the Iowa Writers' Workshop, then to Fellowships at the Fine Arts Work Center in Provincetown, Massachusetts (1990), the Bunting Institute at Radcliffe (1993), and a Guggenheim Fellowship in 1994; sometimes earning her living by teaching or waiting tables, and living with her mother for a time. She characterizes herself as a hardworking "ant," steadily turning out pages, and compares her dedicated writing time to regular exercise at the gym, believing that "regular attendance was half the battle" (*Truth and Beauty* 20, 62). She usually emerged from the writing programs with a significant piece of work: Before graduating from Sarah Lawrence, she had a story published in the *Paris Review;* during her seven-month Provincetown fellowship she completed her first novel, which was sold while she was driving home to Nashville; and her second and third novels appeared during 1993–94, the latter resulting from her time at Radcliffe. Patchett's talent would likely have resulted in fine work in any case, but her oeuvre also represents the positive effect that a stimulating, supportive environment can have on a gifted writer.

Plotting her novels in advance, even years before beginning to write, is essential to Patchett's technique. She compares weaving a storyline to "knitting one of those big, complicated Irish sweaters with 15 needles hanging off the front . . . you've got to have a pattern or you're just going to wind up with a mess." She claims to write stories entirely for herself, trying to create something "complex enough to hold my interest for 5 years" (Siegenthaler).

One of Patchett's dominant themes emerges in her first novel, *The PATRON SAINT OF LIARS* (1992), designated a *New York Times* Notable Book of the year, which illustrates the importance of the nurturing of children, both by blood relations and by those who adopt others out of love. The story follows an unhappy wife who leaves her husband, determined to give her unborn child up for adoption. She changes her mind, however, and the child grows up in a community of nuns, pregnant women, and even fatherly love. Her second novel, *Taft* (1994), also focuses on a diverse community's relationships and evolution. In fact, she insists that the main idea for all her novels comes from Thomas Mann's *The Magic Mountain,* in which "a

group of strangers are thrown together by circumstance and somehow form a family" (Nissley). In *Taft,* John Nickel extends a father's love both to his own absent son and to the employees of his Memphis bar, while feeling imaginative sympathy for a father who has died.

The Magician's Assistant (1997) again explores the idea of constructed family, but with a different focus, here on the connection between a woman who has shared a magician's adult life and those he had long ago abandoned. As in *The Patron Saint of Liars,* a character has decided to make the past disappear. Sabine's journey to reclaim the lost years of her husband's life brings two disparate worlds together: the sophisticated gay community of Los Angeles, with characters named Parsifal and Phan, and that of the heartland characters Dot, Kitty, and Guy, in Alliance, Nebraska. Differences in characters and situations make each Patchett novel distinctive, despite their similar themes. Laurie Parker wrote, "I know of no other writer who is able to—or who is brave enough to—tackle the challenge of creating characters of such varied races and backgrounds, making each one's voice and life so utterly believable."

BEL CANTO (2001) describes a gathering of people with little connection to each other, who under the artificial conditions of a siege, based on the real occupation of an ambassador's residence in Peru in 1996, develop a temporary but intense extended family. Mysteries, intrigues, private feelings, and surprising alliances develop in a situation of danger and forced intimacy. The central character is an opera singer, and the opera is a fitting objective correlative for this highly dramatic situation. The mesmerizing beauty of opera connects the characters through heightened emotionality but also distracts them from each other's real needs and the consequences of their actions. Like characters in an opera, they live for a time in a beautiful, artificial world that cannot survive real life. For Patchett, her idiosyncratic use of the third-person omniscient point of view is a personal achievement, giving her the ability to move "from person to person within a room during the course of a single conversation" (Weich).

Patchett's fifth novel, *Run* (2007), also explores family composition, but its author perceives it as above all a political novel, conceived while her husband considered running for political office. As in *The Patron Saint of Liars* and *The Magician's Assistant, Run* brings a family into contact with individuals they are somehow connected with but who have been invisible to them; however, here the revealed connections raise issues of race, class, and social responsibility. Its three brothers are loosely based on characters in Fyodor Dostoyevsky's *The Brothers Karamazov,* and different family members represent different aspects of running: running for office, running to escape, and running for personal achievement. One of the novel's greatest accomplishments lies in its deft handling of time (Maslin): It takes place over a period of about 24 hours, but incorporates family and friendship histories from several generations, and reveals twin mysteries of interconnection to the youngest of them.

Truth and Beauty (2004), a nonfiction tribute to Lucy Grealy, whose life and career became entwined with Patchett's when they attended the Iowa Writers' Workshop in 1985, has also received critical acclaim, designated a book of the year by both the *Chicago Tribune* and the *San Francisco Chronicle.* Grealy endured a life of serial surgeries to reconstruct her jaw after childhood cancer, and Patchett chronicles Grealy's brave struggle against the limits imposed on her life by her appearance. The narrative does not flinch at describing painful lessons in sexual intimacy, and the book has been both lauded and criticized for this (Cutler). Just as prominent, however, is the intimate portrayal of young writers struggling to find their individual voices, establish effective writing routines, attract attention to their work, and deal with fame when it arrives; and this refreshing candor about the invisible life of an author has been a distinctive aspect of Patchett's own literary career.

Bibliography

Maslin, Janet. Review of *Run.* New York Times on the Web. Available online. URL: http://www.nytimes.com/2007/09/20/books/20masl.html. Accessed April 12, 2008.

Datchett, Ann. "Ann Patchett Hits All the Right Notes." By Dave Weich. Available online. URL: http://www.powells.com/authors/patchett.html. Accessed May 12, 2008.

Parker, Laurie. Review of *The Magician's Assistant.* BookPage.com. Available online. URL: http://www.bookpage.com/9710bp/fiction/themagiciansassistant.html. Accessed May 12, 2008.

———. "BEA 2007: An Early Q&A with Ann Patchett." By Tom Nissley. Omnivoracious' Amazon Blog. Available online. URL: http://www.amazon.com/gp/blog/post/PLNK12MSHH70LUY2U. Accessed May 20, 2008.

———. *Bel Canto.* New York: HarperCollins, 2001.

———. Interview with Ann Patchett. By John Siegenthaler. Available online. URL: http://www.annpatchett.com/about.html. Accessed May 27, 2008.

———. Introduction. *The Best American Short Stories 2006.* Boston: Houghton Mifflin, 2006.

———. *The Magician's Assistant.* New York: Harcourt Brace, 1997.

———. "My Pornography." By Abigail Cutler. Atlantic Online. Available online. URL: http://www.theatlantic.com/doc/200707u/ann-patchett. Accessed May 31, 2008.

———. *The Patron Saint of Liars:* New York: Houghton Mifflin, 1992.

———. *Run.* New York: HarperCollins, 2007.

———. *Taft.* New York: Houghton Mifflin, 1994.

———. *Truth and Beauty.* New York: HarperCollins, 2004.

—Shiela Ellen Pardee

Patron Saint of Liars, The Ann Patchett (1992)

ANN PATCHETT's debut novel tells the touching and often sad story of Rose, a pregnant woman who leaves her life and home, as well as her loving husband of three years, and travels to the rural western Kentucky town of Habit. Here she plans to stay at St. Elizabeth's, a Catholic home for unwed mothers, intending to carry her baby to term and then give it up for adoption. When the time comes, however, she is unable to part with her child, and accepts the unexpected marriage proposal of Son Abbott, the home's groundskeeper and maintenance man, returning to St. Elizabeth's to work in the kitchen while raising her daughter as her and Son's child.

Though *The Patron Saint of Liars* revolves around Rose, her narrative only makes up a fraction of the novel. The story is divided into four sections, each told from a different perspective, beginning with a third-person narration describing the fabled history of St. Elizabeth's. In the second part, Rose tells her own story, beginning with a brief background of her life and ending with her marriage to Son and the birth of her daughter, Cecelia. Son narrates the third part and, like Rose, provides his own brief history before continuing their shared story. The final section of the novel gives voice to Cecelia who, now a teenager accustomed to her parents living apart but desperate for an emotional connection to her mother, begins to suspect that she is adopted. Cecelia concentrates on her own story and, in particular, her attempts to form a connection with her mother. The novel ends with Rose's permanent departure from St. Elizabeth's, preceding the unexpected arrival of her first husband, who intrigues Cecelia with tales of a younger, happier Rose. His true relationship to Cecelia is never revealed, however, and he leaves Son and Cecelia to accept Rose's absence and continue their lives without her.

Patchett shows admirable skill in creating four unique voices that tell one seamless story. Though the lyrical quality of her prose does not waiver from narrator to narrator, it is always clear, through subtle dialogue shifts and emotional reactions, who is narrating each section of the novel. The first section's omniscient narrator, for example, is formal and detached, whereas Rose's narration is marked by crisp statements taut with emotion, such as her initial revelation, "I would be a liar for the rest of my life" (11). There is at times an awkwardness in Son's storytelling that comes from his rough, exposed emotions, most obvious as he watches Rose move out of his and Cecelia's home:

> She didn't say anything else or look back over her shoulder and there was nothing I could do but watch her walking away, getting smaller and smaller in the dark field. . . . She was going and I was letting her go. (230)

While Cecelia's section is just as emotional as Son's, it also has the crispness of Rose's narration; the biting remarks of a teenager are scattered

throughout it, such as her retort toward her mother's attempt to scold her: "You can't be gone all the time and then waltz in here like you're somebody's mother and tell me what I'm allowed to do" (274).

The choice of multiple narrators is most helpful in the treatment of one of Patchett's recurrent themes: unconventional love. Rose's section, for example, ends with her choice to marry Son in order to keep the child she names Cecelia, a name tattooed on Son's arm for another woman. Rose says, "It will be perfect. We'll tell her you had her name put on your arm the day she was born, that you loved her so much you went out and had her name written right here" (124). Her attempt to convince her child of her father's love by a tattoo gives us hope that she can show love, and though none of the following sections provide evidence of that, we are left with that hope for her because the last of her insights we are privy to was one of love for her child.

Another common theme in Patchett's fiction is that of improvised home and family. Rose constantly remakes her home: with her first husband, in her car, at St. Elizabeth's, and in Son's home. Though none of the homes are permanent, or even successful for Rose (she leaves them all), we see them function successfully for others. Rose's roommate at St. Elizabeth's, Angie, makes herself comfortable at the home by taking up knitting and befriending the girls around her. Though she is initially less convinced than Rose that giving up her child is the right thing to do, she remains resolute and later visits Rose to attest to the validity of her choice. Moreover, she seems to reflect on her time at St. Elizabeth's fondly. For her, for a time, it was a home. Patchett uses characters like Angie to attest to the ability to find home and family where and when they are needed.

Underlying each of the main storylines is a search for psychological healing. Rose's search is the most obvious and least successful: though she tries to make amends for her shortcomings through sacrifices (such as giving up her relationship with her mother), she never openly confronts her fears and weaknesses. Conversely, Cecelia exemplifies the most hopeful search for healing. Though she is too young for us to gauge her success, her willingness to deal with confrontation and her attempts to discover the truth make her healing seem more likely.

The Patron Saint of Liars, like much of Patchett's writing, is marked by an allegorical feeling, almost as though the novel were a fable. And its very lack of resolution, its oddly unfinished characters and unresolved plot, merely encourage the reader's imaginative engagement. We are left guessing what will happen to Rose, Son, and Cecelia; and without any certain knowledge about their future, we are more effortful in learning what we can of—and from—them. We can only guess whether Cecelia will become a liar like her mother, or if she will learn from Rose's mistakes, but we can learn from them, whether she does or not.

Though *The Patron Saint of Liars* has not received the critical attention of Patchett's later novels such as BEL CANTO and *The Magician's Assistant,* it was awarded the 1989 James A. Michener/Copernicus award for best novel in progress and was named a *New York Times* Notable Book. In 1997, it was adapted into a made-for-television movie starring Dana Delaney. While the movie remains tied to Patchett's novel, the time-period is changed to the early 1980s, and it deals primarily with Rose, to the exclusion of Son and Cecelia. Also, it explains Rose's poor decisions as the result of a crisis of faith, making it more easy to understand and sympathize with her. As such, the tale becomes a romance full of unquestioning hope and redemption, rather than the allegoristic tale of unconventional love, improvised families, and searches for psychological healing so vividly told in the novel.

Bibliography

Patchett, Ann. *The Patron Saint of Liars.* 2002. New York: HarperPerennial, 2007.
The Patron Saint of Liars. Directed by Stephen Gyllenhaal. Performers: Dana Delaney, Sada Thompson, Clancy Brown. 1997. DVD. Questar, 2005.

—Catherine Altmaier

Peace Like a River Leif Enger (2001)

The *Christian Science Monitor, Denver Post,* and *Los Angeles Times* named *Peace Like a River* Best Book of the Year, and *Time* magazine named it one of its Top Five Books of the Year for 2001. Enger's ability to tell a vivid story in flowing, lucid prose, and to develop realistic, colorful characters has made this national best seller popular with both critics and readers alike.

The story centers on the Land family. The father, Jeremiah, is a man of strong faith and almost inconceivable benevolence, and his deep familial love compensates for the minimal financial support he can provide. Sixteen-year-old Davy has an independent spirit, a strong will, and a love of the outdoors. Reuben, 11 years old at the time of the story, is an asthmatic who should not have lived at birth; he narrates the story with the honesty of innocence. Nine-year-old Swede, a romantic at heart and lover of words, writes narrative poetry about the old West in which situations often parallel those of the Land family's own experiences. Enger makes each of these characters plausible, attractive, and sympathetic.

The central action of the story focuses on a journey Jeremiah, Reuben, and Swede make to find Davy, who has escaped from jail after being charged with the murders of two of the town hoodlums. Jeremiah prays, "Lord, send Davy home to us; or if not, Lord, do this: Send us to Davy." By accident—or, as Reuben might suggest, a miracle—they locate the boy; and while circumstances prevent the family from being physically reunited, they regain their emotional and spiritual unity. Reuben ends his account with a miraculous explanation, which he admits some will not believe: "Is there a single person on whom I can press belief? . . . All I can do is say, Here's how it went. Here's what I saw. . . . Make of it what you will."

Enger complements the novel's affecting plotline with plausible characters whose actions are convincing expressions of their varied personalities. Not only does he make the members of the Land family realistic and winsome, but he also develops a host of memorable minor characters. August and Birdie Shultz harbor Davy at their farmhouse in the Great Plains for a short time during his escape, and give him supplies and a broken-down Studebaker; later they encourage Jeremiah, Reuben, and Swede in their search for their brother. Tim Lurvy, a traveling salesman, stops at the Land home to enjoy lively conversation and good food on his once- or twice-yearly trips through the town of Roofing; he makes the Lands' journey out West possible by providing them with his Airstream trailer. Davy's lawyer, Thomas DeCellar, who believes Davy acted in defense of his family, charms Swede with his vivid accounts of historical events. All grow to love family friend Roxanna and her feisty personality, as well as her lively stories and the cinnamon rolls made according to her great-uncle's recipe; she is, says Reuben, "a lady you would walk on tacks for."

The novel also has its share of colorful villains. Reuben describes Mr. Holgren, the superintendent of schools—whose potted face earned him the name of Chester the Fester among the children—as "the worst man I'd ever seen." Andreeson, a federal agent, earns the disdain of the entire family. Reuben calls him "the king of pukes in most respects," and Swede once hinders his search for Davy by putting syrup in Andreeson's gas tank.

Enger writes to entertain, but at the same time deals sensitively with themes of faith and family. Jeremiah, a spiritual man, rises early each morning to read the King James Bible. He prays often and intensely, and is, as Reuben notes, "so forgiving it almost didn't count." Jeremiah has the power to perform miracles: Christ-like, he gives breath to Reuben when he is a newborn by calling on God's name, turns a small pot of soup into multiple bowls, and mends a torn saddle with his mere touch. One night, Reuben witnesses his father "walking on air" after stepping over the edge of the flatbed of his truck; and the root of all these miraculous events, Reuben concludes, is his father's profound faith.

The novel exalts family. The Lands share a self-sacrificing and forgiving love, and remain loyal to each other despite extraordinarily trying circumstances. Reuben, with Swede's nudging, uses the $25 he earns tearing down a dilapidated corncrib to replenish the family's food supply. Jeremiah searches for Davy, though he believes him guilty. The Lands' love withstands separation by space and time, even death, and expands to include Roxanna and Sara, the latter a young woman whom Davy rescues from a forced marriage with a man who virtually enslaved her until she reached childbearing age.

In themselves, the setting and plot would suggest a sentimental western, but the novel's well-developed characters, lyrical language, and thematic content make *Peace Like a River* a work of literary fiction. The novel speaks eloquently of the power of love—love of God and of family—and confronts the reader with the difficulty, or rather irresponsibility, of labeling people and circumstances as simply good or bad.

Enger calls Robert Louis Stevenson his "favorite writer of all time," praising him for "his great adventure tales, his brand of moral fiction," and his use of language; and Stevenson's humanistic influence is evident not merely in the novel's entertaining narrative and plausible, spirited characters, but above all in its underlying message of love that passes understanding.

Bibliography

Writers and Books. "2004—If All of Rochester Read the Same Book." Available online. URL: http://www.wab.org/events/allofrochester/2004. Accessed November 29, 2009.

Enger, Leif. *Peace Like a River.* New York: Grove Press, 2001.

———. *So Brave, Young and Handsome: A Novel.* New York: Grove Press, 2008.

Mudge, Alden. "Riding the Wave of Leif Enger's Dazzling Debut." BookPage.com. Available online. URL: http://www.bookpage.com/0109bp/leif_enger.html. Accessed November 29, 2007.

—Charlotte Pfeiffer

Peck, Dale (1967–) *American novelist and critic*

Dale Peck is the author of three novels published in the 1990s, MARTIN AND JOHN, *The Law of Enclosures,* and *Now It's Time to Say Goodbye,* but he has enjoyed a secondary career as a nonfiction writer that has arguably brought him more fame during the 2000s. This output included the well-reviewed creative nonfiction work, *What We Lost,* and *Hatchet Jobs,* a collection of book reviews written for the *New Republic.* It is *Hatchet Jobs* that earned Peck the greatest notoriety, including a *New York Times Magazine* profile by James Atlas. Writes Martin Fletcher, reviewing *What We Lost* for the U.K. publication the *Independent:* "Dale Peck has a reputation for cutting literary throats with the ruthlessness of a fox in a chicken-run ... he described Rick Moody as "the worst writer of his generation" and continued the turkey shoot at Faulkner's "incomprehensible ramblings," Nabokov's "sterile inventions," and the "stupid—just plain stupid—tomes of Don DeLillo'" (Fletcher). But after reaping the fruits of his new high public profile—in an era that coincided with the rise of literary and celebrity blogs—the older, mellower Peck has most recently published a classically influenced children's fantasy novel, *Drift House,* and its sequel.

Peck was born in Long Island, New York, and raised in Kansas. He graduated from both Drew University and Columbia University's M.F.A. program. The recipient of a 1995 Guggenheim Fellowship, he currently teaches creative writing at the New School in New York City. Openly gay, Peck has written for *Out* magazine, as well as a series of novels that often deal with sexual themes. He has also edited and been published in several gay fiction anthologies, including the 2007 AIDS fiction anthology *Vital Signs,* for which he also provided a bold, moving foreword.

His first novel was published in 1993, when Peck was 25. *Martin and John* (released in the United Kingdom under the bolder title *Fucking Martin*) is the story of two lovers, one of whom is dying of the AIDS virus. It utilizes postmodern play with time and narrator in order to cast and recast the ill-fated but loving relationship as a series of vignettes between the two men. While written in a tone of unabashed sentiment and unsubtlety, Peck's novel still deserves praise as a product of its time. Taking on practically every issue confronting gay men in the era of Act Up—Peck was a proud member of the organization, and was even among those arrested when they stormed a Dan Rather broadcast (Atlas)—the novel is foremost an activist text. Preceding the wider awareness of gay issues emerging in the 1990s, the novel is a key text of queer fiction. It was widely praised and earned a blurb from no less than Edmund White, though he would later grouse that Peck gave him a lukewarm and "condescending" review of a novel of his three years later (Atlas).

Peck's next novel, *The Law of Enclosures* (1997), turned a finely honed prose sensibility on heterosexual marriage, again told from multiple viewpoints. Intercut with two lengthy contrasting portraits, each of which offers its own precise account of the crumbling marriage, Peck presents intense autobiographical reminiscences of his own childhood. Reflects James Atlas: "It's hard not to suspect that Peck has mythologized his traumatic past to create a vivid, imaginative narrative. Yet the outline is undoubtedly true—the evidence is in his obsessive efforts to come to terms with it by writing the story over and over" (Atlas). The novel's emphasis is on these moments of pain, and the cumulative effect of the retellings is a compelling and unified narrative.

Now It's Time to Say Goodbye (1999) is an uncharacteristic novel, departing from the play with formal and stylistic devices that distinguish Peck's earlier work, and instead exploring race relations between two mythical dustbowl towns marked by a legacy of violence. The issue exists in the novel on a nearly mythic level; rape and murder, long mainstays in the fiction of Faulkner, are cyclically perpetuated in an increasingly disturbing manner. AIDS, too, plays a role in the novel, as the two émigrés visiting the town come from a New York where the virus has run rampant. This nightmarish material did not sit well with some critics, such as the *Washington Post*'s Dwight Garner, who claimed the novel was "as soulless as a rock video and as decadently frenetic as a windup action pimp" (Garner). A milder rebuke published in Salon.com claimed the book was, above all else, "unwieldy" but nonetheless compelling:

> A bit much? Sometimes, yes. But for the most part, the book works surprisingly well, partly because Peck is able to pile up some fantastic sentences. So even as it becomes clear that the town's vast and terrible secrets are neither plausible nor particularly illuminating on matters of race or sex, it's still hard not to get caught up in the onion peeling. (Walker)

What We Lost (2004) eases back from this ambitious pile-up. At times the book seems as if

Peck, well into his career as a harsh reviewer by this time, seems to have internalized some object lessons from his past work. A creative nonfiction work that returns to his childhood by way of an attempt to understand his father's upbringing, it finds Peck discovering that his father's childhood was perhaps just as bad as his own. Yet the author also finds some oblique redemption in reflective passages that praise his father's discovery of "simpler values, an empathy with the land, and the power of silence and reflection that scrub clean wounds of abuse"—even if this is contrasted with a shocking climax of violent retribution performed upon his own abusive father (Fletcher).

By this time, Peck had made serious waves in the literary world with the aggressive forays into literary criticism that made him a household name for many. Collected in *Hatchet Jobs* (2004)—a book whose commercial aspirations seem more obvious than most in its genre—Peck's exuberant outrageousness is on full display. In addition to his sentence-by-sentence assault on Rick Moody's experimental memoir *The Black Veil*, Peck mauls Terry McMillan, Jonathan Franzen, Ian McEwan, Don DeLillo, Thomas Pynchon (as the creator of a big mess that no one cleaned up), and others. Most interesting is his contention that the roots of bad writing can be traced back to the works of high modernism. Responses to the book were predictably hostile, especially in the literary magazine *n+1*, which gave Peck a drubbing of his own. As for Rick Moody, his relationship with Peck had sufficiently cooled in 2008 to the point where he jokingly gave him a pie in the face in a video now widely viewable on YouTube and Gawker.com (Pareene).

Recently, Peck made another striking and widely reported move, partnering with Tim Kring, creator of the popular NBC sci-fi drama *Heroes*, for a massive multimedia project with a popular fiction component. Announced in April 2008, the trilogy of novels, described as a cross between Robert Ludlum and Don DeLillo, will center on a character with LSD-derived superpowers, and plunge into nefarious government intrigue (Neyfakh). In 2005 and 2007, Peck published two *Drift House* children's fantasy novels, time-and-space adventures that owe a debt to C. S. Lewis and Madeleine L'Engle. His 2009 novel, *Body Surfing,* marked yet another dramatic departure: a mixture of supernatural and erotic horror in the thriller genre. It received mixed reviews.

Bibliography

Atlas, James. "The Takedown Artist." New York Times on the Web. Available online. URL: http://www.nytimes.com/2003/10/26/magazine/26PECK.html. Accessed May 12, 2009.

Cityfile New York. "Dale Peck." Available online. URL: http://cityfile.com/profiles/dale-peck. Accessed January 22, 2009.

Fletcher, Martin. Review of *What We Lost.* Independent.co.uk. Available online. URL: http://www.independent.co.uk/arts-entertainment/books/reviews/what-we-lost-by-dale-peck-56 6483.html. Accessed January 22, 2009.

Garner, Dwight. "Small Town, Big Trouble," *Washington Post,* 7 June 1998, sec. X, p. 4.

Neyfakh, Leon. "Dale Peck Partners with *Heroes'* Kring on $3 Million Trilogy." Observer.com. Available online. URL: http://www.observer.com/2008/dale-peck-partners-heroes-kring-3-million-trilogy. Accessed January 28, 2009.

Pareene, Alex. "Everyone Is Friends: Rick Moody Pies Dale Peck." Gawker.com. Available online. URL: http://gawker.com/385919/rick-moody-pies-dale-peck. Accessed January 30, 2009.

Walker, Rob. "Now It's Time to Say *Goodbye.*" Salon.com. Available online. URL: http://www.salon.com/books/sneaks/1998/05/29sneaks.html. Accessed January 30, 2009.

—Chris Smith

Perrotta, Tom (1961–   ) *American novelist*

Perrotta is the author of one collection of stories, BAD HAIRCUT: STORIES OF THE SEVENTIES, and five novels, *The Wishbones,* JOE COLLEGE, *The Abstinence Teacher, Little Children,* and *Election.* The last two he helped adapt to film.

He played football in high school and attended Yale, the setting of *Joe College* (2000), then studied creative writing under Tobias Wolff, Thomas Berger, and Douglas Unger at Syracuse. Mainstream success was elusive, though he published in student and small literary magazines throughout his late teens and early 20s. Some of these stories were collected in *Bad Haircut.*

Perrotta's second novel, *Election* (1998), was optioned in 1996 and subsequently made into the eponymous film by MTV Productions. Only afterward was the novel acquired by a publisher, serving to illustrate indirectly Perrotta's strikingly cinematic style. Inspired by the 1992 presidential campaign, *Election* transposes that setting into a high-school milieu, with an establishment candidate, Tracy Flick (portrayed by Reese Witherspoon), an uncertain but attractive alternate, Paul Warren, and a third-party spoiler critical of the election—and thus high school—system more generally, Paul's sister Tammy Warren.

The novel is told from multiple points of view, including those of adult teachers with interests in sex not dissimilar to their teenage charges. One teacher has sex with Tracy and is subsequently fired, though neither he nor Tracy treats their encounter as being of much consequence on its own, but the repercussions harm the teacher more than the student in an unexpected role reversal typical of Perrotta's work.

Perrota's follow-up novels found steadily wider audiences and received mostly positive reviews. *Joe College* (2000) drew on his student experiences at Yale, exploring the class divide between the wealthy majority of the undergraduates and the working-class minority, which includes the narrator. A richly comic novel, *Joe College* portrays both sides as faintly ridiculous, splicing the mores of college sexual politics onto an engaging story of growing up.

In response to a question about his obsession with youth, Perrotta notes, "It's not just me, you know. The whole culture's obsessed with youth, which makes it a little painful to grow up, something of an exile from the center of things" (Zulkey); and this theme is further developed in *The Abstinence Teacher* (2007), a novel concerning adults whose attempts to understand their own youth are played out against their struggle to control teenage sexuality. A fiery religious teacher takes charge of a class built around abstinence education, while other adults confront their own religious (and other) beliefs in the face of culture wars that generate anxiety and uncertainty regarding social issues, especially those related to sexuality.

Most of Perrotta's novels focus on domestic life in America and are set in contemporary academic institutions (high school or college), or in the anonymous suburban anywhere of *Little Children* (2004). Perrotta both challenges and reifies conventional portrayals of suburban boredom:

> What propels this novel is not sexual passion or spiritual malaise but the exigencies of domestic responsibility. Much of the action takes place not at parties or in adulterous bedrooms but in playgrounds and at the town swimming pool; and when an affair does take place, the lovers are pushed into each other's arms less by an upswelling of Updikean sensuality than by boredom and simple propinquity. . . . (McGrath)

Perrotta's domestic and relational concerns reveal the banality and inertial force of everyday life in the suburbs, exploring the preoccupations of the lower middle class, especially when these come into conflict with larger authority figures and more affluent peers, as in *Joe College.* The novels typically feature emotionally immature characters, whether by disposition or by circumstance, who are buffeted by uncertainties concerning their place in the world and how they came to it. Whether the *Little Children* of that novel refers to literal children or to the adults acting out adolescent fantasies and drives remains ambiguous. In *Election*, Tracy Flick is more mature than the teacher she sleeps with, and Danny, the protagonist of *Joe College,* takes on his father's financial responsibilities by manning a lunch truck during his spring break, when many other Yale students travel to Europe or tropical resorts with the lassitude of upper-middle-class scions.

The experience of societal Others is accentuated by Perrotta's frequent examination of young people, who are typically portrayed as existing outside the adult world, with no entrance available. Most characters have only imperfect, limited vision; as Paul says when he discovers his father's affair, "It was like I'd just opened my eyes after a sixteen-year nap and was wide awake for the first time in my life . . ." (*Election* 4). The painful realization comes earlier for some than for others;

Dave Raymond in *The Wishbones* (1998) is much older but in effectively the same position. Of this persistent interest in the young, Perrotta says:

> Awful as it can be, adolescence is probably the most emotionally intense and illuminating and personally defining period we live through—sadness is part of it, but it's not the whole thing. (Zulkey)

The adults in all his novels save *Joe College* express a melancholic longing for their own adolescence, in part because they feel its reverberations in both their psychological and their social outlook. In *Little Children*, for example, Todd is a former jock known as the "Prom King" who finds release playing midnight football, while Sarah tries to achieve the ideal love life she had dreamt of earlier. But the burdens of responsibility often make these fantasies better left as such, since the complexities of adulthood add elements that easily turn into nightmares. The struggles of growing up in a society obsessed with youth and the dreams of youth are a constant theme in Perrotta's novels, with Dave Raymond in *The Wishbones*, for example, continuing to play in a wedding band in lieu of taking responsibility for himself and his relationship. Sexual relationships often stand in for larger relationships within society, and the extension—or rather distension—of adolescent sexuality is a leitmotif in the novels, reflected in such popular media as Judd Apatow's *Knocked Up* and *Talladega Nights*, or Cecily Von Ziegesar's *Gossip Girl*. The film adaptations of *Election* and *Little Children* have further raised Perrotta's literary profile; Perrotta "loved the movie version of *Election*" (Zulkey), and cowrote the screenplay for *Little Children* with director Todd Field.

Bibliography

McGrath, Charles. "Heading Home to Adultery and Angst; A New Generation of Authors Discovers the Suburbs," *New York Times*, 1 April 2004.

Perrotta, Tom. *The Abstinence Teacher*. New York: St. Martin's Press, 2007.

———. *Bad Haircut: Stories of the Seventies*. New York: Berkley Trade, 1997.

———. *Election*. New York: G. P. Putnam's Sons, 1998.

———. *Little Children*. New York: St Martin's Press, 2004.

———. "Interview with Claire Zulkey." November 12, 2004. Zulkey.com. Available online. URL: http://www.zulkey.com/diary_archive_111204.html. Accessed July 1, 2008.

———. *Joe College*. New York: St. Martin's Press, 2000.

———. *The Wishbones*. New York: Berkley Trade, 1998.

—Jake Seliger

Person of Interest, A Susan Choi (2008)

Susan Choi's third novel focuses on the life of Professor Lee, an Asian-born mathematician whose colleague receives a bomb in the mail. Lee is in his office when the bomb explodes next door, and his close proximity to the scene of the crime propels him to the status of high-profile witness in the case. But as the narrative progresses, Lee exhibits increasingly erratic and violent behavior, partly because of his guilt for not feeling sorrow over the death of his colleague, Hendley; and eventually his alarming behavior piques the interest of agent Jim Morrison and he becomes a "person of interest" in the FBI case on the bombing. Amid a media frenzy and FBI surveillance, Lee must solve the mystery of the "Brain Bomber" before his own career and the tenuous relationships he has with the people in his department and his town are ruined.

More than merely a mystery or thriller about a psychopath modeled on the Unabomber, *A Person of Interest* is a searching exploration of Lee's ordinary, even mediocre life: his failed relationships, his stagnant career, and his misdirected nastiness toward people more successful and happy than himself. The detonation of the bomb in his colleague's office prompts Lee to recall painful and embarrassing memories of his past. In particular, his jealousy of Hendley's popularity and academic brilliance reminds him of the jealousy he once harbored against a peer in graduate school, Lewis Gaither. After receiving an unsigned letter from Washington and a phone call from a former colleague, Frank Fasano, Lee becomes convinced that Gaither is trying to frame him for the bombing because he is still angry over Lee's affair with his former wife Aileen. Yet even after Aileen leaves

Gaither, gives birth to a son, and marries Lee, their relationship is not harmonious. As Lee struggles to unravel the threatening mystery of the bombing— first as witness, then as suspect—he ruminates upon his failed marriages to Aileen, and his second, "freebooting" wife, Michiko. The emotionally hermetic life he leads (symbolized by the physically empty house he returns to daily after teaching) and his suspicious "un-Asian" behavior (his lying and pride) become the main clues in Morrison's investigation, and both he and Lee pull these aspects of his life apart, in vastly different ways, to solve the case.

In the tradition of Leonard Chang, and CHANG-RAE LEE, Choi examines the Asian "Other," here in the role of the detective. But Lee must ultimately resist a host of factors implicating him in the bombing (as well as other bombings of academics) in order to solve the case; and while he sets out on an effortful journey for exoneration, his memories and chance encounters force him to confront previously ignored familial tensions. The case also offers him a chance to explore his callous and ego-driven behavior and to truly consider its effect on people like his ex-wife Aileen, his former graduate-school colleague, Gaither, and his estranged daughter, Esther, as well on as his numerous experiences with racism.

In her novels, Choi anatomizes ethnic and familial tensions, as well as specific elements of American counterculture, to explore and address the contradictory and fragmentary identity of Asians in our society. AMERICAN WOMAN and *A Person of Interest* draw upon actual accounts of violence in American history—the Patty Hearst kidnapping and the Unabomber case respectively—but reframe them by introducing Asian characters who play integral (if not always benign) roles in the narrative. In this way, Choi prompts us to consider the contradictions inherent in all identities, including Asian identity, and reveals the stereotypes we often employ to make sense of the behavior of those who do not belong to the majority. Ironically, it is precisely Lee's "un-Asian" behavior—his solitary existence, his violent and awkward outbursts—that marks him as suspicious. The expectations of Morrison, the townspeople, and his colleagues are frustrated when Lee does not

present himself as a family-oriented, respectful, and humble Asian; and out of frustration he becomes first an object of scrutiny and then a scapegoat for the death of Hendley.

While the complication of ethnicity is a driving force in the case, it is not the only aspect of Lee's life that is explored by Choi. Lee discusses his experiences as an Asian-born man who immigrated to the United States in early adulthood, but insists that he is thoroughly assimilated: "Lee was always insisting he was purely American" (90). He often refutes association with his homeland, which is never explicitly named (except by repeated negations), yet after the bombing he feels as if he is in exile from his once peaceful (albeit emotionally disengaged) American life, and is once again being treated as the suspicious "untypical" Asian. In one particularly frustrating and outlandish scene, agent Jim Morrison tells Lee that his interrogation was inconclusive because ". . . certain persons, of certain racial and cultural backgrounds, are immune to the polygraph test" (199).

After Lee is questioned in connection with Hendley's death he recalls an earlier encounter with the FBI, when he first came to the United States; then the FBI had thought he was Chinese and associated with the Communist Party. The interrogation was both frustrating and insulting, because Lee considered himself American (145). Like Chuck in Choi's earlier *The Foreign Student*, Lee once had issues with speaking English and associating with Americans because of their suspicion of his political intentions; and these issues follow Lee into his adult life, long after he has left Asia, and become a major issue during the FBI case.

Professor Lee thus goes on a journey into his own past to solve a mystery in the present, and his dispassionate inductive reasoning, reminiscent of Sherlock Holmes, reveals at last not merely the identity of the bomber, but his own problematic and often mean-spirited behavior toward friends, colleagues, and family. And although, at the end of the narrative, he is still cranky and easily exasperated, he has redeemed some of his past behavior by extending himself and reaching out to a family he previously shunned. Ironically Lee's behavior, fueled by his selfish desire to be a person of interest, is reformed only when he becomes one, for reasons he neither intended nor foresaw. As in her other novels, Choi complicates ethnicity and crime, and undercuts our expectations of "Asian-like" behavior, succeeding finally, as Francine Prose suggests, in "making us feel deeply for characters who are profoundly flawed" (6).

Bibliography

Choi, Susan. *A Person of Interest.* London: Viking Press, 2008.

American Woman Harpercollins.com. "Book Description" Available online. URL: http://www.harper collins.com/books/9780060542221/American_ Woman/index.aspx. Accessed November 7, 2008.

———. "Book Description [*The Foreign Student*]." Available online. URL: http://www.harpercollins. com/books/9780060929275/The_Foreign_Student/ index.aspx. Accessed November 7, 2008.

Miller, Laura. Review of *Person of Interest.* Salon.com. Available online. URL: http://www.salon.com/ books/review/2008/02/19/choi/. Accessed November 7, 2008.

SusanChoi.com. "About Susan Choi." Available online. URL: http://www.susanchoi.com/about.html. Accessed November 7, 2008.

—Genie Giaimo

Phillips, Arthur (1969–   ) *American novelist*

Arthur Phillips, author of *The Egyptologist* (2004), *Angelica* (2007), and *The Song Is You* (2009), is perhaps best known for his first novel, PRAGUE (2002).

Born in 1969 in Minneapolis, Minnesota, and at one time a child actor, Phillips graduated from Harvard in 1990. After college, he set off for Budapest where he lived for two years, just as the Communist regime began to crumble; and his experiences in Hungary would later serve as inspiration for *Prague.* Prior to the publication of his first novel, Phillips worked as a speechwriter for businessmen, a freelance journalist, a copy editor of pharmaceutical brochures, and a jazz musician; the speech-writing job he has wryly likened to fiction writing, offering him the opportunity to hone his story writing skills. Upon returning to the United States from Budapest, he enrolled in the Berklee School of Music, where he polished his saxophone skills for a year and a half before becoming a professional saxophone player for a short time. He also tried out for the game show *Jeopardy!* and went on to become a five-time champion.

Seven years in the writing, *Prague* vaulted its unknown author into international prominence, winning the *Los Angeles Times*/Art Seidenbaum Award for Best First Fiction in 2003. The novel opens in a familiar European setting, the Café Gerbeaud in Budapest, where five expatriates from North America have assembled. The five (four from the United States and one from Canada) consider their time in Hungary to be temporary, all of them wishing to witness the historic moments of the fall of communism in (then) Czechoslovakia. All five have jobs typical of expatriates living in Hungary: they teach English, write for a newspaper, try to get rich, work for an embassy, or do research.

Charles Gábor is the only one of the five with any previous links to Hungary. With the freeing up of markets there seems every opportunity for those with an entrepreneurial streak to make their fortune, and Gábor, the son of Hungarian immigrants, has come to Budapest to get rich. More central to the novel's core plot, however, is the story of John Price, a 24-year-old American from the West Coast who travels to Budapest to be close to his brother Scott. John takes up a job at the snobbish English-language newspaper, *BudapesToday,* in order to make a living, but it is his idealism and dreams that offer the only real respite from the relentless cynicism of the other four characters. Indeed, bitterness, disillusionment, and escapism are the primary colors of *Prague*'s emotional palette.

Sincerity, a game the five play in *Prague*—wherein each tells four tales in turn, only one of which is true, and the other players must guess which are false in order to collect points—appears in Phillips's second novel, *The Egyptologist.* Set in 1922 when Howard Carter discovers Tutankhamen's tomb, the protagonist Ralph Trilipush is searching for the tomb of Atum-hadu, following his translation of the latter's erotic poetry. While Trilipush is spending his fiancée's fortune searching for the tomb, which may or may not exist, an Australian detective, Harold Ferrell, is trying to hunt down Trilipush and prove the Egyptologist is a fraud and murderer. This would suggest that the novel is a kind of murder mystery, but if so, the genre is profoundly complicated and enriched by the novel's postmodern structure, which, in stark contrast to *Prague*'s thoughtful dialectic, is built from a collection of diary entries, articles, and letters by Trilipush and Ferrell, sweeping from the fields of World War I to Boston, Oxford, Australia, and Egypt.

Phillips's third novel, *Angelica,* is set in 1880s Victorian England, at the height of spiritualism's vogue. It too shows overt traces of genre, here one of the oldest and most hackneyed: the ghost story. But as in *The Egyptologist,* Phillips layers and fragments his plot, weaving in elements of the mystery novel and psychological thrillers. The deeply troubled Barton family appears to be haunted by a restless, sexually charged spirit that is terrorizing the daughter and mother at night; a spirit that may, in the end, be nothing more than a highly suggestive product of the mother's overwrought imagination. Constance Barton is of frail health, sexually timid, and frightened by her husband, the family patriarch, Joseph. Their daughter Angelica, a keenly ambivalent mix of naiveté and cunning, is (apparently) first approached by the specter on the night when she is removed from her parents' bedroom. Issues of sexual repression and gender roles, of private and social identity, of memory, childhood, fear, and fearlessness, are central themes in the novel, and Phillips employs a yet more complicated style, shattering the truth into a narrative hall of mirrors from which the reader is lucky simply to emerge.

Phillips has also contributed the short story "Wenceslas Square" to the important collection, *Wild East: Stories from the Last Frontier* (2003). Set at the end of the cold war, the tale focuses on a CIA agent spying on a Czech woman, who is herself working for the Czech Secret Police and spying on him.

In his latest novel, *The Song Is You* (2009), Phillips fuses two disparate elements of his earlier life—advertising and jazz performance—in a suspenseful love story dominated both structurally and thematically by musical motifs. What at first appears as an escapist maneuver (reminiscent of *Prague*) from a vacuous and inauthentic life into

the rich but unreal "other world" of music, turns out to be an improbable rebirth, on behalf of jaded adman Julian Donahue, into a genuinely musical existence.

Phillips currently lives in New York with his wife and their two sons.

Bibliography

Arthurphillips.com. "*Angelica* synopsis." Available online. URL: http://www.arthurphillips.info/Angelica/synopsis.html. Accessed May 12, 2009.

Phillips, Arthur. *Angelica.* New York: Random House, 2007.

———. *The Egyptologist.* New York: Random House, 2004.

———. *Prague.* New York: Random House, 2002.

———. *Wild East: Stories from the Last Frontier,* edited by Boris Fishman. Boston: Justin, Charles & Co., 2003.

—Victoria Nagy

Picoult, Jodi (1966–) *American novelist*

Jodi Picoult studied creative writing at Princeton University, and received a master's degree in education from Harvard. A prolific writer, she has published 16 novels in 16 years—and her 17th is due for release in 2010. Yet, as pointed out by Louise France in the *Observer,* her novels have received little critical attention from the literary establishment, despite her being Britain's bestselling female writer and having received a host of accolades, including a nomination for Author of the Year in the 2007 British Book Awards. In this respect Picoult is a paradox, a hugely popular, at times controversial writer, ignored by academia, who questions notions of what constitutes literature simply by doing what she does best. She has received great popular acclaim, regularly topping best-seller lists, and criticism for her occasionally excessive sentences. As Janet Maslin in the *New York Times* puts it, Picoult "is a solid, lively storyteller, even if she occasionally bogs down in lyrical turns of phrase." Yet despite—or perhaps because of—her at times quaintly sentimental phraseology, Picoult is a writer with a keen aptitude for exposing the complexities of individual existence.

She is topical and controversial, and does not hide from subjects considered taboo. France suggests that Picoult "has a formula: choose a subject which is soon to become controversial and tell the story through a rotating cast of characters"; yet her tales are not formulaic. She experiments with point of view, narrative level, and leaps in time, all of which ensure that her novels remain fresh and vital. Interestingly, Picoult's first novel, *Songs of the Humpback Whale,* is her least popular but most experimental text, utilizing multiple first-person perspectives from different points—and even directions—in the story. Rebecca, for example, narrates her story backwards, while her mother, Jane, recounts events in a relatively linear manner, suggesting the randomness with which people connect and disengage with others and with life events. It is up to the characters in the novel—like its readers—to find and focus on the most important points of intersection, building up a sensible and meaningful composite of the whole. Picoult employs a similar technique in *My Sister's Keeper.*

Moreover, the range of relevant and often controversial themes that Picoult explores demonstrates not only her accurate and in-depth research, but also her interest in and passion for contemporary issues. *Songs of the Humpback Whale* (1992) treats of adolescent first love and the long-term effects of childhood abuse; *Harvesting the Heart* (1993) is a nuanced look at postnatal depression and the difficulties of learning to mother in the absence of being mothered; *Picture Perfect* (1995) examines issues of domestic violence with tact and sensitivity; *Mercy* (1996) investigates the controversial questions surrounding euthanasia and mercy killing; *The Pact* (1998) opens up the hidden world of teenage suicide; *Keeping Faith* (1999) investigates stigmata; *Plain Truth* (2000) explores the often damaging schism between the Amish community and the United States; *SALEM FALLS* (2001) is a complex novel replete with contemporary concerns such as the struggles of adolescence, interest in pagan religions, and the impossibility of hiding from a past fraught with accusations of child abuse; *Perfect Match* (2002) sensitively examines pedophilia and the extremes that parents will go to in order to protect their children; *Second Glance* (2003) is an eerie excursion into the world of ghosts, lost love, and eugenics; *My Sister's Keeper* (2004) examines stem-cell research and notions of "designer babies"; *Vanishing Acts* (2005) returns to themes of mothering and parenting; *The Tenth Circle* (2006) explores adolescent sexuality and date rape; and *Nineteen Minutes* (2007) investigates the alarming phenomenon of high-school shootings in America. More recently, *Change of Heart* (2008), which, like *Nineteen Minutes,* debuted at number one on the *New York Times* Best Sellers list, explores both mother-daughter relationships and prisoner rights; *Handle with Care* (2009) revisits some of the moral questions in *My Sister's Keeper,* with its tale of parental choice, responsibility, and pediatric care; and the forthcoming *House Rules* (2010) centers on a teenager with Asperger's Syndrome.

Picoult's preeminent gift, perhaps, lies in her suspension of moral judgment regarding characters and situations that typically evoke strident reflex responses. Her protagonists are often flawed but always likable, and her distrust of reflex judgment, in its deference to the complexities of real life, often brings the outré and even incomprehensible within the grasp of our quotidian understanding—a great service in times like these. In her most recent novel, *Nineteen Minutes,* for example, readers who may be swift to condemn the perpetrators of the increasing number of high-school shootings in America are challenged to sympathize with Peter, simultaneously a mass-murderer and a troubled, bullied victim.

Woven among the many moral and legal explorations examined in Picoult's fiction are a number of recurrent topics, among them, mothering and parenting, the challenges of adolescence, and marginalized or clandestine communities such as the Abenaki native American tribe in *Second Glance,* the Yup'ik Eskimos in *The Tenth Circle,* and the Amish community in *Plain Truth.*

Bibliography

France, Louise. "The Great Unknown." *The Observer* (April 15, 2007). Available online. URL: http://books.guardian.co.uk/departments/generalfiction/story/0,,2055466,00.html. Accessed May 14, 2009.

Maslin, Janet. "A Rescuer Retrieves Her Own Lost Past." Review of *Vanishing Acts. New York Times*

(24 February 2005). Available online. URL: http://
www.nytimes.com/2005/02/24/books/24/masl.html.
Accessed May 14, 2009.

Jodi Picoult.com Official Web site. Available online.
URL: www.jodipicoult.com. Accessed May 14,
2009.

Picoult, Jodi. 1993. *Harvesting the Heart*. London: Penguin, 1995.

———. 1999. *Keeping Faith*. London: Hodder & Stoughton, 2006.

———. 1996. *Mercy*. London: Hodder & Stoughton,
2007.

———. 2004. *My Sister's Keeper*. London: Hodder &
Stoughton, 2005.

———. 2007. *Nineteen Minutes*. London: Hodder &
Stoughton, 2007.

———. 1998. *The Pact*. London: Hodder & Stoughton,
2005.

———. 2002. *Perfect Match*. London: Hodder &
Stoughton, 2006.

———. 1995. *Picture Perfect*. New York: Berkley Publishing, 2002.

———. 2000. *Plain Truth*. London: Hodder & Stoughton, 2004.

———. 2001. *Salem Falls*. London: Hodder & Stoughton, 2005.

———. 2003. *Second Glance*. London: Hodder &
Stoughton, 2006.

———. 1992. *Songs of the Humpback Whale*. New York:
Washington Square Press, 2001.

———. 2006. *The Tenth Circle*. London: Hodder &
Stoughton, 2006.

———. 2005. *Vanishing Acts*. London: Hodder &
Stoughton, 2006.

—Charley Baker

Pierre, DBC (1961–) *Australian-born novelist*

DBC Pierre is the author of two novels, VERNON
GOD LITTLE (2003) and LUDMILA'S BROKEN
ENGLISH (2006), and came to international prominence in 2003 when he won the Man Booker Prize
for the first.

Peter Warren Finlay was born to English parents in Australia in 1961, but was raised in Mexico
as his father pursued a career in science, and both
his pseudonym and fiction reflect the uneasy complexity of these roots. He notes, "I grew up with a
real sense of cultural homelessness, I haven't been
successful in fitting in anywhere. I clearly wasn't
Mexican, although I could move in that culture
as easily as anywhere. I'm a British national but
wasn't quite from here. . . . There's nothing I love
more than to just be part of something, for someone to pay you a hello" (Brocke). "Pierre" derives
from an Australian cartoon character whose name
was bestowed on him by a childhood friend, while
"DBC" (Dirty But Clean) refers to the descent
into a drug-induced haze which he describes
as "an unravelling, then an attempt at reravel-
ling . . . From birth to the age of ten, things were
fairly cruising. Ten to twenty, I became pretty corrupted. . . . I was already into every type of drug I
could find" (Weich).

The loss of his father to cancer when Pierre
was 19 merely accelerated this descent, and led
finally to a series of bizarre but colorful escapades.
Pierre has admitted, for example, to being involved
in illegal trading, ploughing his friend's money from
a corrupt house sale into a search for the lost gold
of Aztec emperor Montezuma II (he was later to
return to Mexico in 2006 to film a documentary
exploring the actions of the Spanish conquistado-
res). He claims that he arrived at his 30th birthday
"a couple hundred grand in debt":

> Some of it I'd achieved deceitfully; other
> was just good people who had faith and ei-
> ther invested or loaned me at some point,
> and their faith had been completely dashed.
> (Brocke)

It was at this point, and in the face of his doctor's
assurance that in his present course he had at best
six months to live, that Pierre set about a comprehensive evaluation of his life. The result was an
attempt to "reprogram" himself, an effort that ultimately saw him leave Mexico for Ireland, where he
began to shape *Vernon God Little* from his previous
writings while supporting himself as a part-time
graphic designer.

Pierre's victory in the Man Booker Prize contest
in 2003 was as great a shock to the author as to many
critics. The novels on both the short and long list

were impressive, and many, such as MONICA ALI's *BRICK LANE*, Zoë Heller's *Notes on a Scandal* and MARK HADDON's *The CURIOUS INCIDENT OF THE DOG IN THE NIGHT-TIME*, have gone on to greater international success than *Vernon*. On hearing his name read out by the judges, Pierre's response was "What the fuck have I done now?" He has stated that his prize money will go some way to pay off his debts.

Vernon God Little is primarily concerned with the aftermath of a high-school shooting in small-town Texas, presumably in the present day. The narrative begins three days after the killings have taken place, and the protagonist, Vernon, is being interrogated about his best friend, Jesus Navarro, who has carried out the massacre. The protagonist's diction is reminiscent of J. D. Salinger's *The Catcher in the Rye*, and it is no surprise that Vernon has been described by the *New York Times* as "Holden Caulfield on Ritalin"; but Pierre also encourages us to draw comparisons with the work of Mark Twain, as well as elements of contemporary pop culture, with citations from Dr. Dre and Eminem, and the cartoon South Park. Sam Sifton writes that "in much the same way that noir novelists like James Ellroy seem steeped in the rhythms and textures of jazz, there is a jagged, punk rock sensibility to Pierre's prose, absolutely his own."

Autobiographical touches are everywhere present, from Vernon's casual profanity and drug "storage" to his thoroughgoing dislike of authority; but any attempt to see the novel merely as a diatribe against those who caused Pierre pain would be missing the point. The broad, satirical deconstruction of his milieu, and especially the media that serves and in many ways defines it, is sure and biting. Moreover, Pierre notes that "parts of the book are entirely farcical, totally over-the-top. I think it was the *Guardian* who compared the novel to South Park. I read that and I thought, *Yes*. . . . This was pre-September 11 and the more sobering shift of these last few years. It was the height of unfettered trivia" (Brocke).

Pierre's second novel, *Ludmila's Broken English*, did not meet with the same critical acclaim, although some praised it for its exploration of complex issues of globalization, and its deft parody of the Blair/Brown government in the last years of Tony Blair's leadership.

The work revolves around a series of dramatic dichotomies between Western Europe, especially Britain, and the developing Eastern Bloc, tensions that might appear outdated were it not for Pierre's skilful handling. The most notable of these, contrasts the media-drenched existence of Gordon-Marie and Blair, omphalopagus twins who have recently left the Albion House Institution to take up residence in the community, with the struggles of Ludmila Durev and her family, who carve out a fragile existence on the fictional island of Ublilsk. Somewhat ponderous in the convolution of its two disparate narratives, as well as in its author's acknowledged tendency to "take its characters apart slowly and with great relish," the novel often seems to fall short of its comic potential; but in its sheer youthful energy and political aspiration, as well as its occasionally stinging satire, the work marks a significant development in Pierre's emerging oeuvre.

Vernon God Little has been adapted for the stage.

Pierre is currently working on his third novel.

Bibliography

Pierre, DBC. "DBC Pierre's Strong First Impression—An Interview with DBC Pierre." By Dave Weich. Powells.com. Available online. URL: http://www.powells.com/authors/pierre.html. Accessed May 11, 2009.

———. "'How did I get here?'—An Interview with DBC Pierre." By Emma Brockes, *Guardian*, 16 October 2003.

———. *Ludmila's Broken English*. London: Faber & Faber 2006.

———. *Vernon God Little*. London: Faber & Faber, 2003.

Sifton, Sam. "Holden Caulfield on Ritalin," *New York Times*, 9 November 2003.

—Miles Leeson

Pilgrims Elizabeth Gilbert (1997)

Gilbert's award-winning first book is a collection of short stories about unremarkable people who have embarked on individual, often remarkable pilgrimages. The varied characters that come together in the book are, like Geoffrey Chaucer's original band in *The Canterbury Tales,* a gallimaufry of pilgrims drawn from different walks of life: two young ranch-hands, a female tavern owner, four "kids," a vegetable market worker, Hungarian immigrant, and a woman who is almost 70. M. H. Abrams writes of Chaucer's *Prologue* that each character "grows and is revealed by the story they tell," and a similar process of narrative and psychological development is evident in *Pilgrims* (79).

Each of the 12 narratives that make up the collection begins and ends at an unspecified and apparently random moment in the life of the pilgrim in question. Gilbert's use of this slice-of-life device could easily have resulted in disjointed and desultory storytelling, but this is avoided by her skillful narration and memorable characterization. Influenced no doubt by her journalistic background, she brings the various characters to life in a straightforward and spare manner that focuses on their particular moment in time without any undue preamble. Every chapter is a self-contained tale, and while the agonies and frustrations of these latter-day pilgrims are strongly delineated, the eventual destination of their journeying remains resolutely unspecified. When all the stories have been told, however, it is clear that each person's individual pilgrimage is sustained and enhanced by deep-seated character traits, like strength, determination, or hope, more than any contingent or physical qualities.

Gilbert's storytelling is atmospheric without being oppressive, and the excerpts taken from each of her pilgrims' lives feel timeless, capturing the enduring emotion of the moment more than the ephemeral action. The tales are memorable for their exacting attention to detail, from the (often charged) minutiae of daily life and conversation, to the problems of making ends meet, solving personal dilemmas or, as in "The Names of Flowers and Girls," coming to terms with the inevitabilities of life, decay, and death; and there is a compelling immediacy to the writing, rooted in its sparse dialogue and terse descriptions, neither of which obtrude, or reveal more than is necessary.

The opening story, "Pilgrims," focuses on the burgeoning relationship between Buck, a cowboy, and Martha Knox, a temporary ranch-hand. Beneath the tale's convincing depiction of hard work and hard knocks, lies the seductive notion of the American dream of wild frontiers and freedom. During a tame evening out on the prairie with a group of would-be businessmen hunters, Martha is scornful of their safe adventurism: "Talk about a bunch of pilgrims, Buck," she says, "These guys have never even been in a back yard" (11). To be a pilgrim, Martha implies, is to be a risk-taker. Buck suggests leaving the businessmen to their own devices, stealing a couple of the horses, and heading for the hills, daring Martha to live her words. But Buck himself is only dreaming, and when he begins to fantasize about holding up banks and heading for Mexico, Martha takes the initiative, setting off on a dangerous gallop through the field, riding bareback in the darkness with Buck clinging on for dear life. They fall off the speeding horse, but something firm and real has taken place in Buck. Noticing that Martha "looked as good and important as new grass and berries" as she lies on the frozen ground beside him, he suddenly sees an omen, a shooting star that passes "like a cigarette still burning flung over our heads" (17), and one senses the real pilgrimage has just begun.

"The Finest Wife" focuses on a similarly epochal moment in the life of Rose, who at almost 70 appears to be recalling her youthful heyday as she drives a school bus along its regular route. This time, however, she does not pick up her usual group of children, but all her former lovers and her dead husband, who, as the journey unfolds, fondly recall their memories of her. As the story ends, she falls into a doze "with all of her old men together and behind her and so pleased just to see her again" (210). Gilbert's description of her marriage is typical of the collection's terse and vivid diction: "she ended up eventually married, once again on the basis of a fine walk in a sweet bathing suit," and her husband "bought a musky flock of sheep and a small, tight house" (202).

Pilgrims, then, gives voice to a peripatetic band of disparate (and at times desperate) characters whose stories are told, in the end, almost as accompaniment to a collective journey, as in Chaucer; but instead of traveling toward a common destination, and in the world, they are making a personal journey through the complexities of their own lives, while the ultimate pilgrimage is a composite one, performed by the reader himself.

Pilgrims was selected as a *New York Times* Notable Book, and won best first fiction awards from the *Paris Review,* the *Southern Review,* and *Ploughshares.*

Bibliography

Abrams, M. H., gen. ed. *The Norton Anthology of English Literature.* Vol. 1. 6th ed. London: W. W. Norton, 1993.

Gilbert, Elizabeth. *Pilgrims.* London: Penguin Books, 2007.

—Linda Claridge Middup

Prep Curtis Sittenfeld (2005)

CURTIS SITTENFELD's first novel follows the unexceptional but archetypal outsider Lee Fiora during her four-year tenure at Ault, a New England boarding school. The novel was selected as one of the *New York Times*'s 10 best books of 2005, short-listed for an Orange Prize, and optioned by Paramount Pictures, while drawing honorific comparisons to J. D. Salinger's *Catcher in the Rye* and John Knowles's *A Separate Peace.*

As a 14-year-old arriving in Massachusetts from South Bend, Indiana, Lee quickly discovers that her new world is completely alien to her: She is pensive and exceedingly analytical, and judges herself to be a "dork," thoroughly unsuited to the upper echelons of Ault society; her father owns a mattress store in South Bend, while her classmates are the accomplished scions of investment bankers. Lee is neither athletically nor academically gifted, and she knows it. Some of her classmates, however, see something remarkable in Lee, and their attempts to become close to her drive the central action of the novel. The reader is constantly struck by Lee's complete, almost implausible inability to capitalize on these opportunities for inclusion, handicapped as she is by an unwavering belief in her own ordinariness.

Lee's first year at Ault is largely friendless; she spends her time avoiding her roommates (and Saturday-night dances), and trying to understand the intricacies of the school's social structure. When Gates Medkowski, a senior and the first-ever female prefect at Ault, shows kindness to her, the younger girl is naturally impressed, but is unable to respond with any poise or even courtesy; Lee recalls, "when we made eye contact, [Gates] smiled or said, 'Hey, Lee,' . . . and I usually blushed, feeling caught. I didn't necessarily want to talk to her again because I would probably be awkward, but I wanted to know things about her." This type of interaction is repeated throughout the novel, as Lee becomes increasingly hamstrung by her extreme self-consciousness.

By her sophomore year, Lee has made a few friends, but she has also demonstrated an intriguing and quite plausible capacity for meanness. Though she dolefully claims, early on, that "the best I'd be able to hope for from my classmates would be pity," Lee shows a distinct lack of concern for the feelings of others. She is initially grateful for the friendship of Conchita Maxwell, for example, but devastates Conchita when she decides to become roommates with a mutual friend. Lee tells Conchita, "I'm sorry . . . I really am. But you need to calm down." A disastrous visit with her parents the following fall results in Lee's father slapping her across the face, and calling her an "ungrateful little bitch." In the end Lee comes to occupy a strange kind of social purgatory, unable to fit in at Ault, but now alienated from her old world in South Bend, and her family.

The junior year is consumed by preparation for the senior year for Lee and the other teens of the Ault School. Prefects are chosen, and Lee has a testy relationship with Dave, a local young man who works in the dining hall at the school. Though he shows genuine interest in Lee, she does not have the confidence to acknowledge her relationship with him—especially after another student voices her disapproval: "I'm sure he's okay, but you're an Ault student. Your life is here . . . I don't think you want to separate yourself from the rest of our grade." The irony, of course, is that Lee has been separate from the rest of her grade since her arrival at Ault, while in Dave she found someone from a similar background, who likely would have appreciated her *more* had he known she was not a "typical" Ault student.

Lee's relationship with Cross Sugarman, the most popular boy at Ault, dramatizes the ramifications of her lack of self-esteem. Cross is the aggressor, and makes his interest in Lee clear when he comes to her room one night and climbs into bed with her. Several weeks of late-night trysts commence, during which Cross and Lee cultivate their attraction for and understanding of one another. Their relationship is poisoned, however, by Lee's omnipresent insecurities. Early on she insists, "You're not going to tell people about this, right?"; and later, after the relationship has ended, she tells Cross, "You would never have been my boyfriend . . . I'm sure of it." Cross can only reply, "[It] must be nice to be sure of things."

Lee's unspectacular four years at Ault are concluded by a particularly unpopular *New York Times* article about the Ault School, in which Lee is quoted as saying, "Of course I felt left out. I'm nobody from Indiana." The article focuses on the staid nature of the boarding school, and its unwillingness to relinquish its exclusivity; and carried the subtitle, *What It's Like to be White, Middle-class—and an Outsider*. The Ault community takes Lee's comments as a betrayal, and her father says, "You're lucky it's over . . . because if it wasn't, it still would be over for you." Lee's time at Ault ends much as it began, with her consigned to the fringes of a group to which she never really belonged, and which she could never fully understand.

Prep was rejected by 14 publishers before being finally accepted by Random House, but Sittenfeld's editor there, Lee Boudreaux, claims that he knew *Prep* would be a success when he discovered that "a bevy of young editorial assistants at a glossy fashion magazine . . . [had] taken to referring to good-looking men they know as a 'Cross Sugarman'" (Stuever 2005). While the combination of teenagers and boarding schools has long been a winning one in literary terms, *Prep* is most successful, ironically, because of Sittenfeld's ability to draw the reader into a place that seems make-believe, peopled by teenagers unrecognizable to the majority of the outside world. Sittenfeld is a supremely capable native guide to this other place, one that is difficult to fathom from the outside. Once inside, however, it is clear that these teenagers are tormented by the same trials of maturation as teenagers everywhere;

and it is a mark both of Sittenfeld's skill and her instincts as a storyteller that their travails, familiar and even predictable as they are, never settle into triteness or cliché.

Bibliography

Sittenfeld, Curtis. *Prep.* New York: Random House, 2005.

Stuever, Hank. "Move Over, Holden," *Washington Post*, 23 February 2005, sec. C, p. 1.

Purple Hibiscus   Chimamanda Ngozi Adichie (2003)

CHIMAMANDA NGOZI ADICHIE's debut novel continues the tradition of prominent West African fiction established by Chinua Achebe with his masterpiece *Things Fall Apart*. But whereas *Things Fall Apart* offered a literary chronicle of colonialism's beginnings in Nigeria, *Purple Hibiscus* explores contemporary Nigerian society and its struggle to cope with the devastation that colonialism and its institutions have left in their wake.

Adichie's novel centers on the fraught and complex evolution of a Nigerian family in Enugu, consisting of the story's 15-year-old narrator, Kambili, her brother, Jaja, and their parents, Eugene (Papa) and Beatrice (Mama). Adichie wastes no time in observing her indebtedness to Achebe, opening *Purple Hibiscus* with "Things started to fall apart at home when my brother, Jaja, did not go to communion and Papa flung his heavy missal across the room and broke the figurines on the étagère" (3); thereby resuming Achebe's investigation into the effects of insensitive colonialism on West African society. Papa's strict adherence to the colonizer's religion (Catholicism) and his unbending enforcement of that religion stage much of the novel's action and critique.

In *Things Fall Apart*, Achebe succinctly and memorably articulated the indigenous problematic: "Does the white man understand our custom about land? How can he when he does not even speak our tongue? But he says that our customs are bad; and our own brothers who have taken up his religion also say that our customs are bad. How do you think we can fight when our own brothers have turned against us? The white man is very clever.

He came quietly and peaceably with his religion. We were amused at his foolishness and allowed him to stay. Now he has won our brothers, and our clan can no longer act like one. He has put a knife on the things that held us together and we have fallen apart" (176).

The restrictions placed on Kambili and Jaja as a result of Papa's religious fervor result in these West African children looking and behaving precisely in accordance with the misguided stereotype that Achebe describes. Papa's children are to be stoic, reserved, obedient, and never speak Igbo words; at one point he boasts that his Kambili and Jaja are "not like those loud children people are raising these days, with no home training and no fear of God" (58). Papa thus epitomizes the "converted" West African described in Achebe's dictum, compelling his family to adhere to the oppressive misperception of Africans that was imposed by colonialism.

Though a strict disciplinarian, and deeply tainted by this misperception, Papa is treated with sensitivity and compassion by Adichie. He loves his family and country, and only does what he truly feels is best for both. His love of country prompts him to circulate a political magazine called *The Standard*, which is focused on bringing freedom and harmony to war-torn Nigeria; yet his love of family manifests itself in the near tyrannical imposition of the very colonial standards that have been the major source of Nigeria's servitude and disharmony. This contradiction is pointed out to Papa by another character who, in response to his proud denunciation of "loud children," exclaims, "Imagine what the Standard would be if we were all quiet" (58).

The necessity of voice and sound in bringing about change—whether social or personal—is a major theme in *Purple Hibiscus*. Where *The Standard* serves as an instrument for bringing about social change, the tale of the novel's main character and narrator highlights the critical role of voice and sound in bringing about personal change. When Papa sends Kambili and Jaja to their aunt Ifeoma's house in Nsukka, in order to protect them from the violence of the military coup at home, they are introduced to an entirely new way of being. Aunty Ifeoma is a university lecturer, and her children—Amaka, Obiora, and Chima—are free to laugh, cry, speak Igbo, be loud, and even voice their discontent to adults. Coming of age in this environment allows Kambili to break free of her father's damaging limitations.

In Toni Morrison's *Song of Solomon*, Milkman Dead's aunt Pilate functions as a soul-enriching alternative to his father's oppressive insistence on fostering white values. So here, Aunty Ifeoma's relaxed attitude and openness to both Catholicism and traditional religion allow Kambili a voice to assert her identity as never before. Ifeoma has a purple hibiscus in her garden, whose growth and bloom are echoed in the flourishing of Kambili, as she regains her ability to speak and laugh, and even develops a relationship with the young priest Father Amadi.

With Kambili's new self-awareness comes a heightened sense of the troubles at home and throughout Nigeria. But now, with her roots strengthened and nourished by true freedom, and her father an object of sympathy as much as authority, she can embrace as life-giving what before had seemed life-constricting. Thus, the lowering clouds she muses on at the end of the novel, instead of enclosing and constraining her, are so low she "could reach out and squeeze the moisture from them," and she notes with hard-won hope and maturity that "The new rains will come down soon."

Bibliography

Achebe, Chinua. *Things Fall Apart.* New York: Anchor Books, 1994.

Adichie, Chimamanda Ngozi. *Purple Hibiscus.* New York: Anchor Books, 2003.

Morrison, Toni. *Song of Solomon.* New York: Plume, 1987.

—Gil Cook

Reservation Blues Sherman Alexie (1995)

Reservation Blues, winner of the Before Columbus Foundation's American Book Award, marked poet and short story writer Sherman Alexie's debut as a novelist. While tracing the rise and demise of Coyote Springs, a blues band constituted wholly of Spokane and Flathead Indians, the novel examines the ambivalent, even bittersweet demands that are made on young artists—especially young Native American artists—who aspire to success beyond the often oppressive limits of their upbringing.

The novel ironizes the competing and often conflicting demands for authenticity made upon young Native Americans by the rival mainstream and traditional cultures, by juxtaposing the successful career of (the significantly named) Betty and Veronica with the failure of Coyote Springs. As the novel closes, the two white women have begun an ascent to fame as an Indian band whose first hit insists that one can have blonde hair and white skin but be "Indian in my bones" (294). In lambasting the cosmetically tasteful "Indianness" the two women embody, Alexie employs dark humor to engage readers in his meditation on the exorbitant price that Native cultures have paid in their negotiations with the dominant culture. As Leslie Marmon Silko comments in her review of the novel, "The blues of the novel's title denote more than the style of music that the band plays. The term likewise denotes the melancholy trade-offs that mainstream success demands of the band members, and the long history within which their negotiations with success are situated." Indeed, as

the novel ends, the band members, now veterans of such negotiation, effectively surrender: One member commits suicide, and another spirals into alcoholism. Although the ending seems to suggest that readers should feel hopeful for Chess, Checkers, and Thomas, the three survivors of the band, their survival is enabled only by abandoning the dream both of success for the band and of inclusion on the reservation.

Alexie situates Coyote Springs's misadventures with the music industry at the intersection of two currents that have been largely considered discrete by ethnographers and musicologists: the history of blues music, commonly attributed to black culture and African roots, and that of the subjugation of Native American nations in the 19th century. It is the arrival on the Spokane Reservation of the African-American blues tradition, embodied in the legendary Robert Johnson, which sets the novel in motion. According to legend, Johnson sold his soul to the devil in exchange for virtuosity as a guitarist; in *Reservation Blues,* Johnson is said to have faked his own death to escape his debt, outrunning the "gentleman" ever since. He arrives seeking a woman he has seen in his dreams, Big Mom, who he believes can help him, but he brings with him the possessed guitar, which he leaves in Thomas Builds-the-Fire's van. In building his band around this possessed instrument, Thomas literally incorporates the African-American cultural history of the blues.

Yet, for Alexie, the arrival of Johnson and his guitar marks the *return* of the blues to the place it came from. As we learn more about Big Mom, a character around whom many of the magical realist elements of Alexie's novel center, we discover that she is at least a century old, and heard the screams of the Spokane horses as they were murdered by the U.S. cavalry led by Philip Sheridan. Those screams, which echo at moments when Coyote Springs is facing betrayal by the dominant culture, were distilled by Big Mom into the blues. Later, according to the narrator, she taught those blues to figures like Janis Joplin, Jimi Hendrix, Elvis, and even Benny Goodman's band members. She also takes on Coyote Springs as students before their fateful audition, and heals Robert Johnson by returning him to his true instrument, the harmonica.

Thus, Alexie posits, the blues originated with Native Americans, and as Coyote Springs develops from a cover band to singing its own compositions, the members reinhabit their own cultural history. As M. Celia Cain argues, Alexie is one of a growing number of Native American activists, thinkers, and blues artists who suggest that Native American musical traditions should be understood as the proper source of the blues.

Coyote Springs forms around the guitar, but is driven by the visions and songs of Thomas Builds-the-Fire, who is familiar to readers of "Do You Know What It Means to Say Phoenix, Arizona," a story from Alexie's short story collection *The Lone Ranger and Tonto Fistfight in Heaven*, which he adapted for the film *Smoke Signals*. Victor, Thomas's nemesis as well as the person to whom Thomas assigns the possessed guitar, is also a character from that earlier story, in which the two enemies drive cross-country to recover Victor's father's remains. Here they are joined by the handsome and responsible Junior, Victor's longtime ally, to form the core of the band. At a bar on the Flathead Reservation, their first paying gig, they are joined by sisters Chess and Checkers Warm Water, who sing vocals and play keyboards.

The band enjoys growing success, soon winning a Battle of the Bands competition in Seattle and then receiving an invitation to do a demo in New York City for Cavalry Records. Aptly named, as this is the company that will bring about Coyote Springs's downfall, Cavalry Records is represented by George Wright and Philip Sheridan, who not only share names with the officers who subdued the Spokane and other Northwest tribes, but are in fact the same two men, who have been pursuing the same mission for over a century. At this crucial audition, the guitar rebels and the band fail to secure a contract, effectively ending the band.

The early chapters of the novel dwell on the struggles of the individual band members to work as a collective unit, providing through dreams and voiced and unvoiced recollection many of the pieces of the individuals' pasts that illuminate both their need for and fear of uniting with the rest of the band. Likewise, at the band's demise, Alexie's concern is to show how the individual members deal with the loss of this dream.

Alexie is praised by critics for his witty and passionate interrogation of stereotypes, and the depiction of Thomas embodies this interrogation. Not especially handsome, wearing glasses, and with a bad build, he is nonetheless the lead singer, and thus the person that all who meet or deal with the band want to speak to; yet prior to the band, Thomas was disregarded or even avoided by everyone.

The songs that Coyote Springs performs are a key element both in Alexie's critique of contemporary cultural stereotypes of Native Americans and in fleshing out the complexity of issues facing the latter. Each of the novels' chapters begins with the words to a song that the band performs, and these comment on the chapter's contents, giving voice to an ambivalence that pervades much of Alexie's work. It is clear that Alexie's characters love the ways of the "rez" and long to belong to it, even as they fear being stifled by it. And perhaps, fear they should. Arguing that the novel is in fact a betrayal of Native Americans, Gloria Bird notes that Alexie's reservation is almost wholly devoid of characters who have successfully negotiated a viable way to be a Native American.

Alexie has since written two more novels, adding to his three collections of short fiction, young adult fiction, and more than half a dozen collections and chapbooks of poetry, as well as editorials, articles of cultural commentary, and screenplays. *Reservation Blues* was well reviewed and continues to earn critical praise. Leslie Marmon Silko's review of the novel welcomed Alexie as "one of the best writers we have," praising especially his unsentimental portrayal of living conditions on the

Spokane Reservation, and his nuanced portrayal of the ambivalence of success.

Bibliography

Alexie, Sherman. *The Lone Ranger and Tonto Fistfight in Heaven.* New York: Atlantic Monthly Press, 1993.

———. *Reservation Blues.* New York: Atlantic Monthly Press, 1995.

Bird, Gloria. "The Exaggeration of Despair in Sherman Alexie's 'Reservation Blues.'" *Wicazo Sa Review* 11, no. 2 (Autumn 1993): 47–52.

Cain, M. Celia. "Red, Black and Blues: Race, Nation and Recognition for the Bluez." *Canadian Journal for Traditional Music* 33 (2006): 1–14.

Silko, Leslie Marmon. "Bingo Big," *The Nation,* 12 June 1995, 856–860.

—Danielle Glassmeyer

Right Here, Right Now   Trey Ellis (1999)

Trey Ellis's National Book Award–winning novel depicts the formation of a new religion known as Axe (pronounced "a-shay"), a Brazilian word for power, by self-made billionaire Ashton Robinson. Robinson is a former Yale student and a worshiped motivational speaker, but he grew up in an economically depressed pocket of Flint, Michigan, and had come to perceive himself as worthless. Early in the narrative, he admits to still hiding that persona behind his success, but after his family moved from Michigan to Santa Cruz, California, he took up surfing and skirt-chasing and reinvented himself as a slick entrepreneur, eventually charming his way into the self-help industry with best-selling books, CDs, and pricey seminars.

Like most of Ellis's books, *Right Here, Right Now* employs inventive narrative devices. The compelling tale begins with Ashton relaying thoughts for his next book, an assured best seller, on a microcassette recorder that he carries with him throughout the novel. These are interspersed with sound clips from Ashton's self-help seminars, and the tape becomes the overarching storytelling device of the novel.

Both the narrative and Ashton's life take an outlandish twist one evening at his mansion after he smokes pot and ingests expired cough syrup.

Recorder running, Ashton slips from reality and tumbles into his pool, watching "swimming stars" and "shifting colors, breaking and falling" (Ellis, 89). A Brazilian dwarf then appears, warning Ashton to pursue deeper ideals than financial success; the dwarf turns into a gorgeous woman who Ashton dances with and fondles, powerfully aroused. Then the tape goes silent.

A few days later, Ashton has another bizarre encounter, at a Brazilian restaurant, which leaves him unconscious. He comes to in time to lead a seminar in Chicago but suddenly alters his message, unleashing a tirade about the transforming power of "Axe." Most of the seminar participants leave, but 17 participants of questionable mental power continue the discussion with Ashton in the lobby, and he takes their contact information. Ten of them abandon their current lifestyles, sell their homes, and become Ashton's disciples, relocating to his mansion in Santa Cruz to pursue enlightenment through a regimen of expired cough syrup, wine, tantric sex, family togetherness, and a mishmash of Eastern religions. But as the disciples grow in their trust of Ashton, the outside world becomes suspicious and launches a troubling investigation.

Complementing the novel's inventive plot, Ellis's main characters are skillfully articulated and engaging. Ashton himself is eloquent and manipulative, making plausible his cultlike appeal. He is a classic charismatic narcissist, perceiving himself as a kind of messiah, and his equally powerful grasp of logic proves as compelling, if not persuasive, to the reader as to his "weak-willed" disciples in the story. Readers may even find a hero of sorts in Ashton because of his passionate seizure of the day, without restraint or apology. The characters of his disciples expose the weakness of the human mind in worshiping effective orators who promise transcendence, yet the disciples are sympathetic. They become a family in Ashton's mansion, sharing a general disgust with the monotony and materialism of American life. Ellis is keenly aware of the novel form's capacity to generate empathy even for characters that seem unsavory at first.

One highly ambivalent aspect of Ashton's personality, which survives his conversion, is his almost hysterical pursuit of instant gratification, a central theme of *Right Here, Right Now* explicitly inscribed in its title. Early in the story, Ashton has sex with his assistant, Jill, in her office at company headquarters despite the entire staff eavesdropping. And as the Axe cult progresses, he sleeps with the women regardless of their husbands' feelings, sometimes even encouraging the husbands to listen at the bedroom door. When a disciple named Mr. Tewks is unsettled, Ashton shrewdly characterizes the act, saying, ". . . I am merely giving [her] chills and tickles and perhaps a sense of disembodied dizziness—just centered on particularly sensitive and culturally taboo areas of [her body]" (196). Much of Ashton's gratification and ostensible enlightenment comes from sex, but he also finds it in surfing, which Ellis conveys vividly: ". . . I was high on the shoulder, snapped, and dipped deep into the bowl of the wave, bottom-turned, and drove for the shoulder again, rode and rode, dragged my finger through the flesh of the wave . . ." (152). In fact, the descriptions of surfing are in many ways interchangeable with tantric sex. And once Ashton has found his supposed path to enlightenment through these sensory experiences, he makes it his goal to help the others in his cult achieve it.

Ashton associates enlightenment with disappearance, a nirvana-like transcendence of daily life, and Ellis toys with different forms of disappearance throughout the book. As the cult builds, for example, Ashton, like his disciples, loses all contact with family, friends, and his old job.

Ellis's compelling style is rooted not merely in his formal invention and narrative flair, but in keen observation and an almost childlike fascination with the unknown. Thus he writes with equal assurance and enthusiasm about the world of the self-help guru (Anthony Robbins was the inspiration for Ashton), behind the scenes in the infomercial industry, New Age spirituality, and tantric sex. The result is a richly nuanced and ambiguous but always vivid tale, an exuberant satire, rich in moral overtones but never freighted by them.

Bibliography

Ellis, Trey. *Right Here Right Now.* New York: Simon & Schuster, 1999.

—Reed Stratton

River Angel   A. Manette Ansay   (1999)

The possibility of miracles lies at the center of A. MANETTE ANSAY's novel about the curious circumstances surrounding the death of a young boy in a river in a small town in Wisconsin, and his sudden, unexplained appearance in a barn more than a mile away. In exploring the possibility, Ansay weaves a compelling tale about the power of faith, and the seemingly perennial need to believe in something that operates beyond our physical control. The author's note, in fact, suggests that "[r]eality simply isn't large enough to hold us," and in *River Angel* there is a friendly merger of the spiritual world—the world of belief and faith, including encounters with angelic beings—with the physical reality of quotidian life (9). The story, Ansay points out, is less about what actually did or did not happen in the town, and more about how individuals "make sense" of the world and the often baffling circumstances in which they find themselves (7).

The "river angel" of the title is an angelic presence that purportedly haunts the river running through Ambient, Wisconsin. Young Gabriel Carpenter, bearing a name freighted with meaning, is a nondescript child who arrives there with his feckless father one Christmas Eve. The father hails from Ambient and frames the journey as a kind of glorious homecoming, although Gabriel suspects that his father has made up the story of a river angel to make Ambient seem more interesting than it is (16). Before long the father absconds, leaving Gabriel to his fate and the reluctant care of his uncle and aunt. It is then that Gabriel's supernatural influence on the everyday lives of others is gradually revealed, by means of the first-person accounts of people having dealings with him—people like his Aunt Bethany, or his schoolteacher, or the young woman who helps him one day when he is being bullied, or, indeed, the three teenagers who forcibly take him for a joy ride that goes horribly wrong. Both the physical description of Gabriel and the reactions of others to him are far from positive; the boy is not at all popular because of the way he looks and behaves, and because he has the disconcerting habit of praying openly in front of others. His untimely death, however, shakes the complacent spiritless malaise of the town and reveals the shortcomings of the "godly" folk who live in it.

His death also reignites interest in the river angel story, since his body is found laid peacefully in a barn well over a mile from the snowbound river he fell into, a barn which then lends to the obscure town of Ambient a new celebrity, the building itself becoming a visitor center, and a shrine being dedicated to both the boy and the angel.

Each of Ansay's chapters presents the thoughts and feelings of different characters who have dealings with Gabriel, and with each shift in perception that they offer, the reader is given a cumulative—if inconclusive—impression of the boy. The aunt, for example, has her cosy and ordered life disrupted when Gabriel is left at her house by his father: "Bethany stared . . . she felt her peace of mind torn away like a beautiful scarf caught in a cold snap of wind" (51). Gabriel's schoolteacher resents his presence in her class because "[h]e made her realize all her limitations. He made her realize she should be doing more" (61). Each character has a different encounter with Gabriel and a different tale to tell, their stories gradually amounting to a composite and highly nuanced picture of Ambient and its inhabitants. Added to this are excerpts from the local newspaper, the *Ambient Weekly*, which increases the sense of small-town neighborly familiarity by providing a complex, parallel commentary to the unfortunate incidents disrupting the ordered lives of the townspeople.

The narrative as a whole evinces an ambivalent attitude toward the veracity of people's claims to have seen the river angel, although there is always an underlying "what if . . ." which keeps the reader wondering if the tale is more than myth, right to the end. Even the last sentences of the narrator's coda are delivered almost like a prayer, a plea for there to be something mystical at the end (and edges) of life as we know it. No one knows what really happened to Gabriel when he fell into the river, but perhaps a miracle *did* occur, and it is the questioning of and belief in this possibility that unites the community. More interested in the human response to events than the events themselves, *River Angel* explores this phenomenon in the broader context of the perennial human search for spirituality in the face of recalcitrant corporeality.

In addition to *River Angel*, Manette Ansay has written a host of best-selling and award-winning novels, among which are VINEGAR HILL (1994), *Read This and Tell Me What It Says Stories* (1995), *Sister* (1996), *Midnight Champagne* (1999), *Limbo: A Memoir* (2001), and *Blue Water* (2006). Her latest work, *Good Things I Wish You,* appeared in 2009.

Bibliography

Ansay, A. Manette. *River Angel.* London: Allison & Busby, 2008.

—Linda Claridge Middup

Row, Jess (1974–) *American novelist and short story writer*

JESS ROW's debut novel, *The TRAIN TO LO WU* (2005), met with substantial critical success, including a nomination for the PEN/Hemingway Award (2006); his short stories and nonfiction have appeared in several anthologies (*Best American Short Stories* 2001; 2003) as well as in a range of print and online publications (*Harvard Review, Kyoto Journal, Slate*). Row is currently working on a new collection of short stories and a novel set in Laos during the Vietnam War.

Row was born in Washington, D.C., in 1974. After his graduation from high school in Baltimore, he attended Yale University. Upon graduation from Yale in 1997, he went to China for two years to teach English as a Yale-China Fellow, then returned to the United States in 1999 and completed his M.F.A. in 2001 at the University of Michigan. Row currently teaches English literature at the College of New Jersey in Princeton, New Jersey, where he lives with his wife and daughter (Row Web site). Row is a practicing Buddhist and, since 1994, has been a student of the Kwam Um School of Zen, a Korean school of Buddhist thought ("Eluding"). Described as a Buddhist Chaplain in the Atlantic Online ("Amritsar"), Row spent some time as a community member of the Su Bong Zen Monastery in Hong Kong, and was ordained as a dharma teacher in 2004 (Fox interview).

The stories collected in *The Train to Lo Wu* stem in large part from Row's experiences teaching in Hong Kong, but he has traveled to more than 30 countries in the last decade, all of which have influenced the types of characters and subject matter he explores in his work. The debut collection of seven thematically linked Hong Kong short stories provides vivid and often poignant glimpses into the lives of marginalized drifters ("The Ferry"), cheaters ("The Train to Lo Wu"), survivors ("The American Girl"), artists ("For You"), and general anomalies ("The Secret of Bats"), shaped by often ambitious experimentation in style and perspective (Polley). Through his cast of characters and their geographically diverse back stories Row juxtaposes the surprisingly familiar, with strange and unknown aspects of the city—and of human life in general (Gotham interview); a juxtaposition most evident in the "right now" intersections in his work, where the past meets the present, the familiar meets the foreign, and in many instances hopeful desire meets plangent suffering.

Row is known for deftly capturing situational nuances of his characters' experience, and his work is considered psychologically penetrating by readers and critics on both sides of the Pacific (*Taipei Times* review). Row himself notes that "ultimately the encounter between these characters in this particular situation has to take precedence over everything else (Gotham interview)," lending his work a Chekhovian quality of local intensity, in which universal experience is firmly embedded and alive in the particular. A persistent concern of Row's debut collection is the exploration of identity and culture as experienced by individuals engaged in a process of adapting to their current physical situation ("Many Happy Returns"). Row's explorations of the intersection of individual identity and broader culture reflect current trends in multidisciplinary studies of identity, by suggesting that one's sense of self is intrinsically dynamic, so dynamic, in fact, that it is continually in the process of adapting itself to suit particular social situations, and redefining itself thereby (Jones *Ethnicity*; Diaz-Andreu *Identity*).

Row grew up in a mixed-Protestant household before he converted to Buddhism near the age of 20, which suggests that intersections in faith-based philosophies had an important impact on his life and outlook as a young adult (Fox interview); and this impact is evident in his work, a prominent theme of which is how such intersections can contribute to the ongoing development of individual identity on a spiritual and philosophical level. Row

states that he does not deliberately focus on the philosophical threads often noted by others in his work: "There's no aim there other than to make the material come alive and the language come alive;" but he notably adds that "many of the stories do have some secondary level of intellectual inquiry" (Gotham interview). Whether deliberately inscribed or not, there are prominent spiritual and philosophical undertones apparent in Row's work, with Buddhist structures, for example, clearly framing the narratives in several of *Lo Wu*'s stories such as "For You" and "Revolutions," and also appearing in some of his nonfiction articles ("Many Happy Returns," "Eluding Happiness").

Row makes clear that such intersections in spiritual beliefs need not be sources of destructive tension, claiming of his current perspective, for example, that "Mahayana Buddhism, the larger tradition to which Zen belongs, encourages co-existence among religious traditions" ("Eluding"); but he is aware, like most of the Western world since September 11, 2001, that religious coexistence requires far more than mere abstract toleration. Moreover, excessive zeal in adherence to theoretical concepts motivating an individual to spiritual reform can generate dangerous life practices; and Row considers this very relevant possibility in his new collection of short stories, tentatively titled *The Answer*, which explores how such adherence can manifest itself in instances of religious fanaticism and violence (Fox interview).

Bibliography

Diaz-Andreu, Margarita and Sam Lucy. *Archaeology of Identity*. New York: Routledge, 2005.

Jones, Sian. *The Archaeology of Ethnicity: Constructing Identities in the Past and Present*. New York: Routledge, 1997.

Row, Jess. Atlantic Online. Available online. URL: http://www.theatlantic.com/doc/200808/amritsar. Accessed May 14, 2009.

———. "Eluding Happiness: A Buddhist problem with Christmas." Slate Magazine. Available online. URL: http://www.slate.com/id/2132724/. Accessed May 14, 2009.

———. "Heaven Lake." In Best American Short Stories, edited by Walter Molsey and Katrina Kenison. Boston: Mariner Books, 2003.

————. "Many Happy Returns, Your Holiness: The Dalai Lama Is Turning 71. Where Will Buddhism Be without Him?" Slate Magazine. Available online. URL: http://www.slate.com/id/2145143/. Accessed May 14, 2009.

————. "The Secret of Bats." In *Best American Short Stories,* edited by Barbara Kingsolver. Boston: Mariner Books, 2001.

————. *The Train to Lo Wu.* New York: Dial Press, 2005.

————. "An Interview with Jess Ross." By John Matthew Fox. Book Fox. Available online. URL: http://www.thejohnfox.com/bookfox/2007/05/interview_with_1.html. Accessed May 14, 2009.

————. "An Interview with Jess Row." Gotham Writers' Workshop. Available online. URL: http://www.writingclasses.com/InformationPages/index.php/PageID/268. Accessed May 14, 2009.

Taipei Times. Review of *Train to Lo Wu.* Available online. URL: http://www.jessrow.com/reviews.html. Accessed May 14, 2009.

—Stephanie Laine Hamilton

Roy, Arundhati (1961–) *Indian novelist and essayist*

Arundhati Roy is the author of one novel, *The God of Small Things,* and several nonfiction works that collect her essays and speeches on politics, environmentalism, and activism. She lives in Delhi, India, and since 1997 has been known primarily for her environmental and political activism.

Roy was born in the northeastern Indian state of Assam in 1961 to a Bengali-Hindu father and a Syrian-Christian mother, educationalist, and women's-rights activist Mary Roy. She grew up in Ayemenem, in the southwestern state of Kerala, after her mother returned to her family home following her divorce, and was educated at a school founded by her mother. She trained as an architect in Delhi, where she met her first husband Gerard de Cunha. She turned briefly to acting and filmmaking after meeting her second husband, filmmaker Pradeep Krishen, also working as a production designer and collaborating with her husband on a television series *The Banyan Tree;* in addition, she wrote two screenplays, *In Which Annie Gives It Those Ones* (1988) and *Electric Moon* (1992). She also wrote a series of hard-hitting reviews of Shekhar Kapur's 1994 film *Bandit Queen,* accusing Kapur of misrepresenting the life of Indian outlaw and politician Phoolan Devi.

But it was not until the publication of her first novel, *The God of Small Things,* in 1997, that Roy came to international attention. The novel was described by writer and agent Pankaj Mishra as "the most important Indian English novel since Salman Rushdie's *Midnight's Children*" and was acclaimed by critics in the United Kingdom, the United States, and India as a masterpiece (Tickell, 17). Its reputation was consolidated by winning the United Kingdom's most prestigious literary award in 1997—the Booker Prize is awarded each year to the best novel written in English by an author from the United Kingdom, Ireland, or the British Commonwealth. The novel has since been translated into 40 languages and sales are now estimated to have reached 6 million copies.

The God of Small Things is set in Roy's hometown of Ayemenem in Kerala and reconstructs the events leading up to and following the death of eight-year-old Sophie Mol, framed by the reunion 23 years later of her twin cousins, the novel's main protagonists, Esta and Rahel. The novel opens with Rahel's return to Ayemenem after a period in the United States, to find that her brother Esta has withdrawn into silence. Roy's skillful storytelling allows the childhood events that would shape the later lives of the twins to unfold in parallel with their adult reunion, maintaining two distinct time frames throughout the novel.

Just seven years old when the central tragedy of the novel takes place, the twins are traumatized both by the drowning accident that claims the life of their young cousin, and the fallout from the forbidden relationship between their mother Ammu and Velutha, a low-caste, *dalit* carpenter who works in the family business. As the story unfolds, the private tragedies and transgressions of Esta and Rahel's family become entwined with local political struggles and the deep-rooted social tension that maintains the rigid caste structure, a network of hierarchies that are translated in the novel into the "love laws": "The laws that lay down who should be loved, and how. And how much" (33). The novel illustrates the threat posed by private acts of transgression to the status quo, and equally the lengths to which those in power are prepared to go in order to protect and maintain their interests. The challenge to social norms, and indeed to the concept of transgression itself, culminates in a quasi-incestuous encounter between the adult twins in the closing pages of the novel, an encounter figured more as an act of healing than transgression, but which nonetheless brought charges of obscenity against the author.

The novel is characterized by a linguistic inventiveness that is partly due to the perspective of its child protagonists and partly to the estrangement that the English language itself undergoes in the colonial encounter. Much of its charm and humor emerges from the twins' playful deployment of a variety of registers—their insistence on reading backward, for example, but in their games it is specifically the *English* language that is reassembled to suit their purposes.

Many critics have pointed to the novel's parallels with Roy's own biography—its setting in Kerala, her divorced mother's struggle for recognition, the parallels between Roy and Rahel—but in the light of Roy's subsequent career, its most prominent autobiographical element would appear to be its acute concern with social justice. The novel addresses the injustices of the caste system and the corruption of local politics, singling out Kerala's Communist Party for special criticism, though in an early review, one prominent critic suggested that the novel's emphasis on the personal runs the risk of depoliticizing the very issues it brings into prominence (Ahmad). Nonetheless, its preoccupation with the rights of marginalized groups and with the legacy of India's colonial past and creeping neocolonial present reflect the political issues that would preoccupy Roy in the years after its publication.

While many expected the first-time novelist to capitalize on her newfound literary reputation with subsequent novels, she has instead used it as a platform for her advocacy of environmental and political causes: She donated the substantial financial award from the Booker Prize to a group opposed to the building of dams in the Narmada Valley in India because of the threat they pose to the environment and communities; she famously spent a night

in prison after being found in contempt of court for her part in demonstrations outside the Indian Supreme Court, before settling the dispute with a fine; she has campaigned against the privatization of state resources and utilities in India, and she has been a staunch critic of India's 1998 nuclear tests.

The Cost of Living (1999) brings together some of Roy's writings on these topics, including the eloquent essay "The End of Imagination," in which she expresses her deep opposition to India's nuclear tests. The essay also allows Roy to lay out some of her fundamental values, revealing continuities between her seemingly contradictory roles as writer and activist. In an essay from the volume *Power Politics* (2001) she also takes the opportunity to reflect on the role of the writer, proposing that "there are times in the life of a people or a nation when the political climate demands that we—even the most sophisticated of us—overtly take sides" (12). Since 2001, she has been highly critical of U.S. foreign policy, opposing the wars in Afghanistan and Iraq, and pointing to the potentially destabilizing effects of the growing disparity between rich and poor, the powerful and the disenfranchised. The title essay of the volume *The Algebra of Infinite Justice* (2002) was first published in the aftermath of the September 11, 2001, attacks, and in *The Ordinary Person's Guide to Empire* (2004) she describes her opposition to the Iraq War and what she sees as American neocolonialism. She has also collaborated on a documentary called *DAM/AGE*, opposing the Narmada dam project, and her nonfiction has been adapted for an online documentary entitled *We*.

While great attention was paid to the marketing and media frenzy that accompanied the success of *The God of Small Things*, some critics have noted the "strategic exoticism" on which the novel's critique of India's colonial legacy pivoted, a strategy that paradoxically fueled its global success (Huggan, xi). Roy astutely mobilized her newfound celebrity in the name of an oppositional stance to the dominant political discourses of globalization and the war on terror. Having signaled her intention to return to fiction writing in an interview in early 2007, she commented that 10 years after the publication of *The God of Small Things* "we are in a different world . . . which needs to be written about differently" (Pauli). It remains to be seen what aesthetic strategies she will deploy after more than a decade of political activism.

Bibliography

Ahmad, Aijaz. "Reading Arundhati Roy Politically." *Frontline* 14, no. 5 (August 8, 1997): 103–108.

Bunting, Madeleine. "Dam buster." Guardian Unlimited. Available online. URL: http://books.guardian.co.uk/departments/generalfiction/story/0,,528471,00.html. Accessed May 15, 2009.

Harding, Luke. "India Jails Booker-winner for a Day." Guardian Unlimited. Available online. URL: http://www.guardian.co.uk/world/2002/mar/07/books.india. Accessed May 15, 2009.

Huggan, Graham. *The Postcolonial Exotic: Marketing the Margins.* London: Routledge, 2001.

Pauli, Michelle. "Arundhati Roy Returns to Fiction." Guardian Unlimited. Available online. URL: http://books.guardian.co.uk/news/articles/0,,2012148,00.html. Accessed May 15, 2009.

———. *Power Politics.* Cambridge, Mass.: South End Press, 2001.

———. *The Cost of Living.* London: Flamingo, 1999.

Roy, Arundhati. *The Algebra of Infinite Justice.* London: Flamingo, 1999.

———. *The Ordinary Person's Guide to Empire.* London: Flamingo, 2004.

———. *The God of Small Things.* London: Flamingo, 1997.

Tickell, Alex. *Arundhati Roy's The God of Small Things.* London and New York: Routledge, 2007.

We. A documentary . . . "We. featuring the words of Arundhati Roy." Available online. URL: http://www.weroy.org/. Accessed May 15, 2009.

—Michelle Kelly

Russell, Karen (1981–) *American short story writer*

Karen Russell is the author of the acclaimed short story collection, ST. LUCY'S HOME FOR GIRLS RAISED BY WOLVES (2006). Although the collection is her only current major publication to date, many of her short stories have appeared in respected literary journals, including *Conjunctions* and *Zoetrope.* In 2005, her story "Haunting Olivia" was featured in the debut fiction issue of the *New Yorker,* and she was named one of *New York* magazine's "Top 25 under 25 to Watch." She was also the recipient of the Transatlantic Review/Henfield Foundation Award in that same year.

Russell was born in 1981, and raised in Miami, Florida, where her love of reading began at an early age. Eventually, she earned an M.F.A. from Columbia University and garnered a reputation as a writer who was "poised to become a literary powerhouse" (Ford 64). In interviews following the 2006 release of *St. Lucy's Home for Girls Raised by Wolves,* Russell claimed to be at work on a novel titled *Swamplandia!,* which expands upon "Ava Wrestles the Alligator," the first piece in her collection.

The influence of southeast Florida is everywhere evident in Russell's stories, and the author acknowledges that growing up amid the swamps of the Florida Everglades left a great impression on her: "Southern Florida is a separate universe from the rest of the country. The ocean and swamp offer all sorts of metaphoric seductions, I guess, but they are also, literally, unfathomably mysterious. The Everglades in particular must be one of the strangest places in the world" (BookBrowse.com). She further explains, in the New Yorker Online, that in this area of Florida "the lines between fantasy and reality have all melted together"; and it is in such a realm that her stories are typically set.

Primarily narrated by children and adolescents, the stories often reveal elements of magic realism and are culturally reminiscent of fairy tales where children stumble through forests and find enchantment as well as danger. The protagonists negotiate the territory of loss, longing, and intimacy mostly alone or with other ill-equipped adolescents, whose humorous yet heartbreaking plights have them falling into mammoth seashells, traveling with minotaurs, and living with wolves. Yet, because her characters face thoroughly human conflicts, the reader suspends disbelief and accepts the reality of Russell's worlds, drawn in by characters who search for self, companionship, redemption, and love.

In addition to being ill-equipped for such adversity by their ages, Russell's child and adolescent protagonists consistently find themselves physically or emotionally abandoned by missing or inattentive parents and search to find acceptance with a host of unlikely caregivers and companions. But this absence only helps to increase our sense of immediacy in Russell's stories, and highlights the theme of solitude that permeates the collection. Characters face situations involving peer pressure, sex, and violence in ways that are both darkly comical and unsettling. Although *Publishers Weekly* has called the tales "upbeat and sentimental" (33), the underlying potential for violence, and the characters' consistent failures to find unequivocally happy endings, undercut the humor and sentiment, lending these tales a haunting and sometimes tragic quality.

Yet to ignore the comedic elements in Russell is to overlook an essential facet of her style. For example, in the title story, she describes the differences between Mirabella, the one wolf-girl who has failed tragically to adapt to civilized life, and her well-adapted sisters: "I was wearing a white organdy dress with polka dots. Jeanette was wearing a mauve organdy dress with blue polka dots. Linette was wearing a red organdy dress with white polka dots. Mirabella was in a dark corner, wearing a muzzle" (242). While Mirabella's total failure is communicated here, a reader cannot help but find levity in the juxtaposition of the wild child in her muzzle, and her ridiculously conformist sisters in their frilly dresses. Moments like these provide lightness, and even at times a sort of comic redemption, to stories that deal with otherwise grim situations.

In general, Russell's style is both pithy and poetic, elucidating both setting and character with an economy of words: in "Accident Brief, Occurrence # 00/422," a winter evening in Alaska is encapsulated in three potent lines: "I can hear reindeer rubbing antlers against the fence wood. Snow waits in the high clouds. Our kitchen window fills with cold early stars" (198); in "Lady Yeti and the Palace of Artificial Snows," a boy's unsavory character is revealed in blunt physical description: "Badger's breath smelled like egg sandwich. He had zillions of blackheads on his pug nose" (133); in "The City of Shells," the core of a young girl's personality is captured in a sentence: "She wanted to be beautiful, but she'd had to settle for being nice" (160).

Recognizing the literary quality of Russell's writing, as well as her bold originality, critics have hailed her as one of the best new American voices, comparing her to canonical authors like Flannery O'Connor and Gabriel García Márquez, as well as contemporary writers like Katherine Dunn. She herself claims all three, along with Ray Bradbury, Carson McCullers, Kelly Link, and Stephen King, as literary influences. Although Russell is relatively new to the literary scene, early critical responses suggest that she may on her way to becoming a fixture in the contemporary American canon.

Bibliography

Russell, Karen. *St. Lucy's Home for Girls Raised by Wolves.* New York: Vintage Contemporaries, 2006.
"St. Lucy's Home for Girls Raised by Wolves." *Publishers Weekly* 253, no. 29 (July 24, 2006): 33.

—Lisa Kerr

Russian Debutante's Handbook, The
Gary Shteyngart (2002)

Like his hero Vladimir Girshkin, Shteyngart operates at the fraying border between entertainment and ideology, "part P.T. Barnum, part V.I. Lenin" (3), with a dash of the medieval alchemist Cagliostro (262). New Yorkers by way of late-Soviet Leningrad, both devise a means to capitalize on the tale of "an oppressed immigrant facing systemic barriers to access" (320); on the novel's paperback cover the literary debutante is photographed holding a leashed bear cub.

Handbook's picaresque narrative begins at a cheerless Manhattan nonprofit organization, where "Immigration Facilitator" Vladimir subsists on the schadenfreude of "encountering foreigners even more flummoxed by American society" than he is (11). Vladimir is the listless scion of a Jewish clan that escaped a Brezhnevian bureaucracy in which "even the roaches were small and lacked initiative" (31) to establish a toehold in the Westchester suburbs. His lachrymose mother seizes a piece of "the country's vast floating wealth" (85) as a corporate executive, while his laconic father runs a medical practice dedicated to "defrauding America's paradoxical health care system" (128). The Girshkins have even bankrolled Vladimir's desultory stint at a "progressive Midwestern college" (22). They are not, however, "Normal Americans" like the Ruoccos (94), who slurp brandy and squid in a Fifth Avenue aerie and convene with Vladimir in their daughter's bed to "adjudicate" his postadolescent "crisis" (97–98). Dating Francesca Ruocco becomes Vladimir's entrée into a more fashionable New York, where his status as a "foreigner with an accent" makes him, as she explains, a coveted "signifier" (80).

Vladimir would rather "be patronized than . . . be ignored" (74), but a lifestyle governed by Francesca's "sexy postmodernism" (85) cannot be sustained by credit-card debt alone. A lucrative caper involving a fraudulent SAT score collapses when a drug lord attempts to rape Girshkin and subsequently chases his taxi the length of I-95 with an armada of peach Cadillacs. Marked for death in New York, Vladimir builds an improbable new life in Eastern Europe, where he climbs the administrative ladder of an even tougher syndicate, in the midst of a transition from an older, more prosaic thuggery to the "Americanisms and globalisms" of the "informational age" (283). His base of operations is Prava, "the Paris of the 90s" (20), where "in-your-face" (217) bohemians quaff pints of "Unesko" (212), and signifiers of aesthetic dissent foist their "communal father-hatred" (218) onto a less dedicated set of dilettantes: their "mortal enemies," the backpackers (231). Girshkin schemes to bilk this expatriate clique by peddling stakes in a nonexistent redevelopment project. No trust fund is safe from his "glossy brochures" depicting "smoky factories knocked down to make way for pleasant little corporate parks with recycling bins for glass and newspaper" (200).

Critics have placed Shteyngart's *Handbook* in three principal contexts. Some, like Antrim Taylor, see Girshkin as a "distant cousin" of Jewish-American protagonists like Saul Bellow's Augie March and Philip Roth's Alexander Portnoy. The novel dwells on the "tortures" (116) that assimilation poses to hapless "beta immigrants" (133) and presents a particularly nuanced account of the way that class tensions are encoded in the metropolitan etiquette of dating and mating. As Vladimir's despicable friend Baobob muses of his amour with a frisky 16-year-old, "All love is socioeconomic. It's the gradients in status that make arousal possible"

(51). Vladimir is aroused by gradients of varying steepness: a college girlfriend who drives "The People's Volvo" (64), a bashful dominatrix, downtown "demigoddess" Francesca (82), and finally a "peaceful and generous" WASP tomboy (446) who possesses the unusual and disarming capacity to "admit things . . . no matter how true they are" (267).

Others critics class Shteyngart with the great masters of the prose one-liner. According to Michiko Kakutani, he is "as attuned to the exhilarating possibilities of the English language as Martin Amis, as deadpan as the young Evelyn Waugh," while *Time Out* speculates that "if Henry Miller were Russian . . . he might have written" a novel much like *Handbook.* Thus Shteyngart's boisterous narrator imagines "an airplane drifting through Eastern European clouds rolled together, pierogi-style from the layered exhaust of coal, benzene, and acetate" (62), and quips of a repurposed medieval church, "the only sign of tortured religiosity was the one advertising seared monkfish on a bed of fennel" (211). More vitriolic passages emerge from Vladimir's resentment of an American bourgeoisie "stuck together as if they had all been born in the same Fairfax county pod [and] suckled the same baby-boomer she-wolf" (226). Shteyngart's most distinctive stylistic contribution is his prioritization of smell over imagery and sound. A "Floridian night" reeks of "car exhaust, fast-food onions, and maybe a little something of the sea" (154), while a client's "vodka breath" and "musky aftershave" remind Vladimir of "that certain brisk industrial scent" of "machine oil sprinkled liberally across the gears of a rusted Soviet metal press" (177).

The last group of critics argue, like A. O. Scott, that the *Handbook* belongs to a "Russian satirical-fantastic tradition that stretches from Nikolai Gogol to Mikhail Bulgakov." This angle seems the most valuable in light of Sheyngart's virtuosic send-up of the Halliburton regency in his sophomore effort, *Absurdistan,* which dismisses this lesser novel as *"The Russian Arriviste's Handjob."* Vladimir states a preference for "brief, thoughtful stories where people suffer," as in Chekhov, "quickly and acutely" (26), but the paradigm for *Handbook* and *Absurdistan* is delivered by Joseph Ruocco, a professor of "Humor Studies" who opines that "the serious novel has no future" (92). While

Michael Hirschorn has complained that the contemporary American novel is mired in a broader cultural obsession with minute "quirk," and Melvin Bukiet has accused New York novelists in particular of employing "tropes of wonder" to "write about bad things and make you feel good," Shteyngart uses big and unflinchingly funny narratives to discuss big and undeniably serious ideas, which places him in the contemporary satirical-fantastic tradition of Salman Rushdie and David Foster Wallace.

Shteyngart's Prava, capital of the Republika Stolovaya ("Cafeteria Republic"), satirizes a particular place (Prague) and time (1993); one character explains that its "magical moment" (377) of transformation from "a tabula rasa of retarded post-Soviet mutants" to "Germany in miniature" will take all of three years (70). But it also satirizes a portable phase in the saga of capitalism. The PravaInvest Ponzi scheme that mirrors the real-life exploits of Harvard grad Viktor Kožený, and displays (with a gibe at Milan Kundera) an "unbearable lightness of being" (205), could be retrofitted to Beijing, São Paulo, Mumbai, or (as in *Absurdistan*) to the Persian Gulf and the Caspian Sea.

Handbook suffers from some clumsy dialogue, and seems at times merely cartoonish fiction rather than a revelation of cartoonish reality. Its best episodes—a Scarsdale birthday party, a coffeehouse poetry slam, a Russian gangster's weekly "*biznesmenski* lunch" (192), a "False Naturalization Ceremony Event" performed by an avant-garde film troupe (172), a rousing oration that Vladimir delivers to a lodge of unreconstructed septuagenarian Trotskyites—observe shared rituals from a perspective alien enough to make their formulae transparent, but also invested enough to convey their lived meaning to their participants. Shteyngart offers no easy alternatives to the condition of "postmorality" (308) entailed by the globalist zeitgeist that rationalizes Vladimir's "strange, inglorious path from victim to victimizer" (385). "Identity politics" (271) and "cultural relativism" (273) are marketing tactics in the *Handbook,* rather than ethical injunctions, and its hero's *bildung* terminates at a cheerless accounting firm in suburban Cleveland, the linchpin of a Normal American life in which Girshkin and Morgan will "bring into the world their whimpering replacements" (475) but probably do little else of note. As Vladimir's father suggests, "making compromises may be a necessity, but it's the constantly weighing and reweighing of these compromises that becomes an illness" (133). Shteyngart's stories are afflicted by this illness, and it is, for better or worse, communicable.

Bibliography

Review of *The Russian Debutante's Handbook. Time Out New York,* May 2, 2002.

Antrim, Taylor. "Comic Hero's Russian Roulette: A Spinning Moral Compass." Review of *The Russian Debutante's Handbook. New York Observer* (June 9, 2002). Available online. URL: www.observer.com/node/46107. Accessed October 20, 2009.

Bukiet, Melvin Jules. "Wonder Bread," *American Scholar* (Fall 2007). Available online. URL: www.theamericanscholar.org/wonder-bread/. Accessed October 20, 2009.

Hirschorn, Michael. "Quirked Around," *Atlantic Monthly* (September 2007). Available online. URL: www.theatlantic.com/doc/200709/quirk/. Accessed October 20, 2009.

Kakutani, Michiko. "An Antic Outsider Turns Two Worlds Inside Out," *New York Times,* 7 June 2002, sec. E, p. 41.

Scott, A. O. "In the Shadow of Stalin's Left Foot," *New York Times,* 30 June 2002, sec. 7, p. 8.

Shteyngart, Gary. *Absurdistan.* New York: Random House, 2006.

———. *The Russian Debutante's Handbook.* New York: Riverhead, 2002.

—Aaron Winter

S

St. Lucy's Home for Girls Raised by Wolves
Karen Russell (2006)

KAREN RUSSELL's *St. Lucy's Home for Girls Raised by Wolves* is a rich and illuminating collection of tales that follows a series of primarily adolescent protagonists into territories inhabited by other-worldly creatures and extraordinary people. Russell transforms real-world settings into paranormal realms where ghosts, minotaurs, and werewolves live among human beings. In this hybrid world, children get trapped in the whorls of gigantic seashells and on icy glaciers, and adults regularly disappear on secretive trips and late-night jaunts, leaving their children to fend for themselves. Despite the bizarre worlds in which the characters exist, the struggles they face are vividly, even bitterly human; and themes of belonging, solitude, abandonment, and violence are deftly conjoined with sometimes hilarious, always affecting narrative.

The opening story, "Ava Wrestles the Alligator," sets the tone for the collection, as well as introducing recurrent themes of solitude and abandonment. A young girl feels compelled to save her sister (who is apparently possessed by romantic and sexual desires in ghostly form) and to keep the family's alligator-themed swamp park alive in the wake of their mother's death and their father's disappearance. This is the first in a series of stories in which children lack one or both parents, and are left alone to negotiate the territory of life and loss. In the second story of the collection, "Haunting Olivia," two brothers explore the ghostly waters of an old lake for their sister, whose mysterious death haunts their life. With no adult supervision, they find their own resourceful ways to face their grief, as well as other dangers both natural and supernatural. Building upon the theme of solitude, the third and fourth stories, "Z.Z.'s Sleep-Away Camp for Disordered Dreamers" and "The Star-Gazer's Log of Summer-Time Crime" explore the lure of acceptance, and the capacity for violence, that accompany adolescent peer relationships. These stories find adolescent male protagonists aiding sleepwalking sheep-killers and befriending amateur turtle-kidnappers, while clinging to hopes of gaining acceptance.

As in many coming-of-age novels, the adolescent search for self in Russell's stories is often complicated by a child's growing awareness of his or her parents' limitations. In "Children's Reminiscences of the Westward Migration," a boy and his father, who is a minotaur, head west in a wagon-train with their family. The boy feels a special pride for his father, whom his mother and their traveling companions openly scorn. In contrast, an adolescent boy in "Lady Yeti and the Palace of Artificial Snows" resents his father, who escapes the pressures of caring for the boy's invalid mother by attending bizarre after-hours adult parties held at the local ice rink. The boy's anger and confusion finally explode in an attempt to run his father over with the Zamboni.

Some children in Russell's stories seek out surrogates to replace missing parents. "The City of Shells" features a young girl named Lillith who gets trapped in a giant conch shell with the park's janitor, on whom she makes inappropriate physical advances to win his love. In "Accident Brief, Occurrence #00/422," the protagonist rejects his religious stepfather's attempts to become a father figure in his life; and in "Out to Sea" an old man's attempts to forge a grandfatherly relationship with a female juvenile delinquent fails when she is caught stealing from him. Finally, in "St. Lucy's Home for Girls Raised by Wolves," a number of girls are sent from the homes of werewolf parents to a boarding school, where they are taught to behave civilly and repress their wolfish instincts. Although the girls initially rebel, the school becomes not only a reformatory but also a surrogate home as they leave their old lives behind. The final passage of this story completes the thread that has run throughout the collection, when the narrator, a reformed wolf-girl, goes to visit her former parents and realizes her coming-of-age as a human girl has separated her from them forever. Her realization that calling their cave "home" is her "first human lie" (246) serves as a reminder that all Russell's adolescents struggle with issues of identity and belonging, and often find themselves adrift and anchorless.

Perhaps the greatest strength of this collection is the stories' seamless fit. Although they take the reader from the swamps of the Florida Everglades to frozen Alaska, her characters belong to one world in which the impossible nestles itself next to the familiar, and where the juxtaposition throws into sharper relief the often searching fabulistic moralism. Because of their impeccable construction and nearly pitch-perfect tone, the reader willingly suspends disbelief, drawn in by both the pathos and the humor and eager to follow where the characters lead. The sad absurdity of the characters' situations recalls Flannery O'Connor's misfits and their desperate attempts at love and grace. Yet, the mythologies in Russell's stories are more akin to those of Gabriel García Márquez, where old men with large wings fall from the sky and children are born with pigtails. This association with magic realism also invites comparisons to the work of contemporary writers Katherine Dunn and Gina Ochsner.

Russell's stories might be further categorized as 21st-century updates of the Grimm brothers' tales, in which characters who feel culturally familiar—like Hansel and Gretel or Red Riding Hood—are left to their own devices to survive physically and emotionally perilous conditions. Her settings are populated by lumberjacks, birdmen, child bullies, mysterious strangers, and adults who have no power to defend and protect the child who has wandered off into the proverbial wood. The title of the collection evokes this fairy-tale quality, preparing readers to enter a world where the lines between civilization and wilderness disappear, and we must find a new compass to navigate our way through both narrative and moral terrain.

Bibliography

Russell, Karen. *St. Lucy's Home for Girls Raised by Wolves.* New York: Vintage Contemporaries, 2006.

—Lisa Kerr

Salem Falls Jodi Picoult (2001)

JODI PICOULT's eighth novel is both controversial and thought-provoking. It opens with protagonist Jack St. Bride, recently released from jail for a sexual offense after being forced to take a guilty-plea bargain, drifting into the small town of Salem Falls and taking up a job at Addie Peabody's diner washing dishes. Addie is seen as eccentric, even outright mad, by many of the inhabitants of the town since, despite her daughter Chloe's death, she continues to act as though Chloe is alive and present, leaving food out for her and getting people to "watch" her when Addie is absent. Jack responds sensitively to Addie's psychological state and rapidly gains her strong affection. They commence a relationship fraught with secrets that will not rest. As a high-school student, Addie was gang-raped, and one of her unprosecuted attackers continues to live in the town. When Jack's conviction is inadvertently revealed, a witch hunt commences, with the town's parents determined to drive him out. He is badly beaten and paint is splattered across the door of the home where he is staying.

Simultaneously, a group of four teenage girls—Gillian, daughter of the boss of a pharmaceutical factory that employs many of the town's residents; Meg, daughter of a police officer; and two high-school friends, Chelsea and Whitney—discover the power they wield by forming a coven and practicing Wicca, an increasingly popular form of white witchcraft. After casting a spell, which (they believe) cures minor character Stuart's stroke, the girls begin to use more destructive spells, with Gillian urging the girls to consider "how powerful you felt tonight, healing someone. And then imagine how powerful you'd feel if you could ruin someone's life" (69). Following their celebration of Beltane, a Wiccan festival, Gillian accuses Jack of raping her. What follows is a tale of lies, secrets, personal histories hidden but not forgotten, and the redemptive power of love.

Salem Falls, first published in 2001, encompasses many of Picoult's recurrent themes—the trials of adolescence, rape, courtroom drama, scientific analysis in crime, and the roles and responsibilities of parenthood. Drawing upon Arthur Miller's *The Crucible,* Picoult creates a tale of modern-day hysteria, creating a multilayered story replete with complex and intersecting characterizations. As in all of her work, she focuses on issues that are at the heart of contemporary concerns—in this case rape, child abuse, and, following the introduction of Megan's Law in America and the move toward Sarah's Law in the United Kingdom, the hunting down of those suspected of abusing children. The novel anatomizes with great skill the furor that surrounds such accusations and legal cases, and the devastating ripple-effect that subsequently occurs, summarized by defense lawyer Jordan McAfee: "There's been a witch hunt here in Salem Falls" (462).

Herself a mother of three, Picoult frequently returns to themes of child abuse and rape in her 14 novels—*The Tenth Circle* and *Perfect Match* being perhaps the most memorable. And as ever, her treatment is highly nuanced and multilayered: in addition to Jack being accused of rape by Gillian, Picoult reflects on the attempted rape of Jack himself while in prison and on Addie's experience of being raped.

Typically suspending judgment of her protagonists, Picoult induces the reader to sympathize alternately for a host of conflicting characters, yet this sympathy, like their happiness, is ephemeral, lasting only for a few pages before the story twists, and once again the reader is forced to question the judgments they have made. But the cumulative effect of the novel's many moral, legal, and ethical complexities, rather than baffling the reader, demonstrates the many and mutually dependent shades of gray that constitute our lives. The portrayal of Wicca, for example, is sensitive, factual, and accurate, the girls' involvement in a situation beyond the limits of their emotional and moral maturity being illustrated in their own self-destructive responses. Gillian's self-harming behavior is particularly poignant and instructive.

The roles and reactions of the various fathers in the tale are described with equal assurance and sensitivity; and while many of Picoult's works examine the mother-daughter relationship, mothers are curiously absent here, allowing considerable narrative space for an exploration of the father-daughter bond. The fathers' clouded judgment leads to actions not only immoral but illegal, yet it is easy both to imagine and to forgive their parental anger and fierce protectiveness toward their daughters. The one mother figuring prominently in the tale, Addie, has tragically lost her daughter; yet even this does not stop her *being* a mother. When Meg turns to Addie with accusations of her own against Jack, Addie escorts her to the police herself, despite her innate feelings of defense for her lover. In her view, "it came down to this: Being a mother was something that stayed with you, dormant, ready to flare at a single match-stroke of circumstance. And apparently it didn't matter if the child was one of your body or just one with a place in your heart—instinct was instinct" (340).

This, of course, is the ultimate two-edged sword resting at the heart of our notions of civility and justice, with the same instinct that is nourished and protected by society being itself capable of deeply offending it; and the novel carefully and bravely explores the vanishing point where the one becomes the other. Though it ends, after its greatest and most shocking twist, in a kind of hard-won redemption, *Salem Falls,* like Miller's play before, leaves us in such inescapable perplexity that the light of this very redemption seems almost to illuminate a greater darkness.

Bibliography

Picoult, Jodi. 2002. *Perfect Match.* London: Hodder & Stoughton, 2006.

———. 2001. *Salem Falls*. London: Hodder & Stoughton, 2005.

———. 2006. *The Tenth Circle*. London: Hodder & Stoughton, 2006.

—Charley Baker

Saving Agnes Rachel Cusk (1993)

Saving Agnes is the first novel by RACHEL CUSK, and it won the Whitbread First Novel Award. It centers on Agnes Day, a high-achieving woman in her 20s who is struggling for meaning in her life after university. The novel opens with the local council condemning the London house in which Agnes and her two roommates, Merlin and Nina, are living. The narrative then reconstructs Agnes's formative life—her relationship with her upper-middle-class parents, her time at boarding school, her university career—up to the point of her current realization that she is dissatisfied with her job, insecure in her relationship (with a lover who is never named), and unsure of her friends. The plot then turns on Agnes's attempts to understand her life—in spiritual, political, and practical terms—and gain the courage to achieve some real sense of agency. Her attempts to do so end in a certain degree of ambiguity, since Agnes is essentially saved by circumstance rather than internal change and resolution, but the book closes optimistically as Merlin, Nina, and Agnes together make the decision to buy their house from the council and spend the money to repair it, thus saving it from demolition.

Reviewing Cusk's 2005 novel *In the Fold*, Anna Shapiro described *Saving Agnes* as "the work of a talented and highly clever young person who had nothing much yet to write about" (Shapiro); and indeed, Cusk's narrative focus in *Saving Agnes* is not so much on the plot, which is probably its weakest aspect, but on articulating the interior world of Agnes Day in minute detail. The narrative is often reminiscent of Virginia Woolf's delicate depictions of her characters' interior states. Agnes is intricately constructed, but at the same time oddly passive: She does not seem to actively desire so much as internalize the desires and expectations of others; does not act so much as hope

that things will change by themselves. Moreover, she is repeatedly nonplussed by things that happen to her: "I didn't ask him to come back," she says of one lover. "He just sort of—did" [Cusk 30]. This almost bewildered docility—a characteristic of several of Cusk's protagonists in her story collection, *The LUCKY ONES*, as well—frequently brings her into conflict with Nina, Agnes's roommate and an avowed feminist.

Nina's feminism itself is the source of some bewilderment to Agnes, but Agnes's relationship with feminism is again defined by her lack of agency: "Feminism had discovered Agnes in her first year at university and, recognising in her the potential for prime, dissenting flesh, had been prepared to fight long and hard for her soul," writes Cusk. The tone is ironic, but the irony underscores Agnes's apparent helplessness even in the face of a political movement dedicated in many respects to encouraging and empowering women like her to take control of their lives. Cusk unpacks Agnes's suspicions of feminism by relating it to her equally ambiguous feelings about women:

> What none of [Nina's women's group] knew was that Agnes had lived most of her life in constant fear and loathing of her own sex. The convent school where she had grown up had been red in tooth and claw with female cruelty; and when her new friends spoke of women's community, Agnes was beset by images of hooded nuns, ungodly punishments and peer-group persecution. Unspeakable things had gone on there, things which she had thrown into a cauldron of grief and terror in her heart and which now bubbled like a noxious soup of carping, taunting, bitching, menstruating femininity. Eventually, she could talk of male oppression as freely as anybody; but in those days the cheerful indifference of men and their unemotional talk . . . was something of a relief. (54)

This strategic—and poetic—undermining of one of the central pillars of Agnes's feminist friends' beliefs reflects Cusk's commitment to representing female existence in a way not focused on political or social orthodoxy, a view perhaps most strongly reflected in her fourth book, *A Life's Work: On Becoming a Mother*, which investigates the myths and assumptions surrounding women and motherhood. By contrasting the psychological violence of Agnes's high school environment with the camaraderie of female community assumed by the feminists, Cusk problematizes both the idea of a single valid feminism and the idea of a universal female experience. However, Cusk does not seek to challenge feminist thought so much as to critically investigate the assumptions often made by middle-class, university-educated feminists. Her ironic description of Nina's background is a case in point:

> Nina, for example, had been brought up in a mock-Tudor village in East Sheen, where all her friends called her mother "Margo." But the subtler dramas of country living, with its cruel provincial ways, its sniping observations and censorious unwritten laws which bound young aspiring souls like the feet of Japanese women, could, Agnes later found, compete with the most scarred of childhoods. At university, she was surprised to discover that a background such as her own was almost *de rigueur*: the regimes of the middle classes, she learned, ranked side by side with those of small Central American countries in terms of the abuses they perpetrated. (46)

But although Cusk satirizes student radicalism (a review of Cusk's *A Life's Work* noted that "she dislikes groups and yet pines for a community of feeling" [Kellaway]), much of Agnes's psyche is taken up with the internalization of a series of externally established discourses, which she attempts to reconcile throughout the tale, in striving to construct her own identity. And ultimately it is this search for identity that forms the dynamic center of the novel. Agnes's efforts, in fact, begin when she is still a child, with her creation of a series of aliases: "Agnes Day was her real name," says the narrator, "but this seemed to surprise no one other than herself" (Cusk 13). The obvious play on *agnus dei* ("Lamb of God") again underscores the idea that Agnes is meek, passive, and largely acted upon by those around her. The absence of any cathar-

tic transformation is a curious lacuna in the narrative: Her job improves because her boss finds a satisfying relationship and plans to marry; Agnes's own platonic relationships improve when her lover deserts her; her living situation improves when the roommates decide together to buy their house and save it. But the very absence of such a traditional catharsis may be a clue to the novel's strength, for by avoiding any simplistic, ego-centered resolution, Cusk heightens our sense, vestigial and weakening all the time, of what used to be called fate, and of the nobility inherent in accepting it with grace and good spirits.

Bibliography

Cusk, Rachel. *Saving Agnes.* New York: Picador, 1993.

Kellaway, Kate. "Mother's Ruin." *Guardian Unlimited.* Available online. URL: http://www.guardian.co.uk/books/2001/sep/09/biography.features. Accessed December 13, 2008.

Shapiro, Anna. "Down on the Farm." *Guardian Unlimited.* Available online. URL: http://www.guardian.co.uk/books/2005/aug/27/featuresreviews.guardianreview12. Accessed December 13, 2008.

———Claire Horsnell

Seal Wife, The Kathryn Harrison (2003)

In *The Seal Wife*, author KATHRYN HARRISON revisits themes of obsession, betrayal, and deviant sexuality shared by her earlier works like *The Kiss* (1997), and explores what such forces do to a life suspended in isolation. Set in Anchorage in 1915, *The Seal Wife* follows a 26-year-old man named Bigelow, who has moved to Alaska from Seattle to work for the Weather Bureau. Bigelow arrives unprepared for both the harsh climate and the isolation from his previous life, having to adapt to a life without baths or pie.

Bigelow brings few things with him to Alaska, but what closely attend him are the ghosts of his past, including those of his four lovers: "Karen, to whom he'd written a letter each day; Molly, very pretty, often looking past him to find her own reflection; Rachel, too tall, but it hadn't really mattered; Anne, reading a novel" (Harrison 7). He has few friends or even acquaintances in his new home. Bigelow first sees the Aleut woman at the general store, and his obsession begins as concisely as Harrison describes her: "black braid, black eyes, black buttons on her bodice, and little black lines drawn on her chin" (19). In a review for the *New York Times*, Michiko Kakutani writes, "Like her earlier novels, *The Seal Wife* takes on the subject of passion and its capacity to warp or derail a life. But in this volume Ms. Harrison not only makes us understand the destructive consequences of sexual obsession, but also makes us appreciate its power to shape an individual's sense of self, its ability to inspire and perhaps even to redeem the past." The Aleut woman—the Seal Wife—becomes Bigelow's obsession, shaping his life, though she hardly says a word to him.

Several times a week he visits her, bringing her a gift from the store that she is likely to discard, or wild game that she cooks and serves him. They do not speak the same language, or at least she will not admit to being able to understand him, and so Bigelow tries to complement her the only way he knows how: by asking for more of her food. The Aleut woman, who is never named, does not let Bigelow get close to her. She has an external barrier of control that he cannot penetrate.

First she locks him out of her house, then shuts him out of her life, disappearing and leaving an empty house for him to find. Now truly alone in this frontier land, Bigelow drives himself mad with thoughts of why she left; first thinking she might be pregnant with his child, and then that she might be ill.

Bigelow remains obsessed with this silent woman, but seeks physical satisfaction elsewhere, first visiting a prostitute and later fixating on a dance-hall girl. All the women in his life have some sort of flaw that would keep them on the social periphery in normal society, but in this male-dominated world their defects are deemed exotic and they are fought over. Bigelow eventually courts the shopkeeper's daughter, Miriam, who he had first admired when she sang for the picture shows he frequented. Like the Aleut, Miriam does not speak to Bigelow; but she *cannot*, owing to a serious stammer. Once again

Bigelow is with a silent woman, but Miriam has a far weightier message for him than the Aleut.

All the women Bigelow sees while the Aleut is away prey on his vulnerability. He is acutely lonely in Anchorage, and this loneliness intensifies his obsession, while the physical and geographical isolation that he feels drives him inward, as if through a kind of sexual agoraphobia. Like Harrison's other work, *The Seal Wife* ventures into sexual depravity and its complex relationship to social norms; when the Aleut finally returns, Bigelow reorients himself to her presence in her house and breaks in, smelling her pillows and looking at her belongings, his feelings of betrayal making this violation seem justified. Much of Harrison's work plays with the idea of bending social norms, questioning where feelings of violation start and stop, and whether they are legitimate.

Sadly, such fictive explorations are rooted in autobiographical fact. In *The Kiss*, one of her two memoirs, Harrison chronicles the incestuous relationship she had with her father as an adult, and traces of his exploitation of her can be seen in her novels, like the nude pictures he took of her, which are echoed in *Exposure*, where a photographer's fascination with his daughter affects the rest of her life. In *Envy* Harrison reverses the dynamics but recalls its damaging effects, having the daughter seduce and rape her father.

The Aleut woman stands out from Harrison's typical characters: she is in control of herself, unbuttoning her dress instead of waiting for Bigelow to do so; she does not ask anything of Bigelow, and rejects the gifts he brings to gain her favor. With Bigelow seemingly transplanted from any one of her other novels, this woman is unlike any he has known before, and he is fascinated by the difference. Her silence seems itself a new type of manipulation, which Harrison ponders in her text, asking how someone who keeps to herself could have so much power over another; whether the Aleut woman is indeed passively or actively manipulating Bigelow, and if so, why. The reader is left profoundly uncertain whether her great influence on him is in any way willful, or whether she is simply living her life.

Harrison's writing in *The Seal Wife* is more delicate and thoughtful than in her previous work. She chooses her words carefully, understanding that sometimes silence can mean and matter much more than words ever will.

Bibliography

Kakutani, Michiko. "Sexual Obsession in Frontier Alaska." New York Times on the Web. Available online. URL: http://query.nytimes.com/gst/fullpage.html?res=9C0CE7D81F3EF933A05757C0A9649C8B63 &scp=2&sq=the%20seal%20wife&st=cse. Accessed May 16, 2009.

Harrison, Kathryn. *The Kiss.* New York: Avon Books, 1997.

———. *The Seal Wife.* London: Fourth Estate, 2003.

—Katie R. Watson

Secret History, The Donna Tartt (1992)

Richard Papen narrates DONNA TARTT's best-selling debut novel *The Secret History.* After spending a loveless childhood as the lone offspring of a blue-collar couple in the bleak cultural backwater of Plano, California, he suffers through one year of a pre-med program at a local college, where he finds unlikely joy in the study of ancient Greek. Desperate to escape, and enticed by the glossy brochure of Vermont's elite Hampden College, Richard finagles a scholarship and manages to extricate himself from his uninspired origins.

During his first weeks at Hampden, "where pseudo-intellects and teenage decadents abounded, and where black clothing was *de rigueur*," Richard becomes enamored (from a distance) of five other students (18–19). These students, "magnificent creatures" who share a kind of "cruel mannered charm," are the only five students of Julian Morrow, the enigmatic professor of classics (31). Their leader is the dazzlingly brilliant and anachronistic Henry Winter, who "wore dark English suits and carried an umbrella," and provides the (im)moral and intellectual center of the group (18). Edmund "Bunny" Corcoran is in some ways Henry's foil; the "sloppy blond boy" lacks the intellectual prowess the others share, not to mention the family wealth and sophistication. Francis Abernathy, the "pre-

cariously thin," nervous, and obviously gay dandy, is the only son of an alcoholic but enormously wealthy mother; and Charles and Camilla Macauley are the beautiful, blond, too-close twins. After his first attempt to gain entrance to this mandarin set is rebuffed by Julian's insistence that even six pupils would be far too many, Richard manages to impress several of Julian's disciples with his knowledge of Greek grammar. Soon afterward, Julian admits Richard to the inner circle, which means Richard must take *all* of his courses with Julian. Whatever Richard's initial misgivings about being entirely cut off from the rest of the college, Julian's formidable intellect, as well as the prospect of friendship with his worldly, dissolute students, proves too seductive. To ingratiate himself, Richard fabricates a glamorous childhood of wealth and indolence, and draws closer to these epigones who pepper their conversations with ancient Greek and quote French lyrics verbatim. Parvenu or not, he slowly becomes a part of their hard-drinking, euchre-playing set, even as the heady, drug-induced decadence of 1980s college life swirls around him.

As the holidays approach, though, Richard notices the growing tension between Bunny and the others, particularly Henry. When Henry pays for his and Bunny's extravagant winter trip to Italy, Richard's suspicions increase. Eventually, Henry confesses the group's "secret history." The previous fall, intoxicated with wine and Julian's teachings, four of the Greek scholars (minus the undisciplined Bunny) had decided to reenact a Bacchanal. According to Henry (and later Camilla) it worked: complete with "torches, dizziness, singing. Wolves howling around us and a bull bellowing in the dark. The river ran white . . . the moon waxing and waning, clouds rushing across the sky. Vines grew from the ground so fast they twined up the trees like snakes" (167). But in their Dionysian frenzy, the four students brutally murder a local farmer who happens upon them in the dead of night. When the blood-spattered and dazed celebrants return home, Bunny discovers them and is furious at having been excluded. The murder remains unsolved, but Bunny's initial promises not to betray his classmates gradually give way to veiled hints, threats, and eventually outright blackmail. Bunny becomes such a problem that Henry masterminds a plot to kill Bunny, too—and they do.

For Tartt, who counts T. S. Eliot among her influences, April really is the cruelest month. Not only is it the month of Bunny's murder, but it also features the notoriously capricious Vermont spring. Sunday—the day of Bunny's death—is sunny and warm, but by Monday his body is buried under inches of snow. A stretch of unseasonably cold and snowy weather follows, and Bunny's body remains hidden, thus prolonging the psychological torture of the perpetrators. Even after the discovery of the body, and despite hours of police and FBI interrogation, the remaining five keep mum, through Bunny's maudlin funeral and beyond. The rest of the book chronicles the lethal consequences for the group, as they collectively and individually begin to disintegrate, emotionally, physically, and psychically.

Critics and readers have assigned various generic labels (tragedy, campus novel, bildungsroman, psychological thriller) to this novel, but it is difficult to categorize. However, chapter 1 opens with a discussion of fatal flaws, "that dark show crack running through the middle of a life" which characterizes the protagonist of Greek tragedy. Richard pegs his own fatal flaw as his persistent refusal to see anything but the aesthetic side of everything. As a personality, Richard is almost a nullity; indeed, some critics have called him a "blank slate" or a "recorder" of events, recalling the narrator of Fitzgerald's *The Great Gatsby*. Yet Richard's neutral "confessor" status propels the action of the second half of the book: A message from Richard to Henry precipitates Bunny's murder. At one point, Richard even says that he never saw the whole tragic chain of events as "anything but a game" (276.) Indeed, many of the characters seem strangely amoral, even numb to the evil they have perpetrated. In fact, one of Tartt's greatest achievements in the novel is that she convinces us not only that four disarmingly intelligent college students could manage to whip themselves into a homicidal Bacchanalian frenzy, but also that the subsequent murder of a potential squealer was, if not justified, certainly plausible. Like Richard, we are seduced by the "high, cold" ideals of classical Greek drama and philosophy. And like Richard, we end the book with a sense of tragedy, of young lives wasted, and of the seductive and dangerous pull of ideas.

Bibliography
Tartt, Donna. *The Secret History.* New York: Ballantine, 1992.

—Erin Branch

Seiffert, Rachel (1971–) *British novelist and short story writer*

Seiffert is the author of two novels and a volume of short stories: *The Dark Room* (2001), *Field Study* (2004), and *Afterwards* (2007). The first was short-listed for the Booker Prize in 2001, and won a Betty Trask Award in 2002. Her short story, "Blue," was short-listed for the Macallan/Scotland on Sunday Short Story Competition in 1999, when Seiffert was just 28. She was named one of *Granta*'s 20 "Best of Young British Novelists" in 2003.

Seiffert was born in Oxford to a German mother and an Australian father. She was raised bilingually, and spent time in Berlin teaching English as a foreign language. She returned to Britain in 2003, and now lives in southeast London with her husband and two children.

The Dark Room comprises three novellas, each of which examines the effects of World War II on the lives, memories, and consciences of its protagonists. Helmut was born without a pectoral muscle, and lacks the use of his right arm. Though he is a fervent patriot, his deformity disqualifies him from military service. Instead he photographs the Berlin railway station and the deportation of Jews and Gypsies, and it is clear that his narrow political views are commensurate with the limitations of the camera lens. The second novella juxtaposes Nazism with normalcy, as 12-year-old Lore and her younger siblings try to reconcile their memories of their parents with the monstrous images they are shown. The final novella, set in 1997, witnesses Micha's attempt to find justification for his grandfather's role in the SS. Ultimately *The Dark Room* may be seen as an attempt to exorcise the demons of the German past, and to justify the collective national need to purge itself of pain and guilt.

Seiffert notes that "a preoccupation with guilt comes from being half German," and that "as a child I had a vague feeling that being German was bad. Being a German meant being a Nazi, meant being evil" (Pidd 2007, Holcombe 2004). *The Dark Room* presents three characters who—like many Germans—were not directly involved in the war but are nevertheless profoundly affected by it. The inheritance of a shameful legacy, and the degree to which that legacy can (or should) be cast off, are issues that Seiffert forces the reader to confront. Her representation of the inheritors of guilt, and those who have burdened them with it, makes bold statements about the universality of an experience many consider aberrant or distant from their own lives. Such devastating guilt and shame are not particular to Germans, Seiffert proposes—an idea she expounds in her later work.

Though Seiffert claims that the process of writing about World War II in *The Dark Room* was traumatic, her subsequent novel is no less grim. *Afterwards* (2007) picks up the earlier novel's themes of war, guilt, responsibility, and secrecy, and focuses on the relationship between Alice, a nurse, and Joseph, a laborer who served in Northern Ireland and suffers from posttraumatic stress disorder. His inability to come to terms with his killing of a suspected IRA terrorist creates a cycle of violence and withdrawal that is only interrupted when he meets David, Alice's grandfather, who was in the Royal Air Force in Kenya in the 1950s. David's reminiscences about his time there prove to be distressing for Joseph, whose ongoing silence allegorizes the secrecy, as Seiffert sees it, of Britain's military history.

Seiffert's distinctive prose style has proved controversial, critics alternately lauding her "short, elegant sentences and a Pinterish ability to make what is not said seem more important than what is" (Pidd), and decrying this tendency to pare down her prose "to the point where it has no weight at all" (Chalmers). Seiffert herself has identified her job as a writer as "taking things out" (Holcombe), and claims that she does not like "too much description, full stop, or adjectives. Why do I need to know that someone has a piggy nose, or freckles? Each reader will imagine the piggy nose or the freckles in their own way any-

way" (Pidd). Her economy of phrasing makes her prose sometimes look more like poetry, and has led to comparisons with Katherine Mansfield and James Kelman.

Field Study, Seiffert's volume of short stories, was published in 2004, and continues to unravel some of the threads first introduced in *The Dark Room*. "The Crossing" chronicles an attempt by a woman to get her family across a bridgeless river in an unidentified war-ravaged setting—a journey distinctly reminiscent of that of Lore and her younger siblings. Five of the collection's 11 stories are set in Eastern Europe, the landscape of which stands in for the Germany of Seiffert's earlier novel. It is with her departure from this area—and its accompanying sense of searching and loss—that the author begins to move beyond *The Dark Room*. While Seiffert's economical prose in her first novel was acclaimed by many as reflective of the austerity of her characters' inner battles, her diction provoked still more controversy in reactions to *Field Study*. For some, the sparsity of Seiffert's descriptive voice disjointed the stories, removing from them "colour and range" (Urquhart).

Whether disparaged or commended, Seiffert's distinctive writing style is unquestionably provocative. Her three books have been widely reviewed in Britain, the United States, and Canada, though Seiffert herself remains private about both her work and her life. In addition to being recognized with the Booker Prize nomination and the Betty Trask Award, Seiffert has also won the PEN David T.K. Wong Award (2001) and the *Los Angeles Times* Book Prize (Art Seidenbaum Award for First Fiction) (2002).

Bibliography

Chalmers, Martin. "One Reich, One Volk, One Dimension." Review of *The Dark Room*. *Independent* (London) (June 29, 2001). Available online. URL: www.independent.co.uk/arts-entertainment/books/reviews/the-dark-room-by-rachel-seiffert-752808.html.

Holcombe, Garan. "Rachel Seiffert." British Council Contemporary Writers Database. Available online. URL: http:// www.contemporarywriters.com/authors/?p=auth03A30L020012634903/. Accessed May 16, 2009.

Pidd, Helen. "Unfinished Business," *Guardian* (London), 29 January 2007, sec. G2, p. 12.

Seiffert, Rachel. *Afterwards.* London: Heinemann, 2007.

———. *The Dark Room.* London: Heinemann, 2001.

———. *Field Study.* London: Heinemann, 2004.

Urquhart, James. "Unfinished business in the turmoil of war." *Independent* (London) (March 28, 2004). Available online. URL: www.independent.co.uk/arts-entertainment/books/reviews/field-study-by-rachel-seiffert-56805 1.html. Accessed October 20, 2009.

—Katherine Edwards

Senna, Danzy (1970–   ) *American novelist*

Senna is the author of two novels, CAUCASIA (1998) and *Symptomatic* (2004), exploring the dilemmas faced by mixed-race female protagonists who appear white, but who identify themselves as black or multiracial. She has also written a memoir, *Where Did You Sleep Last Night* (2010).

Senna herself was the child of an interracial marriage, and her complex background fuels and informs her fiction. She was born and raised in Boston, Massachusetts, which provides an important backdrop for her first novel, *Caucasia.* The daughter of poet and novelist Fanny Howe, and journalist Carl Senna, she showed a proclivity for fiction writing early in life, but initially resisted following in her family's literary footsteps by enrolling in pre-med at Stanford University. She went on to receive an M.F.A. from the University of California, Irvine. Before turning full-time to fiction writing, she worked as a researcher and reporter for *Newsweek,* and continues to contribute articles to various magazines. Her experiences as a reporter in New York provided material for her second novel, *Symptomatic,* whose protagonist lives in Brooklyn while working as a journalist at a Manhattan-based magazine. The recipient of an American Whiting Writers' Award in 2002, Senna taught creative writing at the College of the Holy Cross, and held fellowships at the MacDowell Writers' Colony and the New York Public Library's Cullman Center for Scholars and Writers, where she conducted research for a forthcoming nonfiction book that investigates family secrets surrounding her paternal grandmother's alleged affair with a priest. Senna currently lives in California with her husband, African-American writer Percival Everett.

Senna is a part of the most recent generation of African-American women writers, including Rebecca Walker and Emily Raboteau, whose multiracial identities figure prominently in their writing. Because these writers came of age after the civil-rights era, they are often associated with a "post-soul" aesthetic that has come to define Senna's work; thus, while the protagonist of *Caucasia* expresses a strong pride in her African-American heritage that can be attributed to the influence of the black-power movement, she is simultaneously searching for alternative ways to define her identity outside of a black/white binary.

Due to its frank treatment of complex racial issues, *Caucasia* garnered much attention from critics, and numerous accolades, including the Stephen Crane First Fiction Award from the Book-of-the-Month Club, and an American Library Association Alex Award. Soon after its publication, it was adopted in high school and college courses, and was selected for "One Book" Reading Promotion Projects sponsored by the Library of Congress. Critics were less impressed with *Symptomatic,* which many labeled a sophomore effort and accused of retreading ground already covered in *Caucasia.*

Senna's novels are notable for their engagement with race and literary history. In particular, she rewrites established conventions of African-American fiction, such as the novel of passing (in which light-skinned black protagonists cross the color line to pass for white) and the related trope of the tragic mulatto (in which mixed-race characters suffer ill fates due to their exclusion from both black and white worlds). While such themes were often rejected by African-American writers directly affiliated with the civil-rights and black-arts movements, as vestiges of an oppressive past, Senna reinvents these motifs to mark shifts in racial ideologies and attitudes toward mixed-race identity, as well as to indicate where progress still needs to be made. Relationships between women are also central to Senna's work, as she eschews a focus on heterosexual romance in order to prioritize the bonds—and tensions—between mothers and daughters, sisters, and friends.

Despite similarities in subject matter and theme, *Caucasia* and *Symptomatic* reveal Senna's experimentation with different forms. Over 400 pages in length, *Caucasia* is a detailed novel that spans time and place to tell the story of fair-skinned Birdie Lee, who comes of age in the 1970s amid the divisive racial politics that break up her inter-racial family. As Birdie plays at childhood games of spying, goes underground with her radical activist mother, passes for white to elude the FBI, and then embarks on a quest for her lost black father and sister, the novel displays aspects of the suspense genre that Senna would fully exploit in her second novel, *Symptomatic,* a literary psychological thriller.

At half of *Caucasia*'s length, *Symptomatic* is written in a minimalist, *noir* style that is as indebted to filmmakers like Alfred Hitchcock and Roman Polanski (especially in its use of the doppelganger) as it is to African-American literature. Yet, as in *Caucasia*, allusions to past works of the African-American canon abound in *Symptomatic,* whose tale of an obsessive relationship between two mixed-race women owes its origins to Nella Larsen's 1929 *Passing,* a narrative Senna revisits throughout, and especially in the novel's conclusion. Like its predecessors, Ralph Ellison's *Invisible Man* (1952) and James Weldon Johnson's *The Autobiography of an Ex-Colored Man* (1912), *Symptomatic* leaves its protagonist unnamed as a mark of her identity-confusion and invisibility—an invisibility that, as in Johnson's *Autobiography,* derives from the ability to hide her blackness beneath white skin. In contrast to Johnson's fictional protagonist, who remakes himself, *Caucasia*'s Birdie Lee and the nameless narrator of *Symptomatic* rarely define themselves at all, but instead become projections of the identities that others impose upon them. As a novel about a young woman emotionally unraveling in the world of magazine publishing, *Symptomatic* also recalls Sylvia Plath's *The Bell Jar* (1963), with Senna's medical title signaling her metaphorical use of mental illness.

Just as her subject matter deals with characters who defy easy categorization, Senna's style straddles various traditional lines. Her novels do not display the highly innovative and often demanding postmodern aesthetic of contemporary African-American writers like Ishmael Reed and Toni Morrison; nor can they be compared to the easy-reading fare of Bebe Moore Campbell and Terry McMillan. Though engagingly accessible, and often unfolding with page-turning suspense, *Caucasia* and *Symptomatic* are nonetheless self-consciously literary works, thick with allusions both to popular and to literary culture, and characterized by lucid, thoughtful, and evocative prose.

Bibliography
Senna, Danzy. *Caucasia.* New York: Riverhead, 1998.
———. *Symptomatic.* New York: Riverhead, 2004.

—Lori Harrison-Kahan

Sharma, Akhil (1971–) *Indian short story writer and novelist*
Born in New Delhi, India, Akhil Sharma moved to the United States with his family at the age of eight. He was raised by traditionally minded parents and remained connected to his South Asian heritage because of their influence and the family's summer vacations in India. The environs of New Delhi, including its impoverished slums, feature prominently in much of Sharma's fiction, and his work foregrounds taboo themes including incest and adultery, focusing on the impact of stigma on the life of the individual.

Early in his writing career, a number of Sharma's short stories appeared in prominent magazines such as the *New Yorker* and the *Atlantic Monthly,* and many were republished in notable anthologies such as *Best American Short Stories* and the *O. Henry Awards;* among these are the stories "Cosmopolitan" and "If You Sing Like That for Me." After his success in short fiction, Sharma went on to tackle his debut novel, *An OBEDIENT FATHER,* and in 2000, the book was featured on the *New York Times* Notable Book list, the latest in a series of critical awards for his writing.

Sharma graduated from Princeton University with a B.A. in public policy, and later studied both at Stanford University in the writing program and at the Harvard Law School. He is a trained lawyer and investment banker, who won a PEN/Hemingway Award for his debut novel, and took second place in the O. Henry Award of 1995.

In his fiction Sharma dramatizes the attempts of his South Asian protagonists to balance traditional social expectations against the demands of rapid modernization. Equally adroit in his depiction of male and female protagonists, he explores the collision of familial pressure and personal desire in the life of the individual, often demonstrating the ways in which sexist paradigms restrict women's experiences in the South Asian context. In a number of stories Sharma specifically highlights different choices made by two sisters in the same family, choices that function partly as metaphors for the typical options available to Indian women: one leaves India for the West, with its promise of independence, the other remains at home confined by her roles and duties as daughter, wife, and mother. Sharma is stingingly critical of the social attitudes and structures that restrain women struggling to meet the expectations of traditional culture. The sister who remains in India is often subject to abuse, whether physical, sexual, or emotional, by other members of her immediate family, and Sharma is unflinching in his negative portrayal of women conspiring against fellow women by upholding gender roles for the sister who is left behind.

"Cosmopolitan" marks an uncharacteristic foray into the lives of middle-class immigrant Indians who have lived in the United States for a long time, but who find it, after all, no less strange. Gopal, the protagonist, is an unlikely hero whose wife and daughter have abandoned him in the United States while they chase their dreams at an ashram or in Germany, leaving him to languish in an early retirement on his own. Yet, as the abandoned patriarch, Gopal becomes a sympathetic figure; and when he begins an extramarital affair with his American neighbor the story shifts focus from Gopal's personal inertia to glimpses of how his foreignness is constructed by others and his isolation imposed by both kinds of women, Indian and American. His attempts to appear sophisticated and Western are detailed in rehearsed speeches during long evenings alone, in between visits to his neighbor's house. The practiced dialogue never has its intended effect, however, and Gopal remains a man without a meaningful connection to anyone in his proximity. His willingness to overlook conventional boundaries in search of a meaningful

relationship makes of this otherwise simple story of a man's middle-age crisis a narrative eliciting considerable sympathy from the reader. The affair is short-lived and Gopal returns to his solitary existence, more isolated than ever, watching from his house as cars pull into his former lover's driveway. Sharma's willingness to explore the unspoken and unseen in the private lives of his characters makes him a searching storyteller, and reveals nuances in the immigrant experience hitherto unexplored.

"If You Sing Like That for Me" is an early treatment of the major themes that would later inform his first novel, revolving as it does around the tale of Anita, a troubled young woman forced into a marriage but looking for love in spite of her straitened circumstances. The contrast between the two sisters of the family, Anita and Asha, reflects different approaches to the modernization of women's place in the face of traditional practices. Asha ignores her father's wishes and decides to pursue a Ph.D. in the United States, while Anita does not resist when he stops her from going to school. Her subsequent arranged marriage to Rajinder is symptomatic of her life in general, with little choice in her bridegroom and even less influence, after marriage, on her own happiness. Her heartfelt questions about love are summarily dismissed, as only for those in movies, and the lack of feeling merely heightens both the already acute dreariness of her daily life and the seeming pointlessness of her struggle for meaning and agency.

The character of Anita, along with her marriage to Rajinder, resurfaces in the oppressive domestic drama that features largely in Sharma's novel, *An Obedient Father.* Sharma's debut novel centers on the story of a corrupt government official who repeatedly molests his daughter in her childhood, only to live with her as his only family member after she becomes an adult widow. He then becomes sexually tempted by her only child, his granddaughter, and the threat of her child being sexually molested in the same way she was throws Anita into a frenzy: She breaks a lifetime of silence in order to protect her child and tells the entire family what her father had done to her. Yet, in a stunning and disheartening reversal, the family reacts with indifference and even censure to her broaching such an unacceptable topic; and the public exposure of her father's crime ultimately results only in disapproval and rejection of her and not the family patriarch. The frank and unflinching manner in which Sharma explores the hidden life of this troubled household is emblematic of his continuing commitment, evident throughout his oeuvre, to confront the moral underbelly of Indian life.

Bibliography

Alter, Stephen. "*A Few Thoughts on Indian Fiction, 1947–1997,*" *Alif: Journal of Comparative Poetics,* no. 18, Post-Colonial Discourse in South Asia (1998): 14–28.

Rajakumar, Mohanalakshmi. "The Taboo in Indian Literature: Expanded Ways of Reading and Writing Indianness." Submitted for *Indian Writing in English.* Forthcoming.

Rothstein, Mervyn. "India's Post-Rushdie Generation; Young Writers Leave Magic Realism and Look at Reality," *New York Times,* 3 July 2000, p. E1.

Sharma, Akhil. "Chased Away." New Yorker (April 21, 2003). Available online. URL: www.newyorker.com/archive/2003/04/21/030421fa_fact8. Accessed October 20, 2009.

———. "Cosmopolitan." In *Prize Stories, the Best of 1998: The O. Henry Awards,* edited by Larry Dark and Andrea Barrett, 273–296. Garden City, N.Y.: Doubleday, 1998.

———. "Cosmopolitan." *Atlantic Monthly* 279, no. 1 (1997): 62–73.

———. "Debut Fiction Prosperity." *New Yorker,* 19 June 2000, p. 144.

———. "A Heart Is Such a Heavy Thing." *New Yorker,* 8 December 1997, p. 100.

———. "If You Sing like That for Me." In *The Best American Short Stories 1996,* edited by John Edgar Wideman and Katrina Kenison, 282–306. Boston: Houghton Mifflin, 1996.

———. "If You Sing Like That for Me." In *Prize Stories 1996: The O. Henry Awards.* New York: Anchor, 1996.

—Mohanalakshmi Rajakumar

Shell Collector, The Anthony Doerr (2002)

In his debut collection of short stories, ANTHONY DOERR explores the shifting interior landscapes of his characters in relation to the natural landscapes they inhabit. Doerr has lived in Ohio, New Zealand, Africa, and Idaho, and his work reveals his intimacy with these very different landscapes. From the crystalline dreamscapes of a lonely visionary in "The Hunter's Wife," to the abundant cheer of a nameless gang of American fishermen in "July Fourth," Doerr shapes his language so that the sound and tone of each story reflects its setting. The eight short stories in *The Shell Collector* are not connected through characters, events, or geography; yet even while Doerr shows us the profound influence of specific landscapes on individuals, he explores how all places, and all seemingly individual stories, are intricately connected. His characters experience similar moments of wonder at the power of nature. Many have at least some degree of mystical connection to the land, but Doerr's particular style of magical realism is so subtle that the coexistence of magic with reality never distracts from the believability of the stories. Doerr's writing—particularly when his gaze turns toward the natural world—buzzes with dense, ecstatic imagery that blurs the line between prose and poetry.

In the title story, a blind Canadian scientist lives in a remote archipelago in Kenya collecting shells and pondering their mystery. The shell collector's ordered life is derailed when a visitor to the island becomes ill, and is inexplicably cured by the bite of a deadly cone snail. When an important *muezzin* from Lamu demands the same treatment for his dying daughter, and she too is healed, the shell collector's island becomes a hub of miracle-seekers and idealists, including his adult son Josh, whom the shell collector describes helplessly as a "goody-goody." Josh sees in his father's accidental discovery an opportunity to do good in the world. Finally someone dies from the cone shell's poison, and the shell collector settles back into the quiet existence he had known and treasured, but without its former clarity. Only when he himself is bitten—when he is viscerally and violently reunited with his environment—is a sense of order reestablished.

In "The Hunter's Wife," a recluse hunter in Montana falls in love with a young woman who is traveling through a nearby town as a magician's assistant. They live together in an isolated cabin in the mountains, and experience the beautiful and brutal progression of the seasons. During their first winter, the hunter shyly shows his wife a hibernating grizzly bear, and when she touches it she discovers she can read its dreams and longings. The hunter dismisses his wife's gift, but she becomes increasingly attuned to it, seeking out dying animals and channeling their spirits at the moment of their death. When she discovers she can similarly commune with dying people, her being, in a sense, dissolves further into the gift, until at last it cannot be contained by the life she shares with the hunter.

In "So Many Chances," the daughter of Mexican immigrants falls in love in a small town in Maine after her father moves them from Youngstown; but Dorotea's crush on the charming teenage boy who introduces her to fly-fishing ultimately becomes secondary to her love for the landscape of the coast.

"For a Long Time This Was Griselda's Story," narrated by an unknown person who speaks for their small Idaho community, tells the story of sisters Griselda and Rosemary. Tall, beautiful, and mysterious, the older Griselda overshadows the unremarkable, overweight Rosemary, who works at the linen store, marries an uninspiring butcher, and lives with her mother. But after Griselda runs off with a metal eater in the circus, Rosemary slowly picks up the pieces of her own life, and when Griselda's "act" returns to town, Rosemary delivers a powerful performance of her own.

"July Fourth" pokes fun at American bravado as it chronicles a group of American fishermen who challenge a group of their British counterparts to a contest: Each group has a month to catch the biggest fish on each continent. Yet even as the (nameless) Americans drink and bumble thoughtlessly across Europe, the tale ends with a surprising act of empathy on the part of the fishermen.

"The Caretaker" follows Liberian Joseph Saleeby, a man whose personal narrative is inseparable from the horrifying narrative of his country during its turbulent transition into Charles Taylor's regime. He is unable to mend his life as it takes him from Liberia to Oregon and back again, but he finds sparks of redemption in surprising places: in the hearts of beached whales, in a forest garden, in the friendship of a deaf girl.

"A Tangle by the Rapid River" unfolds quietly as Mulligan, a retired fisherman leading a seem-ingly conventional life and in a passionless marriage, accidentally reveals his secret existence to the wrong people.

In the closing story, "Mkondo," a paleontologist named Ward, sent to Tanzania to find a rare fossil, jumps into a river after a woman he has met there. Impressed by his display of bravery, Naima agrees to return with him to his Ohio suburb; but away from Tanzania, her fiery spirit ebbs, and they each retreat into themselves until Naima discovers photography, which takes her away from Ward and pushes him once again to the brink of the unknown.

Anthony Doerr has written a novel, *About Grace* (2005), about a hydrologist who sometimes dreams accurate premonitions, and who runs away from his family after he has visions of his daughter's death. Set in Alaska, Ohio, and the island of St. Vincent, it is written in the same luminous, meditative prose as the stories in *The Shell Collector*.

Bibliography

Doerr, Anthony. *The Shell Collector.* New York: Penguin, 2003.

—Betsy Allister

Shteyngart, Gary (1972–) *Soviet-born American novelist and essayist*

Gary Shteyngart has written one good novel and one superb novel. The RUSSIAN DEBUTANTE'S HANDBOOK (2002), winner of the Stephen Crane First Fiction Award and the National Jewish Book Award, begins with the wearying social climb of a charmless, vaguely Rothian "beta immigrant" (133), takes a detour into Carl Hiassen–style Miami vice slapstick, and concludes with a provocative lampoon of post-Soviet kleptocracy and backpacker ennui in Velvet Revolutionized Czechoslovakia. ABSURDISTAN (2006) focuses *Debutante*'s haphazard satire and warms its hesitant sentimentality. The recipient of a host of accolades including a citation in the *New York Times Book Review*'s annual top 10 list, Shteyngart's second novel is a sweeping yet lovingly detailed survey of post-9/11 political economy, as seen through the eyes of a hip-hopping, Web-surfing, globe-trotting "twenty-first-century Oblomov" (158) exiled in a war-torn Caspian petrol state.

Like his major protagonists, Shteyngart experienced childhood in Brezhnev-era Leningrad and puberty in Koch-era New York City. He has become something of a darling of the Manhattan literary scene, in part by playing what he dismisses as the "professional immigrant game" (*Abs*, 81); in an article for *Esquire*, he explains why his novels present such an unflattering family portrait of his birthland: "Um, because they pay me?" Shteyngart's work is typically marketed with images of stiletto heels and fishnet stockings, which mirror the sexual commodification of New Russia that he analyzed in a 2003 *New Yorker* article about the Moscow lesbian bubblegum pop duo t.A.t.U.

Shteyngart has obliged this branding to an extent by fashioning a literary persona that revels in the juxtaposition of a misogynistic old-world hedonism with the guilt laden third-wave feminist tropes that his characters express in fictionalized versions of his alma mater, Oberlin College, which he mocks as a finishing school for the coastal haute bourgeoisie. The particular timing of his departure from Leningrad becomes a salient issue in a flashback to his "Accidental College" days in *Absurdistan,* in which this persona fragments into three bickering factions—the novel's hero Misha Vainberg (who left at age 18), its villain Jerry Shteynfarb (age seven), and *Debutante*'s Vladimir Girshkin (age 12). These fictional Shteyngarts share the author's conflicted nostalgia for Soviet propaganda, and his unconflicted identification with the secular Judaism of Spinoza, Freud, and Einstein (*Abs*, 251); but the small variances in their date of naturalization assume exaggerated proportions when seen in light of the intricate and often painful process of assimilation that Shteyngart details in *Debutante,* and in biographical articles like "Sixty-nine Cents" and "Immortality." Yet another alter ego named Lionya Abramav, who left Leningrad at age 10, stars in a pair of short stories that Shteyngart penned for *Granta.*

The real Shteyngart is closest in outline to the opportunistic and "perfectly Americanized" (*Abs,* 55) Shteynfarb, who uses Edward Said's *Orientalism* to seduce upwardly mobile minority students in his creative writing classes, and churns out "unfunny short stories chronicling the difference between Russians and Americans" (*Abs*, 176). Shteynfarb gains a measure of revenge for his treatment in *Absurdistan* by writing a review published in the real *Esquire* that skewers the novel's "useless socio-economic observations," and reveals that Shteyngart was a member of the Young Republican Club at Stuyvesant High School. Shteyngart is reportedly working on a novel in which a graying Shteynfarb inhabits "an evangelical community in upstate New York," in a future United States where the vernacular tongue is "a strange hybrid of Korean, Tagalog, Spanish, and English."

Shteyngart has used magazine writing not only for self-promotion and metafictional prankery, but also as a laboratory for his novels, which he views, judging from a number of interviews in which he reserves his highest esteem for the 19th-century Russian canon, as his literary raison d'être. The novels, on the other hand, feed back to the stories: "Several Anecdotes about My Wife" (2002) develops the courtship scenario and nonprofit agency setting of *Debutante,* and offers a variation on the central "screw" metaphor of *Absurdistan;* "Planet of the Yids" (2006) expands the latter novel's whisper of sexual abuse and its anecdote about an anti-Semitic dog.

Debutante was inspired by a collegiate study-abroad term in Prague, and Shteyngart has continued to use travel as a resource for his fiction. Articles on St. Petersburg and Baku (Azerbaijan) in *Travel + Leisure* develop themes that are revisited in *Absurdistan;* and Shteyngart's winning adaptation of the magazine's typical style, an exuberant visual and gustatory American imperialism that alternates between epicurean vignettes of slick cosmopolitan playgrounds and a contemporary version of what Melville once called the *povertiresque,* anticipates the novel's central conceit, which is the protagonist's voracious appetite for love, truth, and justice, and his inability to satisfy these with American-style consumerism. Given this precedent, we should expect Portland, Montreal, Salvador da Bahia (Brazil), and Bangkok to be future ports of call for Shteyngart's fiction. Rome, which he explores in his longest article for *Travel + Leisure,* has already found its way into 2007's "Diaries of Lenny Abramov."

Shteyngart's review essays for *Esquire* and the *New York Review of Books* suggest that he will continue, from both an intellectual and a marketing standpoint, to straddle the line between New York and St. Petersburg, and between the low-middlebrow and the middle-highbrow. They also demonstrate his familiarity with recent Russian satire. Shteyngart classes authors like Vladimir Sorokin, Victor Pelevin, and Maxim Kononenko with American satirists like Brett Easton Ellis, whom he views as creatively frustrated due to the absence of any ideology truly worth subverting, a "satirist's dream" of the sort that the Soviet empire was for Vladimir Voinovich and the czarist empire was for Shteyngart's great-great-grandfather Nikolai Gogol. But though he has mused that he may "ease up on the throttle" in his upcoming fiction, rather than "ramp up the satire," his growing frustration with the impoverishment of literary discourse in the contemporary United States, and the subsumption of his fellow citizens into a "private world of electronic goblins and [muted] sexual urges" (*RDH*, 476) in which the "membrane between adulthood and childhood" becomes ever thinner (*Abs*, 230), suggests that his next Absurdistan, presumably in the Shteynfarb project, may well be the United States itself; indeed, his next novel is said to be set partly in Albany, New York.

Bibliography

Gritz, Jennie. "Same Planet, Different Worlds." Atlantic Online. Available online. URL: http://www.theatlantic.com/doc/200606u/shteyngart. Accessed May 16, 2009.

Shteyngart, Gary. *Absurdistan*. New York: Random House, 2006.

———. "Absurdistan, by Gary Shteyngart." *Esquire* (June 2006). Available online. URL: www.esquire.com/fiction/book&review/ESQ0606ABSURDISTAN-2 Accessed October 20, 2009.

———. "Adventures of a True Believer." New York Review of Books 52, no. 9. May 26, 2005. Available online. URL: www.nybooks.com/articles/article-preview?asterisk_id=17998. Accessed October 20, 2009.

———. "Big Book of the Month: Bret Easton Ellis." Esquire, September 2005. Available online. URL: www.esquire.com/features/ESQ0905BretEastonEllis. Accessed October 20, 2009.

———. "Brazil's Untamed Heart." Travel + Leisure (December 2006). Available online. URL: www.traveland/civic-com/articles/brazils-untamed-heart/4/?comments_page=1. Accessed October 20, 2009.

———. "Hidden Rome." Travel + Leisure (February 2007). Available online. URL: www.travelandleasure-com/articles/hidden-rome/1/. Accessed October 20, 2009.

———. "Hotel Paradise: The Heathman Hotel." Travel + Leisure (June 2008). Available online. URL: www.travelandleisure.com/articles/hotel-paradise-five-writers-stories/1/. Accessed October 20, 2009.

———. "Immortality." New Yorker (June 11, 2007). Available online. URL: www.newyorker.com/reporting/2007/06/11/070611fa_facts_shteyngart. Accessed October 20, 2009..

———. *The Russian Debutante's Handbook*. New York: Riverhead, 2002.

———. "A St. Petersburg Christmas." Travel + Leisure (December 2005). Available online. URL: www.travelandlesiure.com/articles/a-st-petersburg-christmas/1/. Accessed October 20, 2009.

———. "Sixty-Nine Cents." New Yorker (September 3, 2007). Available online. URL: www.newyorker.com/reporting/2007/09/03/070903fa_fact_shteyngart. Accessed October 20, 2009.

———. "Teen Spirit." New Yorker (March 10, 2003). Available online. URL: www.newyorker.com/archive/2003/03/10/030310fa_fact_shteyngart. Accessed October 20, 2009.

—Aaron Winter

Sister Sister Eric Jerome Dickey (1996)

Described on its jacket cover as a "hip, sexy, wisecracking novel"—and it is all of that—ERIC JEROME DICKEY's *Sister Sister* is more substantial than such superficial zingers convey. While certainly not profound, the novel succeeds in capturing the plight of middle-class, professional, young Afro-American women immersed in an urban, materialistic American culture. It chronicles the turbulent lives of three young women in search of love in today's Los Angeles over a period of several months. Two of them—Valerie, called "Red" because of her light brown, "Halle Berry" complexion, and Inda, known as "Black" because of her deep mahogany "Michelle Obama" luster—are biological as well as spiritual sisters. Named by a nurse in a Memphis hospital maternity ward, the third protagonist, Chaquita, becomes a soul sister of Valerie and Inda as the raucous events that draw their lives together interweave and unfold.

While the separate yet enmeshed lives of these "sistahs" seem exciting and groovy, they are in truth unutterably sad, and what makes them especially poignant is the protagonists' quasi-awareness of the shallowness of their individual existence. For all the frivolity of their sexual escapades and romps, their lives are, for most of the tale, empty and fallow, and though in their late 20s and 30s none of the three has children. Valerie's marriage to Walter, a wannabe professional football player and NFL draft reject, is failing, and with its collapse, her self-identity and self-worth languish. Without family, Chaquita is rudderless and drifting; more than Valerie and Inda, she is driven to find and establish family roots, clearly a precondition for the discovery of her self-identity. More realistic than her soul sisters, Inda no longer expects high romance; she will settle for a sustaining love if it can be found in a world where sex is regulated by commerce and is often a mere proxy for love.

Without the stability that self-identity and worth provide, Inda and Chaquita are alternately (unbeknownst to each other) beguiled and bedded by the jaunty philanderer Raymond, whom they later jointly dub "Deputy Dawg," because of his sleazy sexual proclivities. The episode (chapter 17) where Inda and Chaquita accidentally meet and discover Raymond having sex with Gina, another of his provocative playmates, is Chaucerian in the comedic retribution it visits upon Raymond for his brazen infidelity. While Valerie and Inda both come from a loving family, they and their brawny brother, Thaddeus, are the products of a biracial marriage—"Moms" is white—and this is reflected in the children's varying degrees of blackness. Their parents offer no model of parental stability or fidelity, however, as they are (while civil to each other) decorously separated and living their own lives. Without the stability provided by compatible parents in their childhood years, Valerie, Inda, and Thaddeus have learned to support one another, and their consanguinity throughout the trials they each experience accounts for most of the real moments of affirmation in the novel.

Minus the ballast and protection each provides the other, each is easy prey to duplicitous pseudo-lovers and sex merchants, as well as their own wayward inclinations and self-destructive passions. Valerie, Inda, and their friend Chaquita are vulnerable to their own powerful sex drives and are almost glib in the rationalizations of the bad choices they have made in lovers. Valerie's marriage to Walter Sinclair was clearly a misstep. Walter wallows in self-contempt, which he attempts to alleviate by blaming his failed pro-football career on his marriage to Valerie: She has been, he tells her, too complacent in her domesticity and that complacency proved contagious. Similarly, Chaquita rationalizes a relationship turned abusive with Raymond, and at one point even reneges on a potentially positive relationship with Thaddeus in favor of a tryst with morally insolvent Raymond. Her relapse too is attributable to her sense of unworthiness. Inda, however, is nonjudgmental about Chaquita's backsliding, sagely observing, "Sometimes you have to let people change and grow on their own, you have to back off and hope it turns out for the best" (294). Like Valerie and Chaquita, Inda tries to rationalize away her imperfections, but even as she does so she confides to the reader in her asides that she knows she is making excuses for her erratic and sometimes self-destructive behavior. Inda is neither evasive nor delusional. She accepts who she is and is comfortable in her own skin.

Strained and conflicted relationships, however, result in erratic and, if unchecked, even criminal behaviors, as in several scenes when one of the sisters wreaks vengeance on an unfaithful, two-timing spouse or lover. (The slang for this kind of low life is *pie-dog*.) Chapter 23, a retrospective on Inda's failed first marriage to a white man, Andre, has her recapitulating how she scaled up to a hotel balcony, surprised Andre and his mistress in the act of intercourse, and held them hostage with a gun. Chapter 31 begins with Valerie quietly entering her home at night and dousing her sleeping and indigent hubby Walter with gasoline, and ends with her about to strike a match. Although professional, upscale young women, they are still subject to dark and primordial passions that betrayal and rejection summon forth.

The fictional story of the sisters' quest for self-realization is told from three different narrative points of view: Valerie's is exclusively the third-person omniscient, while Chaquita's and Inda's are each in the first person. This dynamic change of point of view has the effect of freezing the narrative in places, enabling the reader to perceive an episode from different perspectives. Along with this technique and serving a similar purpose, each of the chapters features one of the sisters, thereby giving the narrative a sense of simultaneity in the unfolding of events in time. For example, the author can describe what is happening in the *novel's time* to Valerie in downtown Los Angeles (chapter 18) and to Inda in Shoreline Village (chapter 20) without resorting to words like *meanwhile* and *at the same time,* and thereby losing focus or interrupting narrative flow. More important, these techniques, which comprise the form of the fiction, complement the novel's thematic, underscoring the fact that whatever happens to one of the sisters does not happen in isolation from what is concomitantly happening to the others, and that only with the symbiotic support of each for the other(s) will they all realize their quest for selfhood.

Dickey's command of voice is notable, and he creates for Inda a truly memorable one. While Chaquita's voice, feminine and sensitive, also strikes true tinder and is credible, Inda's is resonant with a stature, timbre, and quality that we associate with great characters (here reminiscent of Faulkner's Dilsey). It is a voice consonant with her character: tough, pragmatic, and honest, flinty and flirty by turns, but with a large, capacious heart.

What is most notable, however, about *Sister Sister* is its authenticity. Although written from and about black experience, the novel does not prettify contemporary black culture and the endemic problems that vex it. On the other hand, it does due diligence to the virtues of black culture: the steady emergence of a black professional middle class—in her workaday world Inda is Mrs. Lorraine Johnson-Swift, children's social worker—and a black aesthetic renaissance in music, culture, poetry and the arts that has revivified modern America.

Bibliography
Dickey, Eric Jerome. *Sister Sister.* New York: New American Library (Penguin), 1996.

—Jerome L. Wyant

Sittenfeld, Curtis E. (1975–) *American novelist*

A former high school English teacher, Curtis Sittenfeld is the author of three novels, PREP (2005), *The Man of My Dreams* (2006), and *American Wife* (2008). She is also a frequent reviewer for the *New York Times,* and has had work published in the *Atlantic Monthly,* Salon.com, and *Glamour* magazine. *Prep* was selected by the *New York Times* as one of the 10 best books of 2005, short-listed for the Orange Prize, and optioned by Paramount Pictures.

Sittenfeld is the second eldest of four children born in Cincinnati, Ohio, to Paul and Elizabeth C. Sittenfeld, and is the seventh woman in her mother's family to be called "Elizabeth Curtis," though she goes by the name of "Curtis." The young narrator of *Prep* also has a unisex name (Lee), and like the author, attended boarding school on the East Coast. When the novel was released, its publisher, Random House, encouraged the assumption that the character, Lee, was a thinly veiled version of Sittenfeld herself. Sittenfeld, however, is eager to defend the fictionality of her work: "Is it so easy to believe that I have no imagination and . . . can't invent dialogue or those scenarios?" (Lee).

After attending the Seven Hills School, a preparatory school in Cincinnati at which her mother is a teacher, Sittenfeld enrolled at Groton, a private boarding school in Massachusetts. Before graduating in 1993 she helped form a feminist group, and subsequently wrote an opinion piece for the *Washington Post* about the ways in which female students at the school were treated differently from males. Though this was viewed by some as an act of betrayal against the close-knit Groton community, Sittenfeld's early talent as a writer was apparent. She won the *Seventeen* magazine writing competition in 1992, at the age of 16, during the summer before her senior year at Groton.

Though she initially attended Vassar College, Sittenfeld transferred to Stanford University after her freshman year. At Stanford, she was the editor of the weekly arts magazine of the *Stanford Daily*, and was chosen as one of *Glamour* magazine's top-10 College Women of the Year in 1996. Before becoming a student at the prestigious Iowa Writers' Workshop, Sittenfeld wrote for the *Charlotte Observer* in North Carolina and for *Fast Company* magazine in Boston. While attending the Writers' Workshop she studied under Chris Offutt, Marilynne Robinson, and Ethan Canin. Sittenfeld won the *Mississippi Review*'s fiction contest in 1998, and is a recipient of the Michener-Copernicus Society of America Award.

Sittenfeld graduated from the Writers' Workshop in 2001, and was the writer-in-residence at St. Albans, an all-boys private school in Washington, D.C., for the period 2002–03. Until the publication of *Prep* she taught ninth-grade English at St. Albans, after which she became a full-time writer. (She promised to buy pizza for her students if *Prep* made the *New York Times* best-seller list—and to take them all to Hawaii if the book reached the top of that list.)

Prep centers on Lee Fiora, a girl from South Bend, Indiana, who finds life at a prestigious East Coast boarding school both fascinating and alienating. The Ault School of *Prep*—modeled after Sittenfeld's own Groton—is peopled by teenagers of extraordinary talents, intelligence, and wealth. Lee, who considers herself distinctly ordinary, remains rooted in the machinations of Ault society during her four years there, and *Prep* is remarkable not so much for its plot, which is in keeping with other coming-of-age tales, but for Sittenfeld's vivid portrayal of the insular and exotic character of the boarding school community. "The overall effect [of *Prep*]," writes Hermione Eyre, "is like Sweet Valley High as written by George Eliot" (2005). Sittenfeld infuses the world of rote teenage angst and melodrama with a keen understanding of the subtleties of adolescent interaction, cloaking the minutiae of Lee's story in a deft and supple rendering of the language and life characteristic of teenagers in general, and of boarding school in particular.

Sittenfeld's second novel, *The Man of My Dreams*, was published in 2006, and follows its narrator, Hannah Gavener, from the her 14th summer through a succession of failed relationships with men. The text of *The Man of My Dreams* is larger in scope than that of *Prep*, following its protagonist beyond high school, and allowing glimpses of a more mature, subdued, and meditative Hannah. But like Lee, Hannah is equally fascinated by and terrified of confident and outgoing women; and though Hannah's cousin Fig is a constant source of excitement, Sittenfeld is careful to remind her readers that Fig's adventurousness is not always a positive attribute. Instead, Hannah's contemplative nature provides the context for Sittenfeld's philosophical investigation of the thinking-woman's quest for love. Critics who praised Sittenfeld's ability to create "a believable world you can lose yourself in" (Groskop) through the carefully rendered narrative voice of *Prep*'s Lee Fiora, were less laudatory, however, about *The Man of My Dreams*. Without the backdrop of the New England boarding school—a stock source of fascination to American readers (*A Separate Peace, Catcher in the Rye*)—Sittenfeld's second novel focuses more intently on the sad, teenage character at its fore. Or, as a reviewer for the *New York Times* writes, *The Man of My Dreams* is Sittenfeld's declaration that "all that insiderish preppy stuff was the least important thing about my writing" (Dederer 2006).

American Wife, Sittenfeld's third novel, was published by Random House in 2008, and loosely follows the life of a woman named Alice Blackwell, who is understood to be a fictionalized version of former First Lady Laura Bush; indeed, Sittenfeld's novel takes its inspiration from a biography of Mrs. Bush by Ann Gerhart, called *The Perfect Wife: The Life and Choices of Laura Bush*. Described by Joyce Carol Oates as Sittenfeld's "most ambitious" novel, *American Wife* painstakingly revisits—and reshapes—the events of Laura Bush's/Alice Blackwell's life. Like Bush, the fictional Alice accidentally kills a boy in a car crash when she is 17, is bookish and conventionally middle-class, and marries the future president of the United States, the playboy, alcoholic son of a powerful political family. Just as the media at times obscured the integrity of *Prep* by concerning itself with speculations on an autobiographical slant to Sittenfeld's work, *American Wife* has been more closely scrutinized for its allegorical positioning of Alice Blackwell alongside Laura Bush than for its inherent literary merit.

The question of literary merit has itself been a sore spot for Sittenfeld since 2005, when she reviewed Melissa Banks's *The Wonder Spot* for the *New York Times.* In her article, "Sophie's Choices," Sittenfeld begins by asking, "To suggest that another woman's ostensibly literary novel is chick lit feels catty, not unlike calling another woman a slut—doesn't the term basically bring down all of us?" But she continues, "And yet, with *The Wonder Spot,* it's hard to resist" (Sittenfeld, *NYT*). Her apparent denigration of Banks's novel sparked a minor furor, with some commending Sittenfeld for voicing the prescient concerns of women who write about "female" topics, and others suggesting that Sittenfeld's comments had less to do with an appraisal of Banks's work than with her own insecurities.

Bibliography

Dederer, Claire. "Very Unimportant People," *New York Times,* 21 May 2006. Available online. URL: www.ny/lines.com/2006/05/21/books/chapters/0521-/st_sitt.html. Accessed 20, 2009.

Eyre, Hermione. "I didn't know George Eliot wrote 'Sweet Valley High,'" *Independent,* 2 October 2005.

Groskop, Viv. "My Life as a Full-Time Virgin," *Guardian,* 13 August 2006.

Lee, Felicia R. "Although She Wrote What She Knew, She Says She Isn't What She Wrote," *New York Times,* 26 January 2005.

Oates, Joyce Carol. "The First Lady," *New York Times,* 29 August 2008.

Sittenfeld, Curtis. *American Wife.* New York: Random House, 2008.

———. *The Man of My Dreams.* New York: Random House, 2006.

———. *Prep.* New York: Random House, 2005.

———. Review of *The Wander Spot.* "Sophie's Choices." *New York Times,* 5 June 2005.

Stuever, Hank. "Move Over, Holden," *Washington Post,* 23 February 2005.

—Katherine Edwards

Smith, Zadie (1975–   ) *British novelist, short story writer, and editor*

Zadie Smith is the author of several short stories and essays, and three novels: WHITE TEETH (2001), *The Autograph Man* (2003) and ON BEAUTY (2005). She is also editor of the collections *Piece of Flesh, The Book of Other People,* and *The Burned Children of America.* In 2001, Britain's Masterpiece Theatre adapted *White Teeth* into a successful BBC television miniseries.

Smith, whose given name is Sadie, was born in 1975 in northwest London to Yvonne Bailey-Smith, a Jamaican psychotherapist, and Harvey Smith, a British war veteran. Smith's childhood borough of Brent, along with its surrounding communities of Willesden Green, Cricklewood, and Kilburn, was extremely diverse racially—Pakistani, Indian, Irish, and black—and largely working-class, and the neighborhood serves as the setting for *White Teeth* and portions of *On Beauty.* As a young girl, Smith wanted to star in musicals, and developed a love of tap-dance, which gradually faded as she came of age (though Smith's novel *The Autograph Man* exploits her knowledge of musicals on film). In her teenage years, Smith was overweight and bookish, and spent the vast majority of her time reading classic literature while attending the local state schools in her area. As an undergraduate at Cambridge University, Smith studied English literature, and published several short stories in the university literary magazine. By the time she completed her degree in 2000, at the age of 24, her first novel, *White Teeth,* was already in print. While working on her second novel, *The Autograph Man,* Smith attended Harvard University as the 2002–03 Radcliffe Institute for Advanced Study Fellow. In 2004, shortly before the publication of her third novel, *On Beauty,* Smith married Irish poet Nick Laird, whom she met while studying at Cambridge. She now lives with her husband in Brent, a few blocks from her childhood home.

Though Smith's fiction is not autobiographical in any direct sense, her work does tend to reflect aspects of her experiences as a biracial woman. In an interview with *Fresh Air* radio host Terri Gross, Smith explains that, for those who grow up in a mixed-race household as she did, the experience

is completely normal to you. To me, when I was growing up, all families were mixed-race, and I found going into households where everyone was black or everyone was

white unnerving because it wasn't what I
knew. And also, just as a matter of fact, in
my neighborhood being mixed race was very,
very common, so I felt like I was part of a
very large community of brown girls—they
were everywhere. But I try and show [in my
literature] . . . that this experience isn't ab-
normal at all or in any way different until
sometimes people make you feel that it is,
people outside of your family circle.

Smith's representation of mixed-race families as
viable and functional units, and her belief in the
"normalcy" of mixed-race identity have been
widely recognized as among the most salient features of her work. In each of her novels the reader
is introduced to biracial characters, who are
more often than not central to the novel's plot
and development: Irie Jones, in *White Teeth,* is
the daughter of a Britisher and a Jamaican immigrant—the same as Smith herself; the protagonist
in *The Autograph Man,* Alex-Li Tandem, is Chinese
and Jewish; and Jerome, Zora, and Levi Belsey,
in *On Beauty,* are African-American and white.
Though Smith focuses on the positive aspects of
mixed-race families in her novels, she is likewise
attuned to the difficulties experienced by those
engaged in such relationships—most notably, the
obvious differences in the ways in which blacks and
whites experience and negotiate their race publicly,
outside of the protective realm of the family. Smith
has acknowledged that Howard Belsey, the white
father in *On Beauty* who hates to discuss race with
his biracial children, is based in part on her own
father: "It was very much [my father's] intention,
when we were growing up, to be color-blind . . .
and it was absolutely well-meant and a wonderful
way to grow up, but it doesn't—it's okay inside of
the household, but when you walk outside of the
house there are people who aren't colorblind, who
don't think that way . . . it's a very strange experience. I think I used some of that in the book,
definitely."

White Teeth, Smith's first novel, was published in 2000. The action of the novel spans the
course of the 20th century, and revolves primarily around three families—the Bangladeshi Iqbals,
the British and Jamaican Joneses, and the Jew-

ish and Catholic Chalfens—whose fates, despite
their ethnic and racial differences, are nonetheless intertwined as a result of their inhabiting
the same London community. However, as the
characters travel to and from places as far-flung
as Bangladesh, Jamaica, Bulgaria, Scandinavia,
and Italy, Smith also explores the relationship
immigrants have to their homeland, the complex
of relations immigrants have in their new country, and the ways in which urban life invites—and
at times discourages—cross-racial identification.
Though Smith's novel has often been referred to
as a portrait of "multicultural London" (Squires,
8), Smith herself, in an interview with Masterpiece Theatre immediately following the airing
of the *White Teeth* miniseries, argued that she was
not attempting to make any significant comment
on the racial make-up of London because "this is
what modern life is like. If I were to write a book
about London in which there were only white
people, I think that would be kind of bizarre. People do write books like that, which I find bizarre
because it's patently not what London is, nor has
it been for fifty years."

Her second novel, *The Autograph Man* (2002),
follows the life and times of Alex-Li Tandem, an
obsessive collector of autographs whose search
to find one particularly obscure signature, that
of Kitty Alexander, a former movie star, occupies
much of the plot. Alex-Li is joined by his closest
friends: a black Jewish-American expatriate from
Harlem named Adam Jacobs; Mark Rubenfine,
whose father pushes him into rabbinical studies;
and the British Joseph Klein, whose childhood fascination with both Judaism and autograph collecting initially sparks Alex-Li's interest in the pastime.
Smith's most recent novel, *On Beauty* (2005), represents a departure for Smith. Set in America in a
small college-town in Massachusetts, rather than
in London, the action of the novel revolves around
the lives of two families—the British and American Belseys and the Caribbean Kippses. Despite
the tension between Howard Belsey and Mon-
tague Kipps, both scholars of the artist Rembrandt
who are ideologically and politically opposed, their
wives, Kiki Belsey and Carlene Kipps, are nonetheless able to forge powerful emotional and intellectual bonds. The novel also explores, in a critical

way, the ways in which peoples of mixed race negotiate racial and national boundaries.

Smith's influences are as diverse as her subject matter, ranging from 19th-century British novels to contemporary American works of postmodern fiction. Her work has been favorably compared to that of English playwright Hanif Kureishi and the Indian-British novelist Salman Rushdie, though Smith has denied that she was in any way attempting to answer to or rewrite their novels in the crafting of her own (Squires, 16). Smith acknowledges that Kingsley Amis, George Eliot, Philip Larkin, David Foster Wallace, Charles Dickens, E. M. Forster, Martin Amis, Lawrence Sterne, Jeanette Winterson, and Julian Barnes were all significant authors to her during the crafting of her first novel, *White Teeth*, and she has likewise professed to being a fan of Vladimir Nabokov, Thomas Pynchon, and Raymond Carver (Squires, 20). Smith's last novel, *On Beauty*, takes its title from Elaine Scarry's text *On Beauty and Being Just*, a work of critical philosophy. Smith is also well versed in aspects of popular culture, and makes frequent allusions to hip-hop, rock, and folk music in each of her novels.

Bibliography

Smith, Zadie. *The Autograph Man*. New York: Vintage Books, 2003.

———. Interview. By Terry Gross. *Fresh Air*, National Public Radio. October 17, 2005. Available online. URL: http://www.npr.org/templates/story/story.php?storyId=4961669. Accessed May 16, 2009.

———. "An Interview with Zadie Smith." *Masterpiece Theatre*. Public Broadcasting Service. Available online. URL: http://www.pbs.org/wgbh/masterpiece/teeth/ei_smith_int.html. Accessed May 16, 2009.

———. *On Beauty*. New York: Penguin Books, 2005.

———. *White Teeth*. New York: Vintage Books, 2001.

———, ed. *The Book of Other People*. New York: Penguin, 2008.

———, ed. *The Burned Children of America*. London: Hamish Hamilton, 2003.

———, ed. *Piece of Flesh*. London: Institute of Contemporary Arts, 2001.

Squires, Claire. *Zadie Smith's* White Teeth: *A Reader's Guide*. New York: The Continuum International Publishing Group, 2002.

Walters, Tracey L. *Zadie Smith: Critical Essays*. New York: Peter Lang, 2008.

—Joanna Davis-McElligat

Speed Queen, The Stewart O'Nan (1997)

The Speed Queen is a first-person narrative that begins on Oklahoma's death row, where Marjorie Standiford, sentenced to death for 12 murders and scheduled for execution in a few hours, responds on cassette tape to a list of questions by best-selling horror writer Stephen King, who has bought the rights to her story. Despite this postmodern frame, and a plot so suffused with sadomasochistic sex, severe drug abuse, extremely violent crime, and exceptional car chases that the novel could be a work of genre fiction, *The Speed Queen* is a character-driven work of literary realism that explores the history, material conditions, and mental states that lead Marjorie, her husband, Lamont, and their friend Natalie Kramer—a lover of both husband and wife—to commit "The Sonic Murders." (Sonic is a drive-through fast food chain with carhop service based in Oklahoma City.)

The crimes, committed without a clear plan, as a response to great stress while under the effect of prolonged alcohol and methamphetamine abuse, net the threesome less than $100. Fleeing arrest under the stimulation of remarkable amounts of methamphetamine ("speed") and caffeine, Marjorie drives her husband, lover, and infant son Gainey in a lemon-twist yellow Plymouth Roadrunner through the rural highways and byways of Oklahoma, Texas, and New Mexico, guided only by a vague plan to go west to California or south to Mexico. The high-speed, drugged flight makes Marjorie infamous in the media as "The Speed Queen," and also serves as a metaphorical title for a woman addicted to speed in a variety of forms since childhood: "It's chemical, I think. Everything I used to do just fed into that. When I was using, I didn't have to eat or sleep or anything, just get in that Roadrunner and go" (7).

The Speed Queen is written in four parts, corresponding to the two sides of the two cassette tapes that Marjorie fills for King, and in numbered responses to King's questions. (Though King is never explicitly named, the novel is dedicated to "My Dear Stephen King," and King's novels are referenced by plot and by name.) These questions are not part of the text, and Marjorie largely ignores them, preferring a linear chronicle. She contradicts and criticizes King's questions from the beginning:

> Why did I kill them?
> I didn't kill them. It's not even a question.
> You think you'd start with something like my mom or dad or what I was like when I was a kid. Show me riding my tricycle out behind the chicken house, my hair in pigtails, buckteeth, something cute like that. Then you could say, she was a normal gal and look what happened to her. (5)

Such advice allows O'Nan to comment on the social and genre expectations of how such crimes are told and understood. He makes it clear that genre writers like King are part of the same social milieu of fast food, low-end service jobs, and mass-market art that form the background of Marjorie and her crimes. (Despite such criticism of mass-market writers, O'Nan and King collaborated on a sports book in 2004). A third level of metafictional commentary is achieved through references to Natalie's already-published account of the crimes, *The Sonic Killers.* Marjorie frequently relates and contests Natalie's, the state's, and the press's understanding of her and her crimes, which leaves open the possibility that Marjorie is an unreliable narrator, and adds to the complexity to the text.

One of the novel's strengths is O'Nan's playfulness with the clichéd "reasons" for crimes such as Marjorie's in true-crime and horror novels. As a child, Marjorie witnesses her parents having sadomasochistic sex, the improper disposal of the family pet, and the death of her father. She also sustains several head injuries (one severe) from her love of going fast, and becomes a heavy user of recreational drugs in adolescence. Nonetheless, O'Nan offers no evidence that any of these factors affected her personality or actions, except for the month-long caffeine and methamphetamine binge that coincided with her crimes. Nor does O'Nan present Marjorie's fate as a result of being born

into a "criminal underclass" or a "sick family." Marjorie does seem to have inherited a taste for speed and rough sex from her father, a jockey, but overall her childhood was emotionally and financially stable, though she has friction with her mother as an adult. Marjorie's decision to drop out of college to live with her friends Garlyn and Joy, work menial jobs, and drink as much alcohol and diet Pepsi as possible, is not presented as informed by anything other than her desire for pleasure: "It's easy to blame other people or circumstances, but I won't. I liked to drink, it's that simple. I liked sitting in the booth at the Conoco [a gas station] and taking a tug whenever I felt like it" (49). Neither Marjorie nor the state perceives her as guilty of her crimes by reason of insanity. Instead, she presents herself as a loving and devoted wife, friend, and mother, who eschews drugs throughout her pregnancy, provides Gainey with a high level of care throughout her crimes, and only answers King's questions to leave the child an inheritance.

From the beginning, Marjorie is established as a likable character who has good relations with her guard, Janille; her lawyer, Mr. Jefferies; her spiritual counselor, Sister Perpetua (Marjorie has found Jesus in prison); and the other inmates on death row. She is practical, unpretentious, sophisticated in terms of the legal system and the media, and willing to work hard for what she wants, which is usually excitement and altered states of reality. The contrast between these traits and her horrific actions as part of a "thrill kill" gang, as well as O'Nan's/Marjorie's constant examination of the public perception of such criminals, leads to the surprising humor of the novel:

> Part of the reason why I might die tonight is the eighty-nine times
> [I stabbed my victim.] I know this is going to sound cold, but it doesn't matter if it was eighty-nine times or just one. It doesn't matter that Natalie cut off Kim Zwilich's fingers. Mr. Jefferies disagrees with me; he says that's exactly what matters to a jury. While that might be true, I don't think it's right. Dead is dead.
> But I understand all your readers will want the nasty details. That's what makes

it fun for them. . . . You get to go way over-board with those little gross-out details. I figure that's what you'll want to do here. I'm not sure how you'll do that with real people because it would be hard on their families, but if it's fiction I guess it doesn't matter. You can just change their names. Nobody believes the people in your books are real anyway. That's what makes it fun. (183)

The novel was well received, and the *New York Times* complimented O'Nan for "an unfailing intelligence, a grim and bracing humor, an unblinking eye for the telling detail." It was adapted into a one-character play of the same name, which premiered in 2006.

Bibliography

O'Nan, Stuart. *The Speed Queen.* New York: Doubleday, 1997.

O'Nan, Stuart, and Stephen King. *Faithful: Two Diehard Boston Red Sox Fans Chronicle the Historic 2004 Season.* New York: Scribner, 2004.

Stade, George. "Roadies." New York Times on the Web. Available online. URL: http://www.nytimes.com/books/97/05/11/reviews/970511.11stadet.html. Accessed May 29, 2007.

The Speed Queen. Adapted by Anne Stockton from the novel by Stuart O'Nan. Directed by Austin Pendleton. Performer Anne Stockton. New Jersey Repertory Theatre, October–November 2006.

—Jeff Solomon

Straight Outta Compton Ricardo Cortez Cruz (1992)

A vivid and memorable portrait of indomitable life in the Los Angeles ghetto, RICARDO CORTEZ CRUZ's 1992 novel is narrated straight up from the street, rather than from the safe vantage point of a detached observer. The novel borrows its title from the 1988 album and song by N.W.A. (Niggaz With Attitude). Like the controversial hip-hop hit, Cortez Cruz's debut explores gang life—its drugs, guns, sex, and police brutality—and like the song, pulls no punches. Its hoodlums, prostitutes, and drug addicts speak Ebonics, a Black-Ameri-

can language defined by its ingenuity, dark humor, expletives, cultural reference, and self-conscious autonomy from standardized English. Subtitled "A dive into living large, / a work where characters trip, / talk out the side of their neck / and cuss like it was nothing," *Straight Outta Compton* plunges its readers into the stoops, alleyways, and other transitional spaces of the Compton ghetto. Cortez Cruz does not just talk about the ghetto; he shows it, alive and unpredictable, ultimately perhaps, incomprehensible. Nor does he guide us through it in the manner of a 19th-century narrator, but forces us to wander about unsupervised, unadvised, and unprotected.

Ghetto songs and films typically lionize the violent underbelly of inner-city life. Cortez Cruz, however, criticizes the easy portrayal or dismissive exploitation of black ghettoes, taking pains to distinguish his narrative from the "blaxploitation" (63, 104) that typifies inner-city treatments in music and film; and his problematic heroes, Rooster and Clive, are far from mere players in violent action and its self-destructive repercussions.

Cortez Cruz's narrative style also revitalizes N.W.A.'s depiction of Compton. The groundbreaking song "Straight Outta Compton" features three separate speakers: Ice Cube, MC Ren, and Easy-E, and the novel also incorporates three voices: though at times indistinguishable, they can be roughly discerned as the increasingly detached male adolescent of part one, the progressively more present female prostitute in the first half of part two, and the omniscient, sexually indeterminate reporter of the last two chapters. Moreover, like N.W.A. and other rappers who liberally sample or "quote" song and film clips, Cortez Cruz incorporates a myriad of cultural references into the book. His narrators constantly allude to figures like Public Enemy (15, 115), Rodney King (29, 32, 45, and passim), Yogi Berra (55), Tommy "the Hit-man" Hearns (59), and Larry King (115), and the broader narrative reveals elements of a vast literary heritage, extending the margins of conventional inner-city representation. Among these elements, Compton inscribes, in some form or other, references to Joseph Conrad (25), Shakespeare (36, 37, 38, 103), Toni Morrison (48), Voltaire (89), Karl Marx (104), and Thoreau (108). The novel prizes the protest and innovation of celebrity *and* literary figures.

Beginning with the first chapter, entitled "Tomorrow" in order to evoke a sense of futurity and possibility (instead of the repetition and hopelessness common to blaxploitation), Cortez Cruz urges us to reconsider our assumptions about underprivileged black life in America. We come across "a crowd of Black people ... dramatizing Gwendolyn Brooks' poem 'We Real Cool' and filming it" (14). The young first-person narrator then ironically dismisses—and therefore covertly applauds—this creative act: "It was as if Compton was the mecca for Blacks, another fatherless Black producer trying to produce a blockbuster movie out of the ghetto" (14). Brooks's famous "We Real Cool," this narrator suggests, is not just a portrait of the "real cool" (3) blacks that "left school" (4) to "lurk late," (5) "sing sin," "thin gin" (6) and "die soon" (8). Instead, the 1960 poem may be seen as a critical commentary on simplistic portrayals of black fate itself; or put another way, "We Real Cool" could be conceived as an ironic dismissal of all-too-easy dismissals. This is why the black crowd in *Straight Outta Compton* is engaged in a creative act, not a destructive one: in dramatizing Brooks's poem, the Compton crowd can offer another innovative reading of street life.

Epitomizing the agenda of its publisher, Fiction Collective Two, which launches artistically daring works, *Straight Outta Compton* also extends the stylistic parameters of conventional literary representation. The text is demanding. Multithemed and loose-jointed, it reads like a hip-hop album. Beyond its complex narrative form, it incorporates endless wordplay, syntactical ingenuity, time shifts, and an array of misleading, journalistically inspired subtitles. What the whole buzzing amalgam suggests is that there is no single, straight Compton story, no easy means by which to generalize ghetto life. Emphasizing this point, the novelist offers portraits of two contrasting protagonists: Clive and Rooster. Though childhood friends, their paths diverge as they enlist in rival gangs, and whereas Clive, a former big-brother figure to Rooster, longs to escape Compton, Rooster, his father dead of a drug overdose, finds solace in womanizing.

Perhaps the most innovative quality of *Straight Outta Compton* is its complete rejection of the traditional narrative arc, with its introduction, rising action, climax, falling action, and denouement. Instead, the text is all action, seamless and at times almost undifferentiated, much like a hip-hop number. In this way, it discourages the whole logic of conventional reading, with the latter's progressive, accumulative heuristics. Instead we are welcomed to approach the novel in the same way we do music albums and videos; reading and rereading it, in whole or in part, sometimes seriously, sometimes not, alternately taking up the stance of one or another of the varied countercultures that Ricardo Cortez Cruz privileges; and evolving a sense not so much of convergent truth as of divergent and fecund possibility.

Bibliography

Brooks, Gwendolyn. "We Real Cool." 1960. *The Norton Anthology of American Literature.* Shorter 7th ed. Edited by Nina Baym, 2,540. New York: Norton, 2008.

Cortez Cruz, Ricardo. *Straight Outta Compton.* Boulder, Colo.: Fiction Collective Two, 1992.

—Jason S. Polley

Stripping + Other Stories Patricia "Pagan" Kennedy (1994)

Stripping + Other Stories is a collection of short fiction whose protagonists often seem on the verge of a life-altering epiphany; but rarely does PATRICIA "PAGAN" KENNEDY show the reader the epiphany itself, instead focusing on luminous but easily overlooked moments preceding it. All 10 stories explore efforts to achieve authentic selfhood in a recalcitrant and inauthentic world.

The first story in the collection, "Elvis's Bathroom," presents a young adult narrator struggling to find her place in the world. She moves in with Juan Hombre, a local punk rock star whose 15 minutes of fame have already passed. Together they decide to take a trip to Graceland to see the toilet on which Elvis died, and while in Tennessee, the narrator discovers a place where the reader senses she may at last come into her own.

In "The Dead Rabbit Pocket" the narrator recalls her father and a luminous event on her birthday, when she chooses to ride a horse instead of her usual pony and falls off. The intriguing title arises—never to be explained—when her father "reached into the pocket inside his coat, the pocket in which he used to keep dead rabbits. But all he pulled out was a handkerchief . . ." (27–28). The fragmentary story ends with the young girl drifting off to sleep thinking, "It seems to me that I'm always in that ring now, going around and around on that horse that nothing can stop, not the shutter of a camera, not my father" (28).

The eponymous "Stripping" is told from the perspective of an elderly woman who 60 years ago was raped by an older cousin, Jason. Nannie at last decides to confront her younger cousin, Henry, who had stripped her clothes off and then done nothing while his violent, bullying brother raped her. Yet, confronted by Henry's palliative memories of the rape, Nannie decides to confirm his misrepresentations in order to save him from thinking he is a coward, "And she thought how soon, when the end came, all these things would be stripped away from her, until she was as bare and white as that girl in the barn, not innocent now but hard and smoothed down to nothing as a pearl" (47).

Kennedy explores the contemporary impulse to prescribe away psychological problems in "Shrinks," which describes a mother-daughter relationship filled with psychiatric competition. The mother has recently begun taking Prozac and makes drastic changes to her life while insisting that her daughter, Sara, also take the drug. Sara, who at not quite 30 years of age has already seen 30 different "shrinks," is less than convinced by her mother's Prozac success story. Sara's boyfriend, Andy, realizes, "She was . . . like a person whose wounds never get a chance to heal because she can't stop picking at the scabs" (60). In the end, Sara chooses not to take the drug and finds a more authentic sense of happiness in Andy.

"Underwear Man," the fifth story in the collection, is an unsettling exploration of childhood anxiety. Vicky fears the Underwear Man, a monster with X-ray eyes who can see through her clothes to check if she is wearing underwear. When she breaks her leg and needs X-rays, her fear is exacerbated by a sexual prank call, and that night Vicky makes up a nightmare in order to sleep in her parents' bed. But even her parents cannot save her from the Underwear Man, who smells her out and peels off her skin to get at her bones.

"The Tunnel" also features a young female protagonist, who is here increasingly obsessed with a dangerous tunnel near her house that children sometimes use as a shortcut. Of course this only sharpens her desire to explore it, though this is forbidden by her parents. Along with a neighborhood boy and her best friend, she runs through the tunnel and then, upon returning home, lies to her parents, fearing that they know the truth and will catch her in the lie. But she soon realizes that her parents do not know; and—in one of *Stripping*'s fully realized epiphanies—she suddenly recognizes that she can lie to them without being caught: "What it felt like was another girl inside me, one that didn't come from my parents" (85).

In "Camp," Kennedy explores the same territory on another level. Here the protagonist, Helen, wants nothing more than to become like the teenaged girls she sees at the roller rink. While at camp she experiments with changes to her personality through a rather forced relationship with Jim, a boy she meets at a square dance who would rather be away from the crowd reading *The Hobbit*. Helen pushes them both to move at a faster pace than either is ready for and then abruptly breaks it off: "[W]hen I spoke, I said, 'Yeah, I'm going back.' It was the bored, flat voice of the roller rink girl. She had taken my body; she had possessed me" (103).

"The Black Forest" follows a freshman college student through her obsession with Nietzsche. After enrolling in a seminar on the nihilistic philosopher, Helen becomes so obsessed that she approaches a nervous breakdown. Her friend, Nira, who had introduced her to philosophy, advises her, "If you want to get better, you're going to have to think about superficial things" (121). Helen gradually surrenders her obsession and rejoins her life and self, reflecting dispassionately on what it truly means to be like Nietzsche, the price that must be paid: "Something about him just then reminded me of the mad Nietzsche, who would sit quietly for hours and then suddenly erupt into screams. I had almost forgotten about the screams" (126).

The collection's penultimate story, "UFOs," begins with the witty question: "If they can send a man to the moon, why can't they send them all?" (129). Jenny has been living with her boyfriend, Dave, who is prone to "fits." After a bad "fit," Jenny leaves Dave and moves in with a lesbian, hippie friend. While visiting Jenny, Dave explains that he is from a UFO and reveals his theory of the "Love Universe." Listening to him, Jenny realizes she will never be able to understand him and comes to "a decision" about him that, like most of *Stripping*'s resolutions, is withheld from the reader (148).

For all its lack of explicit resolution, however, there is a sense in the collection's final story of a kind of heuristic key to its enigmatic contents. "The Monument" utilizes a contemplative first-person narration to explore the unspoken linchpin of small-town (and by extension, communal) life. Habit, secular ritual, allows the people in the town to have no need to talk. Silence encompasses the town, and the narrator reflects, "All I can see of the stream is its surface. No, that's wrong, I can't see the surface either; what I see is my own world reflected back . . ." (153).

Bibliography

Kennedy, Pagan. *Stripping + Other Stories.* New York: High Risk Books/Serpent's Tail, 1994.

—Amy Parziale

Swofford, Anthony (1970–) *American novelist and memoirist*

Anthony Swofford is the author of a memoir, JAR-HEAD: A MARINE'S CHRONICLE OF THE GULF WAR AND OTHER BATTLES (2003), a novel, *Exit A* (2007), and both fiction and nonfiction that has appeared in the *New York Times, Harper's, Men's Journal*, the *Iowa Review*, and a host of other popular publications.

Born in Fairfield, California, Swofford was raised on military bases in the United States and Japan. His family has a long military tradition: His father served in Vietnam, his grandfather fought in World War II, and his older brother enlisted in the army.

When Swofford was 17 he joined the U.S. Marine Corps, and three years later his unit was sent to Riyadh, Saudi Arabia, in preparation for the beginning of the First Gulf War. During his time in the Marine Corps, Swofford attained the rank of lance corporal, while also securing a position within the elite STA (Surveillance and Target Acquisition) Platoon, where he was trained as a sniper. Swofford's best-selling memoir, *Jarhead: A Marine's Chronicle of the Gulf War and Other Battles* (2003), focuses on this portion of his life, as well as exploring memories of his life before and after his military service. Vividly capturing the boredom, terror, and loneliness that epitomized life for a soldier involved in America's first large-scale war since Vietnam, Swofford's self-portrait of the contemporary American marine drew wide-ranging critical acclaim. Michiko Kakutani's review of *Jarhead* for the *New York Times* is typical:

> By turns profane and lyrical, swaggering and ruminative, *Jarhead* . . . is not only the most powerful memoir to emerge thus far from the last gulf war, but also a searing contribution to the literature of combat, a book that combines the black humor of *Catch-22* with the savagery of *Full Metal Jacket* and the visceral detail of *The Things They Carried.*

On finishing his military service in 1992, Swofford worked an assortment of jobs before attending the American River College, a community college in Sacramento, where he became interested in writing and edited the award-winning *American River Review*. After finishing at American River College, Swofford earned his B.A. at the University of California, Davis, before attending the prestigious Iowa Writers' Workshop at the University of Iowa, where he completed his Master of Fine Arts. Prior to selling the film rights to *Jarhead*, Swofford taught at the University of Iowa, Lewis and Clark College, and St. Mary's College of California.

In 2005 *Jarhead* was adapted for film, directed by Sam Mendes, who had previously directed *American Beauty* (1999) and *Road to Perdition* (2002). The film, featuring Jake Gyllenhaal in the role of Anthony Swofford, omitted large portions of the memoir and changed a host of details, some of them central to the book. Besides excluding a number of scenes from Swofford's childhood that play a vital role in the literary account, some key elements in the narrative were altered for the filmic version: Swofford is demoted (which never occurred); Troy, one of Swofford's fellow marines who died in a possible drunk driving accident, is depicted as a drug dealer; and the climactic scene in the sniper tower is markedly different from the events of the book. On its own distinct merits, however, the film version of *Jarhead* received largely positive reviews.

Exit A (2007), Swofford's second book, tells the story of Severin Boxx, a young man living on a military base outside Tokyo. Boxx is in love with Virginia Sachiko Kindwall, a young half-Japanese woman and daughter of the base commander. While Boxx's other teenage preoccupation is football (the base commander is also the coach of the team), Kindwall, whose primary heroine is Bonnie from *Bonnie & Clyde,* becomes involved with a local crime syndicate. After Kindwall becomes involved in a serious crime it appears as if she and Boxx are likely to be separated forever, but benign fate intervenes. Although Swofford mined autobiographical material that he clearly knew intimately—details of military culture and daily life on an American military base in Japan, in particular—critics were not impressed with this highly anticipated follow-up to *Jarhead.*

Swofford has also been involved with two major documentaries. He narrated and coproduced *Semper Fi* (2006), a documentary about the U.S. Marine Corps ("Semper fi," from the Latin *semper fidelis*—"Always faithful"—is the motto of the marines, and Swofford makes numerous references to the motto throughout *Jarhead*). Swofford was also featured in Richard E. Robbins's Oscar-nominated documentary *Operation Homecoming* (2007), which focused on a number of soldiers turned writers (including Tim O'Brien and science fiction writer Joe Haldeman), as well as new writers discussing the art of writing war.

In early 2008, Swofford reported on the Iraq Veterans against the War Winter Soldier Event in Silver Spring, Maryland, for *Slate* magazine. He currently lives in Manhattan.

Bibliography

Swofford, Anthony. *Exit A.* New York: Scribner, 2007.
———. *Jarhead: A Marine's Chronicle of the Gulf War and Other Battles.* New York: Scribner, 2003.

—Christopher Garland

T

Tartt, Donna (1963–) *American novelist and short story writer*

Donna Tartt is the author of two novels, *The* SECRET HISTORY (1992) and *The* LITTLE FRIEND (2002); short stories published in the *New Yorker, Harper's,* and *GQ;* and nonfiction. *The Secret History* was released by Knopf in 1992 with wild publicity and an unusual $450,000 advance for Tartt. It was an instant best seller, remaining on the *Publishers Weekly* best-seller list for 13 weeks. Plans to turn the novel into a film have been announced. *The Little Friend* won the 2003 W.H. Smith Literary Award and was short-listed for the 2003 Orange Prize for Fiction. Tartt is reportedly at work on her third novel, and a novella based on Greek myth for the Canongate Myth series.

Donna Tartt was born the elder of two daughters to Don and Taylor Tartt in Greenwood, Mississippi; she grew up in Grenada, Mississippi, near Oxford, where she spent much of her time as a teenager and later attended the University of Mississippi. Tartt is widely characterized as having been a precocious and literary child, writing her first poem at age five and publishing a sonnet at 13. She now divides her time between her farm in rural Virginia and Manhattan's East Side.

Tartt attended the University of Mississippi for one year, where she describes herself feeling like an "oddball" amid her fellow sorority sisters (Kaplan). At Ole Miss she was discovered by Willie Morris, author of *The Last of the Southern Girls* and *The Courting of Marcus Dupree,* and was allowed to enroll in a graduate short story course with Barry

Hannah, author of *Geronimo Rex* and *High Lonesome,* in which she excelled. Sensing her talent, Morris encouraged her to transfer to Bennington College in Vermont for her sophomore year where he felt she could better develop her skills.

At Bennington College, Tartt became friends with future novelists BRET EASTON ELLIS, author of AMERICAN PSYCHO, and JILL EISENSTADT. Tartt began writing *The Secret History* during her second year at Bennington. Ellis, who published the best-selling *Less Than Zero* while at Bennington, read her novel throughout its composition and, when it was nearly finished, introduced Tartt and her novel to his powerful literary agent, Amanda Urban.

The Secret History follows an intellectually arrogant group of classics students at a small New England liberal arts college, which, despite Tartt's objections to the contrary, is generally taken to be modeled on Bennington. Richard Papen, a transfer student like Tartt, works his way into the elite and exclusive group of classics students at Hampden College, only to find out that they have engaged in a Dionysian ritual during which they killed a farmer. When Bunny, the only member of the group absent during the ritual, discovers the accident, he attempts blackmail and ends up murdered. Tartt begins the novel in medias res, revealing Bunny's murder and the identity of his murderers at the beginning of the narrative. The rest of the novel unfolds the reasons, details, and psychological fallout of the murder.

The Secret History combines suspenseful mystery with classical references, an inquiry into values in modern culture, and an exploration of ethical questions. This combination of intellectual richness with an engaging and beautiful style, crafted through her intensive and time-consuming writing process, makes her writing stand out among its contemporaries. The scant scholarly literature on Tartt's fiction has focused on her use of Greek myth in *The Secret History.* As Brian Arkin writes, "Tartt with great skill integrates the mundane existence of the late 20th century in America with the world of ancient Greece. . . . [I]t is the irrational element in Greek life, stressed by Dodds, that produces the undoubted power of this novel" (287). Tartt professes that the success of *The Secret History* was a shock to her; "I really would have bet my life that this was not a commercial book. . . . The book's long," she explains, "it's got Greek phrases, and it's not written in a style that's popular" (Lambert).

Fans impatiently awaited the publication of Tartt's second novel, *The Little Friend,* which was released in 2002. *The Little Friend* finds Tartt returning to her southern roots, being set in a small Mississippi town not unlike the one in which Tartt grew up. Her second novel addresses the aftermath of the mysterious death of nine-year-old Robin Cleves, who is found hanged outside his home on Mother's Day. Years later, his 12-year-old sister Harriet, who was a baby when he died, decides to discover his murderer and avenge his death, with disastrous consequences.

Tartt intentionally employs a different language, diction, and narrative technique in *The Little Friend,* which made her feel that she was writing another first novel (BookPage). Whereas her first novel was written in first-person narrative, *The Little Friend* employs omniscient point of view, incorporates southern dialect, and weaves together multiple storylines. Tartt is intensely interested in style and innovation; "It's a writer's business now, to work at the edges of narrative and different kinds of experience" (Identitytheory, 12/02).

Both novels deal with a theme that Tartt admits is perpetually fascinating to her: the "echoes and repercussions of [murder] and how they play out over time" (Johnson, 189). As Tartt says, "I think that people long for something that will deal with . . . the reality of death in kind of a moral and ethical way, a philosophical way" (Hal-

loween, 10/97). Due to this focus on murder, Tartt has sometimes been categorized as a gothic writer, a label she is not completely comfortable with. She is also often described as a southern writer, or as part of the "New South," but as she points out, her first novel was written and set in New England.

Tartt is currently at work on her third novel, a suspenseful character study in loss, guilt, and obsession (due out in 2012), and on a novella based on Greek myth for the Canongate Myth series.

Bibliography

Arkins, Brian. "Greek Themes in Donna Tartt's *The Secret History.*" *Classical and Modern Literature: A Quarterly* 15, no. 3 (Spring 1995): 281–287.

———. "Donna Tartt." By Robert Birnbaum. Identity Theory. Available online. URL: http://www.identitytheory.com/people/birnbaum77.html. Accessed May 16, 2009.

"Halloween: Gothic Literature." October 30, 1997. Talk of the Nation. Available online. URL: www.olemiss.edu/nwp/dis/tartt_donna/index.html. Accessed October 21, 2009.

Johnson, Sarah Anne. *The Very Telling: Conversations with American Writers.* Hanover and London: University Press of New England, 2006.

Kanner, Ellen. "Murder in Mississippi: A Grisly Murder Haunts the Heroine of Donna Tartt's Long-Awaited Novel." Bookpage.com. Available online. URL: http://www.bookpage.com/0211bp/donna_tartt.html. Accessed May 16, 2009.

Kaplan, James. "Smart Tartt." *Vanity Fair* 55, no. 9 (September 1992): 248–251, 276–278.

Tartt, Donna. *The Little Friend.* New York: Knopf, 2002.

———. *The Secret History.* New York: Knopf, 1992.

———. "Talking with Donna Tartt: A Cinderella Story." By Pam Lambert. *Newsday.* Available online. URL: http://www.geocities.com/soho/8543/dcs.htm. Accessed May 16, 2009.

—Amy Smith

This Book Will Save Your Life A. M. Homes (2006)

A. M. HOMES *This Book Will Save Your Life* is at once a hopeful and apocalyptic story, set in present-day Los Angeles and focusing on the midlife crisis of a day-trader named Richard Novak. An unexpected attack of pain leads him to explore mind/body connections through such New Age activities as seeing a psychological medicine specialist and attending a meditation retreat. He also befriends Anhil, an Indian donut-shop owner whom he lets drive his Mercedes in exchange for free donuts; he starts to spend time with his next-door neighbor, a famous actor/writer who volunteers with the elderly, and with Cynthia, a taken-for-granted housewife who transitions out of domesticity. The novel's moments of real transformation come not from Richard's good deeds (he saves a horse from the sinkhole that swallows his house, he pays for his maid's hip replacement, he rescues Cynthia from a supermarket), but from his relationship with his teenage son, Ben, who comes to visit while on a road trip with his cousin. Despite the fact that Ben is acutely angry with Richard for the latter's seeming abandonment of him and his mother, the two manage to bond and reestablish their relationship.

The novel's satire is a point of contention for many critics. For some it seems that using L.A. as a backdrop for an existential crisis is too easy; for example, when Richard gets hit by a car while walking, the driver complains because she has to wait for the police, and further speculates that if she had hit a woman, the woman would be apologizing to her. But the novel so often casts the metaphorical as the mundane and the mundane as the metaphorical that it becomes hard to tell the difference. "Mr. Dunkin' doesn't even think of me, but I know my donut is better," confirms Anhil, "Mine is the real donut, the human donut . . . I'm very lucky. I count my donuts" (32). Through such humor, *This Book* attempts to desentimentalize moments of tranquility or insight. Richard's son exclaims "nice ocean, calmer than I would have thought. Looking at the water makes me want to pee" (246). In the same way, the meditation retreat that Richard goes on is recollected as a source of profound insight, but the digestive problems caused by its food, as well as the farting in the meditation room, are emphasized as much as any moments of enlightenment.

The novel is a something of a departure for Homes, a well-established New York author who has written six novels, one autobiographical memoir, and two collections of short stories. Her previous books, like *The End of Alice,* written from the perspective of a pedophile, and *Music for Torching,* in which a middle-class couple sets fire to their home, explore darker aspects of the human psyche. However, Homes protests that "it's just as daring and dangerous to write about someone who is trying to find a more positive experience in their lives" (Lindner); and the search for this more positive experience may be one reason why heroism is so central to the novel. Richard achieves his 15 minutes of fame by rescuing an abducted woman from the trunk of a car because he sees SOS signals in Morse code while driving behind them. News coverage refers to him as "the apparent hero," an appropriate epithet because Richard's heroism echoes the sheer randomness found in Albert Camus's *The Stranger.* Yet it is clear that these heroic acts neither resolve his existential angst nor make him more able to reconnect with his family. However, like the donuts Richard is so fond of consuming, it seems that this heroism remains a necessary indulgence. His neighbor explains, "Sometimes you can't do things for the people you should do things for, including yourself, but you can do them for someone else, a stranger" (209).

While Richard's family could not qualify as strangers, it is clear that he feels more estranged from them than the other people he meets. Always a step behind his brother, who is preoccupied with his failure to win the Nobel Prize, Richard also feels disapproval from his mother because of his early retirement. When asked if he had any childhood trauma, he replies "Just my parents—they're Jewish" (50). But the estrangement that is most painful is the one from his son, and as the novel progresses Ben becomes increasingly vocal and provocative in expressing his anger toward his father. When he at last comes to terms with this anger and his feelings of abandonment, Richard too must comes to terms with his failings as a father, as well as his son's homosexuality (a reversal of the plot of Homes's *Jack,* in which a father comes out to his son).

The novel's ending eschews any sentimental moments of realization or reunion, preferring a more hard-nosed and perhaps more valuable pragmatism. But nevertheless readers are left with a sense that however imperfect it may be—or corrupted by the body, L.A., or any other of the countless entropic factors in the novel—transformation (or at least feeling better) is not only possible but desirable. In the end, *This Book Will Save Your Life* is no more prescriptive or lifesaving than a donut shop, but it offers a credible and convincing account of a search for meaning and connection in an otherwise unexamined life, while honestly denying any easy or straightforward resolution of that search.

Bibliography

Homes, A. M. *This Book Will Save Your Life.* New York: Penguin, 2006.

Lindner, Elsbeth. "A M Homes: Reasons to Be Cheerful." Independent (June 9, 2006). Available online. URL: http://www.independent.co.uk/arts-entertainment/books/features/a-m-homes-reasons-to-be-cheerful-481559.html. Accessed May 16, 2009.

—Dominika Bednarska

Toughest Indian in the World, The   Sherman Alexie   (2000)

SHERMAN ALEXIE's second short story collection is a skillful mix of fantasy, humor, and searching social commentary, exploring faultlines in the self, the community, and multiethnic society at large; all common traits of Alexie's broader fictional oeuvre. In the title story, for example, a white man and an Indian woman marry and have children, but the wife still desires to make love with the darkest Indian she can find, and the husband longs for his white high-school sweetheart. In this kind of relationship, they can only talk about race as "a concept, as a foreign country visited . . . or as an enemy that existed outside of their house," and not "as a constant presence, a houseguest and permanent tenant who walked around all the rooms in their shared lives, opening drawers, stealing utensils and small articles of clothing, changing the temperature" (14).

Ron McFarland notes that typically Alexie's humor acts as a kind of catalyst for making the pain and anger easier to tolerate, even if it is "rarely of the gentle, tolerant, urbane variety" (31). For McFarland, it is "essentially a comic vision" that offers "an alternative to the traditionally bleak or at least dark or downbeat ending" in such Native American novels as D'Arcy McNickle's *The Surrounded,* N. Scott Momaday's *House Made of Dawn,* Leslie Silko's *Ceremony,* and James Welch's *The Death of Jim Loney* (37).

Added to this humor is often quasi-surreal imagery and action, employing exaggerated elements of magical realism, as his characters, having been coercively redefined by the dominant forces of American history, struggle to find their own selfhood in a society happy to abandon them to sheer nonidentity (41). Referring to Alexie's first story collection, *The Lone Ranger and Tonto Fistfight in Heaven* (1993), John Newton explains how such stylistic complexity engenders what he calls a "transcultural play of recognitions" in which American Indians are able to create a "counterdiscourse" (421).

This interplay results from the Native subject's "divided consciousness" and creates "a vacillation or ambivalence" within the discourse where "the difference unsettles the binary symmetry of that ritualized moment and reveals both the stereotype itself and . . . an active nonidentity" (421).

Such magical (sur)realism, and its role in Alexie's exploration of identity, is perhaps most apparent in the coyote figure, who dominates the symbolic landscape of "South by Southwest." During their travels, Seymour and Salmon Boy come upon a number of coyotes in extraordinary places: one nailed to a fence post, which they stare at "the way the last two disciples stared at the resurrected Jesus" (61); another "nailed to a speed-limit sign"; one "howling from an overpass" (69); finally, one "drinking a cup of coffee in a truck-stop diner" (69). The coyote is a trickster figure, a survivor on his wits, ultimately a reflection of the Indian's struggle with a dominant culture that refuses to see him or allow him to form and shape his own identity. Like the Indian, the coyote has been crucified on the cross of the dominant society, but this crucifixion makes his resurrection possible, and this resurrection makes it possible, in turn, to shift his identity at will and appear incognito at times. Thus, when an elderly lady asks Seymour and

Salmon Boy if they are real, neither can tell her if they are (68).

Douglas Ford, in his essay, "Sherman Alexie's Indigenous Blues," claims popular culture is another means by which one can recover what has been lost, a means of tracing the false images and histories, of discovering, creating, and re-creating identity: "Popular culture often creates our (mis)conceptions of race, even so, it also provides a storehouse of materials that lend themselves to generating counter-images and new figurations of race" (209); and *Toughest Indian* offers the possibility of "disruption and reconfiguration" (209–210), revealing "a new way of signifying the Indian" (212). Seymour, for example, stares at a Navajo couple at a McDonalds and asks Salmon Boy if he thinks they love each other. Salmon Boy replies that some people say the Navajo are aliens, and "If they do [love each other] . . . then it's alien love. And I don't know anything about alien love" (72). Seymour tells Salmon Boy that Stephen Spielburg knows about alien love, and Salmon Boy says he knows because he is an alien and the "Jews and the Navojos came down in the same ships" (72). He claims Moses was a Navajo and asks Seymour, "Haven't you heard of the lost tribes," to which Seymour answers, "Everybody is lost" (72).

In the interstitial world of *The Toughest Indian,* humor emerges from the empty spaces that exist within the dialectics of race, culture, and class; and with the humor, the magic. Thus, in the title story, the white reporter, who has never thought of himself as gay, finds himself wondering if he would like to stay with a strange Indian fighter about to take on "the toughest Indian in the world." When the fighter leaves the next morning, the driver watches him "rise from earth to sky and become a new constellation" (34). Then, driving home to the place where he was born, he carries with him in his heart the skeletons of a thousand salmon.

The elderly Indian woman in "Dear John Wayne" assures her obtuse white anthropologist interviewer that she is in fact an expert on white people, because all her life she has had "to be white for fifty-seven minutes of every hour" and an Indian for only three; and she promises the anthropologist that he has "no idea, no concept, no possible way of knowing what happens in those three minutes." She tells him—and Alexie's oeuvre attempts to tell us: "You've colonized Indian land, but I am not about to let you colonize my heart and mind" (194).

Bibliography
Alexie, Sherman. *The Toughest Indian in the World.* New York: Grove, 2000.
McFarland, Ron. "Sherman Alexie's Polemical Stories." *Studies in American Indian Literature* 9, no. 4 (Winter 1997): 27–38.
Newton, John. "Sherman Alexie's Autoethnography." *Contemporary Literature* 42, no. 2 (Summer 2001): 413–428.
Richardson, Janine. "Magic and Memory in Sherman Alexie's *Reservation Blues*." *Studies in American Indian Literature* 9, no. 4 (Winter 1997): 39–51.

—Jim Varn

Train to Lo Wu, The Jess Row (2005)

The Train to Lo Wu features seven thematically interrelated stories, each revolving around trauma and alienation. Centered in post-handover Hong Kong (and by extension mainland China), JESS ROW's debut integrates interludes and backstories that reach to South Korea, Thailand, and America. The author's experiments with style underscore his themes; his cast of characters is eclectic and cosmopolitan, his narrative voices wide-ranging. In the collection, the experience of the present is filtered through nostalgia and escapism, with Row's protagonists often lost in undecipherable spaces where the past consumes the present. Moreover, as the title story suggests, such spaces are typically transitional instead of stable and complete. Lo Wu itself is the gateway to Shenzhen, China, a city that, miragelike, metamorphosed from tiny fishing village to frenetic megalopolis in less than three decades.

The opening story, cryptically titled "The Secrets of Bats," is narrated in the first person by a young, white, male English teacher, a persona of the young author himself, who taught English at a Hong Kong university before taking a college position in New Jersey. The confessional narrator evinces the curious mix of amazement and cynicism typical of travel literature: "I've come to see my life as a radiating circle of improbabilities that grow from each other, like ripples in water around a dropped stone. That I became a high-school English teacher, that I work in another country, that I live in Hong Kong. That a city can be a mirage, hovering above the ground: skyscrapers built on mountainsides, islands swallowed in fog for days. That a language can have no tenses or articles, with seven different ways of saying the same syllable. That my best student stares at the blackboard only when I erase it" (5).

An omniscient narrator details the inner and outer lives of blind Chen in "The American Girl." As he taps the streets of busy Kowloon en route to his job as a masseur, Chen's attention repeatedly wanders to his youth in China, where his family was persecuted as "gou zai zi" or imperialist dogs (44). Only Chen survives, but his survival costs him more than his sight. His memories traumatize him, often welling up into violent shouting during his naps. Shaken, he chastises himself for being "afraid of dreams" (35). Such dreams, which are manifestations of his repressed memories, increasingly debilitate him until an American girl, a Blind Services volunteer who reads to Chen regularly, offers him a braille copy of her thesis on the traumatized survivors of the Cultural Revolution. Offended by her invasiveness, he ends their friendship, calling her a "Ghost," a "Dreamstealing woman" (49). Nevertheless, with his story shared he feels "absurdly happy" (50). Once published, the trauma is no longer exclusively his, and Chen surrenders to a present that has eluded him for over 30 years.

Row also makes use of the third person in the stories "For You" and "Revolutions," the first of which deals with the dreams and failures of American photographer Lewis Morgan. Left miserable by his unemployment in Hong Kong and his failing marriage, Lewis has transplanted himself to a Buddhist monastery outside Seoul. Yet the tranquility he seeks does not come easily. Haunted by Hong Kong and nearly paralyzed by depression, he longs for his previous life in Boston, suffering nightmares about his wife in their cramped Hong Kong flat. He reclaims an active stake in his present self, however, when he helps a fellow monk kick a prescription drug habit. "Revolutions" too incorporates a Buddhist backdrop. Its protagonist, Curtis, is in Hong

Kong for more than a year of physical rehabilitation as a result of a motorcycle accident in Bangkok, where he was thriving as a painter, and like Lewis, Curtis cannot work in Hong Kong. Bedridden, he relies on the daily therapy of Ji Shan Sunim, a Buddhist nun from Poland; but at last, still miserable, abandons the sessions. Concerned for his well-being, Sunim travels to his flat and the two end up making love. Their affair lasts until Curtis resumes painting, whereupon Sunim returns to her monastery, and the two stories conclude when the present finally and painstakingly gains ascendance over the past.

The title story is told from the first-person perspective of a Hong Kong man. "The Train to Lo Wu" details Harvey's attempts to decipher the unpredictable actions of Lin, a woman from western China with whom he had an affair in Shenzhen. Their yearlong weekend relationship ends when she abruptly tells him to stop visiting. She has apparently decided to act on her threat to "disappear," to let "China swallow [her] up" (86). But we cannot be certain. Harvey, a self-conscious narrator who seeks consolation in caveats and questions—"I should have mentioned that" (89), "When would I have done that, in my normal life" (109)—resists any simple explanation, and his account complicates (and embarrasses) the kind of dismissive gossip in which we often derive moral comfort and assurance. The single Harvey is not a clichéd Hong Kong male with an illegitimate family in Shenzhen's "Second Wives Village" (92); nor is Lin a Chinese woman in search of any way out of the People's Republic. In the end, Harvey finds a strange, almost Zen-like comfort in his very unknowing, leaving readers to fend as they may.

"The Ferry" is similarly inconclusive. Told in third-person limited omniscience, the story concerns the black Marcel's journey from San Francisco to Hong Kong to parts unknown. Readers have access only to the subjective inner workings of Marcel's complex sensibility, as he arrives in Hong Kong to fire Ford, the black man who hired him in the United States five years earlier. His mission accomplished, Marcel has an epiphany. Mulling over the advice of Ford (who anticipated and accepted his colleague's news with equanimity), Marcel decides to disappear, to escape the blackness that seems to define his actions, at work or play, in

Asia or America. Soaking in rain while sitting alone on a Hong Kong night ferry, he finally experiences the "*relief*" of invisibility (138), and his real story would appear to begin precisely where "The Ferry" ends.

"Heaven Lake" concerns 40-something Liu's remembered experiences as a delivery boy in late '70s New York, when a penniless graduate student. Though he escapes the "sticks and knives" and "machine guns and hand grenades" of the Wuhan, China, of his youth (184), his so-called escape to America ends up proving equally dangerous. He fears New York's crime-ridden streets. He is robbed at gunpoint. He sees a man beaten to near-death. The counterpoint to this traumatic past of memory is the uneventful present with his daughters in Hong Kong. His girls are wholly (and to Liu, regrettably) carefree. For him their music and magazine lives are too easy, too predictable. Now a widower, he has great difficulty relating to them. Unlike their father, they seem to have no individual histories, and thus no means by which to privilege the present; no trauma—no hidden life—from which to recover. But Liu, who is a philosophy professor, finally concedes that perhaps they are just beginning to live, and that maybe "beginnings are enough" (190). And here, as throughout *The Train to Lo Wu*, Jess Row makes a (sometimes hard-won) virtue of the present; to live, if one is to live at all, is finally to embrace the now in all of its wondrous unreadability.

Bibliography

Row, Jess. *The Train to Lo Wu*. New York: Dial Press, 2005.

—Jason S. Polley

True Story Based on Lies, A Jennifer Clement (2001)

In *A True Story Based on Lies*, JENNIFER CLEMENT clothes a simple, almost skeletal storyline with the politics of contemporary Mexico and the language of indigenous folklore, grappling with social injustices still to be found in a country that typically prides itself on being mixed-race and egalitarian. The novel tells the story of "broom-child" Leonora, whose family business is making brooms and whose voice sounds like sweeping, "a long shhhhhhhhh." Silence is constantly thrust up on the protagonist; first by her mother, who instructs her never to speak what she thinks, and later by countless peripheral characters throughout the novel. The story follows Leonora as she leaves her village to become a servant in a Mexico City household, working for a family whose prominent affluence gives the brief illusion that her fortunes have improved. However, she only now becomes fully alive to the dramatic contrast between the status of a rich white family and that of an Indian servant. Mrs. O'Conner questions the newly arrived Leonora's personal hygiene, and tells her she will be regularly checked for parasites. In addition to Leonora, the family is served by Josepha, a cross-eyed maid who answers questions with a single cryptic word, and Sofia, the cook; and all are, in one way or another, voiceless.

Insofar as she can communicate at all, Leonora has been taught never to say "no," which is defined by her mother as "a word for small mouths" (6). Thus, when Mr. O'Conner makes advances toward Leonora, the maid's silence, docility, and invisibility make her the perfect prey; and Clement narrates the scenes of sexual abuse with haunting vividness, using a sparse and at times almost inscrutable diction. We can only infer the internal impact on Leonora from the fact that she has broken four glasses and two plates, and is oversalting the food.

When she discovers she is pregnant, Leonora begs leave to return home, saying that her mother needs her. However, Mrs. O'Conner is quick to put the needs of her own family first, and denies her permission to go, though later, when the truth is out, she berates Leonora for not having been noble enough to leave. Despite the wicked-stepmother elements of Mrs. O'Conner's depiction, Clement allows us to feel sympathy for her. We hear that she increasingly prefers sleep to waking life, and that in a sense she too, as a woman, is one of the dispossessed. The theme of gender inequality cuts across the broader exploration of racial prejudice in the novel, bringing Mrs. O'Conner fleetingly closer to her servants when she is herself mistreated by her husband. Yet ironically it is the servant cook Sofia who voices, sotto voce, the disturbing ideologies internalized by this society, one in which "if a man truly loves a woman he hits her" (89).

When Leonora's child is born, the O'Conners christen her Aura Olivia, and bring her up as their own. Leonora is powerless to resist the decision: doctors and priests help the family steal her daughter, and she is forced to conceal her true relationship or be sent away. As the child of an Indian and a rich white lawyer, Leonora's daughter Aura is a living incongruity, stretched between two worlds—a fate symbolized by her "Autonomous Hand Syndrome," which causes one of her hands to open a drawer, and the other to involuntarily close it. It is interesting to see how others treat Aura, who is, of course, "much darker" than the rest; the servants, for example, teach her to rub lemons on her skin as they do, to try and lighten it. A former student of anthropology as well as English literature, Clement uses Aura partly as an imaginative locus of investigation, to explore the meeting of indigenous and colonial cultures in Mexico.

Following the birth of her daughter, Leonora is living on borrowed time. Mrs. O'Conner's jealousy grows, and pressure for change mounts, eventually leading to the novel's tragic conclusion. But Clement is clearly at pains to ensure we see the events as ultimately part of societal illness rather than personal tragedy. Tales of injustice to indigenous people and women strain at the domestic fabric of the story, establishing a fraught and complex context for Leonora's own misfortunes. As soon as the pregnancy is discovered, for example, Sofia proves a wellspring of anecdotes about other servants who have been impregnated and then cast out by their employers. The author conducted over 30 interviews with Mexican maids in researching the novel (Thompson), and this thoroughgoing cultural anthropology firmly grounds the truth in *A True Story Based on Lies*. The political environment of modern Mexico is also carefully inscribed, and highlighted by student massacres, police corruption, and deaths caused by PEMEX, the state-owned petroleum company, which has a brief cameo as villain in Clement's subsequent novel, *The Poison That Fascinates* (2008).

A True Story reveals a host of affinities with Margaret Atwood's *The Handmaid's Tale* (1985), another searching study of hybridity and gender, with a maid as its protagonist, and with silence—and the abuse of silence—as a central theme.

Clement's style is an intriguing mix of Latin American magic realism and the frank, even polemical narratives of feminist writers like Atwood and Jeanette Winterson. Her objective, pared-down diction, freighted with proverb and (sometimes incongruous) imagery, recalls the work of Gabriel García Márquez, particularly his *One Hundred Years of Solitude* (1967). Indeed, magic realism, which thrives on terrains of social oppression and silence, explicitly appears in the novel, as in the strange connection established between cross-eyed Josepha seeing double and Leonora becoming pregnant.

Prior to publishing this, her second novel, Clement was already a well-established poet and cofounder of the San Miguel Poetry Week. It is thus unsurprising to find intense patterns of language and imagery acting as engines of meaning in *A True Story*, for example in the development of the broom-child trope: Brooms, sticks, and wood are gradually augmented by images of trees, and these then become associated with people, culminating in Leonora's epiphanic realization that "trees were like people, only very quiet" (76). Indians are the quiet people, the invisible maids, raised never to speak their thoughts, useful only as brooms. In the popular media, Indians still tend to be portrayed as maids or gardeners; and this is what makes *A True Story*, for all its universal thematic, stand out as a Mexican novel: It puts a maid on center-stage, and her truth under the spotlight.

A True Story was long-listed for the Orange Prize for Fiction in 2002.

Bibliography
Clement, Jennifer. *New and Selected Poems*. Exeter: Shearsman Books, 2008.

———. *The Poison That Fascinates*. Edinburgh: Canongate, 2008.

———. *A True Story Based on Lies*. Edinburgh: Canongate, 2001.

Thompson, Ginger. "Uneasily, a Latin Land Looks at Its Own Complexion." New York Times on the Web (May 19, 2005). Available online. URL: www.nytimes.com/2005/05/19/international/americas/19mexico.html. Accessed October 21, 2009.

—Heather Child

U

Uses of Enchantment, The Heidi Julavits
(2006)

HEIDI JULAVITS's third novel weaves a tangled tale about the limits of gender identity, narrative authority, and forgiveness in the wake of Second Wave feminism. Set in fictional West Salem, Massachusetts, the narrative shuttles between multiple temporalities as it follows protagonist Mary Veal's quest to explore the murky memories of her own coming of age, on the occasion of her mother's death. Returning home to Massachusetts in 1999, after years of living alone in Oregon, Mary faces a difficult process of mourning the loss of her mother, with whom she has not spoken for years. To repair this loss she must confront not only a broken relationship with her two sisters, but also her own culpability in causing disunion and suffering within the Veal family.

The title of the novel, *The Uses of Enchantment,* refers to a 1976 work of psychoanalytic literary criticism by Bruno Bettelheim in which he posits the reading of fairy tales as a way for children to better understand themselves and the world around them. Yet however reminiscent the novel may be of fairy-tale fantasies such as "Little Red Riding Hood" and "The Girl who Cried Wolf," Julavits's text rejects interpretative or moral pedagogy, challenging singsong visions of female adolescence as either childlike innocence or nymphet deceit. Creating a narrative invested with multiple contradictions, Julavits embraces postmodernism's denial of referentiality, an appropriate style for capturing the self's shifting negotiations of everyday loss.

Mary Veal was once a precocious yet melancholic adolescent girl growing up in the 1980s, who confronted suburban containment and isolation by telling stories about herself and others. In the autumn of 1985, 16-year-old Mary disappears, returning a month later with claims of abduction. Immediately entering therapy with a psychiatrist, Dr. Karl Hammer, Mary follows the trajectory of a former alumnus of Semmering Academy, Bettina Spencer, who 13 years earlier attested to a similar disappearance. Using traditional Freudian psychoanalytic principles, Dr. Hammer concludes that Mary's story of abduction is fictional, symptomatically referring back to a childhood sexual encounter with a family friend named Kurt. Yet after Dr. Hammer publishes *Miriam,* a book that introduces his theory of "hyper-radiance," evidently based on and deconstructing Mary's experiences, a competing feminist psychoanalyst, Roz Biedelman takes on her case and convinces both the Veal family and the psychoanalytic community at large that Mary's story should be understood entirely differently.

An important intertext to Julavits's novel is Sigmund Freud's case study, *Dora: An Analysis of a Case of Hysteria.* Like Hammer's *Miriam, Dora* is an analysis of the real-life Ida Bauer, whose traumatic adolescent sexual encounter with a family friend was undermined by Freud's emphasis on the primary trauma of the Oedipal triangle. Often interjecting common images and themes from Freud's 1905 text into the novel, Julavits experiments with psychoanalytic discourse as a form of storytelling and fictional collaboration. At a number of key

372

points in the narrative, Mary Veal describes the very symptoms Dora presents in Freud's sessions, for example, coughing or clearing her throat, playing with a compact mirror, or, more literally, referring to herself as Ida and her abductor as "K." (playing off of Freud's "Herr K").

Both fictional therapists in the novel fail to take into account the youthful imagination behind Mary's therapeutic story: what the reader, and characters, come to learn is that Mary's fate goes beyond simplistic assumptions of victimization and deceit. Julavits's narrative—and here is the deeper link to Bettleheim—attests to the dangerous, yet recuperative, quality of fantasy and storytelling in women's lives. Its representation of Mary's unbelievable claims of abduction, and the subsequent feminist rescue of her "marginalized" voice, parodies a broader cultural moment in the 1980s where "identity politics" bled into psychiatric therapy and "politically correct" social legislation.

Julavits utilizes multiple narratives to illuminate Mary's decentered subjectivity, a subjectivity that at its core refuses any single fixed identity. Composing secondary plots of doubling (where characters become each other's double), Julavits plays with the divide between subject and object. For example, Mary's adolescent identity mirrors her fellow Semmering alumna and predecessor Bettina Spencer. In fact, Mary comes from a long maternal line of female self-fashioners who used doubling as a tactic for improvisation; her mother and aunt, for example, trade places in key moments of the novel. The reader's confusion as to the different roles Mary's mother, Phyllis, and her aunt, Helen, played in Mary's therapy thus mirrors the protagonist's broader quest to uncover her mother's "true identity" and feelings about her abduction and deceit. Like Mary's performative tale of abduction, Phyllis and Helen's switching of roles brings them excitement and the possibility to at least temporarily remake themselves. Moreover, the importance of Phyllis and Helen in the novel, along with Mary's two sisters, Regina and Gaby, demonstrates

a movement away from the Freudian primacy of the father as the most important figure in a child's coming-of-age.

The Uses of Enchantment can be read as an experimental fictional reply to Freud's *Dora*, replacing the narrative of the omniscient male psychoanalyst with an unreliable and partial voice of an adolescent female patient. In doing so, Julavits imagines a process of maturation that is nonprogressive and alinear, where true therapeutic self-discovery is transformed into a continuous process of fictional self-making. Rather than framing unconscious fantasy as a kind of pathology, interpretable and "curable" by expert therapists, Julavits creates a formally complex novel that merges fantasy with reality, illustrating the individual's power to create not merely alternative stories but also alternative selves.

Bibliography

Bettelheim, Bruno. *The Uses of Enchantment: The Meaning and Importance of Fairy Tales.* New York: Vintage Books, 1976.

Freud, Sigmund. *Dora: An Analysis of a Case of Hysteria.* New York: Simon & Schuster, 1963.

Haaken, Janice. *Pillar of Salt: Gender, Memory and the Perils of Looking Back.* New Brunswick, N.J.: Rutgers University Press, 1998.

Julavits, Heidi. *The Uses of Enchantment.* New York: Random House, 2006.

Soloski, Alexis. Review of *The Uses of Enchantment* "The Vanishing." *Village Voice,* 31 October 2006. Available online. URL: www.villagevoice.com/2006-10-31/books/the-vanishing. Accessed October 21, 2009.

Wittes, Julie Schlack. Review of *The Uses of Enchantment* "Considering Truth and Its Appearance." *Boston Globe,* 19 October 2006. Available online. URL: www.boston.com/ae/books/articles/2006/10/19/considering_truth_and_its_appearance/ Accessed October 21, 2009.

—Jenny James

Vernon God Little DBC Pierre (2003)

Vernon God Little and its author DBC PIERRE came out of nowhere to win the Man Booker Prize in 2003, with controversy surrounding both novel and author. Pierre, born Peter Finlay, qualified for the prize by virtue of his Australian birthplace but has lived most of his life in Texas and Mexico City. The novel's setting is Martirio, a stultifying small town in Texas. When adolescent antihero Vernon Gregory Little is accused of participating in a school shooting, the Mexican border provides a temporary escape, and he effectively dodges martyrdom for the rest of this "wild ride" of a novel, both improbable and compelling (McCarthy).

For DBC Pierre, the book provided his own escape from an avalanche of ill consequences issuing from his troubled youth. The loss of his father when he was a teenager triggered a life of abandon and self-indulgence, including drug use, runaway debt, and the betrayal of friends. Facing a lifetime of penance and straitened circumstances, Finlay risked everything (again) to write a novel he hoped would pay his debts and recover his self-respect, choosing the pseudonym DBC (dirty but clean) to express the paradox of his low position and desperate commitment to a fresh start. The novel was successful but also controversial, some questioning whether the Booker Prize judges' choice of Finlay's provocative satire about the aftermath of a school shooting reflected a mix of horror and fascination with American violence, or even a desire to seem hip, sophisticated, and nontraditional (Daniels).

Others have praised this coming-of-age novel for the convincing voices of its adolescent narrator and small-town characters. Crackling with wry, original humor, *Vernon God Little* is often compared to J. D. Salinger's 1951 classic *The Catcher in the Rye*. Like Salinger's Holden Caulfield, Vernon combines a heightened awareness of hypocrisy and moral complexity with a stunted adolescent image-bank and vocabulary to express his outrage. His all-purpose word is "fucken," and his position in society is "screwed." We first encounter him in the sheriff's office, where female Deputy Vaine Gurie cannot even get past the factual preliminaries without commenting on his "awkward age" (5). The novel's contemporary "punk-rock sensibility" (Sifton) and over-the-top humor have also raised comparisons to TV's *South Park* (Weich).

The juxtaposition of Vernon's searching thoughts with the demented dialogue that stages his observations provides the reader with a wealth of fictional introspection and dramatic consequence. The story is divided into five "acts": "Shit happened," "How I spent my summer vacation," "Against all odds," "How my summer vacation spent me," and "Me ves y sufres" (See me and suffer). The first ends with Vernon in jail, despite his innocence, accused of participating in his friend Jesus' rampage. By the end of the second, he has escaped and is planning to slip across the border to Mexico. In the third, he reaches Mexico and arranges to meet his fantasy girlfriend, Taylor Figueroa, but is apprehended again when she betrays him. He is found guilty and reincarcerated in the fourth act, but stumbles on good fortune (or grace) in the fifth, after learning from a fellow inmate to "give the people what they want" because "intermingling needs make this world go round" (259).

Vernon suffers from occasional incontinence, which figures prominently in the plot. His "shit happened" during the killing rampage, but complications and embarrassment initially prevent Vernon from using his ill-timed evacuation as an alibi. Vernon's failure to control his defecation is set in darkly comic contrast to the failure of the female characters to control their food intake. His mother has in common with her friends (and enemies) a series of failed diets and empty boxes of Bar-B-Chew Barn takeout; Vernon comments that the strip of meat Deputy Gurie tears from a bone "flaps through her lips like a shit taken backwards" (6).

With no father in his life, Vernon is dominated mentally and emotionally by women and female relations; even antagonist Deputy Gurie is an acquaintance of his mother. He keeps them at a distance as best he can with a running mental commentary on their inadequacies, which some readers find "dead-on" and hilarious (McCarthy), but others find offensive and unconvincing. He calls the car in which his mother's friends arrive "the Uterus-mobile from hell" (23), and describes her in ways that seem gratuitously sexual and offensive, as when she offers up a tray of cakes to visitors "like it was a feel of her tits twenty years ago" (Daniels 26), or when (in an echo of Ferris Bueller), having "spent her best whimpery moves," she would "have to shred a tit or something, just to keep up" (60).

At the same time, he is engaged in a life of exceptionally intense sexual fantasy for a 15-year-old boy, which in a peculiar way actually serves to orient him in the world. In keeping with his anxieties about incontinence, his fantasies focus on female underwear—its color, fabric, style, and state of repair. When describing the geographical distribution of wealth and status in his hometown of Martirio, he reaches for his most serviceable metonymy:

All the money, and folk's interest in fixing things, parade around the center of town, then spread outwards in a dying wave.

Healthy girls skip around the middle in whiter-than-white panties, then regions of shorts and cotton prints radiate out to the edges, where tangled babes hang in saggy purple underwear. (13)

Small-town class structure is often savaged, but Vernon is nonetheless held in its grip. Although he can understand and cogently articulate their social destructiveness, his very mode of thought is founded on categories of commodity. After the school shooting, for example, he notices that everyone is wearing black, "except for the Nikes on their feet. I identify the different models while they box up the chicken. They won't even sell certain shoes to outsiders, it's a fact" (14). Remembering how his friend Jesus had been insulted on the way to school the morning of the shooting, he says: "I sting for him sometimes, with his retreaded, second-hand Jordan New Jacks. . . . His character used to fit him so clean, like a sports sock, back when we were kings of the universe, when the dirt on a sneaker mattered more than the sneaker itself" (17).

Another consistent target of the novel's satire is the media. The most obvious villain is Eulalio Ledesma, a small-time hustler trying to reinvent himself as a TV personality and media mogul. After promising to help "Vern" by telling the real story, he seduces Vernon's mother and moves in. He exploits every angle of the story and most of the characters in it, succeeding easily because others are so willing to sell out for the promise of money or fame. Inspired by a glimpse of an Oregon school shooter on TV, the novel riffs on all the expected varieties of media excess, culminating in a reality-TV-inspired game show in which viewers choose which prisoner on death row will be executed.

Vernon God Little is a scathing examination of clichés about small-town life, and the dominance of sleaze-media in the United States. Employing sharp-edged satirical dialogue and the compelling voice of his unreliable narrator, Pierre feels free to describe female characters in viciously misogynistic terms (the most potent being the devouring, ball-breaking mother), deploying a pair of stereotypical sexual predators named Nuckles and Goosens, and shaping a plot that in the opinion of some "careens out of control" and yet is still tied up too neatly at the end (McCarthy).

Bibliography

Daniels, Anthony. "Booker vs. Goncourt; or, when silence is a duty." *New Criterion* 22 (January 2004): 24–27.

Ferris Bueller's Day Off. Director John Hughes. Performers: Matthew Broderick, Alan Ruch, Mia Sara. Paramount, 1986.

McCarthy, Sarah Fay. "*Vernon God Little* by D. B. C. Pierre." *Missouri Review* 27, no. 1 (2004): 183–185.

Pierre, DBC. *Vernon God Little.* New York: Canongate, 2003.

Sifton, Sam. "*Vernon God Little:* Holden Caulfield on Ritalin." New York Times on the Web. Available online. URL: http://www.nytimes.com/2003/11/09/books/r . . ./09SIFTONT.html. Accessed May 16, 2009.

Weich, Dave. "DBC Pierre's Strong First Impression." Powells Books. Available online. URL: http://www.powells.com/authors/pierre.html. Accessed August 14, 2008.

—Sheila Pardee

Vinegar Hill Manette Ansay (2006)

A. MANETTE ANSAY's debut novel is set in 1972, opening just after protagonist Ellen Grier's husband, James, loses his job and lets their savings dwindle, forcing their family of four to move out of their own Illinois home and back to their hometown, Holly's Field, Wisconsin, where James's parents and their small rancher await. Here, Ellen finds herself in a literal glass menagerie of her mother-in-law's creation, to dust and replace in exact position—such rigidity epitomizing the Grier household in general. It is only under the condition that Ellen cook, clean, and care for her in-laws that her family may stay in the elder Grier's house at 512 Vinegar Hill, an address Ansay expressly chose because of its associations with bitterness and the struggle manifest in the landscape of a hill (Ansay 9).

Ansay regularly draws on such sinister natural imagery, capturing the misfortune of James Grier's unexpected lay-off, for example, through "the lilacs in the yard . . . [which] bloomed . . . trust-ing the Illinois winter had passed. The next day, an ice storm trapped the world in crystal" (5). Even flowers here unconventionally symbolize fear and death. Ellen's first doubts of God are refigured as the bloom of a poisonous flower (44), and it is with a reduction of boiled irises that Mary-Margaret considers poisoning her husband. More generally, natural tokens evince a marital divide: Ellen argues for their usual live Christmas tree while James endorses his parent's parsimonious suggestion of an artificial tree; James spends his free time in front of the TV or at the bar, whereas Ellen escapes outdoors for a nightly walk, exchanging the tired odor of pot roasts and lemon oil for the night air that "tastes sweet" (14).

Critics have compared Ansay to Jane Hamilton and Jane Smiley, praising her ability to capture midwestern life and landscape (Bush 567). Ansay's central character, Ellen, loves the land, its agricultural history, and her own farming childhood; for her "there is no bitterness in her memories of these fields . . . the same life that James remembers with such distaste" (47). James has found himself ironically at the heart of agriculture once again, selling farm equipment, which absents him from home for weeks at a time, loosening the ties to his wife and children.

It seems the only connections in the house on Vinegar Hill are made through conflict. Fritz and Mary-Margaret Grier live out the unhappiness that their marriage has always afforded them—she banging on her piano, and he likening her to a cat in heat, joking that "A cat would've made me a better wife" (9). Blindly, Ellen first seeks a kinship in Mary-Margaret because for both so much of "their lives were decided for them by forces they did not recognize in time" (62), but the senior Mrs. Grier rebuffs Ellen's hand of friendship, as does Mary-Margaret's older sister, Salome, who strives to guard the festering Grier family secret. Consequently, Salome grasps the secret so tightly that she can only relive it, creating the rarely seen phenomenon, folie à deux (madness or hallucination shared by two people).

Surprisingly, and increasing the reader's sense of domestic claustrophobia, even Ellen's mother and sisters leave Ellen to her depression and benzodiazepines, advising her to have another baby and "remember that you love him. . . . Sometimes you'll forget, but you do" (21). Ellen watches helplessly as her husband, James, "seemed to grow smaller" (59) under his father's recriminating stare and dictatorial proclamations. James and Ellen quietly work out their own tensions in their cold marriage bed and through mute, angry exchanges around the family table.

In the couple's small front bedroom, fragments of religion cover empty walls: a picture of the Last Supper, a plaster Mary, Palm Sunday fronds, a crucifix. When Ellen was a child, St. Michael's church was "no less familiar than any room in [her] house" (18), but now every choice she makes from buckling her seatbelt to cooking the Christmas goose appears a test of her faith. She has an epiphany one night while holding her rosary, but "She saw not the crucifix but a man, *a dead man*.. . . A sudden feeling of nausea shook her; the rosary slithered away, falling to the floor" (134). At last, Ellen and James's divergent beliefs in Roman Catholicism become themselves a reflection of their disintegrating marriage.

Catholicism has a vice grip on the whole extended family: novenas, statues, and prayer cards abound, and it is the fear of burning in hell that finally keeps Fritz and Mary-Margaret Grier from killing one another. Mary-Margaret, notably, shares her name with the 17th-century nun who first consecrated the worship of Christ's "Sacred Heart," and Ansay deftly shapes a character who is always reminding the family that "I got to be careful of my heart" (32). Ansay demonstrates the ascendant role of St. Michael's in the community, situating it, like a god to be feared, on a mountaintop, and refashioning the steeple's clock as an eye turned inescapably in all four directions. At the St. Michael's school where her two children, Amy and Herbert, attend, Ellen teaches fifth grade. Like Ellen at her age, Amy refuses the sacrament Father Bork offers, but unlike Ellen's mother, Ellen rocks her daughter in her lap and whispers, "Father Bork is wrong. You don't have anything to be sorry for" (122). This is also exoneration for Ellen, and marks a point of reckoning with the patriarchal pressures on her life.

Ellen at last finds the courage to free herself from the pinnings of male dominance in a peculiarly intimate but not less heroic way, through three women: Ann, an admonitory ghost from two generations past; Barb, the wise, brazen friend of the present; and her headstrong daughter, Amy, the voice of a forgiving future. *Vinegar Hill* ultimately proves a memorable lesson in the small, unheralded, but no less honorable or necessary victories, won anonymously behind closed doors.

Bibliography

Ansay, A. Manette. *Vinegar Hill.* New York: HarperPerennial, 2006.

Bush, Trudy. "Vinegar Hill." *Christian Century* 112, no. 18 (1995): 567–571.

"Margaret Mary, Saint." *Columbia Encyclopedia,* 6th ed. New York: Columbia University Press, 2007.

—Katharine Westaway

Virgin Suicides, The Jeffrey Eugenides (1993)

Jeffrey Eugenides is probably best known for *MIDDLESEX* (2002), which earned him a Pulitzer Prize, but his debut novel, *The Virgin Suicides,* is no less impressive. Set in picture-perfect Grosse Point, Michigan, in the 1970s, where Eugenides attended private school, the novel tells the tragic story of five teenage sisters ("the Lisbon girls") who committed suicide, one after the other, during the course of one year, the "year of the suicides" (92). The novel is told from the perspectives of more than one of the middle-aged men, never named, whose lives have been forever changed by the young girls—Therese, Mary, Bonnie, Lux, and Cecilia—and their relentless desire to "find the pieces to put them back together" (249). The narrative voice is particularly interesting because it is a collective one, meant to represent all of the boys (now men) who have never forgotten the girls. Considering the subject matter, one might expect the tone of the novel to be morose or depressing. On the contrary, Eugenides deals with the subject by blending humor, sensitivity, and mystery. It is at once elegiac and strangely lighthearted.

The fact that the narrative is relayed through witnesses is another interesting feature of the novel, as it calls into question the reliability of memory and the influence of time. And while this is undoubtedly a story about the five Lisbon girls, it is as much about the men who have out lived "the year of the suicides" (92); as much about the boys' painful emergence into adulthood as it is about the girls' never reaching it.

The story opens with the suicide of the last remaining Lisbon girl, Mary, who has taken sleeping pills, like Therese. Rather than rush to get inside the house, the paramedics move slowly, knowing exactly what waits for them; they are no strangers to the gas oven, ceiling beam in the basement, or knife drawer. The Lisbon home is completely familiar.

Shortly after this abrupt introduction to its macabre central theme, the novel goes back in time to when Cecilia, the youngest, first attempts suicide by slitting her wrists. She recovers but succeeds a few weeks later by hurling her body from her bedroom window onto the spike of a fence. After her death, and despite gossip and speculation by nosy neighbors and reporters, the Lisbons resume their bizarre lives as best they can. It even looks as if the Lisbon parents, who are both strict and religious, are going to relax their hold on the young girls, so as to avoid the same disaster striking twice. Lux begins a romance with Trip Fontaine, who must get around the strict rules of her overprotective parents. He negotiates a date with her to the school's homecoming dance provided that he can find dates for all of the Lisbon girls. He manages to do so, and they go to the dance under the watchful eye of Mr. Lisbon, a math teacher at the school, who tends to succumb to the demands of his overbearing wife. In the car, the girls' dates are surprised by the fact that they are real people, their neighbors, and not just objects of fantasy.

Not long after being crowned king and queen, Lux and Trip sneak off to the football field where they have sex. Consequently, she misses her curfew and, as a result, the girls all but disappear from the public eye. As punishment for Lux's transgression, all of the girls are removed from school and the house becomes a virtual prison; they are completely cut off from the outside world. Mr. Lisbon is forced to resign from his teaching position because of parent complaints, and the house and yard fall into disrepair; the Lisbons no longer receive grocery deliveries, and none of the girls are ever seen leaving the house, except for Lux, who engages in several sexual trysts on the roof. The house becomes a symbol of the girls' lives.

Just as the boys' interest in the girls begins to fade, they receive communication from them in the form of phone calls and Virgin Mary calling cards (Cecilia had one in her hand when she was found in the bathtub). They are ready to escape their imprisonment, and the boys are willing to go to whatever lengths to help them. Unfortunately, on the night they are meant to help them escape (June 16, one year after Cecilia's attempted suicide), the girls kill themselves in what appears to be a very intricately devised plan.

Just as they lived together, often undistinguishable, so they chose to die. The neighborhood boys, who have always seen the girls as a single unit, are not the only ones who do so. Even their parents assume they are one and the same, and treat them accordingly. Only Mary survives and is taken to the hospital, but she ends her life a few weeks later. Afterward, Mr. and Mrs. Lisbon leave the neighborhood in the middle of the night, and the last that we hear from them is through testimony that the boys provide in their presentation of evidence. What remains in the house is searched through by the boys and becomes more "evidence" for their investigation.

Even the coroner's report, which becomes part of the collection of souvenirs about the girls' lives, observes that they were "'like something behind glass. Like an exhibit.'" It is important to note that Therese, Mary, Bonnie, Lux, and Cecilia were not so much individuals as they were the "Lisbon girls"—mysterious objects who had been hidden away from the world and observed, analyzed, and described by the boys. They were unattainable in life, and now, in death, incomprehensible to the boys. Despite the years of effort to unravel the truth about why they committed suicide, nothing is known for sure. It is all speculation, held loosely together by evidence (testimonies, scraps, interviews, photographs) that amounts to nothing definitive. And herein lies the disturbing appeal of the novel. The keen observations and details provided by the narrator construct the report-like tale, but there is never any resolution. There is no one to blame, no one piece of evidence that completes the puzzle, and no real point to the men's investigation, except for the sheer fact that they loved them but could not save them.

This is a story about that failure, and the enduring questions that remain in the aftermath of suicide; about love, loss, and adolescence; and about the unattainable, and how it can prove more real and enduring than reality itself.

The novel was adapted for film in 1999, directed and with screenplay by Sofia Coppola. Starring Kirsten Dunst as Lux, James Woods and Kathleen Turner as Mr. and Mrs. Lisbon, Josh Hartnett as the teenage Trip Fontaine, and Danny Devito as Dr. E. M. Hornicker, the film adaptation stays true to the novel, despite the challenges of the difficult narrative technique. A few scenes are omitted, including Lux's pregnancy scare; but Coppola, in her directorial debut, earned accolades for the film. In 2001, she won both the MTV Movie Award for Best New Filmmaker and the Young Hollywood Award for Best Director. For her role as Lux Lisbon, Kirsten Dunst was nominated for the Teen Choice Award and YoungStar Award, both in 2000.

Bibliography

Eugenides, Jeffrey. *The Virgin Suicides.* 1993. Warner Books, 1994.

—Sherri Foster

W

Wallace, David Foster (1962–2008) *American novelist and essayist*

Wallace is the author of two novels, *The Broom of the System* (1987) and INFINITE JEST (1996); three collections of short fiction, GIRL WITH CURIOUS HAIR (1989), BRIEF INTERVIEWS WITH HIDEOUS MEN (1999), and *Oblivion* (2004); two collections of literary essays, *A Supposedly Fun Thing I'll Never Do Again* (1997) and *Consider the Lobster* (2004); and a coauthored book on hip-hop, *Signifying Rappers: Rap and Race in the Urban Present* (1990); a layman's introduction to the philosophy of the infinite, *Everything and More: A Compact History of* ∞ (2003); and a slim volume of political reportage entitled *McCain's Promise: Aboard the Straight Talk Express with John McCain and a Whole Bunch of Actual Reporters, Thinking about Hope* (2008). Wallace suffered from depression for much of his life and committed suicide in 2008.

The son of a professor of philosophy and a professor of English, Wallace was born in Ithaca, New York, but spent his childhood and adolescence in central Illinois, near the University of Illinois Urbana-Champaign. In his youth Wallace was a regionally ranked tennis player, a sport he has written about in essays such as "Tornado Alley," "How Tracy Austin Broke My Heart," and "Federer as Religious Experience." Significantly, the better part of *Infinite Jest* is centered around the fictional Enfield Tennis Academy, a setting which Wallace uses to explore issues such as discipline, adolescence, and the construction of the self. Wallace attended Amherst College, graduating in 1985 with a degree in philosophy, a portion of his *The Broom of the System* (a novel about Wittgensteinian language games and a fugitive grandmother) being submitted as his honors thesis. He earned an M.F.A. in creative writing at the University of Arizona in 1987 before moving on to teach English and creative writing at Illinois State University between 1992 and 2002, at which point he moved to California where he became a professor at Pomona College. During the interlude between his time in Arizona and his return to Illinois, Wallace allegedly enrolled in a Ph.D. program in mathematical philosophy at Harvard, which he eventually left to pursue writing full-time. What Wallace describes in *Everything and More* as his "medium-strong amateur interest in math and formal systems" (2) deeply informs much of his fiction, either overtly in stories such as "Here and There," or less directly in the iterative and meta-fictional layerings of *Infinite Jest* and stories like "Octet" and "Good Old Neon."

Wallace referred to writers such as William Gaddis, Don DeLillo, Julio Cortázar, and Cynthia Ozick as literary forebears, though he held a far more strained relationship with figures such as John Barth or Kathy Acker, whose fictions, argued Wallace, so often sacrifice character and real human drama in the name of a-human postmodern play. Recently, many younger writers like Jonathan Franzen have cited Wallace as a formative influence on their own work, helping to foster his slow creep into popular culture. Rumors of an *Infinite Jest* screenplay have been floating around Los Angeles for years, and an independent film adaptation of the story collection *Brief Interviews with Hideous Men* was released in 2009. A recurring reference to Wallace comes by way of the U.S. television show *The Office,* where the mysterious CEO of the Dunder Mifflin paper supply company bears the name David Wallace.

The allusion—likely traceable to John Krasinski, star of *The Office* and director of *Brief Interviews*—is an interesting and ironic one for a number of reasons. Not only is *Infinite Jest* notoriously weighty (1,096 pages, with endnotes) and thus a book demanding a stable supply of great quantities of paper, but Wallace's fiction, particularly the recent *Oblivion,* addresses at length the boredom and paradoxes of corporate culture and office life. Perhaps the greatest irony of the allusion in TV's David Wallace, however, arises from the fact that America's addiction to entertainment, and television in particular, has been one of Wallace's—that is, the author's—most sustained topics of critique. Stories such as *Girl with Curious Hair*'s "Little Expressionless Animals" and "My Appearance," *Brief Interview*'s "Tri-Stan: I Sold Sissee Nar to Eko," and *Oblivion*'s novella-length "The Suffering Channel" all take place either on the sets of television programs or within the media conglomerates that produce them. The "Infinite Jest" in *Infinite Jest,* set within an odd near-future post-television age, is a "tape" that, when watched, becomes so compelling that the spectator forsakes water, food, and human contact in order to continue watching the tape uninterrupted. Like a rat addicted to stimulating its brain's pleasure center, the unfortunate watcher of the "Infinite Jest" tape becomes catatonically suspended in an aggressive feedback loop whose inevitable end is death.

Thus it is no coincidence that perhaps Wallace's most frequently read and cited essay is entitled "*E Unibus Pluram:* Television and U.S. Fiction." Originally published in 1993 in the *Review of Contemporary Fiction,* the essay was later expanded and collected in *A Supposedly Fun Thing.* The essay begins with the startling statistic that "television is watched over six hours a day in the average American household" (22). But then, rather than dismissing "the Average American Household" as a mindless and unthinking enemy of literature, Wallace proceeds to argue that "the most danger-

ous thing about television for U.S. fiction writers is that we don't take it seriously enough as both a disseminator and definer of the cultural atmosphere we breathe and process" (27). Television, in other words, cannot simply be dismissed, nor can it be made fun of in a straightforward way. For Wallace, the peculiar thing about television in contemporary U.S. culture is that any attempt to criticize it ends up either feeding back into its ubiquity or sounding trite and insincere. This is because television has always already mocked and undermined its own alleged authority, because its authority is in fact built upon seeming familiar and willing to take itself unseriously. In other words, television's easy-going self-effacement creates a dependence, or "malignant addiction," in its viewers that is all the stronger because the dependence itself appears so banal and easily dismissible. The downside of all this is thus not merely the per diem six hours the "Average American Household" spends watching television, but the fact that the elaborately orchestrated illusion of television—of, say, beautiful people living far beyond their economic means in posh Manhattan lofts—begins to seem *natural,* and the viewer begins judging his or her own life according to that unattainable illusion.

If the primary target for Wallace's cultural critique is television and the U.S. dependence upon pleasure and entertainment, then his logical tool, if not his entire modus operandi and vivendi, is irony. Put simply, irony is the exploitation of the "gaps between what's said and what's meant, between how things try to appear and how they really are" (65). The problem with irony in contemporary U.S. culture is that it is no longer simply the tool of the satirist and social critic, but has become a primary mode of being and interacting with others. In *Girl with Curious Hair*'s "My Appearance," for example, David Letterman turns out to be exactly the same both on and off camera, sincerely using phrases like "grotesquely nice" and "entertainment dollar" (197). And through our six daily hours of TV we begin to absorb and reflect that performative irony, as though we too were being constantly watched.

In "*E Unibus Pluram*" Wallace suggests that the fiction writer's way out of irony's vicious circle is a simple avoidance of irony and pop-reference: "The next real literary 'rebels' in this country might

382   *War by Candlelight*

well emerge as some weird bunch of *anti*-rebels, born oglers who dare somehow to back away from ironic watching, who have the childish gall actually to endorse and instantiate single-entendre principles. Who treat plain old untrendy human troubles and emotions in U.S. life with reverence and conviction. Who eschew self-consciousness and hip fatigue" (81). Since he made that statement in 1993, Wallace's chosen literary path has oscillated between this brand of American "visceral realism" and an *extreme* self-consciousness that, successfully or not, seeks to lay bare every last artifice of its own production in the hopes of revealing some deeper, human core.

Perhaps the most concise articulation of the difference between these two modes of storytelling occurs in Wallace's first novel, *The Broom of the System*, when its protagonist, Lenore Beadsman, states: "You tell facts, you tell things. These weren't things, they're just a collection of weirdnesses" (103). Recent short fictions like "Incarnations of Burned Children" (2003) and "Good People" (2007) have aimed at facts more or less directly, striving to convey, for example, the immediate panic felt when one accidentally scalds one's child with boiling water. The majority of Wallace's fictions, however, looks more like "collections of weirdnesses" than straightforward facts or things, at least at first glance. His plots and characters are patently bizarre, ranging from *Infinite Jest*'s conspiracy of French Canadian wheelchair assassins to the man in *Brief Interviews* who compulsively screams out *"VICTORY FOR THE FORCES OF DEMO-CRATIC FREEDOM!"* during intercourse (17). But unlike more overtly postmodern, ludic writers like John Barth, Wallace weaves his own ludicrous plotlines in order to strive for a kind of emotional, if not exactly sentimental, truth. As the recovering drug addict Don Gately in *Infinite Jest* knows well, such truths do not come easily. It takes people like him days and months of struggle, of repeating litanies of banal slogans, even "to get a whiff of what's true and deep, almost magic, under the shallow surface of what they're trying to do." Wallace's work moves between this mundane struggle and those ephemeral whiffs because, in the end, "fiction's about what it is to be a fucking *human being*" (McCaffery interview, 131).

Bibliography

Boswell, Marshall. *Understanding David Foster Wallace*. Columbia: University of South Carolina Press, 2003.

Hayles, N. Katherine. "The Illusion of Autonomy and the Fact of Recursivity: Virtual Ecologies, Entertainment, and *Infinite Jest*." *New Literary History* 30, no. 3 (1999): 675–697.

Wallace, David Foster. *Brief Interviews with Hideous Men*. New York: Little, Brown, 1999.

———. *The Broom of the System*. New York: Viking, 1986.

———. *Consider the Lobster: Essays*. New York: Little, Brown, 2005.

———. "*E Unibus Pluram*: Television and U.S. Fiction." In *A Supposedly Fun Thing I'll Never Do Again*. New York: Little, Brown, 1997.

———. *Everything and More: A Compact History of ∞*. New York: W. W. Norton, 2003.

———. "Federer as Religious Experience." *New York Times Magazine*, August 20, 2006. Available online. URL: www.nytimes.com/2006/08/20/sports/playmagazine/20federer.html? Accessed October 21, 2009.

———. *Girl with Curious Hair*. New York: W. W. Norton, 1989.

———. "Good People." *New Yorker*, February 5, 2007. Available online. URL: www.newyorker.com/fiction/features/2007/02/05/070205fi_fiction_wallace. Accessed October 21, 2009.

———. *Infinite Jest*. New York: Little, Brown, 1996.

———. "An Interview with David Foster Wallace." By Larry McCaffery. *Review of Contemporary Fiction* 13, no. 2 (Summer 1993): 127–151.

———. "Kathy Acker's 'Portrait of an Eye: Three Novels.'" *Harvard Review* (Spring 1992).

———. *Oblivion: Stories*. New York: Little, Brown, 2004.

———. *Signifying Rappers: Rap and Race in the Urban Present*. 2d ed. New York: Ecco Press, 1997.

———. *A Supposedly Fun Thing I'll Never Do Again*. New York: Little, Brown, 1997.

—Andrew Warren

War by Candlelight Daniel Alarcón (2005)

DANIEL ALARCÓN's first collection of short stories explores varying contemporary implications of what it means—privately or publicly, at home or abroad—to be "at war." His fiction and nonfiction have previously been published in magazines ranging from the *New Yorker* to the *Virginia Quarterly Review,* and his work addresses themes reflecting both his Peruvian roots and his U.S. upbringing.

Several stories in *War by Candlelight* reference the modern-day immigrant experience in the United States (to which his family emigrated when the author was three), telling of people who become detached by their North American lives from the places and people they are told to call home: "[Rafael's family] was home again, under a Caribbean sun . . . The Spanish they spoke slipped off their tongues too fast, and he couldn't be sure of what he heard and what he misunderstood" (*War,* "a strong dead man," 184). Most of the stories, however, take place in the Peru of Alarcón's birth, addressing the personal and political trauma of repeated cycles of left-wing revolution and military clampdown. The Peruvian tragedy of the 20th century, unknown to many Westerners, is thought-provokingly presented by Alarcón, who places the story of angry South American guerrillas who "made war, fashioned it with our hands, our knives, and our sweat" ("lima, peru, july 28, 1979," 77) alongside that of a reluctant Peruvian visitor to New York on the first anniversary of 9/11 ("absence"). In juxtaposing these narratives, Alarcón unsettles contemporary perceptions of such concepts as "home," "belonging," "war," "nation," and—importantly—"terrorism."

The wars on which Alarcón focuses are vividly brought to life through the formal qualities of his prose. The first story, for example, begins with breathless rapidity, dominated by clipped sentences of tightly packed meaning: "It was the first flood since Lucas had been sent to the University, a year into a five-year bid for assault" ("flood," 1). The reasons behind Lucas's incarceration in "the University" (a jail), so called because "it's where you went when you finished high school" (3), form the basis both of this story—the central episode of which takes place inside the jail—and of many subsequent narratives, as imprisonment and injustice fuel the wars detailed in the collection.

It is not just stories of guerrilla war that feature constricted freedoms and injustices, however. In a later story, a non-Indian man must "disappear" during the visits of his girlfriend's mother to their shared apartment: David comes to recognize "periods of exile" from Reena's life as a result of a "war" over their relationship that "implie[s] all kinds of commitments," and that he cannot hope to win ("third avenue suicide," 57, 60, 72). The title of the collection refers not only to wars that take place in darkness, in which soldiers "'engage the enemy on [their] own terms'" and "neither side sees the other" ("war by candlelight," 118), but to wars that occur in the intimacy of candlelight, in the privacy of living room and bedroom.

Another story of intimate war, "a science for being alone," begins with the same wide narrative view as "the flood:" "Every year on Mayra's birthday, since she turned one, I have asked Sonia to marry me. . . . Each rejection has its own story . . ." (153). This device of collapsing tenses, uniting past and present and viewing both from a remove, is also employed in the first sentence of the title story: "The day before a stray bomb buried him in the Peruvian jungle, Fernando sat with José Carlos and together they meditated on death" ("war by candlelight," 115). It reflects Alarcón's debt both to the short stories of Faulkner and to the Colombian novelist García Márquez, whose *One Hundred Years of Solitude* begins: "Many years later, as he faced the firing squad, Colonel Aureliano Buendía was to remember that distant afternoon when his father took him to discover ice" (9).

Alarcón updates this technique, deploying it in a context in which both the past and the present of his characters involve constant warfare. This is highlighted by the extent to which the title story jumps backward and forward through a life of conflict, beginning and ending with Fernando's final night of guerrilla activity, "th[e] moment [that] was all they had worked for in the last fifteen years" (117). The idea of continuing war, of conflict without resolution—"back then it was possible to imagine the war would never end" (13)—is carried through the collection as a whole, rendering *War by Candlelight* more a fragmented single narrative than a succession of distinct stories. In this way, the form of the work echoes the idea of war itself, replicating the "permanent war psychosis" that Mary Kaldor describes in her analysis of "New and Old" wars, by which "warring parties need more or less permanent conflict . . to reproduce their positions of power" (32, 117).

Many of the stories are set in precise locations, but always with universal significance. Thus the ostensible specificity of "lima, peru, july 28, 1979," merely focuses our attention on an ultimately metaphorical "Lima," in which both the narrator's past (a cheating father, a family destroyed) and present (an aimless life, his desire to join the city's itinerant performers) are constructed as acts in a "city of clowns" (17–56). Alarcón himself has asserted that "the forces shaping the future of a city like Lima are at work in developing countries all over the planet. When I was on tour . . . for *War by Candlelight*, I always found myself saying, 'If Peru was an invented country, and Lima an invented city, many people would still recognize it'" (Olivas).

This outlook also informs Alarcón's first novel, *Lost City Radio* (2007), which focuses on the lost victims of an unnamed South American conflict. Alarcón, however, should not be seen as shying away from the specificity of his earlier work: "I'm Peruvian, the general arc of the war as it unfolds in [*Lost City Radio*] is similar to that of the Peruvian conflict, and everyone will be able to recognize this" (Olivas).

Bibliography

Alarcón, Daniel. "*The Elegant Variation* Guest Interview: Daniel Alarcón." By Daniel Olivas. Marksarvas. blogs.com. Available online. URL: http://marksarvas.blogs.com/elegvar/2007/01/tev_guest_inter.html. Accessed May 16, 2009.
———. *War by Candlelight.* London: Fourth Estate, 2005.
García Márquez, Gabriel. *One Hundred Years of Solitude*, translated by Gregory Rabassa. London: Picador, 1978. (*Cien años de soledad.* Editorial Sudamericana, 1967.)
Kaldor, Mary. *New and Old Wars: Organized Violence in a Global Era.* 2d ed. Cambridge: Polity, 2006.

—Sam Knowles

What Is the What: The Autobiography of Valentino Achak Deng Dave Eggers (2006)

DAVE EGGERS's 2006 novel is a moving, fictionalized account of a real-life Sudanese "Lost Boy's" journey from his war-torn African homeland to life in present-day Atlanta, which succeeds in bringing the plight of African refugees vividly to life for Western readers. The novel's preface is written by Valentino Achak Deng himself, the Sudanese refugee whose story is the inspiration for the tale, and it serves to authorize the novel as a truthful account of a story that might otherwise be written off as too horrific to be true.

The novel's title comes from Dinka folklore, specifically from a creation myth that illustrates the Dinka people's status as the chosen people of God, chosen because they are able to understand and appreciate the *what* that the deity has placed before them, rather than futilely searching for happiness in the unknown. However, as the narrator notes when he hears his father tell this familiar story to an Arab trader shortly before being forced to flee his village, the story can also be told to demonize the other, in this case the Arabs whom God spurns in favor of the Dinka; emphasizing the way religion and culture conspire to create the differences between people that lead to the very kinds of atrocities the novel recounts.

The title also suggests the struggle to forge a new life when the foundations of the old one have been shattered. Deng's Dinka culture is rooted in the connection to the Dinkaland (the southern region of Sudan in which Deng's home village, Marial Bai, is located) and their identity as herders of cattle, God's special gift to the Dinka according to the creation myth. When Deng is forced to flee this place as a child, he is effectively severed from the foundations of his own identity as Dinka, and must seek a new identity as refugee, ironically rendering the rest of his life a search for the *What*, the hidden something that will give his life a purpose. The absence of a question mark at the end of the interrogative title suggests a restless, reflexive paradox in that search—a question answered with a query—when it is uprooted from its assertoric origin in the Dinkan myth.

The story of Deng's flight from southern Sudan to refugee camps in Ethiopia and Kenya is framed by a present-day narrative that calls into question the notion of America itself as a safe haven for those who have been forced to flee their homelands. Indeed, the novel begins with an act of American violence when Deng, after allowing a stranger who is seemingly in distress to use the phone in the Atlanta apartment he shares with a fellow former Lost Boy, finds himself being robbed by the woman and her armed male companion. This betrayal of trust is just the latest in a long line of deceptions that Deng has experienced over the course of his long journey. The two thieves leave a young boy in the apartment to guard the bound and gagged Deng while they cart off his valuables, and the sight of this small boy caught up in forces beyond his control causes Deng to reflect on the long, strange trip that has led him to this point.

The rest of the novel moves freely back and forth in time, from the present, to the recent past, to the long ago moment when young Achak, as he is then known to his friends and family, was first sent literally running from his home village, which is caught in the middle of a brutal battle between forces of the Islamic government in Khartoum and the rebels of the Sudanese People's Liberation Army. Achak falls in with a band of young boys and their leader, the young teacher Dut Majok, all of them in flight from the carnage that has engulfed their homes, setting out on a long and treacherous walk to what they hope will be safe haven in Ethiopia. In the sections of the novel recounting this trek, the reader witnesses firsthand the horrors that such mass migrations of people can involve: Boys eaten alive by lions in the night, death from starvation and disease, all the while struggling onward toward a perceived paradise that they find, when they at last arrive, does not exist. In fact, upon entry into Ethiopia with his group of refugees, which has grown to include thousands of displaced Sudanese, Achak is certain that this desert land, devoid of all the comforts he and the other boys have dreamed were waiting for them, is not Ethiopia at all.

In a striking parable of human resourcefulness, every place in which Achak subsequently seeks refuge will similarly fail to provide him with what he seeks, yet he is able to carve out pieces of what will become his new life in each place. In the Ethiopian refugee camp in Pinyudo, for example, he meets Achor Achor, the friend who will eventually share his home in Atlanta and find him unconscious in the aftermath of the robbery. In Kakuma, the refugee camp in Kenya where Achak and others are resettled after a brutal massacre in Ethiopia forces many of the Sudanese refugees to flee for their lives yet again, he meets Tabitha, a Sudanese girl who will also find a home in the United States and become, for a time, Deng's girlfriend. However, in all these places there is more sorrow and suffering to be endured, and Achak is never able to successfully construct the kind of life he hopes for, even as he achieves some limited, hard-won success, and proves himself to be a motivated and talented leader. For all his achievements, Valentino Achak Deng, like so many others, is ultimately at the mercy of forces beyond his control. Yet unlike many he refuses to give up, and the very act of surviving and telling his story to others becomes a way of making himself and others like him visible to those who would deny or ignore the existence of such suffering and cruelty as he has experienced.

Indeed, the process of storytelling here is part of a broader bearing of witness to the extraordinary but invisible injustice that goes on in the world everyday. The narrative technique, in which Deng directs his internal monologue at various "listeners"—the Atlanta robbers' young accomplice, the intake nurse at the hospital where Deng is taken by Achor Achor in the aftermath of the robbery, a patron of the health club where Deng works—forces the reader into an intimate relationship with Deng. And this results in our being brought face-to-face with one of the faceless refugees who exist for most Americans only as numbers in a news report. In its blend of fiction and reality it resembles Eggers's 2000 memoir, *A Heartbreaking Work of Staggering Genius*, which also begins with an autobiographical foundation but takes creative license with the particulars of its subject's life. Like that work, *What Is the What*'s self-consciousness as a fictionalized memoir enables it to interrogate the act of self-representation itself, and the goals that drive the creation of such narratives; in this case, to aid in the rehabilitation of southern Sudan through the Valentino Achak Deng Foundation, to which all proceeds from the sale of the novel are pledged.

Bibliography

Eggers, Dave. *A Heartbreaking Work of Staggering Genius.* New York: Simon & Schuster, 2000.

———. *What Is the What: The Autobiography of Valentino Achak Deng.* San Francisco: McSweeney's, 2006.

—Elizabeth Davis

Whitehead, Colson (1969–) *American novelist and essayist*

Colson Whitehead, born Arch Colson Chipp Whitehead, is the author of the novels *The INTU-ITIONIST*, *John Henry Days*, *APEX HIDES THE HURT*, and *Sag Harbor*. His nonfiction includes a collection of essays, *The Colossus of New York: A City in Thirteen Parts*, as well as numerous articles in the *New York Times*, *New York Magazine*, *Granta*, *Spin*, Salon.com, and the *Village Voice*.

After graduating from Harvard in 1991, Whitehead was a pop-culture columnist for the *Village Voice*. His first novel *The Intuitionist* (1999) gained immediate critical acclaim. In the *New York Times Book Review* Gary Krist called the book "ingenious and starkly original." It won the QPB New Voices Award and was an Ernest Hemingway/PEN Award finalist. The story follows elevator inspector Lila Mae Watson as she attempts to discover why an elevator plunges into total freefall just days after she inspected it. A faction of the Gotham-like metropolis blames her, and Lila Mae goes into the underbelly of the city to discover what really happened and to clear her name.

Whitehead's second novel, *John Henry Days* (2001), won the Young Lions Award and the Anisfield-Wolf Book Prize, and was a finalist for the Pulitzer Prize. It intersperses numerous versions of the John Henry story with a present-time tale of journalist J. Sutter as he travels on an all-expenses-paid trip to West Virginia for the first annual "John Henry Days" festival, and the celebration of the John Henry postage stamp. Sutter is described as a "junketeer," and he relies on businesses and corporations to pay his bills. In addition to the free food and lodging, Sutter travels to the John Henry Days festival to break the standing record for most consecutive days of attending at least one publicity event.

Apex Hides the Hurt (2006) is the farcical story of an unnamed freelance nomenclature consultant who takes on the job of renaming a town. The town was originally named "Freedom" by ex-slaves who settled the area during Reconstruction, and then the name changed to "Winthrop" after a white millionaire invented a special kind of barbed wire and built a manufacturing company in the town. Now that the Winthrop dynasty has fallen onto hard times, the community wants a new name, and the narrative is propelled by the question of what name the protagonist will choose for the town, what that name will represent, and ultimately what reality that representation will create.

Much of Whitehead's writing is characterized by allegory and social satire. In his early career critics compared his writing with that of Ralph Ellison, Don DeLillo, and Thomas Pynchon, who tackle large, cornerstone books concerning American culture. In each of Whitehead's novels, the main character is black and struggling to situate herself/himself in relationship to surrounding communities that cross not only racial, but gender, economic, and methodological divides. In *The Intuitionist*, Lila Mae encounters prejudice and mistrust because she is the first black female elevator inspector. She is also an Intuitionist, which means she is able to inspect the elevators through her senses alone, without physically taking anything apart to inspect. Intuitionists are mistrusted by many, particularly the Empiricists, the larger and more powerful group of elevator inspectors. After Lila Mae is blamed for an elevator malfunction, she bravely navigates through a Pynchon-like maze of subterfuge and cover-ups to discover the truth. In a review for *Time*, Walter Kirn described the novel as "the freshest racial allegory since Ralph Ellison's *Invisible Man* and Toni Morrison's *The Bluest Eye*." *The Intuitionist* is informed by a mid-20th century New York City atmosphere, but Whitehead never names the specific time or place of its setting, universalizing the tale's mounting racial and political tensions to produce a far-reaching critique of American racism and prejudice.

John Henry Days elaborates Whitehead's signature allegorical style, but ventures further into the realm of social satire. While Lila Mae is a typically sympathetic protagonist, J. Sutter is a more ambivalent figure. The novel introduces him as a spendthrift and freeloader whose primary concern is where his next free meal will come from and whether prime rib will be served. The novel is a stylistic delight that deftly moves between Sutter's meandering existence and versions of John Henry's focused attempt to beat the machine. Whitehead chooses a real event—the first John Henry Days festival, which was celebrated in Talcott, West Virginia, in 1996—as a point of departure to explore dilemmas about representation and identity in postmodern, media-infested America.

Apex Hides the Hurt is Whitehead's shortest and most straightforwardly satirical novel to date. Its farcically brisk pacing and exaggerated characterizations have divided critics, some considering the novel a masterpiece of economy, and some an undeveloped narrative possibility. The unnamed protagonist's job to rename the town spirals into an increasingly complicated affair; informed also by the backstory of his biggest success as a nomenclature specialist: the naming of a bandage that comes in different skin tones, to literally hide people's hurt but not to heal it.

In 2009, Whitehead made what at first appears to be a significant departure from his earlier novels, with the semiautobiographical *Sag Harbor,* a kind of hyper-mimetic chronicle of a young black's "Post-Black" summer among the white elite of the Long Island resort community of Sag Harbor. But a closer look reveals not merely the trademark elements of Whitehead's style but a curious mirror-like reversal of his thematic perspective: Whereas in the earlier work he had explored the hauntingly familiar in alternate realities, here he patiently and skillfully reveals the alternate reality in the hauntingly familiar.

Whitehead is a native of New York, and much of his work is inspired by the city. In his nonfiction work, *The Colossus of New York* (2003), he captures the complicated love New Yorkers have for their city in 13 parts, sometimes inspired by specific locations like "Times Square" and "Central Park," and sometimes by more universal tropes like "Morning," and "Rain." As with his fiction, the prose in the collection moves fluidly within and over boundaries of space and time. Whitehead also read for an audio version of the book.

In 1994, Whitehead moved from Manhattan to Brooklyn, and in the *New York Times* article "I Write in Brooklyn. Get Over It," Whitehead writes a hilarious tongue-in-cheek essay about the move, which both emphasizes and minimizes the differences between the New York neighborhoods. When asked by interviewers what it is like to write in Brooklyn, he answers, "I expect it's like writing in Manhattan, but there aren't as many tourists walking very slowly in front of you when you step out for coffee."

Whitehead has taught at the Tin House Writers' Conference and Brooklyn College. In 2000, he received a Whiting Writer's Award, and in 2002, a MacArthur Fellowship. Currently, he is a Fellow at the New York Public Library's Cullman Center for Scholars and Writers.

Bibliography
Kirn, Walter. Review of *The Intuitionist. Time* (January 25, 1999). Available online. URL: www.time.com/time/magazine/article/0,9171,990080,00.html. Accessed October 21, 2009.

Krist, Gary. Review of *The Intuitionist.* New York Times Book Review (February 7, 1999). Available online. URL: www.nytimes.com/books/99/02/07/reviews/990207.02kristexhtml. Accessed October 21, 2009.

Whitehead, Colson. *Apex Hides the Hurt.* New York: Doubleday, 2006.

———. *The Colossus of New York: A City in Thirteen Parts.* New York: Anchor, 2003.

———. *The Intuitionist.* New York: Anchor, 1999.

———. "I Write in Brooklyn. Get Over It," *New York Times,* 2 March 2008.

———. *Sag Harbor.* New York: Doubleday, 2009.

——— *John Henry Days.* New York: Doubleday, 2001.

—Julie Babcock

White Teeth   Zadie Smith (2000)

White Teeth is the exuberant and ambitious first novel by ZADIE SMITH, who was only 24 when the book was published in 2000. The book's reception by the British press was extraordinary: Smith was lauded as the bright literary light of the new millennium, a first-time novelist with a distinctive, mature voice, whose influences ranged from Dickens to Rushdie, and whose take on multiethnic, postimperial Britain was insightful, comic, and generous. The book was awarded both the 2000 Whitbread First Novel Award and the James Tait Black Memorial Prize for Fiction.

While the novel is broad in its scope, it focuses primarily on three families—the Jamaican Bowdens, English Joneses, and Bengali Iqbals—whose histories, variously shaped by Britain's imperial past, become intertwined in postimperial London. A chance meeting between two soldiers, Archie Jones and Samad Iqbal, in the dying days of World War II, begins a lifelong friendship that is renewed when Samad and his wife, Alsana, emigrate from Bangladesh to London in the early 1970s. Shortly after, Archie's unhappy first marriage ends, and a series of unlikely events lead to his second marriage to the 19-year-old, Jamaican-born Clara Bowden. Children soon follow—a daughter, Irie, for Archie and Clara, and twin sons, Magid and Millat, for Samad and Alsana—and by the novel's end, at the dawn of the new millennium, the families have merged in the form of a child born to Irie and one of Samad's sons. Jumping back and forth in time, Smith's novel reaches further into the families' histories, to the Indian uprising of 1857, in which Samad's great-grandfather, the sepoy Mangal Pande, played a key role, and the colonial history of Jamaica, out of which the Bowden clan emerged.

The postimperial London of *White Teeth* is a multicultural muddle whose hybrid nature is summed up by Archie and Samad's beloved retreat, the greasy café known as O'Connell's, "an Irish pool-house run by Arabs with no pool tables" (183), where a chef named Abdul-Mickey serves up dubious English fare to a small but loyal clientele. Decorated with pictures of Irish racehorses and pages from the Koran, the restaurant is an emblem of the postwar transformation of northwest London. Like so many of the recent novels and films set in contemporary Britain, *White Teeth* looks at the uncertain nature of identity in a nation profoundly shaped by the migration and cultural mixing that are the by-products of empire and its aftermath. The fair-skinned Archie Jones enjoys an easy and unexamined identity as an Englishman, his whiteness placing him beyond the reach of any question regarding ethnicity. However, the situation is different for his dark-skinned daughter as well as Samad's sons, who come up against notions of national identity that offer them no place. When they are asked about their origins, they are not being asked in which part of London they were born, but rather, to account for their dark skin, where they are from *"originally"* (319). The question, obviously, implies that Irie, Magid,

and Millat are less English than their white peers, whatever their own origins. As children and adolescents, Irie, Magid, and Millat all long to identify with "Englishness," but are foiled by its exclusivity. Magid and Millat are informed by an elderly war veteran that their father could not have been a British soldier as they believe, because he shares the general misconception that there were no "Pakistanis" in the war (172); and Irie's hopeful attempt to see something of herself in the "Dark Lady" of Shakespeare's sonnets is foiled by her English teacher, who repeats another familiar misconception, that there were no "Afro-Carri-bee-yans" in Shakespeare's England (270). English history and the sense of identity it underpins are revealed to be highly selective constructs, which are, nonetheless, of central importance in providing individuals with a sense of themselves and their place in the world.

The inability of Irie, Magid, and Millat to find an idea of England that includes them leads them to find imaginary homelands of their own. In the case of Irie, this briefly takes the form of an idealized, edenic Jamaica, comfortably purged of its original Arawak inhabitants. Millat, too, adopts a West Indian pose, occasionally putting on "the Jamaican accent that all kids, whatever their nationality, used to express scorn" (167). More troublingly, the teenaged Millat turns to a rigid form of Islamic fundamentalism, moving through a period as a self-proclaimed "Raggastani" (231) on his way to membership in a group calling itself the "Keepers of the Eternal and Victorious Islamic Nation," whose comic acronym, KEVIN, does not mask the dangerous possibilities such a group represents (295). Millat's youthful activism takes him to the West Yorkshire city of Bradford for the notorious demonstrations against Salman Rushdie's controversial 1988 novel *The Satanic Verses*, whose representation of the prophet Mohammed and the origins of Islam prompted deadly riots and public book-burnings, and led to the author himself having to spend years in hiding. In its invocation of the controversy surrounding Rushdie's novel—another comic account of the hybrid nature of postwar Britain—*White Teeth* reminds us that the blending of diverse cultures is not merely the stuff of comedy.

Another important thematic concern of *White Teeth* is history—its shape and direction, as well as the capacity for individuals to influence it. The lives of the novel's ordinary folk are lived out amid the greater currents of politics—of the Empire and the War—and natural events such as the Jamaican earthquake of 1907. Samad grandly claims descent from Mangal Pande, the rebellious sepoy whose actions are widely seen as the start of the 1857 Indian uprising, in which some historians see the origins of the Indian nationalist movement that finally led to independence for India and Pakistan in 1947. Finding himself in a hopeless "Buggered Battalion" (89) during the war, he desperately seeks a similarly pivotal role for himself and Archie. However, Samad's belief that humans may shape their own destinies is inconsistently held; his more typical view of history is fatalistic: Everything has been foretold by Allah, and human actions merely fulfill a predetermined plan. A very different view is espoused by Marcus Chalfen, a geneticist whose work has culminated in the development of Future-Mouse, a laboratory mouse whose genes have been so precisely engineered that Chalfen claims he can predict the precise moment of its death. Chalfen's goal is to "eliminate the random," and thereby, he adds only half-jokingly, to "rule the world" (341). In a novel that so celebrates the rich confusion of life, the goal of eliminating the random is cause for concern, as becomes very clear when Smith links Chalfen's genetic experimentation with the wartime work of his mentor, Dr. Marc-Pierre Perret, on the Nazis' sterilization program and euthanasia policy. Chalfen and Perret's opponent, and the novel's unlikely hero, is the novel's least thoughtful character, Archie Jones, who instinctively embraces the randomness of existence, making key decisions in his life—even life-or-death decisions—by flipping a coin. Gentle and generous, not very clever but undoubtedly kind, Archie stands up for accidents, shaping his own destiny and others' in ways that none could predict or control.

White Teeth was adapted for television by screenwriter Simon Burke and director Julian Jarrold. The four-part television series was first broadcast on Britain's Channel 4 in 2002, and then in the United States on PBS's Masterpiece Theatre in 2003. The cast included Phil Davis as Archie, Om Puri as Samad, Naomie Harris as Clara, Archie Panjabi as Alsana, and Sarah Ozeke as Irie.

Bibliography
Smith, Zadie. White Teeth. 2000. London: Penguin, 2001.

—Brian Patton

Winegardner, Mark (1961–) American novelist and short story writer

Winegardner is the author of four novels: The Veracruz Blues, CROOKED RIVER BURNING, The Godfather Returns, and The Godfather's Revenge. The last two are sequels to Mario Puzo's The Godfather, authorized after Puzo's death by Random House, who selected Winegardner to continue the saga of the fictional Corleone family. Winegardner has also authored two books of nonfiction, Elvis Presley Boulevard and Prophet of the Sandlots, and a short story collection, That's True of Everyone.

Winegardner was born in Bryan, a small town in western Ohio, and traveled extensively as a youth, experience he recounts and reflects on in his first book, Elvis Presley Boulevard (1988). After completing undergraduate work at Miami University in Oxford, Ohio, he enrolled in the graduate Creative Writing Program at George Mason University, earning an M.F.A. in 1987. Winegardner then taught at George Washington and John Carroll while publishing extensively, later joining the faculty at Florida State University, where he is currently Burroway Professor of English and director of the university's creative writing program.

In The Veracruz Blues (1996), Winegardner revisits the brief success of baseball's Mexican League, which lured several stars away from the American major leagues in 1946. The novel offers fictionalized portraits not only of such outsized heroes as Ernest Hemingway and Babe Ruth, but of journeyman baseball players Danny Gardella, Theolic "Fireball" Smith, and Roberto Ortiz. These players each narrate several chapters, ostensibly as the result of interviews with an aging sportswriter who intertwines their stories with his own experience covering the league. Winegardner returns to the post–World War II era in Crooked River Burning (2001), this time focusing on Cleveland's descent from industrial powerhouse in the 1940s to urban decay in the 1960s. Again, he blends history and fiction, interposing famous Clevelanders into his fictional narrative of two socially mismatched lovers. Set mostly in Nevada from 1955 to 1962, *The Godfather Returns* (2004) faithfully follows Puzo's work, focusing on Michael Corleone's desire to legitimize his family's business while flashing back to his military service in World War II. *The Godfather's Revenge* (2006) continues the saga, as the Corleones deal with government investigation led by the powerful Shea family (explicit avatars for the Kennedys) and threats from rival mob boss Nick Geraci.

Depictions of such icons as Ruth, Hemingway, and Corleone, as well as attention to baseball, organized crime, and rock and roll, illustrate Winegardner's interest in the culture and mythology of American masculinity. In *Elvis Presley Boulevard,* images of Presley are the lone constant as Winegardner roams across America. "Give us this day our daily Elvis," he reports thinking as his friends put Presley's greatest hits album in their tape deck (138). *Prophet of the Sandlots* (1990) follows another archetype of masculinity, Major League baseball scout Tony Lucadello, whose long and seemingly rewarding career ends in unexpected tragedy. As his compelling portrait of Lucadello demonstrates, Winegardner's fascination with such figures does not engender sentimentality; his work is interested in both the limits and the possibilities of American masculinity. Winegardner also cowrote Steve Fireovid's autobiography *The 26th Man* (1991), an account of Fireovid's difficult and ultimately fruitless pursuit of Major League success.

While thorough research is a hallmark of Winegardner's work, his frequent use of multiple narrators suggests a complicated view of history. In an author's note that begins *The Veracruz Blues,* he insists that "A fiction writer must be, to paraphrase Tim O'Brien, more concerned with the story-truth than the happening-truth." In much of his work, Winegardner uses multiple (and at times contradictory) perspectives in order to reframe and question popular historical narratives. His frequent literary forays into the decades immediately following World War II constitute a rich and compelling reading of the midpoint of the 20th century. In Winegardner's work, the same years that witnessed America's industrial dominance and rising standard of middle-class life set the stage for an exodus of baseball players to Mexico and the political corruption sponsored by the Corleone family.

Winegardner has written for a variety of platforms, editing an essay collection about food culture (*We Are What We Ate,* 1998) and a short story anthology for literature courses (*3×33: Short Fiction by 33 Writers,* 2005). He also worked on a video game adaptation of *The Godfather* (2006), serving as script consultant and story editor. This diversity of style and genre is also reflected in the different audiences that have been drawn to Winegardner's work. Both *The Veracruz Blues* and *Crooked River Burning* received a number of literary honors, the former being named a Notable Book of the Year by the *New York Times* and nominated for the *Los Angeles Times* Book Prize; the latter lauded by *Cleveland Magazine* as the best book ever written about the city. After Random House announced he would succeed Puzo as *The Godfather* scribe, Winegardner was interviewed by an extensive array of media outlets; and, as a *New York Times* best seller, *The Godfather Returns* has proven his greatest commercial success.

Bibliography

Fireovid, Steve, and Mark Winegardner. *The 26th Man: One Major League Pitcher's Pursuit of a Dream.* New York: MacMillan, 1991.

Winegardner, Mark. *Crooked River Burning.* San Diego: Harvest, 2001.

———. *Elvis Presley Boulevard: From Sea to Shining Sea (Almost).* New York: Atlantic Monthly Press, 1988.

———. *The Godfather Returns.* New York: Random House, 2004.

———. *The Godfather's Revenge.* New York: Random House, 2006.

———. *Prophet of the Sandlots: Journeys with a Major League Scout.* New York: Simon & Schuster, 1990.

———. *That's True of Everyone.* San Diego: Harvest, 2004.

———. *3×33: Short Fiction by 33 Writers.* Belmont, Calif.: Wadsworth, 2004.

———. *The Veracruz Blues.* New York: Penguin, 1996.

———. *We Are What We Ate: 24 Memories of Food.* San Diego: Harvest, 1998.

—Mark P Bresnan

Y

Yiddish Policemen's Union, The Michael Chabon (2007)

The Yiddish Policemen's Union is a meditation on Jewish identity, shaped with classic tropes of American detective fiction. Detective Meyer Landsman is an alcoholic who spends his solitary evenings with a shot glass and his *sholem,* a "chopped Smith & Wesson Model 39" (Chabon 2). Formerly the "most decorated *shammes* in the District of Sitka" (3), the claustrophobic Landsman is now reduced to two states: "working and dead" (3). He patrols the District of Sitka in northern Alaska, an actual location that Chabon reimagines as a land of exile, a gift from the United States to refugee Jews forcibly removed from Israel in 1948. Chabon's revisionist history does not include the Arab-Israeli War that was sparked by Israel's declaration of independence. Instead, the novel suggests that shortly after this historical event, "the defense of Jerusalem collapsed and the outnumbered Jews of the three-month-old republic were routed, massacred, and driven into the sea" (43). The story begins 60 years after the collapse, just before the Reversion, when the American government will officially take Sitka back. Landsman's drunken defense against memory is interrupted when the body of an executed chess genius is discovered in room 208 of the hotel he calls home. The dead man, who used the pseudonym Emanuel Lasker, turns out to be part of a conspiracy involving the return of the Messiah (the *Tzaddik Ha-Dor*), the Holy Land in Jerusalem, and religious terrorism.

Landsman, his Tlingit-born but Jewish-raised partner Berko, and Landsman's ex-wife Bina, newly appointed inspector of the department, are all thrown headlong into the complex world of the exiled Jews.

This complicated world is shaded with the struggle to define identity, the intricacies of human relationships, and the pressure of history on the present; all reflected in the game of chess, a pastime that haunts Landsman with memories of his father and his childhood, while at the same time serving as an appropriate metaphor for the Sitkan universe. Even death and madness are linked to the game. When Landsman discovers Lasker's body, there is a chess problem set up beside his bed. This propels Landsman to tackle the case, but it is also analogous to his own attempts to solve the problem of self-identity, as he "learned to hate the game of chess at the hands of his father" (38). Indeed, in many ways the novel itself may be seen as a kind of extended chess problem, the problem of self. Landsman "is not a Verbover Jew and therefore is not really a Jew at all. And if he is not a Jew, then he is nothing" (148). His sense of identity is not constructed by an imaginary geography, a foreboding sense of history, or religious duty, and thus he exists outside the Alaskan Jewish experience, "born into the wrong world" (419). The reader learns that Landsman comes from a line of men whose mental struggles resulted in suicide: "Landsman's grandfather threw himself under the wheels of a streetcar in Lodz, which showed a degree of determination that Landsman has always admired. His father employed thirty 100 mg tablets of Nembutal, washed down with a glass of caraway vodka. . . . But when he envisions taking his own life, Landsman likes to do it with a handgun" (227). His struggle with identity, especially through his relationship to his father, signifies the trauma of memory and the oppression of history.

The phrase "These are strange times to be a Jew" recurs throughout the novel with enough regularity to suggest that there has never been a "normal" time. The strangeness is always connected to exile—"Jews have been tossed out of the joint three times now—in 586 BCE, in 70 CE and with savage finality in 1948" (26)—and for Chabon the "exiled Jew" is the most dominant aspect of Jewish identity. The memory of exile defines and confines: "No matter how powerful, every yid in the District is tethered by the leash of 1948. His kingdom is bound in its nutshell. His sky is a painted dome, his horizon an electrified fence. He has the flight and knows the freedom only of a balloon on a string" (435). The Jewish characteristics of strength and determination resonate in Chabon's description of Landsman's ex-wife:

> You have to look to Jews like Bina Gelbfish, Landsman thinks, to explain the wide range and persistence of the race. Jews who carry their homes in an old cowhide bag, on the back of a camel, in the bubble of air at the center of their brains. Jews who land on their feet, hit the ground running, ride out the vicissitudes, and make the best of what falls to hand, from Egypt to Babylon, from Minsk Gubernya to the District of Sitka. (230)

Chabon asserts that the concept of the Holy Land is embodied by the Jewish people, most clearly demonstrated by the description of the old chess teacher: "Litvak's body was a parchment scribed by pain and violence" (507).

The idea of "home" as an imaginary space is manifested in the Boundary Maven who defines *eruvs,* areas throughout the city marked off with string to represent domestic spaces where the rules of Sabbath can be bypassed. The maven, Zimbalist, is a powerful character because he controls the "imaginary ghetto of the Jews" (224). Chabon relates the obsession with imaginary geographies to religious notions of the Promised Land: "The Holy Land has never seemed more remote or unattainable than it does to a Jew of Sitka. It is on the far side of the planet, a wretched place ruled by men united only in their resolve to keep out all but a worn fistful of small-change Jews" (26). The return to Israel defines the Alaskan Jews, but for Landsman the Holy Land is a "fata morgana," a type of mirage common in the Arctic. For him, Jerusalem is a fractured idea that becomes a dangerous reality as the story unfolds.

As he explores the Jewish experience, Chabon also critiques ideas of the American dream and the immigrant experience. He pens a fairly uniform description of the realities of immigration: "The homesteading dreams of a million landless Jews, fanned by movies, light fiction and informational brochures provided by the United States Department of the Interior—snuffed on arrival" (433). Chabon also satirizes frontier mythology in the clash between the Alaskan Jews and the Tlingit Inuits, the "Indians" that fiercely defend their land from the Jewish "pioneers." Landsman's partner Berko embodies the cultural dichotomy, as he is *Indianer* and Jewish: "they catch sight of Berko's yarmulke, and a flutter of fine white fringe at his waist from his ritual four-corner, and you can feel all that giddy xenophobia drain off the crowd, leaving a residue of racist vertigo. That's how it goes for Berko Shemets in the District of Sitka when he breaks out the hammer and goes Indian. Fifty years of movie scalpings and whistling arrows and burning Conestogas have their effect on people's minds" (151).

Indicated by the epigraph to the novel—"And they went to sea in a Sieve," a line from the nonsense poet Edward Lear's "The Jumblies"—the driving motif of the novel is that the return to the Holy Land, the tangible realization of an imaginary geography, would actually destroy the identity of the Jewish people. The obsession creates what Landsman sees as "the deepest, oldest madness of the Jews" (218). As he points out, "A Messiah who actually arrives is no good to anybody. A hope fulfilled is already half a disappointment" (521).

Bibliography

Chabon, Michael. *The Yiddish Policemen's Union.* New York: HarperLuxe, 2007.

—Jared Morrow

You Remind Me of Me   Dan Chaon   (2004)

After enjoying significant acclaim as a short story writer, Dan Chaon exemplifies in his first novel, *You Remind Me of Me,* the way in which a mastery of the former genre may enrich one's approach to the latter. As he did in his collections *Fitting Ends* (1996) and *Among the Missing* (2001), Chaon here demonstrates an extraordinary ability to conjure up a host of immanent worlds in a brief compass, creating the impression of several novels within a novel. Juxtaposing a series of meticulously crafted microcosms set in various towns and cities in South Dakota, Illinois, and New Orleans and covering decades, Chaon follows the fates of a host of down-and-out characters, all antiheros in life stories whose plots they cannot seem to steer. As the tale progresses, the reader develops a sense of the interconnectedness of these seemingly disparate universes, and finally understands that the various protagonists would have formed a family had one of them not given up her baby for adoption at the age of 16. This dispersed family saga thus lays the groundwork for the author's searching investigation of the unusual ways in which lives and identities construct themselves, rarely in accordance with the intentions of the individuals authoring or possessing them.

Although the novelist gives significant weight to each thread of the narrative, the story tends to privilege the point of view of Jonah, a self-conscious, socially inept young man from a small town in South Dakota. Victimized both by his mother's suicide and by a hostile encounter with the family's Doberman pinscher when he was a child, which left his face permanently disfigured, Jonah feels unable to take charge of his own destiny. His awkwardness and pathological tendency to improvise lies in mid-conversation (which seem to "come to him almost supernaturally" [72]) prevent him from forging functional relationships, leaving him alone with his self-help tape, *Fifteen Steps on the Ladder of Success.* In an attempt to regain control of his life and come to terms with his past, Jonah at last sets out on a search for his biological brother, whom his mother gave up before his own birth.

Meanwhile, we are introduced to that mysterious sibling, a man named Troy who, after being charged with small-scale drug-dealing, has lost custody of his son and been placed under house arrest, leaving home only to complete his bartending shifts at a local tavern. Unbeknownst to Troy, Jonah's professional people-search leads him to his brother's place of work, where he goes undercover as a chef to gain proximity to him. Among the other seemingly discrete worlds we enter is that of Nora, Troy and Jonah's mother. During her teens in the 1960s, she is confined to the Mrs. Glass House, a home for unwed mothers. Later in life, she regrets both giving up her first child and keeping her second. We also peek into the life of Judy, Troy's mother-in-law who, deeply affected by her own daughter's plight as a drug addict, is hoping to steal her grandson away from Troy.

Yet what is on the surface a story of broken families and skewed individual histories is at another level a moving tale of the emotional complexities of kinship and the construction of selfhood. What comes across strikingly in the novel is a sense of the uncertain and meandering process— often involving a kind of grace—by which people become who they are. Chaon's representation of subjectivity reflects the fact that by the time we reach adulthood, we are not fully formed individuals located in a given time and place, but always the sum of a multitude of memories, traumas, and events from the past, which constantly call us back to reassess or relive what we have supposedly left behind. In keeping with certain tendencies in present-day autobiographical writing found in the French genre of *autofiction* (practiced by writers such as Nathalie Sarraute, Marguerite Duras, or Annie Ernaux), Chaon writes against a linear conception of the life story, showing how memory may actually move us backward in time in order to modify or reject what we find there (and ultimately here as well). An explicit example of this dialogue between past and present occurs in his 2001 short story "Big Me," wherein a young boy encounters his uncanny double, a man he believes is an older version of himself. He then creates a diary destined for this person—himself in the future—whom he addresses as "Big Me."

In *You Remind Me of Me*, this form of temporal interchange runs in both directions and revolves around the theme of memory. For example, as a young boy Jonah is certain that he saw his biological brother as an infant in a woman's basket at the market, even though this child was in fact born five years before Jonah was. He remembers his mother's reaction upon seeing this baby and how she exclaimed: "Oh, look, there's my baby!" (74). In retrospect, Jonah understands that this was not his brother and that his mother's mistaking the child for her own was due to her anxieties surrounding the abandonment of her first child. We thus observe the transformation of a very real childhood experience into a more "realistic" adult memory.

This vision of subjectivity recalls a subtler version of the concept of *nachträglich,* or "deferred action," a term frequently used by Freud in connection with his portrayal of psychical temporality and causality. For Freud, impressions, events, and "memory-traces" may be revised at a later date to correspond to fresh experiences or the attainment of a new phase of individual development. In such a case, they may be endowed not only with a renewed meaning but also with psychical effectiveness (Laplanche and Pontalis, 111–114).

For Chaon, the tendency for memories and thoughts constantly to shape-shift as they come into contact with new realities is a fundamental component of selfhood. The experiences that determine our personalities can never be narrativized once and for all, which makes it impossible to "come to terms with the past" or be entirely sure of who we are. Jonah's realization midway through the narrative reflects Chaon's vision of the self as the transitory product of both past and present circumstances: "Compared to most people, he barely existed—he was nothing, just a collection of random bits of history and memory he carried along, a series of shifting moods (196)." Chaon's characters are often seeking a sense of unity and stability, which they feel they *should* have, but do not. This impossible quest for self-certainty leads Nora to the conclusion that life is a "cruel puzzle," simply

"a series of echoes, one object mirroring another randomly, emptily, a vast and multiform and mindless series of repetitions" (132–133).

Chaon's extensive use of the present tense, and his tendency to bring the reader into proximity with the dangerously off-kilter psychologies of his characters, make us privy to the more ominous corners of their subjectivities, amplifying his role as omniscient narrator. Writing against the codes of family melodrama, Chaon digs deep into the minds of his protagonists to access hidden repositories of self-conscious anxieties and distorted values. The subtle simplicity of the language, combined with the despondency that haunts certain characters, has the effect of universalizing the woeful plights of these figures. *You Remind Me of Me* thus exposes a bleak undercurrent to the subject's positioning in the contemporary world, bringing the reader to reflect on the uncertainties of her own past and present, which have converged in unforeseeable ways to create the here and now. Yet in this very reflection, and in the empathy that it encourages for the plight of others in the same predicament, there are the makings of genuine healing and redemption.

Bibliography

Chaon, Dan. *Among the Missing.* New York: Random House, 2001.
———. *Fitting Ends.* New York: Random House, 1996
———. *You Remind Me of Me.* New York: Random House, 2004
Laplanche, J., and Pontalis, J.-B., "Deferred action." In *The Language of Psycho-Analysis.* Translated by Donald Nicholson-Smith, 111–114. London: Karnac Books, 1988.

—Daisy Connon

You Shall Know Our Velocity! Dave Eggers (2002)

DAVE EGGERS's debut novel weaves together similar difficulties in otherwise dissimilar social acts, those of mourning and giving away money. Eggers invokes a host of divergent themes in the alternately dark and amusing story of 27-year-old contract builder Will Chmielewski's search for cosmic order and meaning after the most "brutal and bizarre" year of his life. During this year, Will loses Jack, one of his two best friends, in an unlikely car accident, and gains a windfall of money in an equally unlikely stroke of luck. Fueled by anger at this violent yet bathetic series of events, Will takes his other best friend, Francis Wisneiwski (nicknamed "Hand"), on a high-speed mission around the globe to distribute the money to the world's poor. Uncooperative airline schedules and other unanticipated impediments thwart his fantasies of spontaneous charity, yet the trip ultimately helps Will regain the sense of human connectedness that he lost when Jack died.

You Shall Know Our Velocity! animates the trope of "travel as a symbolic act," which Casey Blanton notes for its influence on the American literary tradition (18). One thinks of *Quicksand* (1928), Nella Larsen's story of an African-American woman entrapped by contemporary racial stereotypes whether she finds herself in Alabama, New York, or Denmark; the crippling class-consciousness of James Agee and Walker Evans's New Deal ethnography, *Let Us Now Praise Famous Men* (1936–41); or Jack Kerouac's articulation of the postwar generation's restlessness in the cross-country movement of *On the Road* (1957). The itinerary of Eggers's novel symbolizes Will's efforts to distill some kind of order and purpose from the sense of cosmic chaos and caprice he feels in the wake of Jack's death. Indeed, Will's bitter grief over his bereavement stems less from the irony that Jack was a much safer driver than either himself or Hand than it does from the knowledge that Jack represented the best of the three boys: "[Jack] had calm where I had chaos and wisdom where Hand had just a huge gaping always-moving mouth" (81). When Will loses Jack, he loses the sense that his life, and life in general, has a purpose. Adding to his bitterness is the perceived impotence of the money, totaling $80,000, which Will receives just prior to Jack's fatal accident. The money comes in the form of payment for rights to an image of Will screwing in a light bulb, an image that Will's boss took for a D.I.Y. company brochure and that the Leo Burnett agency wants to use for one of its clients' advertising campaigns. The irony *here* is that Will suspects his boss of taking the original pho-

tograph only to make a joke at his expense: "Was it a joke on me . . . something about Poles—sorry, *Polacks*—and their abilities insofar as lightbulb-screwing goes? My boss insisted it was not . . . then went back to his trailer, muffling a guffaw" (41). The only way to derive meaning from his newfound wealth, which could do nothing to save Jack's life, is to give it to people whose lives it might vastly improve. Thus Will envisions restoring some small measure of purpose and order to the world by bringing his unearned money, love, and thereby (he hopes) a better quality of life, to the impoverished peoples of the globe.

Despite the sincerity behind its conception, Will's plan—to regain the calm and wisdom lost with Jack by dispossessing himself of his small fortune—encounters both practical and theoretical snags. For one thing, Will and Hand find it more difficult to fly from country to country than they had assumed possible before they embarked (without reservations) on their week of spontaneous international philanthropy. Weather, bureaucratic restrictions, and unexpectedly inconvenient commercial travel routes reshape the journey envisioned by the pair of globetrotters (so much so that the reader begins to wonder if the narrator's first name, Will, is an ironic pun on the synonym for "intention"). In the interior monologue that shapes the majority of the novel's narrative into a hybrid of personal retrospective and travel journal, Will confesses that he had

> always assumed, vaguely, that the rest of the world was even better connected than the U.S., that passage between all countries outside of America was constant and easy— that all other nations were huddled together, trading information and commiserating, like smokers outside a building. (52)

While Will and Hand are disappointed when circumstance impedes their access to other nations, they are equally perplexed to discover that America has in some sense already arrived in the countries to which they *do* gain access; other nations, that is, turn out not to be as *other* as they had hoped. Wherever they go, Will and Hand sense the unfettered dissemination of American culture—whether in the Indiana University umbrella they see on the porch of an unfinished condo in Dakar, or in the figure of Taavi, the musician-hitchhiker in Estonia who reminds them "in every way" of the kids they knew in high school. Even geography conspires to foil their expectations, as landscapes they pass on the road from Estonia to Latvia bear uncanny resemblance to the Illinois countryside.

The Americanization of foreign culture undermines Will's attempt to distance himself from the cathected locus of his emotional pain (his home), but it also helps him begin to make meaningful connections with the people that he and Hand encounter on their journey. This is especially significant since Will and Hand often struggle in vain to make the act of giving money away feel purposeful, like an act of communication. They leave wads of American bills in the hands of inscrutable countryside peasants; they speculate wildly about the kind, indigent people who will find the present of money they have furtively taped to the side of their farmhouse; and in one of the most hopeless yet poignant scenes, Will balls up assortments of paper currency he has accrued along the trip and throws them out of the rental car window into the wind. Will's ambivalence toward the act of giving away his money crystallizes early in the novel when he wonders indignantly why a bus driver fails to tell him to ignore a group of insistent beggars by the side of the road. A common interest in professional American basketball that Hand shares with a young man from Dakar, however, grounds one of the most convincing scenes of real charity in the early stages of their journey. And it is precisely Taavi's conversational preference for Western popular culture over "Soviets with tanks stationed in Tallin" that allows Will's mind to drift into one of his boldest confrontations with the traumatic scene of Jack's death. Such mental confrontations allow Will to do the emotional work of mourning that he has not been able to do in the United States. During an imagined dialogue with the deceased Jack toward the conclusion of the whirlwind tour, Will

reflects that giving away money has become his last language of human connection, a medium through which he has ultimately found a way to commune with both the living and the dead.

Eggers's interest in the subject of mourning can be traced back to the publication of his metafictional autobiography, *A Heartbreaking Work of Staggering Genius* (2000), a book that has since garnered this once little-known founder of the literary journal and independent publishing house, McSweeney's (launched in 1998), substantial mainstream notoriety. Though *You Shall Know Our Velocity!* avoids much of the playful narrative conceits found in *Heartbreaking Work,* Eggers added an element of metafictional play when he published an alternative version of the novel under the title *Sacrament* (2003). This version incorporates an additional passage told from Hand's perspective that directly challenges the reliability of Will's narrative voice. McSweeney's offers the incorporated material free at http://mcsweeneys.net/links/faq/download.html.

While continuing his career as a creative writer—he has published *How We Are Hungry* (2004), a collection of short stories, and *WHAT IS THE WHAT* (2006), his second novel—Eggers also directs his energy toward the support of teaching and human rights around the world: in 2002, he opened 826 Valencia, a nonprofit writing and tutoring lab, and cofounded Voice of Witness, a nonprofit oral-history project that draws attention to human-rights crises around the world; and in 2005 he cowrote *Teachers Have It Easy: The Big Sacrifices and Small Salaries of America's Teachers* (2005).

Bibliography
Blanton, Casey. *Travel Writing: The Self and the World.* New York: Routledge, 2002.
Eggers, Dave. *You Shall Know Our Velocity!* New York: Random House, 2002.

—Stacy Lavin

BIBLIOGRAPHY OF WORKS BY MAJOR CONTEMPORARY FICTION WRITERS

Adichie, Chimamanda. *Half of a Yellow Sun.* New York: Random House, 2006.

———. *Purple Hibiscus.* Chapel Hill, N.C.: Algonquin Books, 2003.

Alarcón, Daniel. *Lost City Radio.* New York: HarperCollins, 2007.

———. *War by Candlelight.* New York: HarperCollins, 2005.

Alexie, Sherman. *The Absolutely True Diary of a Part-Time Indian.* New York: Little, Brown, 2007.

———. *Indian Killer.* New York: Warner Books, 1996.

———. *The Lone Ranger and Tonto Fistfight in Heaven.* New York: Atlantic Monthly Press, 1993.

———. *Reservation Blues.* New York: Grand Central, 1996.

———. *The Toughest Indian in the World.* New York: Grove, 2000.

Ansay, A. Manette. *River Angel.* London: Allison & Busby Ltd, 2008.

———. *Vinegar Hill.* New York: HarperPerennial, 2006.

Ali, Monica. *Alentejo Blue.* London: Doubleday, 2006.

———. *Brick Lane.* London: Doubleday, 2003.

Barker, Nicola. *Clear: A Transparent Novel.* London: Fourth Estate, 2004.

———. *Darkmans.* London: Fourth Estate, 2007.

Berne, Suzanne. *A Crime in the Neighborhood.* New York: Henry Holt, 1997.

———. *The Ghost at the Table.* Chapel Hill, N.C.: Algonquin Books, 2006.

Bohjalian, Chris. *Before You Know Kindness.* New York: Shaye Areheart Books, 2004.

———. *The Double Bind.* New York: Shaye Areheart Books, 2007.

———. *Midwives.* New York: Harmony Books. 1997.

———. *Skeletons at the Feast.* New York: Shaye Areheart Books, 2008.

Brockmeier, Kevin. *The Brief History of the Dead.* New York: Pantheon Books, 2006.

———. *Things That Fall from the Sky.* New York: Pantheon Books, 2002.

———. *The Truth about Celia.* New York: Pantheon Books, 2003.

———. *The View from the Seventh Layer.* New York: Pantheon Books, 2008.

Bronson, Po. *Bombardiers.* New York: Random House, 1995.

Canin, Ethan. *America, America.* New York: Random House, 2008.

———. *Emperor of the Air.* 1988. New York: First Mariner Books, 1999.

Chabon, Michael. *The Amazing Adventures of Kavalier & Clay.* New York: Picador, 2000.

———. *Wonder Boys.* New York: Random House Trade Paperbacks, 2008.

———. *The Yiddish Policemen's Union.* New York: HarperLuxe, 2007.

Chaon, Dan. *Among the Missing.* New York: Random House, 2001.

———. *Fitting Ends.* New York: Random House, 1996.

———. *You Remind Me of Me.* New York: Random House, 2004.

Chevalier, Tracy. *Girl with a Pearl Earring.* London: HarperCollins, 1999.

Choi, Susan. *American Woman.* New York: HarperCollins, 2003.

———. *A Person of Interest*. London: Viking Press, 2008.

Clement, Jennifer. *The Poison That Fascinates*. New York: Canongate, 2008.

———. *A True Story Based on Lies*. New York: Canongate, 2001.

———. *Widow Basquiat*. New York: Canongate, 2003.

Cortez Cruz, Ricardo. *Straight Outta Compton*. Boulder, Colo.: Fiction Collective Two, 1992.

Costello, Mark [as John Flood]. *Bag Men*. New York: W. W. Norton, 1996.

———. *Big If*. New York: W. W. Norton, 2002.

Coupland, Douglas. *Generation X: Tales for an Accelerated Culture*. New York: St. Martin's Press, 1991.

———. *Girlfriend in a Coma*. Toronto: HarperCollins, 1998.

———. *JPod*. London: Bloomsbury, 2006.

———. *Life after God*. London: Simon & Schuster, 1994.

———. *Microserfs*. London: Flamingo, 1995.

Cusk, Rachel. *A Life's Work: On Becoming a Mother*. London: Fourth Estate, 2001.

———. *The Lucky Ones*. London: Fourth Estate, 2003.

Danielewski, Mark Z. *The Fifty Year Sword*. Amsterdam: De Bezige Bij, 2005.

———. *House of Leaves*. New York: Pantheon, 2000.

———. *Only Revolutions*. New York: Pantheon, 2006.

———. *The Whalestoe Letters*. New York: Pantheon, 2000.

Danticat, Edwidge. *The Dew Breaker*. New York: Vintage, 2004.

———. *The Farming of the Bones*. New York: Soho Press, 1998.

———. *Krik?Krak!* 1995. New York: Vintage, 1996.

Davies, Peter Ho. *Equal Love*. Boston: Houghton Mifflin, 2000.

———. *The Ugliest House in the World*. New York: Houghton Mifflin, 1997.

———. *The Welsh Girl*. New York: Houghton Mifflin, 2007.

Desai, Kiran. *Hullabaloo in the Guava Orchard*. New York: Anchor Books, 1998, 1999.

———. *The Inheritance of Loss*. New York: Grove Press, 2006.

Díaz, Junot. *The Brief Wondrous Life of Oscar Wao*. New York: Riverhead Books, 2007.

———. *Drown*. New York: Riverhead Books, 1997.

Dickey, Eric Jerome. *Sister Sister*. New York: New American Library (Penguin), 1996.

Doerr, Anthony. *About Grace*. New York: Penguin, 2005.

———. *Four Seasons in Rome: On Twins, Insomnia, and the Biggest Funeral in the History of the World*. New York: Scribner, 2007.

———. *The Shell Collector*. New York: Penguin, 2002.

Due, Tananarive. *Blood Colony*. New York: Atria, 2008.

———. *The Good House*. New York: Atria, 2003.

———. *In the Night of the Heat*. New York: Atria, 2008.

———. *Joplin's Ghost*. New York: Atria, 2005.

———. *The Living Blood*. New York: Simon & Schuster, 2001.

Eberstadt, Fernanda. *Isaac and His Devils*. New York: Random House, 1991.

Egan, Jennifer. *The Keep*. 2006. New York: Anchor Books, 2007.

———. *Look at Me*. 2001. New York: Anchor Books, 2002.

Eggers, Dave. *A Heartbreaking Work of Staggering Genius*. New York: Simon & Schuster, 2000.

———. *Mistakes We Knew We Were Making*. New York: Vintage, 2001.

———. *What Is the What: The Autobiography of Valentino Achak Deng*. San Francisco: McSweeney's, 2006.

———. *You Shall Know Our Velocity!* New York: Random House, 2002.

Eisenstadt, Jill. *From Rockaway*. New York: Knopf, 1987.

———. *Kiss Out*. New York: Knopf, 1991.

Ellis, Bret Easton. *American Psycho*. New York: Vintage, 1991.

———. *Glamorama*. 1998. New York: Vintage, 2000.

———. *Lunar Park*. New York: Vintage, 2005.

Ellis, Trey. *Home Repairs*. New York: Washington Square Press, 1993.

———. *Right Here, Right Now*. New York: Simon & Schuster, 1999.

Enger, Leif. *Peace Like a River*. New York: Grove Press, 2001.

———. *So Brave, Young and Handsome: A Novel*. New York: Grove Press, 2008.

Englander, Nathan. *The Ministry of Special Cases*. New York: Knopf, 2007.

Eugenides, Jeffrey. *Air Mail*. Reinbek, Germany: Rowohlt, 2003.

———. *Middlesex*. New York: Farrar, Straus & Giroux, 2002.

———. *The Virgin Suicides*. New York: Farrar, Straus & Giroux, 1993.

Foer, Jonathan Safran. *Everything Is Illuminated*. 2002. New York: Perennial, 2003.

———. *Extremely Loud & Incredibly Close*. London: Hamish Hamilton, 2005.

Freudenberger, Nell. *The Dissident*. New York: Ecco, 2006 (supplemented paperback edition, 2007).

———. *Lucky Girls*. New York: Ecco, 2003.

Gadol, Peter. *Light at Dusk*. New York: Macmillan, 2001.

———. *The Long Rain*. New York: Macmillan, 2000.

———. *The Mystery Roast*. New York: Picador, 1997.

Gibbons, Kaye. *A Cure for Dreams*. Chapel Hill, N.C.: Algonquin Press, 1991.

———. *Divining Women*. New York: G. P. Putnam's Sons, 2004.

———. *Ellen Foster*. Chapel Hill, N.C.: Algonquin Press, 1987.

———. *The Life All Around Me by Ellen Foster*. New York: Harcourt Trade Publishers, 2005.

———. *On the Occasion of My Last Afternoon*. New York: Perennial, 2005.

Gilbert, Elizabeth. *The Last American Man*. New York: Penguin, 2002.

———. *Pilgrims*. New York: Penguin, 1997.

———. *Stern Men*. New York: Mariner, 2000.

Gold, Glen David. *Carter Beats the Devil*. New York: Hyperion, 2001.

———. *Sunnyside*. New York: Knopf, 2009.

Goodman, Allegra. *Intuition*. New York: Dial Press, 2006.

———. *Kaaterskill Falls*. New York: Dial Press, 1998.

———. *The Other Side of the Island*. New York: RazorBill, 2008.

———. *Paradise Park*. New York: Dial Press, 2001.

Graver, Elizabeth. *Awake*. New York: Henry Holt, 2004.

———. *Have You Seen Me?* Pittsburgh: University of Pennsylvania Press, 1991.

———. *The Honey Thief*. New York: Harcourt, Brace, 1999.

———. *Unravelling*. New York: Harcourt, Brace, 1997.

Haddon, Mark. *The Curious Incident of the Dog in the Night-Time*. New York: Doubleday, 2003.

Hagy, Alyson. *Graveyard of the Atlantic*. St. Paul, Minn.: Graywolf Press, 2000.

———. *Keeneland*. New York: Simon & Schuster, 2000.

———. *Snow, Ashes*. St. Paul: Graywolf Press, 2007.

Hansen, Brooks. *The Brotherhood of Joseph*. Emmaus, Pa.: Modern Times, 2008.

———. *The Chess Garden: Or the Twilight Letters of Gustav Uyterhoeven*. New York: Douglas & Macintyre, 1995.

———. *John the Baptizer*. New York: W. W. Norton, 2009.

———. *The Monster of St. Helena*. New York: Farrar, Straus & Giroux, 2003.

———. *Perlman's Ordeal: A Novel*. New York: Farrar, Straus & Giroux, 2000.

Harrison, Katherine. *The Binding Chair*. New York: Random House, 2000.

———. *Envy*. New York: Random House, 2005.

———. *The Road to Santiago*. Des Moines, Iowa: National Geographic, 2003.

———. *The Seal Wife*. New York: Random House, 2002.

———. *Seeking Rapture: Scenes from a Life*. New York: Random House, 2003.

Hemon, Alexandar. *Nowhere Man*, London: Picador, 2004.

Holman, Sheri. *The Dress Lodger*. New York: Atlantic Monthly Press, 2000.

———. *The Mammoth Cheese*. New York: Atlantic Monthly Press, 2003.

———. *Sondok: Princess of the Moon and Stars*. New York: Scholastic, 2002.

———. *A Stolen Tongue*. New York: Atlantic Monthly Press, 1997.

Homes, A. M. *This Book Will Save Your Life*. New York: Viking, 2006.

———. *Music for Torching*. New York: HarperCollins, 1999.

Hood, Ann. *Somewhere Off the Coast of Maine*. New York: W. W. Norton, 1987.

Hosseini, Khaled. *The Kite Runner*. London: Bloomsbury, 2003.

———. *A Thousand Splendid Suns*. New York: Penguin, 2007.

Hynes, James. *Kings of Infinite Space*. New York: St. Martin's Press, 2004.

Iweala, Uzodinma. *Beasts of No Nation.* New York: HarperCollins, 2005.

Julavits, Heidi. *The Effect of Living Backwards.* New York: G. P. Putnam's Sons, 2003.

———. *The Uses of Enchantment.* New York: Doubleday, 2006.

Kennedy, Pagan. *Confessions of a Memory Eater.* Wellfleet, Mass.: Leapfrog Press, 2006.

———. *The Exes.* New York: Simon & Schuster, 1998.

———. *Spinsters.* New York: High Risk, 1995.

———. *Stripping + Other Stories.* New York: High Risk, 1994.

Kidd, Chip. *The Cheese Monkeys: A Novel in Two Semesters.* New York: HarperPerennial, 2001.

———. *Chip Kidd: Book One: Work 1986–2006.* New York: Rizzoli, 2005.

———. *The Learners.* New York: HarperPerennial, 2008.

Krauss, Nicole. *The History of Love.* New York: W. W. Norton, 2006.

———. *Man Walks into a Room.* New York: Anchor Books, 2002.

Kunzru, Hari. *The Impressionist.* New York: Dutton, 2002.

———. *My Revolutions.* New York: Dutton, 2007.

———. *Noise.* New York: Penguin, 2005.

———. *Transmission.* London: Hamish Hamilton, 2004.

Kurzweil, Allan. *A Case of Curiosities.* 1992. New York: Harvest, 2001.

Leavitt, David. *Family Dancing.* New York: Knopf, 1983.

———. *The Indian Clerk.* New York: Bloomsbury, 2007.

———. *The Lost Language of Cranes.* New York: Knopf, 1986.

———. *Martin Bauman: Or, a Sure Thing.* Boston: Houghton Mifflin, 2000.

———. *While England Sleeps.* New York: Viking, 1993.

Lee, Chang-Rae. *Aloft.* New York: Putnam. 2004.

———. *A Gesture Life.* New York: Riverhead. 2000.

———. *Native Speaker.* New York: Riverhead, 1996.

Lethem, Jonathan. *The Fortress of Solitude.* New York: Doubleday, 2003.

———. *Gun, with Occasional Music.* New York: Harcourt Brace, 1994.

———. *Motherless Brooklyn.* New York: Doubleday, 1999.

———. *You Don't Love Me Yet.* New York: Doubleday, 2007.

Loh, Sandra Tsing. *If You Lived Here, You'd Be Home by Now.* New York: Riverhead Books, 1997.

———. *Mother on Fire: A True Motherf%#$@ Story about Parenting!* New York: Crown Publishers, 2008.

———. *A Year in Van Nuys.* New York: Crown Publishers, 2001.

Martel, Yann. *Life of Pi.* Toronto: Vintage Canada, 2002.

McCracken, Elizabeth. *An Exact Replica of a Figment of My Imagination.* New York: Little, Brown, 2008.

———. *The Giant's House.* New York: Bantam-Dial, 1996.

———. *Here's Your Hat What's Your Hurry: Stories.* New York: Random House, 1993.

———. *Niagara Falls All Over Again.* New York: Dial Press, 2001.

Meloy, Maile. *A Family Daughter: A Novel.* New York: Scribner, 2007.

———. *Half in Love.* New York: Scribner, 2002.

———. *Liars and Saints: A Novel.* New York: Scribner, 2004.

Mendelsohn, Jane. *Innocence.* New York: Riverhead Books, 2000.

———. *I Was Amelia Earhart.* New York: Knopf, 1996.

Mitchell, David. *Black Swan Green,* Great Britain: Sceptre, 2006.

———. *Cloud Atlas.* London: Sceptre, 2004.

———. *Ghostwritten.* London: Sceptre, 1999.

———. *number9dream.* London: Sceptre, 2001.

Moody, Rick. *The Black Veil: A Memoir with Digressions.* New York: Faber & Faber, 2002.

———. *Demonology.* New York: Little, Brown, 2001.

———. *The Diviners.* New York: Little, Brown, 2005.

———. *Garden State.* New York: Little, Brown, 1992.

———. *The Ice Storm: A Novel.* New York: Little, Brown, 1994.

———. *Purple America.* New York: Little, Brown, 1997.

———. *Right Livelihoods: Three Novellas.* New York: Little, Brown, 2007. (British title: *The Omega Force.* London: Faber & Faber, 2008.)

———. *The Ring of Brightest Angels around Heaven.* New York: Little, Brown, 1995.

O'Nan, Stewart. *The Names of the Dead.* New York: Penguin, 1996.

———. *The Night Country: A Novel.* New York: Picador, 2004.

———. *Snow Angels*. New York: Picador, 1994.

———. *The Speed Queen*. New York: Doubleday, 1997.

Packer, Z. Z. *Drinking Coffee Elsewhere*. New York: Riverhead Books, 2003.

Palahniuk, Chuck. *Fight Club*. New York: W. W. Norton, 1996. London: Vintage, 1997.

———. *Haunted*. New York: Doubleday, 2005.

———. *Invisible Monsters*. New York: W. W. Norton, 1999.

———. *Lullaby*. New York: Doubleday, 2002. London: Jonathan Cape, 2002.

———. *Rant*. New York: Doubleday, 2007.

———. *Survivor*. New York: W. W. Norton, 1999.

Parks, Suzan-Lori. *Getting Mother's Body*. New York. Random House. 2004.

Patchett, Ann. *Bel Canto. Run*. New York: Harper-Collins, 2007.

———. *The Patron Saint of Liars*. 2002. New York: HarperPerennial, 2007.

———. *Truth and Beauty*. New York: HarperCollins, 2004.

Pearson, T. R. *Glad News of the Natural World*. New York: Simon & Schuster, 2006.

———. *The Last of How It Was*. New York: Henry Holt, 1996.

———. *Off for the Sweet Hereafter*. New York: Henry Holt, 1995.

———. *A Short History of a Small Place*. New York: Henry Holt, 1985.

Peck, Dale. *Martin and John*. New York: Farrar, Straus & Giroux, 1993.

Perrotta, Tom. *The Abstinence Teacher*. New York: St. Martin's Press, 2007.

———. *Bad Haircut: Stories of the Seventies*. New York: Berkley Trade, 1997.

———. *Election*. New York: G. P. Putnam's Sons, 1998.

———. *Joe College*. New York: St. Martin's Press, 2000.

———. *Little Children*. New York: St. Martin's Press, 2004.

———. *The Wishbones*. New York: Berkley Trade, 1998.

Phillips, Arthur. *Angelica*. New York: Random House, 2007.

———. *The Egyptologist*. New York: Random House, 2004.

———. *Prague*. New York: Random House, 2002.

Picoult, Jodi. 2002. *Perfect Match*. London: Hodder & Stoughton, 2006.

———. 2001. *Salem Falls*. London: Hodder & Stoughton, 2005.

———. 2006. *The Tenth Circle*. London: Hodder & Stoughton, 2006.

Pierre, DBC. *Ludmila's Broken English*. London: Faber & Faber, 2006.

———. *Vernon God Little*. London: Faber & Faber, 2003.

Power, Susan. *The Grass Dancer*. 1994. New York: Berkley Books, 1995.

Row, Jess. *The Train to Lo Wu*. New York: Dial Press, 2005.

Roy, Arundhati. *The Algebra of Infinite Justice*. London: Flamingo, 1999.

———. *The Cost of Living*. London: Flamingo, 1999.

———. *The God of Small Things*. London: Flamingo, 1997.

———. *The Ordinary Person's Guide to Empire*. London: Flamingo, 2004.

———. *Power Politics*. Cambridge, Mass.: South End Press, 2001.

Russell, Karen. *St. Lucy's Home for Girls Raised by Wolves*. New York: Vintage Contemporaries, 2006.

Salzman, Mark. *Lying Awake*. New York: Vintage, 2000.

Seiffert, Rachel. *Afterwards*. London: Heinemann, 2007.

———. *The Dark Room*. London: Heinemann, 2001.

———. *Field Study*. London: Heinemann, 2004.

Senna, Danzy. *Caucasia*. New York: Riverhead, 1998.

———. *Symptomatic*. New York: Riverhead, 2004.

Sharma, Akhil. *The Obedient Father*. New York: Harvest Books, 2001.

Shteyngart, Gary. *Absurdistan*. New York: Random House, 2006.

———. *The Russian Debutante's Handbook*. New York: Riverhead, 2002.

Sittenfeld, Curtis. *American Wife*. New York: Random House, 2008.

———. *The Man of My Dreams*. New York: Random House, 2006.

———. *Prep*. New York: Random House, 2005.

Smith, Zadie. *The Autograph Man*. New York: Vintage Books, 2003.

———. *On Beauty*. New York: Penguin Books, 2005.

———. *White Teeth*. New York: Vintage Books, 2001.

Swofford, Anthony. *Exit A*. New York: Scribner, 2007.

———. *Jarhead: A Marine's Chronicle of the Gulf War and Other Battles*. New York: Scribner, 2003.

Tartt, Donna. *The Little Friend*. New York: Knopf, 2002.

———. *The Secret History*. New York: Knopf, 1992.

Wallace, David Foster. *Brief Interviews with Hideous Men*. New York: Little, Brown, 1999.

———. *The Broom of the System*. New York: Penguin, 1987.

———. *Everything and More: A Compact History of* ∞. New York: W. W. Norton, 2003.

———. *Girl with Curious Hair*. New York: W. W. Norton, 1989.

———. *Infinite Jest*. New York: Little, Brown, 1996.

———. *Oblivion*. New York: Little, Brown, 2004.

———. *A Supposedly Fun Thing I'll Never Do Again*. New York: Little, Brown, 1997.

Whitehead, Colson. *Apex Hides the Hurt*. New York: Doubleday, 2006.

———. *The Colossus of New York: A City in Thirteen Parts*. New York: Anchor, 2003.

———. *The Intuitionist*. New York: Anchor, 1999.

———. *John Henry Days*. New York: Doubleday, 2001.

———. *Sag Harbor*. New York: Doubleday, 2009.

Winegardner, Mark. *Crooked River Burning*. San Diego: Harvest, 2001.

———. *The Godfather Returns*. New York: Random House, 2004.

———. *The Godfather's Revenge*. New York: Random House, 2006.

BIBLIOGRAPHY OF GENERAL SECONDARY SOURCES

Blazek, William, and Michael K. Glenday, eds. *American Mythologies: Essays on Contemporary Literature.* Liverpool, England: Liverpool University Press, 2005.

Bloom, James T., ed. *The Literary Bent: In Search of High Art in Contemporary American Writing.* Philadelphia: University of Pennsylvania Press, 1997.

Brinkmeyer, Robert H. *Remapping Southern Literature: Contemporary Southern Writers and the West.* Athens: University of Georgia Press, 2000.

Bueno, Paulino, Terry Caesar, and William Hummel, eds. *Naming the Father: Legacies, Genealogies, and Explorations of Fatherhood in Modern and Contemporary Literature.* Lanham, Md.: Lexington Books, 2000.

Cunningham, John Christopher. *Race-ing Masculinity: Identity in Contemporary U.S. Men's Writing.* New York: Routledge, 2002.

Cutter, Martha J. *Lost and Found in Translation: Contemporary Ethnic American Writing and the Politics of Language Diversity.* Chapel Hill: University of North Carolina Press, 2005.

Dillard, R. H. W., and Amanda Cockrell, eds. *Twayne Companion to Contemporary Literature in English from the Editors of the Hollins Critic.* New York: Twayne Publishers, 2003.

Eagleton, Terry. *The Crisis of Contemporary Culture.* Oxford: Clarendon Press, 1993.

Fisher, Maisha T. *Black Literate Lives: Historical and Contemporary Perspectives.* New York: Routledge, 2009.

Folks, Jeffrey J., and Nancy Summers Folks. *The World Is Our Home: Society and Culture in Contemporary Southern Writing.* Lexington: University Press of Kentucky, 2000.

Galván, Fernando, and Mercedes Bengoechea, eds. *On Writing (and) Race in Contemporary Britain.* Alcalá Henares, Spain: Universidad de Alcalá de Henares, 1999.

Grimes, Tom. *The Workshop: Seven Decades of the Iowa Writers' Workshop—43 Stories, Recollections, & Essays on Iowa's Place in Twentieth-Century American Literature.* New York: Hyperion, 1999.

Horne, Dee. *Contemporary American Indian Writing: Unsettling Literature.* New York: Peter Lang, 1999.

Keniston, Ann, and Jeanne Follansbee Quinn, eds. *Literature after 9/11.* New York: Routledge, 2008.

Lea, Daniel, and Berthold Schoene, eds. *Posting the Male: Masculinities in Post-war and Contemporary British Literature.* Amsterdam: Rodopi, 2003.

Linguanti, Elisa, Francesco Casotti, and Carmen Concilio, eds. *Coterminous Worlds: Magical Realism and Contemporary Post-colonial Literature in English.* Amsterdam, Netherlands: Rodopi, 1999.

Lohmann, Christoph K., ed. *Discovering Difference: Contemporary Essays in American Culture.* Bloomington: Indiana University Press, 1993.

Madison, D. Soyini. *The Woman That I Am: The Literature and Culture of Contemporary Women of Color.* New York: St. Martin's Press, 1994.

McRuer, Robert. *The Queer Renaissance: Contemporary American Literature and the Reinvention of Lesbian and Gay Identities.* New York: New York University Press, 1997.

Mongia, Padmini, ed. *Contemporary Postcolonial Theory: A Reader.* London: Arnold, 1996.

Mote, Dave, ed. *Contemporary Popular Writers.* Detroit: St. James Press, 1997.

Neumeier, Beate. *Engendering Realism and Postmodernism: Contemporary Women Writers in Britain.* Amsterdam, Netherlands: Rodopi, 2001.

Olster, Tracy. *The Trash Phenomenon: Contemporary Literature, Popular Culture, and the Making of the American Century.* Athens: University of Georgia Press, 2003.

Onega, Susan, and Christian Gutleben, eds. *Refracting the Canon in Contemporary British Literature and Film.* Amsterdam, Netherlands: Rodopi, 2004.

Pack, Robert, and Jay Parini, eds. *American Identities: Contemporary Multicultural Voices.* Hanover, N.H.: Middlebury College Press/University Press of New England, 1994.

Peck, Dale. *Hatchet Jobs: Writings on Contemporary Fiction.* New York: New Press, 2004.

Roorbach, Bill, ed. *Contemporary Creative Nonfiction: The Art of Truth.* New York: Oxford University Press, 2001.

Sauerberg, Lars Ole. *Intercultural Voices in Contemporary British Literature: The Implosion of Empire.* Houndmills, Hampshire, England: Palgrave, 2001.

Schröder, Nicole. *Spaces and Places in Motion: Spatial Concepts in Contemporary American Literature.* Tübingen, Germany: Narr, 2006.

Šesnić, Jelena. *From Shadow to Presence: Representations of Ethnicity in Contemporary American Literature.* Amsterdam, Netherlands: Rodopi, 2007.

Squires, Claire. *Marketing Literature: The Making of Contemporary Writing in Britain.* Basingstoke, England: Palgrave Macmillan, 2007.

Tillett, Rebecca. *Contemporary Native American Literature.* Edinburgh: Edinburgh University Press, 2007.

Zamora, Lois Parkinson. *Contemporary American Women Writers: Gender, Class, Ethnicity.* London: Longman, 1998.

INDEX

Boldface numbers denote main entries.

A

"Abe, between Rounds" (Canin) 48, 119
About Grace (Doerr) 99, 100, 349
"About the Typefaces Not Used in This
    Edition" (Foer) 133
Abrams, M. H. 320
Absalom, Absalom (Faulkner) 142
*Absolutely True Diary of a Part-time Indian,
    The* (Alexie) 8, 198, 199
Abstinence Teacher, The (Perrotta) 311,
    312
Absurdistan (Shteyngart) **1–3**, 334, 349,
    350
"Accident Brief, Occurrence #00/422"
    (Russell) 333, 337
Achebe, Chinua
    Things Fall Apart 3, 322
Acker, Kathy 380
Adichie, Chimamanda Ngozi **3–4**
    "American Embassy, The" 3
    Decisions 3
    For Love of Biafra 3
    Half of a Yellow Sun (novel) 3, 4,
        172–174, 210
    "Half of a Yellow Sun" (short story) 3
    Purple Hibiscus 3, 4, 172, **322–323**
    "You in America" 3
"Admirals" (Chabon) 277
"Adults Alone" (Homes) 282
Adventures of Huckleberry Finn (Twain)
    114
African-American Review 77
"African Immortals" (Tananarive Due) 104
After Life 39
*After the Dance: A Walk through Carnival in
    Haiti* (Danticat) 88
Afterwards (Seiffert) 343, 344
Agamben, Giorgio 181

Agee, James
    Let Us Now Praise Famous Men (with
        Evans) 395
Agni 237
Air Mail (Eugenides) 126
Alarcón, Daniel v, **4–6**
    "City of Clowns" 5
    Lost City Radio 4, 5–6, 384
    "New and Old Wars" 383
    War by Candlelight 4, 5, **382–384**
    "What kind of Latino am I?" 5
"Albertine Notes, The" (Moody) 280
Alentejo Blue (Ali) 8, 9, 38
Alexie, Sherman v–vi, **6–8**
    *Absolutely True Diary of a Part-time
        Indian, The* 8, 198, 199
    Benefit for the Honor the Earth Campaign
        7
    Business of Fancydancing, The 6, 7
    Dangerous Astronomy 7
    "Dear John Wayne" 368
    "Distances" 6
    "Do You Know What It Means To Say
        Phoenix, Arizona" 325
    Face 8
    First Indian on the Moon 7
    Flight 8
    Il Powwow Della Fine Del Mondo 7
    Indian Killer 7, **197–199**
    I Would Steal Horses 6
    *Lone Ranger and Tonto Fistfight in
        Heaven, The* 7, 325, 367
    Man Who Loves Salmon, The 7
    Old Shirts and New Skins 7
    One Stick Song 7
    "Poverty of Mirrors" 6
    Reservation Blues 7, 199, **324–326**
    "Small World" 7
    "South by Southwest" 367
    Summer of Black Widows, The 7

    Ten Little Indians 7
    "This Is What It Means to Say
        Phoenix, Arizona" 7
    Toughest Indian in the World, The 7,
        367–368
    War Dances 8
    Water Flowing Home 7
    "What the Orphan Inherits" 6
Alexis, Jackes Stephen 88
Algebra of Infinite Justice, The (Roy) 331
Alfred A. Knopf Publishing 116, 226
Ali, Monica **8–9**
    Alentejo Blue 8, 9, 38
    Brick Lane 8, **37–38**, 197, 319
    In the Kitchen 8, 9
    "Where I'm Coming From" 8, 9
Aliens in America (Loh) 248, 249
Allen, Joan 279
All Families Are Psychotic (Coupland) 72,
    146
Allison, Dorothy
    Bastard Out of Carolina 115
All the King's Men (Warren) 49
All the Pretty Horses (McCarthy) 226
Allure 65
Aloft (Chang-rae Lee) 239, 240
Amazing Adventures of Kavalier & Clay, The
    (Chabon) **10–11**, 56, 57, 58, 127
America, America (Canin) **11–13**, 49
American Beauty (film) 214, 282, 362
"American Beauty" (short story; Canin)
    120
"American Embassy, The" (Adichie) 3
"American Girl, The" (Row) 329, 369
American Modern (Gadol) 142
American Pastoral (Roth) 49
American Play, The (Parks) 303, 304
American Psycho (Ellis) **13–15**, 115, 116,
    186, 256, 257, 364
American Psycho II: All American Girl 15

American River Review 362
American Short Fiction 58
American Wife (Sittenfield) 353, 354
American Woman (Choi) **15–17**, 64, 65, 314
Amis, Kingsley 357
Amis, Martin 257, 357
Amnesia Moon (Lethem) 242
Among the Missing (Chaon) 58, 59
Anacaona, Golden Flower: Haiti, 1490 (Danticat) 87
Anderson, Sherwood
   "Egg, The" 93
Angelica (Phillips) 315, 316
"Angry Johnny" 85
Annie John (Kincaid) 82
Ansay, A. Manette **17–18**
   Blue Water 18, 328
   Good Things I Wish You 18, 328
   Limbo: A Memoir 18, 328
   Midnight Champagne 17, 328
   Read This and Tell Me What It Says 17, 328
   River Angel 17, **327–328**
   Sister 17, 328
   Vinegar Hill 17, 328, **376–377**
Andersen, Hans Christian 61, 174
Annesley, James 74
"Answer, The" (Row) 329
Antioch Review 278
"Ant of the Self, The" (Packer) 300
Apatow, Judd 313
Apex Hides the Hurt (Whitehead) **18–20**, 204, 386, 387
"Apocalypse Commentary of Bob Paisner" (Moody) 279
Apocalypse Now 213
"Appearance, Disappearance, Levitation, Transformation, and the Divided Women" (Brockmeier) 45
Appendix A: An Elaboration on the Novel the End of Alice 187
Applefeld, Aharon
   Beyond Despair 263
"Aqua Boulevard" (Meloy) 172
Arabian Nights, The 199
Arbus, Amy 187
Artforum 185
Arkin, Brian 365
Arlington Park (Cusk) 83
Arnold, Tom 120
"Around the World" (Graver) 165
Ashbrook, Tom 73
As She Climbed across the Table (Lethem) 242
Atlantic, The 120, 140
Atlantic Monthly 100, 248, 346, 353
Atlas, James 309, 310

At Play in the Fields of the Lord (Matthiessen) 49
"At the Bronx Terminal Vegetable Market" (Gilbert) 152
Atwood, Margaret 162, 241, 251, 266
   Handmaid's Tale, The 371
Austen, Jane 82
Austerlitz, Saul 19
Autobiography of Alice B. Toklas (Stein) 267
Autobiography of an Ex-Colored Man (Johnson) 54, 346
Autograph Man, The (Smith) 295, 355, 356–357
"Ava Wrestles the Alligator" (Russell) 332, 336
Await Your Reply (Chaon) 58, 59–60
Awake (Graver) 164–165
Ayr, Vyvyan
   "Matruschyka Doll Variations" 70

B

Bad Haircut (Perrotta) **21–23**, 311, 312
Bag Men (Costello) **23–25**, 70, 71, 72
Baker, Nicholson 136
Baldwin, James 303
Bale, Christian 117
Bandit Queen 330
Banks, Melissa
   Wonder Spot, The 355
Banks, Russell 133, 272, 286
Banyan Tree, The 330
Barbash, Tom 8
Barker, Nicola **25–27**
   Behindlings 25, 26
   Clear: A Transparent Novel 25, 26, **66–67**
   Darkmans 25, 26, 66
   "Dual Balls" 25
   Five Miles from Outer Hope 25
   Heading Inland 25
   Love Your Enemies 25
   Reversed Forecast 25, 26
   Small Holdings 25, 26
   "Symbiosis" 25
   Three Button Trick, The 25
Barnes, Julian 357
Barnes, Steven 105
   In the Night of the Heat (with Tananarive Due and Underwood) 104
Barry, Brian
   Culture and Equality: An Egalitarian Critique of Multiculturalism 19
Barth, John 40, 92, 156, 380, 382
   Lost in the Funhouse 156
Barthelme, Donald 44
Barthes, Roland 279
Bastard Out of Carolina (Allison) 115

Batman Animated 227
Batman Collected 227
Batman: The Complete History 227
"Batorsag and Szerelem" (Canin) 48–49
Baxter, Charles 123
Beacon Best of 2000: Great Writing of Women and Men of All Colors and Cultures, The 87
Beacon Best of 2001 96
Beah, Ishmael
   A Long Way Gone: Memoirs of a Boy Soldier 28
Beasts of No Nation (Iweala) **27–28**, 209
"Beasts of No Nation" (Kuti) 210
Beatty, Paul 19
Beautiful Ohio (Canin) 48
Beckinsale, Kate 294
Bedtime Stories: Adventures in the Land of Single Fatherhood (Ellis) 117, 118
Before You Know Kindness (Bohjalian) 33, 34
"Beginner's Guide to Hanukkah, A" (Foer) 133
Behindlings (Barker) 25, 26
Behind the Mountains (Danticat) 87
Beigbeder, Frédéric
   Windows on the World 129
Bel Canto (Patchett) **28–30**, 304, 305, 308
Believer, The 58, 110, 178, 218
Bell, Madison Smartt 108
Bell Jar, The (Plath) 221, 346
Bellow, Saul 122, 334
   Henderson the Rain King 49
Beloved (Morrison) 105
Bender, Aimee
   Girl in the Flammable Skirt, The 195
Benefit for the Honor the Earth Campaign (Alexie) 7
Bentley, Wilson
   Snow Crystals 100
Berger, Thomas 311
Berne, Suzanne **30–32**
   Crime in the Neighborhood, A 30, **74–76**
   Ghost at the Table, The 30, 31, 76
   Perfect Arrangement, A 30, 31, 76
Besong, Bate 210
Best American Essays 164
Best American Magazine Writing, The 248
Best American Non-Required Reading 5, 110
Best American Short Stories, The 7, 44, 48, 58, 90, 119, 120, 137, 164, 170, 328, 346
Best of American Voice, The 65
Bet, The (Canin) 49
Bettleheim, Bruno 219, 372
Betting on the Dust Commander (Parks) 303
Between, The (Due) 104
"Between the Pool and the Gardenias" (Danticat) 232

Bewitched 46
Beyond Despair (Applefeld) 263
BH Dani 179
Big If (Costello) 23, 24, **32–33**, 70, 71, 72
Big Sleep, The 289
Big Wave 85
   Binding Chair, The (Harrison) 175, 176
Bird, Gloria 325
Birds of America (Moore) 136
Birnbaum, Ben 164
Black Book 301
Black Clock 142
"Black Forest, The" (Kennedy) 361
*Black Livingstone: A True Tale of Adventure in
   the Nineteenth-Century Congo* (Kennedy)
   225
Black Rose, The (Due) 104
Black Swan Green (Mitchell) 70, 274, 275
Black Veil, The (Moody) 279, 311
Blaine, David 25, 26, 66, 67
Blake, William 97
   Songs of Innocence and Experience 64
   "Tyger, The" 64, 244
Blanton, Casey 395
Blessings (Jackson) 211, 212
Blood Colony (Due) 104, 247
Bloomington Pentagraph 78
Blue Angel (Prose) 57
Blue River (Canin) 48, 49
Bluest Eye, The (Morrison) 69, 386
Blue Velvet (Lynch) 282
Blue Water (Ansay) 18, 328
"Blumenthal on the Air" (Chabon) 276
Body Surfing (Peck) 311
Bohjalian, Chris **33–35**
   Before You Know Kindness 33, 34
   Buffalo Soldier, The 34
   Double Bind, The 33, 34
   Idyll Banter 33
   Killing in the Real World, A 34
   Law of Similars 34
   Midwives 33, 34, **271–273**
   Past the Bleachers 34
   Secrets of Eden 35
   Skeletons at the Feast 34
   Trans-Sister Radio 34
   Water Witches 34
Bohjalian, Grace 325
Bombardiers (Bronson) **35–37**, 46
Bonfire of the Vanities, The (Wolfe) 36
Book of Greek Myths (Ingri D'Aulaire and
   Edgar Parin D'Aulaire) 183
Book of Other People, The 355
"Book of the Dead, The" (Danticat) 96
Bookseller of Kabul, The (Seierstad) 229
Boone (Hansen and Davis) 174
Borges, Jorge Luis 5, 44, 230, 235, 275
Boston Globe 59, 101, 133

Boston Globe Magazine 33, 225
Boston Review 229
Both Ways Is the Only Way I Want It (Meloy)
   265–266
Boudreaux, Lee 322
Bowles, Paul 250
Boyd, Jim 7
Boyd, Terri 180
Boyer, Faidherbe 87
Boyle, T. C. 279
Bradbury, Ray 58, 333
Bradshaw Variations, The (Cusk) 83
"Brave Girl" (Davies) 123, 124
Brave New World (Huxley) 166
Breakfast of Champions (Vonnegut) 19
Breath, Eyes, Memory to (Danticat) 87, 95
Brennan, Carol 211
Brewer, Victoria 34
Brick Lane (Ali) 8, **37–38**, 197, 319
Bridget Jones's Diary (Fielding) 184
Brief History of the Dead, The (Brockmeier)
   38–39, 43, 45
Brief Interviews with Hideous Men (Wallace)
   39–41, 156, 380, 381, 382
Brief Wondrous Life of Oscar Wao, The (Díaz)
   42–43, 97, 98
Briggs, Raymond
   Fungus the Bogeyman 168
Brockmeier, Kevin **43–45**
   "Appearance, Disappearance,
      Levitation, Transformation, and the
      Divided Women" 45
   Brief History of the Dead, The **38–39**,
      43, 45
   "Ceiling, The" 44
   City of Names 43
   "Day in the Life of Half of
      Rumpelstiltskin, A" 44
   "Green Children, The" 44–45
   Grooves: A Kind of Mystery 43
   "Human Soul as Rube Goldberg
      Device: A Choose-Your-Own-
      Adventure Story, The" 45
   "Lady with the Pet Tribble, The" 45
   "March 15, 1997" 44
   "Telephone, The" 45
   Things That Fall from the Sky 43, 44
   Truth about Celia, The 39, 43, 44
   View from the Seventh Layer, The 43, 45
Broderick, Matthew 22
Bronson, Po **45–47**, 49
   Bombardiers **35–37**, 46
   *First $20 Million Is Always the Hardest,
      The* 46
   Nudist on the Late Shift, The 46
   *Nurture Shock: New Thinking about
      Children* (with Merryman) 47
   South of Market 46

What Should I Do with My Life? 46
Why Do I Love These People? 47
Brooklyn Was Mine 65
Brooks, Gwendolyn 78
   We Real Cool" 360
Brooks, Max
   *World War Z: An Oral History of the
      Zombie Wars* 167
Broom of the System, The (Wallace) 40, 201,
   380, 382
Brother, I'm Dying (Danticat) 88
Brotherhood of Joseph, The (Hansen)
   174–175
Brothers Karamazov, The (Dostoyevsky)
   207, 306
"Brownies" (Packer) 299
Buckley, William F. 107
Budnitz, Judy
   If I Told You Once 127
Buffalo Soldier, The (Bohjalian) 34
"Buffalo Soldiers" (Packer) 300
Buford, Bill 136
Bukiet, Melvin 335
Bulgakov, Mikhail 334
Burgess, Anthony 156
Burke, Simon 389
Burned Children of America 133, 355
Burning Bright (Chevalier) 64
Burroughs, Augusten
   Running with Scissors 213
Burroughs, William S.
   Naked Lunch 116
Business of Fancydancing, The (Alexie) 6, 7
Butler, Octavia E. 105, 247
   Kindred, The 105
*Butterfly's Way: Voices from the Haitian
   Dyaspora in the United States, The*
   (Danticat) 88
Buzz magazine 248
Buzzell, Colby
   My War: Killing Time in Iraq 213

C

Caesar's Antlers (Hansen) 174
Cain, M. Celia 325
"Cakes of Baby" (Davies) 124
Callaloo 118
Call It Sleep (Roth) 135
Calvino, Italo 44, 235
   If on a Winter's Night a Traveler 70,
      275
"Camp" (Kennedy) 361
Campbell, Bebe Moore 346
Camus, Albert
   Stranger, The 285, 289, 366
Canin, Ethan 46, **48–50**, 354
   "Abe, between Rounds" 48, 119
   America, America **11–13**, 49

"American Beauty" 120
"Batorsag and Szerelem" 48–49
Beautiful Ohio 48
Bet, The 49
Blue River 48, 49
"Carnival Dog, the Buyer of Diamonds,
    The" 48, 119
Carry Me across the Water 49
"Cathedral" 119
Emperor of the Air 48, **119–120**
For Kings and Planets 49
"Lies" 120
Palace Thief, The 48, 49
"Pitch Money" 120
"Star Food" 48, 119–120
"We Are Nighttime Travelers" 120
"Where We Are Now" 120
"Year of Getting to Know Us, The"
    120
canonic Western literary sensibility (CWLS)
    v, vi
Canterbury Tales, The (Chaucer) 320
Capote, Truman
    In Cold Blood 111
Cappuccino 98
"Caretaker, The" (Doerr) 100, 349
Carey, Edward 265
Carey Harvey, August "Gus" George 265
Carey Harvey, Matilda Libby Mary 265
Caribbean Writer 88
"Carnival Dog, the Buyer of Diamonds,
    The" (Canin) 48, 119
"Caroline's Wedding" (Danticat) 232
Carr, A. A.
    Eye Killers 105
Carroll, Lewis
    Alice in Wonderland 218
Carry Me across the Water (Canin) 49
Carson, Rachel 188
Carter, Angela 164, 278, 279
Carter, Helena Bonham 133
Carter Beats the Devil (Gold) **50–51**,
    159–160
Carver, Raymond 22, 90, 92, 120, 266, 286,
    294, 357
Casanegra (Due) 104
Case of Curiosities, A (Kurzweil) **51–53**,
    234
Catcher in the Rye, The (Salinger) 184, 221,
    222, 319, 321, 354, 374
Catch-22 (Heller) 290, 362
"Cathedral" (Canin) 119
Caucasia (Senna) **53–54**, 345–346
Caught Up in the Rapture (Jackson) **54–56**,
    211, 212
Caveney, Graham 74
"Ceiling, The" (Brockmeier) 44

Ceremony (Silko) 367
Chabon, Michael **56–58**, 159, 241
    "Admirals" 277
    *Amazing Adventures of Kavalier & Clay,
        The* **10–11**, 56, 57, 58, 127
    "Blumenthal on the Air" 276
    *Final Solution: A Story of Detection,
        The* 57
    Gentlemen of the Road 56
    "Halloween Party, The" 277
    "Little Knife, The" 277
    Maps & Legends 56, 57
    "Millionaires" 276
    Model World and Other Stories, A 56,
        276–278
    Mysteries of Pittsburgh 56, 58, 276
    "Ocean Avenue" 276
    "S ANGEL" 276
    "Smoke" 276
    Summerland 56, 57
    Werewolves in Their Youth 56, 57
    Wonder Boys 56–57, 58
    Yiddish Policemen's Union, The 56, 57,
        58, **391–393**
Chamberlin, Jeremiah 92
Chandler, Raymond 24, 57, 166, 241
    Playback 167
Chang, Leonard 65, 314
Change of Heart (Picoult) 317
Channing, Stockard 187
Chaon, Dan **58–60**
    Among the Missing 58, 59, 393
    Await Your Reply 58, 59–60
    Fitting Ends 58–59, 393
    "I Demand to Know Where You're
        Taking Me" 59
    "Safety Man" 59
    You Remind Me of Me 58, 59,
        393–394
Chaplinsky, Josh 302
Charlotte Observer 354
Charms for the Easy Life (Gibbons) 150
Chaucer, Geoffrey 68
    Canterbury Tales, The 320
*Cheese Monkeys: A Novel in Two Semesters,
    The* (Kidd) **60–61**, 226–227
Cheever, John 279
    "Goodbye My Brother" 48
    Stories of John Cheever, The 48, 50
Cherry-Garrard, Apsley
    Worst Journey in the World, The 39
*Chess Garden: Or the Twilight Letters of
    Gustav Uyterhoeven, The* (Hansen)
    61–63, 174
Chevalier, Tracy **63–64**
    Burning Bright 64
    Falling Angels 64

    Girl with a Pearl Earring 63, **153–155**
    Lady and the Unicorn, The 64
    Remarkable Creatures 64
    Virgin Blue, The 63
Chicago magazine 120
Chicago Tribune 59, 150, 306
Children of the Sea (Danticat) 87
"Children's Reminiscences of the Westward
    Migration" (Russell) 336
Child Soldier: Fighting for My Life (Keitetsi)
    28, 209
Choi, Susan 64–66
    American Woman **15–17**, 64, 65, 314
    Foreign Student, The 64, 65–66, 314
    Person of Interest, A 64, 65, **313–315**
"Choice of Accommodations, A" (Lahiri)
    237
Choke (Palahniuk) 301, 302
"Choo Choo" (Goodman) 161
Chosen, The (Potok) 135, 220
Chotiner, Isaac 237
Christian Science Monitor 121, 308
Chronic City (Lethem) 242
"City of Clowns" (Alarcón) 5
City of Glass (Coupland) 217
City of God (Doctorow) 76
City of Names (Brockmeier) 43
"City of Shells, The" (Russell) 333,
    336–337
"Civilization's Ladder" (Mitchell) 70
Clear: A Transparent Novel (Barker) 25, 26,
    66–67
Clement, Jennifer **68–69**
    *Jennifer Clement: New and Selected
        Poems* 68
    Lady of the Broom, The 68, 69
    Newton's Sailor 68
    Next Stranger, The 68
    Poison That Fascinates, The 69, 371
    "Salamander-Child, A" 68
    "This Was When You Could Still Be
        Killed for Love" 68
    True Story Based on Lies, A 68, 69,
        370–371
    Widow Basquiat, The 68
Cleveland Magazine 390
Clifford's Blues (Williams) 173
Close, Glen 187
Closer to the Sun (Gadol) 141, 142
"Closet, The" (Goodman) 161
Cloud Atlas (Mitchell) 45, **69–70**, 274,
    275
Clowes, Dan 227
Coben, Harlan 71
Cold Mountain (Frazier) 298
Cole, Jack 227
Coleridge, Samuel Taylor 40

Collected Short Stories of John Cheever, The 266

Color Purple, The (Walker) 105

Colossus of New York (Whitehead) 206, 386, 387

Comfort, Alex
  Joy of Sex, The 225

Commentary 107, 161

Complete Review, The 137

Confessions of a Memory Eater (Kennedy) 225

"Confinement" (Cusk) 251, 252

Conjunctions 133, 278, 332

Connell, Evan
  Mr. Bridge 49

Connelly, Jennifer 46

Conrad, Joseph 71, 142, 179, 289, 359

Consider the Lobster (Wallace) 40, 380

Convergence of Birds: Original Fiction and Poetry Inspired by the Work of Joseph Conrad (Foer) 133

Cooper, Rand Richards 286

Copernicus, Nicolaus 100

Coppola, Sophia 125, 126, 379

Cornwell, David John Moore. *See* le Carré, John

Cortázar, Julio 40, 380

Cosmopolitan 33

"Cosmopolitan" (Sharma) 346, 347

Cosper, Darcy 186

Costello, Mark
  Murphy Stories, The 70

Costello, Mark A. (Flood) **70–72**
  Bag Men **23–25**, 70, 71, 72
  Big If 23, 24, **32–33**, 70, 71, 72
  Signifying Rappers: Rap and Race in Urban Present (with Wallace) 25, 70, 71

Cost of Living, The (Roy) 331

Country Life, The (Cusk) 82

Coupland, Douglas **72–74**
  All Families Are Psychotic 72, 146
  City of Glass 217
  Eleanor Rigby 72, 74
  Everything's Gone Green 72
  Generation 72
  Generation A 74
  Generation X 72, 73, 216, 217
  Generation X: Tales for an Accelerated Culture 72, **144–146**
  Girlfriend in a Coma 72, 73, 74, 146, 269
  God Hates Japan 72
  Gum Thief, The 72, 74
  Hey Nostradamus! 72, 74, 216
  jPod 72, 73–74, **216–217**
  Life after God 72, 73, 146, 216, 217
  Microserfs 72, 73, **267–269**
  Miss Wyoming 72

"1,000 Years: Life after God" 73
  September 10, 2001 72
  Shampoo Planet 72, 73, 146
  Souvenirs of Canada 217
  Terry 217
  "Wrong Sun, The" 73

Courting of Marcus Dupree, The (Morris) 364

Coyote, Peter 34, 271

Coyote (Gadol) 140, 141

Crane, Stephen
  "Open Boat, The" 207
  Red Badge of Courage, The 210

"Cravings" (Foer) 133

Crazyhorse 58

Creation of Adam, The (Danticat) 87

Crichton, Michael 226

Cricket magazine 65

Crime in the Neighborhood, A (Berne) 30, **74–76**

Crooked River Burning (Winegardner) **76–77**, 389–390

"Crossing, The" (Seiffert) 344

Crucible, The (Miller) 338

Crumb, Robert 224

Cruz, Ricardo Cortez **77–78**
  Five Days of Bleeding 77
  Straight Outta Compton vi, 77, **359–360**

Crying of Lot 49, The (Pynchon) 205

Cuarón, Alfonso 182, 229

Culture and Equality: An Egalitarian Critique of Multiculturalism (Barry) 19

Culture of Narcissism, The (Lasch) 283

Cunha, Gerard de 330

Cure for Dreams, A (Gibbons) **79–80**, 150

Curious Incident of the Dog in the Night-Time, The (Haddon) **80–82**, 168, 319

Cusk, Rachel **82–84**
  Arlington Park 83
  Bradshaw Variations, The 83
  "Confinement" 251, 252
  Country Life, The 82
  "Down on the Farm" 83
  In the Fold 83, 339
  "I Was Only Being Honest" 82–83
  Last Supper, The 83
  Life's Work: On Becoming a Mother, A 82–83, 340
  Lucky Ones, The 83, **251–252**, 339
  "Matters of Life and Death" 251, 252
  "Mrs. Daley's Daughter" 251, 252
  "Sacrifices, The" 251, 252
  Saving Agnes 82, 251, **339–340**
  Temporary, The 82
  "Way You Do It, The" 83, 251

CWLS. *See* canonic Western literary sensibility

D

Da Capo Best Music Writing 2002: The Year's Finest Writing on Rock, Pop, Jazz, Country & More 242

Dahl, Roald 61, 174

Daily Mail 83, 197, 233

DAM/AGE 331

Dangarembga, Tsitsi 4

Dangerous Astronomy (Alexie) 7

Dangerous Joy of Dr. Sex and Other True Stories, The (Kennedy) 225

Danielewski, Annie 85, 192

Danielewski, Mark Z. **85–87**
  Fifty Year Sword 86
  House of Leaves 85, **191–192**, 201, 283
  Only Revolutions 192
  Whalestoe Letters, The 86

Danielewski, Tad 85, 192

Danticat, Edwidge v, 4, **87–88**
  After the Dance: A Walk through Carnival in Haiti 88
  Anacaona, Golden Flower: Haiti, 1490 87
  Beacon Best of 2000: Great Writing of Women and Men of All Colors and Cultures 87
  Behind the Mountains 87
  "Between the Pool and the Gardenias" 232
  "Book of the Dead, The" 96
  Breath, Eyes, Memory to 87, 95
  Brother, I'm Dying 88
  Butterfly's Way: Voices from the Haitian Dyaspora in the United States, The 88
  "Caroline's Wedding" 232
  Children of the Sea 87
  Creation of Adam, The 87
  Dew Breaker, The 87, 88, **95–96**
  Dreams Like Me 87
  Farming of Bones, The 87, 88, 95
  In the Flicker of an Eyelid (with Alexis) 88
  Krik? Krak! 87, 95, **231–232**
  "Missing Peace, The" 231
  Night Woman" 232
  "Wall of Fire Rising, A" 232

D'Arcy McNickle, William
  Surrounded, The 367

Dark Horse Comics 159

Darkmans (Barker) 25, 26, 66

Dark Room, The (Seiffert) **89–90**, 343–344

Darwin, Charles 100

D'Aulaire, Edgar Parin
  Book of Greek Myths 183

D'Aulaire, Ingri
  Book of Greek Myths 183

Davies, Peter Ho **90–91**

"Brave Girl" 123, 124
"Cakes of Baby" 124
Equal Love 90, **123–124**
"Everything You Can Remember in 30 Seconds Is Yours to Keep" 90, 124
"Frogmen" 123
"How to Be an Expatriate" 90, 123, 124
"Hull Case, The" 123, 124
"Next Life, The" 123, 124
"On the Terraces" 124
"Sales" 123–124
"Small World" 123, 124
"Today Is Sunday" 124
Ugliest House in the World, The 90, 124
Welsh Girl, The 91, 124
Davies, Robertson
Deptford Trilogy, The 49–50
Davis, Nick 174, 266
Boone (with Hansen) 174
Davis, Phil 389
Dawson, Rosario 46
Daydream Believers (Debra Eisenstadt and Jill Eisenstadt) 112
"Day in the Life of Half of Rumpelstiltskin, A" (Brockmeier) 44
Dazed and Confused (Linklater) 22
DC 159
"Dead Rabbit Pocket, The" (Kennedy) 361
Deadwood 160
"Dear John Wayne" (Alexie) 368
Death of Ivan Ilych, The (Tolstoy) 261
Death of Jim Loney, The (Welch) 367
Death of the Last Black Man in the Whole Entire World (Parks) 303
Decatur Herald 77
Decisions (Adichie) 3
Debord, Guy 78
"Dejection: An Ode" (Coleridge) 40
Delaney, Dana 308
DeLillo, Don 71, 167, 186, 187, 279, 310, 311, 380, 386
Falling Man 129
Libra 49
Underworld 76
White Noise 19, 283
Demme, Jonathan 87
Demonology (short fiction collection; Moody) **91–93**, 279
"Demonology" (story; Moody) 93
DeMott, Benjamin 165
Deng, Valentino Achek 111, 384
Den of Thieves (Stewart) 36
Denver Post 121, 308
Depeche Mode 85
Deptford Trilogy, The (Davies) 49–50
Depth Takes a Holiday: Essays from Lesser Los Angeles (Loh) 248

Derrida, Jacques 279
Derrida 85
Desai, Anita 94, 97
Desai, Kiran **93–95**, 292
Hullabaloo in the Guava Orchard 93, 94, 201
Inheritance of Loss, The 93, 94, **201–203**
Deshima (Mitchell) 276
Details 278
DeVincentis, D. V. 178
DeVito, Danny 125, 379
Dew Breaker, The (Danticat) 87, 88, **95–96**
Dial Press 162
Diamond, Jared
Guns, Germs, and Steel 70
"Diaries of Lenny Abramov" (Shteyngart) 350
Diary (Palahniuk) 254, 301, 302
Díaz, Junot **96–98**
Brief Wondrous Life of Oscar Wao, The **42–43**, 97, 98
Drown 96, 97, 98
"How to Date a Browngirl, Blackgirl, Whitegirl, or Halfie" 98
Dick, Philip K. 166, 241, 242
Man in the High Castle, The 57
Three Stigmata of Palmer Eldritch, The 166
Dickens, Charles 102, 190, 357, 387
Dickey, Eric Jerome **98–99**
Genevieve 98
Milk in My Coffee 98
Sister Sister 98, 99, **351–353**
Sleeping with Strangers 98
Thieves Paradise 99
Dickinson, Emily 188
Didion, Joan 46
Dillard, Annie 164
Disappointment Artist, The (Lethem) 242
Dissident, The (Freudenberger) 136, 137, 250–251
"Distances" (Alexie) 6
Diviners, The (Moody) 143, 279
Divining Women (Gibbons) 150
Doctorow, E. L. 160
City of God 76
Ragtime 49
Doctor Zhivago (Pasternak) 148
Doerr, Anthony **99–101**
About Grace 99, 100, 349
"Caretaker, The" 100, 349
"For a Long Time This Was Griselda's Story" 349
Four Seasons in Rome 99
"Hunter's Wife, The" 348–349
"July Fourth" 348, 349
"Mkondo" 100, 349
"Procreate, Generate" 101

Shell Collector, The (short story) 100, 348
Shell Collector, The (short story collection) 99, **348–349**
"So Many Chances" 349
"Tangle by the Rapid River, A" 349
"Village 113" 101
Dongala, Emmanuel
Johnny Mad Dog 28
Donleavy, J. P. 113
Dora: An Analysis of a Case of Hysteria (Freud) 372, 373
"Doris Is Coming" (Packer) 300
Dos Passos, John
U.S.A. Trilogy 16
Dostoyevsky, Fyodor 49
Brothers Karamazov, The 207, 306
Notes from the Underground 49
"Dotocomarama" 46
Double Bind, The (Bohjalian) 33, 34
Doubleday 226, 242
Double Take 229
"Double Zero, The" (Moody) 93
Douglas, Michael 58
"Down on the Farm" (Cusk) 83
Doyle, Arthur Conan 24, 80
Hound of the Baskervilles, The 80
"Do You Know What It Means to Say Phoenix, Arizona" (Alexie) 325
"Drawer" (Moody) 92
Dr. Dre 319
DreamWorks 189
Dress Lodger, The (Holman) **101–102**, 182–183
Drift House (Peck) 310, 311
Drinkard, Michael 112
Drinking Coffee Elsewhere (Packer) **102–104**, 299
Drown (Díaz) 96, 97, 98
"Dual Balls" (Barker) 25
Due, Patricia Stephens
Freedom in the Family: A Mother-Daughter Memoir of the Fight for Civil Rights 104
Due, Tananarive **104–106**
"African Immortals" 104
Between, The 104
Black Rose, The 104
Blood Colony 104, 247
Casanegra 104
Good House, The 104
In the Night of the Heat (with Steven Barnes and Underwood) 104
Joplin's Ghost 104
Living Blood, The 104, 105, **246–248**
My Soul to Keep 104, 246, 247
Naked Came the Manatee 104
Dunn, Adam 254

Dunn, Katherine 333, 337
   Geek Love 264
Dunrow, Henry 264
Dunst, Kirsten 125, 379
Duras, Marguerite 393
Dylan, Bob 241

E

Easy-E 359
Eat, Pray, Love (Gilbert) 152, 153
Eberstadt, Fernanda **107–108**
   Furies, The 107
   Isaac and His Devils 107–108, **206–207**
   Little Money Street 107
   Low Tide 107
   When the Sons of Heaven Meet the Daughters of the Earth 107, 108, 207
Eberstadt, Frederick 107
Eberstadt, Isabel 107
Ebony 211, 212
Eco, Umberto 235, 279
"Ecstasy of Influence, The" (Lethem) 242
Edger, David 187
Effect of Living Backwards, The (Julavits) 218, 219
Egan, Jennifer **108–110**
   Emerald City 108–109
   Invisible Circus 108, 109, 224
   Keep, The 108, 109, **223–224**
   Look at Me 108, 109, 224
Egan, Terry 289
"Egg, The" (Anderson) 93
Eggers, Beth 178
Eggers, Dave vi, **110–112**, 229
   Heartbreaking Work of Staggering Genius, A 110, 118, **177–179**, 201, 385, 396
   How We Are Hungry 111, 178
   Teachers Have It Easy: The Big Sacrifices and Small Salaries of America's Teachers 396
   What Is the What: The Autobiography of Valentino Achek Deng vi, 28, 111, 178, **384–385**, 396
   Wild Things, The 112
   You Shall Know Our Velocity! 111, 178, **394–396**
Egyptologist, The (Phillips) 315, 316
Einstein, Albert 350
Eisenberg, Deborah 164
Eisenman, Sara 226
Eisenstadt, Debra 364
   Daydream Believers (with Jill Eisenstadt) 112
Limbo Room, The (with Jill Eisenstadt) 112
Eisenstadt, Jill **112–113**
   Daydream Believers (with Debra Eisenstadt) 112
   From Rockaway 112, 113, **138–139**

Kiss Out 112, 113
Limbo Room, The (with Debra Eisenstadt) 112
Eleanor Rigby (Coupland) 72, 74
Election (Perrotta) 22, 214, 311, 313
Electric Moon (Roy) 330
Elephant Suite, The (Theroux) 293
"Eleven Song Setting" 69
Elkin, Stanley 164, 278
Elle 137
Ellen Foster (Gibbons) **114–115**, 149–151, 298
Eliot, George 165, 354, 357
Eliot, T. S. 343
Ellis, Bret Easton v, 61, 70, 74, 112, 113, **115–117**, 139, 226, 351
   American Psycho **13–15**, 115, 116, 186, 256, 257, 364
   Frog King, The 117
   Glamorama 15, 115, 116–117
   Imperial Bedrooms 117
   Informers, The 115, 116, 117
   Less than Zero 115, 116, 117, 256, 257, 364
   Lunar Park 15, 115, 117, **256–257**
   Rules of Attraction, The 13, 113, 115, 116, 117, 215
   This Is Not an Exit: The Fictional World of Bret Easton Ellis 117
Ellis, Dale 115
Ellis, Robert Martin 115
Ellis, Trey **117–119**
   Bedtime Stories: Adventures in the Land of Single Fatherhood 117, 118
   Home Repairs 117, 118, **184–185**
   "New Black Aesthetic, The" 118
   Platitudes 117, 118
   Right Here, Right Now 117, 118, **326–327**
Ellison, Ralph
   Invisible Man 54, 289, 346, 386
Ellroy, James 24, 61, 226, 319
Eltis, Sos 169
Elvis Presley Boulevard (Winegardner) 389, 390
"Elvis's Bathroom" (Kennedy) 360
"Eluding Happiness" (Row) 329
Emecheta, Buchi 4
Emperor of the Air (Canin) 48, **119–120**
Emerald City (Egan) 108–109
Emerson, Ralph Waldo
   "Self-Reliance" 114
Emigrants, The (Sebald) 261
Eminem 319
Emperor's Club, The 48
Emperor of the Air (Canin) **119–120**
End of Alice, The 185, 186, 366
"End of Happiness, The" (Roy) 331

Enger, Leif (Enger) **120–122**
   Peace Like a River 120, 121, **308–309**
   So Brave, Young and Handsome: A Novel 120, 121
Enger, L. L. *See* Enger, Leif; Enger, Lin
Enger, Lin (Enger) 121
Enger, Robin 120
Englander, Nathan **122–123**, 136
   For the Relief of Unbearable Urges 122, 123, 273
   Ministry of Special Cases, The 122, 123, **273–274**
   "Reb Kringle" 122
   "Tumblers, The" 122
   "27th Man, The" 122
English Patient, The (Ondaatje) 148
Entertainment Weekly 59, 153, 236, 302
Envy (Harrison) 175, 176, 341
Epoch 237
Equal Affections (Leavitt) 238
Equal Love (Davies) 90, **123–124**
Erdrich, Louise 164
Ernaux, Annie 393
Esquire 110, 133, 179, 213, 229, 242, 278, 350
Essence 88
Etiqueta Negra 4
Eugenides, Jeffrey **125–126**, 133
   Air Mail 126
   Middlesex 125–126, **269–271**, 377
   My Mistress's Sparrow Is Dead: Great Love Stories from Chekhov to Munroe 125
   Virgin Suicides, The 125, 126, 271, **377–379**
"E Unibus Pluram" (Wallace) vi, 156, 201, 381–382
Evans, Walker
   Let Us Now Praise Famous Men (with Agee) 395
Everett, Percival 345
Everything and More: A Compact History of ∞ (Wallace) 380
Everything Is Illuminated (Foer) **126–128**, 133, 181
Everything's Gone Green (Coupland) 72
"Everything You Can Remember in 30 Seconds Is Yours to Keep" (Davies) 90, 124
Exact Replica of a Figment of My Imagination, An (McCracken) 264
Exes, The (Kennedy) 225
Exit A (Swofford) 363
Exposure (Harrison) 175, 341
Extremely Loud and Incredibly Close (Foer) 82, 127, **128–130**, 133
Eye Killers (Carr) 105
Eyre, Chris 7
Eyre, Hermione 354

F

Face (Alexie) 8
*Faithful, Two Diehard Boston Red Sox Fans
  Chronicle the Historic 2004 Season* (O'Nan
  and King) 287
Falling Angels (Chevalier) 64
Falling Man (DeLillo) 129
Fallon, Jimmy 120
Family Dancing (Leavitt) 238
Family Daughter, A (Meloy) 172, 265, 266
Family Markowitz, The (Goodman) 161, 220
"Fannie Mae" (Goodman) 161
Farming of Bones, The (Danticat) 87, 88, 95
Farrar, Strauss & Giroux 226, 278
Fast Company magazine 354
Father Comes Home from the Wars (Parks)
  304
Faulkner, William 68, 150, 157, 310, 353,
  383
  Absalom, Absalom 142
  Sound and the Fury, The 81, 142, 169
Fauset, Jessie
  Plum Bun 54
"Federer as Religious Experience" (Wallace)
  380
"Ferry, The" (Row) 329, 369–370
Fiction Collective Two 77
Fiction International 77
Field, Todd 23, 313
Fielding, Helen
  Bridget Jones's Diary 184
Field Study (Seiffert) 343, 344
Fifty Year Sword (Danielewski) 86
Fight Club (Palahniuk) **131–133**, 254,
  301, 302
Final Solution: A Story of Detection, The
  (Chabon) 57
Fincher, David 301
"Finest Wife, The" (Gilbert) 320
Finlay, Peter Warren. *See* Pierre, DBC
Fireovid, Steve
  26th Man (with Windgardner) 390
Firing Line 107
First Indian on the Moon (Alexie) 7
*First Man-Made Man: The Story of Two Sex
  Changes, One Love Affair, and a Twentieth-
  Century Medical Revolution* (Kennedy)
  225
First $20 Million Is Always the Hardest, The
  (Bronson) 46
Firth, Colin 153
Fitting Ends (Chaon) 58–59
Fitzgerald, F. Scott 49
  Great Gatsby, The 56, 343
  This Side of Paradise 184
Fitzhugh, Louise
  Harriet the Spy 246

Five Days of Bleeding (Cruz) 77
Five Miles from Outer Hope (Barker) 25
Five Points 170
Flashpoint Magazine 77
Flatley, Kate 155
Flaubert, Gustave 52, 58, 91
Fletcher, Martin 309–310
Flight (Alexie) 8
Flood, John. *See* Costello, Mark
Flowers for Algernon (Keyes) 81, 169
FoE! (blog) 178
Foer, Albert 133
Foer, Esther Safran 133
Foer, Jonathan Safran **133–134**, 137, 229
  "About the Typefaces Not Used in This
    Edition" 133
  "Beginner's Guide to Hanukkah, A" 133
  *Convergence of Birds: Original Fiction
    and Poetry Inspired by the Work of
    Joseph Conrad* 133
  "Cravings" 133
  Everything Is Illuminated **126–128**,
    133, 181
  Extremely Loud and Incredibly Close 82,
    127, **128–130**, 133
  "If the Aging Magician Should Begin to
    Believe" 133
  Joe (with Serra, Sugimoto) 134
  "My Life as a Dog" 133–134
  "Primer for the Punctuation of Heart
    Disease, A" 133
  "Room after Room" 133
  "Seven Attempted Escapes from
    Silence" 134
  "Sixth Borough, The" 133
  "Very Rigid Search, The" 133
Foer, Sasha 134
Fontaine, Donna 302
"For A Long Time This Was Griselda's
  Story" (Doerr) 349
Ford, Douglas 368
Ford, Richard 266
  *Granta Book of the American Short
    Story* 136
  Independence Day 76
  *New Granta Book of the American Short
    Story* 136
Ford, John 242
"Forecast from the Retail Desk" (Moody)
  93, 279
Foreign Student, The (Choi) 64, 65–66, 314
Foreman, T. E. 249
"Forever Overhead" (Wallace) 40
For Kings and Planets (Canin) 49
For Love of Biafra (Adichie) 3
Forster, E. M. 357
  Howards End 296
  Passage to India 196, 205

Forster, Marc 229
For the Relief of Unbearable Urges
  (Englander) 122, 123, 273
Fortress of Solitude, The (Lethem) **134–
  136**, 242, 282
"For You" (Row) 329, 369
Foucault, Michel 302
"Four Lean Hounds, ca. 1976 (Meloy)
  171
Four Seasons in Rome (Doerr) 99
Fox 2000 Pictures 261
Foxx, Jamie 214
France, Louise 316
Franzen, Jonathan 32, 71, 311, 380
  Twenty-Seventh City 76
Frazier, Charles
  Cold Mountain 298
*Freedom in the Family: A Mother-Daughter
  Memoir of the Fight for Civil Rights* (Due)
  104
Freud, Sigmund 350
  Dora: An Analysis of a Case of Hysteria
    372, 373
Freudenberger, Nell v, **136–138**, 239
  Dissident, The 136, 137, 250–251
  "Letter from the Last Bastion" 137,
    249
  Lucky Girls 136–137, **249–251**
  "Orphan, The" 137
  "Outside the Eastern Gate" 137, 249
  "Real Life" 136
  "Tutor, The" 137, 249
Frey, James 178
  Million Little Pieces, A 208, 213
Friedrich, Molly 182–182
Frog King, The (Ellis) 117
"Frogmen" (Davies) 123
From Rockaway (Eisenstadt) 112, 113,
  138–139
*Frost and the Flower: My Life with Manic
  Depression So Far* (Gibbons) 150
Fucking Martin. See Martin and John (Peck)
Fugitive Pieces (Michaels) 181
*Fugitives and Refugees: A Walk in Portland,
  Oregon* (Palahniuk) 301
Full Metal Jacket 213, 362
Fungus the Bogeyman (Briggs) 168
Furies, The (Eberstadt) 107
Future Dictionary of America, The 133, 229

G

Gaddis, William 40, 156, 380
Gadol, Peter **140–142**
  American Modern 142
  Closer to the Sun 141, 142
  Coyote 140, 141
  Light at Dusk 141–142
  Long Rain 141, 142

Man "Carrying Thing: A Theory of
    Metaphor for Wallace Stevens" 140
    "Modernhaus Projekt-H, 1933" 142
    Mystery Roast 140–141, 142, **284–285**
    Silver Lake 142
Gadol, Normal 140
Gadol, Sybil Rickless 140
Gage, Jenny
    Hotel Andromeda (with Julavits) 218
"Gambit Declined" (Moody) 278
Garcia, Adam 46
García Márquez, Gabriel 229, 230, 333, 337
    One Hundred Years of Solitude 371, 383
Garden State (Moody) 92, **142–144**, 278
Garner, Dwight 310
Gass, William 92
Gates, Henry Louis
    Signifying Monkey: A Theory of African-
    American Literary Criticism, A
Gavron, Sarah 38
Gawker.com 311
Gear 301
Geek Love (Dunn) 264
"Geese" (Packer) 300
Generation A (Coupland) 74
Generation (Coupland) 72
Generation X (Coupland) 72, 73, 216, 217
Generation X: Tales for an Accelerated
    Culture (Coupland) 72, **144–146**
Genevieve (Dickey) 98
Gentlemen of the Road (Chabon) 56
George, Terry 173
Georgia Review 44
Gerhart, Ann
    The Perfect Wife: The Life and Choices of
    Laura Bush 354
Geronimo Rex (Hannah) 364
Gesture Life, A (Lee) **146–148**, 239, 240
Getting Mother's Body (Parks) 303, 304
Gettysburg 85
Gettysburg Review 58
"Ghastly Ordeal of Timothy Cavendish,
    The" (Mitchell) 69
Ghost at the Table, The (Berne) 30, 31, 76
Ghostwritten (Mitchell) 69, 70, 274, 275
"Giant of Cape Cod, The" (McCracken)
    264
Giant's House, The (McCracken) **148–149**,
    263, 264
Gibbons, Kaye, **149–151**
    Charms for the Easy Life 150
    Cure for Dreams, A **79–80**, 150
    Divining Women 150
    Ellen Foster **114–115**, 149–151, 298
    Frost and the Flower: My Life with Manic
    Depression So Far 150
    Life All around Me by Ellen Foster, The
    115, 150

On the Occasion of My Last Afternoon
    151, **297–298**
    Sights Unseen 150–151
    Virtuous Woman, A 150, 151
Gibbons, Reginald 58
Gibson, William 32
Gilbert, Carol 152
Gilbert, Elizabeth **152–153**
    "At the Bronx Terminal Vegetable
    Market" 152
    Eat, Pray, Love 152, 153
    "Finest Wife, The" 320
    Last American Man, The 152, 153
    "Names of Flowers, The" 320
    Pilgrims (collection) 152, **319–321**
    "Pilgrims" (short story) 320
    Stern Man 152
Gilbert, Jan 69
Gilbert, John 152
Ginsburg, Allen 43
Girlfriend in a Coma (Coupland) 72, 73, 74,
    146, 269
Girl in Landscape (Lethem) 242, 282
Girl in the Flammable Skirt, The (Bender)
    195
Girl 6 (Parks) 303
Girl with a Pearl Earring (Chevalier) 63,
    153–155
Girl with Curious Hair (Wallace) 40, 155–
    157, 380, 381
Glamorama (Ellis) 15, 115, 116–117
Glamour 112, 353
Godbersen, Anna 19
Gödel, Kurt 155
Godfather, The (Puzo) 77, 389, 390
Godfather Returns, The (Winegardner) 389,
    390
Godfather's Revenge, The (Winegardner)
    389, 390
God Hates Japan (Coupland) 72
God of Small Things, The (Roy) **157–159**,
    202, 330, 331–332
Gogol, Nikolai 334, 351
Goines, Donald 99
"Going Ashore" (Lahiri) 237
Gold, Glen David **159–160**
    Carter Beats the Devil **50–51**, 159–160
    Sunnyside 159, 160
Gone with the Wind (Mitchell) 298
Goodbye, Columbus (Roth) 22
"Goodbye My Brother" (Cheever) 48
Good House, The (Due) 104
Goodman, Allegra **160–163**
    "Choo Choo" 161
    "Closet, The" 161
    Family Markowitz, The 161, 220
    "Fannie Mae" 161
    Intuition 161, 162

Kaaterskill Falls 161, 162, **220–221**
    "Onionskin" 161
    Other Side of the Island, The 161, 162
    Paradise Park 161, 162, 220
    Total Immersion 161
    "Variant Text" 161
Goodman, Lenn 161
Goodman, Madeline 161
"Good Old Neon" (Wallace) 156, 380
"Good People" 382
Good Things I Wish You (Ansay) 18, 328
Gordinier, Jeff
    X Saves the World: How Generation
    X Got the Shaft but Can Still Keep
    Everything from Sucking 146
Gossip Girl 313
GQ 133, 153, 276, 364
Grand Complication, The (Kurzweil) 52,
    234–235
Granta 90, 101, 133, 137, 197, 229, 232,
    234, 274, 350, 343, 386
Granta Book of the American Short Story
    (Ford) 136
Granta: Best of Young American Novelists
    101, 264, 300
Grass, Günter
    Tin Drum, The 129
Grass Dancer, The (Power) **163–164**
Graveyard of the Atlantic (Hagy) 170
Graver, Elizabeth **164–165**
    "Around the World" 165
    Awake 164–165
    Have You Seen Me? 164
    Honey Thief, The 164, 165, **187–189**
    Unraveling 164, 165
Gravity's Rainbow (Pynchon) 26
Gray, Dorian 14
Great Gatsby, The (Fitzgerald) 56, 343
Green, David Gordon 294
"Green Children, The" (Brockmeier) 44–45
Greene, Graham 141
Greer, Germaine 9
Gregg, Clark 302
Gregory, Sinda 86
Gretlund, Jan Nordby 298
Grishman, John 35
Grooves: A Kind of Mystery (Brockmeier) 43
Gross, Teri 355
Grossman, Austin
    Soon I Will Be Invincible 167
Grossman, David
    See Under: Love 261
Grossman, Lev 241
Grove/Atlantic Monthly Press 121, 226
Guardian 46, 66, 82, 83, 110, 133, 233,
    260, 266, 319
Gumbo: A Celebration of African-American
    Writing 99

Gum Thief, The (Coupland) 72, 74
Gun, With Occasional Music (Lethem) **165–167**, 242, 282
Guns, Germs, and Steel (Diamond) 70
Gyllenhaal, Jake 214, 362

H

Habila, Helon
    Waiting for an Angel 210
Haddon, Mark **168–170**
    Agent Z and the Killer Bananas 168
    Agent Z and the Penguin from Mars 168
    Agent Z Goes Wild 168
    Agent Z Meets the Masked Crusader 168
    Curious Incident of the Dog in the Night-Time, The **80–82**, 168, 319
    Gilbert's Gobbstopper 168
    Spot of Bother, A 168, 169
    Talking Horse and the Sad Girl and the Village under the Sea 168
Hagy, Alyson **170–171**
    Graveyard of the Atlantic 170
    Hardware River 170
    Keeneland 170, **221–223**
    Madonna on Her Back 170
    "Mr. Makes" 170
    "Search Bay" 170
    Snow, Ashes 170, 171
Hagy, Carol Elaine Lindsay 170
Hagy, John Albert 170
Haldeman, Joe 363
Haley, Alex
    Roots 104
Half in Love (Meloy) **171–172**, 265
"Half-Lives: The First Luisa Rey Mystery" (Mitchell) 69
Half of a Yellow Sun (novel; Adichie) 3, 4, **172–174**, 210
"Half of a Yellow Sun" (short story; Adichie) 3
Hallmark Hall of Fame 150
"Halloween Party, The" (Chabon) 277
Hammett, Dashiell 24
Hamilton, Jane 376
Handle with Care (Picoult) 317
Handmaid's Tale, The (Atwood) 371
Hannah, Barry
    Geronimo Rex 364
    High Lonesome 364
Hansen, Ada 175
Hansen, Brooks **174–175**
    Boone (with Davis) 174
    Brotherhood of Joseph, The 174–175
    Caesar's Antlers 174
    Chess Garden: Or the Twilight Letters of Gustav Uyterhoeven, The **61–63**, 174
    John the Baptizer 174
    Monster of St. Helena 174

    Pearlman's Ordeal 174
Hansen, Elizabeth 175
Hansen, Theo 175
Hanson, Curtis 58
"Hardened Criminals, The" (Lethem) 167
Hardware River (Hagy) 170
Hardy, Thomas 100
Harnett, Josh 125, 379
Harper and Row 161
HarperCollins 226
Harper's 5, 178, 229, 241, 242, 278, 362, 364
Harriet the Spy (Fitzhugh) 246
Harris, E. Lynn 99
Harris, Naomie 389
Harrison, Kathryn **175–177**
    Binding Chair, The 175, 176
    Envy 175, 176, 341
    Exposure 175, 341
    Kiss, The 175, 176, 340, 341
    Mother Knot, The 175, 176
    Poison 175, 176
    Road to Santiago, The 175, 176
    Saint Thérèse of Lisieux 175, 176
    Seal Wife, The 175, 176, **340–342**
    Seeking Rapture 175, 176
    Thicker than Water 175, 176
    While They Slept: An Inquiry into the Murder of a Family 175, 176
Harron, Mary 14–15
Harry Potter (Rowling) 183
Harvard Advocate 136, 140
Harvard Review 237, 328
Harvesting the Heart (Picoult) 317
Haslett, Adam 136
Hatchet Jobs (Peck) 309, 311
Haunted (Palahniuk) 254, 301
Haunted (Poe) 85, 192
"Haunting Olivia" (Russell) 332, 336
Have You Seen Me? (Graver) 164
Hawkes, John 278
Hawthorne, Nathaniel
    "Minister's Black Veil, The" 279
Head, Bessie
    A Question of Power 28
Heading Inland (Barker) 25
Heaney, Seamus 140
Heartbreaking Work of Staggering Genius, A (Eggers) 110, 118, **177–179**, 201, 385, 396
"Heaven Lake" (Row) 370
Helicon 58
Heller, Joseph
    Catch-22 290, 362
Heller, Zoë
    Notes on a Scandal 319
Hellman, Lillian 301
Hello 85

Hemingway, Ernest 116
Hemon, Alexandar **179–180**
    Lazarus Project, The 179, 180
    Nowhere Man 179–180, **289–290**
    Question of Bruno, The 179, 180, 289
    "Sorge Spy Ring, The" 180
Hemon, Ell 180
Hempel, Amy 301
Henderson the Rain King (Bellow) 49
"Here and There" (Wallace) 155, 156, 380
Here's Your Hat What's Your Hurry (McCracken) 148, 263–264
Heroes 311
Herskovits, David 108
Hewett, Heather 4
Heyman, David 182
Hey Nostradamus! (Coupland) 72, 74, 216
High Lonesome (Hannah) 364
High Mountains of Portugal, The (Martel) 261
Hirokazu, Koreeda 39
Hirschorn, Michael 335
History of Love, The (Krauss) 127, **180–182**, 229, 230
Hitchcock, Alfred 346
Hollinger, David 54
Holman, Sheri **182–184**
    Dress Lodger, The **101–102**, 182, 183
    Mammoth Cheese, The 182
    Sondok: Princess of the Moon and Stars 182
    Stolen Tongue, A 182, 183
Home Repairs (Ellis) 117, 118, **184–185**
Homes, A. M. **185–187**
    "Adults Alone" 282
    Appendix A: An Elaboration on the Novel the End of Alice 187
    End of Alice, The 185, 186, 366
    In a Country of Mothers 185, 186
    Jack 185, 186, 366
    Los Angeles: People, Places, and the Castle on the Hill 185, 187
    Mistress's Daughter, The 185, 187
    Music for Torching 185, 187, **282–284**, 366
    "Real Doll, A" 186
    Safety of Objects, The 185, 186, 187, 282
    Things You Should Know 185, 187
    This Book Will Save Your Life 185, 186, 187, 282, **365–367**
Honey Thief, The (Graver) 164, 165, **187–189**
Honolulu Star-Bulletin 161
Hopkinson, Nalo 105
Hopkins, Pauline
    Of One Blood 247
Hornby, Nick 32, 178

Hosseini, Khaled **189–191**
 Kite Runner, The 189, 190, **227–229**
 Thousand Splendid Suns, A 189, 190
Hotel Andromeda (Julavits and Gage) 218
Hotel Rwanda 173
Houghton Mifflin 133
Hound of the Baskervilles, The (Doyle) 80
House Made of Dawn (Momaday) 367
House of Leaves (Danielewski) 85, **191–192**, 201, 283
House of Two Three-Legged Dogs, The (McCracken) 264
House Rules (Picoult) 317
Howards End (E. M. Forster) 296
Howe, Fanny 345
How Insensitive (Smith) 146
"How to Be an Expatriate" (Davies) 90, 123, 124
"How to Date a Browngirl, Blackgirl, Whitegirl, or Halfie" (Díaz) 98
"How Tracy Austin Broke My Heart" (Wallace) 380
How We Are Hungry (Eggers) 111, 178
How We Got Insipid (Lethem) 242
Hudson, Gabe 137
Hugo, Richard 266
Hullabaloo in the Guava Orchard (Desai) 93, 94
"Hull Case, The" (Davies) 123, 124
"Human Soul as Rube Goldberg Device: A Choose-Your-Own-Adventure Story, The" (Brockmeier) 45
Human Stain, The (Roth) 54
"Hunger Artist, A" (Kafka) 67
"Hunter's Wife, The" (Doerr) 348–349
Huxley, Aldous 162
 Brave New World 166
Hyde, Lewis 242

I

I Am Charlotte Simmons (Wolfe) 215
I Am Legal 38
Ice Cube 359
Ice Storm, The (Moody) 92, 93, 143, **193–194**, 278–279
"I Demand to Know Where You're Taking Me" (Chaon) 59
Idyll Banter (Bohjalian) 33
If I Told You Once (Budnitz) 127
If on a Winter's Night a Traveler (Calvino) 70, 275
"If the Aging Magician Should Begin to Believe" (Foer) 133
If This Is Kosher 134
If You Lived Here, You'd Be Home By Now (Loh) **194–196**, 248
"If You Sing Like That for Me" (Sharma) 346, 347

Il Powwow Della Fine Del Mondo (Alexie) 7
"Immortality" (Shteyngart) 350
Imperceptible Mutabilities in the Third Kingdom (Parks) 303
Imperial Bedrooms (Ellis) 117
Impressionist, The (Kunzru) **196–197**, 232, 233
In a Country of Mothers 185, 186
"Incarnations of Burned Children" (Wallace) 382
In Cold Blood (Capote) 111
Independent 82, 252, 301
Indian Clerk, The (Leavitt) 239
Indian Killer (Alexie) 7, **197–199**
"Ineluctable Modality of the Vaginal" (Moody) 92, 279
Infinite Jest (Wallace) vi, 40, 71, 156, **199–201**, 283, 380, 381, 382
Informers, The (Ellis) 115, 116, 117
Inheritance of Loss, The (Desai) 93, 94, **201–203**
Innocence (Mendelsohn) 208, 266, 267
Insomnia: If You Lived Here, You'd Be Home Already (Palahniuk) 301
Interpreter of Maladies (Lahiri) **203–204**, 236, 237
In the Blood (Parks) 303
In the Flicker of an Eyelid (Danticat and Alexis) 88
In the Fold (Cusk) 83, 339
In the Kitchen (Ali) 8, 9
In the Night of the Heat (with Steven Barnes and Underwood) (Due) 104
In the Walled City (O'Nan) 294
Intuition (Goodman) 161, 162
Intuitionist, The (Whitehead) 19, **204–206**, 386
Invisible Circus (Egan) 108, 109, 224
Invisible Man (Ellison) 54, 289, 346, 386
Invisible Monsters (Palahniuk) 254, 301, 302–303
In Which Annie Gives It Those Ones (Roy) 330
Iowa Review 362
Iowa Writers' Workshop v, 5, 30, 44, 48, 119, 122, 137, 186, 212, 264, 304, 306, 354, 362
Irving, John 35, 119
Isaac and His Devils (Eberstadt) 107–108, **206–207**
Ishiguro, Kazuo
 Remains of the Day 148, 169
"It's Bad Luck to Die" (McCracken) 264
I Was Amelia Earhart (Mendelsohn) **207–209**, 266, 267
"I Was Only Being Honest" (Cusk) 82–83
Iweala, Uzodinma **209–210**
 Beasts of No Nation **27–28**, 209
I Would Steal Horses (Alexie) 6

J

Jack 185, 186, 366
Jackson, Etna 211
Jackson, Sheneska **211–212**
 Blessings 211, 212
 Caught Up in the Rapture **54–56**, 211, 212
 Li'l Mama's Rules 211, 212
Jackson, Shirley 31, 58
James, Henry 238
Janowitz, Tama 112, 116, 139
Japanese by Spring (Reed) 19
Jarhead: A Marine's Chronicle of the Gulf War and Other Battles (Swofford) **212–214**, 362
Jarrold, Julian 389
Jennifer Clement: New and Selected Poems (Clement) 68
Jeunet, Jean-Pierre 245, 261
Joe (Foer, Serra, Sugimoto) 134
Joe College (Perrotta) **214–216**, 311, 312, 313
Johannson, Scarlett 153
"John Billy" (Wallace) 157
John Henry Days (Whitehead) 19, 204, 205, 386–387
Johnny Mad Dog (Dongala) 28
Johnson, James Weldon
 Autobiography of an Ex-Colored Man 54, 346
Johnson, Samuel 161, 207
John the Baptizer (Hansen) 174
Jones, James Earl 85
Jonze, Spike 111
Joplin's Ghost (Due) 104
Jornada Semanal 68
Joy of Sex, The (Comfort) 225
Joyce, James 123, 157
 Ulysses 262
jPod (Coupland) 72, 73–74, **216–217**
Julavits, Heidi **217–219**
 Effect of Living Backwards, The 218, 219
 Hotel Andromeda (with Gage) 218
 Mineral Palace, The 218
 Uses of Enchantment, The 218–219, **372–373**
Jules & Jim 56
July, Miranda
 No One Belong Here More Than You 195
"July Fourth" (Doerr) 348, 349
"Jumblies, The" (Lear) 392
Jurassic Park 226

K

Kaaterskill Falls (Goodman) 161, 162, **220–221**
Kafka, Franz 180
 "Hunger Artist, A" 67

Kafka Americana 242
Kakutani, Michiko 97, 110, 334, 362
Kaldor, Mary 383
Kamil, Susan 264, 265
Kaplan, Michael Wade 116
Kapur, Shekar 330
Kavadlo 255
Keats, John 161–162
Keeneland (Hagy) 170, **221–223**
Keep, The (Egan) 108, 109, **223–224**
Keeping Faith (Picoult) 317
Keitetsi, China
    Child Soldier: Fighting for My Life 28,
        209
Keller, Marjorie 265
Kennedy, Patricia "Pagan" **224–226**
    "Black Forest, The" 361
    *Black Livingstone: A True Tale of
        Adventure in the Nineteenth-Century*
    "Camp" 361
    Confessions of a Memory Eater 225
    Congo 225
    *Dangerous Joy of Dr. Sex and Other True
        Stories, The* 225
    "Dead Rabbit Pocket, The" 361
    "Elvis's Bathroom" 360
    Exes, The 225
    *First Man-Made Man: The Story of Two
        Sex Changes, One Love Affair, and a
        Twentieth-Century Medical Revolution*
        225
    "Monument, The" 362
    Pagan's Head 224, 225
    *Pagan Kennedy's Living: Handbook for
        Maturing Hipsters* 225
    *Platforms: A Microwaved Cultural
        Chronicle of the 1970s* 225
    "Shrinks" 361
    Spinsters 225
    "Stripping" 361
    Stripping + Other Stories 224–225,
        360–362
    "Tunnel, The" 361
    "UFOs" 362
    "Underwear Man" 361
    *Zine: How I Spent Six Years of My Life in
        the Underground and Finally . . . Found
        Myself . . . I Think* 225
Kerouac, Jack 116
    On the Road 395
Keyes, Daniel
    Flowers for Algernon 81, 169
Khan, Irrfan 236
Kidd, Chip, **226–227**
    *Cheese Monkeys: A Novel in Two
        Semesters, The* **60–61**, 226–227
    Learners, The 61, 226, 227
Kierkegaard, Søren 40, 302

Killing in the Real World, A (Bohjalian) 34
Kim, Walter 386
Kimitake, Hiraoka. *See* Mishima, Yukio
Kincaid, Jamaica 209
    Annie John 82
Kindred, The (Butler) 105
King, Stephen 105, 117, 333, 357, 358
    *Faithful, Two Diehard Boston Red Sox
        Fans Chronicle the Historic 2004
        Season* (with O'Nan) 287, 294
Kingsolver, Barbara
    Poisonwood Bible, The 76
Kirkus Review 46, 212
Kiss, The (Harrison) 175, 176, 340, 341
Kiss Out (Eisenstadt) 112, 113
Kite Runner, The (Hosseini) 189, 190,
    227–229
"Kite Whistler Aquamarine" (Meloy)
    171–172
"K&K" (Moody) 280
Kline, Kevin 48, 279
Klosterman, Chuck
    *Sex, Drugs, and Cocoa Puffs: A Low
        Culture Manifesto* 146
Knocked Up 313
Knowles, John
    Separate Peace, A 321, 354
Kolsch, Kevin 302
Kononenko, Maxim 351
Koontz, Dean 226
Krasinski, John 381
Krauss, Nicole 134, **229–230**
    History of Love, The 127, **180–182**,
        229, 230
    Man Walks into a Room 182, 229–230,
        258–259
Krik? Krak! (Danticat) 87, 95, **231–232**
Kring, Tim 311
Krishen, Pradeep 330
Krist, Gary 386
Krouse, Erika 137
Kuiper, Alice 260
Kundera, Milan 44
    Unbearable Lightness of Being 180
Kunkel, Benjamin 136
Kunzru, Hari **232–234**
    Impressionist, The **196–197**, 232, 233
    My Revolutions 232, 233–234
    Noise 232
    Transmission 232, 233, 234
Kureishi, Hanif 357
Kurzweil, Allen **234–235**
    Case of Curiosities, A **51–53**, 234
    Grand Complication, The 52, 234–235
    Leon and the Champion Chip 235
    Leon and the Spitting Image 235
Kuti, Fela 210
Kyoto Journal 328

L
Lady and the Unicorn, The (Chevalier) 64
Lady Chatterley's Lover (Lawrence) 143
    Lady of the Broom, The (Clement) 68,
        69
"Lady with the Pet Tribble, The"
    (Brockmeier) 45
"Lady Yeti and the Place of Artificial
    Snows" (Russell) 333, 336
Lahiri, Jhumpa 5, 8, **236–238**, 292, 293
    "Choice of Accommodations, A" 237
    "Going Ashore" 237
    Interpreter of Maladies **203–204**, 236,
        237
    "Mrs. Sen" 204, 237
    Namesake 236
    "Once in a Lifetime" 236
    "Only Goodness" 237
    "Sexy" 237
    "Temporary Matter, A" 203, 237
    "This Blessed House" 204, 237
    Unaccustomed Earth 236–237
    "When Mr. Pirzada Came to Dine"
        203, 237
    "Year's End" 236
Laird, Nick 296
Lamb, Mary 35
Larkin, Philip 357
Larsen, Nella
    Passing 54, 346
    Quicksand 395
Lasch, Christopher
    Culture of Narcissism, The 283
Last American Man, The (Gilbert) 152, 153
Last of the Southern Girls, The (Morris) 364
Last Supper, The 83
"Laughing with Kafka" (Wallace) 40
L.A. Weekly 301, 301
Law of Enclosures (Peck) 263, 309, 310
Law of Similars (Bohjalian) 34
Lawrence, D. H.
    Lady Chatterley's Lover 143
Lazarus Project, The (Hemon) 179, 180
Lear, Edward
    "Jumblies, The" 392
Learners, The (Kidd) 61, 226, 227
Leavitt, David 136, **238–239**
    Equal Affections 238
    Family Dancing 238
    Indian Clerk, The 239
    Lost Language of Cranes, The 238, 239
    Martin Bauman: Or, a Sure Thing 238
    Place I've Never Been, A 238
    While England Sleeps 238–239
le Carré, John 142
LeClair, Thomas 199
Lee, Ang 279

Lee, Chang-rae v, 65, **239–241**, 314
   Aloft 239, 240
   Gesture Life, A **146–148**, 239, 240
   Native Speaker 147, 148, 239, 240,
    287–289
Lee, Harper 265
   To Kill a Mockingbird 81–82, 246, 271
Lee, Spike 304
LeFetra, Suzanne 165
L'Engle, Madeleine 311
Lennon, John 180, 290
Leon and the Champion Chip (Kurzweil)
  235
Leon and the Spitting Image (Kurzweil) 235
Leroy, J. T. 208
Lessig, Lawrence 242
Less than Zero (Ellis) 115, 116, 117, 256,
  257, 364
Lethem, Jonathan **241–243**
   Amnesia Moon 242
   As She Climbed across the Table 242
   Chronic City 242
   Disappointment Artist, The 242
   "Ecstasy of Influence, The" 242
   Fortress of Solitude, The **134–136**,
    242, 282
   Girl in Landscape 242, 282
   Gun, With Occasional Music **165–167**,
    242, 282
   "Hardened Criminals, The" 167
   How We Got Insipid 242
   Men and Cartoons 242
   Motherless Brooklyn 135, 136, 242,
    280–282
   This Shape We're In 242
   Wall of the Sky, The Wall of the Eye,
    The 242
   You Don't Love Me Yet 242
"Letter from the Last Bastion"
  (Freudenberger) 137, 249
"Letters from Zedelghem" (Mitchell) 69,
  70
Let Us Now Praise Famous Men (Evans and
  Agee) 395
Lewis, C. S. 311
Lewis, Michael
   Liar's Poker 36
Liars and Saints (Meloy) 172, 265, 266
Liar's Poker (Lewis) 36
Libra (DeLillo) 49
Lienhard, John H. 267
"Lies" (Canin) 120
Lies My Teacher Told Me (Lowen) 45
Life after God (Coupland) 72, 73, 146,
  216, 217
Life All around Me by Ellen Foster, The
  (Gibbons) 115, 150
Life of Pi (Martel) **243–245**

Life's Work: On Becoming a Mother, A (Cusk)
  82–83, 340
Light at Dusk (Gadol) 141–142
Li'l Mama's Rules (Jackson) 211, 212
Limbo (Ansay) 18, 328
Limbo Room, The (Debra Eisenstadt and Jill
  Eisenstadt) 112
Lindquist, Mark 112
Link, Kelly 333
   Magic for Beginners 44
   Stranger Things Happen 44
Linklater, Richard
   Dazed and Confused 22
Lish, Gordon 238, 301
Little Children (Perrotta) 23, 311, 312, 313
"Little Expressionless Animals" (Wallace)
  155, 156, 381
Little Friend, The (Tartt) **245–246**, 364,
  365
"Little Knife, The"(Chabon) 277
Little Money Street (Eberstadt) 107
Little Prince, The (Saint-Exupéry) 267
Liu, Lucy 120
Living Blood, The (Due) 104, 105, **246–248**
Loh, Eugene 248
Loh, Gisela 248
Loh, Sandra Tsing **248–249**
   Aliens in America 248, 249
   Depth Takes a Holiday: Essays from
    Lesser Los Angeles 248
   If You Lived Here, You'd Be Home by
    Now **194–196**, 248
   Mother on Fire: A True Motherf%#$@
    Story about Parenting! 248, 249
   "My Father's Chinese Wives" 248
   Year in Van Nuys, A 248, 249
"London" (David Mitchell) 69
London, Jack 39
London Labor and the London Poor (Mayhew)
  183
London Review of Books 266
Lone Ranger and Tonto Fistfight in Heaven,
  The (Alexie) 7, 325, 367
Long Rain (Gadol) 141, 142
Long Way Gone: Memoirs of a Boy Soldier, A
  (Beah) 28
Look at Me (Egan) 108, 109, 224
Los Angeles: People, Places, and the Castle on
  the Hill 185, 187
Los Angeles Times 76, 90, 121, 133, 140,
  159, 229, 236, 308, 344, 390
Lost City Radio (Alarcón) 4, 5–6, 384
Lost in the Funhouse (Barth) 156
Lost Language of Cranes, The (Leavitt) 238,
  239
Lost Tribe: Jewish Fiction from the Edge 133
Louisville Review 237
Lovely Bones, The (Sebold) 39, 159

"Love Theme of Sybil and William, The"
  (Palahniuk) 301
Love Your Enemies (Barker) 25
Lowe, Chad 48
Lowen, James
   Lies My Teacher Told Me 45
Low Tide (Eberstadt) 107
Lucky Girls (Freudenberger) 136–137,
  249–251
Lucky Ones, The (Cusk) 83, **251–252**, 339
Ludlum, Robert 311
Ludmila's Broken English (Pierre) **253–254**,
  318, 319
Lullaby (Palahniuk) **254–256**, 301, 302
Lunar Park (Ellis) 15, 115, 117, **256–257**
L Word, The 187
Lynch, David
   Blue Velvet 282

M

MacLennan, Michael Lewis 72
Mademoiselle 276
Mad Men 160
Madonna on Her Back (Hagy) 170
Magic for Beginners (Link) 44
Magician's Assistant, The (Patchett) 305,
  306, 308
Mail on Sunday 233
Major, Clarence
   My Amputations 78
Malone, Jena 115
Maltese Falcon, The 235
Mammoth Cheese, The (Holman) 182
Man "Carrying Thing: A Theory of
  Metaphor for Wallace Stevens" (Gadol)
  140
Manifesto (Palahniuk) 301
Man in the High Castle, The (Dick) 57
Mann, Thomas
   Magic Mountain 305
Man of My Dreams, The (Sittenfeld) 353,
  354
Mansfield, Katherine 90
Man Walks into a Room (Krauss) 182,
  229–230, **258–259**
Man Who Loves Salmon, The (Alexie) 7
"Many Happy Returns" (Row) 329
Maps & Legends (Chabon) 56, 57
"March 15, 1997" (Brockmeier) 44
Markham, Beryl
   West with the Night 267
Markson, David
   Wittgenstein's Mistress 38
Martel, Yann **259–262**
   Facts behind the Helsinki Roccamatios
    260
   High Mountains of Portugal, The 261
   Life of Pi **243–245**, 259, 260

Self 259, 260
20th-Century Shirt, A 259–260, 261
"We Ate the Children Last" 260
Martin and John (Peck) **262–263**, 309
Martin Bauman: Or, a Sure Thing (Leavitt) 238
Marvel Comics 99, 242
Marx, Karl 302, 359
Mason, Bobbie Ann 92
Mason & Dixon (Pynchon) 51
Masterpiece Theatre 389
"*Matruschyka Doll Variations*" (Ayr) 70
"Matters of Life and Death" (Cusk) 251, 252
Matthiessen, Peter
　At Play in the Fields of the Lord 49
Maus: A Survivor's Tale (Spiegelman) 127, 181, 261
Maus II: And Here My Troubles Began (Spiegelman) 181, 261
Mayhew, Henry
　London Labor and the London Poor 183
Max and the Cats (Scliar) 245, 260–261
McCaffrey, Larry 86, 201
McCain's Promise: Aboard the Straight Talk Express with John McCain and a Whole Bunch of Actual Reporters (Wallace) 380
McCarthy, Andrew 117
McCarthy, Cormac 58, 226
　All the Pretty Horses 226
　Road, The 226
McClatchy, J. D. 226
McCracken, Elizabeth **263–265**
　Exact Replica of a Figment of My Imagination, An 264
　"Giant of Cape Cod, The" 264
　Giant's House, The **148–149**, 263, 264
　Here's Your Hat What's Your Hurry 148, 263–264
　House of Two Three-Legged Dogs, The 264
　"It's Bad Luck to Die" 264
　Niagara Falls All Over Again 148
　Thunderstruck Not Lightning-Struck 264
McCullers, Carson 157, 265, 333
　Member of the Wedding, A 246
McEwan, Ian 142, 311
McFarland, Ron 367
McInerney, Jay 74, 112, 115, 139, 169
McMillan, Terry 99, 212, 311, 346
　Waiting to Exhale 105, 211
MC Ren 359
McSweeney's 44, 110, 159, 178, 229, 242, 396
Meet the Writers 266
Meloy, Maile **265–266**
　"Aqua Boulevard" 172
　Both Ways Is the Only Way I Want It 265–266

Family Daughter, A 172, 265, 266
"Four Lean Hounds, ca. 1976" 171
Half in Love **171–172**, 265
"Kite Whistler Aquamarine" 171–172
Liars and Saints 172, 265, 266
"Ranch Girl" 265
"Stakes Horse, A" 171–172
Melville, Herman 350
Member of the Wedding, A (McCullers) 246
Men and Cartoons (Lethem) 242
Mendelsohn, Jane **266–267**
　Innocence 208, 266, 267
　I Was Amelia Earhart **207–209**, 266, 267
Mendes, Sam 214, 362
Men's Journal 362
Mercy (Picoult) 317
Merkin, Daphne 264–265
Merryman, Ashley
　Nurture Shock: New Thinking about Children (with Bronson)
Me Talk Pretty One Day (David Sedaris) 195
Meyers, Stephanie
　Twilight 183
Mezlekia, Nega
　Notes from the Hyena's Belly 28
Miami Herald 104, 105
Michaels, Anne
　Fugitive Pieces 181
Microserfs (Coupland) 72, 73, **267–269**
Microsoap 168
MidAmerican Review 58
Middlesex (Eugenides) 125–126, **269–271**, 377
Midnight Champagne (Ansay) 17, 328
Midnight's Children (Rushdie) 197, 233, 330
Midwife's Tale, A (Ulrich) 272
Midwives (Bohjalian) 33, 34, **271–273**
Might magazine 110, 177
Milk in My Coffee (Dickey) 98
"Millionaires" (Chabon) 276
Miller, Arthur
　Crucible, The 338
Miller, Frank 226
Miller, Henry 229, 334
Miller, Mike 248
Million Little Pieces, A (Frey) 208, 213
"Minister's Black Veil, The" (Hawthorne) 279
Ministry of Special Cases, The (Englander) 122, 123, **273–274**
Minnesota Public Radio 120–121
Miracin, André 87
Miracin, Eliab 87
Miracin, Joseph 87, 88
Mishima, Yukio 275
"Missing Peace, The" (Danticat) 231

Mississippi Review 354
Miss Wyoming (Coupland) 72
Mistress's Daughter, The 185, 187
Mitchell, David v, 45, **274–276**
　Black Swan Green 70, 274, 275
　"Civilization's Ladder" 70
　Cloud Atlas 45, **69–70**, 274, 275
　Deshima 276
　"Ghastly Ordeal of Timothy Cavendish, The" 69
　Ghostwritten 69, 70, 274, 275
　"Half-Lives: The First Luisa Rey Mystery" 69
　"Letters from Zedelghem" 69, 70
　"London" 69
　number9dream 69, 274, 275
　"Pacific Journal of Adam Ewing, The" 69, 70
　"Sloosha's Crossin' an' Ev'rythin' After" 69
Mitchell, Margaret
　Gone with the Wind 298
Mitgang, Herbert 261
MIT Press 242
"Mkondo" (Doerr) 100, 349
Model World and Other Stories, A (Chabon) 56, **276–278**
"Modernhaus Projekt-H, 1933" (Peter Gadol) 142
Modern Short Stories 301
Momaday, N. Scott
　House Made of Dawn 367
Money Changes Everything 65
Monster of St. Helena (Hansen) 174
"Monument, The" (Kennedy) 362
Moody, Rick v, 263, **278–280**, 310
　"Albertine Notes, The" 280
　"Apocalypse Commentary of Bob Paisner" 279
　Black Veil, The 279, 311
　Demonology (short fiction collection) **91–93**, 279
　"Demonology" (story) 93
　Diviners, The 143, 279
　"Double Zero, The" 93
　"Drawer" 92
　"Forecast from the Retail Desk" 93, 279
　"Gambit Declined" 278
　Garden State 92, **142–144**, 278
　Ice Storm, The 92, 93, 143, **193–194**, 278–279
　"Ineluctable Modality of the Vaginal" 92, 279
　"K&K" 280
　"Mansion on the Hill, The" 92, 279
　"Pip Adrift" 279
　"Preliminary Notes" 279

"Primary Sources" 279
Purple America 279
Right Livelihoods (Omega Force, The) 279–280
Ring of Brightest Angels around Heaven 279
"Surplus Value Books: Catalogue Number 13" 93
"Willie Fahnstock, *The Boxed Set*" 93
Moore, Lorrie 137
    Birds of America 136
Moore, Rudy Ray 71
More than Human (Sturgeon) 277
Morris, Willie
    Courting of Marcus Dupree, The 364
    Last of the Southern Girls, The 364
Morrison, Toni 34, 97, 99, 103, 105, 292, 346, 359
    Beloved 105
    Bluest Eye, The 69, 386
    Paradise 76, 304
    Song of Solomon 323
Mother Knot, The (Harrison) 175, 176
Motherless Brooklyn (Lethem) 135, 136, 242, **280–282**
Mother on Fire: A True Motherf%#$@ Story about Parenting! (Loh) 248, 249
Mr. Bridge (Connell) 49
"Mr. Makes" (Hagy) 170
"Mrs. Daley's Daughter" (Cusk) 251, 252
Mrs. Dalloway (Woolf) 262
"Mrs. Sen (Lahiri) 204, 237
MSS 58
MTV Productions 312
Mudge, Alden 121
Mulroney, Dermot 187
Munro, Alice 71, 249, 250, 251, 266
    Open Secrets 49
Murakami, Haruki 69, 275
Murphy, Jessica 65
Murphy Stories, The (Costello) 70
Music for Torching 185, 187, **282–284**, 366
Mute magazine 233
My Amputations (Reed) 78
"My Appearance" (Wallace) 381
"My Father's Chinese Wives" (Loh) 248
"My Life as a Dog" (Foer) 133–134
My Mistress's Sparrow Is Dead: Great Love Stories from Chekhov to Munroe (Eugenides) 125
My Revolutions (Kunzru) 232, 233–234
My Sister's Keeper (Picoult) 317
My Soul to Keep (Due) 104, 246, 247
Mysteries of Pittsburgh (Chabon) 56, 58, 276
Mystery Roast (Gadol) 140–141, 142, **284–285**
My War: Killing Time in Iraq (Buzzell) 213

N

Nabokov, Vladimir 85, 266, 275, 289, 310, 357
    Pale Fire 279
    Search for Sebastian Knight, The 180
Nafisi, Azar
    Reading Lolita in the Tehran 229
Nair, Mira 197, 236
Naked (David Sedaris) 195
Naked Came the Manatee (Due) 104
Naked Lunch (Burroughs) 116
Name of the Rose, The 235
Namesake (Lahiri) 236
Names of the Dead (O'Nan) **286–287**, 295
"Names of Flowers, The" (Gilbert) 320
Narayan, R. K. 94
Nash, Ogden 107
National Public Radio 170, 188, 195, 248, 301
    Fresh Air 355
    Marketplace 248
    Morning Edition 46
Native Speaker (Lee) 147, 148, 239, 240, **287–289**
Naylor, Gloria 105
"Negative Reinforcement" (Palahniuk) 301
"New and Old Wars" (Alarcón) 383
"New Black Aesthetic, The" (Ellis) 118
New Granta Book of the American Short Story, The (Ford) 136
New Line Cinema 178
New Republic 263, 309
New Stories from the South 299
Newsweek 133, 209, 242
Newton, Isaac 68
Newton, John 367
Newton's Sailor (Clement) 68
New Yorker, The 5, 39, 44, 58, 65, 88, 107, 110, 125, 133, 126, 137, 161, 179, 185, 187, 203, 225, 229, 233, 236, 237, 238, 240, 250, 264, 278, 299, 332, 346, 350, 364, 383
New York Magazine, The 46, 112, 332
New York Review of Books, The 350
New York Times, The 33, 46, 59, 61, 65, 70, 76, 90, 97, 98, 103, 104, 107, 108, 110, 112, 116, 120, 122, 133, 152, 153, 159, 161, 164, 174, 175, 227, 229, 233, 236, 239, 242, 248, 261, 264, 265, 266, 267, 271, 276, 278, 286, 289, 301, 305, 308, 315, 316, 317, 319, 321, 322, 346, 349, 353, 354, 355, 359, 362, 386, 387, 390
New York Times Magazine, The 107, 108, 118, 309, 386
"Next Life, The" (Davies) 123, 124
Next Stranger, The (Clement) 68

Niagara Falls All Over Again (McCracken) 148
Nietzsche, Friedrich 302
Niggaz With Attitude. *See* N.W.A.
Night Country, The (O'Nan) 287, 295
Night Woman" (Danticat) 232
Nineteen Minutes (Picoult) 317
Noise (Russell Smith) 146
Noise (Kunzru) 232
No One Belong Here More Than You (July) 195
Norton, Edward 132, 282, 301
Norton, W. W. 174
Norton's Anthology of Postmodern American Fiction, A 77
Notes from the Hyena's Belly (Mezlekia) 28
Notes from the Underground (Dostoyevsky) 49
Notes on a Scandal (Heller) 319
Nowhere Man (Alexander Hemon) 179–180, **289–290**
Now It's Time to Say Goodbye (Peck) 309, 310
n + 1 5, 311
Nudist on the Late Shift, The (Bronson) 46
number9dream (Mitchell) 69, 274, 275
Nurture Shock: New Thinking about Children (Bronson and Merryman) 47
N.W.A. 359
Nwapa, Flora 4

O

O 65
Oates, Joyce Carol 8, 31, 32, 35, 133, 272, 292, 354
Obasanjo, Olusegun 209
Obedient Father, An (Sharma) **292–293**, 346, 347–348
Oblivion (Wallace) 40, 41, 156, 201, 380, 381
O'Brien, Tim 136, 294, 363, 390
    Things They Carried, The 210, 213–214, 362
Observer 168, 316
"Ocean Avenue"(Chabon) 276
Ochsner, Gina 337
O'Connell, Jerry 48
O'Connor, Flannery 31, 103, 123, 150, 266, 294, 333, 337
"Octet" 380
Office, The 381
Offutt, Chris 354
Of One Blood (Hopkins) 247
Okonjo-Iweala, Ngozi 209
Old Shirts and New Skins (Alexie) 7
Omega Force, The. See Right Livelihoods
Omega Man 38

O'Nan, Stewart **293–295**
  Faithful, Two Diehard Boston Red Sox Fans Chronicle the Historic 2004 Season (with King) 287
  In the Walled City 294
  Names of the Dead **286–287**, 295
  Night Country, The 287, 295
  Snow Angels 294
  Speed Queen, The 287, 294, 295, **357–359**
On Beauty (Smith) **295–297**, 355, 356, 357
On Beauty and Being Just (Scarry) 296, 357
"Once in a Lifetime" (Lahiri) 236
Ondaatje, Michael 266
  English Patient, The 148
One Hundred Years of Solitude (García Márquez) 371, 383
One Stick Song (Alexie) 7
"1,000 Years: Life after God" (Coupland) 73
"Onionskin" (Goodman) 161
"Only Goodness" (Lahiri) 237
Only Revolutions (Danielewski) 192
On the Natural History of Destruction (Sebald) 129
On the Occasion of My Last Afternoon (Gibbons) 151, **297–298**
On the Road (Kerouac) 395
"On the Terraces" (Davies) 124
"Open Boat, The" (Crane) 207
Open Secrets (Munro) 49
Operation Homecoming 363
Ordinary Person's Guide to Empire, The (Roy) 331
Orlando (Woolf) 267
"Orphan, The" (Freudenberger) 137
Orringer, Julie 136
Osborn, Amy 280
Oscher, Paul 304
Other Side of the Island, The (Goodman) 161, 162
"Our Lady of Peace" (Packer) 300
Out magazine 310
"Outside the Eastern Gate" (Freudenberger) 137, 249
"Out to Sea" (Russell) 337
Ozeke, Sarah 389
Ozick, Cynthia 380

P

"Pacific Journal of Adam Ewing, The" (Mitchell) 69, 70
Packer, Z. Z. v, 136, **299–300**
  "Ant of the Self, The" 300
  "Brownies" 299
  "Buffalo Soldiers" 300
  "Doris Is Coming" 300
  Drinking Coffee Elsewhere **102–104**, 299
  "Geese" 300
  "Our Lady of Peace" 300
  "Speaking in Tongues" 299–300
  Thousands, The 300
Pact, The (Picoult) 317
Pagan's Head (Kennedy) 224, 225
Pagan Kennedy's Living: Handbook for Maturing Hipsters (Kennedy) 225
Pakula, Alan 242
Palace Thief, The (Canin) 48, 49
Palahniuk, Chuck **300–302**
  Choke 301, 302
  Diary 254, 301, 302
  Fight Club **131–133**, 254, 301, 302
  Fugitives and Refugees: A Walk in Portland, Oregon 301
  Haunted 254, 301
  Insomnia: If You Lived Here, You'd Be Home Already 301
  Invisible Monsters 254, 301, 302–303
  "Love Theme of Sybil and William, The" 301
  Lullaby **254–256**, 301, 302
  Manifesto 301
  "Negative Reinforcement" 301
  Pygmy 301
  Rant 301
  "She Breaks Your Heart" 301
  Snuff 301
  Stranger than Fiction: True Stories 301
  Survivor 254, 301, 302
Palahniuk, Frank 302
Pale Fire (Nabokov) 279
Paley, Grace 186, 230, 250
Panjabi, Archie 389
Pantheon Books 227
Paradise (Morrison) 76, 304
Paradise Park (Goodman) 161, 162, 220
Paramount 133
Paretsky, Sara 24
Paris Review 100, 125, 137, 172, 179, 229, 265, 278, 305
Parker, Laurie 305
Parks, Suzan-Lori **303–304**
  American Play, The 303, 304
  Betting on the Dust Commander 303
  Death of the Last Black Man in the Whole Entire World 303
  Father Comes Home from the Wars 304
  Getting Mother's Body 303, 304
  Girl 6 303
  Imperceptible Mutabilities in the Third Kingdom 303
  In the Blood 303
  Ray Charles Live! 304
  Sinners Place, The 303
  365 plays/365 days 304
  Topdog/Underdog 303, 304
  Venus 303
Partisan Review 229
Passage to India (Forster) 196, 250
Passing (Larsen) 54, 346
Pasternak, Boris
  Doctor Zhivago 148
Pasteur, Louis 68
Past the Bleachers (Bohjalian) 34
Patchett, Ann **304–306**
  Bel Canto **28–30**, 304, 305, 308
  Magician's Assistant, The 305, 306, 308
  Patron Saint of Liars, The 29, 305, **306–308**
  Run 305–306
  Taft 29, 305
  Truth and Beauty 304, 306
Patron Saint of Liars, The (Patchett) 29, 305, **306–308**
Patterson, Christina 82
Payne, Alexander 22
Peace Like a River (Enger) 120, 121, **308–309**
Pearlman's Ordeal (Hansen) 174
Peck, Dale 133, 309–311
  Body Surfing 311
  Drift House 310, 311
  Hatchet Jobs 309, 311
  Law of Enclosures 263, 309, 310
  Martin and John **262–263**, 309
  Now It's Time to Say Goodbye 309, 310
  What We Lost 309, 310–311
Pekar, Harvey 224
Pelevin, Victor 351
Pelovits, Pinchas 122
Penguin 182
Penguin Book of Gay Short Stories 238
Penguin/Putnam 226
Penn, Kal 236
Percy, Walker 32
Perfect Arrangement, A (Berne) 30, 31, 76
Perfect Match (Picoult) 317, 338
The Perfect Wife: The Life and Choices of Laura Bush (Gerhart) 354
Perrotta, Tom 311–313
  Abstinence Teacher, The 311, 312
  Bad Haircut **21–23**, 311, 312
  Election 22, 214, 311, 313
  Joe College **214–216**, 311, 312, 313
  Little Children 23, 311, 312, 313
  "Race Riot" 22
  "Snowman" 22
  "Thirteen" 21–22
  "Weiner Man, The" 21
  "Wild Kingdom" 21
  Wishbones, The 214, 311, 313

Person of Interest, A (Choi) 64, 65, **313–315**
Phillips, Arthur **315–316**
    Angelica 315, 316
    Egyptologist, The 315, 316
    Prague 315–316
    Song Is You, The 315, 316
    "Wenceslas Square" 316
Picoult, Jodi **316–318**
    Change of Heart 317
    Handle with Care 317
    Harvesting the Heart 317
    House Rules 317
    Keeping Faith 317
    Mercy 317
    My Sister's Keeper 317
    Nineteen Minutes 317
    Pact, The 317
    Perfect Match 317, 338
    Picture Perfect 317
    Plain Truth 317
    Salem Falls 317, **337–339**
    Second Glance 317
    Songs of the Humpback Whale 317
    Tenth Circle, The 317, 338
    Vanishing Acts 317
Picture Perfect (Picoult) 317
Piece of Flesh 355
Pierre, DBC (Finlay) **318–319**
    Ludmila's Broken English **253–254**, 318, 319
    Vernon God Little 253, 318, 319, **374–376**
Pilgrims (collection; Gilbert) 152, **319–321**
"Pilgrims" (short story; Gilbert) 320
"Pip Adrift" (Moody) 279
"Pitch Money" (Canin) 120
Pitt, Brad 132, 301
Place I've Never Been, A (Leavitt) 238
Plain Truth (Picoult) 317
"Planet of the Yids" (Shteyngart) 350
Platforms: A Microwaved Cultural Chronicle of the 1970s (Kennedy) 225
Plath, Sylvia
    Bell Jar, The 221, 346
Platitudes (Ellis) 117, 118
Platoon 213
Playback (Chandler) 167
Playboy 159, 301
Ploughshares 58, 172, 229, 265
Plum Bun (Fauset) 54
PN Review 229
Pocket Penguin 133
Poe. *See* Danielewski, Annie
Poison (Harrison) 175, 176
Poison That Fascinates, The (Clement) 69, 371

Polanski, Roman 346
Pollack, Sidney 113
Portland Mercury 301
Postcards from the Future 302
Potok, Chaim
    Chosen, The 135, 220
"Poverty of Mirrors" (Alexie) 6
Power, Susan
    Grass Dancer, The **163–164**
Power Politics 331
Prague (Phillips) 315–316
Pratt, Mary Louise 240–241
"Preliminary Notes" (Moody) 279
Prep (Sittenfield) **321–322**, 353, 354
"Primary Sources" (Moody) 279
"Primer for the Punctuation of Heart Disease, A" (Foer) 133
Prize Stories: The O. Henry Awards 164
"Procreate, Generate" (Doerr) 101
Prophet of the Sandlots (Winegardner) 389, 390
Prose, Francine 315
    Blue Angel 57
Proulx, E. Annie 152
Publishers Weekly 34, 59, 271, 289, 333, 364
Puri, Om 389
Purple America (Moody) 279
Purple Hibiscus (Adichie) 3, 4, **322–323**
Pushcart Prize, The 58
Puzo, Mario 390
    Godfather, The 77, 389, 390
Pygmy (Palahniuk) 301
Pynchon, Thomas 40, 156, 167, 311, 357, 386
    Crying of Lot 49, The 205
    Gravity's Rainbow 26
    Mason & Dixon 51

Q

Question of Bruno, The (Hemon) 179, 180, 289
Question of Power, A (Head) 28
Quicksand (Larsen) 395

R

Raboteau, Emily 345
"Race Riot" (Perrotta) 22
Rafkin, Louise 120
Ragtime (Doctorow) 49
"Ranch Girl" (Meloy) 265
Rand, Ayn 229
Random House 264, 322, 353, 354, 389, 390
Rant (Palahniuk) 301
Rather, Dan 310
Ray Charles Live! (Parks) 304
Reader, The (Schlink) 90
Reader's Digest 33

Reading Lolita in Tehran (Nafisi) 229
Read This and Tell Me What It Says (Ansay) 17, 328
"Real Doll, A" 186
"Real Life" (Freudenberger) 136
Real World 177
"Reb Kringle" (Englander) 122
Rechy, John 142
Red Badge of Courage, The (Crane) 210
Redbook magazine 48, 119
Reed, Ishmael 19, 346
    Yellowback Radio Broke Down 78
Remains of the Day (Ishiguro) 148, 169
Remarkable Creatures (Chevalier) 64
Remnick, David 65
Remnick, Dexter 65
Remnick, Eliot 65
Reservation Blues (Alexie) 7, 199, **324–326**
Reversed Forecast (Barker) 25, 26
Review of Contemporary Fiction 381
"Revolutions" (Row) 329, 369
Rice, Anne 105
Rick Moody & One Ring Zero 278
Right Here, Right Now (Ellis) 117, 118, **326–327**
Right Livelihoods (Moody) 279–280
Ring of Brightest Angels around Heaven (Moody) 279
River Angel (Ansay) 17, **327–328**
Road, The (McCarthy) 226
Road to Perdition 214, 362
Road to Santiago, The (Harrison) 175, 176
Robbins, Richard E. 363
Roberts, Julia 153
Robinson, Marilynne 354
Rock Bottom Remainders, The 105
Rockwell, Sam 294
Rolfo, Juan 5
Rolling Stone 133, 241
Romero, George 294
"Room after Room" (Foer) 133
Roots (Haley) 104
Rosenblatt, Roger 14
Ross, Alex 136, 227
Roth, Henry
    Call It Sleep 135
Roth, Philip 122, 229, 257, 334
    American Pastoral 49
    Goodbye, Columbus 22
    Human Stain, The 54
Row, Jess **328–330**
    "American Girl, The" 329, 369
    "Answer, The" 329
    "Eluding Happiness" 329
    "Ferry, The" 329, 369–370
    "For You" 329, 369
    "Heaven Lake" 370
    "Many Happy Returns" 329

"Revolutions" 329, 369
"Secrets of Bats, The" 329, 368–369
"Train to Lo Wu, The" (short story) 369
Train to Lo Wu, The (short story collection) 328–329, **368–370**
Rowling, J. K.
    Harry Potter 183
Roy, Arundhati **330–332**
    Algebra of Infinite Justice, The 331
    Cost of Living, The 331
    Electric Moon 330
    "End of Happiness, The" 331
    God of Small Things, The **157–159**, 202, 330, 331–332
    In Which Annie Gives It Those Ones 330
    Ordinary Person's Guide to Empire, The 331
Rubin, Louis D. 149
Rudin, Scott 133
Rules of Attraction, The (Ellis) 13, 113, 115, 116, 117, 215
Run (Patchett) 305–306
Running with Scissors (Burroughs) 213
Ruocco, Joseph 334
Rushdie, Salman 133, 292–293, 335, 357, 387
    Midnight's Children 197, 233, 330
    Satanic Verses 388
Russell, Karen **332–333**
    "Accident Brief, Occurrence #00/422" 333, 337
    "Ava Wrestles the Alligator" 332, 336
    "Children's Reminiscences of the Westward Migration" 336
    "City of Shells, The" 333, 336–337
    "Haunting Olivia" 332, 336
    "Lady Yeti and the Place of Artificial Snows" 333, 336
    "Out to Sea" 337
    "St. Lucy's Home for Girls Raised by Wolves" (short story) 337
    St. Lucy's Home for Girls Raised by Wolves (short story collection) 332, **336–337**
    "Star-Gazer's Log of Summer-Time Crime" 336
    Swamplandia! 332
    "Z.Z.'s Sleep-Away Camp for Disordered Dreamers" 336
Russian Debutante's Handbook, The (Shteyngart) 1, 2, **333–335**, 349, 350
Russo, Richard
    Straight Man 57

S

Sacks, Oliver 226
Sacrament. See You Shall Know Our Velocity!
Sacred Hunger (Unsworth) 49

"Sacrifices, The" (Cusk) 251, 252
"Safety Man" (Chaon) 59
Safety of Objects, The 185, 186, 187, 282
Sag Harbor (Whitehead) 386, 387
Sahgal, Nayantara
    Storm in Chandigarh 292
Said, Edward 350
Saint-Exupéry, Antoine de
    Little Prince, The 267
"St. Lucy's Home for Girls Raised by Wolves" (short story; Russell) 337
St. Lucy's Home for Girls Raised by Wolves (short story collection; Russell) 332, **336–337**
Saint Thérèse of Lisieux (Harrison) 175, 176
"Salamander-Child, A" (Clement) 68
Salem Falls (Picoult) 317, **337–339**
"Sales" (Davies) 123–124
Salinger, J. D.
    Catcher in the Rye, The 184, 221, 222, 267, 319, 321, 354, 374
Salon.com 5, 137, 241, 250, 278, 310, 386
Sanchez, Sonia 78
San Francisco Chronicle 306
"S ANGEL"(Chabon) 276
Sarraute, Nathalie 393
Sarsgaard, Peter 214
Sartre, Jean-Paul 302
Satanic Verses (Rushdie) 388
Saunders, George 61
Saving Agnes (Cusk) 82, 251, **339–340**
Scarry, Elaine
    On Beauty and Being Just 296, 357
Schiling, Jane 246
Schillinger, Liesl 9
Schlink, Bernard
    Reader, The 90
Scholz, Carter 242
Schoolly D 71
Schreiber, Live 128
Schultz, Bruno 230
Schultz, Charles 227
Scliar, Moacyr
    Max and the Cats 245, 260–261
Scribner Publishing 226
Scott, A. O. 334
Seal Wife, The (Harrison) 175, 176, **340–342**
Seaman, Donna 109
"Search Bay" (Hagy) 170
Searchers, The 242
Search for Sebastian Knight, The (Nabokov) 180
Sebald, W. G. 180
    Emigrants, The 261
    On the Natural History of Destruction 129

Sebold, Alice 159
    Lovely Bones, The 39, 159
Second Glance (Picoult) 317
Secret History, The (Tartt) 214, 245, 246, **342–343**, 364–365
"Secrets of Bats, The" (Row) 329, 368–369
Secrets of Eden (Bohjalian) 35
Sedaris, Amy 294
Sedaris, David 226
    Me Talk Pretty One Day 195
    Naked 195
Seeking Rapture (Harrison) 175, 176
See Under: Love (Grossman) 261
Seierstad, Asne
    Bookseller of Kabul, The 229
Seiffert, Rachel **343–345**
    Afterwards 343, 344
    "Crossing, The" 344
    Dark Room, The **89–90**, 343–344
    Field Study 343, 344
Self, Will 70
"Self-Reliance" (Emerson) 114
Selim, Ali 120
    Semper Fi 363
Sendak, Maurice, 111–112
Senna, Carl 345
Senna, Danzy **345–346**
    Caucasia **53–54**, 345–346
    Symptomatic 54, 345, 346
Separate Peace, A (Knowles) 321, 354
September 10, 2001 (Coupland) 72
Serra, Richard
    Joe (with Foer and Sugimoto) 134
Serrano, Andres 226
Seth, Vikram 292
"Seven Attempted Escapes from Silence" (Foer) 134
Seventeen 88, 353
"Several Anecdotes about My Wife" (Shteyngart) 350
Sex, Drugs, and Cocoa Puffs: A Low Culture Manifesto (Klosterman) 146
"Sexy" (Lahiri) 237
Shackleford, Dale 302
Shakespeare, William 68, 161, 164, 359
Shampoo Planet (Coupland) 72, 73, 146
Shapiro, Anna 83
Sharma, Akhil **346–348**
    "Cosmopolitan" 346, 347
    "If You Sing Like That for Me" 346, 347
    Obedient Father, An **292–293**, 346, 347–348
"She Breaks Your Heart" (Palahniuk) 301
Sheen, Martin 85
"Shell Collector, The" (short story; Doerr) 100, 348

Shell Collector, The (short story collection; Doerr) 99, **348–349**
Shelton, Pamela 87
Shenandoah 170
Shooter, Jim 159
"Shrinks" (Kennedy) 361
Shteynfarb, Jerry 350
Shteyngart, Gary **349–351**
   Absurdistan **1–3**, 334, 349, 350
   "Diaries of Lenny Abramov" 350
   "Immortality" 350
   "Planet of the Yids" 350
   Russian Debutante's Handbook, The 1, 2, **333–335**, 349, 350
   "Several Anecdotes about My Wife" 350
   "Sixty-nine Cents" 350
Sibley, Barbara 68
Sifton, Sam 319
Sights Unseen (Gibbons) 150–151
"Signifying Monkey" 71
Signifying Monkey: A Theory of African-American Literary Criticism, A (Gates) 71
"Signifying Rapper" 71
Signifying Rappers: Rap and Race in Urban Present (Costello and Wallace) 25, 70, 71, 380
Silko, Leslie Marmon 324, 325–326
   Ceremony 367
Silverblatt, Michael 192
Silver Lake (Gadol) 142
Simon & Schuster 212, 278
Sinclair, Upton 46
Singer, I. B. 122
Sinners Place, The (Parks) 303
Sisam, Patrick 120
Sister (Ansay) 17, 328
Sister Sister (Dickey) 98, 99, **351–353**
Sittenfield, Curtis 250, **353–355**
   American Wife 353, 354
   Man of My Dreams, The 353, 354
   Prep **321–322**, 353, 354
Sittenfield, Elizabeth C. 353
Sittenfield, Paul 353
"Sixth Borough, The" (Foer) 133
"Sixty-nine Cents" (Shteyngart) 350
Skeletons at the Feast (Bohjalian) 34
Slate 328, 363
Slaughterhouse-Five (Vonnegut) 290
Sleeping with Strangers (Dickey) 98
Small Holdings (Barker) 25, 26
"Small World" (soundtrack; Alexie) 7
"Small World" (short story; Davies) 123, 124
Smiley, Jane 376
Smith, Betty
   Tree Grows in Brooklyn, A 135
Smith, Dinitia 248

Smith, Harvey 355
Smith, Russell
   How Insensitive 146
   Noise 146
Smith, Zadie 8, 103, **355–357**
   Autograph Man, The 295, 355, 356–357
   On Beauty **295–297**, 355, 356, 357
   White Teeth 38, 197, 295, 355, 3566, **387–389**
Smith, Yvonne Bailey 355
"Smoke" (Chabon) 276
Smoke Signals 7, 325
Snow Angels (O'Nan) 294
Snow, Ashes (Hagy) 170, 171
Snow Crystals (Bentley) 100
"Snowman" (Perrotta) 22
Snuff (Palahniuk) 301
So Brave, Young and Handsome: A Novel (Enger) 120, 121
"So Many Chances" (Doerr) 349
Somewhere Else Entirely v–vi
Sommese, Lanny 60, 226
Sondok: Princess of the Moon and Stars (Holman) 182
Song Is You, The (Phillips) 315, 316
Song of Solomon (Morrison) 323
Songs of Innocence and Experience (Blake) 64
Songs of the Humpback Whale (Picoult) 317
Sontag, Susan
   Volcano Lover, The 51
Soon I Will Be Invincible (Grossman) 167
"Sorge Spy Ring, The" (Hemon) 180
Sorokin, Vladimir 351
Soukhanov, Anne H. 13
Sound and the Fury, The (Faulkner) 81, 169
Sound Unbound: Sampling Digital Music and Culture (Spooky) 242
"South by Southwest" (Alexie) 367
South of Market (Bronson) 46
South Park 319, 374
Souvenance, Rose 87
Spacek, Sissy 34, 271
Spanbauer, Tom 301, 302
Spark, Muriel 275
"Speaking in Tongues" (Packer) 299–300
Spear, Geoff 227
Speed Queen, The (O'Nan) 287, 294, 295, **357–359**
Spender, Stephen 239
Spiegelman, Art 227
   Maus: A Survivor's Tale 127, 181, 261
   Maus II: And Here My Troubles Began 181, 261
Spielberg, Steven 226
Spin 386

Spinoza Baruch, 350
Spinsters (Kennedy) 225
Spooky, DJ
   Sound Unbound: Sampling Digital Music and Culture 242
"Stakes Horse, A" (Meloy) 171–172
Stanford Daily 354
"Star Food" (Canin) 48, 119–120
"Star-Gazer's Log of Summer-Time Crime" (Russell) 336
Starstreet 168
Stein, Gertrude
   Autobiography of Alice B. Toklas 267
Steinbeck, John 46
Steinem, Gloria 116
Step into a World: A Global Anthology of New Black Literature 77
Stern, Laurence 357
   Tristram Shandy 192
Stern Man (Gilbert) 152
Stevenson, Robert Louis 309
   Treasure Island 121
Stewart, James B.
   Den of Thieves 36
Stewart, Martha 225
Stirrings Still: The International Journal of Existential Literature 302
Stolen Tongue, A (Holman) 182, 183
Stone, Richard 92
Stone, Sharon 120
Stories of John Cheever, The (Cheever) 48, 50
Storm in Chandigarh (Sahgal) 292
Story 58
Story Quarterly 237
Straight Man (Russo) 57
Straight Outta Compton (Cruz) vi, 77, **359–360**
Stranger, The (Camus) 285, 289, 366
Stranger than Fiction: True Stories (Palahniuk) 301
Stranger Things Happen (Link) 44
Straub, Peter 58
"Street, The" 46
"Stick or Flip" 46
"Stripping" (Kennedy) 361
Stripping + Other Stories (Kennedy) 224–225, **360–362**
Sturgeon, Theodore
   More Than Human 277
Subtropics 238
"Suffering Channel, The" 381
Sugimoto, Hiroshi
   Joe (with Foer and Serra) 134
Summer of Black Widows, The (Alexie) 7
Summerland (Chabon) 56, 57
Sunday Times (London) 136
Sunnyside (Gold) 159, 160

"Supposedly Fun Thing I'll Never Do Again, A" (Wallace) 200, 380, 381
"Surplus Value Books: Catalogue Number 13" (Moody) 93
Surrounded, The (McNickle) 367
Survivor (Palahniuk) 254, 301, 302
Süskind, Patrick 235
Swamplandia! (Russell) 332
Swofford, Anthony **362–363**
    Exit A 363
    Jarhead: a Marine's Chronicle of the Gulf War and Other Battles **212–214**, 362
"Symbiosis" (Barker) 25
Symptomatic (Senna) 54, 345, 346

T

Tabu 236
Taft (Patchett) 29, 305
Talladega Nights 313
"Tangle by the Rapid River, A" 349
Tanizaki, Junichiro 275
Tartt, Don 364
Tartt, Donna **364–365**
    Little Friend, The **245–246**, 364, 365
    Secret History, The 214, 245, 246, **342–343**, 364–365
Tartt, Taylor 364
Taylor, Antrim 334
Teachers Have It Easy: The Big Sacrifices and Small Salaries of America's Teachers (Eggers) 396
Telegraph 265
"Telephone, The" (Brockmeier) 45
Temporary, The (Cusk) 82
"Temporary Matter, A" (Lahiri) 203, 237
Ten Little Indians (Alexie) 7
Tenth Circle, The (Picoult) 317, 338
Terry (Coupland) 217
That's True of Everyone (Winegardner) 389
Theroux, Paul
    Elephant Suite, The 293
Thicker than Water (Harrison) 175, 176
Thieves Paradise (Dickey) 99
Things Fall Apart (Achebe) 3, 322
Things That Fall from the Sky (Brockmeier) 43, 44
Things They Carried, The (O'Brien) 210, 362
Things You Should Know 185, 187
Thinking about Hope (Wallace) 380
"Thirteen" (Perrotta) 21–22
"This Blessed House" (Lahiri) 204, 237
This Book Will Save Your Life 185, 186, 187, 283, **365–367**
This Is Not an Exit: The Fictional World of Bret Easton Ellis (Bret Easton Ellis) 117
"This Is What It Means to Say Phoenix, Arizona" (Alexie) 7

This Shape We're In (Lethem) 242
This Side of Paradise (Fitzgerald) 184
"This Was When You Could Still Be Killed for Love" (Clement) 68
Thompson, Jean 104
Thoreau, Henry David 359
Thousands, The (Packer) 300
Thousand Splendid Suns, A (Hosseini) 189, 190
Three Button Trick, The (Barker) 25
365 plays/365 days (Parks) 304
Three Stigmata of Palmer Eldritch, The (Dick) 166
3 x 33: Short Fiction by 33 Writers 390
Thunderstruck Not Lightning-Struck (McCracken) 264
Time Machine, The (Wells) 57
Time magazine 46, 153, 241, 308, 386
Time Out 334
Tin Drum, The (Grass) 129
Tin House 65, 101
"Today Is Sunday" (Davies) 124
Today Show 113, 299
To Kill a Mockingbird (Lee) 81–82, 246, 271
Tolkien, J. R. R. 97
Tolstoy, Leo
    Death of Ivan Ilych, The 261
"Too Young, Too Pretty, Too Successful" 137
Topdog/Underdog (Parks) 303, 304
"Tornado Alley" (Wallace) 380
Total Immersion (Goodman) 161
Toughest Indian in the World, The (Alexie) 7, **367–368**
"Train to Lo Wu, The" (short story; Row) 369
Train to Lo Wu, The (short story collection; Row) 328–329, **368–370**
Transmission (Kunzru) 232, 233, 234
Trans-Sister Radio (Bohjalian) 34
Travel + Leisure 2, 350
Treasure Island (Stevenson) 121
Tree Grows in Brooklyn, A (Smith) 135
Trevor, William 249
TriQuarterly 58
"Tri-Stan: I Sold Sissee Nar to Eko" (Wallace) 381
Tristram Shandy (Stern) 192
True Story Based on Lies, A (Clement) 68, 69, **370–371**
Truth about Celia, The (Brockmeier) 39, 43, 44
Truth and Beauty (Patchett) 304, 306
"Tumblers, The" (Englander) 122
"Tunnel, The" (Kennedy) 361
Turing, Alan 238
Turner, Kathleen 125, 379
"Tutor, The" (Freudenberger) 137, 249

Twain, Mark 319
    Adventures of Huckleberry Finn 114
Twenty-Seventh City (Franzen) 76
"27th Man, The" (Englander) 122
26th Man (Winegardner and Fireovid) 390
Twilight (Meyers) 183
Twilight Zone, The 58
"Tyger, The" (Blake) 64, 244

U

"UFOs" (Kennedy) 362
Ugliest House in the World, The (Davies) 90, 124
Ulrich, Laurel Thatcher
    Midwife's Tale, A 272
Ulysses (Joyce) 262
Unabridged Pocketbook of Lightning 133
Unaccustomed Earth (Lahiri) 236–237
Unbearable Lightness of Being (Kundera) 180
"Underwear Man" (Kennedy) 361
Underwood, Blair
    In the Night of the Heat (with Due and Barnes) 104
Underworld (DeLillo) 76
Unger, Douglas 311
Unraveling (Graver) 164, 165
Unsworth, Barry
    Sacred Hunger 49
Updike, John 133, 226, 279, 299
    A&P 119
USA Today 236
U.S.A. Trilogy (Dos Passos) 16
Uses of Enchantment, The (Julavits) 218–219, **372–373**

V

Valby, Karen 302
Vanishing Acts (Picoult) 317
Vanity Fair (magazine) 107
"Variant Text" (Goodman) 161
Vendler, Helen 140
Venus (Parks) 303
Vera, Yvonne 4
Veracruz Blues, The (Winegardner) 76, 389, 390
Vernon God Little (Pierre) 253, 318, 319, **374–376**
Vertigo 289
"Very Rigid Search, The" (Foer) 133
Vienne, Veronique 226
View from the Seventh Layer, The (Brockmeier) 43, 45
Viking Press 239
"Village 113" (Doerr) 101
Village Voice 187, 266, 386
Vinegar Hill (Ansay) 17, 328, **376–377**
Vintage Book of Amnesia: An Anthology of Writing on the Subject of Memory Loss 242

Virgin Blue, The (Chevalier) 63
Virginia Quarterly Review 5, 170, 383
Virgin Suicides, The (Eugenides) 125, 126, 271, **377–379**
Virtuous Woman, A (Gibbons) 150, 151
Vital Signs 310
Vogue 65, 107, 112, 137
Voice of Witness 110
Volcano Lover, The (Sontag) 51
Voltaire 359
Vonnegut, Kurt 19, 167
    Slaughterhouse Five 290
Von Ziegesar, Cecily 313

W

Waiting for an Angel (Habila) 210
Waiting to Exhale (McMillan) 105, 211
Walker, Alice 105
    Color Purple, The 105
Walker, Rebecca 345
Wallace, David Foster v, 32, 71, 85, 110, 178, 186, 335, 357, **380–382**
    Brief Interviews with Hideous Men **39–41**, 156, 380, 381, 382
    Broom of the System, The 40, 201, 380, 382
    Consider the Lobster 40, 380
    "E Unibus Pluram" vi, 156, 201, 381–382
    Everything and More: A Compact History of ∞ 380
    "Federer as Religious Experience" 380
    "Forever Overhead" 40
    Girl with Curious Hair 40, **155–157**, 380, 381
    "Good Old Neon" 156, 380
    "Good People" 382
    "Here and There" 155, 156, 380
    "How Tracy Austin Broke My Heart" 380
    "Incarnations of Burned Children" 382
    Infinite Jest vi, 40, 71, 156, **199–201**, 283, 380, 381, 382
    "John Billy" 157
    "Laughing with Kafka" 40
    "Little Expressionless Animals" 155, 156, 381
    McCain's Promise: Aboard the Straight Talk Express with John McCain and a Whole Bunch of Actual Reporters 380
    "My Appearance" 381
    Oblivion 40, 41, 156, 201, 380, 381
    "Octet" 380
    Signifying Rappers: Rap and Race in Urban Present (with Costello) 25, 70, 71, 380
    "Suffering Channel, The" 381

"Supposedly Fun Thing I'll Never Do Again, A" 200, 380, 381
Thinking about Hope 380
"Tornado Alley" 380
"Tri-Stan: I Sold Sissee Nar to Eko" 381
"Westward the Course of Empire Takes Its Way" 155, 156
Wall-E 38
"Wall of Fire Rising, A" (Danticat) 232
Wall of the Sky, The Wall of the Eye, The (Lethem) 242
Wall Street Journal 46, 155
War by Candlelight (Alarcón) 4, 5, **382–384**
War Dances (Alexie) 8
Ware, Chris 227
Warhol Factory, Andy 107, 108
Warner Brothers 133, 229
Warren, Robert Penn
    All the King's Men 49
Washington, Denzel 118
Washington Post, The 57, 59, 100, 133, 137, 159, 310, 353
Water Flowing Home (Alexie) 7
Waters, John 187
Water Witches (Bohjalian) 34
Watters, Ethan 46, 49
Waugh, Evelyn 266, 334
"Way You Do It, The" (Cusk) 83, 251
"We Are Nighttime Travelers" (Canin) 120
We Are What We Eat 390
Weaver, Sigourney 85
"Weiner Man, The" (Perrotta) 21
Welch, James
    Death of Jim Loney, The 367
Weldon, Fay 251
Wells, H. G.
    Time Machine, The 57
Welsh Girl, The (Davies) 91, 124
"Wenceslas Square" (Phillips) 316
"We Real Cool" (Brooks) 360
Werewolves in Their Youth (Chabon) 56, 57
Western Humanities Review 229
"Westward the Course of Empire Takes Its Way (Wallace) 155, 156
West with the Night (Markham) 267
Whalestoe Letters, The (Danielewski) 86
What Is the What: The Autobiography of Valentino Achek Deng (Eggers) vi, 28, 111, 178, **384–385**, 396
"What kind of Latino am I?" (Alarcón) 5
"What the Orphan Inherits" (Alexie) 6
What Should I Do with My Life? (Bronson) 46
What We Lost (Peck) 309, 310–311
"When Mr. Pirzada Came to Dine" (Lahiri) 203, 237

When the Sons of Heaven Meet the Daughters of the Earth (Eberstadt) 107, 108, 207
"Where I'm Coming From" (Ali) 8, 9
Where the Wild Things Are (Sendak) 111–112
"Where We Are Now" (Canin) 120
While England Sleeps (Leavitt) 238–239
While They Slept: An Inquiry into the Murder of a Family (Harrison) 175, 176
White, Edmund 238, 310
White Boy Shuffle (Beatty) 19
Whitehead, Colson **386–387**
    Apex Hides the Hurt **18–20**, 204, 386, 387
    Colossus of New York 206, 386, 387
    Intuitionist, The 19, **204–206**, 386
    John Henry Days 19, 204, 205, 386–387
    Sag Harbor 386, 387
White Noise (DeLillo) 19, 283
White Teeth (Smith) 38, 197, 295, 355, 356, **387–389**
Whitman, Walt 68
"Whoa Nelly!" 137
Wholphin 110, 178
Who Writes Science Fiction 91
Why Do I Love These People? (Bronson) 47
Widmyer, Dennis 302
Widow Basquiat, The (Clement) 68
Wilcox, James 80
Wild East: Stories from the Last Frontier 316
Wild House, The 168
"Wild Kingdom" (Perrotta) 21
Wild Things, The (Eggers) 112
Wilhelm, Vinnie 5
Williams, John Alfred
    Clifford's Blues 173
Williams, William Carlos 43
"Willie Fahnstock, The Boxed Set" (Moody) 93
Windows on the World (Beigbeder) 129
Winegardner, Mark **389–390**
    Crooked River Burning **76–77**, 389–390
    Elvis Presley Boulevard 389, 390
    Godfather Returns, The 389, 390
    Godfather's Revenge, The 389, 390
    Prophet of the Sandlots 389, 390
    That's True of Everyone 389
    26th Man (with Fireovid) 390
    Veracruz Blues, The 76, 389, 390
Winfrey, Oprah 34–35, 87, 126, 150, 178, 271, 272
Winterston, Jeanette 357, 371
Wired magazine 46, 72, 233
Wishbones, The (Perrotta) 214, 311, 313

Witherspoon, Reese 23, 312
Wittgenstein's Mistress (Markson) 38
Wolfe, Tom
    Bonfire of the Vanities, The 36
    I Am Charlotte Simmons 215
Wolff, Geoffrey 49
Wolff, Tobias 22, 311
Wonder Boys (Chabon) 56–57, 58
Wonderful Town: New York Stories from The New Yorker 64, 65
Wonder Spot, The (Banks) 355
Wood, Elijah 128
Woods, James 125, 379
Woolf, Virginia 165, 252, 339
    Mrs. Dalloway 262
    Orlando 267
World War Z: An Oral History of the Zombie Wars (Brooks) 167
Worst Journey in the World, The (Cherry-Garrard) 39

Writer, The 119
Writing Lost Angeles: A Literary Anthology 248
"Wrong Sun, The" (Coupland) 73
www.themorningnews.org 101

X

X Saves the World: How Generation X Got the Shaft but Can Still Keep Everything from Sucking (Gordinier) 146

Y

Yale Review 125, 266
Year in Van Nuys, A (Loh) 248, 249
"Year of Getting to Know Us, The" (Canin) 120
Year's Best Fantasy and Horror, The 44
"Year's End" (Lahiri) 236
Yeats, W. B. 68
Yellowback Radio Broke Down (Reed) 78

Yiddish Policemen's Union, The (Chabon) 56, 57, 58, **391–393**
You Don't Love Me Yet (Lethem) 242
"You in America" (Adichie) 3
Young, Elizabeth 74
Yourcenar, Marguerite 235
You Remind Me of Me (Chaon) 58, 59, **393–394**
You Shall Know Our Velocity! (Eggers) 111, 112, 178, **394–396**
YouTube 311

Z

Zine: How I Spent Six Years of My Life in the Underground and Finally . . . Found Myself . . . I Think (Kennedy) 225
Zoetrope 332
Zulkey, Claire 245
"Z.Z.'s Sleep-Away Camp for Disordered Dreamers" (Russell) 336